WHY (

PHILIP ROESSLER

HARRY VERHOEVEN

Why Comrades Go To War

*Liberation Politics and the Outbreak
of Africa's Deadliest Conflict*

OXFORD
UNIVERSITY PRESS

OXFORD

UNIVERSITY PRESS

Oxford University Press is a department of the
University of Oxford. It furthers the University's objective
of excellence in research, scholarship, and education
by publishing worldwide.

Oxford   New York

Auckland   Cape Town   Dar es Salaam   Hong Kong   Karachi
Kuala Lumpur   Madrid   Melbourne   Mexico City   Nairobi
New Delhi   Shanghai   Taipei   Toronto

With offices in

Argentina   Austria   Brazil   Chile   Czech Republic   France   Greece
Guatemala   Hungary   Italy   Japan   Poland   Portugal   Singapore
South Korea   Switzerland   Thailand   Turkey   Ukraine   Vietnam

Oxford is a registered trade mark of Oxford University Press
in the UK and certain other countries.

Published in the United States of America by
Oxford University Press
198 Madison Avenue, New York, NY 10016

Library of Congress Cataloging-in-Publication Data is available
Philip Roessler and Harry Verhoeven.
Why Comrades Go To War: Liberation Politics and the Outbreak
of Africa's Deadliest Conflict.
ISBN: 9780190864552

In memoriam of those who died in the killing fields of Central Africa

CONTENTS

CONTENTS

CONTENTS

CONTENTS

CONTENTS

ACKNOWLEDGMENTS

From its very initial stages following a fortuitous encounter between the authors in January 2009 in St Antony's College, Oxford, *Why Comrades Go to War* has benefited immensely from the support of a wide variety of people and organizations. We can only thank some of them here; others, particularly those in Central Africa who provided invaluable assistance to this project but cannot be mentioned because of security reasons, should know how grateful we are to them even if their names are not included in the following pages. This book would not be possible without you.

The genesis of this publication was at the University of Oxford, where we were both affiliated for many years to the Department of Politics and International Relations (DPIR). At Oxford, the collaboration at first revolved around research on Congo for Phil's book *Ethnic Politics and State Power in Africa* (See its Chapter 9, "A Model-Testing Case: Explaining Africa's Great War," from which our book builds). But we quickly realized the story of the outbreak of Africa's Great War could not be confined to a single chapter. As we found ourselves drawn back to Central Africa again and again to pursue even more interviews and greatly expand upon our original research, we set off to write a stand-alone book on this important subject, with greater focus on the regional dynamics of liberation revolutions and the causes of the organizational weakness of the coalition that came together to overthrow Mobutu.

Both the DPIR as an institution and many individuals associated with the department or other university bodies were crucial in getting this project off the ground, sustaining it for almost six years and finishing it in the course of 2015. David Anderson provided encouragement and intellectual stimulation from the start, but also read the entire manuscript and posed incisive questions that forced us to rethink regularly. Ricardo Soares de Oliveira proved invaluable in deepening our understanding of the Congo–Angola link and making sense of the MPLA's complex strategic calculations. Phil Clark was an outstanding sounding board throughout the project. Others with Oxford connections who helped us include Barbara Harrell-Bond, Miles Larmer, Henning Tamm, Sharath Srinivasan and Tony Jackson. The OUP John Fell Fund was crucial in providing seed money that enabled us to begin our research for this book, including our first few research trips together. We are deeply grateful for all this assistance.

After our time in the UK, we both went our separate ways, to American institutions: to the College of William and Mary, which has been unfailing in its support of this project, and to the School of Foreign Service of Georgetown University, based in Qatar. The latter funded a trip to Eritrea and coordination meetings between us as authors, but also—through the financial and logistical aid provided by its Center for International and Regional Studies—a book workshop which brought together academics from across the broader region to discuss our manuscript. The resulting feedback improved our thinking and writing substantially. In this context, we thank Mehran Kamrava, Zahra Babar, Umber Latafat, Sally Moral, Naomi Chazan, Afyare Elmi, Peter Van der Windt, Ibrahim Elnur, Theodor Hanf and C.S.R. Murthy.

The most important funder of our work was the Harry Frank Guggenheim Foundation (HFG), which enabled us to spend two years traveling across the African continent, from Asmara and Addis to Kigali, Kinshasa and Luanda. It was the HFG whose generous aid in 2013 and 2014 allowed us to take the project to the next level and to pursue many loose ends with much greater vigor. Without the Foundation, the research for this book and our understanding of the causes of Africa's Great War would have been much less comprehensive.

We also want to thank several fellow academics who took out many hours of their valuable time to discuss the emerging facts, evidence and conclusions with us between 2009 and 2015: Filip Reyntjens, Tom Turner and Will Reno are outstanding scholars on whose work *Why Comrades Go to War* builds. We are very fortunate to have received such encouraging suggestions from people who are both so familiar with the region we have been studying and with the conceptual frameworks upon which our book draws. Similarly, we much enjoyed collaborating with a number of people at Hurst, where we wish to thank Michael Dwyer, Jon de Peyer, Sebastian Ballard and Tim Page.

In the thirteen countries where we conducted fieldwork, a huge number of people provided extraordinary assistance to help us put together the unprecedented range of interviews on which the core arguments of *Why Comrades Go to War* rely. It is impossible to mention everybody, but to name the most important ones: in Congo, Nadia Ilunga (whose research assistance was exceptional) and Celio Mayembe; in Angola, Manuel Correia de Barros and Charles Delogne; in Rwanda, James Wizeye, Dieudonné Rurangirwa and Frank Begumisa; in Uganda, Tony Otoa; in Tanzania, Koenraad Adam; in Eritrea, Christine Umutoni and Elsa Mussie. We also thank Frank De Coninck, Ian Martin, Johan Swinnen, Mauro De Lorenzo, Marco Jowell, Peter Verlinden, Koen Vlassenroot and Jason Stearns for their direct and indirect contributions to the research. A special mention should be reserved here for two remarkable individuals, both key eyewitnesses to the conflict and sources of measured reflection on the events that constituted Central Africa's killing fields: Frank Rusagara and Alain Ilunga. This book would not be the same had it not been for your insights and time.

We also acknowledge the confidence and courage of our hundreds of interviewees. We are especially indebted to those still in positions where reflecting critically on the past and the ways in which it still shapes the present is often a dangerous endeavor. We wish to pay a special tribute to Lucie Kampinka, whose life was forever scarred by some of the events discussed in this book, but whose fortitude and testimony shook us and inspired us to dig deeper. Visiting Nyamata and Ntarama with her served as an essential reminder of the stakes of how history is studied and written.

Finally, our families and friends have been incredibly understanding of the many sacrifices that writing *Why Comrades Go to War* required. Kate and Maimuna were our lighthouses in the turbulent seas that writing a 430-page book inevitably ends up producing; they were, as ever, irreplaceable. Our parents' love and belief continues to make all the difference, as they always have—we are two extremely fortunate sons. Lucy, Lena and Libby joined this world in 2011, 2013 and 2015 and gave their father yet more motivation to complete the research and manuscript. Lisa, Mike, Steve, Katie, Kim, Dan, Kristen, Ben, Betsy, Paul, Christine, Dennis, Tomovic, Joan, Simu, Matoke, Jorge, Sam, Sofia and Gihad provided much needed laughter, context and comfort at different phases of this project. Luc Verhoeven was a father and mentor to one of us and a friend and fellow football fan to the other. He unexpectedly passed away as the manuscript was being completed, but his imprint is visible in every chapter. We miss him terribly.

ABBREVIATIONS

ADF	Allied Democratic Forces
ADP	Alliance Démocratique des Peuples
AFDL	Alliance des Forces Démocratiques pour la Libération du Congo-Zaïre
AIC	Association Internationale du Congo
ALiR	Armée pour la Libération du Rwanda
AMF	American Mineral Fields
ANC	African National Congress
Balubakat	Association Générale des Baluba de Katanga
BCD	Banque de Commerce et de Développement
BCDI	Banque de commerce du développement et d'industrie
CCM	Chama Cha Mapinduzi
CNL	Comité National de Libération
CNRD	Conseil National de Résistance pour la Démocratie
Conakat	Confédération des associations tribales du Katanga
CPP	Convention People's Party
DGSE	Direction Générale de la Sécurité Extérieure
DMI	Directorate of Military Intelligence
DSP	Division Spéciale Présidentielle
EPLF	Eritrean People's Liberation Front
EPRDF	Ethiopian People's Revolutionary Democratic Front
FAA	Forças Armadas Angolanas
FAC	Forces Armées Congolaises
FAPLA	Forças Armadas Populares de Libertação de Angola
FAR	Forces Armées Rwandaises
FAZ	Forces Armées Zaïroises

ABBREVIATIONS

FDLR	Forces Démocratiques pour la Libération du Rwanda
FLEC	Frente para a Libertação do Enclave de Cabinda
FLN	Front de Libération Nationale
FRELIMO	Frente de Libertação de Moçambique
FRONASA	Front for National Salvation
GSSP	Groupe Spécial de Sécurité Présidentielle
ICI	International Commission of Inquiry
IDF	Israel Defense Forces
JUFERI	Jeunesse de l'Union des Fédéralistes et Républicains Indépendants
LRA	Lord's Resistance Army
MIBA	Societé minière de Bakwanga
MLC	Mouvement pour la Libération du Congo
MNC	Mouvement National Congolais
MPLA	Movimento Popular de Libertação de Angola
MRLZ	Mouvement Révolutionnaire pour la Libération du Zaïre
NALU	National Army for the Liberation of Uganda
NRA/M	National Resistance Army/Movement
PAIGC	Partido Africano da Independência da Guinée Cabo Verde
PALIR	Peuple en armes pour la liberation du Rwanda
PRP	Parti de la Révolution Populaire
RANU	Rwandan Alliance for National Unity
RCD	Rassemblement Congolais pour la Démocratie
RENAMO	Resistência Nacional Moçambicana
RPA	Rwandan Patriotic Army
RPF	Rwandan Patriotic Front
SADC	Southern African Development Community
SPLA/M	Sudan People's Liberation Army/Movement
SWAPO	South West Africa People's Organization
TANU	Tanganyika African National Union
TK	Tigres Katangais
TPDF	Tanzania People's Defense Force
TPLF	Tigrayan People's Liberation Front
UDPS	Union pour la Démocratie et le Progrès Social
UNAMIR	United Nations Assistance Mission for Rwanda
UNITA	União Nacional para a Independência Total de Angola
UNIP	United National Independence Party
UPDF	Ugandan People's Defense Forces

ABBREVIATIONS

USARF	University Students' African Revolutionary Front
WNBLF	West Nile Bank Liberation Front
ZANLA	Zimbabwe African National Liberation Army
ZANU	Zimbabwe African National Union
ZDF	Zimbabwean Defense Forces

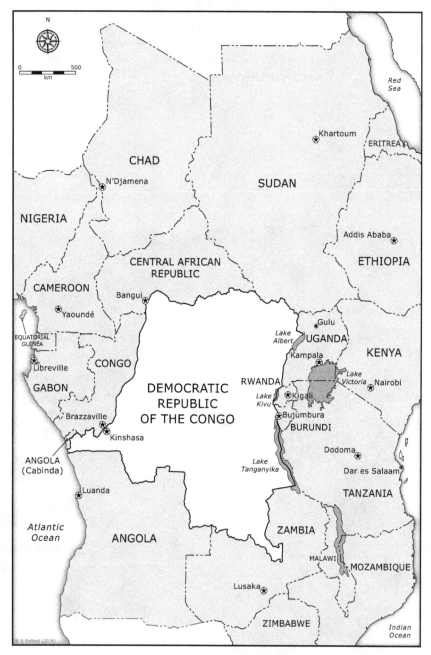

Map 1: Region of Central Africa

Map 2: The Democratic Republic of the Congo

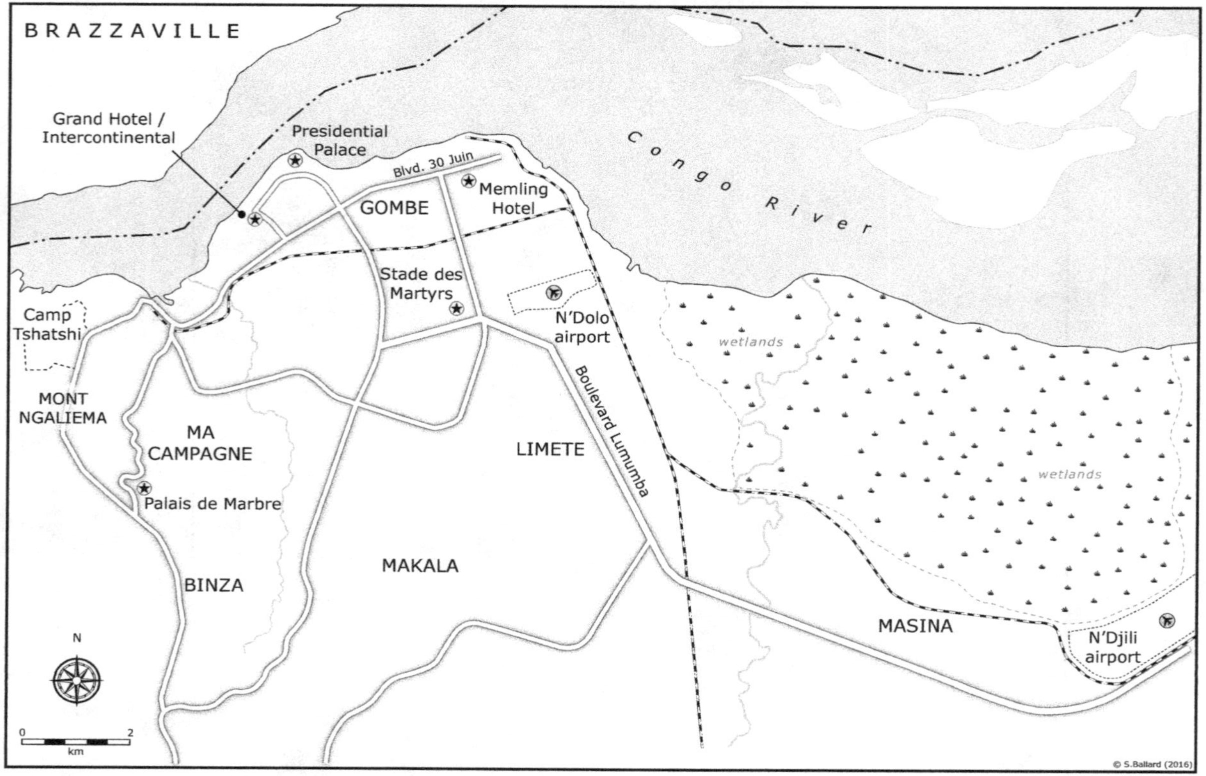

Map 3: Kinshasa and its environs

BRAZZAVILLE

Grand Hotel /
Intercontinental

Presidential
Palace

Blvd. 30 Juin

Memling
Hotel

N'Dolo
airport

GOMBE

Stade des
Martyrs

Boulevard Lumumba

LIMETE

MAKALA

Camp
Tshatshi

MONT
NGALIEMA

MA
CAMPAGNE

Palais de Marbre

BINZA

Congo River

wetlands

wetlands

MASINA

N'Djili
airport

N

km
0   2

© S. Ballard (2016)

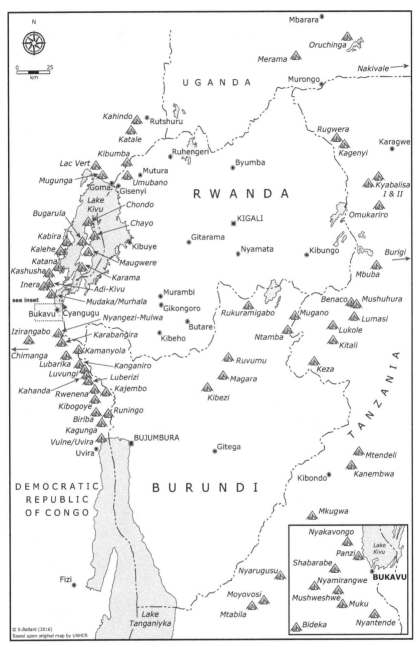

Map 4: Refugee camps surrounding Rwanda in 1995

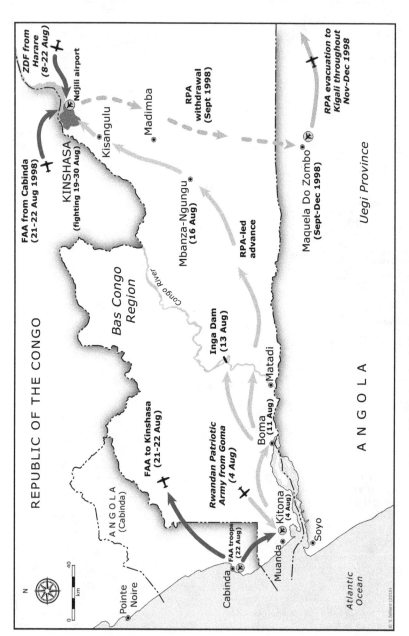

Map 5: The outbreak of Africa's Great War in August 1998

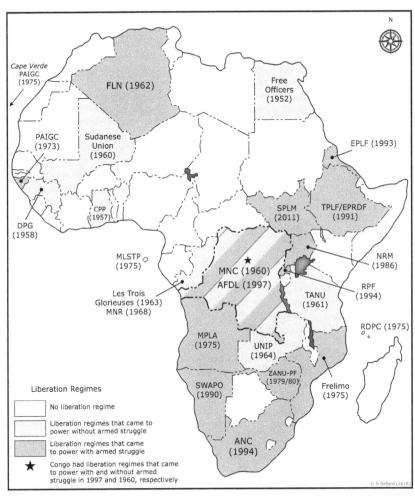

Map 6: Liberation Regimes in Postcolonial Africa

1

INTRODUCTION

The Expulsion Order

Near midnight on Monday, July 27, 1998, less than two days after Laurent-Désiré Kabila, the president of the Democratic Republic of Congo, returned to Kinshasa from a week-long visit to Cuba, a statement was read on Congolese state television:

> The supreme commander of the Congolese national armed forces, the head of state of the Republic of the Congo and the minister of national defense, advises the Congolese people that he has just terminated, with effect from this Monday 27 July 1998, the Rwandan military presence which has assisted us during the period of the country's liberation. Through these military forces, he would like to thank all of the Rwandan people for the solidarity they have demonstrated to date. He would also like to congratulate the democratic Congolese people on their generosity of spirit for having tolerated, provided shelter for and trained these friendly forces during their stay in our country. *This marks the end of the presence of all foreign military forces in the Congo.*[1]

The declaration, which ordered foreign troops to withdraw within forty-eight hours, followed a sudden and secretive decision made by Kabila and only a few of his closest advisers after the Congolese president cut short his visit to Havana and rushed back to Kinshasa. These dramatic developments marked the culmination of months of deepening tensions between two rival forces

---

[1] Emphasis added.

1

who until recently had been sworn allies. On one side was Congo's president, who was affectionately referred to as "Mzee" Kabila[2] by his friends and backed by a redoubtable ethno-political network—the so-called *famille katangaise*. On the other side stood the Congolese Tutsi, and a Kinshasa-based battalion of crack troops of the Rwandan Patriotic Army (RPA) headed by James Kabarebe who, despite his Rwandan citizenship, had doubled as the chief of staff of the Forces Armées Congolaises (FAC) before his dismissal only two weeks earlier. While they remained nominal allies, the relationship between Kabila and Kabarebe had turned poisonous and the two had increasingly heated arguments over restructuring the Congolese army and how to stem the tide of a cross-border insurgency that was infiltrating deeper into Rwanda. But as bad as the situation had become—in which checks for weapons became commonplace even in the Council of Ministers—Kabila's unceremonious decree to expel the very comrades who had carried him to the presidential palace significantly escalated tensions and would light a powder-keg.

The expulsion order represented a remarkable turn of events. Just fifteen months earlier, Kabila anointed himself president after an irresistible military campaign by the Alliance des Forces Démocratiques pour la Libération du Congo-Zaïre (AFDL) overthrew one of Africa's longest running dictatorships, that of Mobutu Sese Seko. In only seven months, the AFDL forces—of which Kabila emerged as the nominal head, but with all military operations orchestrated by James Kabarebe and his RPA deputy Caesar Kayizari— marched more than 1,500 kilometers from Lake Kivu in the east to Kinshasa in the west to end thirty-two years of dictatorship and destabilizing rule. Mobutu was considered the arch-symbol of "Old Africa," a neo-colonial dictator whose legendary appetite for luxury and neo-patrimonial mode of government had turned one of the world's potentially richest countries into one of its very poorest. He had served Western interests for decades, maintaining ties with Apartheid South Africa and operating as a proxy against socialist regimes in the region. To oust the by then cancer-stricken ruler and to give Congo— and Central Africa as a whole—a "second independence," a broad and formidable Pan-Africanist coalition came together in 1996 that was spearheaded by the Rwandan Patriotic Front (RPF) in Kigali, heavily backed by the RPF's closest ally Uganda and under the politico-intellectual patronage of former Tanzanian president Julius Nyerere. Angola, Burundi, Eritrea and Ethiopia also joined the alliance and offered support to a full-scale invasion that

---

[2] Mzee, in Swahili, is a respectful term for elder.

unleashed soaring euphoria as AFDL troops approached Kinshasa. If Nelson Mandela's 1994 election victory had spelled the demise of white supremacist rule in Africa, the liberation of Congo in 1996–7 was supposed to be the death-knell for the neo-colonialism that had cast a long shadow across the region since the assassination of Congo's first liberator, Patrice Lumumba, mere months after the country's independence in 1960.

On Tuesday, July 28, 1998, only hours after the midnight expulsion order was broadcast, James Kabarebe rushed his troops to Kinshasa's N'Djili Airport to leave immediately. The previous day, before the announcement on state television, the former FAC chief of staff had driven with heavily armed guards to the presidential palace, demanding to see Kabila. Congo's president was wary. While Kabila was in Cuba, rumors circulated that Kabarebe was plotting to assassinate the Mzee upon his return by shooting down his plane—an intentionally provocative reference to the events that triggered the Rwandan Genocide in 1994. The RPA commander was determined to set the record straight and try to talk sense into Kabila, but again faced disappointment. Fifteen months after he carried Kabila to power, Kabarebe left the country in disgrace.

Upon his return to Kigali, Kabarebe huddled with his boss, Rwandan Vice-President (and RPF supremo) Paul Kagame, to decide their forces' next steps. As war plans were being finalized, Kabarebe received a desperate call from China. It was Joseph Kabila, Laurent Kabila's son. Kabarebe had appointed Joseph his deputy as head of the Congolese army and the two formed a strong bond. With no military background—save for national service he completed in Tanzania where he grew up—the latter looked up to Kabarebe as a role model, but now Joseph was in China where he had gone for officer training and watched helplessly from afar as his mentor and his father readied for war. The son tried to convince Kabarebe that the alliance and peace could still be salvaged, but to no avail. Kabarebe, who had already decided Joseph's father had crossed the point of no return, hung up the phone. While Kagame instructed his colonels to ready a specialized force for invasion, Kabarebe traveled to northern Uganda to consult with Ugandan President Yoweri Museveni who had also lost all faith in Kabila. Three days later, on August 2, the 10th Brigade of the FAC, the best army unit in Congo and fiercely loyal to Kabarebe, launched a rebellion in the east of the country. Meanwhile, Kabarebe himself commandeered four civilian planes to launch a daring surprise assault on Kitona in western Congo, nearly 2,000 kilometers away on the edge of the Atlantic Ocean, and a gateway to Kinshasa (See Map 5). The offensive forced Kabila to flee to his home region of Katanga and nearly succeeded in capturing Congo's capital but was thwarted at the last minute when Angolan and Zimbabwean aircraft and mechanized troops intervened to halt Kabarebe's forces. The RPF's defeat in the west merely spelled the conclusion of the first chapter of Africa's Great War as anti-Kabila forces continued their advance from the east. Soon the country was nearly divided in half with the Congolese government backed by Angola, Zimbabwe and Namibia holding the western part of the country and Congolese rebels backed by Rwanda, Uganda and Burundi capturing the east and then the north. As the former comrades bitterly fought on the battlefield, the Congolese people suffered immeasurably; millions died from the war and war-related disease and starvation.

* * *

Kabila's expulsion of "all foreign forces" a mere fifteen months after the capture of Kinshasa in May 1997 not only triggered the deadliest war in contemporary African history, but also marked the denouement of the Pan-Africanist project of collective liberation, which had been a central force in the continent's path to independence in the three decades after the end of World War II. In the 1980s and 1990s, the project was rekindled and harnessed by a group of neo-liberation regimes that sought to bring about a "second independence" from neo-colonial forces, of which Mobutu Sese Seko was top of the list.[3] The overthrow of Mobutu was supposed to be one of the greatest triumphs of these neo-liberation forces as they revived the Pan-Africanist project of collective

---

[3] Throughout the book, we refer to both liberation and neo-liberation movements. They are similar in their ideological orientation (leftist to socialist), means of political organization (insurgency or attempts of mass mobilization of excluded or marginalized elements of society), and goals (aim of emancipating the excluded and marginalized and freeing the country from an externally dependent, exclusionary and repressive government). They differ, however, in the type of state which they oppose. Liberation movements operate in and against colonial states or their remnants (e.g., white-minority regimes in South Africa and Southern Rhodesia), whereas neo-liberation regimes operate against "homegrown" governments, but which are perceived to be neo-colonial in character (i.e., authoritarian, repressive, exclusionary and beholden to external or imperial forces). Thus, whereas the AFDL is a neo-liberation movement opposed to the neo-colonial government of Mobutu, the MNC of Patrice Lumumba was a liberation movement opposed to the state of Belgian Congo. When broadly referring to the liberation type of political organization, including both liberation and neo-liberation movements, we simply refer to them as liberation regimes or movements as shorthand.

liberation; yet it ended in its greatest tragedy—a war between comrades. What accounts for this devastating turn in African history? Having fought side-by-side to usher in Congo's second independence, Kabila and his Rwandan brothers had much to gain from forging a lasting partnership. How then can we explain the inability of Rwanda, Angola, Tanzania, Ethiopia, Eritrea and Uganda—the coalition of liberation and neo-liberation regimes that contributed to the overthrow of Mobutu—to craft a new regional order with the Congolese government they installed in power? And, most importantly of all, why did the political fall-out between erstwhile comrades have to lead to a military confrontation that in subsequent years would become the most lethal conflict since the end of World War II, with excess mortality of anywhere between three-and-a-half to six million people?

Africa's Fratricidal War

The return to war in Congo in 1998 represented a heavy blow to the Pan-Africanist dream of a radically different politics on the continent. The downfall of Mobutu had been the capstone of a series of armed rebellions, inspired by Julius Nyerere of Tanzania, that brought leftist revolutionaries to power in Africa: Mozambique (1974), Zimbabwe (1979), Uganda (1986), Ethiopia (1991), Eritrea (1993), Rwanda (1994). The vanquishing of the largest counter-revolutionary threat in the region was, to borrow from that other supposed geopolitical triumph, to be Africa's "end of history" moment—liberation regimes from Asmara to Kinshasa stood virtually uncontested.[4] The hope was that with the AFDL's victory the Pan-Africanist liberation project would be complete, heralding a new domestic politics—a shift away from tribalism and personalist rule to redistribution, state-building and revolutionary democracy[5]—and a new external order marked by regional integration, not endless

---

[4] The one exception was the military-Islamist government in Sudan, which employed mass violence at home to try to hold the Sudan People's Liberation Movement/Army (SPLM/A) at bay, which itself was supported by friendly neo-liberation regimes in Uganda and Eritrea. In turn, Khartoum supported dissident forces in Uganda and Eritrea. By the time of the overthrow of Mobutu, however, the region's neo-liberation regimes had coordinated on a policy to contain the government of Sudan and thwart its expansionist foreign policy.

[5] On revolutionary democracy in Africa, see Patrick Chabal, *Amílcar Cabral: Revolutionary Leadership and People's War*, Cambridge: Cambridge University Press,

proxy wars between revolutionary and counter-revolutionary states. For Africa's liberation movements, internal and external change were mutually dependent: a successful restructuring of domestic affairs would deny forces inside and outside the continent opportunities to destabilize their governments, while a durable regional equilibrium would pave the way for the consolidation of liberation regimes.

It is against this backdrop that one needs to appreciate just how devastating Africa's Great War was from a historical perspective. That the new order was brought down from within by the very liberators who vowed to remake Africa—and indeed had started to do so in their own countries—makes it a double tragedy. This book seeks to account for the implosion of Africa's end of history moment and the calamitous war it would unleash.

We argue that this collapse was no accident but the by-product of a set of internal contradictions and paradoxes that arose from the strategic choices the Leninist-inspired revolutionaries made as they joined forces to liberate Zaire from Mobutu. The protagonists remained largely blind to some of the inherent problems of the liberation project: so much so that an utterly preventable war, in retrospect, struck many scholars as inevitable and overdetermined. Two broad historical forces are often pointed to as the inexorable causes of Africa's Great War. The first posits that Mobutu's Zaire was ripe for violent collapse after the end of the Cold War and that the new government of Laurent-Désiré Kabila subsequently fell prey to a state that had become too weak to govern effectively and vulnerable to the insatiable resource ambitions of regional powers, in particular the RPF. Adherents of an economic theory of Africa's Great War assert that the structure of alliance patterns lends credence to their argument; neighboring states seemed to have joined the side that made it easiest to loot Congo's natural resources. Others root Africa's Great War in the regional cataclysm caused by the Rwandan genocide and its spillover into eastern Zaire, extending the battleground for the war between the RPF and the genocidal forces into Zaire. That Kabila, like Mobutu before him, ended up supporting the *génocidaires*—those who carried out mass killings during the genocide in Rwanda in 1994 and fled to Zaire after the fall of Kigali on July 4, 1994—against the RPF points to the intractability of conflict once it becomes externalized and as dissident forces become ensconced across international borders.

1983; and Patrick Chabal (ed.), *Political Domination in Africa: Reflection on the Limits of Power*, New York: Cambridge University Press, 1986.

Yet what is consistently overlooked in the existing literature is the fratricidal character of Africa's Great War. It is crucial to remember, as the protagonists we interviewed underlined time and again, that the second war was not a conflict between nemeses or distant strangers but a bitter fight between former allies that thwarted their own shared revolutionary ambitions. Kabila's Minister of Information Raphael Ghenda's lament to us in August 2013— *"It was terrible. We began fighting our comrades, brothers"*—was echoed by many of our interlocutors. Revolutionary success presented the slayers of Mobutu with far greater problems than they imagined at the start. Our book proposes that the liberators of Zaire themselves sowed the seeds of destruction in the way they brought about revolutionary change: ignoring the philosophy of Julius Nyerere, the father of Africa's liberation movements, they put the gun before the unglamorous but essential task of building the political forces and organizational structures necessary to safeguard the peace from without but also from within.

The Argument

Why Comrades Go to War argues that the origins of Africa's Great War lay in the struggle against Mobutu—the way the revolution came together, the way it was organized and, paradoxically, the very way it succeeded. While the collapse of the Zairian state and the Rwandan genocide were important antecedents to the Great War, we argue they mattered primarily in the way they shaped the organization and structure of the AFDL. Put differently, if the protagonists in the campaign against Mobutu had organized their revolution and the post-revolutionary order in a different way, Africa's Great War could have been avoided.

* * *

In analyzing the overthrow of Mobutu, we situate it as a *liberation revolution*,[6] which we define as an event in which a political organization, representing excluded or marginalized elements of society and guided by a leftist (often

---

[6] We use the term liberation revolution or liberation regimes as an analytical concept not as a normative evaluation. We are aware that these terms connote multiple political and emotional meanings that may vary over time and differ from the definitions used in this book. To avoid any conceptual confusion about what we mean by these terms, we go to great lengths throughout the book to clearly define and measure them.

anti-imperialist) ideology, captures power through insurgency or popular mobilization with the aim of emancipating the excluded and marginalized and freeing the country from an externally dependent, exclusionary and repressive government. Like other liberation wars in African history, the campaign to displace Mobutu represented both an internal conflict between the incumbent regime and excluded elements of society but also a regional conflict between the reactionary state of Zaire and revolutionary states throughout the region—Rwanda and Uganda most prominently, but Tanzania, Eritrea, Ethiopia and Angola too.[7] We argue that this dual internal–external character is a universal feature of Africa's liberation regimes: it is borne out of the collective Pan-Africanist roots of liberation, which, to paraphrase Kwame Nkrumah, sees no country as free until all of Africa is free.

The collective foundations of liberation, which are at once ideological and strategic, amplified the strength of resistance against European colonialism. But it also had the effect of externalizing the liberation struggle—liberation anywhere on the continent was potentially a threat to colonial regimes everywhere. This leads us to offer a partially revisionist interpretation of Africa's international relations in the twentieth century. The geopolitical environment of post-decolonization Africa was an unforgiving context of rivalry between conservative forces, who defended the international and domestic status-quo, and liberation movements who sought to fundamentally transform domestic political arrangements as well regional relations. The Cold War would exacerbate, but not cause, this polarization. The root cause lay in the fear harbored by reactionary regimes like Mobutu's Zaire and Apartheid South Africa that Pan-Africanist liberation ideology would trigger internal revolution; this led these regimes to pursue both domestic repression and a roll-back strategy vis-à-vis revolutionary states like Ghana, Angola and Mozambique. In turn, fears of the ideological and strategic threat exerted by these reactionary actors led revolutionaries to adopt more violent tactics domestically and, when in power, to export the Pan-Africanist revolution. The key implication of this was that internal conflicts between reactionary and liberation forces became externalized, leading to regionalized civil wars, as both sides would draw on external support—readily forthcoming

---

[7] Similar to our caveat on liberation, we use the term reactionary as an analytical concept not as a normative evaluation. We intend it to connote the existence of a conservative or right-wing government usually aligned with Western powers that opposes political liberalization and social reforms that would undermine its hold on power and strengthen excluded elements of society.

because those intervening feared internal destabilization should the conflict go the wrong way—to try to win the confrontation.

This framework offers a novel lens through which to see the *first* Congo war (1996–7): as a Pan-Africanist coalition of liberation and neo-liberation forces to end once-and-for-all the counter-revolutionary threat posed by one of the relics of the neo-colonial order—the regime of Mobutu Sese Seko. The liberation of Zaire represented the triumph of the revolutionary forces in Central Africa and ushered in a less hostile regional environment for post-liberation consolidation. Our analysis, which posits the centrality in African history of liberation movements and their revolutionary agenda for Africa's international relations, also helps us rethink the outbreak of the second Congo war which had been unthinkable in the minds of the protagonists. The question of why the regional triumph of ousting Mobutu turned into a cataclysmic war between comrades draws our attention to another salient characteristic of liberation movements: their organizational basis.

* * *

We argue the Pan-Africanist coalition that liberated Zaire was, in a sense, a victim of its own success. In dispatching with Mobutu's government in a matter of months, the region's liberation regimes destroyed the dominant counter-revolutionary force in Central Africa, thus ending regional polarization, but in doing the revolutionary heavy-lifting—supplying the force necessary to liberate Zaire—the regional powers, especially the RPF, inhibited the political development and organizational coherence that was the hallmark of their own post-liberation success. The AFDL liberation government lacked the politico-military integration and organizational unity integral to regulating the political uncertainty that arises from the overthrow of the *ancien régime* and the inversion of the power structure that liberation brings about. Moreover, the absence of regional polarization, paradoxically, reduced a major incentive for facilitating intra-regime cooperation and stability—the threat of counter-revolution. While the RPF, National Resistance Movement (NRM), Tanganyika African National Union (TANU)/Chama Cha Mapinduzi (CCM), Tigrayan People's Liberation Front (TPLF), Eritrean People's Liberation Front (EPLF), and Movimento Popular de Libertação de Angola (MPLA) represent some of the strongest politico-military organizations in Africa, explicitly modeled on Leninist structures and principles, the coalition they formed to liberate Zaire was organized principally through informal and personalized channels—with a disproportionate role for an outside power, the

Rwandan Patriotic Front. The organizational structure of the AFDL would prove its fatal flaw.

For the RPF, the informal and asymmetric nature of the revolution was no accident; it was by design. In the face of what Kigali saw as a looming counter-revolutionary threat from the *génocidaires* re-organizing in the refugee camps on its border in 1995 and 1996, the RPF felt it could not afford to spend the time that would be needed to build up the military and organizational capacity of a Congolese force to prosecute the war. Nor was the RPF prepared to delay the intervention in order to formalize the alliance between regional states opposed to Mobutu. The urgency and severity of the threat necessitated the RPF to act decisively to finish off its genocidal enemies and their foreign patron—lest 1994 repeat itself at great cost to its own revolution and millions of Rwandans. But the RPF's militaristic, go-it-alone approach to the liberation of Zaire was also profoundly shaped by its particular worldview and historical experiences, especially the sequential wars it waged in Uganda and Rwanda and the genocide that it fought through to come to power. Its belligerent history predisposed it to military solutions to political problems, and left it deeply mistrustful of outside actors and reluctant to delegate power. The RPF sought to manage the overthrow of Mobutu with its elite troops, while struggling to leverage the presence of a Pan-Africanist team of key political advisers from its own ranks as well as from Eritrea and Ethiopia that was supposed to give the AFDL greater organizational coherence and ideological depth.

The RPF's decision to go it alone in Congo and favor informal, ad hoc means of coordination with other regional states had far-reaching consequences. First, as control and speed were paramount, the RPF sought to streamline the AFDL and minimize the number of Congolese agents it was contracting with; thus despite officially representing a coalition of four different rebel movements, the AFDL would become dominated by a single individual—the RPF's man in Congo—Laurent-Désiré Kabila. Second, in directly participating in the AFDL, it meant that the RPF found itself ensnared in the snake pit of elite politics in a weakly institutionalized regime. Third, it increased the likelihood that any instability within the regime would also be felt regionally and, conversely, regional instability would affect elite bargaining within the Congolese government.

Taken together—the RPF's failure to craft an integrated or formalized regional response to the overthrow of Mobutu and its tolerance of a weakly institutionalized liberation movement, in which it inserted itself—formed an explosive combination. The RPF's privileged place in the post-Mobutu order gave Kigali the capability to quickly and decisively shift the distribution of power within the Kabila regime, but also to alter the regional balance of power, while its secretive nature left other actors in the dark about its intentions. This uncertainty would haunt Kabila—for he always knew that as the RPF put him in power, it could take it away. However, it also alarmed neighboring countries. Fearful of the potential costs to their own relative capabilities, status and influence, this led Zimbabwe, Tanzania and Angola to balance against the RPF in order to minimize such losses.

As we document throughout the book, this internal and external uncertainty reinforced each other. Consequently, as Kabila and the RPF became locked into a security dilemma in which each side saw no way out except eliminating the other, regional states were not neutral bystanders. Angola, facing a resumption of its civil war in 1998, had the biggest stake; its principal fear was that a shift in power in Congo would give its archenemy, União Nacional para a Independência Total de Angola (UNITA), the upper hand. While President Dos Santos had little faith in Laurent-Désiré Kabila as a reliable partner, he did not trust the RPF either due to the emergence of a cold war with the Front that began following the hitherto kept secret Tshikapa incident of April 1997 (Chapter 6). When the RPF and its Congolese allies fell out with Kabila and launched their daring August 1998 raid into Bas Congo, Luanda felt itself forced to choose between cholera and the plague. Ultimately, confronted with the possibility of a rebel and RPF military victory, Angola reluctantly rolled into Kinshasa to repel the invading forces and save the Kabila regime: this would transform the conflict between Kabila and his former patron into the regional cataclysm of Africa's Great War.

Approach

Why Comrades Go to War is not intended as a people's history. It is focused on the winners of the first war and the belligerents of the second: the politico-military elites who intended to liberate Central Africa but ended up plunging it into extraordinary levels of violence. Our book is not about the millions of displaced people or about the excluded masses in Kinshasa or South Kivu; nor is it about the last days of the Mobutists or about the dubious role played by the UN Security Council. It primarily focuses on those who coalesced to form the AFDL and took to the battlefield to fight for a Great Lakes region without Mobutu. We do not claim to provide a full, comprehensive picture of how Africa's Great War was experienced—or what its consequences have been.

Instead, we have taken it as our task to try to explain the complexity and the often contradictory experiences of those former outcasts who rose to the very pinnacle of decision-making in Central Africa.

In placing these transnational elite relationships and interactions at the center of our analysis, *Why Comrades Go to War*, in many ways, represents the antidote to the old adage that all politics is local. In recent years, excellent scholarship on the dynamics of conflict has challenged traditional "big men" or geopolitical accounts of war and reemphasized more parochial sub-national drivers like local ethnic conflict, personal vendettas between villagers, turf wars over grazing pastures or water points and sexual violence. Much of the literature on the Darfur conflict, for instance, while not ignoring elite level politics, underlines the localized nature of the violence,[8] as does the seminal work on insurgency and counterinsurgency of Stathis Kalyvas,[9] and, with particular relevance to Congo, the scholarship of Koen Vlassenroot on ethno-political criminal networks in Ituri and the Kivus,[10] and Séverine Autesserre's analysis of misguided international peace-building efforts.[11] While local dynamics are profoundly important in how violence ultimately plays out and affects the lives of ordinary people, we argue that a grassroots analysis cannot account for the outbreak of Africa's Great War. The tragedy of the conflict is that, in essence, it is the story of the fall-out of only a handful of men; none of the main actors in this story—from Kabila and Dos Santos to Kagame, Kabarebe and Museveni—faced significant popular constraints to their decision-making or ability to marshal lethal coercive power. Both in the political systems they fought and the ones they presided over, power and authority are concentrated at the top among a small group whose members are almost exclusively male. Their ability to work together makes or breaks revolutions, domestically and internationally. And thus, as we show

[8] Julie Flint and Alexander De Waal, *Darfur: A New History of a Long War*, New York: Zed Books 2008.

[9] Stathis N. Kalyvas, *The Logic of Violence in Civil War*, New York: Cambridge University Press, 2006.

[10] Koen Vlassenroot, "Citizenship, Identity Formation & Conflict in South Kivu: The Case of the Banyamulenge," *Review of African Political Economy*, 29, 93 (2002); Koen Vlassenroot and Timothy Raeymaekers, "The Politics of Rebellion and Intervention in Ituri: The Emergence of a New Political Complex?," *African Affairs*, 103, 412 (2004).

[11] Séverine Autesserre, *The Trouble with the Congo: Local Violence and the Failure of International Peacebuilding*, Cambridge: Cambridge University Press, 2010.

throughout the book, when it comes to the outbreak of war, all politics is elite politics, even if in the case of post-Mobutu Congo, these elites were not just Congolese but also Rwandan, Angolan, Ugandan, Tanzanian, Zimbabwean, Ethiopian and Eritrean.

To support our argument about Africa's Great War, we draw on unique first-hand conversations with those protagonists whose fateful decisions between war and peace affected the lives of millions in Congo and beyond. Via hours and hours of interviews with the "comrades" of the Congo Wars we sought to understand their strategic calculus and psychology as well as the personal ties and social relations that connected them to each other. The highly emotional nature of dozens of testimonies about how friends became enemies struck us deeply, pointing to the unmistakable traces these wounds have left in today's regional politics and agendas for domestic state-building. Our interviews revealed how profoundly invested in the dreams of liberation—however illusory these later revealed themselves to be—the comrades were and how these were molded by transnational relationships. As we explain in the appendix (including a long list of the names and affiliations of those interviewed), one of the AFDL's hallmarks was its informal, personalized nature, which hugely influenced the strategic interactions that dominated politics. This book, with its reliance on the voices of those at the center of the liberation project, cannot tell a simple, neutral story: it reflects the subjectivity and acrimony experienced and expressed by the comrades themselves.

The intimacy of the comrades was originally understood by the actors themselves to be a force for peace. Throughout the book, there are many examples of how camaraderie and personal trust provided the fuel for extraordinary cooperation. Perhaps nowhere is this better seen than in the triangular relationship between Laurent-Désiré Kabila, James Kabarebe and Joseph Kabila. After Mzee Kabila lived for nearly a year in Kigali, being fed and clothed by Kabarebe and his aides from the intelligence services, the former two developed an incredible degree of interdependence in which one handled the politics of liberation (which enabled him to become Congo's president) and the other guaranteed the military muscle (making him Central Africa's most famous general). To further lock in this bond, Kabarebe took his ally's son, Joseph, under his wing to mentor him in military affairs, reassuring the Congolese, and especially Mzee Kabila, of the Rwandan's good intentions. In turn, the son would mediate between his father and mentor at times of great stress and, until the very last minute, rejected the notion of having to choose between "Congolese" and "Rwandan" interests, instead insisting on cooperation between revolutionaries. Such personal ties helped to cement the unusual hybrid that was the post-Mobutu order, representing both an ethno-regional coalition of Congolese Tutsi and Katangese and an international coalition of Congolese and Rwandans, with significant input from those in other corners of the continent—the Eritreans of the Horn, the Tanzanians from the Swahili Coast and Angolans from the Atlantic West. However, our research also illustrates the dark side of intimacy: as relationships break down, feelings of betrayal and bitterness dominate and cloud strategic thinking, motivating a desire for vengeance, even at incredible personal risk, such as Kabarebe's daring raid into Bas Congo to get back at Kabila.

Contributions

Why Comrades Go to War builds on outstanding efforts to document and understand our subject by the likes of Fred Halliday, Filip Reyntjens, Christopher Clapham, Rakiya Omaar, Gérard Prunier, Gauthier de Villers, Jean-Claude Willame, Georges Nzongola-Ntalaja, Jason Stearns, and others. The book is explicitly about the why and the how of Africa's Great War, trying to go beyond description and seeking to be more than a simple chronicle of facts. In doing so, it aims to make several contributions to existing scholarship.

First, this book endeavors to re-establish the centrality of liberation ideology, liberation conflicts and liberation movements—in short, liberation politics—to the study of the international relations of Africa. Influential classics tend to focus on the close links between weak statehood, the importance of sovereignty and neo-patrimonialism.[12] While much of Africa's political life is indeed about "the politics of the belly,"[13] "warlord politics,"[14] "the politics of

[12] Robert H. Jackson and Carl G. Rosberg, "Why Africa's Weak States Persist: The Empirical and the Juridical in Statehood," *World Politics*, 35, 1 (1982); Robert H. Jackson, *Quasi-States: Sovereignty, International Relations and the Third World*, Cambridge: Cambridge University Press, 1990; William Reno, *Warlord Politics and African States*, Boulder, CO: Lynne Rienner, 1998; Patrick Chabal and Jean-Pascal Daloz, *Africa Works: Disorder as Political Instrument*, Oxford: James Currey, 1999. Thomas Callaghy, Ronald Kassimir and Robert Latham, *Intervention and Transnationalism in Africa: Global–Local Networks of Power*, New York: Cambridge University Press, 2001; Pierre Englebert, *Africa: Unity, Sovereignty, and Sorrow*, Boulder, CO: Lynne Rienner, 2009; Chabal and Daloz, *Africa Works*.

[13] Jean-François Bayart, *L'etat en Afrique: la politique du ventre*, Paris: Fayard, 1989.

[14] Reno, *Warlord Politics and African States*.

state survival"[15] and the limits imposed by geography and state practice on order creation,[16] we emphasize the importance of the political, ideological and military battle between revolutionary and counter-revolutionary forces. Too often has African international relations been reduced to three key dynamics: first, the obsession with formal sovereignty and the mechanisms by which African elites extract resources—material and discursive—from the global political economy; second, Realpolitik maneuvering around security interests in which African states secure themselves from neighbors sponsoring domestic insurgencies by tit-for-tat reprisals or elite bargains in which incumbents commit to not support each other's enemies; and third, the peculiar nature of the fight against white minority rule in Southern Africa, often analyzed as an exceptional sub-state system because of the racial dimension. Our argument is not so much that these dynamics are incorrect or non-existent, but that they present an impoverished, incomplete picture.

We argue that for lengthy and important parts of modern African history, liberation politics has been utterly central and cannot be subsumed under broader categories of extraversion, the Cold War/the struggle against Apartheid and/or a tautological pursuit of "interests." In that sense, *Why Comrades Go to War* argues that, contrary to the prevailing picture of African states as status-quo players in the international system (given the remarkable absence of inter-state conflict in Africa[17]), an important number of countries—or more pertinently, movements and individuals—have taken both a strongly ideological and strategic view of the continent's international relations and of their own domestic security. They have acted in revisionist ways, believing that the internal consolidation of order was contingent on a transformed regional environment, which, crucially, could not be established by simple elite bargains between older incumbents and newly emergent governments to co-exist: regime change—from "reactionary neo-colonialism" to "Pan-Africanist liberation"—was seen as not merely ideologically desirable, but a necessary condition for survival. In that sense, in accounting for revolutionary change, including the liberation of Zaire, we emphasize the social construction of interests and the entwining of ideology and security—Pan-

---

[15] Christopher Clapham, *Africa and the International System: The Politics of State Survival*, New York: Cambridge University Press, 1996.

[16] Jeffrey Herbst, *States and Power in Africa: Comparative Lessons in Authority and Control*, Princeton, NJ: Princeton University Press, 2000.

[17] Clapham, *Africa and the International System*, pp. 47–50; Herbst, *States and Power in Africa*, pp. 99–106.

Africanism as not merely a set of quasi-unreachable rhetorical ideals, but as an integral component of what liberation movements identify as urgent and actionable in their foreign policies and what trade-offs and options they remain blinded to.

Secondly, our reassessment of Africa's international relations through the development of a new conceptual framework to think about conflict in Africa lead us to challenge the exogeneity assumption that is at the core of some of the literature on revolutions and external conflict.[18] Instead, building from Halliday,[19] we emphasize the importance of unpacking the mutually constitutive effects of the external environment and liberation revolutions. This perspective helps to account for the patterns of regionalized civil war between revolutionary and counter-revolutionary forces that have played out across the continent and led Central Africa's liberation and neo-liberation regimes to come together and oust Mobutu with the hope of consolidating regional peace.

Thirdly, we contribute to the literature on the institutional foundations of regime breakdown and war. This body of scholarship includes classic works such as Samuel Huntington's *Political Order in Changing Societies* (1968) and Theda Skocpol's *States and Social Revolutions* (1979) and a growing recent scholarship on the institutional and organizational sources of regime stability, especially in authoritarian states.[20] While the personalist and informal bases of many African states and political movements has been well documented,[21] important variation has existed across the region, as illuminated in William Reno's systematic exploration of rebel organizations over time and space in Africa.[22] Nowhere is this

---

[18] Stephen M. Walt, *Revolution and War*, Ithaca: Cornell University Press, 1996; Jeff D. Colgan, "Domestic Revolutionary Leaders and International Conflict," *World Politics*, 65, 4 (2013); Jeff D. Colgan and Jessica L.P. Weeks, "Revolution, Personalist Dictatorships, and International Conflict," *International Organization* (2015).

[19] Fred Halliday, *Revolution and World Politics: The Rise and Fall of the Sixth Great Power*, Durham, NC: Duke University Press, 1999.

[20] Jason Brownlee, *Authoritarianism in an Age of Democratization*, New York: Cambridge University Press, 2007; Carles Boix and Milan W. Svolik, "The Foundations of Limited Authoritarian Government: Institutions, Commitment, and Power-Sharing in Dictatorships," *Journal of Politics*, 75, 2 (2013); Steven Levitsky and Lucan Way, "The Durability of Revolutionary Regimes," *Journal of Democracy*, 24, 3 (2013).

[21] Robert H. Jackson and Carl G. Rosberg, *Personal Rule in Black Africa*, Berkeley: University of California Press, 1982; Bayart, *L'etat en Afrique*.

[22] William Reno, *Warfare in Independent Africa*, New York: Cambridge University Press, 2011.

variation better highlighted than in the types of organizations that backed the liberation of Zaire vis-à-vis the type of organizational structure the AFDL became. Thus rather than taking institutions in Africa as given or a certain "type," it is vital to understand and explain the processes driving their development. This represents one of the central goals of this book—to account for the origins and changing character of the revolutionary organization that emerges to dispose of the Mobutu regime. In dissecting the organizational structures of the AFDL, we have not only linked it to the weakness of the Mobutu state but also to the regional strategic environment and the political culture and sociology of its external patron.

Beyond the stabilizing or destabilizing effect of revolutionary organizations, our book also illuminates the effect of regional institutions—or the lack thereof—on internal and external political order after revolution. The role of regional ties has often been understudied in African studies,[23] which is striking given the emphasis much of the conflict literature places on the regionalization of wars on the continent. How the formal and informal linkages between political movements in different countries act as enablers or disablers of state-building projects and visions of regional order is an important theme of the book.

Finally, owing to our hundreds of unique interviews, *Why Comrades Go to War* provides an unprecedentedly detailed account of the rise and fall of the Pan-Africanist coalition against Mobutu. It narrates the extremely violent 1990s in Central Africa from the perspective of the winners of the first war and the belligerents in the second one. The focus is not on the ailing Mobutu regime, the wavering United Nations, the impotent Organization of African Unity or the United States and France, two global powers who loom large in other publications. The book does not aim to provide a "definitive" history of Africa's Great War but rather to explore in great detail the strategic decision-making of the AFDL partners—and the RPF in particular—and to reconstruct, in a theoretically informed manner, a number of key historical junctures. It is thus that we elaborate on and strategically rethink well-known and lesser-

---

[23] For an important exception, see Gilbert M. Khadiagala, *Allies in Adversity: The Frontline States in Southern African Security, 1975–1993*, Athens: Ohio University Press, 1994; Ian Taylor, "Conflict in Central Africa: Clandestine Networks & Regional/Global Configurations," *Review of African Political Economy*, 30, 95 (2003). The onset of the African Union and its more robust collective security regime, however, has motivated a renewed interest in regional institutions. Paul D. Williams, "The Peace and Security Council of the African Union: Evaluating an Embryonic International Institution," *Journal of Modern African Studies*, 47, 4 (2009).

known turning points. These include the "political assassination" of Anselme Masasu Nindaga, Kabila's greatest Congolese rival, in November 1997 (Chapter 7); the political and security implications of the dramatic return to Rwanda of the vast majority of Hutu refugees after the dismantling of the North and South Kivu camps (Chapter 9); and the extraordinary triangular relationship between Kabila, the RPF and the MPLA—already turbulent during the campaign against Mobutu and even more so when in the first days after the outbreak of war in August 1998 both Kabila and Kagame tried to defrost icy relations with Dos Santos to ensure victory (Chapter 11).

This methodology has allowed us to unearth precious new evidence that matters greatly for interpreting the war. We expand on the substantial role played by Eritrea in the coalition to overthrow Mobutu; on the details of how Mzee Kabila was brought out of retirement in Tanzania by RPA special forces to become the AFDL's Congolese face; on the tensions generated by the 1997–8 Northwest Insurgency which returned genocidal violence to Rwanda owing to a major error of judgment by the RPA leadership; and on how Kabila's *famille katangaise* secretly built up a parallel army with the help of Tanzanian officers to replace the key military role played by the RPA after liberation in May 1997. Perhaps most explosively, we provide insights into the relationship between Mzee and the ex-FAR/Interahamwe, the genocidal nemesis of the RPF with whom the Congolese president struck a pact deemed a diabolical *casus belli* by Kagame and Kabarebe. Similarly, we also unveil important evidence on preparations for an anti-Kabila coup d'état by senior Congolese politicians, prior to the July 1998 expulsion and with the help of Rwandan intelligence services. And we show how the seeds of Angola's last-minute intervention to save Kabila's regime from Kabarebe's crack troops were sown in the Rwandan–Angolan cold war that developed during the overthrow of Mobutu.

Plan of the Book

The rest of the book is organized as follows. *Part I: The Argument* is developed in two chapters. Chapter 2, "Liberation, Counter-Revolution and War," offers a theoretical framework to account for patterns of political change and regionalized civil war between revolutionary and counter-revolutionary forces in Africa. The analytical structure crafted in this chapter does not account for Africa's Great War but for the critical events that lead up to it: the Rwandan genocide, the subsequent spillover into Zaire and the origins of the Pan-Africanist coalition that united to overthrow Mobutu. Chapter 2 thus sets up the puzzle of Africa's Great War: if the overthrow of Mobutu marked an "end of history moment" for Africa's neo-liberation regimes—the downfall of the most destabilizing of the neo-colonial relics and the triumph of liberation and neo-liberation forces from Asmara to Kinshasa—why did it all come crashing down?

Chapter 3, "Winning the War, Losing the Peace," lays out the book's central argument. We first address the limitation of existing explanations—war for natural resources, spillover of the Rwandan genocide, anti-foreign resistance and personalization of power. We then develop the building blocks of our argument, which attributes Africa's Great War to the type of revolutionary organization and regional alliance the comrades built to liberate Zaire. In contrast to the strong Leninist political organizations that they built during their own revolutionary struggles, the regional powers, led by the RPF, backed the emergence of a weak, personalized rebel movement heavily dependent on foreign support. This allowed the RPF to maximize its control of the AFDL and pursue its immediate priority of chasing down the *génocidaires* but at the cost of long-term peace. In the absence of strong domestic or regional institutions, the liberators failed to manage the vacuum of power their annihilation of the Mobutu regime brought about. Consequently, despite alignment on the goals of liberating Zaire, the post-Mobutu system would be defined by high levels of internal and external uncertainty among comrades, ending in catastrophic war.

* * *

Part II: The War to End All Wars focuses on the Pan-Africanist alliance that coalesced to overthrow Mobutu. It includes three chapters. In Chapter 4, "The Gathering Storm," we sketch the politico-historical context in which Congo's liberation movement, the AFDL, emerged and the particular circumstances that shaped its character and composition from genesis. We provide background on the nature of the Congolese state, the changing international relations of Africa and the rise to power of the RPF. Importantly, we situate the Congolese experience within the Pan-Africanist liberation project as it was dreamed and godfathered by Julius Nyerere. For the Tanzanian former president and his disciples, the ousting of Mobutu represented the next logical stop in the trajectory of Africa's liberation politics. This was an analysis shared by the RPF whose natural ideological inclinations were supercharged by the security imperative of having the *génocidaires* on Rwanda's doorstep: the Front identified waging war abroad as a precondition for being able to do nation-building at home.

In the subsequent chapter, "Comrades Preparing for War," we analyze the founding of the coalition of revolutionaries to invade Zaire, symbol of "neo-colonial" Africa. We trace the provisions for war by the Pan-Africanist alliance as they helped create a national liberation movement that could transform abstract ideals into a quotidian struggle and political organization. Tasked to front this regime change agenda was Laurent-Désiré Kabila who would develop an extraordinary degree of interdependence with the RPF; their reciprocal relationship would shape the character of the liberation project—and its extraordinarily violent demise—more than any other.

The military operation to unseat Mobutu forms the subject of Chapter 6, "The Campaign." We open with the blistering assault of the Rwandan Patriotic Army on the giant refugee camps outside Goma and Bukavu (See Map 4). Hundreds of thousands were repatriated, but the *génocidaire* hard core escaped into the Congolese rainforest. The failure to eradicate this threat would prove deeply consequential: it meant that the hunt for Interahamwe in Congo competed for Kabarebe's attention with the campaign against Mobutu, leaving little time to focus on the all-important political task of building the AFDL into a true liberation movement. This was further complicated by emerging rivalries inside the AFDL which pitted the Congolese protagonists against each other—notably Kabila versus his fellow Katangese of the Tigres Katangais—but also the RPF against their Angolan comrades of the MPLA. Though the AFDL was a Pan-Africanist affair with military support and political *encadrement* from Eritrea, Ethiopia, Tanzania, Uganda, South Africa and Zambia, the two main providers of hard muscle—Kigali and Luanda—found themselves stumbling into a "race to Kinshasa," when AFDL troops crossed from eastern Congo into western Congo around the border town of Tshikapa. The interdependence between Kabila and the RPF was an arrangement that alienated the MPLA, undercutting the building of regional order that constituted the primary objective of the alliance.

* * *

Part III: From Triumph to Tragedy—The Path to Africa's Great War analyzes the dynamics leading from the great Pan-Africanist victory against Mobutu to the outbreak of Africa's Great War. It represents the heart of the book and covers five chapters. Chapter 7, "The Post-Mobutu Order and Politics after Liberation," tells the story of how the post-Mobutu order was consolidated. Kabila wasted no time in purging the Mobutist elite, circulating a revamped currency and building a new army under the leadership of James Kabarebe to consolidate the partnership with the RPF. However, the commitment problem arose almost instantaneously. Many who had sacrificed during the campaign felt short changed by their limited representation in the new order. None felt more aggrieved than Anselme Masasu Nindaga, who had recruited thousands of *kadogo* fighters (child soldiers) but lost himself in the venal politics of Kinshasa. When Masasu refused to accept the Mzee–RPF duopoly and challenged the president, Kabila moved against him; the arrest of a key comrade transformed the post-liberation atmosphere from euphoria into paranoia almost overnight.

How the surging discontent morphed into full-blown crisis is the focus of Chapter 8, "The Unraveling." The remarkable expression of elite accommodation between Laurent-Désiré Kabila, Army Chief of Staff James Kabarebe and Joseph Kabila, son of the head of state, protégé of Kabarebe and number two in the military hierarchy, began to unravel in early 1998. As the father–president relentlessly sought to increase his political autonomy, he pursued two policies by stealth that inflamed tensions with the RPF: Katangization—the infiltration of the security services and the state bureaucracy by fellow Katangese—and the courting of new allies, not least Tanzania which gave him a bodyguard to replace his Rwandese minders and which sent troops to secretly train a parallel army in Katanga. Relations between the comrades became so poisoned that even Council of Ministers' meetings were preceded by arms searches.

Through the testimonies of civil administrators and security hawks, we demonstrate in Chapter 9, "Back Against the Wall," that the repatriation of nearly a million Rwandans from the camps was not the exorcism Paul Kagame had hoped for, but rather the opposite proved true. The failure to organize screening at the border meant that within months of the return of the refugees the RPF had to confront an insurgency that engulfed the country. With thousands of soldiers deployed in Congo, it could barely stave off the existential menace of the resurgent *génocidaires*. This context informed how the RPF responded to Kabila's Katangization. For Kigali, its shrinking influence in Kinshasa was a disaster, as it came just when Kabarebe needed his authority as chief of staff to send Congolese troops to destroy the resurfaced rear bases of the *génocidaires* in North and South Kivu. The actual divorce was accelerated when intelligence reports began showing the unthinkable was happening: in Kabila's attempts at escaping Kabarebe's embrace, his advisers forged links with the *génocidaires* and supplied them with weapons. This was a point of no return in the security dilemma facing the liberation coalition. Paul Kagame gave the green light to proceed with a regime change strategy in Congo.

The final three weeks before the outbreak of Africa's Great War between comrades are detailed in Chapter 10, "Kabila's Pre-Emptive Strike." We examine "Plan A," a conspiracy involving the RPF, its Ugandan allies and a motley crew of disillusioned Congolese politicians. This coalition of the willing would in August 1998 be recycled into the Rassemblement Congolais pour la Démocratie (RCD) rebellion but was originally meant to dislodge Kabila directly from the presidential palace. However, the de facto coup plot never materialized as the paranoid Congolese president believed the warnings his closest associates were issuing; his expulsion order on July 28 would inevitably trigger war but saved him from a likely death in a sudden strike. While Kabila may have been physically surrounded by his comrades-turned-enemies, his position as head of state enabled him to publicly demand the foreign forces to leave, thus forestalling a coup—if at the cost of triggering Africa's worst war.

The penultimate chapter, "Comrades Go to War," traces the trajectory from the unbearable no-man's-land of waiting for the inevitable to the outbreak of conflict on August 2, 1998, and the ensuing first weeks of fighting. The failure of Joseph Kabila to mediate between his father and James Kabarebe cleared the last obstacle for the bellicose thrust on both sides to take full force. We detail how both Kabila and Kagame sought to obtain the support of the regional bellwether, the MPLA, which fretted over the likelihood of an imminent resumption of the Angolan civil conflict with UNITA. Frantic shuttle diplomacy between Kinshasa, Kigali and Luanda underlined how much the unraveling of the domestic post-liberation order was intimately connected to the reconfiguration of regional order. While Kabarebe launched his audacious air drop in Bas Congo and counted on his intelligence officials to acquire Angola's green light for Rwanda's Blitzkrieg, desperate Kabila emissaries wrote Luanda a blank check. The MPLA waivered for an awfully long time, but ultimately sent its mechanized brigades and air force to the rescue of the beleaguered Mzee. The intervention transformed the initial lightning assault into a protracted war and marked the definitive rupture in the Pan-Africanist coalition that had assembled to overthrow Mobutu and reform Central Africa. Uganda bandwagoned behind Rwanda and the rebels, while Zimbabwe and Namibia joined Congo and Angola; Tanzania, South Africa, Eritrea and Ethiopia remained neutral. Comrades went to war again—but this time they fought each other for four long years.

The conclusion of *Why Comrades Go to War* explores the broader implications of our study. The unraveling of the AFDL happened within the same fifteen-month timeframe that would also see the outbreak of a "war of brothers" between Eritrea and Ethiopia (May 1998) and a violent fall-out between the RPF and Uganda's NRM (August 1999)—on Congolese territory. The fall of Kinshasa in May 1997 marked the last successful violent revolution brought about by liberation movements in Africa (save for the Sudan People's Liberation Movement's (SPLM) partial victory in Sudan). Existing liberation regimes shifted their focus to internal development and a narrow conception of national interest rather than continuing to export revolution and building deep institutional ties with brother countries. Thus, rather than the AFDL triumph ushering in a new era of liberation politics and regional solidarity that would transform Africa, it was in some sense the *Thermidor* of the Pan-Africanist, Nyerere-driven vision of unity and security through regime change campaigns. In the final pages of the book we assess the lasting impact of the liberation project on African politics.

PART I

THE ARGUMENT

2

LIBERATION, COUNTER-REVOLUTION AND WAR

We have done with the battle and we again rededicate ourselves in the struggle to emancipate other countries in Africa, for our independence is meaningless unless it is linked up with the total liberation of Africa.

Kwame Nkrumah, speech upon Ghana's independence, March 6, 1957.

Is it possible that the Congo situation could happen here? It was terrifying. The Congo situation was really frightening for us, we each individually and collectively, we feared what was going to happen in this country ...

Julius Nyerere on the Congo Crisis of the 1960s.[1]

[Nyerere's] hosting with total freedom of action of the majority of communist maquisards who fought in the 1964 rebellion in Zaire, was a permanent threat to Mobutu. In effect, because of the logistical support of Tanzania to them, Zaire suffered numerous aggressions ...

Honoré N'Gbanda, special adviser for security to Mobutu Sese Seko.[2]

---

[1] Cited in Paul Bjerk, *Building a Peaceful Nation: Julius Nyerere and the Establishment of Sovereignty in Tanzania, 1960–1964*, Rochester, NY: University of Rochester Press, 2015, p. 10.

[2] Honoré N'Gbanda Nzambo Ko Atumba, *Ainsi sonne le glas: les derniers jours du Maréchal Mobutu*, Paris: Groupe International d'Edition et de Publication de Presse économique, 1998, p. 33.

27

Forty years after Nkrumah's call for the total liberation of Africa, a Pan-Africanist coalition of Congolese rebels backed by self-styled liberation regimes from Rwanda, Uganda, Angola, Ethiopia, Eritrea and Tanzania blitz-krieged through Congo to overthrow the man who many Africans considered the poster child of neocolonialism. Mobutu Sese Seko was a CIA-backed kleptocrat fêted by successive American and French presidents as he bank-rupted what was potentially one of the richest countries in the world and supported reactionary forces throughout the region, including the anti-communist Angolan rebel leader, Jonas Savimbi, and Rwanda's Hutu chauvinist regime of Juvénal Habyarimana. Regime change in Zaire by a coalition of liberation and neo-liberation regimes—four of which had come to power over the previous eleven years—was a manifestation of the Pan-Africanist ideology championed by Nkrumah. It was also a strategic consequence of the regional polarization that had plagued Central Africa since 1960 when counter-revo-lutionary forces, led by Mobutu, deposed the inaugural prime minister of Congo, Patrice Lumumba. After the ensuing Congo crisis (1960–5) which sucked in neighboring countries as well as the United States, the Soviet Union, Belgium, Cuba and the United Nations, this regional polarization would re-intensify with the seizure of power in Uganda in 1986 by the National Resistance Army/Movement (NRA/M) and the subsequent invasion of Rwanda by the NRA/M's key ally, the Rwandan Patriotic Front (RPF).

In this chapter, we analytically and substantively situate the Alliance des Forces Démocratiques pour la Libération du Congo-Zaïre—the name of the Congolese rebel movement that overthrew Mobutu in May 1997—as a neo-liberation regime.[3] Doing so provides a novel lens to understand the first Congo war and the backdrop of the second Congo war. Like other liberation projects in African history, the violent struggle to displace Mobutu repre-sented both an internal conflict between the incumbent regime and excluded elements of society but also a regional conflict between the reactionary state of Zaire and revolutionary states throughout the region. The central argument we advance is that this dual character is a universal feature of Africa's liberation

---

[3] As explained in the introduction, we use the terms liberation and neo-liberation regimes—defined extensively below—as analytical concepts not as normative evalu-ations. Moreover, in employing these terms, we reflect the way the actors perceive of and express themselves. We are aware that these terms connote multiple political and emotional meanings that may vary over time and differ from the definitions used in this book. To avoid any conceptual confusion about what we mean, we go to great lengths throughout the book to clearly define and measure them.

regimes. It is borne out of the Pan-Africanist roots of liberation, which are at once ideological and strategic. Understanding liberation movements as national-cum-Pan-Africanist forces is critical to explaining patterns of political change and conflict, especially internationalized civil war, in post-World War II Africa.

In doing so, this book highlights the importance of liberation ideology, liberation conflicts and liberation movements to the study of the international relations of Africa. Despite the centrality of liberation processes to African political history, it is surprisingly understudied in the context of interstate relations.[4] We argue that in modern African history, liberation politics has been utterly crucial and cannot just be subsumed under broader categories of extraversion, superpower rivalry during the Cold War and the struggle against Apartheid. Contrary to the prevailing picture of African states as status-quo players in the international system, an important number of countries—or more pertinently, movements and individuals—have taken a strongly ideological view of the continent's international relations and of their own domestic security. They have acted in revisionist ways, believing that the internal consolidation of order was contingent on a transformed regional environment, which, crucially, could not just be established by elite bargains between older incumbents and newly emergent governments to co-exist: regime change—from "reactionary, neo-colonialism" to "Pan-Africanist liberation"—was seen as not merely ideologically desirable but a necessary condition for survival. Whereas liberation movements and ideology are often associated with non-violent resistance, the organizations and experiences analyzed in this book illustrate the pervasiveness and importance of violence to liberation politics in a large number of cases.

Overall, this chapter provides a framework to account for the first Congo war (1996–7) while also offering a unique perspective to understand the Rwandan genocide and its spillover into Zaire (which we extensively analyze in Part II of the book). These events, while often seen as exceptional given the scale of violence and the transnational consequences, very much fit a pattern of revolutionary and counter-revolutionary contests that have defined post-independence Africa. To be clear, however, the argument developed in this chapter does not account for Africa's Great War which broke out in August 1998. Quite the opposite: the first Congo war should have been the war to

---

[4] Exceptions include: Khadiagala, *Allies in Adversity*; Clapham, *Africa and the International System*.

end all wars—exactly as the protagonists saw it. In destroying the last remaining counter-revolutionary threat in Central Africa and bringing to power another neo-liberation regime in the region, the protagonists thought they had ushered in a new era of peace and regional integration. Thus while not explaining the second Congo war, the framework developed here underscores how utterly tragic and devastating Africa's Great War would be: it would be fought among comrades on the heels of what many saw as one of their greatest triumphs—the collective defeat of the final counter-revolutionary regime in the region and the emergence of a neo-liberation bloc from Asmara to Kinshasa. Chapter 3 is devoted to accounting for the great collapse of this neo-liberation peace. But we first provide a theory of liberation, political change and war that accounts for a number of important conflicts in African history, including the war to overthrow the Mobutu regime.

The Liberation Struggle in African History

One of the driving forces in African history has been the dialectic of conquest and liberation. From slave revolts, such as that led by "King" Amador in 1595 on the sugar plantations of São Tomé, to break free of the crushing practices of slavery,[5] to nationalist uprisings, including the Islamo-nationalist rebellion led by Muhammad Ahmad (who proclaimed himself the Mahdi) against the Turco-Egyptian rule of Sudan in the 1880s, to resistance against foreign corporations' ruthless pursuit of mineral riches, such as the Ndebele war in 1893 against the Maxim gun-wielding British South African Company, the struggle for freedom in opposition to European imperialist forces and the trinity of racial subjugation, economic exploitation and political overrule has shaped African history.

The Scramble for Africa and the onset of formal colonialism at the end of the nineteenth century—save for in Liberia and Ethiopia, the latter of which famously defeated Italy[6]—marked the peak of imperial conquest.[7] Colonialism not only entailed the political and economic domination of African societies by outsiders, some of which resembled the worst of the practices of the slave

---

[5] Emmanuel Kwaku Akyeampong and Henry Louis Gates, *Dictionary of African Biography*, vol. 1, New York: Oxford University Press, 2012.

[6] Raymond Anthony Jonas, *The Battle of Adwa: African Victory in the Age of Empire*, Cambridge, MA: Belknap Press of Harvard University Press, 2011.

[7] Thomas Pakenham, *The Scramble for Africa*, New York: Random House, 1991.

trade (see our discussion of Congo Free State in Chapter 4), but it also led to the psychological subjugation of the colonized as they were coerced and socialized to believe in their inferiority to their white colonial masters.[8] The consolidation of imperialist control over Africa, however, would provoke a new form of resistance that demanded the total liberation of the continent and a restructuring of the international system to destroy the underlying conditions that gave rise to imperialism. At the vanguard of this revolutionary change was the liberation movement—a political organization that sought to rally the colonized masses to break free of the physical and psychological prisons that trapped them as well as possessing the material and ideological capabilities to take on (neo-)colonialism.

Pan-Africanism

The rise of liberation activism in Africa formed part of a broader global movement, known as Pan-Africanism, that emerged in the early twentieth century. Spearheaded by black intellectuals, such as the Trinidadian lawyer, Henry Sylvester-Williams, American academic W.E.B. DuBois, Jamaican publicist Marcus Garvey, Trinidadian George Padmore and later by Ghanaian President Kwame Nkrumah and Franco-Caribbean philosopher Frantz Fanon, Pan-Africanism is an ideology that seeks to end both the physical and mental enslavement of people of African descent around the world and of all people living on the African continent—regardless of their skin color, creed or ethnicity. It stresses ideas of self-reliance on an individual level—"none but ourselves can free our minds," in the words of Bob Marley, another Pan-Africanist icon—and for African societies in general, which need to change the way they relate politically, culturally, socially and economically to each other and to the rest of the world. The corollary of looking for liberation from within is all-out outward resistance against the pugnacious trinity of imperialism, colonialism and racism.[9]

In 1900, Sylvester-Williams organized the first Pan-African Conference in London, in which speakers from Africa, the Caribbean, the United States and

---

[8] Frantz Fanon, *Black Skin, White Masks*, New York: Grove, 1967. For insightful analyses of Fanon on this process of dehumanization, see Hussein Abdilahi Bulhan, *Frantz Fanon and the Psychology of Oppression*, New York: Plenum Press, 1985. Pramod K. Nayar, *Frantz Fanon*, London: Routledge, 2013.

[9] Tajudeen Abdul-Raheem (ed.), *Pan-Africanism: Politics, Economy, and Social Change in the Twenty-First Century*, London: Pluto Press, 1996.

the United Kingdom called for increased consciousness, solidarity and organization among those of African descent in order to "improve the condition of their race, to assert their rights and organize so that they might take an equal place among nations."[10] In his speech, W.E.B. DuBois declared "the problem of the twentieth century is the problem of the color line" and called "for the British nation, the first modern champion of Negro freedom ... [to] give as soon as practicable, the rights of responsible government to the black colonies of Africa and the West Indies."[11] Seven subsequent meetings would be held in the form of the Pan-African Congress (Paris 1919; London 1921 and 1923; New York 1927; Manchester 1945; Dar es Salaam 1974; and Kampala 1994). The 1945 conference in Manchester, organized by Nkrumah and Padmore and attended by future independence leaders, Jomo Kenyatta (Kenya), Nnamdi Azikiwe (Nigeria) and Hastings Banda (Malawi), would prove particularly influential as, coming on the heels of World War II, it galvanized African nationalism.[12] It also marked a significant change in the strategy of the Pan-Africanists: there was a growing recognition that independence would not be won through appeals in the metropole but by shifting the battlefront to African soil and mass action against the colonial state.[13]

Ideologically and organizationally, Pan-Africanism and the Pan-Africanist movement instilled in African nationalists the importance of the *collective* foundations of liberation. Transnational solidarity was required to defeat the forces of imperialism and racism but also because the total liberation of Africa was seen as necessary to guarantee the independence of each country.[14] Liberation as a collective struggle motivated African freedom fighters across colonies to share techniques, gain inspiration and solicit material support in

---

[10] This call for solidarity was made in the opening address, entitled "The Trials and Tribulations of the Coloured Race in America," by Bishop Alexander Walters, leader of the African Methodist Episcopal Church in the United States. Cited in Peter Fryer, *Staying Power: The History of Black People in Britain*, London: Pluto Press, 1984, p. 283.

[11] W.E.B. DuBois, "To the Nations of the World," in David L. Lewis (ed.), *W.E.B. DuBois: A Reader*, New York: H. Holt, 1995.

[12] Hakim Adi, Marika Sherwood and George Padmore, *The 1945 Manchester Pan-African Congress Revisited*, 3rd edn, London: New Beacon Books, 1995.

[13] P. Olisanwuche Esedebe, *Pan-Africanism: The Idea and Movement, 1776–1991*, 2nd edn, Washington, DC: Howard University, 1994, Chapter 4, "The Manchester Congress and Its Aftermath."

[14] Kwame Nkrumah, *Africa Must Unite*, London: Heinemann, 1963.

their individual revolutions.[15] The collective foundations of liberation also influenced the way the African states organized the Organization for African Unity and their foreign policies to help those countries that remained under colonial or white settler rule.[16] As we discuss below, this ideological principle would have significant strategic consequences and contribute to the regionalization of the liberation struggle and the counter-revolutionary response.

Socialism

If Pan-Africanism reminded Africans that foreign dominance need not be their destiny, the Russian Revolution and the ascendancy of socialism offered an analytical framework with which to understand and deconstruct imperial rule. With colonialism part and parcel of the global capitalist system, Lenin's critique of imperialism had a powerful impact on African liberators and the political ideology they advanced.[17] Independence required not just self-rule but a transformation of the global economy. This principle reinforced the ideology advanced by Pan-Africanists who were critical of capitalism and the forced integration of African resources into international circuits of capital.[18] For many African intellectuals, socialist thought, and the importance of communal ownership of the means of production and distribution and power in the hands of the people, resonated with the "humanist and egalitarian spirit which characterized African traditional society."[19] Nkrumah, Senegal's Léopold Senghor and Tanzania's Julius Nyerere all connected socialism with African philosophical understandings of communalism, even if these manifested themselves in different national policies and institutions.[20]

[15] Sabelo J. Ndlovu-Gatsheni, "Pan-Africanism and the International System," in Timothy Murithi (ed.), *Handbook of Africa's International Relations*, London: Routledge, 2014.

[16] I. William Zartman, "Africa as a Subordinate State System in International Relations," *International Organization*, 21, 3 (1967).

[17] On the influence of Marx and Lenin on Nkrumah, see Guy Martin, *African Political Thought*, Basingstoke: Palgrave Macmillan, 2009, pp. 88–90.

[18] Walter Rodney, "How Europe Underdeveloped Africa," in Paula S. Rothenberg (ed.), *Beyond Borders: Thinking Critically about Global Issues*, New York: Worth Publishers, 1972.

[19] Kwame Nkrumah, *Handbook of Revolutionary Warfare: A Guide to the Armed Phase of the African Revolution*, New York: International Publishers, 1969, pp. 28–9. Cited in Martin, *African Political Thought*, pp. 88–9.

[20] For an excellent analysis of African understandings of socialism as distinct from

The socialist-bent of Africa's liberation movements was deeply consequential. First, it structured the types of international alliances the liberation movements forged; naturally, many gravitated to and solicited support from the Soviet Union, but also from other socialist regimes, such as Cuba and China. Second, it would influence the economic policies liberation leaders would adopt, such as Nasser's nationalization of the Suez Canal, Nyerere's program of Ujamaa (socialism in Swahili) and Nkrumah's economic lifeline to Guinea after its citizens voted in 1958 against joining the "neo-colonial" *Communauté française* (the French Community that granted France's overseas colonies and territories self-government but only as member states in a French federation). Third, it shaped liberation movements' organizational structures; "organized, militant, mass action" was seen as the blueprint to overthrow colonial governments.[21] To Nkrumah, "the necessity for well-organized, firmly-knit movements as a primary condition for the success of the national liberation struggle" became one of the most important lessons he drew from the Marxist–Leninist model—as stressed upon other Pan-Africanists at the 1945 Pan-African Congress in Manchester.[22]

Nationalism, Mass Political Organization and the Armed Struggle

"The organization of the masses" as a path to liberation[23] directly challenged colonial rule in another fundamental way: it entailed daring to overcome the "containerization" of African societies along ethnic lines.[24] Colonial administrators perfected the art of divide and rule to suppress nationalism and prevent revolutionary change. One of the key policies was indirect rule—the

---

Marxism as well as its bearing on liberation philosophy, see Richard H. Bell, *Understanding African Philosophy: A Cross-Cultural Approach to Classical and Contemporary Issues in Africa*, New York: Routledge, 2002.

[21] Immanuel Maurice Wallerstein, *Africa: The Politics of Independence and Unity*, Lincoln, NE: University of Nebraska Press, 2005, p. 9.

[22] Nkrumah, *Africa Must Unite*, p. 134.

[23] At the 1945 Pan-African Congress, Nkrumah introduced a resolution that would become adopted in the Congress's "Declaration to the Colonial Peoples of the World," stating: "Today, there is only one road to effective action—the organization of the masses." Nkrumah, *Towards Colonial Freedom: Africa in the Struggle against World Imperialism*, London: Heinemann, 1962.

[24] Mahmood Mamdani, *Citizen and Subject: Contemporary Africa and the Legacy of Late Colonialism*, Princeton: Princeton University Press, 1996.

empowerment of traditional authorities to police and control ethnic homelands. Africa's liberators recognized that the path to political independence
required building national organizations that bridged societal divisions.
One of the early adopters of a mass political organization was the African
National Congress (ANC, originally known as the South African Native
National Congress), founded in 1912. Its leaders underlined the need for
unity in the face of tribal divisions:

The demon of racialism, the aberrations of the Xosa–Fingo feud, the animosity that
exists between the Zulus and the Tongas, between the Basutos and every other
Native must be buried and forgotten; it has shed among us sufficient blood! We are
one people. These divisions, these jealousies, are the cause of all our woes ...[25]

Other liberation movements sought to build on the ANC's struggle.
Nkrumah founded the Convention People's Party (CPP) in 1949 to push for
the independence of the Gold Coast (renamed the Republic of Ghana after
1957). The CPP drew support from trade unionists, teachers, petty traders,
bureaucrats and the youth, and organized a series of strikes, boycotts and protests, what Nkrumah described as "Positive Action," based on the principle of
non-violence, to demand "Self-Government Now."[26] Whereas non-violent
resistance proved effective in the Gold Coast,[27] in South Africa it was met
with mass repression. This led the ANC to switch tactics and launch its military wing, Umkhonto we Sizwe.[28] As Nelson Mandela explained in the famous

[25] Pixley ka Isaka Seme, "Native Union," October 24, 1911. Available at http://www.
sahistory.org.za/archive/native-union-article-pixley-ka-isaka-seme-october-24-1911

[26] Kwame Nkrumah, *Ghana: The Autobiography of Kwame Nkrumah*, New York:
Nelson, 1957.

[27] Increasing mass resistance in the late 1940s, culminating in Nkrumah's "Positive
Action" campaign, launched on January 1, 1950, led the colonial government to
employ both repressive and accommodative actions to try to manage political dis-
sent and avoid a revolution. Nkrumah was arrested and a state of emergency was
ordered, but a new constitution was also adopted which permitted the first legislative election under universal suffrage in 1951. Nkrumah's CPP won nearly 90 per
cent of the elected seats, but its leader remained in prison. The CPP refused to cooperate unless Nkrumah was released. The newly appointed British governor-general,
Charles Arden-Clarke, chose to make an implicit pact with Nkrumah for the sake
of stability. Charles Arden-Clarke, "Eight Years of Transition in Ghana," *African
Affairs*, 57, 226 (1958).

[28] Meaning "The Spear of the Nation"—the "simple weapon [with which] Africans
had resisted the incursions of whites for centuries," in the words of Mandela—this

1963–4 Rivonia Trial, in which he and other leaders of the ANC were charged with acts of sabotage and conspiracy against the South African state, it was "unrealistic and wrong for African leaders to continue preaching peace and non-violence at a time when the government met our peaceful demands with force ... [the Apartheid] government had left us with no other choice."[29]

Other liberation movements, such as the Front de Libération Nationale (FLN) in Algeria, had already turned to armed struggle to confront colonial states. The Algerian conflict, which we discuss further below, would have particular resonance throughout the region given the intensity with which it was fought. Contributing to the influence of the revolution beyond Algeria were the writings of Frantz Fanon, the Martinique-born psychiatrist and revolutionary thinker, who lived and worked in Algeria, where he joined the FLN the mid-1950s. Few Pan-Africanists had as much influence on elevating the armed struggle to a central place in the liberation project as Fanon. In *Les Damnés de la Terre* (The Wretched of the Earth), published in 1961, Fanon argued that liberation from foreign rule was impossible without the use of violence to forcefully break free from the institutional and psychological constraints imposed by colonialism.[30] Peaceful or negotiated decolonization, he argued, merely sets the stage for neo-colonialism by the national bourgeoisie, which seeks to retain colonial institutions in order to enjoy the social and economic benefits for themselves; such a system simply reproduces the alienation of the masses. Thus, according to Fanon, a war of liberation is necessary to completely destroy the institutions of colonialism, including the divisive effects of tribalism, and forge a new nation—introducing "into each man's consciousness the ideas of a common cause, of a national destiny, and of a collective history" that contribute to national development after liberation.[31] Beyond its collective effects, "[a]t the level of individuals, violence is a cleansing force. It frees the native from his inferiority complex and from his despair and inaction; it makes him fearless and restores his self-respect."[32]

---

name is emblematic of the continuity that modern liberators saw between their struggle and that of those before them. Nelson Mandela, *Long Walk to Freedom: The Autobiography of Nelson Mandela*, Boston: Little, Brown, 1994.

[29] Nelson Mandela, *No Easy Walk to Freedom: Articles, Speeches and Trial Addresses of Nelson Mandela*, London: Heinemann Educational, 1973, p. 169.

[30] Frantz Fanon, *Les damnés de la terre*, Paris: F. Maspéro, 1961.

[31] Frantz Fanon, *The Wretched of the Earth*, trans. Richard Philcox, New York: Grove Press, 2004 (1963), p. 51.

[32] Ibid.

Fanon's call for armed struggle was most likely to be taken up in colonies with large settler populations, which adopted a hard line against any accommodation of African nationalist movements, as was the case in Algeria and South Africa. In the face of harsh repression, peaceful resistance was deemed non-viable. Instead, these movements, including the Movimento Popular de Libertação de Angola (MPLA), Partido Africano da Independência da Guinée Cabo Verde (PAIGC), Frente de Libertação de Moçambique (FRELIMO), Zimbabwe African People's Union (ZAPU), Zimbabwe African National Union (ZANU) and South West Africa People's Organization (SWAPO), turned to guerrilla warfare and looked to the Soviet Union and China, champions of anti-imperialist movements, for support. The Chinese Communist Party was happy to promote the view that African liberation movements used "Mao Zedong Thought as their primary ideological tool for liberation and revolution,"[33] but it was the Soviet Union which offered the most extensive training and military support for a number of anti-colonial insurgencies, including FRELIMO, ZAPU, SWAPO and the MPLA.[34]

Continuity and Change: From Liberation to Neo-Liberation Movements

In harnessing Pan-Africanism, socialist ideas and strategies of popular mobilization, liberation movements spearheaded anti-colonial resistance in Africa. As we discuss below, decolonization would not be achieved exclusively by liberation movements, but those advocating liberation would exert a powerful influence both domestically and across the region in promoting ideas of Pan-Africanism, socialism and violent struggle. The staggered nature of decolonization helped ensure that these ideas, structures and strategies of political mobilization remained at the forefront of African political thought and practice throughout the 1960s and 1970s. In the 1970s—the peak of violent liberation movements against settler colonies—the Pan-Africanist liberation project would also be adopted by a subsequent generation of dissidents who felt their countries needed a second independence from the national bourgeoisie that Fanon warned about and that continued the extractive, repressive

---

[33] Marcus Power, Giles Mohan and May Tan-Mullins, *China's Resource Diplomacy in Africa: Powering Development?*, New York, NY: Palgrave Macmillan, 2012, p. 37.

[34] Vladimir Shubin, "Unsung Heroes: The Soviet Military and the Liberation of Southern Africa," in Sue Onslow (ed.), *Cold War in Southern Africa: White Power, Black Liberation*, London: Routledge, 2009.

and exclusionary practices of their colonial predecessors.[35] Pitted against these "neo-colonial" rulers, most of whom received extensive external support, regime dissidents saw little alternative than to compel political change through armed struggle. In doing so, they modeled themselves after liberation movements. A paradigmatic example of this is seen through the educational and political experience of Yoweri Kaguta Museveni, the future leader of Uganda and a central figure in this book.

Museveni went to the University of Dar es Salaam in the late 1960s where he was taught by the Marxist and Pan-Africanist thinker, Walter Rodney; voraciously read and debated the works of Fanon; and interacted with fellow budding revolutionaries in a student group Museveni helped to found— University Students' African Revolutionary Front (USARF).[36] Among others, the group included John Garang, future head of the Sudan People's Liberation Army/Movement (SPLA/M), as well as Eriya Kategaya, the future number two of Museveni's rebel movement, NRA/M, and Ugandan foreign minister at the time of the Congo Wars in the 1990s. The members of USARF identified closely with the Mozambican liberation movement, FRELIMO, which was founded in Dar es Salaam in 1962 and maintained its headquarters there under the patronage of Julius Nyerere. In 1968, Museveni and six other members of USARF traveled to FRELIMO's liberated zones in northern Mozambique to learn the nuts and bolts of revolutionary action. Upon his return to Dar es Salaam, Museveni wrote a thesis applying Fanon's theory of revolutionary violence to the case of FRELIMO and Mozambique.[37]

After he graduated, Museveni returned to Uganda to serve with the government. But following Idi Amin's coup in 1971, he fled to Tanzania where he worked with other exiles to oppose the new regime. Over the next fifteen years, Museveni sought to put into practice the lessons he learned from FRELIMO and to lead his own revolutionary movements—first in the form of the Front for National Salvation (FRONASA) and then the more success-

[35] Christopher Clapham, "Introduction: Analysing African Insurgencies," in Christopher Clapham (ed.), *African Guerrillas*, Oxford: James Currey, 1998.

[36] Yoweri Museveni, *Sowing the Mustard Seed: The Struggle for Freedom and Democracy in Uganda*, London: Macmillan, 1997.

[37] Yoweri Museveni, "Fanon's Theory on Violence: Its Verification in Liberated Mozambique," in Nathan M. Shamuyarira (ed.), *Essays on the Liberation of Southern Africa*, Dar es Salaam: Tanzania Publishing House, 1975.

ful National Resistance Army/Movement—against successive Ugandan governments that were just as oppressive and exclusionary as their colonial predecessors. William Reno conceives of Museveni's NRA/M insurgents as "reform rebels," who apply the ideas, practices and techniques of anti-colonial liberation movements to not only liberate their countries from internal colonialism but to transform the state through political and economic reforms with the "recognition that independence alone was not enough to build strong African countries."[38] Crucially, for Museveni, there was no contradiction between the de-ethnicized nationalism the NRA/M espoused and a commitment to continent-wide change: deeply influenced by the Pan-Africanist teachings at Dar es Salaam and the example of Nyerere (see Chapter 4 for an in-depth historical analysis), neo-colonialism in Uganda and elsewhere needed to be combated with the same solidarity between Africans as against white colonial overrule. As for Nkrumah and Nyerere, the ultimate goal was an evisceration of arbitrary borders to give Africa the global autonomy and voice it deserved. Because of these direct ideological and organizational linkages between Africa's independence movements and new revolutionary groups like Museveni's NRM, we conceive of the latter as "neo-liberation movements." As we discuss next, these share all of the same properties of liberation movements, except that they are in opposition to an indigenous elite rather than a foreign one.

Liberation: A Conceptual Framework

To recapitulate briefly: one of the most significant developments in twentieth-century African history was the emergence of the liberation movement which, as an ideological force, was a product of three historical undercurrents—Pan-Africanism, socialism and anti-imperialism (Marxism–Leninism), and nationalism. Liberation movements fought for a complete transformation of the political and economic system to permanently destroy the monopoly of power exerted by the colonial state and their neo-colonial successors; independence could not just be a transfer of sovereignty from white hands to black hands. In this section we develop a conceptual framework to identify the core features of liberation and neo-liberation regimes with an eye toward distinguishing the regime type from other revolutionary organizations.

[38] Reno, *Warfare in Independent Africa*, p. 7.

Defining and Measuring Liberation Regimes

We define liberation governments as any political organization representing excluded or marginalized elements of society and guided (at least initially) by a leftist (and often an anti-imperialist) ideology that captures power through insurgency or other forms of popular mobilization with the aim of emancipating the excluded and marginalized and freeing the country from an externally dependent, exclusionary and repressive government. In other words, liberation entails the inversion of societal power, in which the excluded seize control of the state, and motivated by a socialist ideology, promise to build a more inclusive, representative and autonomous political regime. As explained already, liberation movements may arise in opposition to colonial or indigenous regimes; in the case of the latter, we refer to them as neo-liberation regimes.

Liberation is a subset of regime change, which includes a broad set of processes (e.g., coups, mass uprisings, rebellions, assassinations, negotiated transitions and foreign invasions) in which incumbent, usually non-democratic regimes are forced to relinquish power. Most liberation transitions are revolutionary (though not all), in that, in Huntington's pithy phrase, they unleash an "explosion of political participation" and upend "the dominant values and myths of a society, in its political institutions, social structure, leadership, and government activity and policies."[39] Skocpol defines revolutions as a fundamental change in the way the state is organized, through political upheaval and class conflict—on the one hand, a change in the means by which social inequality is structured and, on the other, in the ways the new social structures are legitimated.[40] Jack Goldstone identifies three key elements that are fundamental to revolutions: (1) a direct challenge to the political institutions and the justifications for political authority in a society; (2) which is brought about by formal or informal mass mobilization; and (3) this mobilization involves non-institutionalized actions (such as mass demonstrations, protests, strikes or violence) that undermine existing authorities.[41]

Liberation revolutions can be distinguished from other types of revolutions in that: (1) they are rooted in social exclusion and represent the revolt of the

---

[39] Samuel P. Huntington, *Political Order in Changing Societies*, New Haven, CT: Yale University Press, 1968.

[40] Theda Skocpol, *States and Social Revolutions: A Comparative Analysis of France, Russia, and China*, Cambridge: Cambridge University Press, 1979, pp. 4–5.

[41] Jack A. Goldstone, "Toward a Fourth Generation of Revolutionary Theory," *Annual Review of Political Science*, 4 (2001).

excluded; (2) the liberators link this social exclusion to the incumbent government's embeddedness in the global system of imperialism or neo-colonialism and see a socialist ideology as the appropriate justification for their political activities; and (3) the hegemonic nature of the *ancien régime* necessitates that any liberation movement's struggle must entail a minimum level of popular mobilization that is not merely spontaneous but politically organized, often in the form of a Leninist-style vanguard party. Thus, while liberation revolutions resonate with Skocpol's definition of social revolutions—"rapid, basic transformations of a society's state and class structures ... accompanied and in part carried through by class-based revolts from below"[42]—they differ in that they require an organizational foundation and that social exclusion needs not purely be class based. The racial nature of colonial oppression and ethnopolitical inequalities of post-independence Africa often meant that class stratification and identity coincided, but not completely.

Following from our definition, we measure liberation governments based on the following indicators.

- *Regime change*: first and foremost, we narrow our focus to liberation governments—those that have actually captured the central government through a process of regime change (including decolonization), in which the incumbent government is forced to relinquish power and hand it over directly (i.e., concede defeat and flee the capital) or indirectly (i.e., accept political changes that empower the opposition, such as through a democratic transition).

- *The revolt of the excluded against reactionary or conservative regimes*: liberation movements arise in opposition to a particular kind of authoritarian regime, one that relies on extractive economic policies to enrich a narrow elite and employs formal or de facto policies of social exclusion to uphold minority rule. We define these authoritarian regimes analytically as conservative or reactionary—in that the ruling oligarchy seeks to preserve the status quo and prevent (often at all costs) a shift in the distribution of power that will allow the marginalized to redistribute wealth and potentially exact revenge for the incumbent's exploitative and repressive policies of exclusion. Whereas reactionary regimes attempt to maintain the status quo, the liberation forces aim to eliminate the exclusionary practices that are the basis of the incumbent regime. Consequently, the marginalized population represents a key support base of the liberation movement (even if they themselves are represented by an elite).

[42] Skocpol, *States and Social Revolutions*.

- *Liberation ideology*: the hegemony of reactionary regimes is rooted in their monopoly control of the state and its levers of coercion. But it also stems from these regimes' links to broader international forces, which its critics conceive as imperial or neo-colonial. One of the central tenets that liberation ideology advances is that internal change alone is not a sufficient condition for independence. Thus liberation states are fundamentally revisionist: they posit that unless the international system changes, independence will remain elusive. The emergence of colonialism as an outgrowth of international capitalist forces led excluded elements to adopt Marxism–Leninism and other anti-imperialist and leftist ideologies as appropriate frameworks to deconstruct reactionary regimes and as a template for a new domestic and international order free from social exclusion and exploitation.
- *Insurgency or popular mobilization*: in claiming to represent the oppressed and to emancipate them from the prevailing government, liberation movements must have a degree of popular support, or at least be effective at mobilizing outside the extant power structure. They rarely come to power through coups d'état or are led by regime insiders.
- *Politically organized*: liberation regimes are rooted in a political organization, often based on Leninist principles of democratic centralism and a complex cell structure, with a clear revolutionary program intended to overthrow the incumbent government. Thus they are distinguished from mass uprisings that also aim to sweep aside oppressive regimes.

Classifying Liberation Governments in Post-Colonial Africa

Table 2.1 reports the application of our coding scheme to all incidences of regime change in Africa from independence to the present. In categorizing governments as liberation regimes, we focus on the presence of these key indicators at the time of the liberation movement's seizure of power. Thus, for example, though they may act only rarely on their liberation ideology, as long as they have formulated one that its leadership and followers believe, this is a criterion for inclusion. We also distinguish between those liberation regimes that come to power through armed struggle or insurgency and those that come to power through more peaceful means. Overall, we code twenty-five liberation regimes. Map 6 at the beginning of the book details the distribution of these liberation regimes in Africa.

A systematic analysis of liberation movements points to three primary groups or classes. The first group, with the exception of the FLN in Algeria, comprises peaceful trailblazers. Commanded by the likes of Nyerere in Tanzania, Nkrumah in Ghana and Kaunda in Zambia, half a dozen liberation movements achieved independence through negotiated transitions, either induced by peaceful mass organization (e.g. TANU in Tanzania) or civil disobedience (e.g. CPP in Ghana, Mouvement National Congolais (MNC) in Congo and United National Independence Party (UNIP) in Zambia).[43] These trailblazers would play a significant role in supporting the total liberation of Africa and supporting other liberation movements.

Table 2.1: Liberation and Neo-Liberation Regimes in Post-Independence Africa

Egypt 1952-Free Officers	Congo-Brazzaville 1968-MNR*	Uganda 1986-NRM (AS)*
Ghana 1957-CPP	Guinea-Bissau 1973 PAIGC (AS)	Namibia 1990-SWAPO (AS)
Guinea 1958-DPG	Cape Verde 1975 PAIGC	Ethiopia TPLF/EPRDF-1991 (AS)*
Mali 1960 Sudanese Union	São Tomé and Príncipe 1975 (MLSTP)	Eritrea EPLF-1993 (AS)*
DRC 1960-MNC	Mozambique 1975-FRELIMO (AS)	Rwanda RPF-1994 (AS)*
Tanzania 1961-TANU	Angola 1975-MPLA (AS)	South Africa 1994-ANC (AS)
Algeria 1962-FLN (AS)	Comoros 1975-RDPC*	DRC AFDL-1997 (AS)*
Congo-Brazzaville 1963-Les Trois Glorieuses*	Zimbabwe 1980-ZANU-PF (AS)	South Sudan 2011-SPLM (AS)*
Zambia 1964-UNIP		

* Neo-liberation regime.
AS = Armed struggle or insurgency.

The second group is mostly concentrated in Southern Africa and in the Portuguese territories in colonies with large settler populations. With massive political and economic stakes in the colony, white settlers took a no-compromise line against any accommodation of African nationalist movements. Settlers' dominance of the colonial government and economy prevented the

[43] Paul Nugent, *Africa since Independence: A Comparative History*, New York: Palgrave Macmillan, 2012.

emergence of an indigenous African constituency that could have developed strong political, economic and cultural ties with the metropole, like that which existed in French colonies.[44] Under these conditions, the resultant nationalist forces were both anti-conservative and revolutionary; they would call for a radical break from the "capitalist imperialism" that they viewed as underwriting these minority regimes. Opposed by repressive minority regimes, these movements, including the MPLA in Angola, PAIGC in Guinea-Bissau and Cape Verde, FRELIMO in Mozambique, ZANU in Zimbabwe, SWAPO in Namibia and the ANC in South Africa, adopted the armed struggle to achieve liberation.

The third group, which we label as neo-liberation movements, is concentrated in Central and East Africa, and arose in opposition to the emergence of a new class of dictators and authoritarian leaders who their critics conceived as neo-colonial for perpetuating policies of social exclusion to advance the interests of the ruling elite.[45] The identified enemies included the conservative regime of Mobutu, one of the most loyal clients for Western interests in Africa, but also the Hutu ethnocracy in Rwanda, sectarian and Islamist governments in Sudan, the leftist regime of Milton Obote in Uganda and even the Marxist–Leninist "Derg" junta in Ethiopia, whose reproduction of traditional social divisions between the Amhara and other nationality groups incited the emergence of popular, leftist resistance.[46] Like their predecessors, these neo-liberation movements were squarely Pan-Africanist and saw their own liberation as connected to the struggle of their comrades.

A Theory of Liberation and Regionalized Civil War in Post-Independence Africa

Liberation movements in Africa have been extensively studied,[47] but mostly through a case-specific or strictly historical approach. Few analyses have pro-

---

[44] Norrie MacQueen, *The Decolonization of Portuguese Africa: Metropolitan Revolution and the Dissolution of Empire*, New York: Longman, 1997.

[45] Clapham, "Introduction."

[46] Bertus Praeg, *Ethiopia and Political Renaissance in Africa*, New York: Nova Science, 2006, p. 72.

[47] W. Scott Thompson, *Ghana's Foreign Policy, 1957–1966: Diplomacy, Ideology, and the New State*, Princeton, NJ: Princeton University Press, 1969; Ngwabi Bhebe and T.O. Ranger (eds), *Soldiers in Zimbabwe's Liberation War*, Portsmouth, NH: Heinemann, 1996; Jocelyn Alexander, JoAnn McGregor and T.O. Ranger, *Violence*

vided a general framework to account for the causes and consequences of liberation change in post-World War II Africa. One exception is the scholarship that analyzes violent liberation struggles in Southern Africa and the role of the Frontline States as an extension of the Cold War and/or socialist–capitalist class conflict.[48] While this supranational conflict had material consequences for conflict escalation and duration in Africa, we argue that the focus on the Cold War has masked the importance of the liberation struggle and the domestic-cum-regional conflicts that erupted between revolutionary and counter-revolutionary forces within Africa.

One of the central arguments we advance in this book is that the liberation project and its counter-revolutionary backlash have been key drivers of transnational conflict in Africa, but, heretofore, the dynamics by which liberation leads to regionalized war have been poorly understood. Our emphasis on the links between liberation, counter-revolution and war has particular relevance for the Congo, because, as is evident from Map 6, the country sits at the interface of two regional hot zones of liberation activity. Few countries would have as significant a stake in the battle between revolutionary and counter-revolutionary forces as Congo/Zaire. In fact, as is the central theme of the book, the reign of Mobutu Sese Seko would be bookended by epic battles between liberation and counter-revolutionary forces—the victory of the counter-revolutionaries ushered Mobutu into power, while the victory of neo-liberation forces three decades later marked his demise.

& Memory: One Hundred Years in the "Dark Forests" of Matabeleland, Oxford: James Currey, 2000; Dale T. McKinley, The ANC and the Liberation Struggle: A Critical Political Biography, London: Pluto Press, 1997; Thomas H. Henriksen, Revolution and Counterrevolution: Mozambique's War of Independence, 1964–1974, Westport, CT: Greenwood Press, 1983; Norma J. Kriger, Zimbabwe's Guerrilla War: Peasant Voices, New York: Cambridge University Press, 1992.

48. Khadiagala, Allies in Adversity; Zaki Laidi, The Superpowers and Africa: The Constraints of a Rivalry, 1960–1990, Chicago: University of Chicago Press, 1990. Hilary Sapire and Christopher C. Saunders (eds), Southern African Liberation Struggles: New Local, Regional and Global Perspectives, Claremont, South Africa: University of Cape Town Press, 2013; Carol B. Thompson, Challenge to Imperialism: The Frontline States in the Liberation of Zimbabwe, Boulder, CO: Westview Press, 1986; Christopher Coker, "The Western Alliance and Africa 1949–81," African Affairs, 81, 324 (1982); Steven R. David, Choosing Sides: Alignment and Realignment in the Third World, Baltimore: Johns Hopkins University Press, 1991.

In accounting for the link between liberation and war in Africa, we take up Halliday's call for revolutionary studies to "establish with some greater comparative perspective and analytical precision the relationship between internal and external."[49] Such a perspective is highly relevant to liberation, as both the underlying conditions that cause revolution in post-World War II Africa (i.e., asymmetric power structures, extractive governments and social exclusion) and the conflict between revolutionary and counter-revolutionary forces are mutually constitutive of the external environment. We argue that understanding the internal–external nexus of liberation politics helps account for the regionalized nature of liberation processes in Africa and the logic by which liberation regimes, after coming to power, faced internationalized civil wars.

In elucidating this dynamic process, we break our argument into four distinct temporal periods. We do this not to suggest liberation is a teleological process, but for analytical clarity. The first period represents the consolidation of colonial rule as a stable equilibrium; the second period is triggered by the shock of World War II and the structural weakening of imperialism leading to the rise of liberation regimes in some countries but the persistence of colonialism in others, especially settler regimes; this shift in the distribution of regimes across the region, however, ushered in an unstable third period as conflict intensified between progressive and reactionary forces internally and externally; the demise of the Apartheid regime marked the end of this period of regional instability and the onset of a more stable regional equilibrium as liberation regimes came to power in Angola, Mozambique, Zimbabwe, Namibia and South Africa.

Period 1: Colonialism

Our theoretical starting point is the consolidation of colonial rule after the Scramble for Africa. The colonial state was at once imperial, extractive, bureaucratic-authoritarian, exclusionary, paternalistic and fundamentally reactionary.[50] As outsiders having established overrule through force, the European colonizers designed the colonial state to stymie revolutionary

[49] Halliday, *Revolution and World Politics*, p. 6.
[50] Crawford Young, *The African Colonial State in Comparative Perspective*, New Haven, CT: Yale University Press, 1994; Mamdani, *Citizen and Subject*; Daron Acemoglu and James A. Robinson, *Why Nations Fail: The Origins of Power, Prosperity and Poverty*, New York: Crown Publishers, 2012.

change; this required the constant threat of violence and psychological subjugation but also divide and rule to thwart mass mobilization. Consistent with an understanding of the connections between internal and external revolutionary dynamics, colonial pro-consuls went to great lengths to buffer their colonies from external forces that could foment revolutionary ideas among their subjects. For example, the emergence of a nationalist movement, the White Flag League, in Sudan in 1924, which was inspired by the 1919 Revolution in Egypt, led the British to expel all Egyptian military personnel and numerous civil servants serving in Sudan as part of the Anglo-Egyptian Condominium.[51]

Beyond these individual policies, however, the European imperial powers collectively created a regional system to reduce the costs of external occupation. As envisaged already by Bismarck back in Berlin in 1884, their peaceful collusion to carve up the continent—what Jeffrey Herbst refers to as the "true colonial achievement ... given the tensions on the European continent at the time and rather remarkable tendency for Europeans to go to war"[52]—and shared interests in averting social unrest led to the creation of a series of regional institutions, such as non-interference in each other's domestic affairs, that upheld exclusionary regimes while suppressing revolutionary change. The outbreak of World War I temporarily challenged this stable order. Not only did it increase external conflict as the battlefield extended to the far-reaches of the African continent, especially those frontiers surrounding German colonies (Togoland, Kamerun, South-West Africa, Tanganyika), the conflict set in motion processes of social change (not least through the mobilization of marginalized populations for the war effort) that could sow the seeds for revolution. Some suggest this "fear that war would provoke revolution" initially tempered South Africa's enthusiasm for joining the war effort but in the end could not prevent it.[53] Although the colonial state would weather global conflict and regional stability was restored, this would not hold a quarter of a century later.

[51] M.W. Daly, *Empire on the Nile: The Anglo-Egyptian Sudan, 1898–1934*, New York: Cambridge University Press, 1986; Heather J. Sharkey, *Living with Colonialism: Nationalism and Culture in the Anglo-Egyptian Sudan*, Berkeley University of California Press, 2003.

[52] Herbst, *States and Power in Africa*.

[53] Hew Strachan, *The First World War in Africa*, Oxford: Oxford University Press, 2004.

Period 2: The Shock of World War II and the Rise of Liberation Regimes in Africa

World War II was a critical juncture in the history of colonial rule. The global conflict would add profound normative and structural consequences for imperial rule. The moral contradictions between a war fought in the name of freedom from foreign conquest and the persistence of colonialism in Africa and Asia were not lost on colonial subjects,[54] nor on liberal constituencies in France and Britain. As Ali Mazrui notes, "When Winston Churchill and Franklin D. Roosevelt signed the Atlantic Charter in August 1941 they were not only denouncing injustice in Europe ... they were also signing the death warrant of the whole idea of 'legitimate colonialism' for the rest of the twentieth century."[55] Pan-Africanists at the Manchester Congress in 1945 seized on the Atlantic Charter as reflecting the moral bankruptcy of colonialism.[56] Simultaneously, the war weakened the structural capacity of European powers to incur the costs necessary to repress local demands for self-rule. These factors would open the door for immediate independence in British colonies in South Asia, which had greater involvement in the war and stronger existing anti-colonial organizations.

The independence of the peoples of the Subcontinent, especially freedom for India, exerted a strong demonstration effect on Africa.[57] In the wake of India's independence, Nkrumah launched his Positive Action campaign of civil disobedience, which reverberated throughout the continent. In Tanganyika, in 1954, Julius Nyerere, founded the Tanganyika African National Union (TANU) as a peaceful nationalist alternative to the Maji Maji rebellion against German colonialism in 1905 (and to the Mau Mau rebellion concurrently raging in Kenya); by 1960, the party, advocating *Uhuru na Umoja* (Freedom and unity), would have more than one million members with TANU flags flying in houses in every corner of the country.[58]

---

[54] As Nyerere notes in an interview with the veteran chronicler, Godfrey Mwakikagile, World War II had the effect of beginning to shift grievances from one of an "inert dissatisfaction that we were not accepted as equals" to the demand for political freedom. Godfrey Mwakikagile, *Life under Nyerere*, Dar es Salaam, Tanzania: New Africa Press, 2006, p. 122.

[55] Ali A. Mazrui, "Seek Ye First the Political Kingdom," in Christophe Wondji and Ali A. Mazrui (eds), *General History of Africa: Africa since 1935*, London: Heinemann 1993, pp. 112–13.

[56] Esedebe, *Pan-Africanism*, Chapter 4, "The Manchester Congress and Its Aftermath."

[57] Martin, *African Political Thought*, p. 90.

[58] Bjerk, *Building a Peaceful Nation*, pp. 40–1.

The end of World War II had similar effects in French colonies. The surrender of Nazi Germany triggered immediate pro-independence demonstrations in parts of Algeria, which Paris had claimed as an integral part of France since 1830. "If it was liberation that a haggard France was feting that May day, that too was the magic word mobilising the Muslim community of Sétif," Alistair Horne poignantly writes. "The difference was that the one was celebrating its return; the other, marching in quest of something it considered to be still denied ..."[59] The heavy-handed government response to protests in Sétif and subsequent nationalist mobilization drove the resistance underground, ultimately culminating in guerrilla warfare to break France's imperial incorporation of the North African territory. The same year TANU was founded, the Front de Libération Nationale (FLN) emerged in Algeria, beginning a seven-year war that claimed more than 100,000 deaths on the road to independence.

From the continent's four corners—the FLN in Algeria, CPP in Ghana, TANU in Tanganyika and the ANC in South Africa—liberation movements led the push for an end to colonial rule and political independence. As discussed above, not all decolonization movements would take the form of liberation movements. In French West Africa, "decolonization through assimilation" was the dominant mode of transition, in which conservative African elites who were integrated into the French polity (many as elected representatives to the National Assembly in Paris) used their strong political and cultural ties with French officials as part of a strategy to neutralize more radical nationalist and leftist forces who threatened their power while fulfilling their people's demands for self-government.[60] Nor did all liberation movements succeed. As Ghana, Tanganyika and even Algeria were able to celebrate their political independence, the quest for majority rule in the settler states of Southern Africa and for self-determination in the Portuguese colonies remained unfulfilled.

Paradoxically, the leaders at the forefront of the export of liberation across Africa were the peaceful liberators Kwame Nkrumah and Julius Nyerere. Their activism was deeply ideological—it was a manifestation of the Pan-Africanist ideals of the collective foundations of liberation. Nkrumah summed up this collective spirit in his speech upon the independence of Ghana: "We again rededicate ourselves in the struggle to emancipate other countries in Africa,

[59] Alistair Horne, *A Savage War of Peace Algeria, 1954–1962*, New York: New York Review Books, 2011.

[60] Tony Chafer, *The End of Empire in French West Africa: France's Successful Decolonisation?*, Oxford: Berg Publishers, 2002.

for our independence is meaningless unless it is linked up with the total liberation of Africa."[61] Nyerere similarly saw unity as a powerful "instrument of liberation" and warned that the "oppressed must not easily give up their unity—only the enemy can rejoice at its loss."[62] But their external fervor was also seen as a strategic necessity and a bulwark against the counter-revolutionary forces that continued to threaten their liberation project domestically. This would be made clear to them with the Congo Crisis that engulfed Central Africa in the early 1960s, as we discuss below.

Period 3: Liberation Revolutions, Regional Polarization and Internationalized Civil War

World War II profoundly disrupted the stable regional equilibrium that existed in Africa after the consolidation of colonial rule by not only weakening the structural and normative pillars of imperialism but by ushering in a regional system polarized between liberation and reactionary regimes (with the remainder emerging as independent but relatively conservative states that neither opposed Pan-Africanism nor actively supported liberation forces in other countries). This polarization proved hugely destabilizing as the continent-wide battle between revolutionary and counter-revolutionary forces would play out over the next several decades. The Cold War and the rivalry between the United States and the Soviet Union would exacerbate, but not cause, this regional polarization.

One of the consequences of a deeply polarized external environment was that it intensified and internationalized both revolutionary and post-revolutionary conflicts, which in turn reinforced regional divisions. The general dynamics of this process can be described as follows:

- The rise of liberation regimes after World War II disrupted the regional order established by the European imperial powers at the Berlin Conference in 1884–5.
- The emergence of a set of liberation regimes committed to Pan-Africanism increased regional uncertainty between the ascendant revolutionary states and the counter-revolutionary holdouts. Each saw the other as an ideological and strategic threat to its own power and survival.

---

[61] Independence speech of Kwame Nkrumah, 1957.
[62] Nawal El Saadawi, "President Nyerere Talks to *El Mussawar* (1984)," in Chambi Chachage and Annar Cassam (eds), *Africa's Liberation: The Legacy of Nyerere*, Kampala, Uganda: Pambazuka Press, 2010, p. 9.

- Fearing an increased domestic risk of revolution led the reactionary regimes to ratchet up repression against revolutionary dissidents, which in turn led the revolutionaries to adopt more violent tactics (e.g., the rising tide of African nationalism coincided with the Sharpeville massacre in 1960 in South Africa, which led the ANC and the Pan Africanist Congress (PAC) to switch from civil disobedience to armed resistance).

- But as the inspiration and support for revolution was also emanating from abroad, the counter-revolutionary states also used force externally to, at a minimum, coerce their liberation rivals to cease assistance or, at a maximum, restore reactionary forces to power (e.g., Mobutu's ascendancy and the demise of Lumumba, Gizenga and the Simba Uprising in Congo).

- This external threat in turn caused the liberation states to accelerate their own interventionist policies abroad (e.g., the Frontline States policy adopted by the liberation regimes of Tanzania, Zambia, Mozambique, Angola and Zimbabwe against South Africa).

This dynamic process—in which regional polarization, revolution and war reinforced each other—helps to account for the prevalence of war, especially internationalized civil war, in Africa's liberation regimes. It thus speaks to the large amount of literature linking revolutionary change to regionalized or internationalized conflicts.[63] However, we challenge the exogeneity assumption that is at the core of some of this literature.[64] Instead, our analysis resonates closely with the thrust of Halliday's theorizing about the endogenous relationship between revolution, war and external polarization:

> The reasons why revolutions lead to war is not ... that revolutionary states are wilfully belligerent, dissatisfied or revisionist, or that their opponents are militaristic and expansionist. Rather, by dint of the very tensions that led to revolution occurring, other states and societies are affected by them. *Thus war is a means by which both groups of states, the revolutionary and the counter-revolutionary, respond to changes in domestic and international politics.*[65]

---

[63] Theda Skocpol, "Social Revolutions and Mass Military Mobilization," *World Politics*, 40, 2 (1988); Zeev Maoz, *Domestic Sources of Global Change*, Ann Arbor: University of Michigan Press, 1996; Walt, *Revolution and War*; Colgan, "Domestic Revolutionary Leaders and International Conflict"; Colgan and Weeks, "Revolution, Personalist Dictatorships, and International Conflict."

[64] See especially Walt, *Revolution and War*; Colgan, "Domestic Revolutionary Leaders and International Conflict"; Colgan and Weeks, "Revolution, Personalist Dictatorships, and International Conflict."

[65] Emphasis added. Halliday, *Revolution and World Politics*, pp. 258–9.

Nowhere is this better seen than one of the first internationalized civil wars in post-independence Africa and the first continental clash of revolutionary and counter-revolutionary forces—the Congo Crisis.

The Congo Crisis as Exemplar

Congo achieved independence on June 30, 1960, led by Patrice Lumumba and his Mouvement National Congolais (MNC). Though the membership of the MNC paled in comparison to TANU in Tanganyika, it represented the first national party in a political landscape dominated by ethnic-based parties. Shortly after the founding of the MNC in October 1958, Lumumba had attended the All-African People's Conference Nkrumah hosted in Accra, where the Congolese nationalist met Frantz Fanon, Gamal Abdul Nasser and Ahmed Sékou Touré.[66] Returning to Congo committed to the "African national project" of "national unity, economic independence and pan-African solidarity,"[67] Lumumba stepped up mobilization efforts and demands for complete independence. Arrested a year later, his incarceration did little to reverse the popular demands for self-determination; Lumumba became the inaugural prime minister of Congo after the MNC won a slim plurality over a fractured party system. At the independence ceremony, Lumumba delivered a rousing speech as the Belgian King Baudouin handed over sovereignty:

> We are proud of this struggle, of tears, of fire, and of blood, to the depths of our being, for it was a noble and just struggle, and indispensable to put an end to the humiliating slavery which was imposed upon us by force ... We are going to show the world what the black man can do when he works in freedom, and we are going to make of the Congo the center of the sun's radiance for all of Africa ... The Congo's independence marks a decisive step towards the liberation of the entire African continent.

The dark clouds of counter-revolution gathered almost immediately, however. Lumumba's advocacy of continent-wide cooperation and integration, global non-alignment and Pan-Africanist values—encouraged by his political mentor Nkrumah—was profoundly threatening to established interests inside and outside Africa.[68] In July 1960, amid an escalating army

[66] David Van Reybrouck, *Congo: Een Geschiedenis*, Amsterdam: De Bezige Bij, 2010, pp. 261–2.

[67] Georges Nzongola-Ntalaja, *The Congo from Leopold to Kabila: A People's History*, London: Zed Books, 2002, p. 84.

[68] Martin, *African Political Thought*, p. 75.

mutiny and anti-settler violence, the mineral-rich province of Katanga, supported by Belgian mining companies and defended by South African mercenaries and Belgian officers, declared its independence from Congo. A few weeks later, the diamond-rich area of South Kasai also pursued secession, also with the support of Belgian mining interests. Lumumba appealed to the United Nations to help preserve Congo's territorial integrity. The Security Council responded immediately but sent UN forces to the country with a relatively passive mandate. The UN mission initially refused to participate in the Congolese government's attempts to crush the secessionists. This prompted Lumumba to turn to the Soviet Union for military support, which alarmed the Americans, who in the words of the CIA director, Allen Dulles, came to the "clear-cut conclusion that if Lumumba continues to hold high-office, the inevitable result will at best be chaos and at worst pave the way to a Communist takeover of the Congo with disastrous consequences ..."[69] Three weeks later, on September 14, 1960, in close coordination with the CIA, the chief of staff of the Armée Nationale Congolais, then known only as Colonel Joseph Mobutu, deposed Lumumba in a coup d'état. Congo's liberation leader was taken to Katanga—to be murdered.

Backed by the United Nations, the new Congolese government retook Katanga and Kasai, but partisans of Lumumba, including his deputy, Antoine Gizenga, refused to recognize the coup and fled to Kisangani—one of the strongest bases of support of the MNC—to set up the "legitimate" Congolese government, which would be recognized by Nkrumah's Ghana, China and the Soviet Union. This maneuver unleashed an internationalized civil war: the arrest of Gizenga helped to subdue the unrest temporarily, but a second rebellion, organized as the Comité National de Libération and led by Lumumba's minister of interior affairs, Christophe Gbenye, emerged in 1964 calling for a second independence for the Congo. This liberation movement—also known as the "Simba Uprising"—received military backing from the liberation regimes of Congo-Brazzaville and Tanganyika as well as from Moscow and Beijing and took control of much of eastern Congo. Ultimately, however, the Simbas and the "second independence of Congo" were crushed by the Congolese army with heavy support from mercenaries, Belgian paratroopers and the CIA.[70]

[69] Larry Devlin, *Chief of Station, Congo: Fighting the Cold War in a Hot Zone*, New York: PublicAffairs, 2007, pp. 62–3.

[70] Nzongola-Ntalaja, *Congo from Leopold to Kabila*, p. 84.

The Congo Crisis sent shockwaves throughout Africa and shook the confidence of even the most ardent Pan-Africanists in the face of the subversion of a liberation regime led by one of their comrades at the hands of a broad coalition of neo-colonial forces—Washington, Belgian mining companies, Apartheid South Africa, Rhodesia, white mercenaries and a tribalist African elite.[71] Nyerere confided to one of his key foreign policy advisers the anguish the Congo Crisis caused him: "Is it possible that the Congo situation could happen here? It was terrifying. The Congo situation was really frightening for us, we each individually and collectively, we feared what was going to happen in this country ..."[72]

For Pan-Africanists, the necessary response to counter-revolutionary forces from within and outside the continent was to forge African unity. Nkrumah in particular formulated bold ideas about a "United States of Africa," but faced opposition from conservative circles who thought the idea premature or a Soviet-inspired plot. The compromise result was the Organization of African Unity, founded in 1963 in Addis Ababa. The OAU charter, signed by thirty-two states, established the bedrock principles that would structure inter-state relations in Africa, namely non-interference in each other's affairs and the recognition of existing territorial borders—a defeat for Nkrumah and his plans for Pan-African unity.[73] Nevertheless, despite the charter's prioritization of national sovereignty over continental cooperation, member states also committed to "eradicate all forms of colonialism from Africa."[74] The OAU set up a Coordinating Committee for the Liberation of Africa, headquartered in Dar es Salaam under the auspices of Nyerere.

The founding of the Coordinating Committee revealed an effort to institutionalize the continued push for the liberation of the continent.[75] Again, the export of liberation was both fundamentally ideological and strategic. As Paul Bjerk writes,

> Nyerere's efforts on behalf of Mozambique and the Rhodesias stemmed from a very real belief not only in the ideals of Pan-Africanism but also in its tactical utility.

---

[71] Kwame Nkrumah, *Neo-colonialism: The Last Stage of Imperialism*, New York: International Publishers, 1966.

[72] Cited in Bjerk, *Building a Peaceful Nation*, p. 10.

[73] Clapham, *Africa and the International System*, pp. 110–12.

[74] OAU Charter.

[75] K. Mathews, "Tanzania's Foreign Policy as a Frontline State in the Liberation of Southern Africa," *Africa Quarterly*, 21, 2–4 (1981).

Nyerere believed that Tanganyika would never be fully sovereign or safe unless the whole of Africa were under majority rule.[76]

Tanzania would host a number of liberation movements, including the United National Independence Party of Zambia, Mozambique's FRELIMO, which was founded in Dar es Salaam in 1962, Angola's MPLA, Namibia's SWAPO, Zimbabwe's ZANU and ZAPU, and the ANC and the Pan Africanist Congress (PAC) of South Africa. Moreover, as we discuss in Chapter 4, the Tanzanian People's Defense Forces provided training sessions to the liberation movements.[77] Working closely with Kenneth Kaunda of Zambia, Nyerere emerged as the great external champion for an end to Apartheid rule in South Africa. As Botswana, Angola, Mozambique and Zimbabwe gained their independence, these states joined Tanzania and Zambia as the Frontline States with the explicit aim of liberating South Africa from Apartheid.[78]

Conclusion: The End of Regional Polarization, Peace and the Puzzle of Africa's Deadliest Conflict

One of the observable implications of our framework—in which regional polarization, revolution and war reinforce each other—is the externalization of internal conflicts between reactionary and liberation forces, leading to regionalized civil wars. Even after a given liberation movement comes to power, the risk of regionalized conflict persists as long as the regional environment is polarized between revolutionary and counter-revolutionary forces as the latter seek to use force to prevent the former's consolidation of power.

Conversely, then, another implication is that the mitigation of regional polarization should help to cultivate peace. This can be illustrated briefly with the case of Southern Africa. Following an arduous and bloody path to self-determination, regionalized civil wars first became a defining feature of the post-liberation politics of Angola, Mozambique and Zimbabwe owing to the ongoing confrontation with Pretoria, which pursued a strategy of defending a regional *cordon sanitaire* of conservative regimes to protect white-minority rule at home. The rise to power of the MPLA and ZANU was thus almost immediately challenged by rebel movements supported by Apartheid South

---

[76] Bjerk, *Building a Peaceful Nation*, p. 192.

[77] Haroub Othman, "Mwalimu Julius Nyerere: An Intellectual in Power," in Chachage and Cassam, *Africa's Liberation*.

[78] Khadiagala, *Allies in Adversity*.

Africa; similarly, Rhodesia's Central Intelligence Organization sponsored Resistência Nacional Moçambicana (RENAMO) against FRELIMO.[79] Two decades of mutual destabilization, however, came to an end with the release of Nelson Mandela and the transition to an ANC-led democracy: not only did this terminate white-minority rule but the dismantling of Apartheid also spawned Namibian independence and created favorable conditions for peace agreements in Angola and Mozambique. While, granted, in the Angolan case the end of the war would only be temporary as post-conflict elections triggered another outbreak of violence, the resumption of war was in part attributable to the support UNITA received from the Mobutu regime—which, like the Apartheid government, supported and propped up reactionary forces and regimes throughout its neighborhood. As we will thus discuss extensively in Chapters 4 and 5, after the overthrow of Apartheid South Africa, the focus of the neo-liberation regimes would shift to Central Africa and regime change in Kinshasa as a necessary condition for regional peace.

As we discuss in detail in subsequent chapters, the inspiration for the renewed focus on Congo after the disappointments of the 1960s came from the disciples of Julius Nyerere, who had turned Tanzania into the launching platform for revolutionary regime change across East and Southern Africa between 1964 and 1990. The rise to power of Yoweri Museveni and the NRA/M in Uganda in 1986, which, as explained above, represented the bridge between the liberation struggle in Southern Africa and the neo-liberation struggle in Central and East Africa, became the catalyst for re-intensified regional polarization and conflict. One of the key constituencies fighting with the NRA/M in its liberation campaign was a group of Rwandan refugees who subsequently turned their attention to liberating their homeland under the banner of the Rwandan Patriotic Front. This represented a direct threat to Mobutu and his regional influence—the Habyarimana regime was one of Zaire's key client states. Consistent with our theoretical framework, both the RPF's liberation struggle and the post-liberation period would play out as a regionalized civil war. Even after the RPF captured Kigali, Mobutu supported the genocidal forces who were welcomed in Zaire, from whence they hoped to return to power. The Mobutu regime's continued destabilizing impact on the region, offering sanctuary to Rwanda's archenemies but also those of Angola's MPLA and Uganda's NRA/M, would mobilize a large Pan-Africanist

---

[79] William Finnegan, *A Complicated War: The Harrowing of Mozambique*, Berkeley: University of California Press, 1992.

coalition against his reactionary rule—an ad hoc alliance that paralleled the Frontline States policy pursued against South Africa. Led by Rwanda and including Uganda, Angola, Ethiopia and Eritrea, with Nyerere as ideological patron, the coalition would indeed succeed in installing another neo-liberation regime—the sixth in eleven years (see Map 6). The hope was that, similar to the end of Apartheid, the overthrow of Mobutu would terminate regional polarization and usher in a period of peace in Central Africa.

Yet in contrast to the expectations of the liberation leaders, regional peace did not ensue; instead, the most cataclysmic war in African history was about to erupt. Why? What happened? We lay out our central argument in the next chapter.

3

WINNING THE WAR, LOSING THE PEACE

THE LIBERATION OF ZAIRE AND THE OUTBREAK
OF AFRICA'S GREAT WAR

*The military preceded the political—we came up with a programme after defining our
security goals. It should have been the other way round ... There was no time for political
organization: it was going too fast. The political organization of the AFDL could not cope
with the rapid military progress ... The military operation was so easy—almost a joke.*

Frank Rusagara, permanent secretary of the Rwandan Ministry of Defense.

In May 1997, during the ultimate days of the first Congo war, as the ADFL
rebels closed in on Mobutu's last strongholds—the capital, Kinshasa, and the
presidential palace in his northern hometown of Gbadolite—the president
despaired about his fate. As "father of the nation" for more than three decades,
he agonized over the unceremonious exit that now seemed imminent.[1] But
Mobutu also worried about the fate of those closest to him, including the
deceased, some of whom were kept in a mausoleum he had built in Gbadolite.
Among them were his late wife Marie-Antoinette and protégé, Juvénal
Habyarimana, the former president of Rwanda whose assassination on April

---

[1] To add insult to injury, he was being forced to relinquish power to a man he regarded
as nothing more than a petty-smuggler and bandit. Michela Wrong, *In the Footsteps
of Mr Kurtz*, New York: HarperCollins, 2001, p. 281.

6, 1994, would immediately lead into the Rwandan genocide. Considering him "like one of his own children,"[2] Mobutu feared what would happen if the embalmed Habyarimana fell into the hands of the rebels or, even worse, the RPF. To prevent such a possibility, Mobutu ordered Habyarimana's body be flown to Kinshasa, but with the rebels advancing on N'Djili Airport as well, there was no time for anything resembling a state funeral and it was hastily decided that the former Rwandan ruler, a famously devout Roman Catholic, would be cremated. Security officials scrambled to find an Indian Hindu priest to officiate the last rite. A mere day before the rebels overran Kinshasa, Habyarimana's body was incinerated—one of the last acts of Mobutu's more than three decades in power.[3]

* * *

With the old order in ashes, a new one was consecrated. From Asmara to Addis Ababa to Kampala to Kigali and finally to Kinshasa, a second genera-tion of liberation leaders had fought their way to power. The overthrow of Mobutu destroyed the principal counter-revolutionary force in the region,[4] and appeared to have broken the axis between the Congolese government and the *génocidaires*. It was a moment of triumph for the RPF and for Nyerere who saw his disciples slay his oldest ideological and geopolitical rival—a success story made in Africa, by Africans.[5] The fall of Kinshasa ended the polarization that had gripped Central Africa since the Congo Crisis in the early 1960s. With remnants of the *ancien régime* posing no major counter-revolutionary threat (Mobutu himself died in Morocco of cancer less than four months after he was removed from power) and the region firmly united in its support for the revolutionary government (save for military-Islamist Sudan, which was isolated and under heavy military pressure from Eritrea, Ethiopia and Uganda), the risk of an externally provoked regionalized civil war like that which plagued Congo in its first five years after independence and consumed post-liberation Angola and Mozambique should have been low.

[2] Howard W. French, "Ending a Chapter, Mobutu Cremates Rwanda Ally," *New York Times*, May 16, 1997.

[3] Ibid.

[4] The lone hold-out in the region was Sudan's military-Islamist regime which was fight-ing a ferocious war against the Sudan People's Liberation Army, led by the pan-Afri-canist and left-leaning Dr John Garang, who had also lived in Dar es Salaam where he would become close to Yoweri Museveni.

[5] Afsane Bassir, "Zaire: Julius Nyerere—Le transfert de pouvoir a été une affaire essen-tiellement africaine," *Le Monde*, May 21, 1997.

Of course, plenty of other challenges to consolidating peace in the new Democratic Republic of Congo existed. As we describe in Chapter 4, the scale of the destruction Mobutu left behind was unfathomable. The country with the richest mineral reserves in the world was bankrupt with effectively no working mining sector. By one estimate, the paved road network that existed at independence had shrunk by 90 per cent.[6] Following the presidential example, civil servants felt license to steal from the state to pay themselves. Mobutu and his henchmen had also perfected the art of stoking local conflicts as a divide-and-rule strategy—a risky game that could easily spiral out of control. Perhaps most crucially, the Zairean military and security forces had become marauding militias that preyed on the population at will. Thus, like in other post-conflict countries, the risk of conflict recurrence was high.[7] But the puzzle is why this conflict would take the form of Africa's Great War—a regionalized civil war with powerful neighboring states, which had previously cooperated to overthrow Mobutu, now on opposing sides of the conflict?

A large body of scholarship has emerged to account for this devastating episode in African history. The most persuasive assessments mix political economy,[8] geopolitical analysis[9] and constructivist insights[10] to narrate the war and to document its consequences, horrors and longevity.[11] These works pro-

---

[6] J.Y. Smith, "Congo Ex-Ruler Mobutu Dies," *Washington Post*, September 8, 1997.

[7] Paul Collier, Anke Hoeffler and Måns Söderbom, "Post-Conflict Risks," *Journal of Peace Research*, 45, 4 (2008); Philip Roessler, "The Enemy Within: Personal Rule, Coups, and Civil War in Africa," *World Politics*, 63, 2 (2011); Barbara F. Walter, "Why Bad Governance Leads to Repeat Civil War," *Journal of Conflict Resolution* (2014).

[8] Jason Stearns, *Dancing in the Glory of Monsters: The Collapse of the Congo and the Great War of Africa*, New York: PublicAffairs, 2011.

[9] John Frank Clark, *The African Stakes of the Congo War*, New York: Palgrave Macmillan, 2002.

[10] Kevin C. Dunn, *Imagining the Congo: The International Relations of Identity*, London: Palgrave Macmillan, 2003; Thomas Turner, *The Congo Wars: Conflict, Myth, and Reality*, London: Zed Books, 2007.

[11] René Lemarchand, *The Dynamics of Violence in Central Africa*, Philadelphia: University of Pennsylvania Press, 2009; Gérard Prunier, *From Genocide to Continental War: The "Congolese" Conflict and the Crisis of Contemporary Africa*, London: Hurst, 2009; Filip Reyntjens, *The Great African War: Congo and Regional Geopolitics, 1996–2006*, Cambridge: Cambridge University Press, 2009; Stearns, *Dancing in the Glory of Monsters*; François Ngolet, *Crisis in the Congo: The Rise and Fall of Laurent Kabila*, New York: Palgrave Macmillan, 2011.

vide valuable descriptive analyses of the events and analyze the permissive conditions leading to the outbreak of conflict. Four main explanations are advanced: (1) state collapse and a war over Congo's natural resources; (2) externalization of the Rwandan genocide; (3) domestic resistance to foreign occupation; and (4) the personalization of power under Kabila. Though existing scholarship on the Great War tends to eschew theory-testing or theory-building, each of these accounts are connected to significant research streams in the conflict literature. These frameworks are important for contextualizing renewed conflict from August 1998 onwards, but we argue they are inadequate to explain the high politics of Africa's Great War—that is, the strategic logic of why the comrades who joined *together* to liberate Zaire would end up fighting *against each other* a mere fifteen months later. Our book fills this gap in the literature and advances an integrated argument to account for both the breakdown of the post-Mobutu order and why it ends in a regionalized conflict—any singular theory of Africa's Great War has to account for both of these dynamics.

Building from Chapter 2, the outbreak of Africa's Great War represents a major paradox. The overthrow of Mobutu ended the regional polarization that had plagued Central Africa since the 1960s and had fueled regionalized civil war in Congo, Angola, Uganda and Rwanda. With the Pan-Africanist coalition's overthrow of Mobutu, liberation regimes reigned from Asmara to Luanda—including now in Kinshasa. This should have been a high point for regional cooperation and regional integration in Central Africa, not conflict. How did the liberators lose the peace?

We argue that their fundamental flaw was the type of revolutionary organization and the structure of the regional coalition the anti-Mobutu forces built to liberate Congo. Despite the ideological affinity between the liberation and neo-liberation regimes that opposed Mobutu, the regional coalition they forged was largely ad hoc and informal; characterized by little information-sharing and coordination between different regional powers; and with an asymmetric, disproportionately influential role played by the RPF. The organizational weakness of the coalition ensured that cracks began to form in the alliance even before Congo was liberated as Angola and Rwanda raced each other to Kinshasa and Tanzania balanced against the RPF. The organizational weakness of the regional effort was mirrored in the structure of the AFDL. In contrast to the strong Leninist political organizations they built during their own revolutionary struggles, the regional powers, led by the RPF, backed the emergence of a weak, personalized rebel movement heavily dependent on foreign support. This was a function of the sheer speed with which the AFDL would advance to Kinshasa, but also a strategic choice made by Kigali. The RPF's policy emerged from its mistrust in delegating power, its attempt to maximize control of the rebel movement, and the imperative of a swift military solution to the counter-revolutionary threat posed by the *génocidaires*, Mobutu and, potentially, France.

While such an approach proved effective in removing the Mobutu regime, the absence of strong coordinating regional institutions and the organizational weakness of the AFDL ensured the liberators failed to manage the vacuum of power their military success engendered. Uncertainty would not only undermine the alliance between Kabila and the RPF as the two sides quickly became locked in a security dilemma but it also unsettled powerful regional states. Fearful of the potential costs to their own relative capabilities, status and influence in the region if the RPF seized on Congo's liberation to provoke a significant shift in the regional balance of power, this led neighboring states to actively subvert the RPF's presence in Congo in order to avert such potential losses, compounding the security dilemma. Ultimately, it was the RPF's direct intervention into the weakly institutionalized liberation regime—the structures of which were of its own making—and the regional uncertainty that it produced, which accounts for why, when the Kabila–RPF alliance eventually collapsed, it unleashed not just a civil war or dyadic conflict between Congo and Rwanda, but Africa's Great War which pulled in Uganda, Angola, Zimbabwe, Namibia and Chad as well.

Existing Explanations

State Collapse and a War for Congo's Natural Resources

As we explain at length in the next chapter, under Mobutu's rule, the Zairian state experienced near total collapse. State failure was largely a function of the kleptocratic policies Mobutu used to "govern" the country. He eschewed formalization of authority for "fear bureaucracies acquire their own interests and power."[12] Predatory policies—looting Gécamines (the state-owned corporation that monopolized copper production in Zaire and represented the largest earner of foreign currency for the state), and forcing the Forces Armées Zaïroises (FAZ) to prey on the population to pay itself—left the state in ruins.

[12] Reno, *Warlord Politics and African States*, p. 147.

As countless observers have noted, there were striking parallels between the personalist rule of Mobutu and Leopold II, the Belgian king whose obsession with acquiring a foreign colony led him to create the Congolese state in the 1880s. As Adam Hochschild writes:

> Aside from the color of his skin, there were few ways in which [Mobutu] did not resemble the monarch who governed the same territory a hundred years earlier. His one-man rule. His great wealth taken from the land. His naming a lake after himself. His yacht. His appropriation of state possessions as his own.[13]

But if Leopold left behind an absolutist "Bula Matari" state,[14] by the end of Mobutu's reign the state became so extensively privatized that state authority ceased to exist on most of the territory. Reno describes how Mobutu followed the classic strategy of "warlord politics," in which political authority is achieved through control over resources and markets and personalized patronage networks rather than through state-building or economic development.[15] Economic decline and the emergence of new market opportunities at the end of the Cold War, however, increased the incentives for strongmen to defect from the president's network and establish their own economic fiefdoms. Numerous scholars thus highlight the decay of the Zairian state and the privatization of violence as a root cause of the regional crisis.[16] They also suggest it left the Zairian state and its economy vulnerable to "Lilliputian states the size of Congo's smallest province, such as Uganda, or even that of a district, such as Rwanda, to take it upon themselves to impose rulers in Kinshasa, and to invade, occupy and loot the territory of their giant neighbour."[17] For John Clark, Congo's opportunistic neighbors in turn used Congo to engage in brutal patterns of violent extortion and the centralization of control over money flows that were reminiscent of the ugly birth of modern European

---

[13] Emphasis added. Adam Hochschild, *King Leopold's Ghost: A Story of Greed, Terror, and Heroism in Colonial Africa*, Boston: Houghton Mifflin, 1998, p. 304.

[14] Bula Matari, meaning "he who breaks rocks," was how Congolese referred to Henry Morton Stanley, who claimed Congo on behalf of King Leopold. During the colonial period it became a general term the Congolese used to refer to the colonial state—reflecting the terror and repression felt under the colonial yoke. Crawford Young and Thomas Turner, *The Rise and Decline of the Zairian State*, Madison, WI: University of Wisconsin Press, 1985., p. 30–31.

[15] Reno, *Warlord Politics and African States*.

[16] Reyntjens, *Great African War*; Nzongola-Ntalaja, *Congo from Leopold to Kabila*.

[17] Nzongola-Ntalaja, *Congo from Leopold to Kabila*, p. 214.

states, as documented by Charles Tilly; resource rents and military intervention in Congo in that sense have had a perversely progressive potential.[18]

The link between Congo's abundance in natural resources and the outbreak of Africa's Great War is important to assess both for theoretical and substantive considerations. Substantively, Africa's Great War would become one of the most notorious resource-fueled conflicts in the modern era; all of its belligerents would reap tremendous profits from the illicit exploitation of gold, diamonds, copper, cobalt, zinc, coltan and much else.[19] Some saw the conflict as reflecting neoliberalism gone wild, with close connections between globalization and state collapse,[20] while others have cited it as the late twentieth-century's most prominent case of neo-imperialism.[21] Theoretically, there is a vast conflict literature linking civil war to economies dependent on natural resource rents.[22] How much, then, was Africa's Great War caused by the abundance of Congo's mineral riches?

Consistent with the large body of scholarship on the pernicious effects of natural resources on governance,[23] the country did indeed fall victim to the "resource curse," in which Congo's rulers from Leopold II to Laurent-Désiré Kabila ruled as rentiers, tapping into the "unearned" income that comes from

---

[18] Clark, *African Stakes of the Congo War*.

[19] Group of Experts, "Final Report of the Group of Experts on the DRC Submitted in Accordance with Paragraph 5 of Security Council Resolution 1952 (2010)," New York: UN Security Council, 2011.

[20] Crawford Young, "Contextualizing Congo Conflicts: Order and Disorder in Postcolonial Africa," in John F. Clark (ed.), *The African Stakes of the Congo War*, New York: Palgrave Macmillan, 2002.

[21] Colette Braeckman, *Les nouveaux prédateurs*, Paris: Fayard, 2003.

[22] For a small sample of this literature, see Philippe Le Billon, "The Political Ecology of War: Natural Resources and Armed Conflicts," *Political Geography*, 20, 5 (2001); David K. Leonard and Scott Straus, *Africa's Stalled Development: International Causes and Cures*, Boulder, CO: Lynne Rienner, 2003; Michael L. Ross, "What Do We Know about Natural Resources and Civil War?," *Journal of Peace Research*, 41, 3 (2004); Macartan Humphreys, "Natural Resources, Conflict, and Conflict Resolution," *Journal of Conflict Resolution*, 49, 4 (2005); Paul Collier, *The Bottom Billion: Why the Poorest Countries Are Failing and What Can Be Done about It*, New York: Oxford University Press, 2007; Massimo Morelli and Dominic Rohner, "Resource Concentration and Civil Wars," National Bureau of Economic Research, 2014.

[23] Excellently summarized by Michael L. Ross, "The Political Economy of the Resource Curse," *World Politics*, 51, 2 (1999).

natural resource extraction to enrich themselves and consolidate their personal power while eschewing or actively suppressing state-building, democratization, economic diversification and other developmental processes that may have disrupted their political control.[24] The dependence on an extractive economy spawned all of the worst features of the rentier state—authoritarianism, repression, corruption, personalist rule, erosion of state capacity and dependence on economic enclaves.[25] When inheriting this political–economic and institutional landscape, Kabila did not hesitate to embrace it: he immediately suppressed opposition parties and arrested civil society activists, extracted rents by selling futures contracts before even coming to power, and personally doled out state resources as patronage. Kabila ruled the Congolese state as he ruled the *maquis*.[26]

But if the resource curse, poor governance and state failure would leave Congo vulnerable to the predations of rapacious neighbors and Africa's Great War would come to resemble hyenas ripping the carcass of an elephant apart, we find no evidence that conflict over Congo's resource wealth was the primary *cause* of the falling out between Kabila and his internal and external allies and thus the trigger of the second Congo war.[27] While the initial intervention of Ugandan and Rwandan forces to overthrow Mobutu led them to activate and strengthen transnational economic networks, as has been reported by Reyntjens[28] and a United Nations panel of experts report,[29] the mass looting occurred *after* the onset of the second war and no formal or informal negotiations seem to have been held prior to August 1998 about the

---

[24] Collier, *Bottom Billion*.

[25] Michael L. Ross, "Does Oil Hinder Democracy?," *World Politics*, 53, 3 (2001). Leonard, *Africa's Stalled Development*.

[26] From the late 1960s onwards, Kabila's Parti de la Révolution Populaire (PRP) controlled an enclave in Fizi-Baraka, South Kivu, from where they continued their resistance to the Mobutu regime. As discussed below, locals resented Kabila's predatory and repressive policies. Erik Kennes, *Essai biographique sur Laurent Désiré Kabila*, Paris: L'Harmattan, 2003, p. 322.

[27] Nor as Prunier extensively discusses was the first Congo war orchestrated by US mining interests working through Museveni and Kagame. Prunier, *From Genocide to Continental War*, pp. 137–43.

[28] See examples cited in Reyntjens, *Great African War*, p. 148.

[29] United Nations, "Final Report of the Panel of Experts on the Illegal Exploitation of Natural Resources and Other Forms of Wealth of the Democratic Republic of the Congo. S/2002/1146," New York: United Nations, 2002.

possible divisions of Congo's spoils between the comrades—which would have been a much less costly way of securing rents than the uncertainty and damage inflicted by conflict. Indeed, as Prunier notes, it is the war itself that leads to the need and the opportunity for Rwanda, Uganda and Zimbabwe— the three most notorious looters—to scale up their extraction of Congo's mineral riches.[30]

This assessment that war caused the mass theft of Congolese riches was corroborated in the extensive interviews we conducted with all sides of the war. It was to be expected that the RPF and Congolese Tutsi would play down the role of natural resources, but, as we will see, what was surprising was the lack of evidence presented on this point by Kabila loyalists and their attribution of the conflict to factors other than foreign greed.

All Roads Lead to Mobutu: Conflict Externalization in Central Africa

If state collapse is one of the most important permissive conditions leading to the 1990s Congo crisis, the key proximate cause of the regionalized conflagration was the Rwandan genocide and its externalization. The classic works of Prunier, Reyntjens and Stearns all begin their macro-level analyses of the Great War with the after-effects of the Rwandan genocide,[31] and rightfully describe how the "genocide and its consequences did not *cause* the implosion of the Congo ... but acted as a *catalyst*, precipitating a crisis that had been latent for a good many years ..."[32]

The regional roots of Africa's Great War align with a stream in the conflict research program on the transnational causes and consequences of civil war. Consistent with the Central Africa conflict system, a major contribution of this body of scholarship is to establish the significant spillover effects from civil war, both in terms of increasing the likelihood of civil war in neighboring countries but also triggering militarized interstate disputes between the conflict-affected country and (usually) its neighbors.[33] Conflict diffusion is attrib-

---

[30] Prunier, *From Genocide to Continental War*, p. 220.

[31] In contrast to Prunier and Stearns who begin in Rwanda, Reyntjens starts with the Kivus and views the consequences of the genocide from the perspective of that critical region. Ibid.; Reyntjens, *Great African War*; Stearns, *Dancing in the Glory of Monsters*.

[32] Prunier, *From Genocide to Continental War*, p. xxxvi.

[33] Idean Salehyan, *Rebels Without Borders: Transnational Insurgencies in Word Politics*, Ithaca, NY: Cornell University Press, 2009; Salehyan, "Transnational Rebels:

uted to "states' efforts to affect the outcome of the civil war through strategies of intervention and externalization and not by an increase in conflicts over unrelated issues."[34] Externalization occurs when the theater of war extends into neighboring countries as rebels seek to exploit international boundaries to establish more secure bases,[35] and the state experiencing civil war tries to deter its neighbor from backing the rebels.[36] Intervention occurs when states directly intervene in civil war to assist the rebels or fortify the government.[37]

This transnational framework maps on well to the web of conflicts in Central Africa that culminated in the ousting of Mobutu. But consistent with our model of regional polarization and regionalized civil war, the externalization of the Rwandan civil war *preceded* the genocide and its diffusion into eastern Zaire. Habyarimana had been a key client of Mobutu and the Zairian president had dispatched his elite forces, the Division Spéciale Présidentielle (DSP), shortly after the RPF invaded Rwanda in October 1990. According to the RPF, this was the real beginning of the conflict with Mobutu: "Congo's struggle might have started in 1964, our quarrel with Kinshasa started in 1990, with the DSP intervention to stop the RPF advance."[38]

As the RPF won the war, the sanctuary Mobutu gave to the genocidal forces as they fled Rwanda can be seen as a continuation of the war effort to reverse the gains made by the Front. But consistent with Idean Salehyan's

---

Neighboring States as Sanctuary for Rebel Groups," *World Politics*, 59, 2 (2007); Kristian Skrede Gleditsch, "Transnational Dimensions of Civil War," *Journal of Peace Research*, 44, 3 (2007).

[34] Kristian Skrede Gleditsch, Idean Salehyan and Kenneth Schultz, "Fighting at Home, Fighting Abroad," *Journal of Conflict Resolution*, 52, 4 (2008), p. 479.

[35] Thus, as Salehyan notes, the institution of sovereignty has profoundly shaped the transnational dynamics of civil war: "although the extreme claim that borders are sacrosanct should be avoided, national boundaries significantly constrain state capacity to repress challengers and raise the costs of counterinsurgency. Sovereignty grants states an advantage in the domestic use of force, but it also confines that force to a given geographic area. Transnational rebels can therefore mobilize in relative safety and escape across the border to avoid the bulk of state security forces." Salehyan, "Transnational Rebels," p. 224.

[36] Gleditsch, Salehyan and Schultz, "Fighting at Home, Fighting Abroad," p. 479.

[37] Ibid.; Kenneth A. Schultz, "The Enforcement Problem in Coercive Bargaining: Interstate Conflict over Rebel Support in Civil Wars," *International Organization*, 64, 2 (2010).

[38] Interview with Frank Rusagara, London, January 2010.

analysis of the transnational dynamics of civil war, the *génocidaires*' retreat into Zaire was also an attempt by the Hutu extremists to exploit an international boundary in order to escape the reach of the RPF and allow them to regroup and prepare for a counterattack.[39] Dissident forces from other countries, including Uganda, Burundi and Angola, also exploited Zairian sovereignty (and Mobutu's willingness to host and support them) to gain a tactical advantage against the governments they fought. In many ways, the first Congo war was effectively the externalization of not just the Rwandan civil war and genocide but also civil wars in Uganda, Angola and, to a lesser degree, Burundi.[40]

The inability of the RPF, the NRM and the MPLA to remotely coerce Mobutu to cease assistance for these dissident forces is one of the primary factors accounting for the first Congo war and the emergence of the AFDL as an instrument to oust Mobutu. Following from Kenneth Schultz's general model of interstate conflict over rebel support, the overthrow of the Kinshasa regime was a bid to resolve the enforcement problem that underpins externalization, in which rival states are unable to make a credible commitment not to support rebel forces challenging the other, leading to inefficient regionalized conflicts.[41] This enforcement problem is rooted in the difficulties of monitoring another state's compliance to not support non-state actors and the uncertainty that comes when that policy is under the unilateral control of the rival state.

This insight also helps to explain why the RPF was reluctant to delegate too much power either to the Congolese rebels or to other regional forces in the overthrow of Mobutu and security operations in post-Mobutu Congo. The RPF's direct intervention as part of the AFDL was intended to reduce the monitoring costs of the *génocidaires* in Congo and their support networks and to mitigate uncertainty about the Congolese government's compliance in not supporting Rwanda's enemies. After all, it was the RPF which controlled the Congolese army after May 1997 through FAC Chief of Staff (and rising star in the RPA) James Kabarebe.

The puzzle that needs to be accounted for is why the RPF's strategy of direct intervention in Congo in 1996–8 failed so spectacularly—such that the very regime they installed to allow them to finish off the *génocidaires* would end up secretly supporting their arch-enemies and move to expel the RPF, once again

---

[39] Salehyan, "Transnational Rebels."
[40] Clark, *African Stakes of the Congo War.*
[41] Schultz, "Enforcement Problem in Coercive Bargaining."

elevating the enforcement problem as the central axis on which the Congo war would revolve. One possibility, of course, is that what makes this enforcement problem so intractable is that direct intervention in a rival state is not a tenable solution because of popular national resistance to such a strategy.

Domestic Resistance to Foreign Intervention

The RPF intervention in Congo was filled with risks. Foremost among these was the peril of deploying forces among a society with long-held and deeply rooted xenophobic views against Tutsi. Few in the RPF High Command harbored illusions about the resentment that self-declared Congolese nationalists would mobilize to combat the nascent "Hima–Tutsi Empire" that the RPF and NRA/M were accused of seeking to build. However, the alternative of allowing the *génocidaires* to continue to promote their ideology and undertake vicious attacks against Tutsi in eastern Congo and Rwanda could not possibly be countenanced.

As we discuss in great detail from Chapter 5 onwards, the reliance on Kabila, a non-Tutsi with strong nationalist credentials, to lead the AFDL was an attempt to mitigate Congolese concerns that the liberation movement was a "Tutsi rebellion." But with Kabila surrounded by Rwandan and Congolese Tutsi bodyguards and advisers, from the beginning the revolutionary was still pegged as a "puppet" or "hostage" of a Tutsi conspiracy.[42] According to one public opinion poll undertaken in Kinshasa in October 1997, 71 per cent of respondents felt Kabila was under "foreign influence" and 62 per cent thought that Rwanda and Uganda were in the process of "recolonizing the Congo."[43]

Opposition leaders, like Étienne Tshisekedi, sought to capitalize on Kabila's heavy reliance on the Rwandan-led, Pan-Africanist coalition to increase pressure on the new leader. A contingent of Tshisekedi supporters heckled Kabila at his inauguration ceremony as the new president of the Democratic Republic of Congo, castigating him for selling the country to foreigners and being a

---

[42] "Hostage" is how one member of the AFDL described Kabila after meeting him in Goma in the early stages of the rebellion. Interview with Mbusa Nyamwisi, Kinshasa, December 2009.

[43] Opinion poll carried out by Bureau d'Etudes, de Recherche et de Consulting International (BERCI). Cited in International Crisis Group, "How Kabila Lost His Way: The Performance of Laurent Désiré Kabila's Government," ICG Democratic Republic of Congo Report, no. 3, May 21, 1999.

puppet of Tutsi interests.[44] Exacerbating anti-Tutsi sentiment was the imperial and abusive manner in which some soldiers behaved, particularly in the eastern part of the country, after overthrowing the Mobutu government. This incited local calls for mobilization against "Tutsi hegemony."[45]

Alien rule need not provoke anti-regime, nationalist resistance, yet it often does when the government it imposes is deemed exploitative and unfair.[46] The Kabila regime was plagued by each of these shortcomings. Thus it is important to consider the degree to which popular resistance to the continued presence of external troops prompted Kabila to expel the RPF—as some journalists conjectured at the time.[47]

Kabila's heavy reliance on the Front was undeniably costly from a political perspective and it also served to damage his legitimacy as a liberator.[48] The expulsion of the Rwandans and other "foreign forces" was popular throughout the country, particularly in Kinshasa, and it is a historical fact that, as the second war erupted, the Kabila regime whipped up xenophobic sentiment—in some cases using anti-Tutsi propaganda that resembled the hate speech used during the Rwandan genocide—to mobilize the population in the war effort. But we do not see these popular sentiments as the primary reason for the decision to expel the RPF or the cause of the fallout. If anti-Rwandan sentiment was strong, popular political pressure was weak. While Tshisekedi was a thorn in the side of Kabila and railed against the alliance with the RPF, there were no mass demonstrations or other forms of opposition mobilization that threatened to unseat the Kabila regime or even minimally destabilized it unless the president expelled the RPF.[49] Thus this line of argument cannot account for the suddenness and urgency—extensively dissected in Chapter 10—with which Kabila forced out his former comrades after returning from his visit to Cuba in July 1998. If the expulsion was a mere function of Kabila's

[44] James C. McKinley, Jr, "Kabila Sworn in as President, Promises Transition to Democracy," *New York Times*, May 30, 1997.

[45] Reyntjens, *Great African War*, p. 149.

[46] Michael Hechter, *Alien Rule*, New York: Cambridge University Press, 2013.

[47] See, for example, "Kabila Ends Foreign Military Presence in Congo," Panafrican News Agency, July 28, 1998 and Howard W. French, "Congo Replay," *New York Times*, August 5, 1998.

[48] See discussion in Reyntjens, *Great African War*, pp. 166–7.

[49] Moreover, the protests that Tshisekedi did instigate occurred in the first few weeks and months after the overthrow of Mobutu, but they did not lead Kabila to cut his ties with the RPF.

domestic legitimacy problem, why could Kabila and the RPF not come to some negotiated arrangement that would resolve the foreign occupation problem and address the RPF's security concerns but avoid a devastating regionalized civil war that nearly led to Kabila's ouster from power?

Another limitation of this argument is that the personalist nature of Kabila's rule largely insulated him from domestic pressure. The population—or the opposition—had few levers to hold Kabila accountable for his dependence on the Rwandans aside from popular demonstrations, which, as mentioned, never materialized or were close to materializing during this period. In sum, "occupation" as the cause for Africa's Great War lacks an empirical basis.

Fleeting Liberation: The Personalization of Power and Africa's Great War

Beyond natural resources and the legacy of the Rwandan genocide, another factor often presented to account for Africa's Great War was the disastrous rule of Kabila, which alienated just about everybody inside and outside the country.[50] If Mobutu followed Leopold II's playbook for ruling Congo, Kabila "simply replaced Mobutu with Mobutism," in the words of one European observer.[51] Historically, in personalist regimes the biggest threat comes from those within the regime. And for Kabila, that threat was the RPF and its Congolese allies.

From the moment of his auto-proclamation in Lubumbashi in May 1997, in which Kabila anointed himself president without consulting his allies in the liberation movement, Kabila was consolidating power in his own hands, subordinating key organs, such as the AFDL as a political party, to himself, and weakening the horizontal constraints on his authority. Few would disagree that the road to Africa's Great War was paved by Kabila's authoritarian, repressive and arbitrary governing style. In adopting a personalist type of rule that relied heavily on secrecy, the personal distribution of patronage (literally handing out bags of diamonds and dollars to clients), personal loyalty and ethnic ties, Kabila mirrored Mobutu. Yet in contrast to Mobutu's skillful use of the rotating-door of politics, in which he effectively reshuffled his clients to ensure none ever became too powerful but neither did they ever feel they were permanently out of the game, Kabila did not hesitate to liquidate rivals he

[50] Ngolet, *Crisis in the Congo*, pp. 3–19.
[51] Cited in Wrong, *In the Footsteps of Mr Kurtz*, p. 308.

feared. In particular, his elimination of Masasu Nindaga, one of his co-conspirators in the AFDL, would shake the foundations of the regime, as we document in detail in Chapter 7.

Crucially, however, as a growing body of scholarship suggests, the personalist regime constructed by authoritarian leaders is neither accidental nor anomalous. Not only did Kabila reflect the institutional environment of the Congo itself,[52] but revolutionary regimes often give rise to personalist rulers. Jeff Colgan and Jessica Weeks argue that this selection effect works in two ways:

> [R]evolutions are unlikely to succeed unless they are led by a charismatic, forceful, risk-tolerant, politically savvy, and ambitious leader, and these are precisely the types of individuals most likely to create personalist dictatorships ... Second, because revolutionary movements by their very nature overturn the political institutions of the previous government, revolutionary leaders are especially likely to be able to consolidate a personalist dictatorship. Such leaders face few, if any, limits on their formal legal powers in the immediate aftermath of the revolution, and therefore often have the opportunity to structure the regime as they wish.[53]

The rise of risk-acceptant, unconstrained rulers in post-revolutionary regimes is significantly more likely to lead to war than non-personalist and non-revolutionary rulers. Such rulers tend to be more bellicose due to their leadership qualities (i.e., high-levels of risk tolerance and willingness to challenge the status quo),[54] but also because of the weak institutional constraints in personalist regimes (i.e., they are less likely to be held accountable domestically for disappointing war outcomes, and less likely to face horizontal constraints from other elites for foreign policy adventurism).[55]

This framework is a powerful lens through which to interpret the outbreak of Africa's Great War. It offers an institutional explanation as to how Kabila could get away with his bold and reckless steps to reach out to the *génocidaires*, quite possibly as early as March or May 1998 (Chapter 9) and expel the Rwandans in late July 1998—the *casus belli* of the Second Congo War. But the model equally applies to the RPF and the other governments that would

---

[52] Reno, *Warfare in Independent Africa.*

[53] Colgan and Weeks, "Revolution, Personalist Dictatorships, and International Conflict," p. 23.

[54] Colgan, "Domestic Revolutionary Leaders and International Conflict."

[55] Jessica L. Weeks, "Strongmen and Straw Men: Authoritarian Regimes and the Initiation of International Conflict," *American Political Science Review*, 106, 2 (2012).

[56] Prunier makes this point in his concluding chapter. Prunier, *From Genocide to Continental War*, pp. 335–6.

throw themselves into the Congolese abyss.[56] Though the RPF was much less personalized than the Congolese regime James Kabarebe installed in power, there was nonetheless an incredible concentration of power in a single decision-maker—Rwanda's vice-president and minister of defense, Paul Kagame. Even if Kagame faced stronger elite-constraints inside his liberation movement (especially from the so-called "Council of Colonels"), the sociology of the RPF and the movement's violent history, which inculcated its members "with systematic beliefs about the necessity, effectiveness, and appropriateness of using military force,"[57] increased its willingness to accept war as a legitimate, frequently usable policy tool.[58]

One limitation of this institutional model of external conflict is that it fails to account for the origins of personalist rule and how the underlying factors that shape personalism may also increase the risk of conflict. The Congo case highlights two potential sources of endogeneity and points to the need for a more comprehensive theoretical framework that accounts for the internal–external nexus of revolutionary regimes, as we discussed in the previous chapter.

The first source of endogeneity is that personalist rule is a function of the strategic environment in which violence specialists operate and their decision to purge rivals who threaten their political authority.[59] This uncertainty and the shifts in power it brings about within a revolutionary or liberation movement are rarely self-contained but often have external repercussions. Given the personalization of foreign policy, in which foreign states rely on personal ties with different clients in a regime rather than all operating through the same formal channel, the shifting fortunes of key members of a regime's elite increases regional uncertainty.

[57] Todd S. Sechser, "Are Soldiers Less War-Prone than Statesmen?," *Journal of Conflict Resolution*, 48, 5 (2004). Cited in Weeks, "Strongmen and Straw Men."

[58] Harry Verhoeven, "Nurturing Democracy or into the Danger Zone? The Rwandan Patriotic Front, Elite Fragmentation and Post-Liberation Politics," in Maddalena Campioni and Patrick Noack (eds), *Rwanda Fast Forward: Social, Economic, Military and Reconciliation Prospects*, Basingstoke: Palgrave Macmillan, 2012. See also Michael C. Horowitz and Allan C. Stam, "How Prior Military Experience Influences the Future Militarized Behavior of Leaders," *International Organization*, 68, 3 (2014).

[59] Roessler, "The Enemy Within: Personal Rule, Coups, and Civil War in Africa"; Koga, June 2013. "Accountability, Leadership Survival and Personalization in Dictatorships," unpublished manuscript, Department of Political Science, University of Strathclyde.

The second source is that external support for revolutionary or liberation movements can weaken internal governance structures and undermine institutionalization. This works at multiple levels. At one level, as Jeremy Weinstein notes, the presence of an external patron that is willing to finance and arm a rebel movement affects the type of individuals who join a rebel movement (attracting not just the most committed to the cause but also opportunists who seek the immediate benefits doled out by the external sponsor). Moreover, it reduces the rebel movement's need to "strike cooperative bargains with noncombatant populations," leading to more predatory rebel strategies.[60] External dependence can also weaken elite constraints at the top of the rebel organization as the foreign patron, intent on maximizing its influence and reducing coordination costs, empowers a single individual who is accountable to the outside actor rather than to the organization or other elites within the rebel movement. As we explain at length, Kabila's consolidation of power was impossible without the support provided by the RPF, a trend which worried other members of the Pan-Africanist coalition. In fact, some within the AFDL go as far as to accuse the RPF of eliminating Kabila's rivals on his behalf. Promoting Kabila within the coalition was in the RPF's short-term interest as it increased his dependence on Rwanda while preventing the emergence of rivals who could threaten Kigali's interests. The RPF, however, overlooked how this strategy came at a cost internally (Kabila's terrible governance record) and externally (as it contributed to the cold war between Rwanda and Angola).

In sum, the personalization of power under Kabila *is* a key contributor to the outbreak of Africa's Great War. Yet, rather than wholly attributing it to Kabila's erratic personality or idiosyncratic management style, we root it in the institutional and strategic environment in which he operated. Kabila's power grab was a direct result of the RPF's attempt to maximize control over the AFDL and eliminate the number of agents it had to work with; it preferred dealing with one interlocutor over which it held huge sway, rather than a quartet of contenders with links to other foreign patrons. The re-emergence of personalist rule in Kinshasa after May 1997 was thus abetted by the Front in that Kabila skillfully exploited the organizational structure the RPF had created to first become head of the AFDL and then to systematically remove challengers to power. While initially welcomed tacitly by Kagame and Kabarebe, they would soon come to regret this costly mistake.

---

[60] Jeremy M. Weinstein, *Inside Rebellion: The Politics of Insurgent Violence*, New York: Cambridge University Press, 2007, p. 10.

Our Argument: Sowing the Seeds of Its Own Destruction

State collapse, the externalization of the Rwandan civil war, domestic resistance to foreign occupation and the personalization of power under Kabila are important contributing factors, yet they fail to fully account for the high politics of Africa's Great War: why the core of the Pan-Africanist project for Congo—the RPF–Kabila–MPLA alliance—ended up fracturing and pitting Kabila and ultimately the MPLA against the RPF and their Congolese allies.

The overthrow of the Mobutu regime brought an end to regional polarization in Central Africa, but, ironically, this success compounded a fundamental challenge that arises from revolution: how to manage the vacuum of power following the removal of the *ancien régime*. This was a major concern for the AFDL stakeholders and their foreign supporters, as each invested in overthrowing Mobutu with an eye to remaking the Congo and the broader regional system in a way that advanced their political interests. The challenge thus was how to rebuild order in Central Africa in accordance with each stakeholder's strategic interests and collectively sustain the new distribution of power in the absence of a supranational authority. This of course represents one of the fundamental problems in international politics;[61] uncertainty about other actors' future commitments to upholding the balance of power is a key source of war, both internationally[62] and domestically.[63] Risk of war is theorized to be particularly high after revolution owing to an increase in information asymmetries and fluidity in the distribution of power.[64]

[61] A vast literature exists on this subject. Seminal works include: Robert Jervis, "Cooperation under the Security Dilemma," *World Politics*, 30, 2 (1978); Kenneth Neal Waltz, *Theory of International Politics*, Reading, MA: Addison-Wesley, 1979; Robert Gilpin, *War and Change in World Politics*, New York: Cambridge University Press, 1981; Robert O. Keohane, *After Hegemony: Cooperation and Discord in the World Political Economy*, Princeton, NJ: Princeton University Press, 1984; Alexander Wendt, "Anarchy is What States Make of It: The Social Construction of Power Politics," *International Organization*, 46, 2 (1992).

[62] James D. Fearon, "Rationalist Explanations for War," *International Organization*, 49, 3 (1995); Dale C. Copeland, *The Origins of Major War*, Ithaca: Cornell University Press, 2000; Robert Powell, "War as a Commitment Problem," *International Organization*, 60, 1 (2006).

[63] Philip Roessler, *Ethnic Politics and State Power in Africa: The Logic of the Coup–Civil War Trap*, New York: Cambridge University Press, 2016.

[64] Walt, *Revolution and War*; Maoz, *Domestic Sources of Global Change*.

In post-Mobutu Central Africa, the cooperative nature of the revolutionary change and the ideological affinity of the protagonists should have helped to mitigate information asymmetries and concerns about shifts in the future distribution of power. As we explain at length in the chapters that follow, there was an incredible strategic interdependence between the AFDL and its primary foreign backer—the RPF. Similarly, though to a lesser degree, a strong alliance of regional powers had coalesced to usher in a "second independence" for Congo and the continent. Why could they not sustain this cooperation and convert it into a regime of collective security that advanced each state's strategic interests? We attribute the breakdown of cooperation and the outbreak of Africa's Great War to the weakness of the organizational structures that underpinned the AFDL and the Pan-Africanist alliance. Forged through informal and ad hoc agreements and characterized by an organizational asymmetry with the RPF playing a dominant role, there were few mechanisms to share information about each contributing state's military activities or even to agree upon basic issues such as each state's role in Congo after the overthrow of Mobutu. The absence of such channels increased the risk of misperception about each other's intentions. Just as critically, the dominance of the RPF and the weak organizational constraints it faced both within Congo and regionally gave it incredible leverage to bring about a future shift in the distribution of power. This possibility haunted Kabila—who feared that, just as the RPF had put him in power, it could also take it away. But it also worried regional powers like Angola's MPLA who were unsure how the RPF would exploit its upper-hand in Congo and the implications this would have for their own strategic interests. These information problems and uncertainty reinforced each other and, given the RPF's deep and direct involvement in Congo, this had both internal and external consequences. As we show extensively throughout this book, one of the ultimate consequences of the information asymmetries and uncertainty that dominated the post-Mobutu order was that it locked Kabila and the RPF in a security dilemma that has bedeviled other co-conspirators in Africa's weak states.[65] The upshot in the case of Congo was that, due to the regionalization of the AFDL, the security dilemma could not be contained to a dyadic conflict between the Kabila regime and the RPF but ensnared powerful regional states and gave way to Africa's Great War.

Following from this, the fatal flaw of the revolutionaries and their Pan-Africanist allies was the vehicle they built to vanquish the Mobutu regime and

---

[65] For an analysis of this security dilemma and the Congo case in comparative perspective, see Roessler, *Ethnic Politics and State Power in Africa*.

that would fill the post-revolutionary vacuum of power—an organizationally weak, externally dominated rebellion. Ironically, the AFDL looked very different from the set of Leninist movements that would back its rise to power. The RPF, NRM, MPLA, TPLF, EPLF and TANU/CCM represented some of the most durable and effective politico-military organizations in postcolonial Africa. Their organizational structures helped minimize, though not avoid, the devastating internecine elite infighting that often plagues those regimes that come to power by force[66] and has all too regularly co-engendered state failure in Africa.[67] So what went wrong in Congo? Why did these strong regimes install one of the weakest, opening the door to Africa's Great War? How can we explain the failure of the AFDL's backers to draw on the lessons they learned from their own liberation struggles? We attribute the weakness of the AFDL to three key factors: the fragility and dysfunctionality of the *ancien régime*, the end of regional polarization, and, perhaps most importantly, the strategic outlook and political culture of the AFDL's primary sponsor—the RPF. A sequential discussion of these below concludes this chapter.

* * *

In *Warfare in Independent Africa*, William Reno notes that the degree of organization and mobilization that liberation movements develop during the revolutionary struggle is a function of the strength of the enemy.[68] He goes on to argue that insurgents often tend to organizationally mimic the state they seek to overthrow, and merely need to outperform the foe they are fighting to gain power; this means that defeating a strong incumbent regime (e.g., the Derg, backed by thousands of heavily armed Soviet "advisers" in Ethiopia between 1974 and 1991) will necessitate a formidable insurgency, but that taking on a fledgling, unraveling government seldom compels rebels to reach highly sophisticated levels of politico-military organization.[69] The nature of the Zairean state at the end of Mobutu's reign meant that the AFDL faced exactly the latter scenario: "what passed for a government structure was so rotten that the brush of a hand could cause it to collapse."[70] The upshot of this,

---

[66] Roessler, "Enemy Within"; Milan W. Svolik, *The Politics of Authoritarian Rule*, New York: Cambridge University Press, 2012.

[67] Roessler, *Ethnic Politics and State Power in Africa*.

[68] Reno, *Warfare in Independent Africa*.

[69] Ibid.

[70] Prunier, *From Genocide to Continental War*, p. xxxi.

as Prunier goes on to say, is "a few mortar shells dislocated it beyond recognition."[71] Though this is hyperbolic, it reflects the minimal resistance the AFDL faced as its fighters marched through the country. Frank Rusagara, the permanent secretary of the Rwandan Ministry of Defense, acknowledged the unintended consequence of the weakness of its foe: "There was no time for political organization: it was going too fast. The political organization of the AFDL could not cope with the rapid military progress ... The military operation was so easy—almost a joke."[72] Moreover, it was the regional powers, especially the RPF, which did the revolutionary heavy-lifting in providing the firepower necessary to liberate Zaire. Consequently, the powerful organizational structures—especially integrated and hierarchical military institutions—that liberation movements have historically forged amid protracted and violent revolutions never materialized.[73]

Some of these emerging problems were temporarily veiled by the euphoria engendered by the sheer success of ousting the enemy within less than a year of the start of the campaign. The overthrow of Mobutu ended the regional polarization that had dominated Central Africa since the 1960s, ushering in a less hostile environment for post-liberation consolidation. Ostensibly, this was exactly the game-changer Nyerere, Kagame, Dos Santos and Museveni had been hoping for. However, the Pan-Africanist coalition failed to anticipate one key change that did not work in favor of regional peace. Although in the past regional polarization had indeed contributed to devastating cycles of conflict *between* revolutionary and counter-revolutionary forces, often it had also helped to foster organizational coherence and unity *among* the revolutionaries.[74] A formidable counter-revolutionary menace necessitated the building of powerful national and regional political coalitions, as well as fostering unity after liberation to ward off the continued threat to its survival.[75] Out of this process emerged some of the most durable and effective politico-military organizations in post-colonial Africa—FLN, ANC, TPLF, EPLF, MPLA, FRELIMO, NRM and RPF—and regional security efforts—the

---

[71] Ibid.

[72] Interview in London, January 2010.

[73] On revolutions and organizational strength and coherence, see Huntington, *Political Order in Changing Societies*; Levitsky and Way, "Durability of Revolutionary Regimes."

[74] On the analytical importance of regional polarization on revolutionary coherence, we have benefited from discussions with Lucan Way.

[75] Levitsky and Way, "Durability of Revolutionary Regimes."

OAU Liberation Committee and Frontline States policy. Their organizational strength proved essential in resisting the counter-revolutionary onslaught, but it also served as a powerful regulator of political competition and uncertainty within their own liberation regimes.

The AFDL, however, would be a clear outlier in this regard. It lacked the military integration, organizational coherence and political unity that characterized other violent liberation regimes in African history. Thus, it did not have the institutions necessary to manage the uncertainty that arises from the violent seizure of power and that increase the risk of regime infighting and factionalism. With the melting away of what was left of the Mobutu regime and the end of the major counter-revolutionary threat in the region, there was little internal cohesion. Therefore, even as a high-degree of strategic interdependence developed between Kabila and the RPF, it was not institutionalized and was highly asymmetric.

The final factor that shaped the AFDL and helps to explain its fatal institutional weakness was the strategic outlook and political culture and sociology of the organization spearheading the charge against Mobutu—the Rwandan Patriotic Front. For the RPF, the informal and asymmetric nature of the AFDL, as its chosen vehicle for regime change in Kinshasa, was no accident; it was by design. This strategic choice by the RPF was profoundly shaped by the imminent counter-revolutionary threat it faced from the *génocidaires*, backed by the Mobutu regime, in the first two years after the genocide. Facing what it perceived as a continual existential threat, the RPF felt it had to act immediately to pre-empt the looming counter-revolution; it could not afford to take the time to cultivate a strong, locally rooted rebel organization or institutionalize an anti-Mobutu coalition.

But the RPF's strategic approach was also experiential and profoundly shaped by the sequential, successful wars it fought and the genocide it faced. Its success in helping Museveni come to power in Uganda and then overthrowing the genocidal regime in Rwanda—even as the Habyarimana government received extensive support from France—reinforced its towering self-confidence and its absolute belief in the transformative power of force when confronted with an impasse.[76] This made it predisposed to military solutions to political problems,[77] and left it deeply mistrustful of outside actors and reluctant to delegate power

---

[76] Verhoeven, "Nurturing Democracy or into the Danger Zone?"

[77] As one member of the RPF described it: "The military preceded the political—we came up with a program after defining our security goals. It should have been the other way round." Interview with Frank Rusagara, London, January 2010.

to anyone but itself. This mindset helps account for why the RPF sought to manage the war and the post-Mobutu order with its elite troops, while struggling to take advantage of the presence of a Pan-Africanist team of key political advisers that was supposed to strengthen the AFDL's organizational coherence and ideological depth. It also helps to explain why the Front readily accepted Kabila's invitation for James Kabarebe, the commander of the RPF's crack units that led the AFDL military operations in Congo, to become chief of staff of the new Forces Armées Congolaises.

The RPF's decision to go it largely alone in Congo and favor informal, ad hoc means of coordination with other regional states undermined the Front's strategy in the longer term even if it initially seemed advantageous to Kagame and his officers. First, it undermined the development of a strong, integrated Congolese military that was necessary for long-term stability. Second, it meant the RPF would find itself sucked into Kinshasa politics in a way it had never considered, without any of the requisite political institutions to regulate the intensifying competition between different regime factions. Third, the disproportionate role of the RPF vis-à-vis other, less involved regional comrades increased the likelihood that any instability within the AFDL would also be felt regionally and that the RPF would be held responsible for it. Conversely, regional instability would affect elite bargaining within the Congolese government, of which the Front had essentially become a part with the appointment of Kabarebe as head of the army.

Overall, the RPF's failure to formalize the regional response to the overthrow of Mobutu and its tolerance of a weakly institutionalized, poorly integrated liberation movement in which it inserted itself proved highly destabilizing. The RPF's privileged role gave it the capability to quickly and decisively shift the distribution of power within the Kabila regime, but also to alter the regional balance of power, while its secretive nature would increase others' suspicions about its "real" objectives. This uncertainty haunted Kabila—whose dependence on the RPF also left him highly vulnerable if Kigali decided to move against him. However, it would also preoccupy regional players—Tanzania and Zimbabwe but especially Angola. The mistrust between the RPF and the MPLA reached a first peak following the Tshikapa incident of April 1997, which triggered a kind of cold war between the two regional powers that would later prevent the two movements from cooperating to remove Kabila, even as both came to see him as a liability in the region. Ironically, the RPF was thus unwittingly sowing the seeds for renewed regional conflict after sacrificing so much to rid Central Africa of the cancerous Mobutu regime.

PART II

THE WAR TO END ALL WARS

4

THE GATHERING STORM

MOBUTU'S ZAIRE, THE AFRICAN LIBERATION PROJECT AND THE RWANDAN PATRIOTIC FRONT

Africa is reeling ... Recall that Zaire is more than a state: it is a continent. It has never been governed. It has always been looted.

Laurent-Désiré Kabila, internal AFDL memo, November 23, 1996.[1]

By the early 1990s, Africa was ripe for transformative change. The Cold War and the post-colonial consensus not to alter the borders as they came out of the imperialist century had kept the continent's international relations in a straitjacket for decades. The demise of the Soviet Union hastened the collapse of its Marxist–Leninist allies, such as Mengistu Haile Mariam's military dictatorship in Ethiopia. It also forced left-wing ruling parties and opposition movements to reassess their guiding ideology and the external backing for their projects. Growing signs that the West would revisit its relations with the continent and extend the economic conditionality of "structural adjustment" in the neoliberal 1980s to the political realm (insisting on democratization

[1] Gauthier De Villers and Jean-Claude Willame, *République démocratique du Congo: chronique politique d'un entre-deux-guerres, octobre 1996–juillet 1998*, Tervuren and Paris: Institut Africain—CEDAF/Editions L'Harmattan, 1999, pp. 43–4.

and liberalization) gave Africans a strong sense that a new era was dawning. South Africa's Apartheid regime had never been so isolated and Nelson Mandela was released on February 2, 1990. Not since 1960 had there been such anticipation of change from Cairo to the Cape.

The dreams of a "second independence" coincided with a dramatic upsurge in violence, mostly within, rather than between, African states. From the late 1980s onwards, seemingly stable countries—Algeria, Liberia, Sierra Leone, Somalia—were engulfed by conflicts that sank economies, created huge refugee flows and saw the deaths of hundreds of thousands of citizens at the hands of their fellow countrymen. Neither the United Nations nor the Organization of African Unity was able to prevent, contain or resolve spiraling wars in these states, nor in places like Angola, Chad, Sudan and northern Uganda, where protracted conflicts persisted, bringing famine and misery to the war-ravaged populations. The birth pangs of the New Africa were more disruptive than expected; for every new election organized, a new war seemed to erupt or an old one intensified.

While so many on and off the continent were confused as to whether they should be optimistic or pessimistic about the future of the continent, one group of actors remained resolutely hopeful. They would play a defining role in redrawing the political landscape of Africa in the years to come. From Asmara in the far northeast to the halls of the presidential palace in Kampala to Robben Island off the southern shores, self-declared Pan-Africanists were exhilarated by the opportunities they saw emerging from Africa's new geopolitics. This revolutionary group, which united both newly inaugurated presidents as well as ageing opposition leaders and youngsters from sprawling refugee camps, did not formally work together under the banner of a unified political force but was an amorphous movement built on personal networks and a vision of transforming Africa. Each (neo)liberation movement would pursue change in its homeland first and then lend a hand to its neighbors, but there could be no doubt that the ultimate objective was the crushing of all imperialist intervention on the African continent and the definitive break with the era of colonialism, which, in their eyes, had been perpetuated by a number of African leaders who all too readily served as neo-colonial proxies.

This book tells the story of the most ambitious transformation project the Pan-Africanists of the 1990s pursued. This chapter sketches the politico-historical context during which a Congolese liberation movement, the AFDL, and its international backers coalesced. It does so by describing a gathering storm, with the Congolese theater as its eye, as three inter-related historical processes converged by the end of 1995: the weakening of the Mobutist state and the inability of the ageing ruler to maintain the system of regional order he had so successfully exploited for years; the growing momentum for a revival of Pan-Africanist liberation politics that identified regime change in Kinshasa as an indispensable goal in the quest for a "New Africa"; and the rise to power of the Rwandan Patriotic Front, which ousted the genocidal government run by Hutu extremists in July 1994 but remained locked in a war with these forces as they retreated to Mobutu's Zaire. In analyzing these three core dynamics, we explicate the domestic and regional conditions that shaped the AFDL's character from its genesis and which we discuss in greater detail in the next chapter. From the perspective of the self-styled revolutionaries, the achievements of domestic liberation would be continuously imperiled if they did not also overhaul the regional architecture, which aided and abetted oppressive neo-colonial governments in their home states. The establishment of a more stable and "progressive" internal equilibrium was intrinsically linked to a more conducive external environment and vice versa. And this transition was, invariably and inevitably, tempestuous.

The State of Congo: Mobutu and "Neo-Colonial Africa"

The territory of Africa's second biggest state covers an area of more than 2,300,000 square kilometers; an area the size of Germany, France, the Benelux, the Iberian Peninsula, Italy, Denmark, Greece and the British Isles *combined*. On a continent popularly associated with state failure, grinding poverty and devastating conflict, no country's history has become more coterminous with misfortune than that of the Congo. Commentators invariably cite geography and the idea of a national destiny-as-tragedy when seeking to account for misery and violence amid what should be a land of abundance. In 1892, a Belgian geologist, Jules Cornet, exclaimed upon visiting Katanga, the country's massive southern region, that the territory the Belgian sovereign Leopold II had acquired was nothing less than a *"geological scandal"*: it was so impossibly rich in mineral riches and other natural resources—from rubber and timber to ivory and hyper-fertile soils—that it seemed like God himself favored the king's Congo Free State project as it had begun a decade earlier in 1885.[2] Leopold immediately understood the economic potential and the political dangers of Cornet's geological discoveries. He reiterated promises to

[2] Cited in Nzongola-Ntalaja, *Congo from Leopold to Kabila*, p. 28.

Europe's Great Powers that his Free State would act as a stabilizing, neutral buffer between British, French, German and Portuguese colonial rivalries and that no country would enjoy a more privileged relationship with it than the others,[3] just like the Belgian state was supposed to do in Western Europe. However, independence in 1960, at the height of the Cold War, led to a resurfacing of the idea that Congo's resources would simply prove too tantalizing to be left alone. For Afro-Caribbean revolutionary Frantz Fanon, *"Africa is shaped like a gun and Congo is the trigger."*

While Congolese history is infinitely more varied than tropes of geographical determinism and an omnipresent (potential for) violence suggest, the political annals are nevertheless replete with cynical power games and ruthless processes of extraction that have ensured that what should be one of the world's wealthiest nations was, according to the 2013 UNDP Human Development Report, in effect its least developed country.[4] The state was first erected by the Belgian monarch's agents to allow King Leopold to benefit from the largest piece of private property in history: the Free State was not his because of his title as king of the Belgians, but rather as owner of the Association Internationale du Congo (AIC) which at the 1884–5 Berlin Conference was endowed with sovereignty over large swathes of Central Africa. With no involvement of or oversight by the Belgian government and hence no Belgian public funds available to the AIC bar one loan in 1890, every franc invested in Congo either had to be raised there, or paid back to an external investor. Thus, to make the Free State a financial success, an exploitative reign of terror was installed that caused the deaths of hundreds of thousands of people—perhaps millions—owing to harsh labor requirements, arbitrary violence and displacement-induced hunger and disease.[5] The Leopoldian years have been described as an "African Holocaust."[6]

The Free State was neither a colony, nor a protectorate, nor a Belgian province but the personal estate of an individual, Leopold von Sachsen-Coburg, who never set foot on Congolese soil. The institutions and dis-

---

[3] Pakenham, *Scramble for Africa*, pp. 239–55.

[4] United Nations Development Programme, "Human Development Report: The Rise of the South," New York: UNDP, 2013.

[5] Jean Stengers and Jan Vansina, "King Leopold's Congo," in G.N. Sandersen, J.D. Fage and Roland Oliver (eds), *The Cambridge History of Africa: From 1870 to 1905*, Cambridge: Cambridge University Press, 1985.

[6] Hochschild, *King Leopold's Ghost*.

courses produced by this highly unusual polity would change in appearance as the country evolved from colony to formal, sovereign state, but they retained their defining characteristics a century after its founding:[7] alien, in that the "national" institutions were utterly unrepresentative of the vast majority of Congolese subjects/citizens; highly authoritarian, with sovereignty a product of the brutal imposition of authority; exclusionary, with the state dominated by a handful of enclaves (Leopoldville/Kinshasa, Matadi/Boma, Elisabethville/Lubumbashi, Jadotville/Likasi), where capital and coercive power were concentrated; and externally oriented, because its connections with global markets and diplomatic capitals were much closer than with its own vast hinterland.

Neither Leopold II's "generous bequest"—a year before his death he "donated" the Free State to the Belgian state amid international criticism of the atrocities and financial difficulties plaguing the royal family—nor the advent of "colonial developmentalism" in the 1940s and 1950s fundamentally transformed the nature of the state. Despite reforms to the labor regime, an expansion of social services (with a major role for the Catholic Church) and a post-war economic boom,[8] the state remained authoritarian, exclusionary, alien and externally oriented. What did change, however, was the discourse surrounding Congo, so much so that by the 1950s it was widely considered a model colony by many British and French observers who criticized their own governments.[9]

If London prioritized indirect rule and Paris organized its African possessions along the Republican model—both of which seemed to have gone badly wrong as made evident by blood-soaked (counter)insurgencies in Kenya and Algeria—then the Belgian strategy of extreme paternalism in Congo and in the post-1919 "mandate territories" of Ruanda–Urundi seemed to generate higher economic growth and greater political stability. The Congolese were not considered citizens and had barely any civil or political rights; there were no Congolese lawyers, architects or engineers. The motto of Governor-General Pierre Ryckmans (1934–46) was *dominer pour servir*—dominate in order to serve.[10] This was reflected in an education policy that produced one of the highest percentages of primary school enrolment in Africa, but only six,

---

[7] Young, *African Colonial State in Comparative Perspective*.

[8] Gaston Vandewalle, *De Conjuncturele Evolutie in Kongo en Ruanda-Urundi, van 1920 tot 1939 en van 1949 tot 1958*, Ghent: Rijks Universiteit, 1966.

[9] John Gunther, *Inside Africa*, New York: Harper, 1955.

[10] Pierre Ryckmans, "Belgian 'Colonialism'," *Foreign Affairs*, 34, 1 (1955).

fourteen or twenty-eight (depending on the source) university graduates at independence. Being able to read and write your own name and execute basic orders was considered useful; independent thought most certainly was not.

This highly oppressive system of colonialism—born out of the megalomania of a European sovereign and perpetuated by a racist bureaucracy and mining conglomerates towering over the economy—would be one of the main grievances motivating the leadership of the AFDL decades later. But the anger of Laurent-Désiré Kabila, Paul Kagame and their comrades would be even more directed at the post-independence policies pursued by African elites. No one embodied the notion of "neo-colonialism" better than Mobutu Sese Seko, the ruler of Congo (or "Zaire," as he renamed it in 1971) between 1965 and 1997. No president was more loathed in leftist circles than the sergeant-major turned commander-in-chief with the leopard-skin hat.

Mobutu was born in 1930 by the banks of the Congo River in Lisala in the equatorial forest to a father who died before his son reached adolescence. Mobutu's hard-working mother, who was absent for much of his childhood, sent him to school in the bustling towns of Leopoldville (seat of the colonial government) and Coquilhatville, later known as Mbandaka, capital of Mobutu's beloved but marginalized Equateur region in the northwest. Mobutu excelled academically and his wit and physical prowess impressed many of the priests, teachers and other officials he met.[11] Belgians were astonished by the ability of this "forest boy" to adopt Western, urbanized manners. It was a dialectic Mobutu would use all his life: to impress people with his cosmopolitan charm, yet claim to be a humble son of the land, distrustful of the corruption of the big town; to shun the "sin city" of Kinshasa as president by residing most of his time in his jungle hideout in Gbadolite, yet to live there in unimaginable luxury with all urban amenities. Similarly, both before and during his political career, Mobutu was keen to stress his image as a faithful Roman Catholic and quoted biblical passages extensively, but he also clashed with the Church and deliberately spread rumors about his sexual voracity and his dabbling in witchcraft.[12] For Mobutu and his admirers, there was no contradiction: merely the irresistible dominance of his personality.

Mobutu was a key beneficiary of the paternalism of Belgian rule as well as someone who would virulently denounce colonialism. Among fellow

[11] Michela Wrong, *In the Footsteps of Mr Kurtz: Living on the Brink of Disaster in Mobutu's Congo*, London: Fourth Estate, 2000, pp. 68–73.
[12] Van Reybrouck, *Congo: Een Geschiedenis*, pp. 351–84.

Congolese in the Force Publique, the formidable colonial army in which he served for almost a decade, he would castigate Belgian occupation, yet instrumentalize all the connections and training that working for the Force Publique provided. Later, as a journalist, he became a confidant of the leftist nationalist leader Patrice Lumumba and simultaneously flirted with the Belgian intelligence services and the CIA. While many sources report Mobutu to have been a pawn of the latter two, the charmer from Equateur bet both on the nationalist and the imperialist horse to further his options and was happy for things to evolve either way, as long as he would be at the center of developments.

By June 30, 1960, Congo's independence, Mobutu was Leopoldville's coming man. Prime Minister Lumumba appointed him first as a negotiator with the Belgian *haute finance* and then as army chief of staff; within twelve months of independence, he had stamped out a mutiny, confronted the Katangese secession, turned on his former mentor and had Lumumba sent to his death, having become de facto ruler of his country after a coup d'état in September 1960.[13] Mobutu tolerated President Joseph Kasavubu as his nominal superior until he reached for the presidential crown he believed to be rightfully his in 1965. To many urban Congolese, he was a nationalist hero who helped save the country from disintegration; to citizens from impoverished hinterland provinces, he was a guarantee that Congo would not just be dominated by the elites from Leopoldville, Elisabethville (Lubumbashi, Katanga) or Stanleyville (Kisangani, Province Orientale); to Western spy agencies, he was the only man strong enough to keep the Soviet Union out of Central Africa and ensure that business would continue as usual.[14]

The regime that would persist for thirty-two long years is a study in personal rule—Mobutu has rightly been described as Africa's archetypal dictator, dominating a classic "kleptocracy."[15] It is hard to overstate the devastating decline in living standards under his reign and the complete reversal of perceptions: if, after the roaring 1950s, Congo was widely considered Africa's great future prospect, under Mobutist rule it experienced quasi-total collapse of formal economic

---

[13] Ludo De Witte and Ann Wright, *The Assassination of Lumumba*, London: Verso, 2002.

[14] Ludo De Witte, *Huurlingen, Geheim Agenten en Diplomaten*, Leuven: Uitgeverij Van Halewyck, 2014.

[15] Daron Acemoglu, Thierry Verdier and James A. Robinson, "Kleptocracy and Divide-and-Rule: A Model of Personal Rule," *Journal of the European Economic Association*, 2, 2–3 (2004).

activity and associated runaway inflation and sky-high unemployment. The number of teachers was halved, from 285,000 to 126,000, between 1982 and 1985. Zaire's leader had millions of dollars printed for his personal use by the central bank in Kinshasa and habitually reserved a third or more of the government's budget for the presidency, a hefty sum topped up by nearly 15 per cent of unaccounted state expenditure that he directly controlled too.[16] In 1992, Mobutu's reported personal fortune of more than US$6 billion exceeded the total output of the Zairian economy. The following table, compiled by William Reno from various reports of the Banque du Zaire, shows the extent to which the president personally dominated the state budget—and the resultant loss of state capacity to provide even basic public goods.

Table 4.1: Zairian Government Expenditure, 1972–92 (%)[17]

Year	President	Agriculture	Social Services
1972	28	29.3	17.5
1974	26	32.1	12.4
1976	29	30.9	13.2
1978	29	41	11
1980	33	42	11
1982	35	32	10
1984	39	30	9
1986	39	29	7
1988	49	18	4
1990	80	11	2
1992	95	4	0

World Bank estimates describe a fall by two-thirds of income per capita for a Zairian between 1960 and 1995; the Economist Intelligence Unit reported inflation of 23,000 per cent in the same year. One of countless classic Mobutu jokes captured his disinterest in even maintaining the basics of state infrastructure: one day in the 1980s, Mobutu receives a phone call in Gbadolite from a fellow African leader who has long sought his patronage. He is obviously in distress and in a panicked tone tells Mobutu that rebels have invaded his land

[16] Steve Askin and Carole Collins, "External Collusion with Kleptocracy: Can Zaïre Recapture Its Stolen Wealth?," *Review of African Political Economy*, 20, 57 (1993), pp. 77–8.

[17] William Reno, "Sovereignty and Personal Rule in Zaire," *African Studies Quarterly*, 1, 3 (1997), pp. 43–4.

and are marching to the palace. What to do, he asks the Zairian/Congolese president. "Did they come by land?" Mobutu asks. "Non, *patron!*" the younger leader says. Mobutu tries again: "Perhaps by sea, with Soviet help?" The response comes swiftly: "Not at all. They are coming by road." "Aha!" Mobutu exclaims. "I see you did not follow my advice from years ago. You should do what I do. Never ever build roads."

The previously symbiotic relations between government and big business that formed the bedrock of Congo's extraordinary growth in the 1950s turned into parasitic leeching of the private sector, particularly from the second half of the 1970s onwards.[18] The mining conglomerates of Katanga stood among global record-beaters prior to Mobutu; by the 1990s, they produced one-tenth of their peak. Under colonialism, five gigantic holding companies lorded over two-thirds of the Congolese economy, with Union Minière—the jewel in the Belgian crown—perhaps paying up to half of the total taxes collected in the entire country. Under Mobutu, one man overshadowed all other economic players.

Legal economic activity beyond subsistence scale outside the system became nigh-impossible: either one partnered with a senior Mobutist and accepted political appointees in the company, or assets would be seized or closed down. By 1994, state-owned Gécamines, the successor company to Union Minière and the single biggest source of foreign exchange inflows in the 1970s and 1980s, barely managed to produce 32,000 tons of cobalt and copper rather than the more than 450,000 tons which for years was its average.[19] The plantation sector too, once a great employer and source of export earnings, declined steeply, shrinking on average by 3 per cent per annum from 1978 onwards.[20] Direct theft by the dictator—the transfer of public goods into his personal hands—contributed substantially, but the root cause was Mobutu's extreme form of patrimonial politics, which heavily disincentivized productive activity.

The mutation of Congo/Zaire from economic powerhouse into a "lame Leviathan,"[21] where the state lost even the most basic capacity to execute pol-

[18] Young, *Rise and Decline of the Zairian State*.

[19] J.E. Ikos Rukal Diyal, *La générale de carrières et des mines (gcm): une culture et une civilisation*, Lubumbashi: Editions Baobab, 2007.

[20] Fadjay Kindela and Laurens Rademakers, "Recycling the Past: Rehabilitating Congo's Colonial Palm and Rubber Plantations," http://news.mongabay.com/bioenergy/2006/09/recycling-past-rehabilitating-congos.html

[21] Thomas Callaghy, "The State as Lame Leviathan: The Patrimonial Administrative

icy, did not happen overnight but was the product of the logic of survival that Mobutu seemed to master to perfection. According to CIA Station Chief Larry Devlin, with whom he worked closely to remove Lumumba and to end the Simba Uprising in eastern Congo in 1963–4, he was nothing less than a "political genius."[22] Mobutu's golden rule was that absolutely no threat to his personal rule was to emerge—no individual, no elite, no class—and that he would be ready to sink the economy to do so.[23] The "forest boy" from Equateur distrusted the security forces above all and, like in so many other dictatorial regimes from Nazi Germany to Haile Selassie's Ethiopia, he organized chaos among them by pitting one against each other: the military intelligence spied on the secret service, which in turned confronted the gendarmerie, the leaders of which could not bear the border security, and so on. All sought his favors, busying themselves with endless fake or half-true reports on plots hatched, supposedly against the president, by their rivals. Mobutu also starved the armed forces of resources, to the point that he would cease salary and maintenance payments altogether under the motto of the infamous but formally non-existent constitutional principle "*article 15: débrouillez-vous*" (sort yourselves out). Soldiers were told to be an "army of the people" and to provision themselves, erecting roadblocks and engaging in licit and illicit businesses. This reduced the scheming against Mobutu as officers and recruits were too busy trying to survive; the context of deepening resource scarcity worsened the collective action problem across the security services.

A similar logic of divide-and-rule through neo-patrimonialism and permanent insecurity of their formal and informal positions in the Mobutist networks characterized politics under the omnipresent tyrant.[24] The system was best described as a game of political "musical chairs" in which incumbents could only be certain of a particular post—MP, army commander, director of a state-owned company—for a short period of time, after which Mobutu would organize a reshuffle that could land one an ambassadorship, a similar post in a different province, a stint in jail or nothing at all. The

State in Africa," in Zaki Ergas (ed.), *The African State in Transition*, New York: St. Martin's Press, 1987.

[22] Devlin, *Chief of Station, Congo*, p. 265.

[23] Michael G. Schatzberg, *The Dialectics of Oppression in Zaire*, Bloomington: Indiana University Press, 1988.

[24] Winsome J. Leslie, *Zaire: Continuity and Political Change in an Oppressive State*, Boulder: Westview, 1993.

strategic logic of these permanent rotations was that it discouraged any organized opposition: no one was in charge of a post long enough to build up an autonomous power base, and currying favors with the president was the best guarantee not to find oneself in exile or facing bankruptcy. It encouraged massive corruption—such short time-horizons incentivized the looting of as much as possible as quickly as possible—and an irreversible decline in maintenance of public assets. As such, Mobutu's logic of survival torpedoed any chance of the emergence of a vibrant middle class, a corporatist sector or a Hamiltonian bureaucracy.[25]

As the economy contracted, the kleptocratic system could only be sustained with inflows of foreign capital.[26] Congo's sheer mineral wealth (e.g., more than two-thirds of the world's cobalt reserves) still attracted multinationals and foreign entrepreneurs for years, even in an extremely hostile investment climate. Mobutu's pivotal role in the Cold War ensured that IMF and World Bank support and bilateral aid from the United States, France and Belgium kept gushing, no matter how glaring the human rights and financial governance abuses. Zaire's debt was rescheduled nine times between the 1970s and late 1980s, despite the government's manifest disastrous management of public finances.[27] As documented in painstaking detail by a former IMF official,[28] the international financial institutions and bilateral partners engaged in a mixture of self-delusion, absurd optimism and strategic blindness each time another technical mission concluded that none of the promised reforms had been implemented and that rent-seeking was not being addressed, but was actually escalating. Money kept flowing to Zaire.

The chief reason for the enduring tolerance of the most egregious forms of graft was simple. Mobutu had risen to power and consolidated his dominance by selling himself to Western powers as the only force who could guarantee stability in the "heart of darkness," quashing the rise of communism domestically and helping to roll it back in Angola where a bloody civil war pitted the Soviet-backed MPLA government against the pro-American UNITA and

---

[25] Jean-Claude Williame, *L'automne d'un despotisme: pouvoir, argent et obéissance dans le Zaïre des années quatre-vingt*, Paris: Karthala, 1992.

[26] Michael G. Schatzberg, *Mobutu or Chaos? The United States and Zaire, 1960–1990*, Lanham: University Press of America, 1991.

[27] Winsome J. Leslie, *The World Bank and Structural Transformation in Developing Countries: The Case of Zaire*, Boulder: Lynne Rienner, 1987.

[28] Erwin Blumenthal, "Zaïre: rapport sur sa crédibilité financière internationale," *La revue nouvelle*, 77, 11 (1982).

Frente Nacional de Libertação de Angola (FNLA) rebels. Mobutu's elite Division Spéciale Présidentielle (DSP), consisting largely of his Ngbandi co-ethnics from Equateur, was trained and armed by Israeli specialists;[29] French, Belgian and Moroccan troops stood ready as a last-resort to save the president if an uprising somewhere spiraled out of control. Though many despaired of Mobutu's eccentric personality and his ruthlessness in squeezing his patrons, he hugged Muhammad Ali, hosted Pope John Paul II and received weapons from Ariel Sharon. His circle of political friends was virtually unmatched in Africa: US Presidents Ronald Reagan and George H.W. Bush; Belgium's King Baudouin; televangelist Pat Robertson; the Netherlands' Prince Bernhard; Bavarian conservative giant Franz-Josef Strauss; French Presidents Valéry Giscard d'Estaing and François Mitterrand; and, last but not least, Romanian tyrant Nicolae Ceauşescu.

For more than three decades, Mobutu lorded with great pomp amid an impoverishing population. Yet as the "King of Zaire" accumulated gastronomical, sexual and financial excesses, the world was changing and Africa's best-known consumer of pink champagne struggled to keep up. When it was announced at the France–Africa summit of La Baule of June 1990 that Paris would make aid flows to its African partners dependent on steps towards democratization—"*and there are not 36 ways towards democracy*," warned François Mitterrand[30]—Mobutu first ignored the admonition, but then quickly had to deal with the surfacing of the Conférence Nationale Souveraine back home which ushered in an unprecedented degree of openness and even power-sharing with an autonomous prime minister.[31] Moreover, Belgium, the old colonial power whose post-1960 hangover Mobutu continually exploited, decided to suspend all official development assistance following the smashing of protests on the campus of the University of Lubumbashi in May 1990.[32] Mobutu badly miscalculated when he subsequently expelled all Belgian technicians from Zaire and closed all but one Belgian consulate: Canada and the EU followed Brussels' lead,

[29] Benjamin Beit-Hallahmi, *The Israeli Connection: Who Israel Arms and Why*, London: I.B. Tauris, 1987.

[30] For the full text of the La Baule speech of the French president see: http://www1.rfi.fr/actufr/articles/037/article_20103.asp

[31] Gauthier De Villers and Jean Tshonda Omasombo, "An Intransitive Transition," *Review of African Political Economy*, 29, 93–4 (2002), pp. 400–3.

[32] Turner, *Congo Wars*, pp. 29–30.See also Emizet F. Kisangani, *Civil Wars in the Democratic Republic of Congo, 1960–2010*, Boulder: Lynne Rienner, 2012.

ending all non-humanitarian assistance for Kinshasa, and even in the US Congress the Zairian regime was now loudly criticized, including by US Assistant Secretary of State for Africa, Herman Cohen. The World Bank also suspended all cooperation over corruption allegations. And by 1992, French aid was a third of what it had been prior to 1989.

Mobutu did what he could to outwit, bribe and intimidate the sovereign national conference led by Archbishop Laurent Monsengwo and the opposition-leader-cum-premier Étienne Tshisekedi, but in the post-Cold War environment time was running out.[33] The lavish external flows on which his kleptocratic style of governance and game of political musical chairs vitally depended were simply no longer available to him—with serious strategic consequences. Mobutu was forced to fragment political authority and cede power to his previously subservient clients; senior security service figures like his cousin Nzimbi Ngbale (commander of the DSP) and Kpama Baramoto (head of the Garde Civile) spun their own sprawling patronage webs that dabbled in licit and illicit cross-border trade of gold, timber, diamonds and luxury goods, while a weakening grip on Katanga's politics and resources became a self-reinforcing cycle that further shrank Mobutu's grip. Even the pretense of Mobutist rule and its extractive state now withered, as the skeletal bureaucracy had done years before.[34] Like in the final days of the Soviet Union, political violence along ethnic lines raged across the territory in the Kivus, in Kasai, in Katanga. While the president could still deny the different politico-commercial emergent forces the ability to coalesce and reach for Gbadolite and Kinshasa, he could only manage the escalating forest fires but no longer douse them.

The shrinking of Mobutu's time-horizons and his loss of patronage resources also had important consequences for Zaire's external relations. The president still incarnated formal sovereignty and made official foreign policy decisions, but the growing autonomy of his clients allowed them to conclude separate business and armament deals with rebel movements in Uganda and Angola and governments in South Africa, Sudan and Rwanda. This undercut Mobutu's credibility in the eyes of his peers, as he was increasingly unable to deliver mutual security guarantees. This was not so much a matter of rendering Mobutu irrelevant—de jure sovereignty continues to count dearly in post-

---

[33] Gauthier De Villers and Jean Tshonda Omasombo, *Zaïre: la transition manquée (1990–1997)*, Paris: Editions L'Harmattan, 1997.

[34] John F. Clark, "The Nature and Evolution of the State in Zaire," *Studies in Comparative International Development*, 32, 4 (1998).

1989 Africa, as before—as one of making him ever more vulnerable to an externally backed assault. His weakness threatened their security—foreign rebels found weapons, rear bases, foreign currency, passports and much more in Zaire, even if the Kinshasa government promised not to tolerate such activities—and therefore compelled action. For Mobutu's neighbors, who for years had to suffer his meddling in their domestic politics and waltzed to his diplomatic tune in Central Africa, payback time was coming.

The Pan-Africanist Liberation Project: Tanzania, Uganda and Beyond

According to Larry Devlin, the CIA's iconic chief operative in Congo in the 1960s,

> While far from democratic, Mobutu's style of governing was no worse than most African leaders and probably better than many. Mobutu inherited all the trappings of a parliamentary democracy, but he ruled as a tribal chief, the only form of government he really knew. He merely extended the role of chief on a national basis.[35]

To many on and off the continent, Mobutu incarnated the post-independence dilemmas faced by African societies in the first years after 1960; given the turbulent international waters of the Cold War in which the new-born African state was to navigate after independence, the logic of reproducing the discourse of stabilizing authoritarianism proved irresistible.[36] It was a view that echoed Leopold's portrayal of the stabilizing role of the Congo Free State in an era of Great Power rivalries. Even if proponents of this analysis understood the self-serving character of Mobutu's *spiel*, his arguments about continuity and pragmatism trumping democracy and policies to reduce Africa's dependency on the global economy were seen as ultimately more realistic than the radical alternative. With neighboring Uganda and Central African Republic suffering the horrors of Idi Amin Dada and "Emperor" Jean-Bédel Bokassa, and with Angola and Sudan ensnarled in civil war, Mobutu's reign appeared comparatively benign—an anchor of stability at the heart of the continent.

However, if the Mobutist state of the 1960s and 1970s was seen as a model for some, to others it symbolized the worst pathologies of the conformist postcolonial state—the very reason for the shattered dreams of African independence. This critique was formulated most cogently by the Pan-Africanist movement (see discussion in Chapter 2), an amorphous

[35] Devlin, *Chief of Station, Congo*, p. 262.
[36] Dunn, *Imagining the Congo*, p. 123.

ensemble of activists, intellectuals and politicians struggling for "liberation" in the tradition of Garvey, DuBois, Nkrumah, and Fanon. At the coming of independence in the late 1950s, early 1960s Pan-Africanists warned of the perils of continuity: Africans themselves would need to reset the terms of trade, rely on themselves for the protection of their sovereignty and actively assist peoples around the world still struggling for freedom.

Mobutu's rise to power through the assassination of Lumumba, a prominent Pan-Africanist and democratically elected prime minister, and his intimate ties with Washington, Paris and Brussels made him into the prime target of Pan-Africanist criticism: he was the symbol of the "Old Africa," to be replaced with a "New Africa." The Leopard King represented all the problems arising from neo-imperial intervention in Africa during the Cold War, making his ouster into an obsession for many on the left.[37]

Mobutu's most important Pan-Africanist detractor was Julius Nyerere. As president of Tanzania he organized the 1974 Fifth Pan-African Congress in Dar es Salaam, the first to be held in Africa and a follow-up to the legendary 1945 meeting in Manchester that called for mass mobilization in their home countries to gain the freedom fought for in World War II (see Chapter 2). It is hard to think of two leaders more different in personal lifestyle, geopolitical orientation and philosophical approach than Mobutu and Nyerere. If the former was a degree-less, self-made man from a rural backwater whose love for luxury was known around the world, the latter was a former schoolteacher of royal pedigree who lived a life of Spartan austerity, despite having enjoyed a privileged education, including at the University of Edinburgh. Mobutu exasperated his Western allies, but always remained fundamentally loyal to their interests; Nyerere was loved in Europe, but always refused to align himself with any outside power. In Kinshasa, the administration continued to work in French, and ministers, generals and company managers were selected through a careful balancing of ethnicity, region and language; in Dar, the central government did everything it could to erase ethno-regional affiliations and promote a national Tanzanian identity by privileging the Swahili language, not the "colonial" English.

The fundamentally different worldviews of both heads of state were reflected in their diametrically opposed foreign policies too.[38] Mobutu fur-

---

[37] Ludo Martens, *Kabila et la révolution congolaise: panafricanisme ou néocolonialisme?*, vol. 1, Antwerp: EPO, 2002.

[38] On the historical animosity between Nyerere and Mobutu, and the Mobutist system of regional order, see N'Gbanda, *Ainsi sonne le glas*, pp. 28–34.

thered American and French interests by refusing to join the anti-Apartheid coalition, backing the FNLA and UNITA rebels in Angola, buttressing the Habyarimana dictatorship in Rwanda and sending his elite DSP to Chad to thwart Qaddafi's intervention in the civil war. By contrast, Nyerere turned his country into a revolutionary regional hub from which to fight imperialism and neo-colonialism.[39] Tanzania became a leader of the Frontline States which sought majority rule and the end of segregation in Southern Africa, and it provided political support, training camps and financial assistance to South Africa's African National Congress (ANC), Namibia's South West Africa People's Organization (SWAPO), the Movimento Popular de Libertação de Angola (MPLA), the Zimbabwe African National Liberation Army (ZANLA) and the Frente de Libertação de Moçambique (FRELIMO).

The Tanzanian president's greatest concern was that, even after formal independence, African states would remain locked into deeply unequal relations with the outside world.[40] The "Mwalimu" (teacher) warned that the kind of armed forces that Britain, France and Belgium had bequeathed to states like Congo served as fundamental impediments to nation-building, democracy and development. Militaries such as the King's African Rifles in East Africa were, according to Nyerere, ideally suited for neo-colonial purposes as their recruitment had been ethnically stratified, deepening the divisions that colonial powers needed to subjugate Africans and which would allow them to play different population groups off against each other after 1960 too; his personal experience with the 1964 mutiny in Tanganyika, when two battalions of the King's African Rifles (still under white British command) revolted, reinforced this conviction. Nyerere believed that in (neo-)colonial militaries, the loyalty of ordinary recruits and their commanders resided not with the nation, but with petty individual and ethno-regional interests: hence the series of coups and civil wars in Congo, Uganda, Burundi, Sudan and elsewhere that enabled London, Paris and Brussels to maintain influence in Africa.

The colonial Force Publique and its Mobutist successor, the Forces Armées Zairoises (FAZ), were archetypal examples of the disease Nyerere identified. The Force Publique consisted of West African mercenaries and Congolese soldiers whose military doctrine was deterrence through terror; it was not an

---

[39] Julius K. Nyerere, "America and Southern Africa," *Foreign Affairs*, 55 (1976).
[40] Julius K. Nyerere, "Third World Negotiating Strategy," *Third World Quarterly*, 1, 2 (1979).

army that intended to protect the population:[41] its practice of decimating rebellious communities—literally killing or severely beating every tenth man in a village—set the tone for more than a century of totally dysfunctional relations between the Congolese security forces and its population. Troops served under white officers who did not shy away from physically abusing their own men; in turn, these uneducated recruits, deployed far away from their home areas and in regions where they spoke neither the language nor understood the culture, took revenge on civilian targets. The problem of large-scale sexual violence by soldiers is hence by no means specific to eastern Congo in the early twenty-first century. It is a malice that has existed as long as the Congolese army itself.

The FAZ emerged as Mobutu's rebranding of the Force Publique and its successor, the Armée Nationale Congolaise. The latter was the force of which Lumumba had made him chief of staff but which mutinied at independence and massacred hundreds in Luluabourg in an attempt at stamping out the Kasai secession. It lacked skilled officers, logistical and intelligence capacities and, above all, unity of purpose and leadership. These problems deepened when Mobutu became president and had the Armée Nationale Congolaise turned into his FAZ. Mobutu's idea of the role of the armed forces was to render them too preoccupied with material survival to be involved in politics. The army competed incessantly with rival security bodies and was obliged to get what it needed from the population—*article 15*. Mobutu had his recruiters raise men across the territory, but deployed them in such ways that troops would not serve in their home areas. Moreover, the continuous rotation of command positions rested on the tenuous ethno-regional balance Mobutu played at, further encouraging rivalries. The frustration of officers at having to serve in such a shambolic force was compounded by the knowledge that real power lay with the DSP, dominated by Mobutu's Ngbandi co-ethnics. Divided, uneducated, tribalized and ill-disciplined, the FAZ embodied all the ailments associated with post-colonial African armies.

The model force Julius Nyerere had in mind as the cornerstone of a progressive African nationalism was the diametric opposite of the Force Publique and FAZ "doctrine." The Mwalimu's answer lay in "People's Defense Forces." The army would cease to be an apolitical institution—or worse an ethnicized institution: both ordinary soldiers and their officers would receive in-depth ideo-

---

[41] Bryant P. Shaw, "Force publique, force unique: The Military in the Belgian Congo, 1914–1939," University of Wisconsin–Madison, 1984.

logical training to heighten their political consciousness.[42] The partnership with China's People's Liberation Army and its experience of revolution, popular war and rural mobilization reinforced the views of the leadership of Tanzania's ruling TANU party.[43] Political commissars helped the army fulfil its duty, with commanders also functioning as TANU chairmen in their area. The armed forces were not only to safeguard the nation's borders, but to reform its political economy as it sought to delink from Western-imposed patterns of unequal trade—a "developmental militia," the Mwalimu called it. As guardians of the revolution, they would confront imperialist enemies from within and from without, but also incarnate a model of integration of tribes, regions and classes that could unite the young nation in the face of neo-colonial *divide et impera*.[44] Nyerere envisaged that the People's Defense Forces would mark the transformation of the army as a source of instability in post-independence Africa into a catalyst of progressive modernization and cross-ethnic and trans-regional integration.[45] All soldiers were given TANU party membership, and to this day, the Tanzania People's Defense Force (TPDF) created by Nyerere has never tried a coup; equally remarkably, Tanzania has also never experienced civil war.

That this success was no question of pacifism is made clear by the radical foreign policy the Mwalimu pursued—and the key role for People's Defense Forces in it. The TPDF invaded Uganda in 1979 to unseat Idi Amin's despotic rule—a policy concomitant with the regime change Nyerere promoted across Eastern and Southern Africa. He advised the revolutionaries sheltering and training in Tanzania to wage a true people's war in their homelands against Apartheid and imperialism—with no artificial boundaries between the activities of the incipient People's Defense Forces and those of the civilian wing of a liberation movement. Military cadres, foreign and domestic, read development studies at the University of Dar es Salaam; at this hotbed of Pan-Africanist thought in the 1960s and 1970s, leftist professors like Walter Rodney (author of *How Europe Underdeveloped Africa*) combined academic writing with political praxis. The intention was for officers and recruits to

---

[42] Henry Bienen, *Tanzania: Party Transformation and Economic Development*, Princeton, NJ: Princeton University Press, 1970, pp. 374–80.

[43] Martin Bailey, "Tanzania and China," *African Affairs*, 74, 294 (1975).

[44] Ali A. Mazrui, "Anti-Militarism and Political Militancy in Tanzania," *Journal of Conflict Resolution*, 12, 3 (1968).

[45] Elise Forbes Pachter, "Contra-Coup: Civilian Control of the Military in Guinea, Tanzania, and Mozambique," *Journal of Modern African Studies*, 20, 4 (1982).

understand not just the international economic context of their soldiering, but their fundamentally political vocation.

The ideas of the People's Defense Forces and their role in African development were inculcated into scores of rebel leaders who passed through Dar es Salaam. According to Yoweri Museveni, a Dar es Salaam student of Rodney's who would lead Uganda's liberation movement and used his university days to expose himself to revolutionary thought and military training in Mozambique:

> Our role in the student movement had three effects: it radicalised and deepened the ideological content of our thinking; it made us quite well known on the African scene, especially in liberation movement circles; and it reinforced our Pan-Africanist views and enabled us to make Pan-Africanist contacts such as President Nyerere.[46]

Slowly but surely, Nyerere's efforts paid off: after Tanzanian forces ousted Idi Amin and Zimbabwe celebrated its independence from white colonialism, momentum for a revived Pan-Africanist liberation gathered in the 1980s. In January 1986, for the first time in African history, a rebel movement managed to overthrow an incumbent government and capture the capital. Museveni's National Resistance Army/Movement (NRA/M) was based on the Nyerere–Maoist model of organization, having waged five years of bitter guerrilla struggle from the countryside under a banner of anti-tribalism, redistribution and a progressive new politics.[47] In South Africa, Nelson Mandela was released, the Apartheid system was disintegrating and declining support for the RENAMO insurgents signaled the definitive victory of Nyerere's comrades of FRELIMO in Mozambique in 1992. Meanwhile, Museveni turned Uganda into the nerve center of a campaign to usher in a new Pan-Africanist regional order. With Kampala's support, in 1990, the Rwandan Patriotic Front of Fred Rwigyema and Paul Kagame invaded its homeland from southern Uganda to end the despotism of Juvénal Habyarimana.

To the north, the Sudan People's Liberation Army/Movement (SPLA/M) of John Garang (another alumnus of the University of Dar es Salaam) intensified its struggle, with Ugandan support, against the military-Islamist "Al-Ingaz" regime in Khartoum. To up the pressure, Garang in turn reached out to two other Pan-Africanist rural insurgencies which had stunned Africa in the early 1990s by vanquishing the continent's most formidable army: the defeat of the

---

[46] Museveni, *Sowing the Mustard Seed*, p. 31.

[47] Nelson Kasfir, "Guerrillas and Civilian Participation: The National Resistance Army in Uganda, 1981–86," *Journal of Modern African Studies*, 43, 2 (2005).

military dictatorship of Mengistu Haile Mariam at the hands of the Tigrayan People's Liberation Front (TPLF) of Meles Zenawi and the Eritrean People's Liberation Front (EPLF) of Issayas Afewerki led to the liberation of Ethiopia in 1991 and Eritrean independence in 1993 after two decades of civil war. Mozambique, Uganda, Ethiopia, Eritrea, South Africa, Rwanda: in one country after another, young new incumbents admiring Nyerere and speaking a broadly similar progressive discourse captured power.

The rise to prominence of a generation of leaders flying the Pan-Africanist flag and carried forward by a phalanx of disciplined youngsters whose world-views were shaped by the violent struggle and leftist teachings was a sign that the time of cozy relations under the umbrella of the Cold War between the region's incumbents had come to an end. The implications of the NRA/M example—rebels ousting a sitting regime—changed the political calculus for everybody in the Horn of Africa and Great Lakes region. Those in the Pan-Africanist camp wanted to actively export their political model and felt it a duty—as well as legitimate self-defense—to support armed movements against "neo-colonial" and/or right-wing regimes in Rwanda, Sudan and Zaire. Contrary to wildly optimistic predictions in the early 1990s, the end of the US–Soviet confrontation thus did not turn Africa into a more peaceful place; instead, the rise of Garang, Issayas, Meles, Museveni and Kagame would lead to an interlocking of conflicts from the Red Sea to the Atlantic, unleashing a series of violent confrontations between neo-liberation movements and conservative regimes that had come to power before the fall of the Berlin Wall.

Two opposing trends thus constituted darkening geopolitical skies for Mobutu back in his jungle palace in Gbadolite: on the one hand, his own relative loss of power back home, as he had to concede greater autonomy to the clients in his system and was increasingly unable draw on external resources to buttress his autocratic rule; and on the other, the emergence of a potent, strongly militarized enemy in the form of various neo-liberation regimes who, for reasons ranging from ideological opposition, their own personal security and revenge for Mobutu's patronage of their enemies, were spoiling for a fight if the opportunity presented itself. Just when the "King of Zaire" seemed at his weakest and most distracted by the fight against prostate cancer and the democratizing impulses of the sovereign national conference, an extremely hostile regional environment emerged.

Africa's international relations between 1960 and 1990 had legally been governed by the Charter of the Organization of African Unity (OAU) which had intended to stabilize politics between African states.[48] At the founding meeting of the OAU in Addis on May 25, 1963, the heads of state and government resolved that the borders that had emerged out of the Scramble for Africa would remain unaltered: to decide otherwise risked opening a Pandora's Box of population transfers, secessionist and irredentist claims and opportunities for the former colonial powers to continue meddling. The corollary of the inviolability of borders was that African leaders also promised to stick to the principle of non-interference in each other's internal affairs—undisputed sovereignty over one's own territory entailed respecting that of others. While this system was often criticized for recognizing African governments irrespective of their governing and human rights records,[49] it did contribute to relative stability in the form of institutional continuity (the juridical state survived intact) and a remarkable absence of inter-state war across Africa—even as proxy wars flourished between ideological rivals (see Chapter 2). However, the (externally assisted) military victory of leftist rebels over the sitting governments in Uganda and Ethiopia as well as the demise of the Cold War and the associated security-cum-stabilization lens of Western powers heralded the end of one era of Africa's international relations and the dawn of a different regional strategic environment.

Especially after the withdrawal of support by Belgium, the EU and the World Bank, Mobutu anxiously looked to Washington and to how it would use its military, economic and political supremacy to influence the changing balance of forces on the continent. The first signs were not promising: President George H.W. Bush, despite his past as a Cold Warrior, was keen to put some distance between himself and the less than glamorous history of US policy in Africa. Associating with an Apartheid regime on its last legs and a decadent Mobutu did not fit the administration's New World Order discourse; while the United States refrained from cutting off all ties with Kinshasa, its green light for World Bank disengagement and its open support for Archbishop Monsengwo, head of the sovereign national conference, worried Mobutu greatly. The ageing president had been supremely humiliated

[48] Clapham, *Africa and the International System*.

[49] Eric G. Berman and Katie E. Sams, "The Peacekeeping Potential of African Regional Organizations," in Jane Boulden (ed.), *Dealing with Conflict in Africa: The United Nations and Regional Organizations*, New York: Palgrave, 2003, pp. 52–6; Jeffrey Herbst, "African Peacekeepers and State Failure," in Robert I. Rotberg et al. (eds), *Peacekeeping and Peace Enforcement in Africa*, Washington, DC: Brookings Institution Press, 2000.

when the Belgian government—previously his country's biggest donor, ahead even of the Americans—did not invite him to attend the funeral in August 1993 of King Baudouin, the devoutly Catholic monarch with whom Mobutu had an intense emotional relationship.[50] He was particularly worried when the United States also denied him visas and Bush administration officials identified him as the "biggest obstacle to change" in the country. The killing in Kinshasa of the French ambassador in terrible riots earlier in January 1993 had also weakened his bond with his other traditional ally and left him dangerously isolated.[51] According to Belgian Ambassador Frank De Coninck (envoy first to Kigali (1994–7), then to Kinshasa (1997–2000)), Mobutu became "*infrequentable*," to be shunned at all costs.[52]

The growing foreign policy assertiveness of Uganda's Yoweri Museveni on his eastern flank and the civil war in Rwanda augured more bad weather. In the latter conflict, Zaire's DSP troops had failed to stem the advance of the Kampala-backed RPF following which French paratroopers had to save Mobutu's friend, President Juvénal Habyarimana; it exposed the rapidly diminishing utility of the Zairian president in helping out those closest to him. With the advent of Bill Clinton as forty-second commander in chief of the United States, Mobutu tried to regain leverage: he committed to reforms and welcomed back the flamboyant Kengo wa Dondo as prime minister in early 1994, after having served in the same position between 1982 and 1990. Kengo was the son of a Rwandese Tutsi mother and a Belgian Polish Jewish father who had emigrated to Congo; more importantly, like Mobutu, he was born in Equateur, and his neoliberal economics made him a favorite of the IMF. But no matter how hard Kengo tried to emphasize liberalization and stabilization, the political imperatives of the Mobutist system meant that his room to make substantive changes was all too limited. The Clinton administration was not impressed and felt that only democratic elections could legitimize a serious structural adjustment program which would get to grips with decades of mismanagement.

The fundamental problem for Mobutu's attempted comeback was that Central Africa was simply no longer a geopolitical priority for Washington. After the downing of two Black Hawk helicopters over Mogadishu led to the

---

[50] Gauthier de Villers, *De Mobutu à Mobutu: trente ans de relations Belgique–Zaïre*, Brussels: De Boeck Université, 1995, pp. 239–40.

[51] "French Envoy in Zaire Killed as Troops Rampage," *Los Angeles Times*, January 29, 1993.

[52] Interview in Rome, May 2009.

death of eighteen American servicemen in Somalia in 1993, Clinton's Africa policy intended to extricate Washington from costly entanglements and potential embarrassments. The democratization process in South Africa was the top priority, followed by the counter-terrorism agenda regarding Sudan, which hosted a range of Islamist dissidents, some of which were openly jihadist and almost all of whom were used by the Al-Ingaz regime to export its Islamic revolution to the wider neighborhood.[53] Crucially, Washington's Sudan agenda pointed towards improved relations with the very movements Mobutu was beginning to fear the most: the leftist Pan-Africanists who had taken power in Eritrea, Ethiopia and Uganda and were seeking to do so in Rwanda and Sudan. Western unipolar dominance had undercut the Marxist-inspired reform programs they had proposed during their long struggles, and their pragmatism upon coming to power was not lost on the State Department and Pentagon, who argued for engagement of these movements as key allies to isolate military-Islamist Khartoum.

Faced with this bleak regional predicament, Mobutu would for the last time play the card that had so often saved him on previous occasions: his *"après moi, le déluge"* argument still held some sway, particularly when pogroms against Kasaien migrants in Katanga and escalating inter-ethnic violence in the Kivu province raised the specter of a new Somalia should the Mobutist state collapse entirely.[54] As the president's grip weakened, politico-military entrepreneurs surfaced everywhere, ready to feast like vultures on the carcass of the Zairian state. This fragility received an additional jolt when neighboring Rwanda exploded in genocidal conflict in April 1994, following the eruption of civil war in Burundi in 1993. Mobutu argued that by virtue of geography and his political proximity to key belligerents he could once again assume a stabilizing role and that shunning him would have devastating consequences for regional security; this was his chance to reassert control of the region's geopolitics after having been on the defensive for half a decade. Mobutu was certainly right in suspecting that the Rwandese genocide would be a geopolitical game-changer. But rather than restoring him to his formerly elevated position of Central Africa's *primus inter pares*, it would act as a catalyst for his downfall.

---

[53] Harry Verhoeven and Luke A. Patey, "Sudan's Islamists and the Post-Oil Era: Washington's Role after Southern Secession," *Middle East Policy*, 18, 3 (2011).

[54] Bill Berkeley, "An African Horror Story," *Atlantic Monthly*, 272, 2 (1993).

The Banyarwanda Question and the Rise to Power
of the Rwandan Patriotic Front

On New Year's Day, 1994, coverage of Africa in newsrooms only really revolved around one topic. There was the Algerian civil war where jihadists and government death squads outperformed each other in grizzly violence exacted against tens of thousands of citizens. There was also the succession of Africa's eldest statesman, Félix Houphouët-Boigny, who, after a career that included a decade in the French Assemblée Nationale, four years as minister in Paris and being the fifth-ranked signatory to Charles De Gaulle's 1958 constitution, died as head of state of Côte d'Ivoire, a post he had occupied since independence. But the eyes of the world rested above all on South Africa, which entered the last phase of its democratization with the 1994 election. The earlier optimism that had followed Nelson Mandela's release and the unbanning of his African National Congress (ANC) had begun to dissipate as the country was mired by unrest involving white supremacists, the Inkatha Freedom Party and ANC militants. Bombings, prison breaks and ethno-racial attacks in the weeks before the vote formed the context for warnings about an imminent war. With international attention so seized by South Africa, Mobutu, whose regional influence was waning and whose domestic authority was severely tarnished, looked forward to a quiet year during which his old mantra of stability at all costs was likely to gain traction once again. The only potential threat on his radar seemed to be the Kinshasa political elite who the 64-year-old tyrant would, surely, continue to divide-and-rule just as he had before.

Yet it was not from within, but from without, that Mobutu's ultimate nemesis would emerge. This movement, which Mobutu consistently underestimated, read the changing tectonic plates of geopolitics better than he did and would make use of the unique re-alignment of forces in Africa to launch an attack on Kinshasa three years later. United in a comparatively small but extraordinarily well-organized group of refugees influenced by Pan-Africanist ideas of liberation struggle, the cadres and foot soldiers of the Rwandan Patriotic Front grew up in exile from their homeland passionately hating Mobutu and everything he stood for. Ideologically and in terms of political praxis, his politics were seen as the model that other African autocrats copied. One of these was Juvénal Habyarimana, the president who had governed Rwanda since 1973, partnered with Mobutu in business deals and, on the advice of his Zairian mentor, had developed a close military and diplomatic relationship with Paris since 1975 which consolidated his grip on power. For one RPF commander, "Mobutu represented everything we did not want in Africa ... Corruption, dictatorship, tribalism—whatever. He was neo-colonial. These were our problems in Rwanda, in Uganda, [in] Congo. His system was to make change impossible outside Zaire—to protect himself."[55] In the eyes of the Rwandan refugees, the alliance between Mobutu, Habyarimana and the Élysée was the central obstacle to change in their country of origin, more than eighty times smaller than Congo; the RPF believed that liberation and the return of the diaspora would be inevitable once Habyarimana and his "fascist" government were forced to fight on their own against the RPF's highly motivated and increasingly experienced combat force.[56]

The Long Shadow of Colonial History

The RPF's assessment of Rwanda's "neo-colonial" predicament and the importance of the regional security environment in changing its situation were determining factors for why its cadres found a Nyerere-inspired political framework so attractive to embed their own struggle in. However, it also stemmed from the RPF's reading of Rwandan history, which fused leftist ideas with strongly worded generalizations rooted in the experiences of its core members and social base: to fight Habyarimana and later Mobutu, the RPF interwove the historical trajectory of its main constituencies with a broader Pan-Africanist narrative. Hence, from its inception in the late 1980s, the Front has sought to free itself of colonial historiography and associated subjects and objects of political agency. The Hutu–Tutsi divide—so salient in any discussion of the country—is, in the RPF's reading, essentially a foreign construct. Rwanda, like the rest of the continent, was doing fine until the Scramble for Africa in the last quarter of the nineteenth century, during which Europeans re-invented notions of tribalism to divide-and-rule Africans.[57] The tragedy of Rwanda as the divided nation with its forcibly exiled diaspora was depicted as a post-independence crime that emerged out of the seeds sown by colonialism. To subvert the once mighty kingdom, German and Belgian impe-

---

[55] Interview with Frank Rusagara in London, January 2010.
[56] Interview with Frank Mugambage in Kampala, March 2013.
[57] Mamdani, *Citizen and Subject*; Mahmood Mamdani, *When Victims Become Killers: Colonialism, Nativism, and the Genocide in Rwanda*, Princeton: Princeton University Press, 2001.

rialists had enlisted a handful of local auxiliaries who allowed ideas of race and ethnicity to obscure a more fundamental process of exploitation and class formation—and this continued after sovereignty was transferred to Rwandans in 1962.

The RPF's rather rosy views on precolonial Rwanda—the inevitable political counterpoint of its denunciation of imperialism and the division of the imagined Rwandan nation—have not been substantiated by much independent scholarship. They also conveniently de-emphasize patterns of feudalism and aristocratic oppression associated with some family lineages of dominant members of the Front. However, the RPF's analysis of the heart of the problem and its origins do echo much of what we know about recent Rwandan history. This book cannot do justice to the complexity of processes of social, economic and political change and continuity in Ruanda–Urundi under colonialism.[58] Nevertheless, it is important to briefly explore some of them here and the ways in which they fed into regional politics in the early 1990s.

The issue of the displaced Banyarwanda (people who speak Kinyarwanda) in the Great Lakes was indeed a poisonous legacy of the imperialist thrust of the late nineteenth and early twentieth century and the disastrous impact of the colonial confrontation between Europe and Central Africa. The root of the Rwandan question could be found in the political economy of Belgian colonialism. Thousands of Banyarwanda were transported as cheap labor to work in "underpopulated" Belgian Congo, while the mandate territory of Ruanda–Urundi, transferred from Germany to Belgium after World War I,

---

[58] For some excellent scholarship see: Alison Des Forges, *Defeat is the Only Bad News: Rwanda under Musinga, 1896–1931*, Madison: University of Wisconsin Press, 2011; Jean-Paul Harroy, *Rwanda: de la féodalité à la démocratie, 1955–1962*, Brussels: Hayez/Académie des Sciences d'Outremer, 1984; Catharine Newbury, "Ubureetwa and Thangata: Catalysts to Peasant Political Consciousness in Rwanda and Malawi," *Canadian Journal of African Studies/La Revue canadienne des études africaines*, 14, 1 (1980); Newbury, *The Cohesion of Oppression: Clientship and Ethnicity in Rwanda, 1860–1960*, New York: Columbia University Press, 1988; Newbury, "Ethnicity and the Politics of History in Rwanda," *Africa Today*, 45, 1 (1998); David Newbury, "Precolonial Burundi and Rwanda: Local Loyalties, Regional Royalties," *International Journal of African Historical Studies*, 34, 2 (2001); Filip Reyntjens, *Pouvoir et droit au Rwanda*, Tervuren: Musée Royale de l'Afrique Centrale, 1985; Jean Rumiya, *Le Rwanda sous le régime du mandat belge (1916–1931)*, Paris: Editions L'Harmattan, 1992; Jan Vansina, *Antecedents to Modern Rwanda: The Nyiginya Kingdom*, Madison: University of Wisconsin Press, 2005.

perfected the age-old principle of using an ethno-political minority to domi-nate a much larger population. Drawing on a nineteenth-century paradigm that classified people into hierarchies of races, each with their own "nature," levels of intelligence and diligence, propensity to lead or serve, and so on, colonial officials favored the Tutsi nobility at the expense of Hutu elites and the vast majority of Banyarwanda. Control was maintained by outsourcing administrative functions to loyal Tutsi chiefs in whom disproportionate pow-ers were vested. Rwanda's Belgian overlords evoked racial difference between Africans—a colonial fantasy of incredible consequences—to justify this brutal system of oppression. According to Pierre Ryckmans, the governor-general of Belgian Congo whose philosophy of *dominer pour servir* was quoted earlier: "The Batutsi were destined to reign, their mere appearance alone gives them considerable prestige over the inferior races by which they are surrounded ... There is nothing surprising about the fact that those dapper Bahutu, less clever, more simple-minded, more spontaneous and more trusting, have let themselves be enslaved."[59]

Neither early German colonizers nor Belgian administrators invented inequalities between Hutu and Tutsi, nor did colonialism establish a central-ized state for the first time, but their policies did fundamentally change pro-cesses of subjugation and the structuration of power, identity and social difference. Not all Tutsi were the fabled intelligent pastoralists that Ryckmans and others identified (some were, others preferred to farm) and not all Hutu were the subservient peasants who worked for Tutsi lords (some were, others had livestock and still others were chiefs). Previously fluid categories of Hutu and Tutsi were rendered immutable by the colonial administration who issued identity cards in the 1930s permanently labeling a citizen "Hutu," "Tutsi" or "Twa." Tutsi chiefs were entrusted with unprecedented control over agricul-tural land and the (mainly Hutu) peasants working on them, as well as with tax collection and the implementation of the reviled corvée system. To be Hutu (or, even worse, a Twa "pygmy") under colonial rule was to be a third-class citizen, devoid of political rights and most opportunities for socio-eco-nomic advancement. To be Tutsi was not necessarily to be privileged (the vast majority remained poor and all were still considered inferior to white resi-

[59] Jean-Pierre Chrétien, *Le défi de l'ethnisme: Rwanda et Burundi, 1990–1996*, Paris: Karthala Editions, 1997. This is our translation of the original quote, as cited by Chrétien, of Pierre Ryckmans, *Dominer pour servir*, Brussels: Librairie Albert Dewit, 1931, p. 26.

dents of the mandate-territory), but to be at least one class above a Hutu and often to enjoy access to government jobs and better education.

As momentum for independence gathered in the late 1950s, economic and social factors had begun to undermine the racialized edifice through which Belgian officials had ruled Rwanda. Society was increasingly polarized and prone to violence, with Tutsi elites seeking a transfer of sovereignty before the less-educated, predominantly Hutu masses had the chance to organize politically. Their efforts were paralleled by a vociferous group of Hutu intellectuals who presented their demands through colonial ideas and terminologies of inherent racial antagonisms and Tutsi hegemony. Their 1957 *Hutu Manifesto* saw an independent Rwanda as a chance to usher in democracy, which was understood as Hutu rule: if the majority of the population is Hutu, then a Hutu ruler must mean Rwanda is a democracy. As David Newbury notes about both elitist Tutsi royalists and the nascent Hutu counter-elite, "The fact that their positions were often articulated in 'school-based knowledge' suggests that these positions were not representative of the population as a whole but of the colonial culture that promulgated it."[60]

Tensions exploded in 1959 with the so-called Social Revolution. In the eyes of Grégoire Kayibanda, the country's first president drawn from the emerging Hutu elite, this was an overdue correction of the nexus between Tutsi feudalism and Belgian colonialism that would lead to the liberation of the peasant masses as lands were re-confiscated and "collaborators"—a worryingly broad category that could include the majority of Tutsi—punished. Building on deep-seated grievances in rural Rwanda, the conflict forced tens of thousands of mainly Tutsi citizens to flee during a long season of turbulence Kinyarwanda speakers metaphorically refer to as a capricious, destructive wind, the *muyaga*. The *muyaga* drove perhaps half a million presumed Rwandan accomplices and beneficiaries of Belgian rule into Burundi, Congo, Tanzania and Uganda between 1959 and 1964.[61] The traumatic winds of these years would reverberate for decades to come: it would be the children of these refugees who formed the Rwandan Patriotic Front twenty-five years later to return home by any means.

[60] David Newbury, "Canonical Conventions in Rwanda: Four Myths of Recent Historiography in Central Africa," *History in Africa*, 39 (2012), p. 50.

[61] Gérard Prunier, *The Rwanda Crisis: History of a Genocide*, New York: Columbia University Press, 1995.

The RPF Liberation Project

In RPF ideology, the *muyaga* became synonymous with a final stab at the Rwandan nation by the departing colonial administrators, paving the road for continued exploitative relations after independence, in the form of neo-colonialism for which governments obsessed with ethnicity were perfect auxiliaries.[62] This was a selective reading of history that had little to say about Rwandans who did benefit from collaboration with the Belgians or about the frustrations and aspirations of the predominantly Hutu rural population. But no matter how stylized a view historians have argued this is, it proved deeply consequential in terms of political action and the formation of alliances. The Kayibanda (1962–73) and Habyarimana (1973–94) regimes were seen by the exiles in a similar light as the Mobutist system in Congo: the product of colonially orchestrated violence at the cusp of freedom, during which innocents and progressive voices opposing Western machinations were targeted, leading to the establishment of governments that divided their nation to stay in power and serve foreign paymasters. Nothing exemplified the betrayal better in the eyes of the exiles than the celebrations of the tenth anniversary of Rwanda's independence during which Belgian colonial officials like Guy Logiest and Jean-Paul Harroy were feted for the good work they and the system they served had done in Africa.[63] Diaspora communities considered the institutionalized discrimination of a quota system stipulating maximum numbers for Tutsi in government service as another example of the same pathology. The Kayibanda and Habyarimana governments claimed to protect the nation against a return of feudalism and Tutsi supremacy,[64] but in reality a small clique of relatives and confidants around the president (commonly referred to as *akazu*) kept the vast majority of both Hutu and Tutsi dirt-poor—the real issue was the concentration of wealth and power in the hands of a tiny cabal.

As the years went by and exile seemed to take on a more permanent character, the nostalgia in the diaspora deepened and many of the differences between the Kayibanda and Habyarimana governments were overlooked. Attempted returns

---

[62] The following paragraphs are based on in-depth interviews, conducted between 2009 and 2015 in a range of different locations, with about a dozen of the RPF's most senior commanders and politicians.

[63] Harroy, *Rwanda: de la féodalité à la démocratie, 1955–1962*.

[64] For an anatomy of the Habyarimana government's discourses: Philip Verwimp, "Development Ideology, the Peasantry and Genocide: Rwanda Represented in Habyarimana's Speeches," *Journal of Genocide Research*, 2, 3 (2000).

via armed *inkotanyi* incursions into Rwanda in the 1960s only yielded disappointments and increased inflows of Tutsi refugees into neighboring states. Through the 1970s and 1980s, the outside world seemed to forget about the plight of the Rwandan displaced—the UN was uninterested—and Rwanda was the *enfant chéri* of development workers and the Belgian and French government who maintained close ties. There was simply no appetite among African or Western governments to overthrow what the RPF would describe as ethnofascist regimes. Habyarimana in particular followed the example of his mentor Mobutu and cultivated the image of a loyal ally in the Cold War and a devout Catholic. He never strayed from the implicit bargain Mobutu had with the heads of state of Congo's neighbors: no support for Zairian rebel movements if you do not want to be destabilized yourself. Development assistance to Rwanda, like Zaire considered to be a beacon of stability, increased and Presidents Giscard d'Estaing and Mitterrand expanded cooperation, including through the 1975 military agreement between Paris and Kigali.

This deep sense of alienation was particularly strong among refugees in Zaire and Uganda.[65] In Mobutu's Zaire, the displaced joined the ranks of the already present Banyarwanda communities (mostly in North and South Kivu) whose fragile co-existence with other population groups was determined by the extent to which they were able to secure favorable treatment and protection from dominant figures in the political system. In a context of resource scarcity and competition over land and grazing pastures for cattle, legislative changes or altering informal political winds could have a dramatic impact on the ability of the Banyarwanda—new arrivals and older settlers—to survive. Faced with quotidian discrimination and harassment—bullying of Rwandophone children, prejudiced jokes, demands by "autochthonous" communities that they be excluded from any citizenship rights—they had little choice but to seek a powerful patron. For years that role was played by Barthélémy Bisengimana, a Tutsi who was born in the 1930s near the Congolese–Rwandan border in Cyangugu and graduated as an engineer from Kinshasa's colonial university, Lovanium. Bisengimana benefited from Mobutu's policy of employing individuals without a strong ethno-regional constituency in key positions (rendering them completely dependent on his patronage and unable to ever aspire to the presidency itself) and ran both some of the Big Man's and his own business affairs as the president's chef-de-cabinet.[66]

---

[65] Rachel Van der Meeren, "Three Decades in Exile: Rwandan Refugees, 1960–1990," *Journal of Refugee Studies*, 9, 3 (1996).

[66] Young, *Rise and Decline of the Zairian State*, pp. 167–8.

Bisengimana worked arduously to get labor migrants, who had been brought from Burundi and Rwanda into Belgian Congo, recognized as Congolese citizens and to improve the plight of more recent arrivals as a result of the *muyaga*. As Mobutu's decade-long office manager he brought a degree of stability to the Banyarwanda and some of their local allies in eastern Congo—an overdue reprieve from the pogroms and evictions in Rwanda and the chaos of the post-Lumumba civil war in Congo during which thousands of citizens perished; especially in South Kivu, lands belonging to Tutsi pastoralists and peasants had been violently seized.[67] But Bisengimana also hardened existing stereotypes of the Tutsi as foreign schemers, conspiring to obtain ever more wealth: as chef-de-cabinet, he ensured that many of the fertile lands and plantations that the exodus of white settlers and Mobutu's Zairization campaign had left behind fell into the hands of Banyarwanda businessmen.[68] For Bisengimana and other refugee leaders, there was no problem—merely a survival strategy in a xenophobic climate. This was not a specifically Tutsi conspiracy: other communities, he argued, would have done the same if presented with the opportunity. But for many Zairians and the Hutu elite in Rwanda, it confirmed old prejudices of Tutsi greed. Bisengimana's fall from grace in the late 1970s led to the undoing of the nationality laws and heralded fifteen years of increased bitterness and growing Banyarwanda vulnerability, leaving them at the mercy of the disintegrating state and local powerbrokers who did not take a kind view of the "outsiders."

Failed assimilation, harassment and rejection by the host population were also the experiences of the Banyarwanda in Uganda—both post-1959 refugees and earlier arrivals. In the context of Uganda's own turbulent post-independence politics, they became scapegoats for mounting economic and political problems and were caught up in the tensions between the traditional power bloc rooted in central and southern Ugandan society—the old Buganda Kingdom—and the northern politico-military elites around President Milton Obote. Following the failure of their *inyenzi* incursions in the 1960s to force a return to Rwanda, they had little choice but to try to integrate into their host society, yet Obote's description of the Banyarwanda as "temporary guests" made them easy targets of frustrated local politicians and soldiers. Cornered, some Rwandan youth rallied behind Field Marshal Idi Amin Dada,

---

[67] Stearns, *Dancing in the Glory of Monsters*, pp. 60–2.

[68] René Lemarchand, *The Dynamics of Violence in Central Africa*, Philadelphia: University of Pennsylvania Press, 2011, pp. 211–13.

whose dictatorship (1971–9) relied heavily on members of minority groups to maintain control over society through a reign of terror. Thus, while the vast majority of Banyarwanda feared the arbitrary violence of Amin's security forces in equal measure as the rest of the country, in the popular imagination the regime was as run by Sudanese (Amin's Kakwa tribe also lives across Uganda's northern border) and Rwandans. This association of the refugee population with the atrocities of personal rule was one for which they would pay a heavy price after 1979. The return to power of Milton Obote and key anti-Tutsi security advisers triggered reprisals across southern Uganda where both youth in the refugee camps and upwardly mobile Banyarwanda were targeted in a spree of killings, rape and confiscation of property.

Materially, the Banyarwanda refugees had struggled greatly after their arrival, but one avenue in Ugandan society that remained open to them was education. It was an opportunity that thousands of young men and women seized with relish. Banyarwanda adolescents spent their holidays helping younger boys from the camps improve their English, get better results at school and excel in sports as well as academically. Patrick Mazimhaka and Frank Rusagara, later respectively a senior RPF minister and the post-genocide permanent secretary of the Ministry of Defense, exemplified this and took the lead in pushing each other and scores of other bright youngsters to do better and to exploit the only visible route for social mobility and the empowerment of the exiled community to its maximum. The "Ugandan" nexus between education, camaraderie and socialization into the idea of a unique Banyarwanda destiny remains essential to understanding the RPF and its worldview today.

Access to education allowed the youngsters to connect their personal trajectories as pariahs in Rwanda and Uganda with emancipatory discourses from across East Africa. Nyerere's ideas about rejecting ethnicity as a foundation in African politics and his promise of trans-regional solidarity against "neo-colonial" regimes inspired the increasingly leftist Rwandophone youngsters. This was all the more the case because Amin, to burnish his credentials as chair of the OAU, had allowed dozens of young Namibians, Zimbabweans, South Africans and others into Uganda to study at Makerere University, where they built close friendships with the Rwandan exiles: deep ties were forged under the banner of student politics and in university dormitories, with young progressives finding parallels to their own predicament in the situation of other African comrades. The embrace of Pan-Africanism became even tighter when scores of Banyarwanda joined the anti-Obote struggle of the National

Resistance Army (NRA) of Yoweri Museveni, a leftist alumnus of the University of Dar es Salaam. The latter preached revolution and a non-ethnic politics, arguing that the struggle for freedom and emancipation in Uganda was no different from that elsewhere in Africa. This was music to the ears of the Rwandophone exiles, not least because it came from a blood-relative: Museveni hails from the cattle-herding Bahima community which frequently intermarries with their Rwandan cousins. These kinship ties, the fact of having grown up together in southwest Uganda where most of the refugee camps were located and the shared progressive ideology of anti-tribalism, anti-imperialism and rural development proved powerful bonding material.

The NRA experience would prove the crucible in which the hard core of the Rwandan Patriotic Front was formed. For a generation of youngsters it offered a psychological and political liberation. Internalized beliefs of being second-class citizens and unwanted refugees were transformed into a self-recognition as primary actors, able to shape their own destiny through the armed struggle. The bulk of the NRA fighting force was Ugandan, but many of its intelligence cadres and shock troops were of Rwandan origin, engaged in the most sensitive operations, from the initial raid on the Kabamba School of Infantry by twenty-seven rebels on February 6, 1981, to the killing fields of the Luwero Triangle in central Uganda and the bloody post-liberation pacification campaign in northern Uganda. Thousands of youth enrolled and acquired military skills and a growing self-belief, as well as an enduring conviction that it would pay to fight when confronted with a political impasse. Back against the wall, pushed by an apparent threat to their survival and by a liberation ideology that promised social mobility and freedom, they defied expectations and proved to be superb soldiers. Having grown up in the same refugee camps (especially Nyakivara and Rucinga around Mbarara) and attended the same educational institutions (notably Ntare Secondary School and Makerere University), the Rwandan recruits of the NRA were further bound together by the formidable glue of mutual sacrifices, shared paranoia about the outside world and frontline camaraderie.

The leadership of the Rwandan contingent of the NRA rested with Fred Rwigyema, a nom de guerre the exile from Gitarama had acquired during his time in the late 1970s in Mozambique with FRELIMO and Tanzania in the company of Museveni.[69] Together with Paul Kagame, a brilliant intelligence

---

[69] Yoweri Museveni, "Museveni Explains Great Lakes' Crisis," *The Monitor*, May 30, 1999.

officer with a flair for organization and strategy, Rwigyema formed part of the famous group of twenty-seven who launched the NRA rebellion with the attack on Kabamba. Not all of the youngsters who were subsequently mobilized by them shared the same ethnic background as Rwigyema and Kagame, as is conventionally assumed. What later became the RPF is often wrongly seen as coterminous with a "Tutsi force," at least according to RPF sources: a non-negligible chunk of the refugees who left Rwanda in the late 1950s and early 1960s were pastoralists, but they were Hutu rather than Tutsi. In Uganda, their children went to the same schools as Tutsi exiles and over time the label "Tutsi" became part of the resistance identity developed in exile. Many of these displaced joined the NRA, as did large numbers of Banyarwanda who had lived in the Luwero Triangle for decades and who had been alienated by Obote's brutal policies. It is through this latter group that James Kabarebe, later Paul Kagame's aide-de-camp, foremost general and liberator-cum-conqueror of Congo, would also join the struggle.

However, despite the NRA's success and the crucial role the Banyarwanda played in the fall of Kampala in January 1986, the liberation of Uganda would prove an anti-climax. It was made clear by the new government and an increasingly hostile public that their sacrifices would not lead to Ugandan citizenship. In the words of Frank Rusagara, "Every day that went by showed you that you were not wanted in Uganda, that you were not Ugandan."[70] The NRA officer corps was disproportionately dominated by Banyarwanda—Fred Rwigyema had even been appointed as deputy minister of defense, second only to Museveni in the chain of command—and combined with the growing role played by Rwandan exiles in the economy, this produced widespread resentment among the Baganda and wavering northerners and easterners who were thinking of joining the new regime.[71] Having been socialized in Ugandan schools and having fought for Uganda's political future, this rejection by Ugandan society was a huge blow for the Banyarwanda and their warrior youngsters, who internalized the lesson: never trust anyone, bar your own.

As Museveni embarked on a reform of the Ugandan economy and trimmed the army—he awkwardly portrayed the release of Rwandans from the armed forces as an inevitable consequence of engaging the World Bank and its structural adjustment ideology—the post-1986 disillusionment of the Banyarwanda morphed into a renewed embrace of an old project: the return to Rwanda. The

---

[70] Interview in London, February 2011.

[71] Gérard Prunier, "The Rwandan Patriotic Front," in Christopher Clapham (ed.), *African Guerillas*, Oxford: James Currey, 1998, pp. 71–2.

instruments to successfully do so were available: plenty of eager recruits and cadres; a reservoir of diaspora further afield, from Congo to Belgium, wanting to return home; a Pan-Africanist ideology to restructure domestic and regional politics; and the experience of participating in a victorious uprising, built as a rural insurgency from the ground up, against a sitting president. The dormant Rwandan Alliance for National Unity (RANU), founded as the successor to the Rwandan Refugee Welfare Foundation but exiled in Kenya between 1981 and 1986, was revived and became increasingly political in character, attracting greater numbers of Banyarwanda—including many women and youngsters who had not been able to participate in the struggle. In December 1987, RANU was re-baptized as the Rwandan Patriotic Front; with this transformation the leadership advanced the military option in case the Kigali government rejected the right to return of all exiles.

Museveni, aware of the growing militarization of the Banyarwanda on his territory, urged Habyarimana to find a way of accommodating them and allowing the diaspora to reintegrate. Habyarimana came to Kampala and was ironically protected by Ugandan–Rwandan escorts during his visit, but refused to budge: Rwanda is full, he repeated. This would prove the final straw—with no chance of integration in Uganda, with the doors of peaceful return to Rwanda shut and with increasingly bullish reports by informants and the international press regarding the weakness of the Habyarimana regime (particularly now that France, after the La Baule conference, seemed to have made continued support for its clients conditional on democratization), the path of war beckoned. On October 1, 1990, the RPF invaded, taking everybody, not least Habyarimana's Forces Armées Rwandaises (FAR), by surprise.

The War of Liberation

The RPF's armed return to Rwanda in 1990 marked a major turn for regional order. Partly inspired by the Pan-Africanist liberation project of Julius Nyerere, it was a direct challenge to an important ally of Mobutu,[72] and thus to the Mobutist system of protecting his grip on power through mutual deter-

---

[72] Mobutu's chief political adviser summed up the alliance between Zaire and Rwanda. "If Marshall Mobutu was strongly invested in the stability of his colleague and friend Habyarimana, it was not solely because of the sincere friendship that the two men had, but it was above all because Habyarimana guaranteed in his eyes predictability and moderation in the unstable equilibrium of the Great Lakes region." N'Gbanda, *Ainsi sonne le glas*, p. 84.

rence: if you do not harbor any rebels of mine, I will not support your foes. Mobutu had been wary of Museveni's ascent to power in Kampala given his ties with Tanzania and Mozambique, but Zaire's president had not been particularly close to Milton Obote—regime change in Uganda did not have to be threatening and co-existence with Museveni appeared possible. Rwanda, however, was different: as a French client state headed by a personal friend of Mobutu's but now threatened by an invasion by Anglophone rebels, it needed to be defended. Moreover, given the presence of Banyarwanda communities in Zaire, Mobutu feared spillover and a destabilization of his eastern border, which together with Katanga had been the historical source of serious challenges to his rule. He suspected that even if the RPF had invaded independently, Museveni would not be far behind, offering support to let another "neo-colonial" domino fall. Mobutu thus ordered the only decent troops he still controlled in battle: the DSP helped the FAR and counter-attacked within days of the October 1 invasion. When DSP forces failed to reverse the rebel tide, 600 French paratroopers were flown in to prevent a possible collapse of the Habyarimana regime in the face of the presumed Ugandan–Rwandan Tutsi advance.

As it became clear that high international stakes were involved in the conflict, Rwandan society also received a high voltage shock due to the confluence of a chronic economic crisis, donor demands for democratization and the outbreak of war.[73] The convergence of these trends poisoned Rwandan politics and pushed it into an all-consuming vortex that would ultimately lead to the 1994 apocalypse, which began after the downing of Habyarimana's plane over his residence in Kigali on April 6. The Rwandan civil war and the genocide have been amply documented in outstanding research.[74] What we focus on

---

[73] Alison Des Forges, *"Leave None to Tell the Story": Genocide in Rwanda*, New York: Human Rights Watch, 1999.

[74] Ibid.; Timothy Longman, *Christianity and Genocide in Rwanda*, Cambridge: Cambridge University Press, 2009; Linda Melvern, *Conspiracy to Murder: The Rwandan Genocide*, London: Verso, 2006; Prunier, "Rwandan Patriotic Front"; Filip Reyntjens, "Rwanda: Genocide and Beyond," *Journal of Refugee Studies*, 9, 3 (1996); Scott Straus, *The Order of Genocide: Race, Power, and War in Rwanda*, Ithaca: Cornell University Press, 2006; Philip Verwimp, "An Economic Profile of Peasant Perpetrators of Genocide: Micro-Level Evidence from Rwanda," *Journal of Development Economics*, 77, 2 (2005); Omar Shahabudin McDoom, "Who Killed in Rwanda's Genocide? Micro-Space, Social Influence and Individual Participation in Intergroup Violence," *Journal of Peace Research*, 50, 4 (2013).

here is how civil war and genocide shaped the character of the "liberators" and the nature of their post-July 1994 grip on power, including their foreign policy vis-à-vis Zaire once sovereignty had been wrested from the genocidal regime.[75]

Almost nothing about the Rwandan civil war unfolded as the RPF's top commanders—Fred Rwigyema, Paul Kagame, Sam Kaka and Stephen Ndugute (a veteran who had already served under Idi Amin)—had foreseen. Two scenarios had been discussed among the High Command: a rapid collapse of the state, leading to a capture of power within weeks, or a prolonged liberation war on the "Ugandan" model of 1981–6 that would allow the RPF to further develop organizationally and ideologically but to ultimately emerge victorious. The French intervention and the time it bought the FAR to reconstitute itself precluded the first option, but the second scenario too quickly became a lot less plausible. Following the October invasion, the RPF had conquered a narrow zone beyond the Ugandan border, but the conflict in northern Rwanda was anything but a classical guerrilla war—the region emptied before the RPF, driven in flight not just by violence on the frontline but reports of rebel atrocities. It remains difficult to ascertain the veracity of the reported killings by the RPF and the scale at which these took place, but most likely the stories that emerged from the warzone were cannibalized by government propaganda in an attempt at depriving the rebels of a popular base and rallying the population in the rest of Rwanda behind the Habyarimana regime: depicting the RPF as murderers bent on bringing back the monarchy, feudalism and colonialism was a very effective propaganda message. The fears it evoked ran deep and would be crucial in mobilizing the masses in 1994 for the genocide against Tutsi and their presumed Hutu accomplices.[76] By contrast, from a strategic perspective, RPF atrocities in the Ruhengeri–Byumba area made no sense as these would deprive them of a key asset they had counted on to win the war: the support of ordinary Rwandans.

This is an all the more pertinent point to keep in mind when remembering that the RPF in its historiography and ideology continued to frame Rwanda as a fundamentally consensual nation, diverted from its path to progress by imperialist divide-and-rule and neo-colonial regimes that reproduced colonial terminologies and hierarchies. Prior to October 1990, RPF ideologues had

---

[75] Like the previous sections, the following paragraphs are based on in-depth interviews, conducted between 2009 and 2015 in a range of different locations, with about a dozen of the RPF's most senior commanders and politicians.

[76] Straus, *Order of Genocide*.

expected the population to side with them enthusiastically, casting off the yoke of dictatorship and joining the Front in its establishment of non-ethnicized democracy.[77] The Rwanda they remembered—but which they had not stepped foot in for decades, if ever—was an imaginary land of milk and honey that had been wrecked by comprador elites. The RPF had thus not only no strategic reason to alienate the population by large-scale excesses but it was actually counting on popular backing to propel its insurgents to power. Yet what happened after the invasion baffled both its leadership and foot soldiers: more than a million Rwandans fled the north within weeks of the operation, leaving the RPF with little or no possibilities to get food and shelter in the villages, or able to organize a local administration that could levy taxes, spread its ideology and serve as a test-run for future government. It was a tremendous military and political blow, which forced the rebellion to operate from cold mountains and remote forests (including Zaire's Virunga Park), rather than fight the "Maoist" insurgency amid the people it had planned for. Frank Rusagara, a mid-ranking officer at the time, expressed the frustrations of many of his comrades and commanders: "We were never able to fight a guerrilla war. We never had the support of the population."[78]

Not only would the civil war be fought in a very different way from what it had originally envisaged, but the Front was also forced to do so without its most able soldier, the heart and soul of the RPF: Fred Rwigyema died on the second day of the invasion. In him, the rebels lost their closest ally to Museveni, an excellent motivator and a man of military experience who maintained good contacts with foreign embassies. This second major blow forced Paul Kagame—who rushed back to the front after three and a half months at Fort Leavenworth in the United States where he had been receiving training in his capacity as an experienced NRA officer—to dramatically restructure the liberation struggle. A tactical withdrawal allowed the RPF to dig in for the long haul and to first win militarily; convincing the population of the blessings of RPF rule would be something that would mostly happen after liberation, or so the leadership told itself. Moreover, in its initial thrust the RPF had largely counted on waging its liberation war autonomously from any foreign force, but the military predicament made it impossible not to turn to Uganda for supplies, recruitment, access to diplomatic channels and weaponry. Kagame

---

[77] Gérard Prunier, *The Rwanda Crisis: History of a Genocide*, London: Hurst, 1998, p. 152.

[78] Interview in London, November 2010.

himself, as the new commander of the Rwandan Patriotic Army (RPA), was given several of Museveni's armored vehicles to move around northern Rwanda and Uganda.

With the conflict unfolding in such unexpected ways, the RPF/RPA demonstrated a remarkable ability to radically change tack: instead of waging a Maoist insurgency, its campaign would be more Leninist in nature. The Front engaged opposition politicians, launched counter-propaganda and assuaged the fears of those layers of the Rwandan population it did meet, yet it also imagined itself as a righteous vanguard that had the right recipes for Rwandan society even if the latter may not yet be aware of it. The Leninist model suited Kagame's cerebral, aloof style of decision-making and he increasingly manifested himself as the *primus inter pares* in the High Command. Under his aegis, the RPA developed formidable organizational capabilities, a Spartan discipline and a highly flexible doctrine. Bolstered by a policy of actively recruiting outside its traditional base (it was obvious that the image of the Front as a Ugandan Tutsi movement hurt it considerably and played into the hands of Habyarimana's propaganda), hundreds of exiles from Congo, Burundi, Europe and elsewhere joined the struggle. Many of these had benefited from a considerable degree of education: not only did this boost the RPF's financial and logistical operations but it also meant, for example, that the RPA was able to field forty qualified medical doctors against only four or five on the side of the FAR.

Between 1991 and 1994, the RPF's political leadership forged coalitions with emerging actors in the democratization process, talked regularly to the French about the Front's intentions and even engaged the Habyarimana regime and Hutu extremist parties in peace negotiations in Arusha. And while the RPF saw some value in these processes with the goals of facilitating the return of exiles to Rwanda, opening up the political landscape and securing as much influence as possible for itself in the national institutions, its increasingly Leninist outlook and the disappointments of a civil war that refused to go according to plan meant that its leaders assumed a fight to death between FAR and RPA would be the most likely outcome. The RPA High Command held the upper hand vis-à-vis the politicians—a dynamic that did not change with the promotion of senior Hutu figures like Colonel Alexis Kanyarengwe (who even became the Front's nominal chairman), Pasteur Bizimungu, Colonel Théoneste Lizinde and Seth Sendashonga in RPF ranks. As the war continued and a peaceful solution remained elusive, this imbalance worsened further. The exigencies of the struggle—keeping ranks closed, prioritizing security, acquiring the strongest possible negotiation position through on the ground advances—did not thwart lengthy and intense internal debates within the RPF and RPA about which course to follow, but did imply that, ultimately, the armed wing of the Front always had the final say. Kagame's unique position as virtually the only senior military officer well versed in politics and the only political figure with the necessary military gravitas to sway the other commanders gave him unique authority. His motto throughout the campaign remained *si vis pacem, para bellum*: if you want peace, prepare for war.

Post-Genocide Rwanda

What many RPA officers had long expected materialized from April 6, 1994 onwards. Departing from Tanzania, Habyarimana headed home in a Falcon 50 jet with Burundese President Cyprien Ntaryamira and three key members of the Rwandan military elite aboard, refusing to heed the intelligence reports that warned of dangers upon return to Kigali. He also ignored the usual precautionary measures of ensuring the Rwandan president and his Army Chief of Staff Déogratias Nsabimana never traveled together in order to maintain the continuity of command in case of an attack. Two days earlier, Habyarimana had met with his close friend Mobutu in Gbadolite to gauge the latter's reaction to his decision to share power with the RPF and cede half of all officer posts in the reformed national Rwandan armed forces to the RPA as well as the sensitive position of the minister of the interior.[79] Allegedly drawing on French intelligence, Mobutu told Habyarimana to continue playing for time and to consult further with Paris regarding the Arusha Peace Accords, but to certainly not travel to Dar es Salaam. The Rwandan head of state did not heed his mentor's advice and went anyway. When the aircraft was downed over the gardens of Habyarimana's own residence at 20:26, the *akazu*, led by Théoneste Bagosora and other FAR officers, grabbed power in a coup, ordered roadblocks to be erected across the city and began a process of eliminating the interim prime minister, members of parliament, party leaders, judges, human rights activists and moderate Hutu members of the security services. Genocide followed.

The murder of around 800,000 Rwandans in 100 days—with the vast majority of the victims exterminated within the first six weeks—was a horror of indescribable proportions. To give but one example, consider what hap-

---

[79] N'Gbanda, *Ainsi sonne le glas*, pp. 75–7.

pened in Gikongoro. On April 16, ten days after Habyarimana's assassination, thousands of Rwandan citizens flocked together on the hilltop of Murambi, in the southwest of the country. They gathered around a dozen or so school buildings, following the instructions of local authorities who had warned the Tutsi population of the Gikongoro Prefecture that they would not be able to protect them in their villages. The Tutsis of Gikongoro were petrified but fled to Murambi, believing local *bourgmestres'* vows of help and security.[80] Mere days after their arrival, the trap closed behind them: the mayors and gendarmerie commanders who had promised to bring humanitarian assistance aided the encirclement of the hill by the Interahamwe militia. At dawn on April 21, the assault was launched by the Interahamwe and thousands of ordinary Hutus, armed with machetes, clubs, sticks and broken bottles. Up to 50,000 men, women and children were killed in Murambi.[81]

The hunt for Tutsis and their presumed Hutu accomplices—those who were opponents of the Habyarimana regime, those who refused to join the massacres or simply those whose economic assets made them targets of violence under the cover of war and genocidal anarchy—was waged in churches and in schools, in swamps and in forests, in homes and in deserted streets. The killing spree was the product of a heavily centralized state, the vicious "Hutu Power" ideology it promoted and key officials' orders to exterminate, but it was also driven by local mobs, parochial greed and individual initiative to murder. Jean Hatzfeld, whose fieldwork in southern Rwanda provides us with a unique micro-perspective on both perpetrators and victims, quotes a school teacher, Jean-Baptiste Munyankore from Ntarama, to capture a sliver of the madness:

> What happened in Nyamata, in the churches, in the marshes and the hills, are the supernatural doings of ordinary people. Let me tell you why I say this. The headmaster and the school inspector in my area took part in the killings, striking blows with spiked clubs. Two teacher colleagues with whom I used to exchange beers and pupil assessments got stuck in too, if I may put it like this. A priest, the magistrate, the assistant chief of police, a doctor, killed with their own hands. ... These intellectuals had never lived in the time of the Batutsi kings. They had never been robbed of anything nor bullied, they were under obligation to no one. They wore pleated cotton pants, they had proper time to rest, drove around in vehicles or on

---

[80] Local officials had a lot of control over their municipalities and, following the politico-administrative system of Belgium, the *bourgmestre*—a powerful mayor—sat at the pinnacle of that local hierarchy.

[81] African Rights, "'If You Die, Perhaps I Will Live'": A Collective Account of Genocide and Survival in Murambi, Gikongoro, April–July 1994," Kigali: African Rights, 2007.

mopeds. Their wives wore jewels and knew city ways, their children frequented white schools.[82]

Another survivor, Innocent Rwililiza from neighboring Nyamata, offers his testimony:

> While we, on the other hand, bolted at the slightest noise, we scrabbled through the earth on our bellies in search of manioc, the lice guzzled us, we died cut by machetes like goats in the market. We looked like animals, since we no longer resembled the humans we used to, and they had grown accustomed to see us as animals … When an Interahamwe caught a pregnant woman, he would start by piercing her belly with the help of a blade. Not even the spotted hyena could dream up such cruelty with his fangs …

> Those responsible for the Rwandan genocide are not poor and ignorant farmers, no more than they are ferocious and drunken Interahamwe—they are the educated people. They are the professors, the politicians and the journalists who expatriated themselves to Europe to study the French Revolution and the Humanities. They are those who have travelled, who are invited to conferences and who have invited Whites to eat at their villas. In Nyamata, the Interahamwe president's Christian name was Jean-Désiré. He was a good teacher. Sometimes we would share a Primus together, out of friendship. He would say to us: "Alright, if the inkotanyi [RPF] come into Rwanda, then we will have to kill you," and suchlike. But because he was kind, we laughed about it and offered him another beer. This man, with whom we exchanged jokes, became one of the three or four leading promoters of genocide in the region.[83]

How the 1994 Cataclysm Shaped the Front

The terror of the genocide fortified the dominant characteristics the RPF had developed during four years of conflict with the FAR.[84] The first key takeaway, from the Front's perspective, was that compromise is a dangerous strategy; by contrast, violence, when confronted with a political impasse, is essential to achieve one's objectives. RPA forces had been instrumental in overthrowing two incumbent military regimes and thus the transformative power of force had been underlined yet again, because once the genocide was underway, the RPA counter-offensive was unstoppable and liberated Rwanda in three months' time. Whereas the confidence of the RPF in its own ability to succeed

---

[82] Jean Hatzfeld, *Into the Quick of Life: The Rwandan Genocide—The Survivors Speak*, London: Serpent's Tail, 2005, p. 73.

[83] Ibid., pp. 73, 77–8.

[84] Verhoeven, "Nurturing Democracy or into the Danger Zone?"

militarily was sky high, its belief in empathizing with opponents was at its nadir following the collapse of the Arusha Accords and the extermination of 75 per cent of the Tutsi population inside Rwanda. In other words, what peace negotiations could not achieve, bold military strategy did deliver. A martial approach to political problems, while not devoid of messiness and difficulties either, could lead to a wholesale transformation of the situation and allowed one to dictate terms. Unsurprisingly, therefore, the military and intelligence wing of the Front came to almost completely dominate the senior civilian figures in the movement.

Second, the RPF's underwhelming reception in much of liberated Rwanda disappointed the Front. This was no classic liberation triumph. As Rose Kabuye, mayor of Kigali after the genocide, noted, "There was no celebration of our victory."[85] The population was traumatized and anxious after the waves of extremist propaganda about the return of Tutsi feudalism and *inyenzi* atrocities.[86] For years, urban and rural citizens alike had been bombarded with depictions of the RPF as devils, and stories of presumed atrocities in northern Rwanda were widely believed; many Hutu peasants feared that retribution was inevitable given widespread popular involvement in the killings. Both ordinary Rwandans and arriving RPA soldiers reported extreme degrees of tension whenever the rebels would take over another half a dozen hills and stumble upon survivors and a disoriented Hutu population. The RPA had hoped to be hailed as liberators, or at the very least to receive extensive cooperation from society in tracking down remaining pockets of Interahamwe and FAR. Instead, many peasants withdrew into their villages in a sort of passive non-commitment, waiting to see how the Front would govern. The RPF considered this as incredulous ingratitude on the part of a population of which large swathes had been involved in massacring the relatives of advancing RPA troops. In the words of the head of the UN Human Rights Field Operation in post-genocide Rwanda, "The tensions in the countryside were virtually unmanageable."[87]

The third lesson then was that the RPF would continue to have to rule as a misunderstood but rightly guided vanguard. Part of the Front's disappointment stemmed from the fact that it was not just the hostile "Hutu" rural areas who failed to hail the RPA as liberators. Many *rescapés* (genocide survivors) too, while obviously relieved at having survived the Interahamwe death

---

[85] Interview in Kigali, July 2014.
[86] Mamdani, *When Victims Become Killers*, pp. 6–7, 186–9.
[87] Skype interview with Ian Martin, December 2014.

squads, lacked enthusiasm for the liberation project. Some blamed the Front for being intransigent in the negotiations or argued that the 1990 invasion had unleashed the genocidal winds; others were bewildered by the urbanized and Anglophone character of their protectors, which contrasted with their own modest, Kinyarwanda-only rural backgrounds; still others could not understand why RPA units were showing such leniency and did not embark on a massive retaliation campaign against any Hutu they could find; and a final group were just too psychologically and physically scarred to carry on and be of any use to the nation-building task. Kagame himself recognized this gap between *rescapés* and the RPF but still felt the Front's 1990 decision to fight for liberation was totally justified:

> As we saw it, that was a very narrow way of looking at things. It was not in dispute that people were being oppressed. In some way, that tends to draw a line, as if those of us outside were different from those here. Yet some of those opposed to us were also part of us. They were our relatives. There was not a single Rwandan outside who did not have relatives inside. We were a family. Yes, in some cases there was a feeling by some people here that things were better left the way they were. But the way things were was simply unacceptable.[88]

Apart from the countless dead, more than a million people were internally displaced and more than two million had fled abroad; Rwanda was left with around 500,000 orphans and 400,000 widows. For the RPF leadership, only a strong, paternalistic hand could pick up the broken pieces that constituted Rwandan society and bring back order and direction. This undoubtedly strengthened the RPF's self-perception as a vanguard that may not be widely appreciated, but would be legitimized in its actions by history.

The fourth key trait of the Front that had already emerged in previous years, but was amplified by the genocide, was its distrust of the Western-led international community. As a clandestine movement fearing infiltration, the Front had long assumed the default insurgent position of suspicion vis-à-vis outsiders. The confrontation with France, Habyarimana's loyal ally, and the unwillingness of the UN Security Council to respond to growing violence before April 1994 and then to the genocide itself, persuaded the RPF that depending on the outside world when in need, makes things worse. Kagame's High Command rebuffed the UN's unchanging insistence on a ceasefire and peace talks after the United Nations Assistance Mission for Rwanda (UNAMIR)

---

[88] Stephen Kinzer, *A Thousand Hills: Rwanda's Rebirth and the Man Who Dreamed It*, Hoboken: John Wiley & Sons, 2008, p. 99.

had been reduced to a skeletal force of 200 in April 1994 following the assassination of ten Belgian blue helmets. The RPF had lost all trust in an external solution and continued full steam ahead with the only answer it saw to the war and genocide: a total RPF takeover, not a UN deal that would separate the belligerents and allow the Interahamwe to finish their extermination campaign under the cover of a political process. The Front vehemently opposed the Security Council resolution of May 6 (which would have deployed a force of 5,500 under Chapter VII) and even more so the UN-mandated *Opération Turquoise* of the French army, which ostensibly created safe zones for refugees in the southwest of Rwanda, but allowed the collapsing genocidal government and tens of thousands of FAR and Interahamwe militia to escape into neighboring Zaire in June–July 1994. From the RPF perspective, the international community had not just chosen to be a bystander to genocide; it had assisted the *génocidaires* in escaping so that they could fight another day.

Governing a Scorched Land

If the genocide was a drama of unspeakable proportions, the weeks and months after the hecatomb ended in Rwanda in July 1994 presented mindboggling challenges too. In the space of three months, the entire country had been ravaged. Industrial production had fallen to zero, the workforce had been decimated, agricultural output crashed. Barely any medical facilities, already in desperately poor condition before the tragedy, functioned and the National University in Butare had been the scene of grotesque massacres in which students and professors hunted their peers. The water and sanitation system in cities had broken down, and with hundreds of thousands of disintegrating bodies, the public health situation was extremely alarming. Markets stopped functioning; a food crisis of catastrophic proportions seemed inevitable.

The capital was a ghost town where only RPA soldiers and orphans appeared to roam and all normal life had ceased; the newly appointed RPF mayor, Rose Kabuye, described it as follows: "It was like the whole of Kigali was an orphanage."[89] There were no offices to resume government work from; phone lines were dead; the vast majority of judges and other justice officials had been killed, fled or compromised in the genocide; and the prisons around the country would soon be bulging with 120,000 suspected *génocidaires* who were kept in such overcrowded conditions that gangrene and death by suffoca-

[89] Interview in Kigali, July 2014.

tion were common occurrences. In a bid to restore some degree of normality, Kabuye encouraged survivors and exiles to return as soon as possible, to help the physical reconstruction and, however slightly, to revive public life—football games, taxi rides, market sales. However, this created its own problems as repatriated refugees, having been expelled from their ancestral villages themselves, settled into vacated houses. As the RPF tried to also return surviving relatives of these owners, or the owners themselves who might have fled to a neighboring country, this inevitably led to intense confrontations in which the Front was asked to arbitrate and constantly stood accused of either failing to promote national reconciliation (with an alleged bias towards exiles) or to turn its back on its long-standing supporters (favoring "Hutu murderers").[90]

The learning curve was extremely steep. As discussed earlier, the RPF had never been able to wage the anticipated Maoist liberation war and garner the experience of governing rural areas. It excelled in raising money and military-organizational matters, but they mostly pertained to intra-movement matters, not to interacting with the population. Moreover, its cadres were extremely young. Most of the dominant figures were in their thirties: Kagame, who assumed the post of minister of defense and vice-president, was thirty-six, the new head of the gendarmerie, Kayumba Nyamwasa, was thirty-two, and Fred Ibingira, commander of the RPA storm troops who had won the war (the 157th Mobile Force), was thirty. Pasteur Bizimungu, the 44-year-old Hutu politician whom the RPF nominated as president of the Republic, Patrick Mazimhaka, minister of reintegration at forty-six, and the Minister of the Interior Seth Sendashonga (forty-four) were already considered "veterans." The task of rebuilding Rwanda as a state and a nation would have been overwhelming for even the best prepared government in the world. It certainly was for the young liberation warriors of the RPF/RPA.

To pacify the rural areas in western Rwanda and to boost its numbers after losses during the war, the RPA recruited thousands of survivors and returning exiles. This influx of less disciplined new troops—pushing the army's size well above 25,000—rapidly compounded an escalating problem of RPA "excesses,"

---

[90] For perhaps the best account by a Rwandan of the impossible post-genocide context, see André Sibomana, *Hope for Rwanda: Conversations with Laure Guilbert and Hervé Deguine*, London: Pluto Press, 1999, pp. 101–20. Many of the human rights, economic, political and security challenges were also documented by the UN. UN Special Rapporteur of the Commission on Human Rights, "Report on the Situation of Human Rights in Rwanda," New York: UN Commission on Human Rights, 1997.

the euphemism the Front leaders adopted to downplay the large-scale killing of civilians in the countryside. Army units discovering churches, schools or public latrines full of human remains would sometimes be overcome by emotion and kill any Hutu civilian they could find in the vicinity; at other times, special teams would return to zones of *génocidaire* atrocities at night, round up all the remaining men and murder these "Interahamwe." The advance of Ibingira's 157th Mobile Force—from the east, passing through the Bugesera into southwest Rwanda—was particularly brutal and resulted in the destruction of the town of Kibungo in May 1994 *after* FAR and Interahamwe had withdrawn. One former officer of the 157th Mobile Force testified that "some Hutus couldn't afford to be bystanders. We essentially killed civilians."[91] According to the same witness, after the genocide, units within the same force (now renamed the 305th Brigade) organized nocturnal "black ops" in which they systematically targeted "hostile populations," killing hundreds.

This pattern of post-genocide violence by the RPA and the Directorate of Military Intelligence (DMI) was first mapped in the so-called "Gersony report," written by a team built around US army veteran Robert Gersony, after a month-long fact finding mission in the Rwandan countryside in August 1994. While initially tasked by the UN high commissioner for refugees, Sadako Ogata, to establish whether the large-scale repatriation of refugees could commence, the human rights violations they came across were too disturbing to ignore. Rory Beaumont, one of the authors of the Gersony report, recalls the discovery of one such incident, and its context, in Butare Prefecture:

> In early August [1994], Gersony and I arrived in a deserted village. No living soul to be seen but approximately 150 bodies were stacked up in piles. They were neatly organized inside brick buildings and perhaps only seven—or maximum ten—days old. When we then got back in our car and drove on, we got to a church. Something was lying on the ground. As we got there, I saw that these were clearly bodies. Totally shriveled bodies. We then entered the church and found other remnants of an older massacre where the Interahamwe had clearly broken into the holy place and murdered everybody. The bodies were everywhere and in all kinds of positions. When we walked back to the car, Gersony asked me how many bodies were there—I said fifty or sixty; Gersony told me it was thirty exactly.[92]

The RPF leadership has never denied the "excesses" but rejects the idea that the killing was a centrally organized policy. One of Kagame's most senior advisers remarked: "Of course there was revenge. But you need context. This

---

[91] Interview in Kampala, March 2013.
[92] Interview in Oxford, December 2014.

is very emotional for us."[93] This argument was echoed by six high-ranking political and security officials in interviews conducted between 2012 and 2014: that RPA discipline partly broke down; that the RPF's grip on remote rural areas where it had never operated was more tenuous than its politicians could publicly admit and that this explains why so many killings happened there rather than in the cities, where revenge was largely absent; and that the purges targeted Interahamwe cells and sympathizers, keeping in mind that participation in the genocide by ordinary civilians was the rule, not the exception, in much of Rwanda.[94] The scale of the killing has led some observers and RPF critics to allege that this was a double genocide, even if empirical research points in another direction.[95] According to RPA officers, most of the violence hence occurred in the south and southwest, where the genocide killed the highest number of Tutsi and the insurgent potential initially was greatest, with the northern region largely spared of revenge killings or lethal search operations. The Gersony report, which estimates the death toll of RPA activity between 25,000 to 40,000 people in the April–August 1994 period, confirmed this when commenting on Ruhengeri Prefecture (where the RPF had been present since 1990):

> In striking contrast to the southern and southeastern regions described above, refugee returnees from Zaire ... and local residents in part of western Ruhengeri ... reported overwhelmingly that conditions in their area were secure, stable and peaceful ... A liberal border-crossing policy by local authorities permitted families to walk home for brief exploratory visits, confirm for themselves the security situation and return to Zaire to bring back their families.[96]

The violence that continued to rage in the Rwandan countryside after July 1994 was related to the incomplete defeat of the *génocidaires*' forces and ideology. *Opération Turquoise* turned the southwest of Rwanda into a site of sprawling refugee camps home to hundreds of thousands of mainly internally displaced Hutu and was not brought under the same strong grip that the RPF

[93] Interview in Kigali, July 2014.

[94] Interviews in Kigali, London and one withheld location elsewhere in Africa, April 2012–December 2014.

[95] Des Forges, *"Leave None To Tell the Story"*, pp. 692–735; Philip Verwimp, "Testing the Double-Genocide Thesis for Central and Southern Rwanda," *Journal of Conflict Resolution*, 47, 4 (2003).

[96] "Summary of UNHCR Presentation before Commission of Experts, 10 October 1994: Prospects for Early Repatriation of Rwandan Refugees Currently in Burundi, Tanzania and Zaire," Geneva: UNHCR, 1994, p. 10.

was able to establish over northern, central and eastern Rwanda. Even more importantly, the entire genocidal government, the military and security command structure and many of the economic elites had been assured a hasty but safe passage into the Zaire of Habyarimana's former patron, Mobutu. The objective was to set up a state outside the state, literally just across the Rwandan–Zairian border, and to take Rwanda's population along in an attempt at preparing their return to power in Kigali.[97] As the FAR chief of staff, Augustin Bizimungu, said from Goma, just across the border: "The RPF will rule over a desert." Hundreds of thousands of Rwandans, many of them ordinary citizens who may or may not have had blood on their hands, were herded into eastern Zaire through a mixture of propaganda-induced fear of RPA reprisals and government compulsion. Just as northern Rwanda had emptied before the RPF advance during the war and had greatly frustrated the Front's plans and ability to overcome its political and psychological distance from the population, so now western and southern Rwanda were largely cleared of rural masses for the RPF to rule over. This was a major blow for the new government domestically—and would ultimately lead to regional war.

The Refugee Camps in Zaire

About one-and-a-half million refugees had crossed the western frontiers of Rwanda in July 1994, with everything they could transport in cars, trucks or on their backs. This sea of displaced people would have been virtually impossible to stop even if the Zairian border guards had wanted to, but the cozy ties between the Rwandan establishment and the Mobutist regime assured that support from Gbadolite was forthcoming. As discussed earlier, Mobutu had correctly identified the post-genocide refugee crisis as a golden opportunity to maneuver his way back into international politics. The outcry over Rwanda in international humanitarian circles was so deafening and the needs of the refugees looked so overwhelming that the Zairian despot would play the sovereignty card to maximum effect: using the weakness of the Zairian state as an asset to extract resources and legitimacy from the international system had been a key recipe of Mobutu's political longevity all along and the need to feed, vaccinate and shelter the Rwandan masses on his territory offered him an opportunity to cash in.

Mobutu's return to prominence on the international stage began during the genocide when Jacques Foccart, grandmaster of France–Africa relations as key

[97] John Rucyahana, *The Bishop of Rwanda*, Nashville: Thomas Nelson, 2007, p. 134.

adviser to French Presidents De Gaulle, Pompidou and Chirac, patronized a visit in April 1994 to Gbadolite by Herman Cohen (former US assistant secretary of state for African affairs), Max-Olivier Cahen (son of Alfred Cahen, the Belgian ambassador to Paris and formerly Brussels' envoy to Mobutu) and Robert Bourgi (a Lebanese-French Gaullist lawyer) to discuss the Rwandan crisis and impress on Mobutu that the West, represented by the three lead nations on Zairian/Congolese matters, needed him.[98] Days earlier, the Habyarimana family had been safely evacuated to Paris via Zaire. Mobutu's green light for French supplies and reinforcements for the FAR, his subsequent hosting of the camps and even his involvement in violating the UN arms embargo by letting Zaire act as the conduit for external weapon deliveries to the *génocidaires*[99] were rewarded with an invitation to return triumphantly to the French–Africa summit of November 1994 in Biarritz. His African peers were also busy rehabilitating him, with Mandela inviting Mobutu to play a role in the Angolan peace process, given his privileged contacts with the rebels of Jonas Savimbi's UNITA. The genocide and the Rwandan refugees were thus valuable political currency in the hands of the old leopard, but also lucrative business for the local officials in North and South Kivu for whom the aid flows to the displaced proved a bonanza.

The camps that were set up along the shores of Lake Kivu around Goma and Bukavu and around Uvira and Lake Tanganyika—about forty in total (see map)—were by no means ordinary zones of protection, rest and service delivery. Perhaps best known to the world because of the terrible cholera outbreak in July–August 1994 that claimed the lives of more than 40,000 people—a public health emergency that led to a dramatic mobilization of humanitarian assistance by hundreds of NGOs and international organizations[100]—the camps quickly became central pillars of legitimacy for the exiled regime. Supported by a massive influx of aid into the camps, the old Rwandan authorities reorganized at astonishing speed. As the former ruling elite recreated Rwanda's administrative structures, the government apparatus functioned as if the war had never happened: regular salaries were paid to civil servants for the first eighteen months after July 1994; government decrees were issued;

---

[98] See declassified document, American Embassy Kinshasa to Secretary of State, Washington, DC, "Former A/S Cohen Meets Mobutu," P181554Z, April 1994; Martens, *Kabila et la révolution congolaise*, vol. 1, pp. 110–11.

[99] Letter dated March 13, 1996, from the secretary-general addressed to the president of the Security Council, S/1996/195, March 14, 1996.

[100] Ray Wilkinson, "Cover Story: Heart of Darkness," *Refugees Magazine*, 110 (1997).

agricultural and foreign policy was debated and then implemented by farmers and diplomatic envoys alike. When the collapsing regime had withdrawn from Kigali, it had emptied the vaults of the Central Bank of all foreign reserves and taken massive amounts of Rwandan francs with it—the RPF found the treasury literally empty.

The outstanding organization of the Rwandan refugees enthused aid organizations initially as it made delivery of programs so much easier.[101] Many humanitarians were delighted to work with Africans who "got it" and were taking initiatives themselves. The image of cholera-induced squalor was rapidly replaced by tales of self-reliance and economic dynamism:

> When it came to adapting to adversity, the Rwandan refugees could teach even their inventive Zairian neighbours a thing or two about article 15. In 1995, a UNHCR survey listed nearly 82000 thriving enterprises in the camps, including 2324 bars, 450 restaurants, 589 general shops, 62 hairdressers, 51 pharmacies and 25 butchers. Cinemas rubbed shoulders with photographic studios. The refugees even ran their own transport service between the camps and Goma and Zairians sometimes headed to the settlements to do their shopping.[102]

Whereas tens of thousands had been killed by disease immediately after arriving, the combination of the gigantic aid operation and the "self-organization" of the refugees produced remarkable results, such as a rapid improvement in nutritional intake, high vaccination rates and a stabilization of prices inside the camps. Life was, in many ways, considerably better in the camps of Kahindo, Kashusha and Katale than in the dead-end villages of North and South Kivu.

However, there was another side to the extraordinary levels of organization of the displaced. One afternoon in September 1994, Jean Kambanda, prime minister of the Rwandan government during the genocide, visited the sprawling INERA camp in South Kivu outside Bukavu and urged hundreds of refugees who gathered around him not to get too used to Zaire, where they had arrived some weeks earlier. Kambanda, who was escorted by several FAR officers, pressed on the Hutu peasants that there was no point in getting too comfortable on the land they now occupied and sowing for too many harvests: "Don't try to cultivate too many crops here in Zaire ... We will soon

---

[100] For an excellent introspective discussion by MSF of its presence in the camps in 1994–5, see Laurence Binet, *Rwandan Refugee Camps in Zaire and Tanzania, 1994–1995*, Geneva: Médecins sans Frontières, 2005.

[102] Wrong, *In the Footsteps of Mr Kurtz*, p. 239.

return to Rwanda."[103] The idea of an imminent comeback "to finish the work" took center stage in the formal and informal communications of the exiled regime; the state outside the state expected to fight its way back soon and complete the unfinished labor of the genocidal project.

The hate-radio broadcasts urging the population to be vigilant against *inyenzi* (cockroaches) and to prepare to return violently to Rwanda never ceased. Propaganda predicting RPA massacres and a genocide of the Tutsi against the Hutu anchored fears in the hearts of the refugees. Those who explored ways of going back peacefully to Rwanda—a common feature of camp life in the early weeks, with individuals freely crossing the border several times—faced violent reprisals, including the murder of those queuing outside UNHCR tents to register their interest in repatriation programs.[104] The old state re-erected its pyramidal *commune* system that allowed central authority to mobilize individual households with dazzling speed; it also re-established its military chain of command. As the Interahamwe enforced genocidal ideology inside the camps and received the formal military training they had lacked during the massacres and conflict in Rwanda, the FAR—which had fled with its heavy artillery, vehicles and ammunition supplies intact—readied itself for open battle with the RPA. Augustin Bizimungu, FAR chief of staff, lorded over North Kivu and had tens of thousands of men under his command; Gratien Kabiligi, the main FAR authority in South Kivu, had fewer troops and armaments than Bizimungu but organized a guerrilla infiltration campaign into southern Rwanda, the region the RPA knew and controlled least of all. Thus, in effect, the success of the humanitarian activities helped resurrect a politico-military monster that was preparing to invade.

The trouble began in late 1994 and escalated into 1995. Stories—some true, some fictitious, some embellished—of RPA reprisals against presumed Interahamwe cells and Hutu civilians, together with *génocidaire* intimidation in the camps, had reduced the return of refugees back into Rwanda into a trickle. Incidents like the operation in Camp Busanze near the border with Burundi, where 9,000 displaced Hutu had gathered and were attacked on January 6–7, 1995, by RPA soldiers seeking revenge for a grenade attack by Interahamwe, hardened suspicions. The deaths of anywhere between sixteen

---

[103] Eyewitness account by Olivier Rukundo, then a secondary school student, interviewed in April 2014.

[104] UN Special Rapporteur of the Commission on Human Rights, "Report on the Situation of Human Rights in Rwanda," New York: UN Commission on Human Rights, 1997, pp. 31–3.

(according to the US embassy in Kigali[105]) and 750 people (according to reports by the American ambassador in Burundi[106])—the incredible range as testament to the difficulty of establishing hard facts amid propaganda efforts on both sides—helped strengthen the perception of IDPs as either the first line of resistance (for RPF opponents) or Interahamwe sleeper cells (the RPA).

The camps in southwest Rwanda were increasingly a source of tension too between international aid workers and the RPF because growing infiltration of weapons and fighters into them made the new government anxious as it struggled to connect with the rural masses and persuade people to return to their villages. Caesar Kayizari was the RPA brigade commander in southern Rwanda and witnessed first-hand the rapidly deteriorating security situation: Tutsi survivors of the genocide were killed, RPA officers were murdered, public transport was ambushed. Apart from the proximity of the camps—"a cancer from our perspective"—the other root problem of the growing insecurity was, according to him, that "most of the population was with the other side."[107] The insurgency affected Cyangugu, Nyungwe Forest, Gikongoro, Butare and Kibuye as well as parts of Gisenyi and Ruhengeri. Its codename, *Opération Insecticide*, made clear what its final purpose was.

The situation became untenable. Tutsi *rescapés* complained to the RPF that international NGOs were feeding *génocidaires* in Rwanda and Congo instead of bringing them back to the hills to till the land. The totally traumatized survivors had no electricity, barely any schools and remained angst-ridden, while they saw the camps as a place where the killers were protected and received free services. In an attempt at responding to these stinging criticisms, reasserting sovereignty vis-à-vis the internationals it resented and improving the security situation, the RPF unilaterally decided in early 1995 that all IDP camps would be closed down. Three-quarters of all IDPs had already gone home, more-or-less voluntarily, from locations in Kibuye and the north, but nine camps remained with 250,000 people in them in Gikongoro Prefecture. The Ministry of Rehabilitation and Social Welfare knew it would be overwhelmed by the sudden closure of the camps, but the military and political

---

[105] American Embassy Kigali to Secretary of State, Washington, DC, "RPA Attack on IDP Camp," 121456Z, January 1995.

[106] Robert Krueger and Kathleen Tobin Krueger, *From Bloodshed to Hope in Burundi: Our Embassy Years during Genocide*, Austin: University of Texas Press, 2009, pp. 100–7.

[107] Interview in Kigali, April 2013.

urgency meant that even an imperfect return of the civilians to the country-side appeared better than the status-quo.[108] However, what happened in Kibeho in April 1995 made things a lot worse in the short-to-medium term.

The Kibeho camp was situated in Gikongoro, less than an hour north of Butare and outside Kibeho town itself which had gained international visibility because of claimed apparitions of the Virgin Mary in 1981–2 to several adolescents; Notre Dame de Kibeho was recognized by the Vatican as the first location on the African continent where the Virgin spoke directly to humanity. In 1994, Gikongoro was a hotbed of *génocidaire* activity: Tutsis were massacred in April in Kibeho's local parish church and, not far from there, in Murambi, thousands of Tutsis were killed after having been given assurances about protection by their *bourgmestres*. Tutsis had only a 25 per cent chance of surviving the hecatomb in Gikongoro.[109] After *Opération Turquoise*, Hutu refugees ended up in a camp outside Kibeho that by April 1995 accommodated nearly 100,000 people, including Zambian and Australian UN troops, around the riverbed, a church and a hospital complex. On April 18, RPA Chief of Staff Sam Kaka gave the orders to surround Kibeho (Kagame was on a medical visit in Germany after a car accident, kept secret so as not to embolden the RPF's enemies), in the hope that displaying force would persuade the refugees to go home and separate themselves from *génocidaire* elements. This backfired when a resulting stampede led to an impossible situation in which 80,000 IDPs sought refuge on the hilltop around the church, a giant mass clustered together on a tiny space. Kaka promised the refugees safe passage, but for the next four days barely anyone quit Kibeho, with Interahamwe leaders vowing to kill anyone leaving the hill. Appalling hygienic conditions meant that time was running out for everybody—the *génocidaire* commanders who were trapped; the UN troops who could not cope; and the RPA, which had the international media and embassies observe its every move but could not withdraw given the domestic political and military pressure on Kaka and his officers.

Kibeho exploded at 10:30 a.m. on April 22, 1995: after a first attempted break-out and subsequent stampede, the whole day was mired in panic, confusion and extreme violence. The RPA failed to control either the frenzied crowd or its frightened soldiers who had no more experience with the situa-

---

[108] Interview with Christine Umutoni, chef-de-cabinet of the minister, August 2014.
[109] Marijke Verpoorten, "The Death Toll of the Rwandan Genocide: A Detailed Analysis for Gikongoro Province," *Population*, 60, 4 (2005).

tion than the refugees or Interahamwe. Gunfire raged late into the night, with waves of people breaking out north and south of the hilltop and the military operation largely collapsing. Some RPA soldiers remained disciplined and fired strategically in an attempt at securing the population and neutralizing Interahamwe trying to escape and join their brethren in the area around Nyungwe Forest from whence the camp had been infiltrated for months. Other RPA troops panicked and shot wildly into the crowds, mowing down everything that moved. By the end of the day, Kibeho was littered with bodies. Numerous investigations, including an International Commission of Inquiry (ICI), never settled on the total death toll. The ICI claimed it was 338, the UN said 1,500–2,000 (an estimate shared by US Chargé d'Affaires Peter Whaley in confidential communication with Washington[110]) and informal estimates by Australian and Zambian servicemen suggested that 4,000 to 8,000 people had been killed.[111]

For the RPA/RPF, Kibeho was a political disaster. Much is made by critics of the Front[112] of the impunity enjoyed by Kagame and his generals regarding the deaths at Kibeho and scores of other incidents. But, while it is certainly true that the United States in particular decided to privately express concern yet ultimately gave the RPF a politico-legal pass, even more consequential for RPF policymaking—and underappreciated in the existing literature—was how the episode shaped the Front's strategic outlook. This point was made by, among others, Christine Umutoni, directeur-de-cabinet of the minister of reintegration and Rwandan representative on the ICI who had to deal with a suspicious international community, a population which more than ever distrusted the Front and an RPA command structure that understood the debacle revealed a much wider internal and external problem.[113] The hope that early resistance against RPF rule would melt away, among the population and internationally, had not been borne out—quite the contrary. Kibeho was a turning point for the RPF leadership in that it convinced those still wavering among the most senior echelons that the war was not over. The enemy was regrouping, security had worsened after the closing of the IDP camps and the

---

[110] American Embassy Kigali to Secretary of State, Washington, DC, "Analysis of Kibeho Commission Report," 221116Z, May 1995.

[111] Shaharyar M. Khan, *The Shallow Graves of Rwanda*, London: I.B. Tauris, 2000, pp. 104–19.

[112] Prunier, *From Genocide to Continental War*, pp. 37–42; Reyntjens, *Great African War*.

[113] Interview with Christine Umutoni, Asmara, August 2014.

hearts and minds of the rural masses remained as elusive as ever: the killings at Kibeho strengthened the hand of Hutu extremists who seized on this "proof" of the RPA's intent to wipe out Hutu refugees to rally forces inside and outside the country.

Moreover, from the perspective of the RPF, the international community failed to comprehend the gravity of the threat and, as always, foreign empathy and goodwill proved fickle. It may not have pressed for the International Criminal Tribunal on Rwanda to include killings by the RPA into the latter's prosecuting mandate, but the Security Council still refused to disarm the refugee camps in Zaire and stop the extensive aid flows into them that allowed the *génocidaire* menace to reconstitute itself. For James Kabarebe, who would lead the RPF's military response to the camps, Kibeho's fallout taught that a bleak situation was likely to worsen further: "By 1995, we knew we would be attacked in a devastating way. We were afraid."[114] In the words of Jack Nziza, a key operative in the Directorate for Military Intelligence, "[It was] no longer possible for us to be patient when the Interahamwe used to be on the border and would cross to plant in their gardens, to sleep with their wives and to attack our people."[115] After Kibeho, war clouds again darkened over Central Africa.

Conclusion

As Africa emerged from the end of the Cold War, a rapidly evolving political and security context severely challenged domestic and regional order. This chapter described how, at this critical juncture, the Zairian state had all but withered away: Mobutu's governance style had ensured the virtual collapse of public services and infrastructure, the destruction of the nation's fiscal base and the dismantling of the state's coercive apparatus. In the context of shrinking patronage opportunities and reduced Western tolerance of his predatory reign, Mobutu played his old divide-and-rule card, fanning the flames of ethnic conflict and trying to reclaim international relevance after the Rwandan civil war spilled-over into Zaire. Playing host to the biggest refugee camps the world had ever seen, the cancer-stricken ruler gambled that aid would give him a new lease of life and allow him to re-assume the role of patron to Rwanda's Hutu elite, who plotted the resumption of their genocidal project from Zairian hideouts.

[114] Interview in Kigali, April 2013.
[115] Interview in Kigali, July 2014.

This strategy may well have worked if it had not been for the strategic shift by the United States in the direction of his nemesis, the Pan-Africanist movement. The end of the Cold War had not triumphantly ushered in liberal democracy and free markets; Africa saw an upsurge of violent conflicts and political instability. In this context, Washington found new allies in the leftist youngsters who took power in Uganda, Eritrea, Ethiopia, and Rwanda and who promised a radical restructuring of regional and domestic order, making their peace with the international financial institutions but getting *carte blanche* from America for their militarized approach to international relations. Inspired by the *éminence grise* of Pan-Africanism, Julius Nyerere, they sought security for their projects of internal transformation in overthrowing regimes hostile to them. And no regime held greater symbolic value as a relic of the hated "neo-colonial" era than Mobutu's.

The proximate cause of the liberation campaign in Mobutu's Zaire—the subject of the next chapter—would be the spill-over of the Rwandan civil war. The Rwandan Patriotic Front, the core members of which had adopted Pan-Africanism and its professed blindness to ethnicity after being rejected as citizens of Rwanda and Uganda, had managed to become the new government in Kigali, but governing the post-genocide country was a daunting task. Not only was meeting the material challenges of food security, public health and economic recovery nigh-impossible but the RPF had also overestimated the amount of popular support on which it could draw and had not foreseen the exodus of more than two million Rwandans into Zaire and Tanzania, nor the growing insecurity that made its hold on power tenuous. On the one hand, RPF officials reached out to the masses, urging them to return to their hills and to pragmatically cooperate with the Front, despite the widespread involvement of the population in the killings. On the other hand, frustration with the hostile reception the RPF received meant that the shadow of calamitous violence hung over much of rural Rwanda in the period after July 1994. The tragedy in Kibeho symbolized the unbridgeable gap: whereas the RPF felt that it had done everything it could to peacefully and patiently dismantle overcrowded and increasingly infiltrated camps, its enemies accused it of trying to wipe out all displaced Hutus.

It was through the combination of the ravenous Zairian state, the RPF's membership of the informal coalition of belligerent Pan-Africanist states and the dangerous impasse in which it found itself in Rwanda after one year in power that the gathering storm against Mobutu turned into a hurricane. Its ideological prism, the advice of its close friends and, most importantly, its assessment of a looming counter-revolution outside its borders combined with an untenable politico-security situation at home led the RPF leadership to believe, by the summer of 1995, that it should launch a pre-emptive strike to consolidate its revolution. Acquiring the ability to govern at home would mean waging war abroad.

5

COMRADES PREPARING FOR WAR

THE ALLIANCE TO OVERTHROW MOBUTU

Organize, don't agonize! My own recommendation is that we should analyze the internal weaknesses that make us vulnerable to foreign dominion, rectify them, and make other demands as we go along. We can change our destiny, so let us concentrate on that instead of moaning and pleading. It is true that the western powers are responsible for what happened to Africa, and it is a moral obligation on their part to rectify this historical injustice, but I am not going to make it my primary method of emancipation: I shall emancipate myself with or without their sympathy.

Yoweri Kaguta Museveni, April 4, 1994.

The war in the east was not and is not about natural resources. It's about security ... The security of the Tutsi is the heart of the Eastern Question ... Of course the resources were useful and people looted them, but they were not the cause. Of course I am talking about the interpretation of "security" and "power" by Rwanda. That may be right or wrong— but it matters hugely.

"Shé" Okitundu, Laurent Désiré Kabila's chief diplomatic adviser.[1]

The end of Apartheid unleashed a tremendous wave of optimism among many on and off the continent in the mid-1990s. Economically, Africa was experiencing another "lost decade" following the advent of the debt crisis of the

[1] Interview in Kinshasa, August 2013.

143

1980s, the stagnation of agricultural production and the imposition of structural adjustment programs by the World Bank and International Monetary Fund. But given that the liberation of Southern Africa from white-minority rule had been a top priority for the Organization of African Unity and Pan-Africanist activists since the 1960s, the transfer of power to the ANC was a moment of growing self-belief: Africans could indeed confront the oldest, fiercest of foes—and win. For the leaders of the largely amorphous Pan-Africanist movement, this was a moment pregnant with opportunity, while simultaneously fraught with danger. As we previously discussed, the democratically mandated ascent of Nelson Mandela to the presidency coincided with the horrors of the Rwandan Genocide and the failure of Africa to help arrest it. Moreover, with the genocide unfolding in the backyard of leading members of the Pan-Africanist movement and because of the intensifying ties between the RPF and like-minded forces on the continent like the Ethiopian People's Revolutionary Democratic Front and the Eritrean People's Liberation Front, a consensus began to emerge among these ambitious rebels-turned-governments. On the one hand, the liberation of South Africa reinforced their belief that it was *possible* to eradicate neo-colonialism, on the condition a united front was maintained and the "enemies of Africa" were isolated; on the other, the 1994 genocide underscored that it was *necessary* to accelerate the liberation project and for Africans to control their own destiny to ensure such outrageous tragedies would not be repeated.

By mid-1995, the sense of urgency of entrenching the revived liberation project deeper into the African soil and protecting its spectacular advances in East Africa in the preceding years was growing. An old adversary seemed poised to make a comeback and a new one launched an ideological, military and political challenge to African leftists. The new foe was Sudan's military-Islamist regime whose efforts to export its own revolution reached its zenith in June 1995 when Egyptian jihadists, armed and funded by Sudanese intelligence, tried to assassinate Egyptian President Hosni Mubarak in Addis Ababa. Khartoum's aggressive Islamization push and its hostile relations with the United States led the latter to help forge a regional alliance involving Cairo, Asmara, Addis and Kampala to isolate and militarily contain Sudan's Salvation Revolution. Spearheading the pushback was the Sudan People's Liberation Army/Movement (SPLA/M), the leader of which, John Garang, was an alumnus of the University of Dar es Salaam and Nyerere's Pan-Africanist teachings. But the intensification of the conflict in and around Sudan was only one battlefront for the Pan-Africanists. The old enemy back in the ascendency was Mobutu whose governing style and friendships with the

West had seemed an anachronism, only for him to use the aftermath of the Rwandan genocide to reclaim international relevance. Moreover, with the resurgent ex-FAR/Interahamwe in the Zairian refugee camps preparing a counter-revolution with Mobutu's backing, Paul Kagame had a strong case with which to convince Yoweri Museveni, Julius Nyerere, Meles Zenawi and Issayas Afewerki that a regional war was approaching rapidly.

This chapter narrates and analyzes the emergence of a regional coalition of self-styled revolutionaries to overthrow the Mobutu regime, symbol of the "neo-colonial" Africa of the 1970s and 1980s. It begins with the situation in Rwanda and on the Zairian–Rwandan border after the tragedy in Kibeho and it traces the RPA's provisions for war. One crucial step in these preparations was the search and identification of a "Congolese front" for the invasion of Zaire/Congo. The man selected to play this role was a character forgotten by most, but not by the leaders of the Pan-Africanist movement. Thousands of kilometers from Mobutu's jungle palaces in Gbadolite, an old Lumumbist foe from the 1960s, "Mzee" Laurent-Désiré Kabila, had retired from rebellions and smuggling in Zaire's Kivu provinces and was living a modest life in Tanzania. It was there in late 1995 that he received a visit from Patrick Karegeya and Dan Munyuza, intelligence officers for Rwanda's External Security Organization. Karegeya and Munyuza wanted to reactivate the Mzee and his old Marxist–Leninist networks for the purposes of invading Congo. In the next few months, Kabila was joined by other rebels enlisted for the twin task of destroying the bases of *génocidaire* terror and ousting Mobutu. The chapter concludes with an analysis of the strategic objectives of the AFDL and the calculus of its driving forces: as lengthy quotes from the protagonists reveal, the link between the internal equilibrium of a post-liberation regime and its external relations was understood as pivotal by the actors themselves.

The RPF's Dilemma, Laurent-Désiré Kabila and the Road to War

On the eve of Monday, September 11, 1995, a junior officer of the Rwandan Patriotic Army was shot by an unknown assailant in Kanama, Gisenyi Prefecture, near the Zairian border, less than twenty-five kilometers from the sprawling refugee camps that hosted hundreds of thousands of Rwandan civilians and the *génocidaire* forces.[2] Within hours of the incident, RPA troops surrounded Kanama village and went on a nocturnal rampage that by early

[2] Donatella Lorch, "At Edgy Border, Rwanda Army Kills 100 Hutu," *New York Times*, September 14, 1995.

morning left more than 110 people, mostly youngsters, dead. Little effort was made to identify the actual perpetrator(s) of the assassination of the RPA lieutenant; in the words of the UN observer based in the Gisenyi area, who investigated the killings: "Kanama was cold blooded execution of civilians."[3] Following an outcry by local human rights groups and the United Nations Assistance Mission for Rwanda, the RPA chief of staff, Sam Kaka, and the minister of defense and vice-president of Rwanda, Paul Kagame, visited Kanama and denounced the "excessive force" used by the RPA. Both Kaka and Kagame were mindful of the Kibeho debacle and in no doubt about how the massacre would be used by their enemies in the camps to scare the civilian Hutu population. However, while a handful of ordinary soldiers were court martialed, no senior officers were publicly held to account for the deaths at Kanama. And in the months after September 1995, RPA search operations would push the death toll of counterinsurgency into the four digits.

As reported by the same UN human rights monitor, what had happened in Kanama would become a template for a pattern of extreme retaliation: "They emptied the villages of young men."[4] The already bulging prisons swelled further as the RPF High Command gave orders to the Directorate of Military Intelligence (DMI) to develop a policy of incommunicado detention to address the increasing insecurity. In regions where the insurgency's momentum was especially hard to reverse, like in Gisenyi, Ruhengeri and Cyangugu Prefectures, lethal force was used with ever greater frequency and against an ever wider range of targets, sometimes leading to the wholesale executions of young men.[5] Bernard Lapeyre, head of Médecins sans Frontières France, wrote a letter to the RPF leaders Paul Kagame, Joseph Karemera and Patrick Mazimhaka detailing yet another incident:

> On Monday, November 6, in the health center of Runyombi ... in Gikongoro Prefecture, an RPA soldier entered the compound and opened fire on people waiting for a consultation. Our team arrived moments later and counted thirteen deaths, five men, six women and two children. Eighteen wounded persons were transferred by our carers to the hospital of Kabutare. One woman died during the transfer and another succumbed to her injuries shortly after arriving there.[6]

[3] Interview with Homayoun Alizadeh, December 2014.

[4] Ibid.

[5] UN Special Rapporteur of the Commission on Human Rights, "Report on the Situation of Human Rights in Rwanda," pp. 27–8.

[6] Our translation, original in French. Médecins Sans Frontières France, "Lettre au ministre de la santé," Kigali, November 8, 1995.

MSF's outspokenness about the large-scale human rights abuses it witnessed in Runyombi, in Kibeho and many other locations around the country ultimately led to the expulsion of MSF France from Rwanda in December 1995.[7] Many inside the RPA were uncomfortable with these expanding "reprisals" and "excesses," but dared not protest publicly. For Okwiri Rabwoni, a Ugandan volunteer who had joined the RPF, married a Tutsi woman and served as an officer of the 305th Brigade of the RPA, "It was not a double genocide but it was disgusting … There was a deliberate policy of terrorizing the Hutu countryside so you would never think again about rising up against the regime or another genocide."[8]

Inside the UN, both in New York and Geneva, but also among the UN Human Rights Field Operation in Rwanda, key actors were increasingly convinced of the systematic and deliberate character of RPA violence. Reflecting back on almost a year of investigations under his watch, the head of the field operation in Kigali, Ian Martin, wrote the following confidential analysis to the UN commissioner for human rights, José Ayala-Lasso:

> Most RPA killings of recent months were, in our view, attributable to individual acts, indiscipline or low-level decisions: we have had no reason to believe that they were sanctioned at high levels of the chain of command, and believed on the contrary that the Ministry of Defence was making efforts to prevent human rights violations in the face of real problems of communication with local commanders. I believe we now have a new situation in which troops have been given the message that a tough crackdown has been ordered and have at best not been given instructions to confine killings to legitimate targets.[9]

What accounts for the ratcheting up of RPA operations and indiscriminate reprisals against Rwandans? As discussed in Chapter 4, revenge was an important motivating force. But the killings were also a function of the uncertainty and information problems that plagued the RPF as it sought to consolidate power over a deeply mistrustful society and combat an escalating insurgency.[10]

---

[7] For a self-critical overview of MSF's operations in Rwanda in 1994–5, see Binet, *Rwandan Refugee Camps in Zaire and Tanzania*.

[8] Interview in Kampala, March 2013.

[9] Message from Ian Martin to José Ayala-Lasso, "Developments in Rwanda II," Kigali, UN Human Rights Field Operation in Rwanda, July 15, 1996.

[10] On the link between weak societal ties and indiscriminate violence, see Kalyvas, *Logic of Violence in Civil War*; Jason Lyall, "Are Coethnics More Effective Counterinsurgents? Evidence from the Second Chechen War," *American Political Science Review*, 104, 1 (2010); Roessler, *Ethnic Politics and State Power in Africa*.

It is crucial to keep in mind just how much of the rural population had been indoctrinated, mobilized and militarized by the Habyarimana (and later the genocidal) government, but also that the RPF was facing criticism from genocide survivors, in its own RPA ranks and in the population as a whole, as it failed to protect them adequately. Targeted killings of *rescapés*, a clear statement of the Interahamwe's intent to "finish the job" begun in 1994, proved particularly traumatic. Moreover, by October 1995, the RPA was dealing with an average of one attack on its border troops a day; its capture of Iwawa Island in Lake Kivu on November 11, 1995, from whence 300–400 *génocidaires* launched strikes on Rwandan territory, did little to solve the fundamental problem.[11] Societal relations remained impossibly tense and few local informers stepped forward to volunteer intelligence on the insurgents. The RPA lacked non-lethal coercive technology like tear gas and other police equipment to handle out-of-control crowds (cf. Kibeho) and was forced to rely on poor information, all-or-nothing displays of force and a weak understanding of the political networks of its foes. It was a recipe for a deepening political and security crisis.

The RPF continued its policy of outreach to the rural masses and organized a long-lasting series of public meetings in Rwanda's hills during which the RPA, national ministries and local authorities would try to address the fears of the peasant communities and sought to convince them of the Front's benign intentions. For hours, RPF officials would lecture the largely silent masses and reassure them that they had nothing to fear if they cooperated. But these efforts spearheaded by individuals like Kayumba Nyamwasa, as head of the gendarmerie, and Patrick Mazimhaka and Christine Umutoni, in charge of resettlement and reintegration, appeared futile. One UN human rights field officer captured the terrible predicament the RPF and the population found themselves in: "Sometimes, they would take us to the communes, from house to house and point at some homes. They would go 'enemy, enemy, enemy, enemy, enemy ...' They saw themselves as an occupying force in enemy territory."[12] Not only was the security situation worsening but the flow of returnees from the camps in Zaire was reduced to a trickle by late 1995, with only about 15,000 people crossing back into Rwanda in the entire seven-month period between November 1, 1995, and May 31, 1996, according to UNHCR's June

---

[11] Thomas Paul Odom, *Journey into Darkness: Genocide in Rwanda*, College Station: Texas A&M University Press, 2005, pp. 260–8.

[12] Interview with Konrad Huber, January 2015.

1996 information bulletin. The prominent minister of the interior, Seth Sendashonga, had earlier resigned over what he perceived as the deliberate killing of Hutus.[13] And, controversially, UN Secretary-General Boutros Boutros-Ghali, known for his close ties with France and difficult relationship with the United States, stated that "everybody is afraid that a new genocide may happen, this time not by the Hutu against the Tutsi, but by the Tutsi against the Hutu."[14] Critique from within and from without was further dissuading refugees from returning, the population from collaborating and donors from providing much-needed cash. The RPF was losing politically, as it felt unable to gain the legitimacy it so eagerly craved, and it knew that the harder it cracked down, the greater its long-term problem would be.

The flipside of the failure to win politically was that it made the military track the only feasible option, both because it resonated with the militarized socialization of the RPF leadership and its self-belief and because there seemed to be no other way out of the impasse. With the UN Security Council failing to come to any agreement on the disarmament and relocation of the refugee camps—more than forty governments approached by Boutros-Ghali turned down his request for peacekeepers[15]—the clock was ticking. Kigali argued that time was running out as the enemy was growing stronger and better organized by the day.[16] International aid flows to the camps formed a crucial part of the controversy. This was recognized by the Joint Evaluation of Emergency Assistance for Rwanda:

> Of the more than US$2 billion estimated to have been spent on the Rwanda crisis since April 1994, the vastly larger share has gone to the maintenance of refugees in asylum countries ... it appears to Rwandese who have lived through the horror of genocide that the international community is more concerned about the refugees than the survivors.[17]

By contrast, the amount the government received was merely counted in the millions, despite the immense needs; even when US$530 million was

[13] Prunier, *From Genocide to Continental War*, pp. 365–8.

[14] "Transcript of Press Conference by Secretary-General Boutros Boutros-Ghali Held at United Nations Headquarters," SG/SM/5854, December 18, 1995. Available at http://www.un.org/press/en/1995/19951218.sgsm5854.html

[15] Khan, *Shallow Graves of Rwanda*.

[16] Richard Orth, "Rwanda's Hutu Extremist genocidal Insurgency: An Eyewitness Perspective," *Small Wars & Insurgencies*, 12, 1 (2001), pp. 86–7.

[17] Joint Evaluation of Emergency Assistance for Rwanda, "The Rwanda Experience: International Response to Conflict and Genocide," Copenhagen, 1994.

pledged at the first Round Table Conference on aid to Rwanda in Geneva in January 1995,[18] this was still only a quarter of what was poured into the refugee camps. The imbalance infuriated the RPF leadership, which saw its enemy regaining strength.

This belligerent attitude was further deepened by the RPA's nascent engagement with the Israel Defense Forces (IDF) between 1994 and 1996, which resulted in a growing embrace of the concept of offensive, pre-emptive war as IDF instructors worked with RPA officers and special forces.[19] The High Command developed the notion that it should never have to fight in Rwanda but should keep the enemy as far away as possible from its borders. The RPF was particularly worried about the threat to Kigali in the face of a well-coordinated surprise attack from the *génocidaires*—remember that the RPF itself nearly won the war before the genocide in this manner—and so a new doctrine had to be developed. This meant imminent action, re-seizing the offensive. As Okwiri Rabwoni of the RPA's 305th Brigade said: "In Kagame's mind, the end of the genocide was just the end of phase two of the war. Fighting in Congo would become part three, just another chapter in the war. He saw this as a long conflict."[20]

Thus, at some point in the second half of 1995 (the exact date remains unknown), the RPF leadership took the decision to prepare for all-out war, which would inevitably mean invading Zaire to neutralize the ex-FAR/ Interahamwe threat and to return the refugee population home so it could finally begin ruling like a normal government over its people. But while in initial deliberations the emphasis was very much on a high intensity operation of limited geographical reach, voices inside the Front began arguing that crossing the border would have to involve armed confrontation with Mobutu's forces and a much deeper push into Zaire to defeat the RPF's enemies. This was perceived as highly risky in international political terms and possibly militarily, but did the RPF have another choice given that time was not on its side? At least for now it could still determine the timing of the resumption of direct war, or so the argument went.

[18] Khan, *Shallow Graves of Rwanda*, p. 93. See also Christian P. Scherrer, *Genocide and Crisis in Central Africa: Conflict Roots, Mass Violence, and Regional War*, Westport, CT: Praeger, 2002, pp. 182–3.

[19] Interview with an RPA/RDF general and with a member of the special forces, Kigali, July 2014.

[20] Interview in March 2013.

Moreover, many senior RPF leaders believed that Paris had by no means reconciled itself with the Front's takeover of Kigali. France, they reasoned, would continue to prop up Mobutu, bolster the *génocidaire* threat and perhaps even try to intervene militarily, seeking to reverse the new order in Rwanda. In the words of Dr. Emmanuel Ndahiro, RPA spokesman at the time and political adviser to Paul Kagame: "We didn't think it was wise for us to wait for the French on our territory. They underrated our capabilities."[21] The RPF sought contact with Paris and sent President Bizimungu and his chef-de-cabinet Frank Mugambage to Mobutu in Gbadolite to talk to him directly in late 1994,[22] but its case was not getting heard and external support for its archenemy persisted. Karake Karenzi, director of military intelligence between 1994 and 1997, argued that the failed engagement of Mobutu and the realities inside Rwanda meant that invading Zaire could not just be a matter of quickly liberating the refugee camps and returning home; a much bigger campaign needed to be prepared: "It was not terribly clear how difficult or easy it would be but there would have been no justification to do it half way."[23]

While the RPF could not quite resolve what the endgame would look like of their planned offensive on Zairian soil, it began looking for a Congolese front for its operations. Outright unilateral invasion would stand a much greater chance of being condemned by the Security Council and triggering a counter-operation by France, while hiding behind a new, locally rooted rebel movement would provide Kagame and his advisers with the cover required to dismantle the camps and teach Mobutu a lesson.[24] As we will see in the next section, this was an idea that was explicitly promoted by the RPF's regional friends in Addis, Asmara, Dar es Salaam and Kampala; the Front listened to their advice and initiated conversations about possible plans of attack on the Kivu region of Zaire as well as readying itself, by late 1995, militarily and financially for a massive assault on its nemesis.

The Mzee and the RPF: The Genesis of a Partnership

Not long before the 1996 New Year, a handful of intelligence officers, supported by a small elite unit of the RPA, drove up the yard of a house outside

[21] Interview in Kigali, December 2014.
[22] Interview with Mugambage in Kampala, April 2013. Discussions between the RPF and Mobutu are confirmed by the latter's key security adviser: N'Gbanda, *Ainsi sonne le glas*, pp. 89–97.
[23] Interview in London, November 2014.
[24] Interview with Caesar Kayizari in Ankara, June 2015.

the center of Butiama, a small town in northern Tanzania's Mara region of perhaps 10,000 inhabitants. Butiama was a hot, sleepy place that was mainly known for the fact that it was where Julius Nyerere, the country's founding president and Pan-Africanist icon, was born in 1922. The Rwandan team had not come to pay tribute to the Mwalimu, but on his advice sought out an ageing lion from the 1960s who had all but retired from frontline politics. Scores of chicken were scuttling around as Patrick Karegeya, head of Rwanda's External Security Organization, entered the not particularly luxurious compound and looked around to find the man he had been tasked to bring back to Kigali with him to lead a war that would change Africa. His name was Laurent-Désiré Kabila.[25]

Kabila was born in 1939 in one of the enclaves of Belgian Congo, in the wealthy South Katangese town of Jadotville (today's Likasi), far from his tribal homelands in north Katanga around Manono where his Luba father grew up. Kabila's education and his youth, which were mostly spent in Katanga, remain shrouded in a haze that even his most determined biographer has not been able to clear up.[26] But the profile that does emerge suggests, unmistakably, that he was a man with huge ambition. He possessed neither Mobutu's good looks and ability to maintain an enigmatic silence, nor Lumumba's oratorical charisma and intelligence, but instead an unusual type of charm that entailed a mixture of flattery, determination to pursue his goals, and a working-class Congolese humor that enabled him to connect with, and endear himself to, broad sections of society. As a young adult, Kabila joined the Association Générale des Baluba de Katanga (Balubakat), a party that defended the interests of the Luba and north Katanga more generally, but simultaneously, as the son of a Lunda mother and a long-time resident of the Likasi–Lubumbashi (Elisabethville) area, he also maintained good cross-ethnic ties in South Katanga.

Kabila's personal relations and nascent political convictions were tested severely during the crisis in which Congo was plunged after independence on June 30, 1960, and which was touched upon in Chapter 2. As the Force Publique mutinied, Belgian and UN troops intervened and Premier Lumumba and President Kasa-Vubu battled for political supremacy, the

---

[25] Stearns suggests a different pick-up location, claiming—through the testimony of ESO supremo Karegeya—that Kabila was met in Dar es Salaam. See Stearns, *Dancing in the Glory of Monsters*, p. 86. However, our key source in the RPA special forces—who also traveled to meet Kabila—was adamant that it was in Butiama.

[26] Kennes, *Essai biographique sur Laurent Désiré Kabila*.

wealthiest province of the Congo declared itself independent under the leadership of the Confédération des associations tribales du Katanga (CONAKAT) of Moïse Tshombe, who was a representative of the growing Katangese bourgeoisie. In the eyes of both Tshombe and Kabila, an independent Katanga would really mean the dominance of South Katanga—where the vast majority of geological riches are concentrated. And given the extensive support of Belgian and South African business interests for secession, it would also guarantee that the state's geopolitical orientation would point solidly towards Brussels, Pretoria and Salisbury (the capital of the Federation of Rhodesia and Nyasaland). Yet whereas this was a highly desirable scenario for the federalist and staunchly anti-socialist Tshombe (based on the understanding that electorally challenging the national powerbase of the left-wing Lumumba would keep CONAKAT marginalized and Katanga in its role as the Congolese state's cash cow), Kabila disapproved wholeheartedly. He envisaged a strong, united Katanga in a strong, united and socialist Congo that would not be the puppet of Western mining conglomerates but would follow the route of leftist governments in Algeria, Ghana and Guinea. To oppose the secession and to reverse a military putsch in Kinshasa, Kabila first joined the Balubakat's youth militia and connected from 1963 onwards to Lumumbist revolutionary circles who were trying to regroup in eastern Congo and on the western shores of Lake Tanganyika. His choice for the path of armed resistance would be one of serial disappointments, but the burning hope that his ideals could one day be realized was kept alive.

National prominence came with Kabila's alignment to the Comité National de Libération (CNL), a coalition of four nationalist movements who contested the legitimacy of the flailing Leopoldville/Kinshasa government and who demanded the full decolonization of Congo, including the final settlement, to the advantage of the Congolese people, of the immense *portefeuille* of financial and mining assets that was skewed in favor of Belgium at independence. The CNL rejected the state of emergency imposed by the rightwing cabal dominated by Mobutu, and from its political seat in neighboring Congo-Brazzaville, it sent two envoys to Kivu and north Katanga—Gaston Soumialot, a widely recognized provincial politician from Maniema, and the unknown populist organizer Laurent Kabila. Within weeks of their arrival, the nationalist ideology they preached led to the recruitment of hundreds of youngsters who, with the help of the Burundese government, began launching attacks on police stations and government officials in April 1964. Uvira, Fizi and Albertville/Kalemie (the latter a highly strategic city on Lake Tanganyika) all fell within weeks; the insurrection spread like bushfire.

What would soon become known as the Simba Revolt led to the "liberation" of more than one-third of the Congolese territory by the CNL and the nationalist rebels. The revolt sent shockwaves through the West. Despite the considerable organizational weaknesses of the Simbas, their advance seemed unstoppable, resulting in the fall of Stanleyville/Kisangani in August 1964. Kabila, who had risen to become vice-president of the CNL and its provisional government in Albertville, traveled around the region and predicted an imminent march on Leopoldville. It was only when the Belgian Minister of Foreign Affairs Paul-Henri Spaak and the Central Intelligence Agency in Langley, Virginia, provided not just support to Mobutu's Armée Nationale Congolaise but also organized hundreds of mercenaries, including exiled Cuban fighters who had participated in the failed Bay of Pigs invasion,[27] in the infamous *Opération l'Ommegang* that the Simbas were pushed back and defeated. The end result was the death of many thousands and the consolidation of Mobutist rule over Congo.[28]

The Simba Revolt was more than just Laurent Kabila's first revolutionary experience. The memories of the emancipatory promise of the CNL would remain a nostalgic background refrain that he cherished and interwove with more contemporary ideas and actions throughout his career: the sense that the capitalist world had trembled before the advance of home-grown Congolese rebels, co-organized by the young Kabila, increased his self-confidence and gave him a life-long sense of entitlement as the surviving incarnation of Africa's first military challenge to "neo-colonialism." The Simba Revolt was a political–ideological awakening that shaped the rest of his career. Pan-Africanism was not initially part of Kabila's political universe, but emerged gradually as Congo exploded onto the international agenda and progressives around Africa railed against the Belgo-American alliance and its local henchmen and in favor of Patrice Lumumba, who was claimed as a martyr of the Pan-Africanist movement. Many Congolese and Africans believed that Tshombe, Kabila's Katangese rival, was Lumumba's chief assassin when the latter was executed by white mercenaries outside Elisabethville/Lubumbashi on January 17, 1961—and rightly so, as evidenced by the investigative report of a Belgian parliamentary commission.[29] The assistance pro-

---

[27] Frank R. Villafana, *Cold War in the Congo*, New Brunswick, NJ: Transaction Publishers, 2009.

[28] De Witte, *Huurlingen, Geheim Agenten en Diplomaten.*

[29] Daniel Bacquelaine, Marie-Thérèse Coenen and Ferdy Willems, "Parlementair

vided by Algeria, Cuba, Egypt, Ghana, Guinea and Tanzania to the Simbas transformed Kabila's parochial outlook and gave meaning to slogans of international solidarity and collective resistance to imperialism. As a Katangese diametrically opposed to Tshombe and as one of the CNL leaders who had lit the revolutionary fuse in 1964, he had gained respect, name recognition and valuable contacts in Pan-Africanist and socialist networks, on and off the continent. No connection would prove more valuable to him than that with the Mwalimu in Dar es Salaam.

Even after the ruthless crushing of the Simba Revolt by mercenaries, Belgian paratroopers and Mobutu's army, Kabila—contrary to many other nationalists—refused to give up the armed struggle. He withdrew to the *maquis* of Fizi-Baraka in South Kivu, where he would continue to represent an on-and-off security nuisance for the next decade. Despite relative international obscurity, the Parti de la Révolution Populaire (PRP) survived via lucrative smuggling activities and regular resupplying through speedboat deliveries from western Tanzania across Lake Tanganyika to Zaire.[30] Kabila and his closest PRP aides also continued to invest in the networks they had built during the 1963–5 uprising. An extensive web of contacts covered the Congolese diaspora in Western Europe and North America, which ensured that Kabila—despite controlling barely any territory and never having had a base in Kinshasa—remained on the radar of intelligence services. Rejecting offers by Mobutu to be made minister or ambassador, he maintained an aura of uncompromising resistance and commitment to Pan-Africanism, and a long-lasting relationship with Julius Nyerere. Thus, when the RPF began looking for a "Congolese face" to the invasion it began plotting in the second half of 1995, and asked its mentors in Kampala and Dar es Salaam who would possess enough nationalist credentials to shrug off criticism of being a foreign puppet, one man was repeatedly mentioned: Kabila.

The youngsters of the RPF belonged to a different generation. The Cold War and the Congo Crisis in the 1960s were not their central reference points; Kabila was a name from a previous era and his personality and vision were only really known to a number of Congolese Tutsi elders who had fought in the *maquis* of South Kivu alongside him in 1965. What Kabila and the

---

Onderzoek met het oog op het vaststellen van de precieze omstandigheden waarin Patrice Lumumba werd vermoord en van de eventuele betrokkenheid daarbij van Belgische politici," Brussels: Belgische Kamer van Volksvertegenwoordigers, 2001.

[30] Interview with Didier Kazadi, Kinshasa, August 2013.

RPF did share was a general commitment to Pan-Africanism, a mutual loathing of Mobutu—for both Kabila and the RPF, Mobutu was the physical embodiment of neocolonialism and its evils on the continent—and a relationship with Julius Nyerere. And the word of the latter, particularly when reinforced by Yoweri Museveni's nod of approval, persuaded Kagame to send his intelligence chief Patrick Karegeya to Tanzania to pick up Kabila without any delay. There was no official appointment of Kabila as the future head of the RPF-created Congolese rebel movement, nor did Karegeya and his boyish deputy on the mission, Dan Munyuza, give guarantees to the old warrior regarding a march to Kinshasa.[31] This was corroborated by one of Kabila's closest confidants as handler of the trafficking across Lake Tanganyika, Didier Kazadi, who was involved in discussions with the RPF right from the start. Although Kabila and Kazadi quickly learned that the High Command had not yet made a final decision regarding the extent of the proposed military campaign in Zaire—"They had apprehensions ... Not sure they would go all the way to Kin"—they felt this opportunity to return to frontline politics was too good to miss.[32] Upon his arrival in Kigali after traveling via Kampala, Kabila met with Kagame and Ndahiro, who persuaded him further that a partnership with the Front represented a unique opening at a time when Mobutu was frailer than ever before.

For months, Kabila shared a house on the hill of Kimihurura in central Kigali. Except for brief interludes at the residence of two other young RPA officers, James Kabarebe and Caesar Kayizari (the very commanders who would take Kabila to Kinshasa the next year), most of his time was spent in the home of Dan Munyuza, the inexperienced but much trusted junior intelligence officer who had been part of the team that picked Kabila up in Tanzania. In-between lavish meals, the "Mzee" entertained his hosts with theoretical monologues and anecdotes about his exploits confronting Mobutu, the CIA and the Belgian establishment in the 1960s, boasting to his young bodyguards that they had experienced nothing like it. His RPF political handlers chuckled quietly, seeing them as the ramblings of an old guerrilla who seemed oblivious to the calamity that had just ravaged Rwanda and to the two wars the Front had successfully concluded by ousting incumbent regimes.[33]

---

[31] Interviews with Rwanda's head of mission at the embassy in Washington, DC, Joseph Mutaboba (October 2010), in London, and James Kabarebe (April 2013) and Emmanuel Ndahiro (July 2014) in Kigali.

[32] Interview in Kinshasa, August 2013.

[33] Interviews in Kigali, December 2009, July 2014.

There was no meeting of the souls between Kabila and the RPF, but that seemed to matter little to either side. The Mzee needed his "naïve" Rwandan partners, for without them he stood no chance of playing a role in ending Mobutu's tyranny; and the RPF needed Kabila because, as the domestic security situation worsened, the urgency of using a Congolese figurehead and the Congolese force he could mobilize to address the menace of the camps grew. It was a mutual dependency that both sides pragmatically accepted and would be the key ingredient in the overthrow of Mobutu, but also later of the extremely violent dissolution of their alliance in August 1998.

Washington and the "New Bull in Central Africa"

The alliance that was struck between Laurent-Désiré Kabila and the Rwandan Patriotic Front would only be as historically consequential as the comrades intended it to be because of the changing global geopolitics of Africa already introduced in Chapter 4. The first years after the end of the Cold War were characterized by a decline of US interest in the continent—a process epitomized by the Black Hawk Down debacle in Somalia and Washington's shameful passivity during the Rwandan genocide. In its first term, the Clinton administration focused on Europe, North America and East Asia and saw Africa mainly as a potential domestic liability. But the disengagement from Africa was reversed when influential constituencies lobbied for targeted outreach to the region: Madeleine Albright, the US ambassador to the UN (and from January 1997 onwards secretary of state), and National Security Council director for African Affairs, Susan Rice, joined other voices in America's national security establishment in arguing that the continent was too important to be left alone and that US policy could positively affect several key dossiers.

The rise of Albright and Rice became closely associated with the so-called "new generation of African leaders"-policy, which was rooted in the belief that the development of deep, personal ties with a group of youngish former rebel leaders who had captured state power could help the United States shed the negative image it had acquired in Africa as a result of its policies during the Cold War.[34] Albright and Rice did not share the Marxist–Leninist-inspired worldview of Meles Zenawi, Issayas Afewerki and Yoweri Museveni (see discussion in next section), but found these new incumbents intelligent, flexible

---

[34] Peter Rosenblum, "Irrational Exuberance: The Clinton Administration in Africa," *Current History*, 101, 655 (2002).

and willing to implement their domestic agendas in collaboration with America, rather than in opposition to it like previous generations of radical Pan-Africanists. If the State Department was keen to rid itself of the popular perception of cozy ties with ageing tyrants like Mobutu, then it made sense to partner with those who were explicitly targeting the "neo-colonial" consensus. The appeal of doing so continued to grow owing to an increased convergence of US interests with those of the new leaders. As Sudan's military-Islamist regime emerged as a pariah state,[35] Albright and Rice helped form an alliance in the Horn of Africa for the containment and roll-back of Khartoum's export of the revolution.[36]

The second constituency catalyzing a change in Washington's approach—to Africa generally and the Great Lakes specifically—had related, but different concerns. The withdrawal from Mogadishu after the loss of eighteen American lives in 1993 had left many in the Pentagon and CIA frustrated—as they saw it, the end of communism did not necessarily lead to a safer Africa. Instead, greater American involvement would be required to combat the growing menace of terrorism and Islamism in North and East Africa. In more than thirty African countries, US special forces began training new African units, and a series of initiatives, some congressionally mandated, some not, were launched to bolster ties between African armies and the Pentagon.

The RPF offered a prime example of how far-reaching the impact of the heightened interest and support of these two constituencies could be. The combination of post-genocide guilt about the fateful choices of the Clinton administration and the identification of a valuable new ally in the disciplined RPA phalanx underpinned the rapid development of a partnership between Kigali and Washington. This began with Operation Support Hope in July 1994, which mostly contributed to feeding the refugee camps in Zaire, but also brought about 200 American troops into direct contact with the RPA. Through the Pentagon's links with Museveni's Uganda, individuals like Fred Rwigyema and Paul Kagame were already known as formidable military and intelligence officers but the intense collaboration from July 1994 onwards between the US Army and the RPA led key individuals in the former to develop a profound sympathy for the cause of the RPF and the challenges

---

[35] American Embassy Khartoum to Secretary of State Washington, DC, "Sudan's Turabi on 'Internationalism of Islam,' Al Bashir on 'a Nation of Message,'" 23089Z, September 1992.

[36] Verhoeven and Patey, "Sudan's Islamists and the Post-Oil Era."

facing the new Rwanda. The Front's passion for soldiering, its Anglophone culture and its martial and bureaucratic efficiency created the impression among US officials that they had stumbled upon a white tiger, deserving of protection and support. Kagame's first visit to Washington as minister of defense in December 1994 was a tremendous success, impressing all whom he met. In the words of William Odom, the US defense attaché to Rwanda from 1994 to 1996: "We knew the RPA were a different kettle of fish ... The RPA was the new bull in Central Africa."[37]

Odom and his successor Rick Orth, as well as the US Ambassador to Rwanda Robert Gribbin and Deputy Chief of Mission Peter Whaley would all relentlessly engage and socialize with the RPF; these men spent virtually every spare hour in the RPA mess, on the tennis courts with Kagame or sharing beers with the military elite of the new government. They invariably explained and often defended the Front's policies in Washington, which, in the unimaginable context of post-genocide Rwanda, they saw as exceptional and deeply misunderstood. While diplomatic envoys often develop great affection for their host country, Gribbin, Odom, Orth and Whaley pushed the limits of what was acceptable.[38] The US embassy in Kigali favored minimalist casualty reporting on the Kibeho tragedy; helped put huge pressure on the International Criminal Tribunal for Rwanda not to examine war crimes committed by the RPF; set up special forces training for the RPA (some of these units would later lead the hunt for ex-FAR/Interahamwe in Congo and elsewhere in Central Africa); and gave RPF leaders access to leading US decision-makers, much beyond what a tiny African country without a particularly strategic location or large natural resource endowment is usually able to obtain.

Thus, even if the RPF leadership continued to feel insecure because of the ongoing domestic insecurity and the menace represented by the genocidal government in exile in the Zairean refugee camps, US engagement substantially boosted its self-confidence and gave it diplomatic wriggle room vis-à-vis France and the UN. Both these elements would be crucial in the confrontations to come in the next year. But most importantly, perhaps, the pro-RPF advocacy of the Pentagon and the US embassy in Kigali further bolstered the militarist instincts already so dominant in the ranks of the Front: it meant little substantial push-back over excesses by RPA units as well as a further

---

[37] Odom, *Journey into Darkness*, pp. 195, 269.

[38] For a critical but comprehensive overview of facts and rumors regarding US support for the RPF and AFDL see Reyntjens, *Great African War*, pp. 66–79.

legitimation of and boost for the military elites in the new government, at the expense of the civilian politicians. The new American policy thus contributed to the development of a decision-making context in which renewed war with the *génocidaires* and attacking Zaire were not only seen as necessary for RPF survival but also as actually politically feasible. Increasingly, Paul Kagame and other RPA commanders began to believe that the bold military operation they were planning, in which Kabila would serve as the Congolese figurehead, might even receive the blessing of the planet's only remaining superpower.

The Pan-Africanists Come on Board: The Role of Eritrea, Ethiopia, Tanzania and Uganda

Growing sympathy and support in the Clinton administration for its cause would not be the only vital assurances that the RPF High Command would receive as it plotted the coming offensive. In parallel to the development of relations with influential players in the Pentagon and State Department, Kigali also found a listening ear among its ideological and politico-military peers around the continent. Within two years of the Front's capture of Kigali and the establishment of formal state-to-state ties, these comrades would provide troops, political advisers, weapons and diplomatic legwork in a grand bid to both help resolve the RPF's short-term security concerns and to remake Central Africa. To understand how this alignment came about in the mid-1990s and why it would prove so consequential, we must briefly return to our conceptual framework.

For decades after independence, the dominant fault-lines in Africa's international relations were, on the one hand, that of the relationship between the state and its former colonial power and, on the other, the positionality of African governments in the context of the Cold War. Much of African politics was reduced to these two main axes—including by African rulers themselves who found these categories materially and discursively useful to work with and drew legitimacy and resources from these dynamics and juxtapositions.[39] Pan-Africanists accepted that these constructs were seen as real and were therefore real in their consequences, but argued that true liberation would entail a politics in which Africans themselves reset their relationship with the outside world and would stop being intellectually, politically and financially dependent on the global political–economic sys-

---

[39] Clapham, *Africa and the International System*.

tem. And to do so would mean rejecting all vestiges of colonialism and imperialism—whether of an American, a French or a Soviet type—through resistance and armed struggle.[40]

This was the vision of Julius Nyerere who, for a long time after formal decolonization, lived a fairly lonely life on Africa's international stage, surrounded by Washington, Paris and Moscow's client states as well as by the white-minority regimes of Southern Africa. This was the reason why he turned Tanzania into a nerve center for regime change and liberation across the east and south of the continent—a lifelong project that began to bear fruit in the second half of the 1970s with the independence of Angola, Mozambique and Zimbabwe and gathered steam when Museveni took power in Uganda. The defeat of the Soviet-backed Derg in Addis, leading to Ethiopian and Eritrean independence, had less to do with Nyerere's direct input, but the new rulers there also joined their progressive comrades elsewhere in clamoring for a new era: if Africa's underdevelopment was the result of the imposition of the straitjacket of the Cold War and the perfidious role of neo-colonial henchmen, then the collapse of the Soviet Union and the growing Western disinterest in the continent generated space for a revival of Pan-Africanist thought and action. Armed with this ideology and with the military, bureaucratic and economic machinery of the states they had captured, the Eritrean, Ethiopian, Rwandan and Ugandan neo-liberation movements saw themselves as a new generation of African leaders, long before Bill Clinton famously toasted them as such.[41]

As mentioned earlier, the Rwandan genocide was a watershed for these movements. Not only did the massacres take place in their very region, with the failures of the international community underlining their message of self-reliance, but the hecatomb also occurred as the Pan-Africanist movement was organizing a major moment of action-oriented soul-searching. In April 1994, as the genocide began, the 7th Pan-Africanist Congress was taking place in Kampala, the first meeting of its kind since the 1974 gathering in Dar es Salaam. Held from April 3 to 8, the list of attendees was wide ranging: John Garang, leader of the SPLA/M; Libya's Colonel Muammar Qaddafi (who sent in a taped video message and helped fund the Congress); huge government delegations from Tanzania, Ethiopia and Cuba; Chairman Alexis Kanyarengwe, Patrick Mazimhaka, Emmanuel Ndahiro and Christine Umutoni for the RPF;

---

[40] Godfrey Mwakikagile, *Nyerere and Africa: End of an Era*, Pretoria: New Africa Press, 2010, pp. 352–8.

[41] Dan Connell and Frank Smyth, "Africa's New Bloc," *Foreign Affairs* (1998).

the widows of Malcolm X, Samora Machel and Walter Rodney; the Botswanan socialist opposition leader Kenneth Komo; the Sudanese Second Vice-President George Kongor Arop; intellectual beacons like Ali Mazrui and Ngugi wa Thiong'o; and even the Somali warlord Mohamed Aideed (of *Black Hawk Down* fame).

In his opening speech, Ugandan President Museveni received rapturous applause when he told the audience that the time had come to reverse Africa's malaise by taking matters into its own hands and eradicating the obstacles to a true post-colonial future:

> Organize, don't agonize! My own recommendation is that we should analyze the internal weaknesses that make us vulnerable to foreign dominion, rectify them, and make other demands as we go along. We can change our destiny, so let us concentrate on that instead of moaning and pleading. It is true that the western powers are responsible for what happened to Africa, and it is a moral obligation on their part to rectify this historical injustice, but I am not going to make it my primary method of emancipation: I shall emancipate myself with or without their sympathy.

Museveni was explicitly casting himself as Nyerere's torch-bearer; that his words were more than rhetorical platitudes but foreshadowed a revived campaign of neo-liberation in Congo would soon become evident.

Museveni proposed creating a permanent secretariat to breathe new life into the movement. The selection as congress chairman of Kahinda Otafiire, the national political commissar of the NRA/M during the bush war (and as such close comrade of Rwigyema, Kagame, Kayumba and others) and, in 1994, the director-general of Uganda's External Security Organization, symbolized the imperative of translating Pan-Africanist ideology into militant action. Otafiire, a Munyankole (Bahima) co-ethnic of the president, brought a degree of political clout, ideological credentials and security expertise, which underlined that the 7th Congress was much more than a talking shop; as one of the NRA/M's key Congo policy-makers, Otafiire would be working closely with Kabila and the RPF to overthrow Mobutu less than two years later. His behind the scenes convening and public orchestration of the Kampala congress helped his boss make a pitch for regional leadership. Museveni's open support for the SPLA/M and the RPF (both of which were given prominent slots at the congress to state their cause in Pan-Africanist terms) was a clear statement of Uganda's intent to become the center of a new generation of liberation struggles.

Although the timing of the conference on the eve of the Rwandan genocide was coincidental—the 7th Congress had been prepared for a long time and postponed from its scheduled 1993 date to April 1994—the decision to move the date on which it was held proved to have important consequences. The assassination of Juvénal Habyarimana and the subsequent massacres took everybody by surprise, but for the more militant congress participants (including Museveni himself) it resoundingly confirmed the urgency of combating the ethnic divide-and-rule policies of right-wing African incumbents that were held responsible for the tragedy. The combination of the onset of the killings in Rwanda and the re-intensification of the Sudanese civil war strengthened Museveni's tidings of a transition to a new era through struggle. Both in 1994 and the years that followed, it provided a frame of reference and a powerful memory that would be used by the de facto leaders of the Pan-Africanist movement to garner support for their campaign to defeat the *géno-cidaires* in Zaire, oust Mobutu and write a more emancipatory next chapter for Central Africa. Fighting its liberation war amid genocide would bring the RPF to power in Kigali but would also prove the fulcrum of an informal alliance between the new Rwanda, Uganda, Ethiopia and Eritrea, with Nyerere as the symbolic patron, that marched on Kinshasa three years later.

Uganda

In January 1986, Yoweri Museveni's National Resistance Army/Movement successfully ended its five-year-long campaign against the Obote government (1981–5) and the military dictatorship of Tito Okello (1985–6). Since independence in 1962, the country's politics had been plagued by conflict between the ambitious Obote and the northern Ugandan generals surrounding him, on the one hand, and the economic elites of central and southern Uganda on the other, many of whom were close to the Buganda Kingdom and the traditional ruler of Buganda, the kabaka. In the eyes of Museveni (himself from the southwest, but not a Baganda), the cycle of coups, war and failed democratization was the result of a poisonous imperialist legacy: the British, by recruiting men from the Acholi, Kakwa and Langi ethnic groups from the north into the King's African Rifles but reserving most economic and political privileges for the Baganda, divided and ruled Africans and pitted population groups against one another even after their departure.

Inspired by Nyerere's teachings, the NRA/M promised a post-ethnic future and a leftist restructuring of politics.[42] Its Maoist-style insurgency, in which

---

[42] Museveni, *Sowing the Mustard Seed.*

vilified communities like the Banyarwanda played a major role and participatory governance in remote rural areas was prioritized, was to be the launching platform for inclusive nation-building on the Tanzanian model, rather than the divisive neopatrimonialism of Zaire, Rwanda or pre-1986 Uganda.[43] The appeal of Museveni's anti-tribalist discourse was reinforced by his pragmatism once in power. On the one hand, he compromised on his radical socialist promises and dealt efficiently with the IMF and World Bank; on the other, he dramatically expanded primary school enrolment and, in the 1990s, became an outspoken advocate of combating HIV/AIDS. At a time when so much of Africa was affected by kleptocratic misrule and deepening poverty, the NRA/M seemed a rare enlightened partner for the West.[44]

The degree to which Yoweri Museveni turned himself into a loyal American ally, particularly during the Global War on Terror with Ugandan forces combating Al-Shabab in Somalia,[45] may cloud observers' interpretation of NRA/M's foreign policy identity—Kampala's pragmatic dealing with Washington in the post-1989 international order should not be mistaken for a total embrace of that order in Africa. Uganda under Museveni has proven to be a revisionist state in East Africa and eager to contest long-existent equilibria. A case in point was the friendship with Libya's Muammar Qaddafi, with whom it shared a dislike of military-Islamist Sudan and a commitment to Pan-Africanism. It was Qaddafi who provided some of the seed money and weaponry for the NRA/M to launch its rebellion by attacking the Kabamba barracks in 1981—which a grateful Museveni never forgot. Resentment of Western hegemony and the impact of the Cold War on Africa was an ideological framework shared with the Libyan colonel:

> Qaddafi is a nationalist: Qaddafi has conducted an independent foreign policy ... I am not able to understand the position of Western countries, which appear to resent independent-minded leaders and seem to prefer puppets ... I am totally allergic to foreign, political, and military involvement in sovereign countries, especially the African countries. If foreign intervention is good, then, African countries should be the most prosperous countries in the world, because we have had the greatest dosages of that: the slave trade, colonialism, neo-colonialism, imperialism, etc. But all those foreign-imposed phenomena have been disastrous. It is only

---

[43] Kasfir, "Guerrillas and Civilian Participation." See also Weinstein, *Inside Rebellion*.

[44] Edward A. Brett, "Rebuilding Organisation Capacity in Uganda under the National Resistance Movement," *Journal of Modern African Studies*, 32, 1 (1994).

[45] Jonathan Fisher, "Managing Donor Perceptions: Contextualizing Uganda's 2007 Intervention in Somalia," *African Affairs*, 111, 444 (2012).

recently that Africa is beginning to come up, partly because we are rejecting external meddling.[46]

Critical as Museveni was of outside intervention and the legacy of the Cold War for Africans, his revisionist critique was by no means sovereigntist, but rather a plea for *African* interventionism. The Ugandan president's counterpoint to external support for reactionary regimes was not an embrace of the OAU's non-interference in domestic affairs but a strategy of encouraging regime change through a popularly rooted armed struggle. If Nyerere's Tanzania had taken the lead in organizing the rollback of Apartheid and resistance against neo-colonialism, than Museveni defined the challenge of his generation of Pan-Africanists as clearing the neo-colonial rubble from the African political theater and confronting new threats. And while revisionist rhetoric and financial support are two instruments the NRA/M has often used for this task, it has also engaged in political violence and direct intervention—in Sudan, in Congo, in Somalia, in the Central African Republic and most recently (since 2013) in South Sudan.

Museveni's ideological disposition has continuously shaped his responses to real world events—highlighting certain developments disproportionately, blinding him to others—but these same events have also profoundly affected his ideological compass.[47] His militant Pan-Africanism made him sympathetic to leftist rebels across East and Central Africa and this generated tensions with incumbent regimes in neighboring countries who threatened Uganda, in turn reinforcing its beliefs about the need to wage proxy wars to make the NRA/M's domestic transformation project safe from external detractors. Museveni never stopped seeing the safeguarding of his own reign at home as intimately linked with external relations. What this meant in concrete terms in the mid-1990s was that his ideological criticism of the Mobutist state and the military-Islamist Al-Ingaz in Khartoum as illegitimate, externally imposed regimes (by the Cold War protagonists and Islamist Arabs respectively) coincided with the conviction that Zaire and Sudan could not countenance the NRA/M experiment in Uganda: co-existence could, at best, be temporary, and ultimately, (in)direct military confrontation would be inevitable.[48] Put differently, the

---

[46] Emphasis in original. Yoweri Museveni, "The Qaddafi I Know," *Foreign Policy*, 24 (2011).

[47] Aili Mari Tripp, *Museveni's Uganda: Paradoxes of Power in a Hybrid Regime*, Boulder: Lynne Rienner, 2010.

[48] Interviews with Wilson Muruuli Mukasa (March 2013) and Jeje Odongo (April 2013) in Kampala.

domestic equilibrium of liberation politics was and is determined by a "pro-liberation" external political and security environment and vice versa.[49]

By the time of the 7th Pan-African Congress in Kampala in April 1994, the initial years of co-existence with Uganda's neighbors had ended. The NRA/M leadership maintained ties with Sudanese, Zairian and Rwandan rebels and was in turn increasingly convinced that Zaire and Sudan were serving as rear bases for its foes as they escalated their attacks to undermine the Ugandan government's legitimacy. The NRA/M faced its most lethal challenge in the form of Joseph Kony's Lord's Resistance Army (LRA), successor to the Holy Spirit Movement of Alice Lakwena in the late 1980s. Extremely brutal attempts at pacifying northern Uganda through Operation Iron Fist and the displacement of hundreds of thousands of Acholi into squalid camps failed to either foster widespread acceptance of NRA/M rule or to break the LRA.[50] After Kony was introduced to members of the Khartoum security apparatus in 1993 by the Southern Sudanese warlord Riek Machar, which led to the Ugandan rebels acquiring bases in Sudan's Equatoria region and extensive armaments, the LRA morphed into a potent force that engaged in deadly ambushes across northern Uganda against the Ugandan People's Defense Forces (UPDF) and held the population hostage.[51] The LRA threat was compounded by the activities of the National Army for the Liberation of Uganda (NALU) and the West Nile Bank Liberation Front (WNBLF) which shared Kony's view of Museveni as an illegitimate usurper and used the Zairian–Ugandan borderlands as launching pads for strikes that were meant to expose the inability of the UPDF to protect the territory and the Ugandan people.[52]

---

[49] Rene Lemarchand, "Foreign Policy Making in the Great Lakes Region," in Gilbert M. Khadiagala (ed.), *African Foreign Policies: Power and Process*, Boulder: Lynne Rienner, 2001, p. 101.

[50] Heike Behrend, *Alice Lakwena and the Holy Spirits: War in Northern Uganda*, Oxford: James Currey, 1999; Adam Branch, "Neither Peace nor Justice: Political Violence and the Peasantry in Northern Uganda, 1986–1998," *African Studies Quarterly*, 8, 2 (2005).

[51] Interview with a former officer of Sudan's National Intelligence and Security Service in Kampala, March 2013. The officer in question helped organize the initial Kony–Machar encounter.

[52] Gérard Prunier, "Rebel Movements and Proxy Warfare: Uganda, Sudan and the Congo (1986–99)," *African Affairs*, 103, 412 (2004).

After the Rwandan genocide, the sense of Zaire as a security threat grew in Kampala. Museveni and Mobutu had long distrusted each other,[53] with the latter seeing the former as a populist demagogue and the former regarding the latter as the emblem of "Old Africa." Yet as the Sudanese civil war spilled southwards and Uganda's involvement in it grew, there was a qualitative change in Museveni's perception of Zaire—from a latent, chronic worry to an acute challenge.[54] Kampala was not blind to the fact that the growing weakness of Mobutu and the increased independence of key clients of his like General Nzimbi of the DSP and Baramoto of the Garde Civile meant that Zaire's Province Orientale and Kivu were now used by armed groups in the region as smuggling routes and staging posts for military strikes. Nzimbi and Baramoto were involved in arms dealing and the delivery of supplies to the highest bidder; together, the Ugandan rebel forces were unable to muster more than 10,000–15,000 fighters, but they had a destabilizing effect as they had entrenched themselves in the no man's land of northeast Zaire. This problem was compounded by Mobutu's mounting assistance to two of Museveni's enemies: the Sudanese government and the Rwandese *génocidaires*. Whereas the former was given permission to use Zairian territory to pursue John Garang's SPLA/M and to supply anti-Museveni insurgents, principally the LRA and the militant Islamists of the Allied Democratic Forces (ADF) entrenched in the Rwenzori Mountains, the latter denounced the NRA/M–RPF axis as a Tutsi conspiracy against Bantu Africa and built their state-outside-the-state in the Zairian refugee camps around Lake Kivu and Lake Tanganyika.

In 1993, Museveni and Mobutu had tried to prevent a security dilemma between them from spiraling out of control. Honoré N'Gbanda, the Zairian president's closest security adviser and nicknamed "Terminator," was sent to Kampala to express his worries about Uganda's strategy of war by proxy. He brought up the subject of Museveni's past relationship with Laurent Kabila, warning Uganda not to back such a dangerous rebel. According to N'Gbanda, an evasive Museveni expressed his belief in correct neighborly relations and reassured him that Kabila had retired from frontline politics and was probably merely smuggling coffee and gold.[55] However, the shift in

---

[53] For a Mobutist perspective on this mistrust see N'Gbanda, *Ainsi sonne le glas*, pp. 104–11.

[54] Interviews with ESO chief David Pulkol and Museveni's chief political adviser Moses Biyaruhanga, Kampala, April 2013.

[55] N'Gbanda, *Ainsi sonne le glas*, p. 119.

regional politics in 1994 undid this uneasy co-existence. From Mobutu's point of view, it was Museveni who was fanning the flames by helping the RPF win the Rwandan civil war and by backing the SPLA's renewed offensive in Sudan's Equatoria and Bahr al-Ghazal regions. His convening of the 7th Pan-African Congress and renewed contact with various old Mobutist foes like André Kisase Ngandu were perceived as preparing another proxy war. Seen through Museveni's eyes, it was Mobutu who was destabilizing the equilibrium, because the rising insecurity inside Uganda came not just from the LRA on the country's northern border but also emanated from the western frontier with Zaire where the ADF, NALU and WNBLF had bases, with Sudanese intelligence and army supplying them, directly or indirectly, through Mobutu's clients.[56]

Against this background, Museveni entered into discussions with Nyerere and the RPF in early 1995 about the worsening regional outlook. The RPF's ascent to power had created opportunities for a second wave of liberation in East Africa. However, given the escalating tensions with Sudan—the Ugandan embassy in Khartoum and the Sudanese embassy in Kampala would remain closed until 1999—and the explosive situation on the Zairian–Rwandan border, a far bleaker outcome seemed equally possible, according to Museveni's Minister of Security Wilson Muruuli Mukasa and David Pulkol, from 1996 onwards head of Uganda's External Security Organization (ESO).[57] Kagame, Museveni and Nyerere all agreed that the security "cancer" in eastern Zaire had to be removed—a necessary condition for the liberation regimes in Uganda and Rwanda to survive and for momentum for the SPLA/M in the Sudanese civil war to be generated. Of the three leaders, Museveni hesitated the most about an all-out military operation that would lead to the de facto occupation of large swathes of a neighboring country—he feared international condemnation, possibly imperiling American goodwill vis-à-vis the NRA/M and RPF and triggering a French military reaction that could swing the balance against the Pan-Africanist forces.[58] Following further discussions with the leaders of recently liberated Ethiopia and Eritrea, it was decided that the offensive into Zaire would need to be on a massive scale; the possibility of going all the way to Kinshasa would be explored, but, regardless of the ulti-

---

[56] Prunier, *From Genocide to Continental War*, pp. 80–7.

[57] Interviews in Kampala, on March 27 and 29, 2013, respectively.

[58] Interviews with Karake Karenzi, Patrick Mazimhaka, Emmanuel Ndahiro, David Pulkol, Kampala and Kigali, April 2013–December 2014.

mate objective, the leaders resolved that the operations would have to be led by a Congolese movement to be successful. In the words of Didier Kazadi, Mzee Kabila's right-hand man: "Kagame and Museveni needed a facade and we needed them."[59]

On the Ugandan side, the preparations for the coming war on the western border were delegated to a small group of trusted operatives led by Kahinda Otafiire (chair of the 7th Pan-African Congress and former ESO supremo), General Kale Kayihura (former national political commissar), General James Kazini (commander of the UPDF's Fourth Division based in Gulu, northern Uganda) and Museveni's half-brother Salim Saleh (presidential adviser on defense and security). Otafiire began organizing the training of several thousand Congolese rebels of the Conseil National de Résistance pour la Démocratie (CNRD) of André Kisase Ngandu who was a veteran of the Simba rebellion and had returned to Kampala in 1990 after a long exile in Sudan and Berlin. After spending three years at a military academy in Uganda and having launched some strikes against Mobutu's FAZ and against Ugandan rebels in the Ruwenzori Mountains, Kisase was considered reliably pro-NRA/M.[60] Simultaneously, Ugandan intelligence worked with its Rwandan counterparts headed by Patrick Karegeya to enlist Laurent-Désiré Kabila into the nascent anti-Mobutist front. Apart from facilitating the pick-up of Mzee in Tanzania by the Rwandan covert unit, Kampala also spoke directly to several of Kabila's closest comrades in Dar es Salaam, including Didier Kazadi, to ensure they had a second channel of communication, parallel to the Rwandans.

Museveni decided that Uganda would remain cautious and act as a secondary force assisting the coming offensive, given his fears about France and commitment to the Sudanese civil war and anti-LRA operations. But because he yearned to retain as much overall strategic influence over the "Congolese" rebellion as possible, his lieutenants attempted to build and promote a network of insurgents intensely loyal to Uganda at the heart of the emergent new force. Most of these came from Kisase's CNRD and were eastern Congolese. Museveni, Otafiire and the others were doubtful of Kabila's capacity to successfully emerge from retirement and actually lead a serious insurrection; they also fretted that his relationships in Tanzania and the RPF's control over him would render him beholden to Kigali and Dar es Salaam. As the planning for war intensified in 1996, Kisase and his Ugandan-trained troops were by far the

---

[59] Interview in Kinshasa, August 2013.
[60] Martens, *Kabila et la révolution congolaise*, vol. 1, p. 171.

best prepared Congolese contingent and represented an implicit alternative to the "pro-Rwandan" Kabila as the spearhead of the movement.

Tanzania, Ethiopia and Eritrea

While Rwanda and Uganda faced the most acute security threat from Zaire and would take the military lead when war broke out in 1996, the final plan for the conflict and the political structure of what would later become Congo's liberation movement, the AFDL, were to a substantial degree shaped by Tanzania, Eritrea and Ethiopia as junior partners in the push to overthrow Mobutu. As the RPF prepared for a direct, unilateral intervention behind a Congolese front and Museveni favored a slow-burning proxy war, Julius Nyerere, Issayas Afewerki and Meles Zenawi would advocate a hybrid model. All three leaders argued for a Congolese liberation movement that would receive fast-track assistance to morph into a significant military force and be aided through extensive political *encadrement* by veteran Pan-Africanists to nurture a strong organizational discipline and ambitious political–ideological program.

For Julius Nyerere, the war against Mobutu and the defeat of the "negative forces" in eastern Zaire were to be the epilogue to an impressive, drawn-out career on the African stage. As discussed in the previous chapter, Mobutu and Nyerere were polar opposites in terms of personality and political vision. The Mwalimu fought for decades for African unity[61] and against what he saw as Western interventionism and its local henchmen on the continent, seeking to roll-back Apartheid and neo-colonialism in Southern and Eastern Africa.[62] He had voluntarily given up the Tanzanian presidency in 1985 and the chairmanship of Chama Cha Mapinduzi (Swahili for "Party of the Revolution," and the 1977 successor to the old TANU party) in 1990 and publicly declared he was done with politics: a new generation should continue his revolutionary efforts in the changing international order. But despite Nyerere's official retirement to his native Butiama, his travel schedule proved he remained a crucial force behind the scenes of African politics. Freed from the official formalities of the presidency, he accepted the mantle of *éminence grise* of the informal Pan-Africanist movement,[63] which underwent a renaissance with the coming

---

[61] Julius K. Nyerere, "A United States of Africa," *Journal of Modern African Studies*, 1, 1 (1963).

[62] Julius K. Nyerere, *Crusade for Liberation*, Oxford: Oxford University Press, 1978.

[63] Mwakikagile, *Nyerere and Africa*, pp. 432–9.

to power of many of its sympathizers in Ethiopia (1991), Eritrea (1991/3), South Africa (1994) and Rwanda (1994). The elder statesman was sought out by the mostly youthful new rulers of these states, craving both his practical advice and the legitimacy associating with him would bring. It was a role Nyerere relished and which constituted a crucial dimension of African liberation politics in the final decade of the twentieth century.

Nyerere sensed that the changing international order in the 1990s presented important opportunities, yet he also recognized that the expansionist fundamentalism of military-Islamist Sudan and the 1994 disaster, about which he wrote a little-known booklet called *Genocide in Rwanda*, were pivotal moments that could either smother the Pan-Africanist momentum or propel it forward. He traveled around the world explaining the imperative of a new politics and the revitalization of his life-long project. In an interview with *The New York Times*, the 74-year-old Nyerere argued that the genocide had irrevocably reshaped regional relations and made it necessary for a whole new paradigm to take center stage. Sovereignty should not be a straitjacket that constrains Africans while allowing bankrupt regimes and their neo-colonial overlords to get away with murder, according to Nyerere: "There is a new leadership developing in Africa," he said. "They are saying 'What does this mean? This non-interference. What does it mean? Who is sovereign in the country. The people? Or the junta?"[64]

The Tanzanian government took a different stance from the Mwalimu, remaining rather hostile towards the Front as long as Ali Mwinyi was head of state and blaming the RPF's thirst for absolute power for the failure of the Arusha Peace Accords. The government allowed hundreds of thousands of refugees, including high-profile Interahamwe leaders, to settle in sprawling camps in western Tanzania and was slow to follow Nyerere's lead in calling the extermination of Tutsi and their presumed Hutu accomplices "genocide." According to a revealing cable sent to Washington by the US embassy in Dar es Salaam, influential circles in Tanzania saw the RPF as a "Tutsi force" that needed to be balanced, with the Rwandan refugees as potentially useful assets to help establish a Hutu Burundi to offset "Tutsi" Rwanda.[65] However, the election of a new president in 1995, Benjamin Mkapa, resulted in a more pragmatic policy of engaging the RPF and more tacit support for Nyerere's

---

[64] James C. McKinley Jr, "As the West Hesitates on Burundi, Leaders in Africa Make a Stand," *New York Times*, August 24, 1996.

[65] American Embassy Dar es Salaam to Secretary of State, Washington, DC, "The Refugees are Here To Stay," R 240543Z, July 1996.

personal diplomacy. Mkapa ruled out the contribution of Tanzanian troops in the coming war but endorsed the enlistment of Laurent Kabila as rebel spokesman. The government also ended the open door policy for refugees.[66] Contrary to Zaire, Tanzanian security forces did what they could to depoliticize the camps, move them away from the border and peacefully return those who wished to go back home.[67] Mkapa pledged full cooperation with the International Criminal Tribunal for Rwanda—to be based in Arusha after a UN decision in February 1995—and began ordering the arrests of suspected *génocidaires*. This contrasted strongly with the Kenya of President Daniel arap Moi, which retained close ties with Mobutu's Zaire and quickly became a sanctuary for leading members of the former genocidal regime. Nyerere kept Moi out of all East African deliberations of any consequence on the issue of the Zairian refugee camps and Mobutu's role in the region.

If Kenya was shunned, that certainly did not apply to Eritrea and Ethiopia. Both the Eritrean People's Liberation Front (EPLF, nicknamed *Shabia*) and the Ethiopian People's Revolutionary Democratic Front (EPRDF), the alliance dominated by the Tigrayan People's Liberation Front (TPLF, nicknamed *Woyane*) played secondary but nevertheless important roles in the story of liberating Zaire/Congo. Although the struggles of the EPLF and TPLF/ EPRDF were overwhelmingly processes situated within the specific contexts of center–periphery tendencies in Ethiopia and the geopolitics of the Horn of Africa, their undisputable achievements—overthrowing what was perhaps Africa's most brutal regime, one which could draw on the continent's biggest army, armed to its teeth by the Soviets—resonated in progressive circles. Both were Marxist–Leninist-inspired movements with few organizational links to the Pan-Africanist movement prior to May 1991, but their ability to organize the peasantry from the ground up and to fight for two decades in a brutal guerrilla war against a superpower-backed military government impressed Nyerere. This formidable degree of organization and the intellectual brilliance of their leaderships earned the EPLF and TPLF/EPRDF respect, as became evident in the desire of other Pan-Africanist forces to work together on a new regional liberation agenda.

[66] Bonaventure Rutinwa, "The Tanzanian Government's Response to the Rwandan Emergency," *Journal of Refugee Studies*, 9, 3 (1996), pp. 291–302.

[67] According to a high-ranking Tanzanian security official at the time, the shadow of an RPF intervention to close the refugee camps in Tanzania motivated them to address the refugee problem systematically. Interview in Dar es Salaam, June 2015.

The convergence of the trajectories of the Eritrean and Ethiopian liberation fighters and those of the Great Lakes began about a year after the fall of the Derg. It was in 1992, as the Al-Ingaz regime in Khartoum unleashed a full-blown jihad against domestic opposition and threatened neighboring states, that Haile Menkerios—the right-hand man of Issayas Afewerki in foreign affairs—traveled to Uganda to get a sense of Kampala's view of the Sudanese civil war. Sudan had supported the Eritrean struggle for years, but the fiery Islamist rhetoric of Hassan Al-Turabi unsettled the region, including an Eritrean government nervous about its own Muslim population.[68] Haile was received by Museveni, who was bullish on the Eritrean–Ethiopian plan to breathe new life into the defunct sub-regional organization, the Intergovernmental Authority on Development (IGAD). The Ugandan president asked Asmara and Addis for help in dealing with what he described as a growing isolation of progressive forces in the Great Lakes. Claiming he was surrounded by enemies (Turabi's Sudan, Mobutu's Zaire, Habyarimana's Rwanda, but also Moi's Kenya), he urged an alliance of leftist governments, with immediate support to be given to a small group of Rwandan exiles "to help break the siege on Uganda and further the Pan-Africanist cause." After the encounter, Museveni introduced Haile to RPF leader Paul Kagame. In a conversation about African politics that dragged on for hours, the latter two had a true meeting of the minds that set in motion the development of a deep relationship between Eritrea, Ethiopia, Rwanda and Uganda who together would end up taking on the regional cancers of Sudan and Zaire.[69]

When the Sudanese conflict spilled over to northern Uganda in 1994 and the Rwandan genocide occurred, Meles and Issayas were asked for urgent help by Museveni and Kagame. The latter duo asked the former two whether it was possible to do more than organize mutual visits and lend political support to the cause of liberating Rwanda. Ethiopia was still on reasonably good terms with Khartoum and held off on the Sudanese front, but immediately decided to deploy peacekeepers as part of the post-genocide United Nations Assistance Mission for Rwanda. Meles agreed to the dispatching of the troops in one of the most sensitive parts of the country, the southwestern border region of Cyangugu Prefecture, in close proximity to the Zairian refugee camps around

---

[68] Gaim Kibreab, "Eritrean–Sudanese Relations in Historical Perspective," in Richard Reid (ed.), *Eritrea's External Relations: Understanding Its Regional Role and Foreign Policy*, London: Royal Institute of International Affairs, 2009, pp. 82–90.

[69] Interview with Haile Menkerios in Addis Ababa, November 2014.

Bukavu, the border with unstable Burundi and the prefectures of Butare and Gikongoro where the mass murders had been particularly intense; in taking on this difficult task, the Ethiopian UN peacekeepers were the only blue helmets who ever confronted the ex-FAR/Interahamwe militarily during their deployment in Rwanda.[70]

Eritrea, for its part, was already being placed on the defensive by Al-Ingaz's backing of the Eritrean Islamic Jihad and enhanced its support for John Garang's SPLA/M while also declaring its willingness to develop military cooperation with the RPA. Issayas traveled to Rwanda in early 1995 and was profoundly moved during his visit to the hilltop of Murambi, where, as we saw earlier, thousands of Tutsi civilians had perished at the hands of the Interahamwe. He vowed that this would never be repeated and that Eritrea would do all it could to protect Rwanda from a return of the genocidal project; according to Yemane Gebreab, the Eritrean president's most senior political adviser, this alliance was further consolidated by a follow-up visit Kagame made to Eritrea and its sacred mountain site of anti-Derg resistance at Nakfa.[71]

After 1995, the meetings between the different elements constituting this emergent Pan-Africanist bloc became increasingly characterized by high excitement and grand ambitions. The Islamist threat from Sudan remained a major topic but consensus rapidly transpired on an even more urgent project that could unlock so much energy that had it the potential to transform Africa: the elimination of Mobutu. In the words of Yemane Gebreab: "The genocide in Rwanda had a catalytic role ... [There was] an understanding on the part of our region that there was a huge opportunity for change. It was the time of the 'Greater Horn,' we wanted to make changes."[72] Eritrean-born Yemane Kidane, chief-of-staff of the Ethiopian foreign minister, Seyoum Mesfin, echoed this sentiment: "We wanted to support revolutionaries across Africa—Rwanda, Uganda, Congo. We believed in new African states. We were so excited and wanted to change everything."[73] Neither Eritreans nor Ethiopians had ever fought the Zairian leader directly, but the political importance for Africa of regime change in Kinshasa was on their minds. It would help to solve Rwanda and Uganda's security problems, contribute to putting

---

[70] Richard Orth, "African Operational Experiences in Peacekeeping," *Small Wars & Insurgencies*, 7, 3 (1996), p. 319.

[71] Interview in Nakfa, August 2014.

[72] Interview in Asmara, March 2015.

[73] Interview in Addis Ababa, November 2014.

Khartoum on the defensive and provide a highly symbolic reckoning with the continent's past. According to Haile Menkerios:

> No regime was more divisive in Africa than Mobutu's ... Mobutu had given sanctuary to everybody's enemies. He had to go ... We very much believed in a new era ... We thought we were opening up Africa. It's simply that we were looking at Congo as an extension of our own struggle. Many of us had little empathy with the specific Congolese struggle and context.[74]

Hence, when Kagame asked Meles and Issayas for advice and assistance regarding the refugee camps issue, the response from Asmara and Addis was unambiguous: they agreed that the Canadian idea of an intervention force that would merely separate the *génocidaires* from the RPF through a buffer zone along the border would be disastrous and lead to a resumption of the civil war. Rather, they argued for maximum Rwandan support to a Congolese liberation movement that would oust Mobutu. In doing so, Meles and Issayas counseled against a unilateral RPF invasion of eastern Zaire, fearing a massacre in the camps and associated outcry of the international community: *"it would have turned the victim into a victimizer."*[75] Instead, they subscribed to the earlier advice of Nyerere (who had received a high-level Eritrean delegation in Butiama just prior to the Issayas–Meles–Kagame meeting to discuss Zaire and Rwanda) of a two-level maneuver that invoked the protection of the Tutsi in eastern Zaire and relied on a domestic Congolese force, enabling public support by Eritrea and Ethiopia for the offensive.

Thus, while the coming war in military terms would largely be an operation of Rwandan firepower and tactics, fronted by Congolese rebels and aided by Ugandan intelligence, the final shape of the offensive was largely a product of the political strategy proposed by Nyerere, Meles and Issayas. Their shrewdly phrased counsel swayed the RPF planners to divert from their initial thinking about the inevitable conflict against Mobutu. The Tanzanian, Ethiopian and Eritrean role would become particularly visible in two aspects of the battle plan. First, the RPF continued to hesitate throughout 1995 and 1996 about how far into Zaire the operations would have to reach to crush the enemy, as is evident from conversations with the RPA's most senior officers;[76] Museveni's warnings about a possible virulent French reaction made them hesitate about being too ambitious. But Nyerere—and later Meles and Issayas too—pleaded strongly for

---

[74] Ibid.

[75] Interview with Haile Menkerios, November 2014.

[76] Interviews with James Kabarebe (April 2013) in Kigali, Karake Karenzi (October 2014) in London and Caesar Kayizari in Ankara (June 2015).

a much deeper push that would remove the roots of the problem and affect the underlying pathologies, as they saw them, of Central Africa's dysfunctional politics. As Yemane Gebreab put it on behalf of Eritrea in discussions with the RPF: "Once momentum was created, we argued we should go all the way."[77] Clamoring for the removal of Mobutu was not immediately successful, but swayed the entire RPF High Command soon after hostilities commenced. By the time the weakness of the host of the ex-FAR/Interahamwe was revealed in November 1996, objections were no longer raised to the idea of marching on Kinshasa.

The second dimension in which the role of Issayas, Meles and Nyerere became evident was the choice of the instrument: a united and integrated Congolese liberation movement, extensively assisted by its Pan-Africanist backers, but with strong local support. While for Nyerere this was a tried and tested recipe he had promoted in Mozambique, Rwanda, Uganda and Zimbabwe, for the TPLF/ EPRDF and EPLF it was a natural template based on their own liberation experiences.[78] What would make matters a little different in the Congolese context was the degree to which external actors would help carry the burden, but its proponents argued that there was no time to wait for a more slowly growing organic rebellion to emerge given the urgency of the security situation for the Tutsi in Congo and the threat of counter-revolution: history would have to be speeded up a little. The problems this would cause—such as the absence of Gramscian "organic intellectuals," strong levels of ideological awareness among the recruits and sufficient political organization—would be remedied by a Pan-Africanist taskforce instructed to assist the rebellion through political *encadrement*: Haile Menkerios and Yemane Gebreab for Eritrea, Yemane Kidane for Ethiopia and Claude Dusaidi for Rwanda (a political adviser close to Kagame) were to form the core, with occasional further support provided by Seyoum Mesfin (Ethiopia), DMI officer Charles Karamba and Christine Umutoni (Rwanda) and Kahinda Otafiire and Okwiri Rabwoni (Uganda). As the security situation came close to boiling point in the summer of 1996, these highly influential individuals started gathering in Kigali. Only one final step had to be undertaken before war was to begin.

Conclusion: The Alliance des Forces Démocratiques pour la Libération du Congo-Zaïre and the Lemera Agreement

On Friday, October 18, 1996, four men met to sign a terse but unambiguous declaration of war on the Mobutu regime. Having concluded that the state of

---

[77] Interview in Asmara, March 2015.
[78] Interview with Yemane Kidane, November 2014.

Zaire had been damaged beyond repair by its greedy ruler, they committed their respective movements to the armed struggle and created a "political framework" called the Alliance des Forces Démocratiques pour la Libération du Congo-Zaïre (AFDL) as the vehicle to pursue regime change. They held out the promise of a democratic and free nation and announced that the formation of alliance structures and a more detailed political program were to follow soon. Finally, the four appointed one among them as the *porte-parole* [spokesman]: Laurent-Désiré Kabila. The site at which the founding protocol of the AFDL was allegedly signed—Lemera—was highly symbolic: this small commune on the Ruzizi Plateau of South Kivu was close to the historical *maquis* of Kabila but also lay in the heartland of the Congolese Tutsi living in the region. As such, it was meant to thoroughly establish the AFDL as a Congolese movement, firmly rooted in the long history of the struggle against Mobutu, but also connected to the contemporary threat against Tutsi in the region of the Great Lakes of Africa.

The four leaders, brought together by Paul Kagame, Yoweri Museveni and Julius Nyerere, represented various aspects of the tragedy that had befallen Congo and united different constituencies from across the country under the umbrella of the overthrow of Mobutu. The first "genitor" of the AFDL was of course Mzee Kabila of the Parti de la Révolution Populaire. As the most recognizable among the Congolese leaders of the rebellion, he was a logical choice as spokesman. His clear links with the anti-imperialist cause, his refusal to ever be bought by Mobutu and his Katangese ethnicity were crucial in framing the liberation war. The second signatory, André Kisase Ngandu, was a Tetela from Kasai Oriental in the heart of Congo—an ethno-linguistic ancestry he shared with the Pan-Africanist martyr Patrice Lumumba, in whose footsteps he had followed by joining the Simba Revolt in the 1960s. He brought the most significant Congolese force to the AFDL, the Conseil National de Résistance Démocratique, which—as we saw earlier—consisted of several thousand recruits who had been trained by Ugandan instructors. Despite his age, his links with Tanzania and Qaddafi's Libya as well as his overall pro-Ugandan orientation and connection to Lumumba made him an important asset for the liberation struggle.[79]

The third founder of the AFDL was Déogratias "Douglas" Bugera, a Congolese Tutsi architect from North Kivu whose parents had been murdered in 1965 by Mobutu's soldiers during the Simba Revolt.[80] Bugera had

---

[79] De Villers and Willame, *République démocratique du Congo*, pp. 21–2.
[80] Email correspondence with Déogratias Bugera, March 2010.

been a co-founder of the Alliance Démocratique des Peuples (ADP), a move-ment which sought to protect the Tutsi from growing inter-communitarian violence in the early 1990s in North Kivu. He had helped recruit youngsters from across eastern Zaire to join the RPF from 1991 onwards, and his inclu-sion in the AFDL underscored both his community's ties to Rwanda as well as the venomous ethno-politics threatening the survival of Tutsi after the ex-FAR/Interahamwe moved to the Kivus. The final representative signing the "Lemera Accord" was Anselme Masasu Nindaga, who aged twenty-seven was much younger than his companions. Masasu came to symbolize the aspira-tions of the young masses of Zaire who were mired in abject poverty, violence and repression. Charismatic, dynamic and trained as a professional soldier by serving in the RPA, he was the dashing figure who ensured the rebellion was not just a cast of historical characters but could present itself as forward-looking. The Belgian ambassador to Rwanda and later, Congo, Frank De Coninck, captured his role perfectly: "To most, he represented something new from the East."[81] Masasu was born and raised in Kabare, South Kivu, as the son of a Mushi father and a Tutsi mother, and had experienced discrimina-tion and prejudice all his life; the fact that he subsumed his complex identity in the nationalist-cum-Pan-Africanist cause of ousting Mobutu was an exam-ple to the legions of unemployed youngsters across the region. Masasu was officially the head of the Mouvement Révolutionnaire pour la Libération du Zaïre (MRLZ), but this organization only existed on paper. His real contribu-tion lay in the thousands of youngsters, the *kadogo*, he would soon recruit in villages across eastern Congo for the march on Kinshasa. The signing of the AFDL's founding act by Kabila, Kisase, Bugera and Masasu was the capstone of two years of increasingly frantic preparations for an all-out war against Mobutu and the genocidal forces in eastern Zaire.

* * *

This chapter began by describing how catastrophic violence continued to ter-rorize the Rwandan countryside after the genocide and how the increasing insecurity led to ever more ruthless counterinsurgency operations by the RPA. The aftermath of the killings at Kibeho, Kanama and elsewhere in Rwanda pointed in the direction of a game-changing resumption of direct confrontation with the ex-FAR/Interahamwe across the border. What exact shape the coming conflict would take was a matter of discussion among the

---

[81] Interview in Rome, June 2009.

RPF High Command, but all agreed that as long as hundreds of thousands of Rwandans were living with the *génocidaires* outside the country, neither the political nor the security situation could be fundamentally ameliorated. UN representatives tried to marshal member states behind a proposal to relocate the camps away from the border and to deploy a force of 3,000 well-trained soldiers—2,500 Zairians, to get Mobutu on board, and 500 UN blue helmets—which, it was estimated, would only cost about US$55 million for a six-month period.[82] However, UN Secretary-General Boutros-Ghali could not persuade even a single country to commit personnel or financial assistance for what was probably the only alternative to war.

The RPF's search for a way out of this unexpectedly lethal conundrum led it to partner with its old Ugandan comrades and a range of Pan-Africanist movements, who shared the Front's loathing of Mobutu and each had their own strategic, ideological and personal reasons for supporting military action in eastern Zaire. Starting at the 7th Pan-African Congress, it was the RPF's continuous dialogue over a period of two years, with Museveni's Uganda, Meles's Ethiopia, Issayas's Eritrea and Julius Nyerere of Tanzania, that shaped the battle plan. Initial RPF designs of a unilateral attack on the camps, with limited hot pursuit operations inside Zaire, were replaced with a far more extensive strategy of using a Congolese liberation movement to oust the hated dictator. What Museveni, Meles, Issayas and above all the Mwalimu were suggesting was that the dire situation in which Rwanda and Uganda found themselves could be transformed into a tremendous opportunity for Central Africa as a whole: domestic liberation projects could be consolidated if the external context became much more benign with the departure of Mobutu. To this end, they endorsed the RPA's coming onslaught on its foes and pledged varying degrees of political and military support, as well as suggesting some of the Congolese individuals the Front should partner with.

The most important of these was Laurent-Désiré Kabila, the old rebel of the 1960s, who was plucked from retirement in Tanzania and taken to Kigali where he entered into a remarkable partnership with a new generation of comrades. Their relationship was defined by mutual dependence from the start. The RPF needed a Congolese spokesman and a nationalist symbol to counter international criticism, get the full backing of its Pan-Africanist mentors and challenge Mobutu. Kabila had no troops of his own and no organizational infrastructure to harbor any prospects of playing a major role in Zairian politics in the future— the RPF offer was a godsend which was impossible to turn down if he still

---

[82] Khan, *Shallow Graves of Rwanda*, p. 79.

wanted to realize his dream of starting a Congolese revolution and replacing Mobutu. While other Congolese leaders were brought on board and enabled the nascent AFDL to reach out to constituencies across the country, at the very heart of the struggle would be Kabila and the RPF. This strategic alliance would represent the linchpin of the liberation movement—and later its extraordinarily violent unraveling—more than any other.

6

THE CAMPAIGN

THE SPRINT TO KINSHASA AND THE RWANDAN–ANGOLAN COLD WAR

Congo has liberation with no Congolese liberation story. The Congolese politicians knew it. The Congolese military knew it. The Congolese people knew it. Rwanda had carried them on its back. They hated us for it.

Caesar Kayizari, deputy force commander of the Rwandan Patriotic Army in Zaire.

In October 1996, after weeks of rumors about troop maneuvers and an impending invasion of Rwanda by the *génocidaire* forces or of Zaire by the RPA, war broke out in eastern Congo as thousands of Rwandan soldiers and Congolese auxiliary forces crossed the border for a blistering assault on the region's main towns and sprawling refugee camps. Under the umbrella of the AFDL, they broke through the resistance of ex-FAR and Interahamwe units and captured Goma, Uvira and Bukavu, liberating most of North and South Kivu within weeks. Mobutu's FAZ troops simply melted away. Almost one million Rwandan Hutus were shepherded back to their homeland, but the hard core of killers escaped and fled into the Congolese rainforest, with at least 300,000 civilians following in their wake. The failure to eliminate the *génocidaire* organization would prove deeply consequential: it meant that the hunt for Interahamwe in Congo and elsewhere in Central Africa would compete for the RPF's attention with the campaign against Mobutu, leaving little time to focus on the all-important political task of building the AFDL into a true liberation movement.

Much of this remained hidden from view to outsiders and insiders alike: the blistering advance of the AFDL under the command of the RPA officers James Kabarebe and Caesar Kayizari astonished the world and engendered a sense of euphoria about the end of the Mobutist era—just as the Mwalimu had predicted. Angola's entry into the Pan-Africanist coalition further accelerated the march on Kinshasa; the MPLA's artillery and transport capacity made military defeat for Mobutu inevitable. Jubilant crowds in Kisangani, Mbuji-Mayi and Lubumbashi greeted the Congolese foot soldiers, their Rwandan commanders and the AFDL "founding fathers." However, what the cheering masses and television crews did not see was the merciless hunt by RPA units for their enemies in the jungle, a hot pursuit that led to innumerable deaths—some of them combatants, many others civilians. The RPF's comrades were stunned into silence by the ferocity of the continuation of the Rwandan civil war, but the exhilaration of impending triumph and the associated division of spoils preoccupied them more than the future of the *génocidaire* threat and the humanitarian tragedy inside Zaire/Congo.

In the final approach towards Kinshasa, a stark contrast emerged between the undeniable military prowess of the alliance—the capital was taken in seven months, after a march of almost 2,000 kilometers—and the political divisions that plagued the movement even before the entire country was liberated. The murder of André Kisase Ngandu marginalized the influence of his constituencies in the AFDL while Kabila's skill at recruiting his "friends and pals" to join the revolution weakened the Banyamulenge's initial dominance. As the Mzee increasingly imposed himself as the revolution's leader, this process created myriad tensions, internally as well as externally. The AFDL was a Pan-Africanist affair with support from Angola, Eritrea, Ethiopia, Rwanda, Tanzania, Uganda, South Africa and Zambia, but little seemed to have been agreed upon among the protagonists, apart from the removal of Mobutu. The two main providers of military muscle—Kigali and Luanda—found themselves stumbling into a *"race to Kinshasa,"* when AFDL troops crossed from eastern Congo into western Congo around the border town of Tshikapa in Kasai Occidental. Angolan troops and Luanda-backed Congolese reinforcements, the so-called Tigres Katangais, contested James Kabarebe's military leadership and sought to launch the final assault themselves, which the RPA rejected. Both armies set out on a parallel advance to Kinshasa, with the RPF winning the "sprint" by accelerating the deployment of advance forces to infiltrate the Congolese capital. The rivalry between the RPF and MPLA also acquired an intra-Congolese dimension; the Angolan preference for the former secessionists from South Katanga—rather than the obstinate Mzee Kabila who seemed to be too close to Kigali and his Rwandan bodyguard—led to a power struggle weeks before Mobutu was driven from office. Even before the military victory had been completed, the promise of regional peace was already at risk of being lost.

Zero Hour: The Invasion of Zaire and the "Liberation" of the Refugee Camps

By September 1996, regional war in the Great Lakes had become inevitable. The members of the UN Security Council had failed to return from their summer holidays with a realistic plan to get to grips with worsening insecurity inside Zaire and Rwanda and to dismantle the ticking time bomb of the refugee camps. Humanitarian organizations were sounding alarm bells, but the Security Council failed to act—despite ominous reports from UN staff on the ground. On July 5, the UN commissioner for human rights in Geneva, José Ayala-Lasso, was told by his most senior field coordinator that more large-scale violence lay in store:

> I wish to draw to your attention the major implications of recent killings of Tutsi genocide survivors and others by Hutu insurgents infiltrating across Rwanda's borders ... From my own conversations with senior Ministry of Defence officials yesterday, I gained the impression that a decision may well already have been taken on a cross-border response to these incidents.[1]

In August, UNHCR officials began moving some of the nearly 50,000 refugees, on the largest island in Africa, Idjwi Island on Lake Kivu (which at some points is only a kilometer removed from Rwanda's territory) to the Zairian interior. Daily reports of infiltrations into Rwanda and growing *génocidaire* rhetoric was unsettling observers on the ground, who also heard rumors of an impending RPA counterstrike. Patrick de Sousa, head of UNHCR in South Kivu, commented:

> Idjwi was always a potential base ... Today it is said quite openly there are attacks. There are no denials and no defensiveness. It reflects the fact that the forces of extremism are gaining the upper hand. By this I mean those who say that all the Tutsis are oppressors and the only approach is to reclaim the homeland, and on the other side those who say that all the Hutus are killers who deserve to be killed.[2]

---

[1] Message from Ian Martin to José Ayala-Lasso, "Developments in Rwanda I," Kigali, UN Human Rights Field Operation in Rwanda, July 5, 1996.

[2] UN Integrated Regional Information Network, "IRIN Situation Report on Idjwi Island, South Kivu," 1996.

Escalating flames across the region were merging into a much bigger fire-storm. Guerrilla operations from Idjwi resulted in the murder of Tutsi civilians and Hutu "collaborators" in Kibuye, Kigali Rural and Gisenyi.[3] Pre-existing disputes over land, cattle and nationality in North Kivu had fused with the Rwandan conflict and had led to the expulsion of nearly all Congolese Tutsis from the Masisi territory; in Kichanga, more than sixty people lost their lives on June 22 when Congolese and Rwandan Hutus clashed with the "autoch-thonous" Hunde over control of this strategic enclave where thousands of IDPs had taken refuge. In South Kivu, local officials—the governor, district commissioners and Anzuluni Mbembe, who was head of Zaire's transitional parliament in Kinshasa—demanded a census of all Banyamulenge and their property in the province—a barely veiled call for imminent pogroms and expulsions. Tutsi pastors were attacked with bayonets, and goods belonging to Banyamulenge were confiscated or destroyed. NGOs documented the displacement of an estimated 250,000 people, accusing Mobutu's FAZ of working with Hutu extremist militia to cleanse eastern Zaire of unwanted ethnic groups.[4] Back in Rwanda, RPA counter-insurgency operations at Gasake, Giseye and Karago in Gisenyi Prefecture between July 9 and 25 killed at least 100 civilians. On the night of July 9 and during the day on July 10, another search operation in Ruhengeri concentrated on the village of Nyamutera, long a source of recruitment for the FAR. As government troops closed off the area, any sign of people fleeing was taken as an admission of guilt; RPA soldiers shot an estimated sixty to eighty people, before burning the bodies of the deceased—it was only when wounded survivors started piling into local medical centers and health posts set up by Médecins Sans Frontières that reports of the Nyamutera incidents reached the UN.[5] According to US Ambassador Robert Gribbin, in July 1996 alone, 365 people were summarily executed by the RPA.[6]

---

[3] UN Special Rapporteur of the Commission on Human Rights, "Report on the Situation of Human Rights in Rwanda."

[4] Fédération Internationale des Ligues des Droits de l'homme, *Zaïre: forcés de fuir—violence contre les Tutsi au Zaïre*, Paris: Fédération Internationale des Ligues des Droits de l'homme, 1996.

[5] Interview with the investigating officer of the UN Human Rights Field Operation, January 2015.

[6] Robert E. Gribbin, *In the Aftermath of Genocide: The US Role in Rwanda*, Lincoln, NE: iUniverse, 2005, p. 162.

After two years of recovery and reorganization, the senior command of ex-FAR and Interahamwe believed it was ready to scale up from the hit-and-run attacks of *Opération Insecticide*, which were part of its continued psychological warfare against RPF rule. Paul Rwarakabije, who had been a gendarmerie commander in Kigali during the genocide and was part of the reconstituted FAR officer corps, testified that: "We wanted to show that the RPF couldn't govern. We knew people in the interior backed us."[7] The senior leadership proposed a much more extensive, conventional military operation: "We were preparing a big strike in 1996 inside Rwanda."[8] The idea was to carry out a surprise attack, not dissimilar to the one the RPF launched in October 1990 against the Habyarimana government, with troops attacking Gisenyi and Cyangugu from Virunga Park and Nyungwe Forest and raids inside western Rwanda launched from Idjwi Island where a battalion stood ready. While few written documents of these designs for the re-conquest of Rwanda survived the war, at least one eminent scholar confirms these plans and possesses copies of some papers.[9]

Point of No Return: The Final Preparations

As the threat coming out of Zaire intensified, the RPF leadership hastened its own preparations for all-out war. The man selected to lead the operations was James Kabarebe, the formidable 37-year-old head of the Republican Guard and a confidant of Paul Kagame as his former aide-de-camp. Kabarebe was born and raised in Uganda, not as a refugee from the 1959–62 *muyaga*, but as the great-grandson of Rwandan economic migrants to the north. When the Obote regime's xenophobic campaign against the Banyarwanda intensified in 1982, Kabarebe, who attended Makerere University, became a foreigner in his own country and increasingly (re)identified as a Rwandan. Despite playing no major role in the fight against Obote as part of the NRA/M, Kabarebe's sacrifices during the later Rwandan war of liberation—including at the time of the genocide—and his personal loyalty to Kagame ensured a stellar rise through RPF ranks to the position of Republican Guard commander in 1994.[10] His professionalism as a soldier was complemented by hawkish views

---

[7] Interview in Kigali, April 2013.

[8] Ibid.

[9] Reyntjens, *Great African War*, p. 47.

[10] Interviews with senior RPF politicians and leading defense and intelligence cadres, December 2009–December 2014.

on security matters; he emerged as one of the earliest post-1994 advocates of the need to keep on the offensive against the *génocidaires*. In Kabarebe's view, pre-emptive war had become a necessity after Kibeho. Rwandan intelligence estimated that total enemy strength hovered between 80,000 and 100,000 ex-FAR and Interahamwe of which perhaps half were considered serious fighters—a quasi-unstoppable force if they invaded tomorrow: "We risked an even bigger wave of genocidal hatred if we didn't disarm and liberate the camps: the second genocide would finish us off."[11]

Kagame's decision to favor James Kabarebe as force commander for the coming war was rooted in the need to portray the campaign as a Congolese affair—as counseled by the RPF's Pan-Africanist friends. As he did not command any of the regular army brigades and was barely known to people outside the RPF inner circle, putting "James" in charge of the military operation seemed a safer bet than delegating to more well-known RPA officers, such as Kayumba Nyamwasa, Sam Kaka or Karake Karenzi. To further obscure RPF involvement in the AFDL, rebel officials and Rwandan intelligence deliberately misspelled Kabarebe's name throughout the war as James Kabare[12]— because "Kabare" carried quasi-mythical connotations with the memory of a nineteenth-century Tutsi military commander who had been instrumental in guaranteeing freedom of movement and relative peace in what is now eastern Congo prior to the advent of Leopoldian colonialism.[13]

It was Kabarebe who throughout 1996—and with increasing intensity in July, August and September of that year—began convening meetings of the AFDL founding fathers and their international backers on the hilltop of Kimihurura, very close to where Mzee Kabila was residing and a stone's throw away from the RPA mess where officers socialized in the evenings and on weekends. It was there that Kabarebe, with the assistance of ESO chief Patrick Karegeya, laid out the plans of the RPF for Congo and kept them abreast regarding the Ugandan, Eritrean and other Pan-Africanist support for the emerging coalition. As war drew closer and shortly before Kabila was officially designated as the AFDL's spokesman at a Kimihurura meeting, other Rwandan commanders joined in.

[11] Interview in Kigali, April 2013.

[12] Kabare became the name widely—but erroneously—reported by journalists and other observers at the time. For example, even one of the earliest and most authoritative accounts of the war uses it whenever referring to him, see De Villers and Willame, *République démocratique du Congo*.

[13] Interview with Frank Rusagara, Kigali, July 2014.

One of these was Caesar Kayizari, who Kagame appointed as Kabarebe's deputy given his extensive experience in fighting the ex-FAR/Interahamwe after the genocide. Kayizari was born in eastern Rwanda but grew up as an impoverished refugee in Uganda where he managed to assemble funds to study at Makerere University, together with his friend and fellow resident of Lumumba Hall, Theogene Rudasingwa, later Rwanda's first post-genocide ambassador in Washington. Daily harassment by Obote's army and the sense of not being wanted in Uganda pushed Kayizari to join the struggle in 1985. During the 1990–4 Rwandan civil war, he suffered a gunshot wound in the jaw, but somehow managed to extricate himself out of enemy territory into the RPF-controlled zone.[14] Enduring immense pains, Kayizari's courage and sociability ensured his rise into the upper echelons of the officer corps. In May 1995, after the Kibeho debacle, he was appointed brigade commander in south Rwanda, where he witnessed first-hand the rapidly deteriorating security situation in Cyangugu and Nyungwe Forest as well as parts of Gikongoro and Butare. His tough approach to the threat, good relationship with the Ethiopian UN peacekeepers in his sector and grasp of the links between the insurgents and the refugee camps in South Kivu and north Katanga led Kagame to identify him as the perfect complement to Kabarebe's leadership.

Kayizari shared Kabarebe's hawkish views. He advocated a massive pre-emptive strike that would give the RPA the advantage of keeping the war outside Rwanda: "All intelligence showed we were about to be invaded. Rwanda has no strategic depth it can use to defend itself. Mobutu had indirectly declared war on us. We needed to strike first."[15] The former Belgian ambassador to Rwanda, Frank De Coninck, remembers a conversation in September 1996 with Kayizari on the terrace of the legendary Hotel Ibis in Butare, mere weeks before the invasion: "Caesar said to me, 'Listen, it's simple. These guys in the camps need to be disarmed. If you [the international community] don't do it, we will find another solution for the problem.'"[16]

Kabarebe, Kayizari and Karegeya worked around the clock to put the final provisions in place. From late 1994, on the grounds of Gako camp about 50 kilometers south of Kigali, the RPA trained more than 6,000 Congolese Tutsi who had initially been intended as either a self-defense force, an auxiliary arm

---

[14] Interview with Christine Umutoni in Asmara, August 2014.

[15] Interview in April 2013, Kigali.

[16] Interview in Addis Ababa, January 2014.

of the RPA or a future division within the new Rwandan government army.[17] However, as the scenario of a liberation war became the preferred one, the instructors began preparing them as the nucleus of the future AFDL—Congolese units at the heart of the rebellion, but with strong pro-RPF loyalties. Many of the arms for these troops were provided by Ethiopia and Eritrea which sent a plane full of light weapons and grenades to Kigali.[18] Asmara also allowed Kigali to purchase a number of T-55 tanks at a fraction of the international market price and sent trainers to help out in Gako.[19] Kisase Ngandu and his mentors in Ugandan intelligence prepared their own troops, massing at the border to cross into the *Grand Nord* of North Kivu—the area around Beni and Butembo—and the southern parts of Province Orientale; this was intended to be a secondary force that would close off key escape routes for the ex-FAR/Interahamwe and FAZ soldiers who had not been defeated around the refugee camps. They would simultaneously also attack the Ugandan rebel movements hiding in these territories.

Throughout the summer of 1996, hundreds of advance troops—Congolese Tutsi and Rwandan—infiltrated South Kivu, bringing weapons and supplies into presumed safe zones (not least on the Ruzizi Haut Plateau) and fetching intelligence for Kigali; with Caesar Kayizari as brigade commander in charge of Cyangugu Prefecture—the crossroads in and out of Congo and Burundi—there was an unmistakable link with the AFDL's preparations for war. These infiltrations served as an excuse for Hutu extremists, radicalized politicians and Zairian commanders to intensify their persecution of local Tutsi populations and to expel and kill large numbers of innocent civilians.[20] In turn, reports of these atrocities legitimized the increasingly bellicose tone of the RPF in public fora, including its refusal to sign a non-aggression pact between Central African states in Yaoundé. By late September 1996, RPA, FAZ, FAR and AFDL units engaged in worsening skirmishes all along the Congo–Rwanda border zone, with the bulk of the fighting in South Kivu.[21] Despite attempts at formally de-escalating the crisis, including a cease-fire agreed

---

[17] Interviews with James Kabarebe, Kigali, April 2013, and Richard Orth, Washington, DC, February 2015.

[18] Interview with Yemane Kidane in Addis, November 2014.

[19] Interview with Yemane Gebreab in Asmara, March 2015, and with Richard Orth in Washington, February 2015.

[20] Amnesty International, "Amnesty International Condemns Human Rights Violations against Tutsi," September 27, 1996.

[21] Reyntjens, *Great African War*, pp. 45–51.

between Kinshasa and Kigali on September 25, the situation went from bad to worse. Banyamulenge citizens were lynched or executed in cities and villages every day; Zaire accused Rwanda of seeking to destabilize it through ethnic Tutsi militias who crossed over via Burundi; and on October 11, the Zairian army chief, General Eluki Monga Aundu, declared in Goma that his country was at war.[22] Under heavy international pressure, on October 15 Mobutu stated that the Banyamulenge were undeniably Zairian citizens and not foreigners but, as roadblocks appeared in cities like Bukavu to hunt for Tutsis, the RPF concluded once again that the Zairian tyrant was unwilling to reverse course and cease support for the *génocidaires*. On October 18, 1996, the AFDL issued its Lemera Declaration. A war that had already killed several thousands in the preceding weeks now officially began.

Dismantling the Camps

The war which had been two years in the making started with deception. The primary target remained the refugee population. Kabarebe and Kayizari were ordered by the High Command to militarily destroy the enemy bases and bring as many Rwandans back home alive as possible: victory was defined as breaking Mobutu's determination to fight on and returning the population back to Rwanda for the new Kigali government to rule over. This was a massive task and one fraught with dangers. As we saw earlier (see also Map 4), almost forty camps had been set up all along the shores of Lake Kivu around Goma and around Bukavu as well as further inland along the Walikale–Masisi axis in North Kivu, along Lake Tanganyika in South Kivu and even inside Maniema: a huge area. In North Kivu alone, UNHCR estimated there was a total of 718,000 refugees concentrated in Katale (202,000), Kibumba (195,000) and Kahindo (113,000) camps north of Goma and Mugunga (156,000) and Lac Vert (50,000) less than 10 kilometers to the west.[23] Yet whereas the *génocidaire* forces with their heavy artillery, reconfigured command structure and thousands of fighters expected a conventional fight with the RPA on the Zairian–Rwandan border, the plan Kagame, Kabarebe and Kayizari crafted relied on distracting the FAZ and ex-FAR/Interahamwe, only to then attack when their encirclement was complete.

---

[22] UN DHA Integrated Regional Information Network, "Update on the Conflict in South Kivu, Zaire," October 11, 1996.

[23] UN DHA Integrated Regional Information Network, "Zaire: UNHCR Population Statistics as of 26 September 1996," 1996.

The central concept of the operation[24] was for elite RPA troops to bypass the closest camps and to take up positions across North and South Kivu so they could effectively encircle the refugees and enemy troops; sporadic attacks before the main assault would create chaos and a sense that strikes could pierce their ranks from anywhere. Rwandan forces would subsequently shell enemy positions—on the outskirts of the camps and sometimes inside them—but leave an "eastern" corridor out of the encirclement—a road that led back to Rwanda and offered civilians the possibility of going home and combatants of surrendering. Those who tried to make their way north, west or south would thus implicitly confess their guilt and signal continued resistance to the RPF: the mechanism of the corridor would be used as an informational short-cut by Kabarebe's forces to separate enemies from those willing to return. While it is hard to see how any military operation in the refugee camps could have been humane and solved the impossible situation in a just way without significant civilian casualties, the RPA strategy would prove highly effective in some senses and lethally counterproductive in other ways.

According to James Kabarebe,[25] the High Command originally estimated that the operations to liberate the camps would take about a month, but they were completed in two weeks—a stunning success in the short-term that owed much to the surprising weakness of the FAZ, the RPA strategy of choosing the battlefield (the terrain handed a big advantage to whoever struck first) and overwhelming the ex-FAR/Interahamwe from the onset, a maneuver Kagame's troops excelled at and its enemies hated. In North Kivu, the force led by Kabarebe bypassed the three biggest camps north of Goma—Kibumba, Katale and Kahindo—which drew ex-FAR troops out in pitched battles that were largely fought outside the camps—and hence generated unexpectedly low casualties.[26] However, because the encirclement was not complete, the vast majority of refugees headed to the camp of Mugunga in the west. It was there that the genocidal forces of Augustin Bizimungu were headquartered: hundreds of thousands of people congregated, including new arrivals from South

---

[24] Interviews with James Kabarebe, Caesar Kayizari and Jack Nziza, April 2013, July 2014.

[25] Interview in Kigali, April 2013.

[26] This was confirmed by interviews with Rwandan refugees who were in the North Kivu camps and who observed deaths and injuries attributable to general fighting and shelling, but no generalized targeting of the civilian population. The experience of those who trekked westwards, however, would quickly be different.

Kivu, chased by the advance of Kayizari's forces. This is James Kabarebe's own description of what happened:

> We deployed forces in Mushaki, beyond Mugunga. We dislodged ex-FAR there and those fighters fled into the camp. I personally led the Mugunga operation—it took one day to conquer all hills surrounding the camp with a battalion of about 1,000 troops. When we entered, it was total chaos. People were scared, disorganized, we could do what we liked. Once the first people started going back after we told them to move in the direction of Rwanda, the entire mass followed them. It was crazy. We did not fire a single shot in Mugunga camp. I moved in with my escorts, walking around. No one touched us. People walked towards Rwanda.[27]

Hundreds of thousands of people, the very same masses who had left Rwanda with everything they could carry as the genocide had come to an end, now lumbered back to the country of their birth. More than fear, it was total confusion that characterized the perplexed, eerily silent masses crossing the border. The blitzkrieg-style shelling of previous days and the subsequent encirclement of the camps paralyzed them. Predictions by ex-FAR/Interahamwe leaders of either an imminent defeat of the RPA or of assured extermination of the Hutu population in case of a victory of Kagame's troops proved unfounded. As noted by Paul Rwarakabije, a senior FAR officer, who led forces in North Kivu: "If they wanted to exterminate us in Mugunga and the other camps, they could have. But they wanted people to go back alive."[28] The rudderless masses, who had suffered two years under the spell of the genocidal leadership, did not know what to do and in total quiet followed the orders of Kabarebe's forces to head in the direction of Rwanda. At one of the border posts, ESO chief Patrick Karegeya stood with Yemane Kidane, the envoy of Meles Zenawi to the AFDL, watching in disbelief as tens of thousands of Rwandans trundled home. No screenings or security checks of any kind took place as the wave of human beings rolled into the interior. Kidane remembers: "I never saw anything like it, I never saw so many people in my life. A sea of people walking, from the morning until the evening time. They walked without stopping, it just kept going on."[29]

About 800,000 Rwandans of all ages and walks of life returned to Rwanda in the following days, weeks and months. To call this a voluntary return is a gross misrepresentation and denial of anti-RPF sentiment; to call this simply a violent, forced return ignores the complexities and trade-offs involved in wresting

[27] Interview in Kigali, April 2013.
[28] Ibid.
[29] Interview in Addis Ababa, November 2014.

191

people from the clutches of a genocidal cabal and its militias. A significant minority of refugees, however, did not head back to their homeland: possibly up to 400,000 Rwandans headed west in the direction of the Congolese rainforest as one camp fell to the AFDL advance after another and the *génocidaire* forces staged a retreat, hoping to fight another day. Thousands of ex-FAR/ Interahamwe broke through the position of Kabarebe's army in the Sake hills, overrunning a small number of RPA units, which enabled them to sneak into the jungle—even if most civilians were shepherded back east by RPA soldiers. The hemorrhage was even worse in South Kivu: tens of thousands of people escaped the advance of Caesar's units, in part because the resistance was more intense, the geography more demanding and rumors of RPA death squads—not exactly dispelled in the eyes of civilians terrified by incessant mortar fire on roads out of Bukavu and Uvira—panicked the refugees.

The events around Bukavu between October 21 and November 3, 1996, were particularly sordid and will probably never be fully understood. The ADI–Kivu, INERA, Kamanyola, Kashusha and Lubarika camps were protected by outer fortifications as well as inner defenses. The command of this sector was in the hands of perhaps the most skilled FAR general, Gratien Kabiligi.[30] It had been Kabiligi—a professional soldier but also an ideological hardliner—who was key in holding the RPA back in the salient around Kigali for almost three months during the genocide; now he faced the same opponent as back in 1994—Caesar Kayizari—and fought him with everything he could muster. Kabiligi's "*no pasaran*"-attitude forced the RPA to use heavy artillery, killing many hundreds of people, including, undoubtedly, large numbers of civilians. As Kayizari's forces finally overran the last lines of defense on November 2, Kabiligi's units, in a final act of defiance, opened fire on Kashusha camp near Bukavu airport. Anti-aircraft guns were used to blaze the tents with fire to cover the *génocidaire* withdrawal and to punish those civilians who had not obeyed earlier orders to retreat with other ex-FAR/ Interahamwe units. According to one Congolese eyewitness, Kabiligi ordered that the wounded and the elderly should be left behind; all infrastructure and material, including buses and petrol supplies, were consumed by a gigantic blaze. Hundreds of people were burned alive.[31]

As ex-FAR/Interahamwe positions were destroyed by the advancing RPA forces and as non-Rwandan AFDL troops increased their operational radius

[30] Interviews on these events with Caesar Kayizari, Kigali, April 2013 and in Ankara, June 2015.

[31] Interview in Butare with Bshimbe Bantuzeko, August 2010.

by establishing control over the entire border region by December 1, 1996, the withdrawal became a de facto collapse of authority, according to interviews conducted in Brussels and Liège with ex-FAR officers still in hiding today.[32] Some ex-FAR/Interahamwe tried to hold their ground and move in parallel with the civilian population that had not been willing to take the RPA corridors to Rwanda—in that sense, they sought to provide protection to a population many of them genuinely believed was at risk of extermination. But others, not least the higher echelons and best troops (including overall FAR commander Augustin Bizimungu, the presumed genocidal mastermind Théoneste Bagosora and Tharcisse Renzaho, the former mayor of Kigali), either melted away into the forest or fled via vehicle or plane to Kisangani, Lubumbashi or Kinshasa. The plan of the *génocidaires* had utterly failed; within two weeks, their dreams of reconquering Rwanda went up in smoke.[33] Once their original positions had been abandoned, these forces were barely able to mount a fight and preferred to run, leaving the Hutu population to fend for itself in the Congolese rainforest against the RPA.

The initial weeks of "Congo's liberation war" were thus by and large dominated by Rwandans, not by the Congolese. The bulk of the fighting and the strategic priorities were unmistakably a reflection of the RPF's most pressing concerns, but it also gave the AFDL and its Congolese political leadership time to prepare for the longer campaign ahead: organizing political rallies in liberated areas; developing a national and international media presence challenging Mobutu; training newly enlisted recruits; and gaining military experience on secondary fronts, away from the fighting with the ex-FAR/Interahamwe. Some Congolese AFDL soldiers did see action in the camps: hundreds of Banyamulenge, many of whom had already been prepared at Gako for two years, accompanied RPA units into the camps, while others were used as storm troops to capture the main towns of the Kivus: Uvira (October 24), Bukavu (October 31), Goma (November 1), Masisi (November 20) and Butembo (November 26).[34] Early victories and the unwillingness of Mobutu's FAZ to put up much resistance—without salaries and without proper supplies (mostly looted by their commanders, if they ever arrived on the frontlines)—boosted the confidence of the AFDL tremendously.

Whereas, in the earliest stages, most analysts thought of the war as a Rwanda–Zaire border conflict or another wave of ethnic cleansing limited to the Kivus,

---

[32] Interviews with "Eugène" and "Jean-Marie," December 2009.

[33] Interview with Paul Rwarakabije, Kigali, April 2013.

[34] Interviews with low-ranking AFDL soldiers in Butare, August 2010.

by the end of 1996 that picture had started to change. The liberation rhetoric of Mzee Kabila, as the movement's spokesman, had to be taken seriously, not least because thousands of youngsters—some barely in their teens—had begun joining AFDL ranks. The charismatic Anselme Masasu Nindaga, one of the AFDL's official founders and a South Kivu native, went from village to village urging the voiceless and unemployed to join the march to Kinshasa. Masasu promised the so-called *kadogo* (little ones) US$100, a gun, food and above all dignity: a hugely successful call to arms that shifted the ethnic (if not the regional) composition of the bulk of AFDL troops and gave it less the aura of a Tutsi force. Rains slowed the AFDL down more than Mobutist resistance; few in number were the observers who did not have a growing sense that major change in Zaire/Congo was imminent when they saw these thousands and thousands of Swahili-speaking youth covering sometimes more than 40 miles in a day on foot.[35] Recalling the description of Belgian Ambassador Frank De Coninck, this truly did seem "something new from the East."[36]

Angola Enters the Ring: The Pan-Africanist Alliance Expands

As the first phase of the war drew to a close, there was renewed discussion among the AFDL's Pan-Africanist supporters about the conflict and the strategy to be pursued. The initial offensive had been a stunning success and resulted in a sharp drop in insecurity inside Rwanda. AFDL troops and foreign auxiliaries (including the UPDF, which had helped complete the capture of North Kivu in late November and which took Bunia in Province Orientale on Christmas Day 1996, together with Congolese forces under André Kisase Ngandu's command) now controlled "a buffer zone of about 800 kilometres long and some 100 kilometres deep ... along the Ugandan, Rwandan and Burundian borders."[37] The "liberation" of this territory was an obvious humiliation to Mobutu, but not yet an existential threat. According to NRM National Political Commissar Kizza Besigye and ESO chief David Pulkol, Museveni in particular still feared a reaction from Paris;[38] in the Francophone media, Kampala was seen as the spider in the web, using Rwandan and Congolese proxies to push back the Francophonie.[39] Both Rwanda and

---

[35] Stearns, *Dancing in the Glory of Monsters*, pp. 120–2.

[36] Interview in Rome, June 2009.

[37] Reyntjens, *Great African War*, p. 55.

[38] Interviews in Kampala, March–April 2013.

[39] Asteris C. Huliaras, "The 'Anglosaxon Conspiracy': French Perceptions of the Great Lakes Crisis," *Journal of Modern African Studies*, 36, 4 (1998).

Uganda, incredulously, kept issuing public denials of any involvement in what had become widely (if mistakenly) known as the "Banyamulenge rebellion," a term that the AFDL's Rwandan commanders also kept using in order to create confusion.[40] Even if these statements persuaded few veteran observers, they helped forestall a possible UN-mandated intervention into Zaire/Congo under a humanitarian cover. What troubled Museveni and Kagame was the risk of a repeat of France's UN-mandated *Opération Turquoise* that had let the *génocidaires* escape into the Kivus in June–July 1994.

Any doubts that still existed within the coalition about what the end game might look like were superseded by the pace of developments on the ground; Kinshasa remained the ultimate goal. First, UPDF troops took on a more prominent role in combat operations, doing the bulk of the fighting alongside Congolese AFDL units as the entire stretch of border from south of Lake Edward to an area north of Lake Albert was cleared of FAZ troops and Ugandan rebels backed by military-Islamist Khartoum. Secondly, Rwandan intelligence breathed a sigh of relief that the immediate threat to RPF rule had been neutralized but was convinced that the war was far from over; in the analysis of the senior DMI officer tasked with dealing with the *génocidaires* in Congo, Major Jack Nziza, the imperative to pursue the enemy and dislodge his main supporter was still acute: "Despite the liberation of the camps, the center of gravity of the enemy remained, the leadership was intact ... Some of the most dangerous elements escaped us. Mobutu was also organizing and wanted to rearm the Interahamwe."[41] Thirdly and lastly, the reports of Mobutu's forces melting away encouraged the coalition to push for a rapid implosion of the regime. The terrain ahead was tough—hundreds of miles of rainforest and the cities of Kisangani, Mbuji-Mayi and Lubumbashi which the DSP was expected to defend fervently—but the quicker the advance of the AFDL, the more Mobutu's departure would become a self-fulfilling prophecy, as domestic and external supporters would abandon the cancer-stricken ruler.

Angola and the Pan-Africanist Context

To settle his long struggle with Mobutu and all but guarantee the AFDL's military triumph, Nyerere proposed to Kagame and Museveni to enlist a new partner into the alliance. They, in turn, briefed their intelligence chiefs as well as

---

[40] Interview in Ankara, June 2015.
[41] Interview in Kigali, July 2014.

Meles and Issayas.[42] Burundi was too small to make a difference outside South Kivu; South Africa was preoccupied with its own consolidation of democracy; and the Kenya of Daniel arap Moi remained distrusted. Instead, the Mwalimu insisted on Angolan participation: particularly as the battle for Zaire's main cities and the western half of the country drew closer, the heavy artillery of Angola's mechanized brigades was considered invaluable. Moreover, Angola occupied a special place in the imagination of many Pan-Africanists.

It was partially on Angolan soil that one of the greatest causes of Pan-Africanism was achieved—the defeat of Apartheid—as the combination of Soviet-backed Angolan government forces and thousands of Cuban soldiers routed South African troops and their rebel allies of the União Nacional para a Independência Total de Angola (UNITA). This happened most famously in the Battle of Cuito Cuanavale, the greatest military confrontation in Africa since World War II, fought by thousands of belligerents between September 1987 and March 1988: it was in Cuito Cuanavale that the image of Pretoria's martial superiority was shattered, triggering the withdrawal of the South Africa Defense Force from Angola and decisively shifting the balance of power in the region. Less than two years later, Madiba was released from prison; the politico-military machine of Apartheid started falling apart. In the words of Nelson Mandela himself, Cuito Cuanavale was "a turning point for the liberation of our continent and my people."[43]

Since Angolan independence from Portugal in 1975, Pretoria had maintained hostile relations with the Movimento Popular de Libertação de Angola (MPLA) of President Agostinho Neto (1975–9) and José Eduardo dos Santos (in power since 1979). The MPLA's Marxist–Leninist ideology, its alliance with Moscow and its ties with Apartheid's nemesis, the African National Congress (ANC), set it on a collision course with John Vorster and P.W. Botha: the latter in particular pursued a policy of creating a "cordon sanitaire" in the Southern African region to protect white-minority rule at home through proxy regimes that resisted the ANC's and the Dar es Salaam-based Frontline States alliance's attempts to expunge Apartheid.[44] To this end, Pretoria fought leftist nationalists in Mozambique, Rhodesia/Zimbabwe (a settler regime until 1979) and South West Africa/Namibia (formally occupied by South

---

[42] Interview with David Pulkol in Kampala, March 2013.

[43] Vladimir Shubin, *The Hot Cold War: The USSR in Southern Africa*, London: Pluto Press, 2008, p. 105.

[44] James Barber and John Barratt, *South Africa's Foreign Policy: The Search for Status and Security, 1945–1988*, Cambridge: Cambridge University Press, 1990.

Africa until 1990). Nowhere was military confrontation of this type more intense—due to extensive American, Cuban and Soviet involvement—than in Angola.[45] South Africa's most important ally there, UNITA, led by the charismatic Jonas Savimbi, drew maximum benefit from the Cold War logic to build a daunting war machine and offer an alternative vision of regional relations, nation-building and economic development.[46] While a highly opportunistic movement that changed its ideological discourse depending on the political weather, the tens of thousands of troops under its command, its control of most of the Angolan countryside and its financial entanglement with Mobutu's Zaire (not least through the diamond trade) made it a formidable enemy. By contrast, the MPLA state was effectively limited to coastal enclaves and was "incapable of performing a host of sovereign functions."[47]

The war between the MPLA and UNITA survived the Cold War's demise. The failure of the 1992 elections to bring peace led to a resumption of the conflict during which the MPLA state was no more than an archipelago of cities and towns as UNITA effectively denied the government control of three-quarters of Angola. While the drying up of South African and American support left UNITA reliant on revenue from its lucrative diamond smuggling operations, the end of the Soviet and Cuban presence rendered the MPLA more than ever dependent on petrodollars from offshore oil exploitation. Tens of thousands of people died in the renewed fighting until a peace process—the Lusaka Protocol (1994)—froze the battle lines and heralded an uneasy twilight period, with an enhanced role for the UN.[48] Both the government and the rebels rearmed, each distrusting the commitment of the other to a negotiated final solution.

Particularly troublesome, from the MPLA's point of view, were the enduring ties between UNITA and Angola's neighbors. Zambia entertained an ambiguous relationship with Dos Santos and Savimbi. On the one hand, Zambian President Kenneth Kaunda (1964–91) had always supported the ANC's struggle and hosted its leadership in Lusaka, as well as numerous train-

[45] Piero Gleijeses, "Moscow's Proxy? Cuba and Africa, 1975–1988," *Journal of Cold War Studies*, 8, 4 (2006).

[46] Justin Pearce, "Control, Politics and Identity in the Angolan Civil War," *African Affairs*, 111, 444 (2012).

[47] Ricardo Soares de Oliveira, "Illiberal Peacebuilding in Angola," *Journal of Modern African Studies*, 49, 2 (2011), pp. 290–1.

[48] Norrie MacQueen, "Peacekeeping by Attrition: The United Nations in Angola," *Journal of Modern African Studies*, 36, 3 (1998).

ing camps for ANC fighters and the military wing of the MPLA, the Forças Armadas Populares de Libertação de Angola (FAPLA). On the other hand, many post-1991 Zambian security officials and politicians had also developed close business links with UNITA, and Savimbi had many friends in the country, where he lived for years. Tensions between Luanda and Lusaka took on a bellicose tone. Bomb explosions on Zambian territory were followed by warnings from the Angolan ambassador to Zambia, Emanuelle Augusto, that Luanda did not tolerate hostile, pro-UNITA regimes in Brazzaville and Kinshasa and would not tolerate them in Lusaka either.[49]

However, the most tumultuous regional relationship was with Zaire. Among Angolan Cold Warriors, Mobutu, who built his international reputation on a self-declared struggle against tropical communism, had been a long-hated figure. Zaire had invaded Angola in the early 1970s. It supported yet another Angolan insurgent group, the Frente Nacional de Libertação de Angola (FNLA) of Holden Roberto, and had been a crucial partner of Washington and Pretoria in assisting UNITA offensives. In response, FAPLA units crossed into Zairian territory to pursue UNITA assailants and the MPLA lent extensive backing to the Shaba rebellions in Katanga in 1977 and 1978. In the late 1980s, as the Cold War ended and the New York Agreements changed the geopolitical equation in Angola, Mobutu had briefly desired pragmatic rapprochement with Luanda; he organized the Gbadolite summit during which the Zairian president hosted Dos Santos and Savimbi in the hope of bringing stability to his southern border. But the unmistakable immersion of Mobutu's clients in diamond smuggling throughout the 1990s—UNITA's life-line, with Kinshasa as the marketplace where UNITA representatives could freely meet Lebanese, Israeli and Western diamond traders—infuriated Dos Santos and his generals.

Killing the Wounded Animal: The MPLA Joins the War Effort

When Julius Nyerere began notifying old friends in the MPLA (Tanzania had hosted training camps for Angolans to fight Portuguese colonialism and shared Luanda's loathing of Apartheid and Mobutu), he found them extremely receptive to the idea of a regional coalition supporting a Congolese liberation movement to oust the ageing dictator. While one prominent scholar claims Nyerere's outreach to Dos Santos to join the alliance had already occurred

[49] Anthony Mukwita, "Relations with Zambia Not So Cordial," Inter Press Service, March 6, 1998.

back in 1995,[50] evidence in support of this assertion has not been forthcoming in documents or interviews. What senior Angolan military and diplomatic officials did reveal was an informal military agreement brokered between Angola and the AFDL allies that led to the Angolan army playing a prominent role only from early 1997 onwards.

The then head of Angola's military intelligence, Lieutenant-Colonel Mario Placido Cirilo de Sa "Ita," was particularly candid: as the RPF and NRA/M finalized preparations for the offensive, Museveni and Kagame flew to Luanda in an Angolan military aircraft in the summer of 1996 to discuss their plans—another sign that this was not a war that was meant to remain limited to security operations in eastern Zaire.[51] Dos Santos, Kagame and Museveni were joined by several aides who would mold the Rwandan–Angolan relationship over the next two years: Patrick Karegeya, head of Rwanda's External Security Organization; Colonel Joseph Karemera, minister of education and later Rwanda's ambassador to South Africa; Lieutenant-Colonel Ita; General Kopalipa, Luanda's top security chief; General Miala, head of Angola's External Intelligence Services; and Miguel Neto, Dos Santos's roving diplomatic envoy for the Great Lakes. A joint decision was taken that the AFDL and its foreign backers would keep the MPLA abreast of the campaign against Mobutu but that no immediate Angolan military assistance would be forthcoming, even if a bigger future role remained a probable option to all parties around the table.

Angola's choice to play a cautious, discreet role in the liberation of Zaire was not coincidental. The MPLA had long distrusted external forays, was not an enthusiastic practitioner of regional diplomacy and continuously proclaimed sovereignty to be a cardinal principle of international relations. Its focus was mainly on UNITA and a possible resumption of the civil war; distractions from this agenda appeared dangerous, especially because the MPLA remained unsure of the extent to which the United States would tolerate an anti-Mobutu campaign and how strong the Gbadolite-based ruler really remained. Much better then, in the assessment of the senior leadership, to wait and see in the conflict's initial stages and keep all options open.[52]

This calculation changed as the first phase of the war ended in late 1996, following the creation of the 800-kilometer long and 100-kilometer deep

---

[50] Prunier, *From Genocide to Continental War*, p. 67.
[51] Interview with General Ita, Luanda, May 2014.
[52] Ibid.

"buffer zone" between Zaire, Rwanda and Uganda. The spontaneous dissolution of FAZ units as the AFDL advanced boosted the voice of those in Luanda advocating for Angola to join the coalition in quickly killing the wounded animal that was the Mobutist regime: not only would this remove a historical foe at a relatively low cost but it would also ensure the MPLA had a seat at the table when the post-Mobutu order was put together, which was important for safeguarding Angolan political and security interests. Betting on what seemed like a winning horse would help lock in the gains of Mobutu's removal, whereas staying out risked letting others set Kinshasa's new priorities. From December 1996 onwards, Soviet-manufactured transport aircraft flew into Kigali with heavy material as well as specialized units of the Forças Armadas Angolanas (FAA, the rebaptized FAPLA)—engineers, technicians, intelligence officers, rather than ordinary foot soldiers. Within weeks of the airlift commencing, Angola became the second biggest foreign contributor, after Rwanda but before Uganda and Eritrea, to the war effort. However, the FAA refrained from directly attacking Zaire from its own territory to keep its role covert as long as possible and not to give UNITA an excuse to restart the Angolan civil war. Regime change was best advanced, in this analysis, through the mechanism of the AFDL: "We wanted Kabila to take power, not the MPLA."[53]

While Angola's contribution to the conflict was managed from Luanda by General Kopelipa and General Miala, two extremely influential confidants of President Dos Santos, their on-the-ground representative was military intelligence chief Ita, whose long service to the MPLA and good command of English made him a logical choice. As the head of reconnaissance for FAPLA back in 1988, Ita had had the distinct pleasure of announcing to the international media that all South African troops had withdrawn from Angolan territory following the battle at Cuito Cuanavale.[54] Moreover, after nearly a decade as head of military intelligence, Ita had been closely involved in mapping the use of Zairian airstrips and other infrastructure by UNITA, crucial for the rebels' resupplying of weapons and ammunitions. He was known as a trusted hawkish presidential adviser who did not believe in a peaceful resolution of the conflict with UNITA.[55] His dealings with US intelligence and diplomatic interlocutors during the 1993–4 Lusaka peace talks further

[53] Ibid.

[54] James Brooke, "Angola Confirms Pullout by Pretoria's Forces," *New York Times*, September 1, 1998.

[55] Paul Julian Hare, *Angola's Last Best Chance for Peace*, Washington, DC: United States Institute of Peace Press, 1998, p. 19.

equipped him with highly valued contacts and knowledge of the international context of the AFDL's offensive.

Apart from organizing the on-the-ground logistics of helping the AFDL liberate Congo, Ita had been given two main tasks by the MPLA leadership. The first was to complete a political assessment of the AFDL and its Congolese leaders and to find ways of maximizing Angolan influence within this context: who could be key interlocutors, which Congolese liberators were particularly close to Rwanda, Uganda, Tanzania or any other outside force and how to lock in an anti-UNITA agenda once they reached Kinshasa. His second mission was a more urgent military one: to help the AFDL capture the great city on the Congo River, Kisangani. Kisangani was a place of tremendous historical significance as it was here that in 1883 Henry Morton Stanley had established the first trading post for King Leopold—the start of the colonization of Congo. It was also in Kisangani (formerly Stanleyville) that Lumumba's popularity had peaked and where the Simba Uprising of 1964–5 had reached its climax: the city, founded close to the seven cataracts of Wagenia/Boyoma Falls, had been the stage for the paramount dramas of Congolese history.[56] Mobutu, who was highly cognizant of its symbolism and knew that the fall of Kisangani would entail losing the entire east, therefore proclaimed it to be the site whence his counteroffensive would roll back the AFDL "aggression." FAZ troops were joined by some of the president's best DSP units as well as a multinational mercenary force composed mainly of veterans of Serbia's genocidal campaign in Bosnia and led by Belgian Christian Tavernier (who was one of the *affreux*—the so-called "horrific ones"—who had fought Kabila and his fellow rebels in the 1960s and had remained close to security circles in Paris).[57] Equipped with airpower and plenty of ammunition, the confrontation would seriously test what the AFDL was really worth.[58]

However, the grand battle that was intended to become the conflict's turning point and the iconic image future generations would associate with the AFDL war never materialized. The pace and firepower of the AFDL units proved simply irresistible. Angolan artillery bombardments, RPA encircle-

---

[56] Walter Zinzen, *Kisangani: Verloren Stad*, Leuven: Van Halewyck, 2004.

[57] Stephen Smith, "L'armada de mercenaires au Zaïre: commandés par un belge, 280 'affreux' mènent la contre-offensive," *Libération*, January 24, 1997.

[58] Howard Adelman and Govind C. Rao, *War and Peace in Zaire–Congo: Analyzing and Evaluating Intervention, 1996–1997*, Trenton: Africa World Press, 2004, pp. 154–5.

ment maneuvers and Congolese storm troops, armed by Luanda, caused the Zairean units to disintegrate even before the fighting began. Furthermore, Tavernier's Serbians spoke no French, refused to accept orders from the FAZ command and failed to put their light fighter bombers and Russian Mi-24 helicopters to the destructive use for which they were intended.[59] *Le Léopard*, and his last remaining international friend, France, had gambled and lost. Kisangani fell on March 15, 1997, without serious combat. The end was nigh for Mobutu.

Washington's "Green Light": Limited but Influential US Support for the AFDL

One old ally whose backing the Zairean dictator had lost long before France came to see that Mobutu could no longer be rescued, was, of course, Washington. The brisk development of US–RPF relations, with influential individuals in the State Department and the Pentagon seeing the Front as "the new bull" in Central Africa, had a major impact on the AFDL liberation struggle, as already indicated in Chapter 5. Famously, in August 1996, mere weeks before zero hour, Kagame met with US Secretary of Defense William Perry in Washington. According to almost all RPF sources we spoke to—and according to Ambassador Gribbin[60]—the enthusiastic reception Perry had in store for Kagame was interpreted in Kigali as an American green light for the RPA-led AFDL invasion of Zaire. From September 1996 onwards, the US embassy in Rwanda parroted the RPF's official policy that no Rwandans were involved in the "Banyamulenge rebellion," even though it knew more than any other foreign mission about the extent of RPA involvement in the war. There can be no doubt that Washington approved of military action against the refugee camps in eastern Zaire and concurred with the logic behind dismantling them. It is harder to ascertain when exactly the Clinton administration was informed about the regime change agenda of the Pan-Africanist coalition, but testimonies of the major players indicate it was early on: Bizima Karaha, the rebellion's most important Banyamulenge and later Kabila's foreign minister, testified that "We got a go ahead ... to remove Mobutu on the condition that we were going to respect certain things."[61] Similar statements about

[59] Prunier, *From Genocide to Continental War*, p. 129.
[60] Gribbin, *In the Aftermath of Genocide*, p. 176.
[61] Interview in Goma, December 2009.

Washington's "blessing" of the AFDL, as Moïse Nyarugabo (Kabila's private secretary)[62] and two contemporary RPF ministers put it,[63] were also made by Shé Okitundu (Kabila's key diplomatic adviser), Raphael Ghenda (minister of information from May 1997 onwards) and other protagonists. Even if Gribbin claimed William Perry had told Kagame in August that his empathy with Rwanda's security predicament did not amount to an endorsement of a unilateral strike on Zaire,[64] the AFDL comrades all clearly understood it as such.

Our evidence suggests that Washington did not limit itself to green-lighting the dismantling of the camps and the attempt at ousting Mobutu. According to Mwenze Kongolo (the American–Congolese diaspora returnee who became minister of justice in the post-Mobutu government), Kabila officially encountered Assistant Secretary for State George Moose and NSC Director for African Affairs, Susan Rice, for the first time in Cape Town in February 1997, but had frequently been meeting the CIA bureau chief in Kigali from the start of the rebellion onwards.[65] Kabila's contacts with the Americans were marked by suspicion and anxiety on the part of Mzee,[66] but left Washington with little doubt about the nature of the rebellion, its regional backers and its ambitions. And even though Kabila did not really endear himself to his interlocutors, this did not dampen growing American support for the rebellion.

The Pentagon helped provide aerial reconnaissance and radio intelligence to the RPA, which allowed it to quickly build a comprehensive picture of the weakness of Mobutu's FAZ but also of movements of the ex-FAR/Interahamwe and refugees—with lethal consequences for both.[67] This was particularly effec-

[62] Ibid.

[63] Names withheld at the sources' request, interviews in Kigali, December 2009.

[64] Gribbin, *In the Aftermath of Genocide*, p. 177.

[65] There is a possibility Kongolo was actually referring to Peter Whaley, but even if he confused or identified Whaley with a CIA operative, this remains quite telling; interview in Kinshasa, August 2013.

[66] Didier Kazadi recalls the mixture of distrust and excitement Mzee exuded in the days before and after the meeting with CIA Director George Tenet, US Ambassador to the UN Bill Richardson and US Ambassador to Zaire Daniel Simpson in April 1997 in Lubumbashi; interview in Kinshasa, August 2013.

[67] Interview with a senior UN official who saw the photos and was preoccupied by what they meant for the fleeing refugees. The source requested anonymity, interview in London, May 2015. None of the senior US policy-makers we interviewed for this book denied that the American government did such intelligence gathering over

tive given the Clinton administration's simultaneous efforts at blocking the deployment of a "Multinational Intervention Force" (MNF). The MNF was backed by France and Mobutu's African allies—Cameroon, Morocco, Togo—but was described by Rwandan Ambassador to the UN Gideon Kayinamura as a "second *Opération Turquoise*" intended to let the *génocidaires* once again escape and save the crumbling Mobutu regime.[68] Washington's delaying effectively aborted the MNF proposal. As such, it helped clear the road to Kinshasa for the AFDL, because a last-minute UN or French intervention was the nightmare scenario Kagame, Museveni and Dos Santos worried about.

US diplomatic maneuvering and military assistance to the RPA in a handful of key areas in which the alliance was deficient—training of special forces and high-tech intelligence gathering—made a difference to the campaign. Pentagon officials were also on the ground to observe the AFDL–RPA attack on the camps in North Kivu,[69] and sightings of them at different locations in eastern Congo seem too plentiful to be without basis. We interviewed a senior UN official who clearly recognized one American security official in Kisangani in March 1997, whom he knew personally from previous work in Africa and who appeared to be functioning in an advisory/liaising capacity with the RPA, as part of a dozen-strong US team.[70] However, such assistance does not mean that this was a campaign bankrolled, planned or even driven by the Clinton administration; for all its engagement, Washington actually had little impact on the course of the conflict and the choices made by the comrades who created *faits accomplis* all along the way.

Some branches of the US government provided assistance, but they struggled to shape the AFDL or the RPF and failed to turn them into proxies that would behave predictably, much more so than is recognized in conspiratorial accounts.[71] Several scholars and journalists reported the "decisive" involvement of American "advisers"/mercenaries, with the Pentagon's blessing,[72] and

---

Zaire/Congo and shared it with the RPF. See also Reyntjens's extensive discussion of the US role, Reyntjens, *Great African War*, pp. 66–79.

[68] Interview in Kigali, December 2009.

[69] Name of the source at the Defense Intelligence Agency withheld, interview in Washington, DC, February 2015.

[70] Name of the source withheld; interview in London, May 2015.

[71] See, for instance, Wayne Madsen, *Genocide and Covert Operations in Africa, 1993–1999*, Lewiston, NY: Edwin Mellen Press, 1999.

[72] Jacques Isnard, "Des 'conseillers' américains ont aidé à renverser le régime de M. Mobutu," *Le monde*, August 28, 1997.

the extensive supplying of AFDL troops with high-tech American weaponry through Entebbe and Kigali—the supposed plot being that America's unused arsenal for its operations in Somalia was handed to the UPDF, RPA and AFDL to oust Mobutu.[73] The main problem with such accounts is that they overlook several important historical facts. Rather than US advisers accelerating Mobutu's demise, the campaign would be highly decentralized as the RPA commanders on the ground faced incredible difficulties in liaising and communicating with their comrades—to the point that several units got lost, commanders disappeared for days on end and the AFDL advance units were chronically short of supplies of all kinds.

Moreover, for all the claims about heavy American equipment (lethal or non-lethal) supplied to the alliance, this was an extraordinarily low-tech war: no tanks or air support were used by the RPA/AFDL, hardly any trucks got through and Caesar Kayizari described his elation when the Tigres Katangais made it to the frontlines because they brought Angolan rocket-propelled grenades and machine guns with them;[74] until February–March 1997, his advance force had to make do with basic automatic rifles. Similarly, sightings of US agents "running" the AFDL war—like that of "Tim," a "CIA pilot" flying between Congo, Rwanda and Uganda to resupply frontline troops and evacuate the wounded[75]—turned out to have a rather different explanation: Tim was indeed American, but was actually employed since 1996 by Didier Kazadi, Mzee's chief security adviser. The flights carried out by this pilot were AFDL operations, but often deliberately kept off the radar of the RPA as part of Kabila's attempts at gaining greater autonomy and building political and financial capability for himself.[76]

The comrades were grateful for American support to the AFDL but they were also wary of any undue US influence on their liberation project. Kabila was most obviously ambivalent about cozying up to the Pentagon and State Department, but so were the MPLA and even the RPF. Thus when the Angolan FAA finally began sending supplies and the Tigres Katangais to eastern Zaire via Kigali, both the RPA and FAA tried to hide this important development from the United States.[77] Washington, in turn, maintained its

[73] N'Gbanda, *Ainsi sonne le glas*, pp. 105–11.
[74] Interview in Ankara, June 2015.
[75] Reyntjens, *Great African War*, p. 68.
[76] Interview with Didier Kazadi in Kinshasa, August 2013.
[77] Interview with a senior RPA officer in Kigali, July 2014; interview with Richard Orth in Washington, DC, February 2015.

policy of not selling the RPA or FAA any lethal military equipment—to the frustration of the Rwandans in particular who privately and publicly complained. Moreover, the AFDL partners were gravely irked by the flow of statements by spokesmen for the Clinton administration warning that those responsible for atrocities committed during the campaign would be held to account. Kabila perceived these statements as especially inflammatory because they cast doubts on his credentials as Congo's future leader.[78]

To this day, important questions remain unanswered regarding the extent of Washington's involvement in the AFDL campaign. Much of the confusion clearly stems from the contradictory signals given by different branches of government—a problem plaguing the Clinton administration not just in Congo, but in other African countries too.[79] A combination of improvisation, naïvety and wishful thinking characterized Washington's relationship with the AFDL project which would, as we will see in the next section, seriously limit US policy options vis-à-vis the movement and its quixotic president. Unwittingly, the cumulative effect of the efforts of US policymakers to "engage and influence" was to further strengthen RPF militarism; to help install a new authoritarian leader in Kinshasa; and to sentence thousands in the Congolese rainforest to their deaths. In Reyntjens's words: "the incoherent involvement of the only remaining superpower has generated dynamics of which it insufficiently measured the consequences. In Central Africa like elsewhere, the United States has been an apprentice sorcerer incapable of accompanying a process, which span out of control, with ... disastrous consequences."[80]

The March to Kinshasa: Diverging Priorities and Emerging Fault-lines

As the AFDL continued its advance in the first months of 1997, it was greeted in the liberated towns by teeming crowds who came to see the AFDL leaders. Kabila and Masasu in particular excelled on these occasions: they would pepper their speeches with a mixture of optimistic promises, Mobutu-style jokes (with the punch-line, this time, at the dictator's expense) and calls to arms to

---

[78] For example, "Misgivings about Zairian Rebel—U.S. Believes Laurent Kabila Is No Democrat," *Seattle Times*, May 1, 1997.

[79] William Minter, "America and Africa: Beyond the Double Standard," *Current History*, 99, 637 (2000).

[80] Reyntjens, *Great African War*, p. 79.

youngsters. So many volunteers swelled the ranks that it became impossible for even the commanders to provide—then or today—a definite number of the size of the liberation army: anywhere between 25,000 and 60,000 "fighters" enlisted with the AFDL, though perhaps only 10,000 or so actually led the offensives to take Congo's main cities. With the military campaign going so well—Angolan participation and the fall of Kisangani made victory in the near future a very plausible scenario indeed—a sense of euphoria gripped the victors; the sky seemed the limit and AFDL protagonists began thinking their hopes for the future were already an inevitable reality. However, underneath all the camaraderie and elation, three crucial dynamics of tension emerged, months before the final capture of Kinshasa. One was the continuation of the Rwandan civil war in Congo, which culminated in a blood-soaked hunt by the RPA for ex-FAR/Interahamwe and their presumed refugee associates. A second fault-line pertained to the mounting rivalries among the Congolese liberators about who would call the shots once Mobutu was ejected. And a third and final axis of tension developed between the AFDL's two main foreign backers: Rwanda and Angola. As first Kasai, then Katanga and ultimately Bas Congo fell into AFDL hands, the RPA and FAA became ensnarled in a cold war that nearly led to open conflict near the town of Tshikapa, less than 50 kilometers from the Angolan border, in April 1997. Both Kigali and Luanda saw acquiring decisive influence in the new Kinshasa as vital to their own domestic security equilibrium—and were blinded by their own paradigm to that of the other. The AFDL won Congo, but was already sowing the seeds of its own demise.

Death in the Rainforest

The implosion of any serious resistance against the Pan-Africanist campaign of pursuing regime change was a source of ecstasy for many Congolese who, for the first time in decades, cautiously imagined a political landscape that was not utterly dominated by Mobutu Sese Seko. For the RPA, the approaching demise of Mobutu heralded the likelihood of a more stable, predictable security environment in the medium to long term, but the pressing short-term concern of the *génocidaire* forces reconstituting themselves remained. The walk-over against the FAZ meant that RPA troops and special units of the DMI could focus on hunting down the remnants of the exiled population—an estimated 300,000 to 400,000 people who did not head home as Kabarebe and Kayizari, commander and deputy commander of the RPA in Zaire/Congo, dismantled the refugee camps.

As mentioned earlier, the RPF High Command had come to a consensus that a failure to return and a continued attempt at escaping RPA forces was an admission of genocidal guilt: fleeing westwards was used as an informational short-cut for where one's allegiances lay. The official policy remained to bring as many people as possible back safely to Rwanda—in some cases to face trial, in other cases to "emancipate" them from "genocidal thinking" as "ideological hostages". The UN special rapporteur for Rwanda, René Degni-Ségui, confirmed that the first phase of return was remarkably peaceful: "Few cases of deaths or killings were reported during repatriation. By 6 December 1996, the Human Rights Operation in Rwanda had received confirmation of 12 deaths. Those deaths are, of course, to be deplored, but the number, relative to the total of 600,000 returnees, was lower than had been feared."[81] According to Caesar Kayizari: "We even had soldiers dying of cholera and diarrhea because they worked with sick Hutus, carrying them on their backs. We wanted to save our people."[82] Yet for those who did not accept this "assisted" return, another fate lay in store.

Based on dozens of interviews with the RPA leadership, with their AFDL allies and with UN eyewitnesses at killing sites like Ubundu in Province Orientale, we feel confident in asserting that instructions were given from the very top to the frontline troops and the special forces to extinguish the *génocidaire* menace to the country, by any means. What began happening from December 1996 onwards—escalating in March and April 1997—was a ferocious campaign to "neutralize" all possible enemies—in effect a license to kill large numbers of people, even if they were infants, elderly, famished or sick. And this is precisely what happened, from Shabunda and Tingi-Tingi to Boende and Mbandaka.

Despite the secrecy surrounding the disappearance of tens of thousands of Rwandans in the forest between November 1996 and May 1997, extensive efforts at documenting the horrors of this retribution campaign have been undertaken by survivors, eyewitnesses and international organizations.[83] And

---

[81] UN Special Rapporteur of the Commission on Human Rights, "Report on the Situation of Human Rights in Rwanda," p. 37.

[82] Interview in Kigali, April 2013.

[83] Amnesty International, "Deadly Alliances in Congolese Forests," London: Amnesty International, 1997; Emizet N.F. Kisangani, "The Massacre of Refugees in Congo: A Case of UN Peacekeeping Failure and International Law," *Journal of Modern African Studies*, 38, 2 (2000); Human Rights Watch, "Attacked by All Sides: Civilians and the War in Eastern Zaire," New York: Human Rights Watch, 1997; Médecins sans Frontières, "Forced Flight: A Brutal Strategy of Elimination in Eastern Zaire,"

while it is true, as the RPF publicly retorts, that much of the evidence is sketchy, incomplete and sometimes internally contradictory, there can be no doubt as to the overall pattern of violence and the order of magnitude of these crimes against humanity. Refugees were strangled, their skulls were bashed in, they were bayonetted, hacked to death or shot. It is impossible to provide a single number of people murdered, but the death toll, in all likelihood, totals six digits. The opaqueness of the massacres and the decentralized nature of the way the RPA waged war in Congo (with extraordinary autonomy for field commanders because of logistical and communication difficulties) has made it notoriously hard to identify the individuals responsible for these crimes. Nevertheless, scholars such as Filip Reyntjens and organizations like Human Rights Watch have put forward evidence that implicates Force Commander James Kabarebe, Jack Nziza of the DMI and RPA field commander Godfrey Kabanda as well as a range of other RPA officers often only known by their first names or *noms de guerre*—Wilson, David, Richard, and so on.[84]

According to statistics from July 1997 provided to us by Filippo Grandi, the field coordinator of the UNHCR in Congo who traveled in parallel to the AFDL and who remains convinced that these imperfect estimates[85] are the best

---

Geneva: MSF, 1997; Pierre-Claver Ndacyayisenga, *Voyage à travers la mort: Le témoignage d'un exilé Hutu du Rwanda*, Montréal: Groupe Ville-Marie Littérature, 2012; Marie Béatrice Umutesi, *Surviving the Slaughter: The Ordeal of a Rwandan Refugee in Zaire*, Madison: University of Wisconsin Press, 2004; United Nations Commission on Human Rights, "Report on the Situation of Human Rights in Zaire," New York: UNCHR, 1997; United Nations Security Council, "Report of the Investigative Team Charged with Investigating Serious Violations of Human Rights and International Humanitarian Law in the Democratic Republic of Congo," New York: UNSC, 1998.

[84] Human Rights Watch, "What Kabila Is Hiding: Civilian Killing and Impunity in Congo," New York: Human Rights Watch, 1997, pp. 40–6; Reyntjens, *Great African War*, pp. 80–99.

[85] Official registration numbers in eastern Zaire before and after the return from Mugunga may be inflated or deflated for a number of reasons including a desire not to be identified, refugees registering multiple times to receive more rations, and so forth. Grandi, however, is very confident that the numbers of people repatriated from Congo through trucking operations and air-lifts is accurate, as every single individual was counted by the UNHCR. Note that the original registration numbers and those after the operations in Mugunga almost certainly comprise high numbers of Interahamwe.

available, more than a quarter-of-a-million people remained unaccounted for (see Table 6.1). This certainly does not mean that all these Rwandans were murdered: tens of thousands reached neighboring Congo-Brazzaville, Central African Republic, Zambia and Angola, while unknown numbers of others stayed in Zaire/Congo (unlikely to be less than 30,000) but escaped the AFDL–RPA whether through peaceful integration with local communities or by hiding to fight another day in Rwanda (see Chapter 9). Many thousands of refugees also starved or succumbed to infections on the road or in the forest.

Table 6.1: Refugees in Zaire and Returnees to Rwanda in 1996–7

Description	Total Number of People
Officially registered refugees with UNHCR in the refugee camps in eastern Zaire	1,100,000
Mass return from Mugunga[86]	600,000
Repatriated through trucking operations from North and South Kivu after December 1996	180,000
Repatriated through air-lift from Province Orientale and Equateur, April–June 1997	54,000
Refugees unaccounted for	266,000

The RPF has never categorically denied that "excesses" took place and that many people, including civilians, died in the rainforest—whether of hunger and disease on their march fleeing the AFDL advance, or during combat, the shelling of make-shift camps or executions. As early as 1997, Paul Kagame recognized that killings happened, but denied that this was systematic policy; moreover, he offered an alternative reading of the murders in Congo: "These are not genuine refugees. They're simply fugitives, people running away from justice after killing people in Rwanda—after killing! They were still killing."[87] Two decades on, RPA commanders still officially maintain this position and highlight that it was impossible for Kigali to oversee the actions of units who operated with great autonomy deep inside Congo; however, they also provide

[86] Though not all refugees in eastern Zaire that returned to Rwanda in November 1996 came from Mugunga, most did, because, as mentioned earlier in the chapter, as the RPA onslaught began, almost all those staying in North Kivu headed to Mugunga as the RPA overran the camps closer to the border and closed off alternative escape routes.

[87] Philip Gourevitch, "Continental Shift," *The New Yorker*, August 4, 1997.

more context and recognize that Minister of Defense Kagame was kept in the loop about all "issues of strategic importance," including the "*génocidaire* menace." Caesar Kayizari tried to explain the fiendishly risky and impossible mission he was given regarding the refugees:

"Bring them back" had tragic choices. We knew damage was inevitable but our situation was not exactly a normal one ... Rwanda has never denied excesses might have occurred because of command and control issues. Revenge killings happened, yes ... These guys were not seeing the images you and I see now. [During the genocide], they saw the bodies, fresh bodies. Can you blame them for taking revenge when this [was] done by their neighbors, people they knew? That is war.[88]

Jack Nziza of the Directorate for Military Intelligence also testified as to why "excesses" happened: "People fleeing to the forest, so many of them ... Military and civilian were mixed. But everybody had more or less been militarized. There was no demarcation between them. There was also no command structure."[89] He categorically rejected, however, that this was, in any way, part of an effort to exterminate a population implacably hostile to the RPF: "There is no way we could have reached Kinshasa in seven months if we had tried to kill everybody. Our force was too small and we were on foot."[90] Similar statements (and private admissions of large-scale killing) were made by other senior members of the RPF and RPA in a range of interviews.

One particularly important informant, François, a special forces operative who still loyally works for the RPF but whose real name is changed here to protect his identity, detailed the existence of a separate, specialized unit within the RPA that was tasked with the hunt for *génocidaires* and *génocidaire* sympathizers across Central Africa. Advanced training for these commandos was provided by Israel (in 1995) and the United States (in 1996), according to François, even if neither the Israeli nor the American trainers knew what exactly these troops were to be used for. The *Washington Post* reported in 1998 that

from July 17 to Aug. 30 [1996], a U.S. Army Special Forces team from Fort Bragg instructed Rwandan army soldiers in small-unit leader training, rifle marksmanship, first aid, land navigation and tactical skills, such as patrolling ... Rwandans studied camouflage techniques, small-unit movement, troop-leading procedures, soldier-team development, rappelling, mountaineering, marksmanship, weapon maintenance and day and night navigation.[91]

[88] Interview in Kigali, April 2013.
[89] Interview in Kigali, July 2014.
[90] Ibid.
[91] Lynne Duke, "U.S. Faces Surprise, Dilemma in Africa," *Washington Post*, July 14, 1998.

Upon the return of the commandos to Kigali, newly arrived US Defense Attaché to Rwanda Richard Orth was told by Kagame himself that "we'll keep them together and put them to good use."[92] Their real purpose was kept secret.

While the AFDL campaign was ongoing, the special unit would travel around Congo, operating both behind enemy lines and in liberated territory, but would also be on stand-by to travel abroad to apprehend or neutralize suspects.[93] Between September 1996 and May 1997, missions took place in Cameroon, Gabon, Congo-Brazzaville and Southern Sudan.[94] François himself headed an eight-man team that traveled around the nebulous border zone of Congo, Sudan and Central African Republic with operations taking place in Aba, Bangassou, Doruma, Garamba, Kaye, Yambio and Yei. The formidably tough terrain—dense forests, sweltering temperatures, steep climbs—was partly overcome with vital logistical support by Ugandan intelligence and SPLA commanders. Asked to estimate the number of presumed Interahamwe liquidated during all these missions, François refused a direct answer: "Many. Just many."[95] François accepts that such assassinations contravened international law and that they ended up killing unarmed civilians as well as Interahamwe, but he points to a context of "total war" in which the RPF was trying to secure its survival and that of the Tutsi population against a genocidal opponent. Its ruthless strategy was intended to ensure "we would not have to fight again, at a time that suited us less."[96]

The continuation of the Rwandan civil war had important political consequences for the AFDL as a liberation movement. The RPA's preoccupation with the fleeing Hutus did not slow down the AFDL's advance; the routes taken by James's brigades (a "northern" advance from Goma and Walikale to Kisangani, through the forest, to Bumba and Mbandaka in Equateur) and those commanded by Caesar (a "southern" march from Bukavu and Kindu into Kasai, Katanga and Bandundu) were strongly oriented vis-à-vis ex-FAR and refugee movements but also coincided with a logical military approach towards Mobutu's equatorial stronghold, the key mining areas around Mbuji-Mayi and Lubumbashi and ultimately Kinshasa. The real upshot of the RPA obsession with refugees was political: for all its commitment at meetings with Pan-Africanist leaders to organizationally and ideologically deepen the AFDL,

---

[92] Interview in Washington, DC, February 2015.
[93] Interview in Kigali, July 2014.
[94] Interview in Kigali, December 2009.
[95] Interview in Kigali, July 2014.
[96] Ibid.

immense energy was spent on matters other than consolidating the alliance with its Congolese comrades and other foreign comrades. Despite the glaring fragility of this "Congolese" liberation front, the RPA was happy to exploit its inability to stand on its own feet to pursue Rwanda's own military objectives. As would become clear after the fall of Kinshasa, this was a decision with disastrous consequences: the organizational weakness of the AFDL would become a major security menace in its own right. However, the conviction of Kagame, Kabarebe and other RPA leaders was that letting the *génocidaire* enemy escape would contravene the very purpose of the intervention in the first place.

A second problem emanating from the ongoing Rwandan civil war was situated predominantly on the Congolese side of the AFDL equation. The AFDL's "founding fathers" were naturally aware that it was the convergence of their dream of ousting Mobutu with Rwanda's post-genocide security predicament that had brought the RPF on board and that had caused it to commit six brigades to the war effort—the decisive input that was about to secure victory. Direct communications by the RPF leadership and waging war on the side of the RPA had given them first-hand insights into the Front's number one priority. But the RPF's allies, no matter how much violence they themselves had engaged in over the years, were still stunned by the ferocity with which the RPA hunted down ex-FAR/Interahamwe and civilian refugees alike. Within the AFDL a kind of *omertà* was observed regarding the "excesses" of their Rwandan allies; everybody knew that something deeply troublesome was happening, but few bothered to find out more details. Those involved in operations with RPA units—like Faustin Munene who advanced with them at Tingi-Tingi and Kisangani—enjoyed the camaraderie but remained tight-lipped throughout the campaign about what their comrades did. But in interviews conducted between 2009 and 2014 many expressed their disgust, regardless of whether they would currently consider themselves RPF allies or not.

Rwanda's Eritrean and Ethiopian friends—Yemane Gebreab, Haile Menkerios and Yemane Kidane of the Pan-Africanist team for political *encadrement* of the AFDL—contacted Issayas and Meles back home when they understood what was happening in the forest. Their own experience in fighting a "total war" meant that the "excesses" were far from unrecognizable. "I don't know what happened in the forest, but we could guess," said Yemane Kidane, the chief Ethiopian envoy to the AFDL who traveled with Kabila.[97] The Angolan head of military intelligence, Ita, was in a similar,

---

[97] Interview in Addis, November 2014.

uncomfortable situation of not wanting to withdraw support for the AFDL, but sensed the danger presented by the RPA's clandestine operations to the reputation of the liberation campaign. Raising the issue of these missions, which after a while seemed to serve no military point to him, he questioned his Rwandan peers about their intentions: "We asked them several times. What is the goal? Kinshasa is there. The reason is because they wanted to kill these people."[98] Shé Okitundu, one of Kabila's close advisers and who after the fall of Mobutu would handle the dossier of the massacres for the Congolese government, remembered his awkward discussions with Kabila and Kabarebe on the subject: "James was physically present during the killings in Equateur ... They did what they could not to involve us in Mbandaka."[99] It is important to underline that Okitundu offered this testimony not as a post-factum kick in the teeth but that he actually tried to empathize with their policy, much as he disagreed with it: "The war in the east was not and is not about natural resources. It's about security ... The security of the Tutsi is the heart of the Eastern Question."[100]

As had been the case in eastern Zaire, it was only after the AFDL's storm troops—often RPA units—had captured a town that Kabila and other Congolese politicians would move in to announce the blessings of the revolution. But with increasing frequency, local populations would question them about the horrendous stories of Rwandans killing Rwandans and abuse of Zairian citizens at the hands of the foreign backers of the AFDL as well as the retreating ex-FAR/Interahamwe; some of this was intermingled with decades-old anti-Tutsi prejudice (often expressed in heinous jokes about Tutsi deviousness and secret assassinations), but many were genuinely expressing outrage at the slaughter of what seemed to be innocent civilians. This was particularly the case in North Kivu, Province Orientale and Equateur. Mzee instinctively understood the cloud these actions were casting over his nationalist credentials: the first impression of the revolution of a significant number of Congolese, happy as they were to be rid of Mobutu, was that it appeared to be a cover for a Rwandan/Tutsi revenge campaign in Zaire or outright takeover of the country. In response, Kabila sought to silence discussion and assuage fears. By all accounts, this was totally ineffective but he and other Congolese

---

[98] Interview in Luanda, May 2014.

[99] Interview in Kinshasa, August 2013.

[100] Ibid.

[100] Prunier, *From Genocide to Continental War*, pp. 124, 31; Reyntjens, *Great African War*, pp. 107–8.

AFDL leaders could do little else. Given how tight control of their personal security by the RPA was (nigh-all bodyguards appointed to them were Rwandan or Congolese Tutsi trained in Rwanda), turning this into an issue with Kabarebe was not an option. They quietly hoped the matter would go away and that an anxious outside world and the Congolese people would forget about the killings. But as liberation drew ever closer, and after the fall of Mobutu, the dossier came back to haunt the AFDL, and especially Kabila.

The Rise of the "Famille Katangaise": The AFDL's Changing Composition

Although the official AFDL founding fathers—Bugera, Kabila, Kisase Ngandu and Masasu—had profiles that connected them to different constituencies in the Congolese population, neither they nor the movement as a whole could plausibly claim to be representing the entire nation. The AFDL was above all a movement of easterners and, within that category, of Congolese Tutsi—it was they who provided the bulk of the fighters and the early cadres. Gradually, the balance changed as Kisase brought in fighters through his Ugandan connection, Masasu recruited the *kadogo*, and Kabila enlisted his "friends and pals," who mainly came from the North American and European diaspora. This shift deepened as Kinshasa beckoned, increasing uncertainty and tension within the AFDL.

The four chief comrades shared little, whether in terms of political experience, age, regional background or vision for Zaire/Congo. Beyond a vague ideological commitment to revolutionary change and Pan-Africanist principles to be implemented in post-Mobutu Congo, what united them was the fact that Nyerere, Museveni and Kagame had brought them together to front the AFDL, first in Kigali and then in Goma. This meant that collaboration between them was difficult and that each man looked after his own interests, those of his key constituency and those of his key external ally. Any changes in the composition of the fighting force, corps of cadres and external backing of the movement would therefore affect the relative weight of a specific founding father in the alliance and his ability to shape the AFDL in line with his vision and interests.

Of the four, Kisase's role wilted the quickest. Kisase was the one least comfortable with the huge external dimension to the liberation of his homeland and maintained an arm's length relationship with his Ugandan patrons. At several instances he argued with James and other Rwandan commanders, frustrated at being excluded from strategic decisions and actual military operations, but also complaining about the suspected asset-stripping by RPA soldiers in Congolese cities, as vehicles, generators and valuable furniture were transported to Rwanda. The two most authoritative accounts of the war[101] allege that Kisase, for this reason, was lethally ambushed by RPA hitmen on January 7, 1997—a move condoned by Kabila. The RPA has always denied any involvement in the killing; Kayizari (who was himself ambushed, unsuccessfully, several times in South Kivu) suggested he was actually the most respected of the four Congolese AFDL bosses because of his martial credentials: "He was at least a tough fighter. I liked him better."[102] Interviewed extensively, most Congolese protagonists of the AFDL, regardless of whether they later fell out with the RPF or not, made no accusations implicating Rwanda nor did they wish to discuss the matter much. There were, however, four important exceptions: Mutomb Tshibal,[103] a refugee recruited by Kisase in Uganda who used to travel with him during the campaign and last saw him with Rwandan officers who were supposed to be providing his security at the time of his death; Lunda Bululu,[104] a former prime minister of Mobutu's who was in Kinshasa at the time of the killing but would later ally with the RPF against Kabila (i.e., certainly not a rabid anti-Rwandan); Shé Okitundu,[105] Kabila's foreign policy adviser who did not form part of the AFDL advance in eastern Congo; and Godefroid Tchamlesso,[106] a pro-Cuban adviser to Kabila who distrusted the RPF from the start. None of them provided any specific evidence on the exact circumstances of Kisase's assassination on the Goma–Beni road, but they pointed to an obvious motive for the killing. All cited the logic of liquidating an openly autonomous commander who did not easily obey RPA orders and who fatally traveled in an area which RPA forces were said to have declared safe.

This opinion seems to have been shared by Ugandan intelligence. Kahindo Otafiire (Museveni's point man on Congo who convened the 7th Pan-African Congress in Kampala in 1994) and David Pulkol (director of Uganda's ESO) suspected a Rwandan DMI hand in the assassination. According to Okwiri Rabwoni, an influential Ugandan intelligence official (and former officer in the RPA): "The Rwandans wanted someone who would allow them to carry out full-scale movement of troops and give them a free hand in their opera-

---

[102] Interview in Kigali, April 2013.
[103] Interview in Kinshasa, August 2013.
[104] Interview in Kinshasa, December 2009.
[105] Interview in Kinshasa, August 2013.
[106] Interview in Kinshasa, August 2013.

tions."[107] Pulkol made the same analysis, adding: "He was our man [in the AFDL] ... Kisase [should] have been president."[108] Their views are dismissed by Congolese and Rwandan protagonists who suggest it was either a genuine ambush by local Mai Mai militias (James Kabarebe and Emmanuel Ndahiro),[109] or a plot hatched by Kabila. According to Moïse Nyarugabo, Mzee's private secretary, Kabila ordered the killing to secure his position at the helm of the AFDL.[110] This internal power dynamic was also cited by Émile Ilunga, a fellow Katangese close to Angola who fell out with Mzee even before Kinshasa was liberated: "Kabila lost his last real rival for leadership. The permanent competition was over."[111] However, Mbusa Nyamwisi, a Nande of North Kivu who worked for both Rwandan and Ugandan intelligence during the war years, points out that Kabila barely had any men at his disposal, let alone the capability to liquidate a rival in this manner.[112]

The murder of André Kisase Ngandu remains an unsolved mystery. But what is crystal-clear is how his disappearance weakened Uganda's relative influence within the AFDL and strengthened the positions of Kabila and Anselme Masasu Nindaga. Déogratias Bugera, the Congolese Tutsi from North Kivu, lacked both the troops and the political wherewithal to be a major player and was widely perceived to be a Rwandan stooge (and therefore unable to assume the absolute, formal leadership of the AFDL). Kabila and Masasu, however, did have a substantial following and saw their star rise further in the wake of Kisase's assassination.

Masasu's popular touch and personal connection with the thousands of *kadogo* he recruited into the AFDL made him probably the most loved personality of the revolution. He became widely known as *afande* ("commander" in Swahili), reflecting his pre-eminent, informal status among the rank and file: with Kisase dead, he was seen as the de facto Congolese military leader of the AFDL, not so much owing to great battlefield victories (despite his years in the RPA, Kabarebe and Kayizari barely used him in operations) but because he expanded the army, warmed the population to the revolutionary project and kept troop morale high throughout the campaign. His energy and

[107] Interviews in Kampala, March 2013.
[108] Ibid.
[109] Interviews in Kigali, April 2013 and July 2014 respectively.
[110] Interview in Goma, December 2009.
[111] Interview in Kinshasa, August 2013.
[112] Interview in Kinshasa, December 2009.

charisma contrasted with the unobtrusive Bugera, who never seemed to stray too far from his Rwandan protectors.

Ultimately, however, it was not Masasu but Laurent-Désiré Kabila who would emerge as the de facto head of the revolution. The official RPF line may have been that it had no preference regarding the internal hierarchy of the movement and that this was to be left to the Congolese, but many of its actions considerably strengthened and emboldened Kabila: the fact that he had been the first invited to Kigali; his prominent Rwandaphone bodyguard, visible for all to see; the mentoring of his son, Joseph, by James Kabarebe and Caesar Kayizari during the campaign; and the liaising between Kabila and the Eritrean and Ethiopian members of the AFDL political support team, facilitated by the RPF. Kabila had used these expressions of support to consolidate his role as spokesman and understood that he needed to stay close to Kabarebe, ESO chief Patrick Karegeya and Dan Munyuza, the intelligence officer traveling with the AFDL who had picked Mzee up in Tanzania and subsequently hosted him in Kigali. As one RPA commander tellingly conceded, the favoring of Kabila had been the plan all along for obvious reasons: "Corporal Masasu was like Mzee—we brought him. But at least Kabila had a name."[113] Simultaneously, however, in order to gain more leverage within the movement vis-à-vis the RPF and to strengthen his profile as a nationalist lion, Mzee rapidly infiltrated his own networks into the AFDL.

The story of Raus Chalwe, later head of the Congolese National Police, exemplifies the trajectory of what became commonly known as "Kabila's friends and pals," a group of mostly (but not exclusively) Katangese diaspora returnees who rapidly gained informal influence and became a vital instrument in offsetting the influence of Kabila's nominal allies. Raus's father had been a successful fish merchant in the northeastern part of Katanga—the region between Pweto, Kasenga and Manono (Mzee's home area)—who knew the Kabila family well. He financially supported early efforts by Laurent-Désiré Kabila to fight the Leopoldville/Kinshasa government. His son, Raus Chalwe, grew up in Lubumbashi and originally joined the Mobutu regime through the Garde Civile, but was forced into exile in the Belgian town of Bastogne after the new corps commander, General Baramoto, purged the ranks. In Belgium, Raus immersed himself in the Katangese diaspora community, which provided a valuable network for social contacts and political activism and which often hosted Kabila during his European visits. Émile Ilunga, who would also join the AFDL and later rebel against Kabila after the

---

[113] Name withheld at the source's request, interview in June 2015.

fall of Lubumbashi in April 1997, led the so-called Katangese "circle" or "family." Gaëtan Kakudji, a childhood friend of Kabila's and from late 1997 onwards the Mzee's minister of the interior, served as Ilunga's deputy and Raus was the circle's treasurer. Also involved were the children of Moïse Tshombe (the "neo-colonial" traitor in the eyes of many Pan-Africanists) and Célestin Lwanghy, whose mother was Tutsi and who would later become Kabila's minister of justice.

With the end of the Cold War and the steady deterioration of Mobutu's health and political fortunes, Raus Chalwe returned to Central Africa as a pharmaceutical trader but also to explore whether the evolving geopolitical landscape might facilitate a comeback of the Katangese "family." He moved between Zaire, Zambia and Rwanda and looked into potential sources of funding for a rebellion: cassiterite, later instrumental in fueling conflict in eastern Congo,[114] appeared for the first time on Raus's radar as one possibility. Seed money for preparing this project was provided by a young Zambia-based Katangese businessman, Moïse Katumbi.[115] However, the real scaling-up only came when Kagame, Museveni and Nyerere began building the AFDL. From Kigali, Mzee phoned his European network; Ilunga, Kakudji, Lwanghy and Raus flew in as the campaign commenced. Raus co-founded some of the advance intelligence teams that Kakudji coordinated, operating them independently from the RPA. These teams infiltrated big cities even before their formal capture by the AFDL and allowed the movement to not only more rapidly place them squarely under its control but also gave Kabila a financial and political edge over his Congolese comrades-cum-rivals, Masasu and Bugera. Raus and others leveraged their Zambian connections in particular to build up a war-chest for Kabila, not to be used for the campaign against Mobutu, but for the consolidation of Mzee's number one position before and after Kinshasa.[116]

---

[114] Global Witness, "Under-Mining Peace—Tin: The Explosive Trade in Cassiterite in Eastern DRC," London: Global Witness, 2005. Cassiterite is a mineral that is by far the most important tin ore; Congo's most valuable deposits are to be found in North Kivu, around Walikale. Cassiterite has been mined since the early colonial period in the Kivus but following a production slump in the Mobutu era, exploitation made a come-back after regional war re-erupted in August 1998.

[115] From 2006 onwards, Moïse Katumbi became governor of Katanga and one of the most powerful men in the country.

[116] This entire section is based on discussions with Raus Chalwe in Kinshasa, August 2013 as well as with other prominent Congolese AFDL leaders.

While the AFDL advance westwards allowed it to enlist non-easterners into the ranks of its growing army, the closer the movement came to Kinshasa, the more open it had to become about its governance structures and who exercised formal authority. Inevitably, this revealed the main power axes of the Congolese body of the AFDL and highlighted the dominance of the Congolese Tutsi on the one hand and Kabila's "*famille katangaise*" and his "friends and pals" on the other. As the following table shows, the Executive Council—the AFDL's highest organ, which was supposed to work with porte-parole/spokesman Kabila—was an entirely male affair composed of four Tutsis; three Luba; three members of the European (Belgian) diaspora; two members of the North American diaspora; four comrades hailing from South Kivu; two from Katanga; and two from Kasai. Almost everybody spoke Swahili. No one hailed from Kinshasa or Equateur, Mobutu's fief. And not a single "commissar" had ever served at a senior level in government or assumed any major military or financial responsibilities in a rebel movement.

The composition of the AFDL's Executive Council underlines the pivotal alliance between the Banyamulenge, who still provided the bulk of AFDL fighters, and the mostly Katangese and diaspora networks of Mzee, who proved increasingly adept at occupying strategic political positions. But whereas the former group lacked a clear, experienced leader to rally around—Bugera was from North Kivu and lacked political acumen, Masasu was too young and had no experience, and Bizima Karaha had no military credentials—the latter was tied in various ways to Kabila who they looked up to. This shift boosted Mzee's ability to translate his ambitions into actual power. Moreover, whereas the Tutsi group felt understandably rather sheepish about openly embracing ethnic politics and thus confirming stereotypes of being "Rwandan" puppets, Kabila's circle had no such hesitations and both openly courted RPF support and divided the spoils among ethno-political insiders.

With Kabila steadily accumulating influence and emerging ever more clearly as the AFDL's leader, both to those within the movement and to American diplomats and spooks,[117] the unease grew among his comrades—even before Mobutu had finally been removed. Many felt this was a power grab by stealth, without formal decisions or consultations, but more a kind of "inevitable" imposition by Mzee of himself on the movement, through shrewd

---

[117] Mzee's rise to power is obvious from the way the US ambassador to Zaire, Daniel Simpson, already talks about a "putative Kabila government" on April 2, 1997, more than six weeks before the fall of Kinshasa: See American Embassy Kinshasa to Secretary of State Washington, DC, "Kabila Government," 021206Z, April 1997.

maneuvering and, allegedly, the carefully calibrated use of violence. According to Azarias Ruberwa, chef-de-cabinet of Bizima Karaha: "Kabila manipulated, intimidated, killed. The idea was 'we'll correct the mistakes later, war has priority.'"[118] The growing euphoria of liberation and the frantic pace of the approach to Kinshasa veiled festering frustrations. When the moment came at which Kabila formally threw his cards on the table and proclaimed himself both the AFDL's top dog and Congo's president, it had become impossible for Kabila's comrades-cum-rivals to stop him and put forward an alternative, especially as he retained unequivocal RPF support. But in that unacknowledged discontent laid a ticking time bomb.

Table 6.2: Executive Council of the AFDL before the Capture of Kinshasa

Name	Position	Background
Déogratias Bugera	AFDL Secretary-General and Commissar for North Kivu	Tutsi, from North Kivu
Raphaël Ghenda	Commissar for Information and Propaganda	Tetela, from Kasai; Belgian diaspora
Paul Kabongo	Commissar for Internal Security	Luba, from Kasai; Belgian diaspora
Gaëtan Kakudji	Commissar for External Relations (Europe and Asia)	Luba, from Katanga; Belgian diaspora
Bizima Karaha	Commissar for External Relations (America and Oceania)	Tutsi, from South Kivu; graduate from Lubumbashi University
Mwenze Kongolo	Commissar for Justice	Luba, from Katanga; North American diaspora
Samson Muzuri	Commissar for Education	Tutsi, from South Kivu; graduate from Lubumbashi university
Mawapanga Mwana Nanga	Commissar for Finances	Bakongo, from Bas Congo; North American diaspora
Joseph Rubibi	Deputy Commissar for Finances	Tutsi, from South Kivu
Anselme Masasu Nindaga	Commissar for South Kivu and "Afande"	Bashi, with a Tutsi mother, from South Kivu

[118] Interview in Kinshasa, December 2009.

The Rwandan–Angolan Cold War: Tshikapa and the First Confrontation between the Comrades

The mounting tensions among the AFDL's core Congolese members in the final sprint towards Kinshasa were compounded by brewing trouble within the broad Pan-Africanist coalition that had come together to remake Central Africa. The overarching ideological principles and rhetorical convergence notwithstanding, the allies found rather quickly that there was no automatic agreement on what international priorities the "new" Congo they midwifed should pursue as part of a post-Mobutu regional order. "Security" for the liberation regimes of Angola, Rwanda and Uganda was easy enough to agree on, but given the vital connection Luanda, Kigali and Kampala identified between a stable internal equilibrium and a safe external environment, how exactly this was to be achieved remained unclear. The MPLA and RPF in particular directly linked who was in power in Kinshasa with their chances of countering a (resurgent) rebellion. This compelled them to seek to maximize their influence in the post-Mobutu domestic order and to promote rival candidates for the top position as the AFDL advanced at breath-taking speed. In the absence of much intimate knowledge of each other and of formal institutional mechanisms to regulate AFDL decision-making, the resultant informal politicking set them on a collision course which nearly resulted in a break-up of the Pan-Africanist project for Congo.

The month was April 1997. The biggest city in Kasai and great diamond mining center of Congo, Mbuji-Mayi, had fallen on April 5, with Mzee and 3,000 Congolese AFDL soldiers making a triumphant entry after an advance force of 300 RPA crack troops had cleared the surrounding areas of possible resistance. Kinshasa was still more than 800 kilometers away, but from here on the terrain would be less tough than in preceding months. Caesar Kayizari ordered his units to march on Kananga—the other big Kasaien city and historical military training center in the middle of the country—and, after its seizure on April 12, from there onwards into Bandundu and Bas Congo; the objective was to secure the Zairian–Angolan border region to prevent reinforcements of Angola's UNITA rebels from joining the last stand Mobutu was putting together. One strategically important town that lay before the AFDL was Tshikapa, less than 50 kilometers from the Angolan border, situated in an area known for diamond smuggling as well as, more recently, arrivals of Rwandan refugees. Kayizari commanded the same 300-strong elite force to move immediately to Tshikapa, following a worrying phone call with Kabarebe who was in Lubumbashi and had alerted him that the MPLA was secretly massing troops at the border.[119]

The following day, Kabarebe, who had rushed to Kananga, and Kayizari boarded a small plane for an aerial tour of the region. But what they saw half an hour after take-off was their biggest shock so far of the war. According to Kayizari:

> James, Alex [Alexis Kagame, another RPA commander] and I were flying in a plane from Kananga together with a white priest over the Tshikapa area, which our forces had just captured ... From the sky, we saw an incredible force rolling into Zaire from Angola, thousands and thousands of soldiers ... The Tigres Katangais moved in first, the FAA were behind ... It was impressive.[120]

Out of nowhere, on April 23, 1997, a force that must have counted at least 5,000 men moved from the Angolan frontier post at Dundu into Zaire after lying in wait for weeks. It was a mechanized brigade that brought heavy artillery into the southern theater of the war and was spearheaded by several thousand Congolese fighters, the so-called "Tigres Katangais." They were heading to occupy Tshikapa and then into the neighboring province of Bandundu to commence the final attack on Kinshasa. This was the most impressive war machine to be deployed in the conflict thus far, and its show of force left little to the imagination. Crucially, nobody had told Kabarebe, Kayizari or other Rwandan officials about this "strengthening of the liberation effort." The signal was unmistakable.

On the previous day, Kabarebe and Kayizari had been invited by Angolan military intelligence official Paulo Cesar and the FAA chief of staff of the terrestrial forces, António Emílio Faceira, to a strategic "coordination meeting" in northern Angola with the FAA's most senior officers. While phrased in courteous language and extensive flattery of the RPA's performance, the Angolan officers who had traveled to Kananga to extend the invitation told Kayizari that he lacked the troops to break through the UNITA defenses in Bandundu and Bas Congo and that neither the RPA's special forces nor the swelling AFDL army of *kadogo* had the capacity to capture and control a city of millions like Kinshasa. By contrast, the mechanized FAA/Tigres Katangais brigade and its experience in urban warfare made it a much more suitable army to finish the job of liberation, according to the Angolans. The RPA was thanked for its efforts in eastern and central Zaire but was now asked to

---

[119] Interview in Ankara, June 2015.
[120] Interview in Kigali, April 2013.

assume a secondary role. The MPLA proposed a unified command, under Angolan leadership.

If Kayizari disliked the tone of the Angolan "notification" (which gradually led to awkward and tense exchanges) but saw some military sense in what was proposed—he had been instrumental in the capture of Kigali during the genocide and knew the complexities of urban combat well—James Kabarebe took the MPLA's admonition badly. From his perspective, Angola was trying to snatch a victory from the very forces that had made the greatest sacrifices and taken on the boldest missions during the campaign. The suggestion that he lacked the wherewithal to finish the job gravely offended the RPA *esprit de corps* of invincibility and exceptionalism that had been so deeply internalized by Kabarebe. And finally, there were the major political consequences Kabarebe knew would result from an Angolan conquest of Kinshasa. Whoever took the capital and was seen to have ousted the dictator would have a vital advantage in structuring the post-Mobutu order, domestically and regionally. The RPA had fought too hard to give away such a prize.

Kabarebe was outraged, but played for time in discussions with his FAA interlocutors. In the meantime, he commanded his advance force to move away from Tshikapa (which was left in the hands of the Tigres) to Kikwit in Bandundu. Time was of the essence: what Kayizari termed "the race to Kinshasa" had begun. Within less than four weeks, the RPA and the most trusted AFDL units reached their ultimate objective, steamrolling through southwest Congo and approaching the capital through a pincer movement. Pumped up with adrenaline and a desire to end the war with a decisive statement of Rwandan military prowess, the RPA-led AFDL forces reached the gates of Kinshasa believing its greatest challenger at this point was no longer Mobutu but the FAA which was seen as capable of undoing so much the RPF had patiently worked for.

From the Angolan perspective, it was the RPF's behavior—not the MPLA's scaling-up of its contribution to the war—that triggered the stand-off at Tshikapa and unleashed tensions within the AFDL. The Front had always signaled that it would welcome others carrying part of the burden and it had recognized in international meetings that other liberation movements, like the MPLA, had major interests in Zaire/Congo too, which required their involvement. Western Congo was Angola's backyard, a strategic zone that played a crucial role in the Angolan civil war—like Kivu did for Rwanda. But Kabarebe's unilateral decision-making left the MPLA in the dark and suggested to the Angolans that the RPF's liberation rhetoric was a veneer for maximizing regional power at the expense of other alliance partners. For General Ita, who had worked closely with Kabarebe as Angola's most senior envoy to the AFDL in Congo over the preceding months, Kabarebe's orders to begin a race to the capital suggested an alternative agenda: "They wanted to come first to Kinshasa … Kinshasa is here, Rwanda is there. They wanted the power."[121] According to Colonel Manuel Correia de Barros, another senior military intelligence officer, this completely ignored the Angolan viewpoint: "We needed a strong government to control everything inside Zaire … The problem with the Rwandans is that they had other interests than ousting Mobutu … They thought they were going to be commanding Congo."[122] Ita underlined how the arrogance implicit in the RPA's refusal to insert their forces into a unified, Angolan-led army was not appreciated by the FAA, which had been at war for two decades, from a time when Kabarebe and Kayizari where still at school: "James was right. We would only accept one unified command: ours. Of course we refused to serve under him, we were better. We had much more capabilities than he did."[123]

The tensions the Tshikapa incident created between the RPF and the MPLA heavily affected the intra-AFDL (Congolese) equilibrium too. As mentioned earlier, the army which moved into Kasai from Dundu was spearheaded by at least 2,000 Tigres Katangais (TK), a heavily armed force that presented a credible alternative to Masasu's *kadogo* or Mzee's *famille katangaise*. Led by General Delphin Muland and his deputy, General Vindicien Kiyana, 700 TK had already been active from February 1997 onwards in eastern Zaire following their drop-off by massive Angolan Ilyushin planes in Kigali, from whence they moved to Goma, Bukavu and then the frontline;[124] according to Mobutu's intelligence services, another 1,000 or so Tigres joined their comrades shortly thereafter with plenty of equipment, including much-feared Katyusha rocket launchers, otherwise known as "Stalin's organs."[125] From Tshikapa, this initial force of around 2,000 was reinforced by a bigger brigade that operated with full Angolan backing.

An important historical dimension exacerbated the lack of trust between Mzee Kabila and the recent Katangese arrivals: not only did they contest his

[121] Interview in Luanda, May 2014.
[122] Interview in Luanda, March 2014.
[123] Interview in Luanda, May 2014.
[124] De Villers and Willame, *République démocratique du Congo*, pp. 51–2.
[125] N'Gbanda, *Ainsi sonne le glas: les derniers jours du Maréchal Mobutu*, pp. 207–8.

leadership of the AFDL and Katanga from the moment they crossed into Tshikapa, but during the troubles of the 1960s they had taken the side of the "neo-colonial" Katangese secession of Moïse Tshombe. The Tigres, also known as the "Gendarmes Katangais," were, as their name suggests, the security force of the would-be Katangese state and carriers of a serious nation-building project.[126] They fled into Angola after the implosion of the secessionist project. There they became guns for hire in the civil war, learning Portuguese, intermarrying and fighting on the side of the MPLA, which needed all the reinforcements it could get to keep UNITA at bay. Years of service in MPLA ranks gave them significant expertise and experience, as was evident when they launched the Shaba invasions against Mobutu in 1977 and 1978.[127] Hence Kabila was acutely sensitive to the threat they posed right from the start.

In a rapidly evolving context, their entry into liberation politics led to an immediate counter-reaction by Kabila and the RPF who feared that unless they re-established control quickly, the victory they were so close to scoring might elude them. An opportunity came after the Tshikapa incident when RPA–AFDL troops completely secured Katanga, rolling back the Mobutist state from the lucrative mining areas and capturing Kolwezi, Likasi and Lubumbashi. After receiving a bogus invitation several weeks later, Muland made his way to the Katangese capital but was unexpectedly placed under arrest on May 9 by twenty Rwandan soldiers who charged him with insubordination. While Muland had indeed been behaving in an overly confident way—believing the TK's old Katangese networks might prove stronger than those of Kabila who had been away for so many years—there is little evidence to suggest he was preparing to usurp the AFDL leadership, as some of Kabila's close advisers have suggested. As even Mwenze Kongolo, the Mzee's commissar for justice, admitted, his arrest was above all related to the "fear that he would spread disobedience among the soldiers."[128] Rather than the RPF manipulating Kabila, this was a case of Mzee instrumentalizing his Rwandan protectors: by portraying Muland as an insubordinate, unpredictable Angolan stooge, Kabila succeeded in having his main Katangese rival incarcerated. About a month earlier, the Angolan security forces themselves had already arrested another

---

[126] Miles Larmer and Erik Kennes, "Rethinking the Katangese Secession," *Journal of Imperial and Commonwealth History*, 42, 4 (2014).

[127] Miles Larmer, "Local Conflicts in a Transnational War: The Katangese Gendarmes and the Shaba Wars of 1977–78," *Cold War History*, 13, 1 (2012).

[128] Interview in Kinshasa, August 2013.

potential Katangese challenger in the form of Émile Ilunga, formerly head of the Belgian–Katangese diaspora "circle" to which Raus Chalwe and Gaëtan Kakudji also belonged. This left Mzee stronger than ever before. Neutralizing Muland was a high-stakes gamble by Kabila and the RPF, but a calibrated one. Kabarebe and the RPA still shared intelligence with Generals Kopelipa and Ita and did not purge the Tigres Katangais already serving in the AFDL from their ranks in the movement, but kept them.[129] Jack Nziza, who had operated mostly out of Kisangani, working for months with Angolan liaison officers, did what he could to reassure his counterparts: "We did not have the intention of staying in Congo but they kept asking why we were behaving like this was our country."[130] Most crucially, to prevent a full-scale rupture, Kabila reassured Luanda that despite recent tensions he was committed to keeping key pro-Angolan figures in positions of influence. Irung Awan was an ethnic Lunda—historical rivals of Kabila's Luba group—who had spent many years in Angola working for the political arm of the Tigres after the failure of the Shaba invasions. When Kabila visited Luanda in 1996 after the start of the AFDL liberation project, the MPLA organized a meeting for Mzee with the Katangese diaspora. Lacking Congolese soldiers who could balance the RPA and Banyamulenge, Kabila charmed the TK whom he praised as professional fighters and invited them to join him in eastern Congo. While President José Eduardo Dos Santos was still apprehensive about a direct attack on Mobutu, fearing a backlash and resumption of the war with UNITA, he endorsed the idea of proxy warfare and organized for hundreds of TK to be flown with Angolan intelligence and technical specialists to Kigali via Zambia. Upon arrival, Irung Awan thus became diplomatic counselor to Kabila, a role in which he worked closely with the rising Banyamulenge star Bizima Karaha who was the AFDL's commissar for external relations. After Muland's arrest, Kabila by no means marginalized individuals like Awan but, to the contrary, empowered them further and gave them important responsibilities—albeit on his terms.[131]

For its part, the MPLA reciprocated by not pushing for an all-out confrontation either. Its trust in Muland had been limited and Kabila's recent signals suggested that some kind of collaborative relationship was likely to emerge out

[129] Interviews with James Kabarebe and Caesar Kayizari in Kigali, April 2013.

[130] Interview in Kigali, July 2014.

[131] Interviews with Irung Awan, Émile Ilunga and Godefroid Tchamlesso in Kinshasa, August 2013.

of the liberation campaign—the Angolan analysis was that Kabila would be happy to rebalance his extreme dependence on the RPF in a pro-MPLA direction once he assumed the presidency, as now seemed inevitable. According to Ita, with his Tutsi bodyguard surrounding him at all times, "He was in jail."[132] Moreover, though bitter about losing the "race to Kinshasa" to the RPA, Luanda decided it had too much to lose from derailing the anti-Mobutu campaign at the last minute. A pre-emptive assault on Kinshasa from the Cabinda enclave, which would effectively outpace the RPA–AFDL force, was rejected as an option because it risked triggering a major conflict with the RPA and uniting all Congolese against the MPLA and TK: Angola would be dangerously exposed and isolated and the story spun for the international press of a Congolese liberation movement freeing its own people would go up in smoke, forcing Angolans to handle the mess they had created. A further reason to back off somewhat was provided when Rwandan forces routed UNITA troops in the weeks after Tshikapa—news the MPLA obviously welcomed. Yet despite Luanda's decision to de-escalate and try to turn a page, there was no denying among Angolans or Rwandans that severe damage had been inflicted on the Pan-Africanist coalition: the matter had not been existential enough to merit open conflict, but a cold war between the RPF and MPLA emerged after Tshikapa and the Muland arrest. The honeymoon was over even before the wedding cake had been consumed.

Conclusion: The AFDL and the Fall of Kinshasa

With neither the RPF, nor the MPLA, nor Kabila, nor the remaining Tigres wishing to let the "race for Kinshasa" spiral into full-scale confrontation between the comrades, energies were re-concentrated on finishing the ambitious project that had been launched eight months earlier. The most important part of the final push came from southeast of Kinshasa, where Kabarebe and Kayizari crushed the last resistance offered by the DSP and a battalion of UNITA fighters around the town of Kenge, where hundreds had died on May 5 and 6 in the only serious battle of the war. Kabarebe then headed north, to lead RPA special forces, who had been hunting ex-FAR/Interahamwe and refugees, while a small, specialized Eritrean unit traveled by barge down the Congo River from Mbandaka, the capital of Equateur. Katanga had already been secured with the capture of Lubumbashi on April 9. Kikwit was taken on April 30, and Mbandaka fell on May 13.

[132] Interview in Luanda, May 2014.

The writing of the very final chapter of liberation was entrusted to Caesar Kayizari's leadership. Mobutu's FAZ chief of staff, General Mahele Lieko Bohungu, one of the few competent officers in the FAZ, blew up the Mai Ndombe bridge to cross the Kwango River (the final natural obstacle before Kinshasa) and held his forces back to counter any amphibian assault. An excited Mahele called Mobutu to report that they had effectively trapped the RPA–AFDL between two escarpments, right by the stream. But the 3,000 or so RPA–AFDL troops sought and found an alternative way of crossing the river—50 kilometers down the road, still in the escarpment, where smugglers used an old, barely functional bridge made out of loose-hanging wires. Kayizari sent a deception force past the bridge destroyed by Mahele but ordered the bulk of his troops to use the smugglers' crossing. The transit took more than two days, as all the RPA–AFDL soldiers needed to go one at a time, traversing the fast-flowing river; barbed wire cut into the hands and uniforms of the fighters, including Kayizari's own. However, once the strategic crossing was made, the final sprint to Kinshasa—only 68 kilometers away— was initiated at lightning speed; intelligence reports suggested Mobutu was still in the city. Less than a day later, the AFDL was in the outskirts of Kinshasa, taking everybody by surprise as its advance forces, commanded by Kayizari, overpowered the contingent at N'Djili Airport on the evening of May 16, coming perhaps fifteen minutes too late to capture Mobutu whose plane took off as the RPA approached the terminal building. The next day, on May 17, 1997, all resistance collapsed. DSP and FAZ troops took off their uniforms and tried to cross the Congo into Brazzaville or hide among the population. The Mobutist state finally received its formal obituary. The war of liberation was complete.

While Congolese AFDL soldiers were given the honor of marching down Kinshasa's streets in the hope this would lead the population to recognize them as liberators, the city was divided into military sectors where security was the responsibility of different Rwandan commanders, whom Kayizari instructed to provide intelligence reports to a handful of FAA officers. The RPA immediately proceeded to create a Congolese military police which was to stop any possible looting and acts of revenge—widespread fears about a bloodbath and sacking of the city once the AFDL moved in proved unfounded.[133] From Luanda to Asmara, congratulatory phone calls were exchanged by the Pan-Africanist comrades who had contributed to the end of the

[133] Wrong, *In the Footsteps of Mr Kurtz*, p. 274.

Mobutist era. From Kinshasa's Stade Kamanyola (the national football stadium which had the same name as Mobutu's yacht), an exhausted James Kabarebe called Laurent-Désiré Kabila, who had stayed in Lubumbashi, to share the good news.

The retired rebel leader, so often ridiculed by references to Che Guevara's unflattering description of his time with him in the South Kivu *maquis*,[134] was about to become president of Africa's collapsed giant. Despite a turbulent campaign in which the greatest challenge had not been defeating Mobutu's forces but maintaining unity among the alliance partners, particularly following the death of Kisase and the Tshikapa incident, everything seemed to fall into place at the last minute. The chances of a Mobutist insurgency were low, the problem of the ex-FAR/Interahamwe and Rwandan refugees seemed to have been solved and the RPF and MPLA appeared ready to settle things pragmatically. The revolution was ready to take off and transform Central Africa for the better. Or was it?

---

[134] Guevara felt that, despite Kabila possessing "genuine qualities of a mass leader," he lacked "revolutionary seriousness, an ideology that can guide action, a spirit of sacrifice that accompanies one's actions ..." He concluded: "I have grave doubts about his ability to overcome his defects in the environment in which he operates." Ernesto "Che" Guevara, *The African Dream: Diaries of the Revolutionary War in the Congo*, London: Havill Press, 2000, p. 244.

PART III

FROM TRIUMPH TO TRAGEDY

THE PATH TO AFRICA'S GREAT WAR

7

THE POST-MOBUTU ORDER
AND POLITICS AFTER LIBERATION

President Laurent Kabila will assume from now on the functions of head of state ... I am happy, very happy to succeed.

Laurent-Désiré Kabila's autoproclamation as president of the (new) Democratic Republic of Congo, Lubumbashi, May 17, 1997.

Mzee had struggled for forty years—they never understood this. The PRP did not start in 1996. They overstayed their welcome ... Every liberation movement receives foreign help—it does not diminish their achievement. But in any case our friends stayed on permanently, which we did not ask for.[1]

Jaynet Kabila, daughter of Laurent-Désiré Kabila and twin-sister of Joseph Kabila.

The date was May 17, 1997. The orderly procession of Rwandan and *kadogo* soldiers in the streets of Kinshasa contrasted sharply with the chaos of the Zairian state in the final years of Mobutu's reign and signaled the ambitions of the Pan-Africanist coalition to put the country back on its feet. While Caesar Kayizari marched his men across the city to seal the revolution's victory and to deter possible looting, Laurent-Désiré Kabila remained 1,500 kilometers to the southeast, in Lubumbashi, capital of the mineral-rich province of Katanga and the rebels' headquarters since capturing the city on April 9. Hitherto the AFDL's spokesperson, Mzee called a press conference at the governor's mansion. Seated behind a table covered with the old Congolese flag not used since

[1] Interview in Kinshasa, August 2013.

233

the 1960s, he declared the end of the Mobutu regime and triumphantly pro-claimed, "President Laurent Kabila will assume from now on the functions of head of state" of the Democratic Republic of the Congo, renamed from Zaire. According to the reporters in attendance, Kabila, still in disbelief at his rever-sal of fortune from washed-up revolutionary living in exile in Tanzania to following in the footsteps of Lumumba as Congo's liberator, burst out, "I am happy, very happy to succeed" followed by a deep-throated laugh.[2]

Kabila's announcement, however, unsettled his comrades in the AFDL—not because of his ascension to the presidency per se, but because of the way in which he became president.[3] The decision was made outside the organs of the liberation movement and without consulting other AFDL leaders, who had tried to put in writing a "governance proposal with criteria to choose the new leadership team, especially the conditions to choose the new president," but which Mzee had an "allergic" reaction to.[4] They never discussed the mat-ter; instead, two parallel tracks emerged. One was pursued collectively and the other was pursued "behind our backs" by Kabila, "his Katangan courtesans ... and the Rwandese generals."[5] Kabila's bombshell proclamation even caught his own speechwriters, like Azarias Ruberwa, dumbstruck when they heard him systematically change "we" to "I."[6] In this interpretation, it was nothing short of a "mini-coup" and "the birth of a new dictatorship" on liberation day. To those closest to Kabila, however, their comrades' resentment was misplaced. Henri Mova, a former human rights activist who had joined the rebellion and would become minister of transport, opined that Kabila's critics were not willing to accept that "[Mzee] had a will of his own and was determined to chart his own course."[7]

---

[2] James C. McKinley Jr, "Zairian Rebel and His Plan Puzzle West," *New York Times*, May 18, 1997. See also Karin Davies, "Rebel Leader Claims Presidency, Renames Zaire," Associated Press, May 17, 1997.

[3] Other than wryly noting that the Mzee once declared during the early days of the rebellion that he had no ambition to be president, those foreigners witnessing Kabila's claim to the throne found it did not strike a discordant note. After all, Kabila had been the AFDL's public face from the beginning and subsequently the one to meet with foreign diplomats and lead the rebel delegation in the failed negotiations with Mobutu convened by Nelson Mandela.

[4] Email communication with Deogratias Bugera, secretary-general of the AFDL, February 2010.

[5] Interview with Azarias Ruberwa in Kinshasa, December 2009.

[6] Ibid.

[7] Interview in Brussels, April 2011; Mova went on to explain his perspective on the

With the AFDL divided over Kabila's unexpected move, the role of its foreign backers was decisive. No alliance partner had more influence than the RPF—and its evaluation determined how Uganda, Eritrea, Ethiopia and others involved in liberating Congo would perceive the announcement. Emmanuel Ndahiro, one of Paul Kagame's closest advisers, asserted that the RPF was also surprised: "[Kabila's] *autoproclamation* was a complete shock to all of us. We were not in league with Kabila on this. Everyone asked James [Kabarebe] what is this? He said he didn't know."[8] According to Ndahiro, discussions unfolded in Kigali and Kinshasa among the RPA commanders to assess the situation, but ultimately they came to the conclusion that not much could be done, given how heavily the Front had invested in its relationship with Mzee and how poorly it rated the other AFDL "founding fathers": "The option of Kabila for Rwanda was not the first choice or the last choice, it was the only choice."[9] The RPF's non-reaction—which some in the AFDL interpreted as complicity—proved crucial in the first step of Kabila's personalization of power.

This chapter narrates how the new regime was consolidated following the removal of the old dictator and how the liberators were consumed by the uncertainty they had unleashed with the overthrow of the Mobutu regime. Kabila's proclamation announcing himself as the new president was both the first moment in the creation of the post-Mobutu order but also, in the minds of many comrades, the first step towards authoritarianism and an unraveling of the ties that bound the AFDL together, internally and externally. Misunderstandings, mistrust and tension arising from the absence of strong organizational structures to regulate the distribution of power would recur throughout the brief interwar period of May 1997 to August 1998, while the lack of military integration compounded the uncertainty arising from political divisions. It would poison the relations between comrades and pit all sides against each other—Kabila and his allies against the Congolese Tutsi; the Congolese Tutsi against Kabila; and both Kabila and the Congolese Tutsi mistrusting, to different degrees, the RPF. For its part, the RPF sought to engage in the art of the

---

pronoun changes in the speech. "In Ruberwa's version there was not a single mention of Kabila, everything was collective and the role of supporting foreign forces was exaggerated; Kabila ignored this however and used a speech written by Maître Langwi, who later became Minister of Justice ..."

[8] Interview in Kigali, 2014.

[9] Ibid.

impossible—staying above the fray while controlling everything. At the very moment of the triumph of liberation, the alliance began turning in on itself.

Building Post-Mobutu Congo: Elite Accommodation and Order Creation

The RPF Stays On

The stunning victory of the AFDL, as orchestrated by James Kabarebe and Caesar Kayizari, was marked by a small party among the RPF High Command back in Kigali. While Western journalists reported on the RPA–AFDL atrocities committed in Shabunda, Biaro and Tingi-Tingi in previous months and during the final days of the offensive around Mbandaka in Equateur,[10] most press attention was devoted to the fact that anarchy did not grip the sweltering metropolis of Kinshasa. Foreign diplomats and the MPLA had warned that the AFDL would find it impossible to control the mass rioting and looting of the city that was predicted once the Mobutist regime dissolved. But the speed with which Rwandan soldiers deployed in strategic spots to prevent a meltdown proved impressively effective. There was no bloodbath; in the words of Jaynet Kabila, this was to be a *"révolution pardon,"* a magnanimous revolution.[11] Among RPA officers there was a huge sense of pride about winning yet another war—the third successful regime change they had helped orchestrate in eleven years. With Mobutu gone, an old score had been settled. An elated but exhausted Caesar Kayizari spent his first night in Kinshasa, in the company of Joseph Kabila, sleeping on the sofas of the VIP lounge at the giant Stade Kamanyola (later renamed Stade des Martyrs)—a fitting if somewhat bizarre celebration for the football-fan-cum-victor who had led the campaign together with James Kabarebe.[12]

The RPF, as the leader of the Pan-Africanist coalition that had created this critical juncture in African history, knew it had to take some crucial decisions that would determine whether this opportunity would be seized or not. Kagame and his advisers were faced with a fundamental strategic dilemma: either withdraw all RPA forces and manage the AFDL from afar in the hope that the revolution would be strong enough to realize the yearned-for trans-

---

[10] "Evidence Mounts of Mass Killings by Kabila's Forces in Congo," *International Herald Tribune*, June 12, 1997; Dianna Cahn, "Evidence Mounts of Massacres in the Congo," Associated Press, June 27, 1997.

[11] Interview in Kinshasa, August 2013.

[12] Interview in Ankara, June 2015.

formation of Central Africa or maintain a large RPA presence in Congo to bolster the AFDL project and hunt down *génocidaire* enemies, but thus incur the costs of what would surely be described as a foreign occupation by its critics.[13] The choice before the RPF Council of Colonels had already been debated on several occasions but was revisited one more time, as Kabila suggested to Kabarebe that he stay to help with the formation of a new Congolese army and to secure the revolution against reactionary enemies from within and without.

On one side were those like Emmanuel Ndahiro, who argued that the coalition had done what it had to do and that anything more risked backfiring. Ndahiro and a few others noted that there was little appetite among their Ethiopian, Eritrean, Tanzanian and Ugandan comrades to be permanently involved in the day-to-day implementation of the AFDL project. They were keen to offer training and political assistance, but not to have boots on the ground. Thus, Ndahiro said, the RPF should adopt a strategic approach to its own long-term security and pull out Kabarebe and Kayizari with their forces. In his words: "Africa was on our side—we did not want to lose this moral high ground."[14]

Yet this camp favoring withdrawal and delegation was outflanked by those who counseled that the stakes were simply too high for the RPF to play a secondary role. The argument that there were some *génocidaires* who had managed to remain hidden in the Congolese rainforest and could quickly regroup once the RPA left was advanced by hardliners in the security services, the ESO and DMI, notably Patrick Karegeya and Jack Nziza. Moreover, there was a risk of re-infiltration; with thousands of kilometers of porous borders and countless ex-FAR/Interahamwe having fled into Sudan, Central African Republic, Congo-Brazzaville and Cameroon. Instead, the hawks proposed using Congo as a base to gather intelligence and launch clandestine missions across Central Africa to fight the enemy far from Rwanda's borders.[15]

Kabarebe, whose own career and reputation were intimately tied to the success of the AFDL project, supported this policy. The triumph in Congo had given his career as military commander a major boost, elevating him from a second-tier officer in the RPA to becoming its latest hero and entering the

---

[13] On the delegation problem that arises when foreign governments sponsor rebel movements, see Idean Salehyan, "The Delegation of War to Rebel Organizations," *Journal of Conflict Resolution*, 54, 3 (2010).

[14] Interview in Kigali, July 2014.

[15] Interview with Jack Nziza, July 2014.

top circle of decision-making. A potential counter-revolution or *génocidaire* resurgence threatened the status he had acquired. A similar logic, in which personal ambition and the necessity of stabilizing Congo were intertwined, also applied to other key officials—Kayizari, Alexis Kagame, Dan Munyuza— who had been involved in the AFDL saga. Given the informational advantage these commanders in Congo held over the RPF bureaucracy in Kigali on the situation on the ground and the importance of the (virtually incontestable) intelligence they contributed to the policy discussion on the benefits and perils of pulling out, it is perhaps not surprising that the debate ended in their favor. The RPF resolved its dilemma and decided to stay on.

As a life-long nationalist, Kabila resented his dependence on outside actors. However, he knew he could not have taken Kinshasa without them and, having witnessed their overwhelming military firepower first hand, recognized the benefits of continuing to have such a force at his disposal.[16] Given the difficult task of consolidating order in light of possible attempts by Mobutists to reclaim power or challenges from the street by the leader of the non-violent opposition, Étienne Tshisekedi, Kabila did not oppose a continuation of the partnership with the Front. He lacked an army—his leftist and Katangese networks mostly consisted of people in their fifties and older—and the *kadogo* could hardly be relied upon to defend Africa's third largest state. Kabila thus gambled and invited Kabarebe and the RPF to stay on to form an integrated new army, capable of protecting the regime and playing a major role in the region. Mzee knew this would not be without political costs. In particular, it would give his primary political foe, Tshisekedi, nationalist ammunition with which to attack him. But he felt he had little choice and decided to turn this problem into an opportunity to deepen the alliance with the very people who had handed him the presidency. In the words of Patrick Mazimhaka, "Kabila recognized his own forces were not yet ready. He asked us [the RPF] for protection; asked for James [Kabarebe] as chief of staff. He felt he could trust us more than any other force available to him."[17]

The presence of James Kabarebe as chief of staff, Dan Munyuza as Rwandan spymaster in Kinshasa, and the Rwandan-American national Alfred Kalisa as the Kabila regime's top banker, helped the RPF avoid information-asymmetries that would have arisen from delegation. Now the RPA elite faced the practical problem of where to set up base and live—an important decision

---

[16] Interview with Mwenze Kongolo, August 2013.

[17] Interview in Kigali, December 2009.

given nationalist sensitivities in Congo and the simultaneous need to maintain control of the revolution. To manage these twin priorities, they wasted no time in occupying key properties as well as in developing local networks to assist them with their mission. Munyuza moved around the plush Gombe neighborhood and took over the homestead of Kengo wa Dondo (prime minister under Mobutu), while other officers resided in the Binza area. Most remarkably, Kabarebe himself decided to settle into the house of Jean Seti Yale, who had served as Mobutu's top security adviser. In return for not permanently expropriating the residence and for some influence in the new order, Seti Yale's son, Jeannot, traveled with a team of RPA special forces to Cameroon, Central African Republic and Chad to help them hunt down ex-FAR/Interahamwe. By putting the contacts of the old Mobutist regime at the service of the RPA's best and toughest, these secret operations proved highly effective in arresting or neutralizing suspected *génocidaires*.[18]

The Father, the Son and His General

As part of the elite compact to fill the vacuum of power after Mobutu had been removed, Kabila not only appointed a foreign Tutsi as head of his armed forces—he also gave the RPF carte blanche to deal with its enemies. He permitted ongoing Rwandan "black ops" in the Congolese rainforest against those who had escaped the refugee camps and, as we will see later, blocked UN attempts at investigating accusations of AFDL–RPA massacres in Equateur and eastern Congo. In the accommodative spirit of the new regime and to reassure Kabila of the RPF's friendly intentions, Kabarebe named Kabila's son, Joseph, as his deputy. Overall, Kabila's Congo was not so different from Mobutu's Zaire—formal institutions remained weak and virtually non-existent; instead, the distribution of power was governed by the exigencies of elite bargaining in which military clout, individual cunning, personal ties and informal deals determined appointments.

In this system, one of the most intriguing and politically consequential set of relationships was between the father, his son and his general. This trinity was fraught with personal complexities. While his life story remains shrouded in mystery, Joseph Kabila Kabenge was born to Sifa Maanya, along with his twin-sister Jaynet, in 1971. Joseph's birth came as Laurent-Désiré Kabila was trying to rebuild momentum for an insurgency in eastern Congo after the

<hr />

[18] Interview with the head of this RPA special forces team, Kigali, July 2014.

failed Simba Uprising and Che Guevara's disastrous venture into Africa's Great Lakes region. Sifa was already at least the fourth woman to give birth to a child of the 32-year-old Kabila.[19] Having grown up in Maniema, she had been the companion of Michel Lukoma, a comrade of Mzee's who disappeared during an operation in the *maquis* (Lukoma later resurfaced and learned that his second wife had been involved in sexual relations with his boss who, like Mobutu, had a habit of taking his aides' spouses as mistresses). While the Sifa–Kabila marriage was marked by turbulence, for many years it was arguably the most stable of Kabila's six unions. After the bush years, Joseph and Jaynet—often inseparable in childhood—went to live with their mother in the Oyster Bay neighborhood of Dar es Salaam as guests of Nyerere. It was in Tanzania that they spent most of their adolescent lives (with the exception of a few years in Uganda), receiving an education at the École Française Arthur Rimbaud and at Anglophone schools.[20] Joseph then underwent military training in Tanzania and became known for the cars, taxis and *dala dala* minibuses he sought to make money from; his relationship with his father, whom he did not see often, was not overly close, but nor was it characterized by confrontation,[21] even though it seemed to have deteriorated by the time that the AFDL was created. He was a taciturn, introverted young man who trusted few people, apart from Jaynet.

In order to assist his father, Joseph traveled to Kigali as the preparations for the AFDL began in late 1995 and stayed at the house of Dan Munyuza (Jaynet joined her father and brother later).[22] Showing little noticeable interest in the coming AFDL campaign, his focus mainly seemed to rest on personal issues; he acquired a Rwandan girlfriend in 1996 but this relationship proved politically untenable. According to their hosts in Rwanda's Department of Military Intelligence and External Security Organization, Joseph was withdrawn, silent and did not appear particularly close to his father—Joseph respected his duties as a son but, given their differences in personality, Joseph often seemed more at home with the more introverted Rwandan officers surrounding him than with Mzee's boisterous Congolese clique.

---

[19] Kennes, *Essai biographique sur Laurent Désiré Kabila*, pp. 298–9.

[20] C.K. Lumuna Sando, *Histoire du Congo: les quatres premiers présidents*, Kinshasa: Editions SECCO & CEDI, 2002, pp. 186–7.

[21] Kennes, *Essai biographique sur Laurent Désiré Kabila*, p. 300.

[22] Interview with James Kabarebe and an officer of the RPA's special forces; the timing of the arrival seems to be confirmed by Kennes's witness cited on (ibid.) p. 319.

This impression was confirmed by the two most senior Rwandans who traveled on the campaign trail with him and adopted him as their younger brother: James Kabarebe and Caesar Kayizari. While initially it was mainly Kabarebe who took Joseph under his wing in the first months of the campaign to gain his trust, teach him military tactics and expose him to battlefield operations, the latter stages of the military campaign were spent mostly with Kayizari. As Kayizari's forces smashed through the last resistance around Kenge and found a solution to the demolished bridge over the Kwango, the ultimate obstacle before Kinshasa, Joseph had to cross the river, like all other RPA–AFDL troops, by holding onto the ropes and barbed wire. For the first time, Joseph was exposed to real hunger and thirst—by far the biggest challenges for the RPF on the journey from eastern to western Congo—a world away from the gentle life of Oyster Bay. He shared an old mattress to sleep on with Kayizari and Alexis Kagame along the road and his last breakfast before reaching Kinshasa consisted of no food but several bottles of *Tembo* beer, courtesy of several trucks carrying beer supplies from which the RPA served itself during the final approach. Such hardships allowed for a real camaraderie to be forged. Reflecting back, Kayizari still talks fondly of his old comrade, whatever politics may have come in-between them since 1998: "[During and after the campaign] I always joked with him that I would send him the bill for my efforts and my food he ate later."[23]

According to RPA sources and Congolese nationalists like Paul Kabongo,[24] Henri Mova[25] and Mwenze Kongolo, this camaraderie between Joseph, Kayizari and Kabarebe was encouraged by Mzee, who felt that through his son he could develop an even greater level of strategic interdependence with the RPF. While accounts differ as to whether Mzee wanted Joseph to take part in any AFDL operations or preferred him to focus on the politics of relationship-building with RPA commanders, Kabarebe insisted two days after the liberation of Congo that the son be made his deputy chief of staff in the FAC. Kabarebe was explicitly trying to lock in the elite bargain too, as Joseph's appointment obviously had no military rationale: "I wanted cover."[26] This was also the impression back at the Ministry of Defense in Kigali, where Permanent Secretary Frank Rusagara noted that "James' support and training

[23] Interview in Kigali, April 2013.
[24] Interview in Kinshasa, August 2013.
[25] Interview in Brussels, April 2011.
[26] Interview in Kigali, April 2013

of Kabila the son was a kind of guarantee for the Congolese about Rwanda's good intentions."[27]

The meteoric rise of Joseph Kabila offered him a seat at the highest tables of the revolution without having any military, financial or political credentials. The gap between his formal position and his skillset quickly became painfully evident. Moreover, Joseph gave the impression of not really wanting to play a prominent role, and the relationship with his father remained difficult; he preferred to spend time with his mother and sister, both of whom lived separately from Mzee, even in Kinshasa. According to Jack Nziza of Rwanda's DMI: "He was a prisoner in the barracks."[28]

Under these circumstances, it was decided that Joseph should be formally schooled in military affairs. According to Yemane Gebreab (one of Asmara's key envoys to Congo), in order to consolidate the Pan-Africanist alliance, Joseph had earlier been sent for a brief period of training at the reputed Sawa camp in western Eritrea. However, as Issayas quickly developed doubts about Mzee Kabila and as the EPLF was widely regarded as the RPF's second closest ally after the NRM, Congo's new president did not want to further pursue the option of his son undergoing additional Eritrean military training.[29] The RPF's subsequent suggestion was to continue working within the context of the Pan-Africanist alliance and have Joseph travel to Zambia for a one-year training course with the experienced Jack Nziza of Rwanda's DMI. But Mzee Kabila feared that this risked bringing him too close to his main ally; an intelligence operative of the caliber of Nziza—who had run into numerous arguments with Jaynet Kabila while they were both in Kisangani during the campaign—might be able to manipulate his son and divide the first family. Instead, he looked for an alternative: on the advice of Kabarebe, US Ambassador Daniel Simpson had made preparatory arrangements to enroll Joseph in an American military academy,[30] but at the last minute Mzee decided Joseph would train in China.[31]

As already alluded to, elite accommodation with the RPF was necessary, yet at the same time it also created a set of strategic problems for Kabila. The first was the foreign occupation perception. The prominence of foreigners in the

---

[27] Interview in London, January 2010.

[28] Interview in Kigali, July 2014.

[29] Interview in Nakfa, August 2014.

[30] American Embassy Kinshasa to Secretary of State Washington, DC, "President's Son Studying in Cuba?," 190852Z, May 1998

[31] Interviews with Abdoulaye Yerodia and Irung Awan, Kinshasa, August 2013.

post-Mobutu regime served as a consistent source of political pressure for Kabila; for certain Congolese constituencies, the AFDL went from being hailed as liberators to being resented as foreign pawns. "President Kabila saw this and knew this," Shé Okitundu stated, "but was in no position to do anything about it because the Rwandans could remove him at any moment."[32] This qualifier represented the second, and more threatening, strategic problem that came from sharing power with the Front: what assurances did Kabila have that the RPF and their allies would not exploit their overwhelming offensive advantages—control of the military, security and even Kabila's personal bodyguard which was headed by RPA officer Francis Gakwerere[33]—to replace him when it suited them? The fear of being taken out by the very conspirators who put you in power is the essence of the commitment problem rulers of irregular regimes face. The first priority for Mzee was to strengthen his position and chip away at the stranglehold. Kabila started to consolidate his power, but only "slowly," as it was "very dangerous to provoke the Rwandans."[34]

From Liberation Movement to Sovereign Government: Kabila's Balancing Act

The Distribution of Spoils and the New Cabinet

Having concluded his deal with the RPF of continued Rwandan protection in exchange for a free hand to deal with the *génocidaires*, Mzee carefully prepared the appointment of a "revolutionary" government that would have to realize the promises of democracy, national sovereignty and economic development the AFDL had made during the struggle. Faced with pressures from the unarmed opposition over the prolonged Rwandan presence and the delicate task of balancing regional representation with the need to reward those who had sacrificed most to oust Mobutu, Kabila nevertheless managed to form a cabinet that served his overarching goal: political survival and a reinforcement of his presidential authority. The composition of the new government reflected this imperative in multiple ways.

First, he appointed a cabinet consisting almost entirely of ministerial novices: only Thomas Kanza (in the 1960s) and Paul Bandoma had any prior

---

[32] Interview in Kinshasa, December 2009.

[33] "Kabila was like a hostage inside. Tutsi were all around him. Very dangerous sign for Kabila." Interview with Mbusa Nyamwisi, Kinshasa, December 2009.

[34] Interview with Kabila's minister of human rights, Léonard "Shé" Okitundu, Kinshasa December 2009.

Table 7.1: Composition of the AFDL Government, July 1, 1997[35]

Name	Ministerial Position	Background
Mwenze Kongolo	Interior	Luba, Katanga
Deputised by Faustin Munene		*Former colonel in the MPLA; Bandundu*
Raphael Ghenda	Information and Culture	Tetela, Kasai Oriental
Deputized by Juliana Lumumba		*Daughter of Patrice Lumumba; Tetela, Kasai Oriental*
Bizima Karaha	Foreign Affairs	Banyamulenge, South Kivu
Mawapanga Mwana Nanga	Finance	Bakongo, Bas Congo
Thomas Kanza	International Cooperation	Old partisan of Lumumba; Bas Congo
Justine Kasa-Vubu	Public Office	Daughter of Congo's first president, UDPS; Bas Congo
Replaced on August 14 by Paul Kapita Shabangi		*UDPS; Luhua, Kasai Occidental*
Henri Mova Sakanyi	Transport	Lunda, Katanga
Paul Bandoma	Agriculture	UDPS; Ngbaka, Equateur
Pierre Victor Mpoyo	Economic Affairs	Luba, Kasai Oriental
Kambale Mututulo	Mines	Nande, North Kivu
Jean Moreno Kinkela VI Kan'si	Post and Telecoms	Bakongo, Bas Congo
Jean-Baptiste Sondji	Health and Social Affairs	Bandundu
Augustin Kamara Rwakaikara	Education	Hema, Province Orientale
Célestin Lwanghy	Justice	Kusu, Maniema
Etienne-Richard Mbaya	National Reconstruction	Old Lumumbist; Luba, Kasai Oriental
Anatole Bishikwabo Chubaka	Public Works	Bashi, South Kivu
Pierre Lokombe	Energy	Kusu-Tetela, Maniema
Edi Angulu	Environment and Tourism	Bandundu
Mutomb Tshibal	Youth and Sports	Lunda, Katanga

[35] De Villers and Willame, *République démocratique du Congo*, pp. 86–8.

government experience. This ensured that while many ministers were still figuring out how to govern and build a minimum degree of bureaucracy, almost all decisions of any consequence would be taken by the president. Secondly, Kabila did more than merely transfer the AFDL hierarchy into the state apparatus. He used the appointment of a Council of Ministers to marginalize a number of potential rivals. Only four of the ten members of the AFDL Executive Council (see Chapter 6) were given ministerial responsibility, while Anselme Masasu Nindaga—despite being a widely popular "founding father" of the liberation movement—was kept out of the official hierarchy altogether. Instead, Kabila rewarded some of his oldest "friends and pals," designating Mwenze Kongolo (Interior), Pierre Victor Mpoyo (National Economy) and Célestin Lwanghy (Justice) to important positions, while also including various individuals with clear links to the 1960s to mostly symbolic positions (Justine Kasa-Vubu, Thomas Kanza, Juliana Lumumba).

Thirdly, whereas it was to be expected that Mobutu's home province of Equateur would be subject to some degree of punishment (its previous over-representation was reversed, with barely one representative in the new cabinet), Kabila surprised many by handing only a handful of positions to the Banyamulenge (even if one of those was Minister of Foreign Affairs Bizima Karaha) and other groups from the Kivus. For months, the AFDL had been referred to in the international press as the "Banyamulenge rebellion," but in the cabinet there was little to substantiate this. Tellingly, the Congolese Tutsi were outnumbered by dissident members of Tshisekedi's Union pour la Démocratie et le Progrès Social (UDPS)—a canny move by Kabila to debunk claims of him serving as a figurehead for a Tutsi takeover of Congo. Finally, Mzee also used the formation of the first AFDL government to shift the political center of gravity away from Equateur and Kinshasa to a new axis between Katanga and Kasai, which together held almost half of all ministerial portfolios.[36] Both were not only key mining regions but had historically been hotbeds of anti-Mobutu sentiment. They were to form the political backbone of a new Congolese nationalism.

Unsurprisingly, Kabila did not stop at the distribution of ministerial seats to consolidate personal power and to exploit fault-lines in the political landscape. He handed the governorships of Kasai Occidental and Kasai Oriental to the UDPS to counter Tshisekedi's critiques and brought a new guard in to

[36] Stephen Smith, "Au nouveau Congo, les cent jours du pouvoir éclaté de Kabila: Radioscopie du régime du tombeur de Mobutu," *Libération*, August 26, 1997.

Table 7.2: Other Key Appointments July 1997[37]

Name	Function	Background
Pascal Tshiroka Ngalamuleme	Governor of Kasai Occidental	UDPS
Mbuyi Mulomba	Governor of Kasai Oriental	UDPS
Gaëtan Kakudji	Governor of Katanga	Luba
Deputized by Meli Kakongo		*Mutabwa; Former chief of staff of Tshombe and secretary-general of CONAKAT*
Léonard Kanyamuhanga	Governor of North Kivu	Tutsi, from Rutshuru
Deputized by Balume Tusi		*Hunde, from Masisi*
Jean Charles Magabe	Governor of South Kivu	Havu, from Idjwi Island[38]
Deputized by Benjamin Serukiza Nkunda Bantu		*Banyamulenge*
Anicet Kashamura	Constitutional Commission (established to deal with nationality question)	From Idjwi Island, South Kivu
Deputized by Delphin Banza		*Luba, Katanga*
Aubert Mukendi	Chief of Staff of the President	Luba, Kasai
Emile Kanengele	Deputy Chief of Staff of the President	North Katanga
Moïse Nyarugabo	Private Secretary to the President	Banyamulenge
Michel Rudatenguha	Economic Counselor to the President	Banyamulenge
Didier Kazadi Nyembwe	Political Counselor to the President	Burundese/Adopted Kasaien
Alfred Kalisa	Banker of the President	American-Rwandan
Georges Mazili Fundi	Head of the ANR in Katanga	Kabila's half-brother; Lunda
Nelly Tambwe and Régine Kambali	Personal Assistants to the President	Luba, North Katanga and Tutsi
James Kabarebe	Chief of Staff of FAC	RPA/Rwandan
Joseph Kabila	Deputy Chief of Staff of FAC	Luba, Katanga
Célestin Kifwa	Chief of National Police	Hemba, Katanga
Francis Gakwerere	Head of Presidential Guard	RPA/Rwandan
Paul Kabongo	Head of the ANR	Luba, Kasai
Shabani Sikatenda	Head of the Détection Militaire des Activités Anti-Patrie (DEMIAP)[39]	Bembe, South Kivu
Jean-Claude Masangu	Governor of the Central Bank	Katanga

[37] De Villers and Willame, *République démocratique du Congo*, pp. 91–101.

[38] As mentioned in Chapter 6, Idjwi Island was strategically situated between Rwanda and Congo and was a base for the ex-FAR/Interahamwe between 1994 and 1996.

[39] DEMIAP was another security service that was a carry-over from Kabila's old PRP and headed by an old Kabila loyalist.

run the Kivus. In Katanga, he appointed his childhood friend and leading figure in the Katangese diaspora, Gaëtan Kakudji, as governor while having his own half-brother run the provincial wing of the Agence Nationale de Renseignements (ANR—the national intelligence service)[40] to keep an eye on any disturbance caused by the disaffected Tigres Katangais who were virtually leaderless since Delphin Muland's arrest in May 1997. The governor of the Central Bank (Jean-Claude Masangu) and the head of the National Police (Célestin Kifwa) were Katangese too, as were the president's chiefs of staff and their deputies. A handful of Tutsi individuals were named as presidential collaborators to reassure the Banyamulenge constituency and the RPF that Mzee was not turning his back on them. Thus, with the Council of Ministers and informal positions of influence taken together, the AFDL regime—which claimed to be blind to ethnicity and region—was essentially an act in power-sharing between Katanga, Kasai and the Kivus, with a crucial Rwandan presence in the coercive apparatus of the state.

The Revolution and Its Foreign Backers

With the formation of the government complete, the governorships distributed and the key positions in finance and security filled, the last remaining piece of the puzzle of the post-Mobutu order was to determine the role to be played by the regional governments that had supported the liberation of Congo. Uganda had been involved with the AFDL from the start and offered to train the new Congolese national police. Mzee accepted the proposal without hesitations but failed to pay Kampala for its services, which quickly led to tensions.[41] Yoweri Museveni thus chose to mainly rely on his close relationship with the RPF for his security concerns in Congo. As had been the case during the AFDL campaign, a small but dedicated group of advisers to Museveni were tasked with Congo policy: Minister of Local Government Kahinda Otafiire, the president's half-brother Salim Saleh, UPDF General James Kazini and his brother, Colonel Jet Mwebaze, ESO director David Pulkol, and MP Okwiri Rabwoni sought to deny the rebels of the Lord's Resistance Army and the Allied Democratic Forces a sanctuary in Province Orientale and kept an eye on the general geopolitical orientation of Congo's liberation movement. Uganda's Congo cabal concentrated

---

[40] Augustin Katumba Mwanke, *Ma vérité*, Nice: Imprimerie Toscane, 2013, pp. 97–100.
[41] Interview with David Pulkol, Kampala, March 2013.

principally on obtaining influence in the intelligence services where it managed to get several of its protégés appointed, like Kasereka Kibatondwa Moses (a Ugandan-Congolese Nande from North Kivu on Kampala's pay list) who became the number two in the nation's top spy service, the ANR.[42]

To offset the dominance of the Rwandan–Ugandan axis in the security sector, Kabila also asked others to assume strategic roles. The Tanzanian government of Benjamin Mkapa and his foreign minister Jakaya Kikwete and the Tanzanian People's Defense Forces (TPDF) had become increasingly weary of the RPF and sought to reduce Kigali's influence in Kinshasa. TPDF trainers were deployed to the old military base of Kamina in Katanga to train new army units and officers, where James Kabarebe's gaze struggled to penetrate.[43] Zimbabwe, which shared Dar es Salaam's doubts about the RPF, offered to provide weapons and equipment to these recruits. Finally, South Africa looked into what could be done on the economic side to help revive the ailing economy.

All in all, the assistance offered to the AFDL was modest, particularly in comparison to the high expectations that the Pan-Africanist mobilization for the AFDL in 1996–7 had generated. One reason for this was the preoccupation of the most fervent advocates of exporting liberation regimes in Asmara, Addis Ababa and Kampala with the internationalized civil war in Sudan. The EPLF, TPLF/EPRDF and NRM gave all-out support to the SPLA/M of John Garang and sent thousands of soldiers into Sudan to confront the military-Islamist Al-Ingaz regime which also sought to export its ideological model, having already backed regime change in Chad in 1990 and tried to assassinate Egyptian President Hosni Mubarak in 1995.[44] This epic fight was prioritized over further involvement in Congo.[45] A second reason for the downscaling of the collective, Pan-Africanist element of post-liberation consolidation was that Julius Nyerere's health permitted ever less involvement in furthering the cause. Nyerere would make one trip to Kinshasa in September 1997, but Kabila's personalization of power would leave the Mwalimu deeply disap-

---

[42] Interviews with Faustin Munene and Mwenze Kongolo, December 2009.

[43] Interviews with Jean-Claude Yav in Kinshasa, July 2013 and with Caesar Kayizari in Kigali, April 2013.

[44] Harry Verhoeven, "The Rise and Fall of Sudan's Al-Ingaz Revolution: The Transition from Militarised Islamism to Economic Salvation and the Comprehensive Peace Agreement," *Civil Wars*, 15, 2 (2013).

[45] Interviews with Jeje Odongo in Kampala, March 2013 and Yemane Kidane in Addis, November 2014.

pointed,[46] and instead he devoted his attention to mediation efforts in the Burundese civil war. Nyerere's withdrawal opened the way for the Tanzanian government and security services—which had an increasingly divergent view of Congo and Rwanda—to dominate its Congo policy, which they leveraged to counter-balance the RPF.

A final factor undoubtedly lay in the swift disillusionment of regional players with the AFDL project. Already at Kabila's official inauguration on May 27, 1997, the heads of states in attendance—Pasteur Bizimungu (Rwanda), Pierre Buyoya (Burundi), Frederick Chiluba (Zambia), José Eduardo Dos Santos (Angola) and Yoweri Museveni (Uganda)—were unpleasantly surprised that Kabila could spare the Pan-Africanist alliance that had brought him to power only one small sentence: "We cannot end this speech without thanking all the countries that supported us during our long liberation struggle."[47] Bizimungu, Museveni and Dos Santos understood that Mzee had to bolster his nationalist credentials and was mainly addressing the Congolese nation. However, he did not even bother to name the movements and leaders who had made all the difference; moreover, his terseness regarding international security concerns worried them. It would be the first in a series of early disappointments.

One of the first allies to be directly alienated by Kabila was Angola. After the overthrow of Mobutu, dozens of technical specialists and intelligence officers operated in the country under the command of Mário Plácido Cirilo de Sá "Ita." The MPLA had hoped that even if Luanda would not be able to play a major role in the new Kinshasa government, it could at least continue operations to deny UNITA the use of its old Congolese bases and networks. However, after the Tshikapa incident of April 1997 and the open rivalry with the RPF, compounded by Kabila's distrust of the Tigres and the arrest of Muland (see Chapter 6), the relationship had soured to the point that Mzee asked the Angolans to leave Congo in June 1997—Kabila's first (and least well-known) expulsion order. The MPLA accepted the decision without much drama, but did not forgive or forget, suspecting Rwandan manipulation—an element that would prove crucial after the outbreak of war in August 1998. As RPF veteran Patrick Mazimhaka recalled: "They were expelled before us: they were con-

---

[46] At the end of the trip, Nyerere is alleged to have warned the new president: "Our support was not for you; it was for the Congolese people. If you don't watch out, the same thing will happen to you as happened to Mobutu." Quoted in Stearns, *Dancing in the Glory of Monsters*, p. 203.

[47] De Villers and Willame, *République démocratique du Congo*, p. 77.

vinced Rwanda engineered the expulsion."[48] In the words of Ita: "Mzee asked us to leave but Rwanda imposed their will to stay in Congo."[49]

Angola's ignominious exit after its contribution to the liberation struggle had a ripple effect around the region. Mandela and Nyerere were disappointed to hear the news of the Angolan departure, but not surprised. Mandela had already developed the impression that Kabila would be a mediocre president at best after his personal dealings with him in the weeks before the fall of Kinshasa, during South Africa's attempts at getting Mobutu to relinquish power voluntarily;[50] Nyerere's September 1997 visit to Congo was an even greater let down when the Mwalimu witnessed the dysfunctionality of the AFDL and growing tensions between the comrades. Neither the RPA officers, nor the Congolese Tutsi, nor the ordinary population appeared satisfied with the way things were going. Kabila's habit of managing Congo's government the way he managed the *maquis*—in some cases turning PRP organs that he created in Fizi-Baraka into state institutions—revealed itself as a potentially lethal liability.[51] At the Memling Hotel in Gombe, Nyerere thus whispered to a group of AFDL cadres that "Congo was not lucky with its leaders."[52]

This sentiment of disappointment and resultant disengagement was also shared in Eritrea and Ethiopia. Haile Menkerios, who led the Pan-Africanist team for political encadrement of the AFDL and organized Issayas's visit to Kabila's Congo in June 1997, lived for five months in Kinshasa's Gombe area but felt increasingly frustrated at being ignored. His team's ideas for a constitution were left unimplemented by Kabila who met with them less and less frequently. Haile saw Mzee's new government not so much as a milestone, but a step in the wrong direction: "He was joined by so many predators—we saw it happen, but could do nothing."[53] The non-existence of a Congolese army left him gravely worried; if it were not for the RPF, the revolution could quickly collapse: "I told Meles and Issayas that Kabila was not listening to any advice ... We were a military success but a political disaster. There was no ideological army, no real cohesion. Without transformation I feared it would be a predatory army—with the same mistakes of the Mobutu mind-set."[54] Haile

---

[48] Interview in Kigali, July 2014.
[49] Interview in Luanda, May 2014.
[50] Reyntjens, *Great African War*, 130.
[51] Kennes, *Essai biographique sur Laurent Désiré Kabila*, p. 322.
[52] Interview with Moïse Nyarugabo in Kinshasa, December 2009.
[53] Interview in Addis Ababa, November 2014.
[54] Ibid.

Menkerios's fellow Eritrean envoy Yemane Gebreab reached the same conclusion: "The biggest problem was the Congolese internal weakness. The Rwandans were not all too problematic. Kabila did not make use of the Rwandan presence to consolidate power. The Congolese lacked the organization and the focus to manage it themselves. Sorry."[55]

The growing concerns among the comrades are best captured by an anecdote dating back to several months after the liberation, when Yemane Kidane, Ethiopia's special envoy for the Great Lakes, traveled to Congo in the hope of seeing Mzee. When it became clear that the latter had numerous commitments on multiple days in a row, Kidane told Joseph Kabila he would return to Addis with the official plane, as this was needed in Ethiopia. Upon hearing this, Mzee, however, implored Kidane to stay, saying he would arrange transport back to Addis if he would stay another day. Kabila finally met his Ethiopian comrade the next afternoon and they spoke for hours; they then drove together to N'Djili Airport where a private jet was waiting. Two Russian pilots, standing on the tarmac, were expecting Kidane and greeted the Congolese president with a quick salute. To Kidane's utmost surprise, Mzee responded to their gesture by handing them a big Samsonite bag full of US dollars. "Don't worry Yemane!" he said. "The jet is paid for by me." In his report to Ethiopian Prime Minister Meles Zenawi upon his return, Kidane could barely disguise his disgust: "Administration was completely non-existent. There was no finance department to organize my ticket, no administrative procedure to pay the Russians, no official receipt, no protocol officer to do it. He personally gave the money for fuel."[56]

Going It Alone: The Mzee Consolidates Power

One of the more apt descriptions of Kabila as president is Prunier's classic line that he was "a political Rip van Winkle whose conspiratorial political style had been frozen at some point back in the 1960s ..."[57] This had also been the impression of Haile Menkerios when Mzee lectured him on imperialism, the dangers of the comprador bourgeoisie and the problems with electoral democracy, notwithstanding the fact that Kabila had never been close to managing a state and Menkerios was a key shaper of the (then) Eritrean success story of national lib-

---

[55] Interview in Asmara, March 2015.
[56] Interview in Addis Ababa, November 2014.
[57] Prunier, *From Genocide to Continental War*, p. 149.

eration: "Kabila lived in a dream ... He did not try to see the world's from any-body else's perspective."[58] Western diplomats echoed this perception too; according to Frank De Coninck, who met Mzee in March and April 1997 for the first time, "It was like the Berlin Wall did not fall for Kabila."[59]

Kabila's Cold War-tinted glasses blurred his political vision in a number of ways but it nearly blinded him to Washington's "New World Order," which hailed democracy as the silver bullet to Africa's political and economic woes. At a minimum, incumbents, especially those dependent on foreign aid to grease their patronage networks, were expected to do the democracy two-step: embrace multi-party rule and hold elections. Across the continent, autocrats from Daniel arap Moi in Kenya to Idriss Déby in Chad and Hastings Banda in Malawi succumbed to this pressure—in the case of the latter at the cost of his political survival. But even if the incumbents were unwilling to allow an even playing field, merely going through the motions and "taking steps down the path to democracy" were often enough to get a pass from donors, espe-cially in the wake of the democratization debacles that littered Africa from Algeria to Angola. Kabila's refusal as president to even engage in such token-ism was the first major sign of the coming frustration of US policy-makers vis-à-vis Congo, despite the close coordination between Washington, the RPF and the AFDL that we discussed in Chapters 5 and 6.

Kabila's Refusal to Entertain the "Charade of Democracy"

On Wednesday, March 25, 1998, Bill Clinton and Yoweri Museveni hosted a highly unusual summit by the shores of Lake Victoria in Entebbe: at the request of his American counterpart, the Ugandan leader brought together Presidents Bizimungu (Rwanda), Moi (Kenya), Mkapa (Tanzania), OAU Secretary-General Salim Salim, Ethiopian premier Meles and, last but not least, Laurent-Désiré Kabila. The informal but much publicized gathering was intended as the highlight of Clinton's unprecedented voyage to Africa and for the United States to boost what it saw as a new generation of African leaders. With the attendance of several leading lights of the Pan-Africanist coalition that had overthrown Mobutu, it also served as recognition of the new regional order ushered in by the comrades. Clinton famously toasted Kabila who visibly relished the irony and triumph of having a US president recognize his leadership.

[58] Interview in Addis Ababa, November 2014.
[59] Interview in Rome, June 2009.

Yet if Washington seemed to embrace Kabila and endorse his government publicly one year after liberation, privately Clinton sternly lectured Mzee about the state of Congo's political institutions.[60] Whereas the AFDL's statements during the campaign had incessantly lambasted Mobutu's dictatorial tendencies, the democracy it once deemed inalienable turned out to be negotiable. Upon capturing Kinshasa, Congo's new sovereign immediately banned opposition parties and political demonstrations; when Tshisekedi's UDPS party defied the order, security forces forcefully dispersed the demonstrators. A constitutional decree released on May 27, 1997, attributed all powers to the president. At his official swearing in on May 29, Kabila announced that his government was "not in a hurry" to hold elections and promised them within two years at the earliest. At first, the Clinton administration appeared happy to give Kabila some breathing room given the "severe problems" the country faced.[61] "We'll give you some time to put the house in order" had also been the understanding on the side of Kabila and his advisers when in April 1997 Mzee met CIA acting director George Tenet, US Ambassador to the UN Bill Richardson and US Ambassador to Zaire Daniel Simpson in Lubumbashi.[62] Around the same time, he also met senior Belgian envoys who requested reassurances that there would be no large-scale revenge when the AFDL moved into Kinshasa.[63] Kabila's fellow African heads of state were even more accommodating. For example, Nelson Mandela stated publicly that "It would be suicidal for him to allow the operation of parties before he has a firm grip on the government of the country. ... I think therefore that we can trust him, on the basis of his record, to keep his word."[64]

However, Kabila's track record did not bode well for the future of democracy in Congo. Numerous journalists, in seeking to learn about the man who had appeared out of nowhere to end Mobutu's thirty-two years in power, dug into Kabila's past and interviewed people in Fizi-Baraka, the location of the *maquis* that the revolutionary set up in the late 1960s. The reports were not flattering. According to one *Guardian* exposé:

[60] Interview with US Ambassador David Scheffer, March 2015.
[61] Andrew Maykuth, "Kabila Assumes Office amid Accolades, Anger," *Philadelphia Inquirer*, May 30, 1997.
[62] Interview with Didier Kazadi in Kinshasa, August 2013.
[63] Interview with Frank De Coninck in Rome, June 2009.
[64] Scott Straus and Inigo Gilmore, "Congo Ban on Political Parties Wins Praise: First Things First, African Leaders Say," *Globe and Mail* (Canada), May 28, 1997.

Not many Kinshasans waiting to see their new president can say with confidence what life will be like under Laurent Kabila. A year ago, hardly anyone under the age of 40 had heard of him ... But buried deep in the east of the country are a group of people who have first hand experience of Mr Kabila's rule, and they would not recommend it to anyone ... Mr Kabila armed and ruled the Bembe people on and off from 1964 until the late 1970s. They were rallied in the name of Marxist revolution, and villages were run on similar ideological lines. But many Bembe grew to despise him ... They paint him as a violently authoritarian opportunist who was more interested in profiteering and running his own fiefdom than fighting from his outlying headquarters of Hewa Bora. The Bembe accuse Mr Kabila of brutal killings, such as burning alive at the stake those he suspected of betraying him, or of using witchcraft. They say he used them to mine gold which ostensibly went to fund his obscure and, at the time, futile revolution.[65]

To the exasperation of his American would-be allies, Kabila did not change course and, even worse, made a mockery of Washington's calls for political reforms, including in a notorious joint press conference with US Secretary of State Madeleine Albright in December 1997. In response to a critical question from a journalist about freedom of association in Congo, Kabila reaffirmed his government's right to jail political agitators and enemies of the state before exclaiming in a sarcastic tone: "Long live democracy. Ha-ha-ha!"[66] A few weeks later, in February 1998, Clinton's special envoy to Africa, Jesse Jackson, visited Kinshasa to further push for political reforms but Mzee rebuffed him. Jackson met Tshisekedi, however, which prompted Kabila to exile the opposition leader to his native village in Kasai Oriental. This measure disappointed some of the president's own supporters too, who felt he was delegitimizing the government in resorting to some of Mobutu's tried-and-true tactics.[67] A general crackdown on all kinds of dissident voices ensued, including against the Kasaien sociology professor (and UDPS secretary) Mathieu Kalele who was manhandled and sentenced to two years in prison for publishing a document entitled "100.000.000$ US to Steal Our Country and Give It to the Tutsi and Nilotics," which claimed that Congo had become "the exclusive property of

---

[65] Chris Mcgreal, "Worrying Past of a Rebel In Crocodile Shoes," *The Guardian*, May 21, 1997. For a more academic but no less scathing account, also Wilungula B. Cosma and Jean-Luc Vellut, *Fizi, 1967–1986: Le maquis Kabila*, Brussels: Institut Africain CEDAF 1997.

[66] Howard W. French, *A Continent for the Taking: The Tragedy and Hope of Africa*, New York: Alfred A. Knopf 2004, pp. 247–8.

[67] Interview with Henri Mova Sakanyi, April 2011.

Eritreans, Ugandans and Rwandans ... At will they confiscate our vehicles, our houses, our women!"[68] Kabila's clumsy reaction to Washington's calls for even the weakest of signals demonstrating a commitment to democratic reform belied the deeper strategic considerations that motivated his whole-hearted embrace of authoritarianism. The first was his fixation on the potential threat posed by Tshisekedi and the Kinshasa-based opposition. Unlike the AFDL, the opposition leader had extensive networks of supporters in the capital; moreover, opinion polls in the first months after the overthrow of Mobutu showed that Tshisekedi was more popular than Kabila (33 per cent support to 11 per cent).[69] As Minister of Human Rights Shé Okitundu stated at the time, "We cannot trust that person ... Don't believe we are going to fight for 37 years and then say, 'Tshisekedi, take the power.'"[70] The neutralization of Tshisekedi was effective (or at least the suppression of the willingness of the Kinshasa residents—known as the Kinois—to state their support for him): by July 1998, the opinion polls showed Kabila outpaced his opposition rival—33 per cent to 20 per cent.

Even as he sidelined his main rival in Kinshasa, Kabila rejected calls to open the political system. Assured of the RPF's support and with the council of ministers entirely beholden to him, there was little to be gained, and much to lose, from rushing to hold elections. His decision to favor the consolidation of power through authoritarianism rather than democracy mirrored the approach of his main foreign patron[71]—but without the organizational apparatus necessary to prevent the political instability that arises from the concentration of power.

In many ways, Kabila's rejection of multi-party rule was much less destabilizing than his emasculation of the AFDL as a political organization and the elimination of the constraints it placed on his personal power. The political longevity of Africa's liberation and neo-liberation regimes has resulted from their control over the military as well as the strength of the politico-military

---

[68] De Villers and Willame, *République Démocratique du Congo*, p. 108.

[69] Opinion poll carried out by Bureau d'Etudes, de Recherche et de Consulting International (BERCI). Cited in International Crisis Group, "How Kabila Lost His Way: The Performance of Laurent Désiré Kabila's Government," Brussels: ICG, 1999.

[70] Lynne Duke, "Only the Faces Change; Kabila's 1st Year Resembles Congo's Former 30-Year Dictatorship," *Washington Post*, May 17, 1998.

[71] Filip Reyntjens, "Rwanda, Ten Years On: From Genocide to Dictatorship," *African Affairs*, 103, 411 (2004).

organizations they built during their rise to power. The political organizations of these liberation movements have been essential in insulating them from existential threats from within and from without—Angola's MPLA and Mozambique's FRELIMO, for instance, have both been in power since 1974. However, in the case of the AFDL, the organizational bases for both single-party rule and multi-party rule were non-existent. The AFDL was an empty shell and Kabila exploited this in anointing himself president. When the post-liberation government was formed, Mzee was perfectly content with letting Déogratias Bugera—a Tutsi from North Kivu recruited by Patrick Karegeya's ESO, but with even less of a political base than Kabila himself—run the party. In giving Bugera a major stake in the new order, Kabila was outwardly hoping to be seen as recognizing the sacrifices made by the Congolese Tutsi during the struggle. But inwardly he intended the appointment to be largely symbolic, not substantive.[72]

The tensions between Bugera and Kabila dated back to the AFDL campaign when the former hoped that, with the RPF's help and by partnering with Masasu, he would have a credible shot at the top position—a notion that was not up for discussion as far as Mzee was concerned.[73] Kabila's decision to anoint himself president went down badly with Bugera, but in the face of what he saw as RPF collusion, he sat tight with the hopes his accommodative approach would pay off with a position of real influence in the new government.[74] It was in this context that Kabila appointed Bugera to more or less stay on as secretary-general of the AFDL—seeking to appease his comrade, while giving him little power. But if Kabila gambled that this would be seen as a pacifying gesture, it turned out to be a recipe for additional trouble. Bugera sought to elevate the party as a primary locus of influence, and strengthen its political networks parallel to that of the presidency. Tellingly, however, when he attempted to use the (empty) Office of the Prime Minister as the party's headquarters, Kabila's inner circle prevented him from doing so by claiming that this was an anti-democratic usurpation of state property. Thus by the time the prominent young Banyamulenge business man Thomas Nziratimana joined Bugera's staff in October 1997, only a semblance of cooperation

---

[72] Interview with Henri Mova in Brussels, April 2011.

[73] Interview with Deogratias Bugera, March 2010, and Jean-Baptiste Sondji, December 2009.

[74] Stephen Smith, "Au nouveau Congo, les cent jours du pouvoir éclaté de Kabila. Radioscopie du régime du tombeur de Mobutu," *Libération*, August 26, 1997.

remained between Kabila and the AFDL. This increasingly evident rupture in Kinshasa, combined with growing complaints from the Kivus about Kabila's disinterest in their problems, Nziratimana could only conclude with them that "We had started realizing that Kabila was not the guy we thought he was."[75] The discontent among comrades within the AFDL was about to take a chilling turn.

The Political Assassination of Masasu

By late 1997, it was becoming glaringly obvious that the incredible divergence in the fortunes of the AFDL's four founding fathers was a profoundly destabilizing factor in Congolese politics, one which threatened the revolution itself. With Kisase dead and Bugera ever less relevant, only one other individual in the movement retained the capability to challenge the growing concentration of power in the president. However, Anselme Masasu Nindaga,[76] the charismatic, 27-year-old AFDL commander from South Kivu who had played a significant role in the first months of the campaign with his wildly successful recruitment drive in the Kivus, was struggling greatly in adapting to life in Kinshasa, both personally and politically. While he had acquired a stunning house in the exclusive neighborhood of Mont Fleury/Ngaliema, his lack of political experience and rural upbringing left him overwhelmed by life in the metropolis and sapped his authority. When forming a government, Kabila had not felt the need to appoint him to any formal position, merely informally signaling to Masasu that he was the AFDL military commander—*afande*—and that, because no one challenged this fact, there was no need to formalize it. Masasu disliked this fiercely, but with the RPF so solidly aligned with Kabila, he seemed to have little option other than resignation.

Like Bugera, Moïse Nyarugabo and others in the alliance, Masasu had been dismayed when Kabila flouted the movement's deliberations on who would be president and assumed the position unilaterally.[77] As time went by, Masasu's companions encouraged him to show Mzee that he should not be taken for granted. Moreover, fearing that Kabila might even deprive him of his role as "*afande*," Masasu created a parallel security force consisting of loyal easterners.

[75] Interview, March 2013.

[76] For incredible insights into the rise and fall of Masasu, see Lieve Joris, *The Rebels' Hour*, trans. Liz Waters, New York: Grove Press, 2008.

[77] Communication with Deogratias Bugera, March 2010.

This move, unsurprisingly, was badly received in the circles around Kabila, who saw Masasu as a rival center of authority. The latter's frequent travel to the Kivus to maintain close connections with his armed supporters and recruit extra *kadogo* was a thorn in the side of Mzee's project of concentrating power in the presidency.

Matters came to a head when, on November 25, 1997, following a six-day trip to China, Kabila made his move. Fearing the *afande* was building himself up to pose a credible threat to Kabila's hold on power, Mzee had him arrested. In characteristic style, Kabila taunted Masasu publicly as nothing more than a Rwandan corporal who had played a marginal role in the struggle—a slap in the face to one of the heroes of the revolution. Masasu was accused of providing intelligence to foreign enemies, running a private militia and creating a shadow state in the east.[78] His brother was also arrested and condemned to twenty years imprisonment for inciting rebellion in Bukavu; Masasu himself would face the same verdict before a military court in Lubumbashi in May 1998.[79]

Kabila's neutralization of one of the AFDL's most popular leaders shook the movement to its core. Violence erupted almost immediately in military camps in Kinshasa between forces loyal to Masasu and Kabila's Katangese soldiers, killing dozens;[80] the shooting only stopped when the *afande* called his men and ordered them to lay down their arms.[81] Bugera released a statement two days after the arrest saying that he trusted that Masasu would be found innocent before a judge—to which Kabila responded by barring the AFDL secretary-general from attending Council of Ministers' meetings.[82] Enock Ruberangabo Sebineza, a community leader from South Kivu commented that, "His arrest triggered great discontent in the east. There was a feeling that Kabila was picking off his enemies one by one."[83] Malick Kijege, a Tutsi officer in the FAC, also expressed his outrage and dismissed the pretext for Masasu's arrest: "It was his entourage which told Mzee that Masasu wanted to kill him—which was a fabrication. They wanted more power and used

---

[78] "Kinshasa Denounces Arrested Security Adviser," AFP, November 30, 1997; interviews in Kinshasa, eastern Congo and Rwanda, December 2009–August 2010

[79] De Villers and Willame, *République démocratique du Congo*, p. 126.

[80] "Tough Tactics in Ex-Zaire Evoke Ghost of Mobutu," *New York Times*, November 30, 1997. "Le Congo d'abord," *Jeune Afrique*, December 16, 1997.

[81] Interview with Bshimbe Bantuzeko, one of Masasu's lieutenants, Butare, August 2010.

[82] Interview in Kinshasa with *Philomène* Omatuku, December 2009.

[83] Interview in Kinshasa, December 2009.

Masasu to grab it."[84] Belgian Ambassador Frank De Coninck interpreted the bottom-line in similar terms: "the political elimination of Masasu was another key sign that the influence of the east was shifting away to Katanga."[85]

Masasu's "political assassination"[86] had a profound impact on trust between Kabila and the other co-conspirators. As Lieve Joris describes it through the eyes of Assani, her young Tutsi protagonist who sees Masasu, the man who personally recruited him to join the revolution, shackled and imprisoned: "Assani ... felt crushed. It was as if everything he'd once believed in was finished. Kabila had turned his back on the men who'd helped him to power and decided to rule by himself."[87] To contain the growing backlash, Kabila let his national security adviser, Didier Kazadi, read out a statement on national television on December 1 in which he admitted that indiscipline and tribalism had seeped into the national revolutionary forces and that a zero-tolerance policy would be implemented against excesses and disloyalty.[88] Informally, however, Kabila reached out to the RPF, knowing its reaction to the entire episode would be critical. James Kabarebe was under no illusion as to why Masasu was arrested:"He went after him because he saw him as a rival. That's all there was to it."[89] But tellingly, the RPF did little to save the former RPA corporal Masasu (whose relationship with Kabarebe had deteriorated independently of his problems in Kinshasa[90]), instead accepting—for the time being—Kabila's continued commitment in the form of carte blanche to pursue the ex-FAR/Interahamwe. The renewed elite bargain was highlighted by a public announcement in December 1997 which finally confirmed to the population that James Kabarebe was the FAC chief of staff and would be ruthlessly intolerant of insecurity and indiscipline on Congolese territory.

Yet if Mzee's appeasement worked vis-à-vis the RPF, his own people were less reassured. Even close advisers were rattled by Masasu's incarceration. Shé Okitundu, Kabila's main foreign policy counselor, admitted that this was a power struggle, not a question of criminality: "[Masasu] was a military threat

[84] Interview in Kinshasa, August 2013.

[85] Interview in Rome, June 2009.

[86] This is how a top official in the AFDL described Masasu's arrest. Interview Kinshasa, December 2009.

[87] Joris, *Rebels' Hour*, p. 126.

[88] Martens, *Kabila et la révolution congolaise*, vol. 1, pp. 262–3.

[89] Interview in Kigali, April 2013.

[90] Interview with Bshimbe Bantuzeko, one of Masasu's lieutenants, Butare, August 2010.

to Laurent-Désiré Kabila, given his support among the young. He and Mzee had a huge sense of entitlement."[91] Henri Mova, a fellow Katangese and the minister of transport, described Masasu's incarceration as a "shock"[92] while Chikez Diemu, a Katangese member of the Constitutional Commission, saw the arrest as "a turning point ..."[93] Others echoed this analysis: "One of the biggest mistakes the president made was to arrest Masasu," Faustin Munene, one of Kabila's lieutenants for security matters and vice-minister of the interior, reflected. Revealing the degree to which the move increased uncertainty and mistrust in the regime, he then commented: "I could have been Masasu."[94]

Conclusion

Despite the initial euphoria, the consolidation of political order after the liberation of Congo presented major difficulties. This chapter dissected how the AFDL coalition went about laying the foundations of the revolution it had promised, but within a few months of promulgating a new state, cooperation turned to discord and members of the alliance attempted to block each other at every turn. Two of the most influential actors within the AFDL, however, remained in lockstep—Mzee and the RPF. Each continued to help the other pursue its post-Mobutu agenda, even as doing so eroded the goodwill and trust of their alliance partners—as well as sowing the seeds for their own falling out.

The RPF had decided after an internal debate to stay in Congo and become part of the liberation regime, with all the risks this entailed. In light of what they saw as a continued existential threat posed by the *génocidaires* hiding in neighboring countries and the Congolese rainforest, Kagame and his security chiefs calculated that the AFDL remained all too weak as a politico-military force and that the situation was thus too critical to entrust to anyone but the RPA elite forces. The overthrow of the old tyrant of Zaire had been the third total military victory for the RPF in less than ten years; partly deceived by its own hubris, the Front underestimated the political costs of occupation and overestimated its own ability to shape the post-Mobutu order in Central Africa.

In doing so, the RPF deepened its partnership with Kabila, whose overriding ambition was to consolidate his authority and gradually build autonomy vis-à-

---

[91] Interview in Kinshasa, August 2013.

[92] Interview in Brussels, April 2012.

[93] Interview in Lubumbashi, August 2013.

[94] Interview in Kinshasa, December 2009.

vis his Rwandan allies. Mzee showed scant interest in multi-party democracy or the building of a strong party, relying instead on a growing personalization of power. Appointing the first post-liberation government was a crucial step in the affirmation of the hierarchy he envisaged; in dividing and ruling the opposition, as well as forging a new politico-regional axis between Kasai and Katanga, he swiftly managed to take major strides towards his objective. This generated angst among Congo's regional friends, who were increasingly unimpressed with how Mzee had squandered the unique opportunities of the honeymoon months of liberation. Eritrea and Ethiopia pulled out of Congo altogether, Angola was asked to leave and Uganda managed its interests from a distance. The shine of the Pan-Africanist triumph was wearing off precipitously.

A similar sense of disappointment emerged among the Congolese comrades, particularly as Mzee marginalized Déogratias Bugera and had Anselme Masasu Nindaga preventively shackled. Discontent was rapidly spreading. Kabila's attempts to strengthen his grip on power soured the trust that had developed between the conspirators in their victorious campaign against Mobutu. Constituents of the AFDL from eastern Congo protested as the balance of power within the regime was tilted away from them in favor of the Katangese. As their prominence waned, Congolese Tutsi worried that Kabila would backtrack on his promise to resolve the nationality question. The RPF questioned the reliability of Kabila as well, because even if their elite deal remained in place, his treatment of the young *afande* suggested he might turn on his other comrades too: "We lost hope in Kabila when they arrested Masasu—he represented our interest more than anyone else."[95] The conspirators no longer took it for granted that their partners preferred mutual cooperation. Instead, suspicion and fears of betrayal weighed on the comrades and the mistrust came to dominate strategic interactions.

---

[95] Interview in Kigali with key Rwandan security operative based in Kinshasa in 1997–8, December 2009.

INTERLUDE

A RWANDAN FOLKTALE

As long as anyone could remember, humans and hyenas had been sworn enemies. Whenever a hyena was spotted, the villagers would alert each other and defend their children and their village against possible incursions of the hunter. This took up a lot of the villagers' energy, but it paid off: no villager had been killed in years and fewer and fewer hyenas tended to come close to the village.

One day, however, an arrogant young farmer, Umwirasi, bumped into a hyena in the forest outside the village. Umwirasi had been living on his own, even before getting married, which was very unusual but he did not care much for the critique of his elders. Sure of his own decisions, he lived a carefree life and when he met the hyena, he saw no reason to change that attitude. Umwirasi and the hyena spoke and spoke—and both seemed to like each other. The next day they met again. The hyena was not that young and seemed not dangerous at all; and Umwirasi had never cared much for the warnings of those villagers that nothing good could come of a hyena. To prove them wrong, he decided to try to tame the hyena. When on the third day he returned from another trip to the forest and the elders admonished him for such a dangerous idea, Umwirasi laughed. What did they know about hyenas? All they had ever done was fight them. Umwirasi would show that hyenas could be useful for the village—and everybody would, eventually, be grateful to him for providing the community with such a valuable service.

For a month, Umwirasi and the hyena lived together, and every day he would urge the animal to help him carry out important tasks to support his livelihood. The hyena appeared full of goodwill, but was not very effective in

his assistance. Umwirasi, mindful of the scorn he faced from the other villagers, refused to give up and told people that the hyena was learning and would
soon surprise them all.

One day, the hyena came running towards Umwirasi. "Umwirasi!" he said,
"There are beautiful pastures on the other side of the forest where we can take
some of our cows to graze. The grass there is so good that the cows simply
refuse to eat anything else once they have tasted it!" Umwirasi's eyes shone
with pride—the hyena was giving him invaluable advice. Soon his cows would
be bigger and stronger than everybody else's. This was an exciting thought.

The following afternoon, Umwirasi set out with the hyena on a journey to
see those pastures before taking his cows there. As he was about to leave, many
of the villagers stood silently at the village's edge watching them. Umwirasi did
not say anything but his triumphant expression spoke volumes: soon everybody would envy him. He walked into the forest with the hyena by his side.
"How long before we reach the pastures, hyena?" he asked. "Perhaps four
hours," the hyena said.

After an hour of walking under the canopies, the hyena suddenly stopped.
"I can't go on anymore, Umwirasi, I'm tired," he complained. "The walk is
more difficult than I remember." Umwirasi was still euphoric and refused to
let this dampen his spirit. "Why don't you rest for five minutes and then we
continue?" The hyena demurred somewhat: "Okay, but could you carry me on
your back for a while so we reach the place as soon as possible? I'm sure I'll be
well rested after a bit and then we can walk together again." Umwirasi told the
hyena to jump on his back.

The two covered more ground and climbed and descended a hill in the
forest, but with the heavy animal on Umwirasi's back, the progress made was
less and less impressive. Umwirasi was exhausted and the forest seemed endless. He had a hard time admitting that he was lost and could no longer think
clearly. The hyena, by contrast, looked very fit and jumped off Umwirasi's
back. "Come on, Umwirasi, we need to get there soon. Let's move a bit
quicker!" the hyena shouted. "If you're tired and lost, why don't you let me
carry you and lead us?" Before Umwirasi knew it, the hyena had pulled him
onto his back and quickened the pace.

A stunned Umwirasi was led into a different direction by the hyena. The
forest grew thicker and thicker and every time he asked the hyena where they
were, the animal chuckled and told him not to worry—their destination was
not far anymore. The trees seemed to become ever taller, until Umwirasi and
the hyena arrived at another hill in the forest, with big rocks now dominating

the landscape. The hyena threw the hapless man off his back; Umwirasi fell onto the ground and realized the animal, which he thought he had tamed and put at his service, had remained wild and fiercely independent all along. He was far away from the village, all alone and his cries for help could not reach anyone. The hyena had deceived him—and he had deceived himself—and now it was too late.

8

THE UNRAVELING

INTERNAL AND EXTERNAL STRAINS ON THE ALLIANCE

The killings of the refugees was a very destabilizing issue for us ... We took the blame. There was no other way we could deal with it—we couldn't accuse Rwanda.

Mwenze Kongolo, minister of justice in the Kabila government.

We were a bit naive: we thought that if South Africans could live together, as black and white, so could we in Congo. This was a big mistake.

Bizima Karaha, minister of foreign affairs in the Kabila government.

The one-year anniversary of the liberation of Congo was intended to be celebrated with much fanfare. Sixteen heads of state from across Africa were invited to partake in the festivities. Concurrently, a two-day summit entitled "Solidarity and Development in the Great Lakes Region" was to be held in Kinshasa to give the country, in the words of the state-owned radio station, "a new credibility in the African continent."[1] But if "Kabila's swearing in was a bit like an OAU summit—everybody wanted to attend, everybody wanted some stardust,"[2] one year later, the region, including Kabila's staunchest allies, Rwanda and Uganda, started to treat the Congolese leader as a pariah. Most heads of state—except for Robert Mugabe of Zimbabwe and Ange-Félix

[1] "Security Summit Postponed in Kinshasa," Associated Press, May 15, 1998.
[2] Interview with Caesar Kayizari, Kigali, April 2013.

Patassé of Central African Republic, both of whom had not been part of the Pan-Africanist alliance that had handed Kabila the presidential crown—shunned the anniversary celebrations. At the last hour, the Congolese government was forced to "postpone" the Great Lakes summit until a later date.

The foreign minister, Bizima Karaha—one of the few Banyamulenge who maintained a close relationship with the president and was referred to by many as "Mzee's son"—had to break the news to a "stunned" Kabila that "nobody wanted to come and that everybody was disappointed."[3] The government scrambled to save face and attributed the summit's postponement to the outbreak of war between Eritrea and Ethiopia, which, according to an official Congolese statement, had been integral to the summit's preparation and organization.[4] In the eyes of one of Kabila's ministers, Edi Angilu, the canceled summit marked "the point of no return ... It was clear that the Ugandans and Rwandans wanted him gone."[5] The government-owned Ugandan newspaper, the *New Vision*, ended a critical editorial, entitled "Wake Up, Kabila!," with a not-so-subtle warning that "[i]t is not too late [for Kabila] to rescue the situation but he must start listening to friends both at home and abroad ... Otherwise he may go the way of his predecessor, sooner rather than later."[6]

* * *

In the face of this humiliating affront, Mzee opted for a familiar stance: defiance. With or without the regional heads of state, the show would go on. The main event was a parade and presidential address in the country's largest sports stadium where Caesar Kayizari had spent his first night in Kinshasa in 1997. It had now been renamed as the Stade des Martyrs, in honor of former Congolese prime minister, Évariste Kimba, and three of his ministers who were hanged on the site in the first year of Mobutu's reign on conspiracy charges. In his speech, Kabila railed against the "international embargo" imposed on Congo on the false pretext of "the respect of human rights."[7] The acrimonious relationship with the "international community" primarily stemmed from Kabila's stonewalling of UN investigations into atrocities committed during the liberation war; even if the relations with the Pan-Africanist

---

[3] Interview with Bizima Karaha, Goma, December 2009.
[4] "Kabila to Mark One Year in Power Minus Key Allies," Reuters, May 17, 1998.
[5] Interview in Kinshasa, December 2009.
[6] "Wake Up, Kabila!," *New Vision*, May 19, 1998.
[7] Michel Cariou, "DRCongo President Celebrates One Year in Power," AFP, May 17, 1998.

comrades were at an all-time low, the Mzee and his speechwriters publicly retained their part of the elite bargain with the RPF.

Privately, however, that bargain was by now severely strained and nearly came to a breaking point just as Kabila was to give his presidential address. The incident involved Kabila's security detail and Dan Munyuza, the senior RPF intelligence officer stationed in Kinshasa who was described by one of his RPF colleagues as Mzee's "shadow for two years."[8] A low-ranking intelligence operative at the time, Munyuza was among the delegation that picked Kabila up from Tanzania in 1995, as we saw in Chapter 5. He then hosted him at his house where he acted as Mzee's "caretaker," "feeding him *ugali* and chicken" and "arranging plenty of girls" for him.[9] The time Munyuza spent with Kabila landed the former—"who was totally unknown before 1996"—"the position of the top intelligence operative of the RPF in Congo."[10] With his star rising, Munyuza was seemingly second only to James Kabarebe in terms of the importance of foreign agents stationed in Congo.

At the Stade des Martyrs on May 17, 1998, "the Rwandan Mr Congo," as some Congolese referred to Munyuza,[11] made his way to the stage with other members of the RPF delegation to listen to the speech. In the absence of Paul Kagame, Yoweri Museveni or José Eduardo Dos Santos, the RPA contingent was the lone representation among the regional allies who had underwritten the AFDL's triumph. But the presidential bodyguards, which were only a short while ago changed over from RPF-trained Congolese Tutsi to Tanzanians and Tanzanian-trained Katangese, had strict orders not to allow anyone with weapons near the main stage. According to a number of witnesses, an altercation ensued as Kabila's bodyguards grabbed Munyuza by the belt, violently searched him and confiscated his weapon.[12] Munyuza was incensed; a highly combustible situation was at risk of detonating then and there, according to Henri Mova. "I was afraid ... He was going to fight. It was so tense, they were furious."[13] Munyuza and the RPA delegation stormed out of the largely empty

[8] Name withheld at the source's request, interview in Kigali, July 2014.

[9] Interviews with an ESO intelligence operative, name withheld at the source's request, March 2013.

[10] Interview with Frank Rusagara, London, February 2013.

[11] Interview with Enock Rubenrangabo Sebineza in Kinshasa, December 2009.

[12] Interview with Henri Mova in Brussels, April 2011 and April 2012; interview with Thomas Nziratimana, March 2013; interview with James Kabarebe, Kigali, April 2013.

[13] Interview with Henri Mova, April 2012.

stadium. Many in the AFDL cited this incident as a turning point. "The real rupture with the Rwandans was not the dismissal of James," Mova said, "but the trouble with Dan."[14]

The confrontation revealed the explosive conditions that emerged at the highest levels of the revolution as trust dissipated between the RPF and those around Kabila but in which the RPA contingent remained armed and stationed in Congo with access deep inside the regime. Munyuza's manhandling represented the palpable consequences of this uncertainty and was a devastating indication of the critical condition the alliance was now in: the man who served as Mzee's caretaker, protector and cook could no longer be trusted to carry a weapon in his presence. This uncertainty worked both ways, of course. As Kabila moved to protect himself from the RPF, he increased their insecurity. Kabarebe was tremendously unnerved about the incident in the stadium as, in his words, it came "on the back of Katangization and the promotion of many people who hated our guts and would do everything to see the backs of us."[15] He doubted whether it was merely a misunderstanding and feared if it happened again, the consequences would be much more severe.

* * *

This chapter analyzes the internal and external factors leading to the unraveling of the alliance that underpinned the post-Mobutu order. The events surrounding the one-year anniversary of the liberation would set the stage for a frantic seventy-five days in which extreme uncertainty would take over the regime (detailed in Chapter 10). Here, we analyze three of the most important factors that contributed to the breakdown of the strategic interdependence between Kabila and his internal and external allies. The first was the mounting international pressure on Kabila for blocking UN investigations into the massacres committed in the refugee camps and the equatorial forest during the overthrow of Mobutu. Kabila's intransigence was both a function of his alliance with the RPF and his anti-UN worldview; it would have significant consequences for his government's access to desperately needed foreign aid and be seen by many close to Kabila as a major destabilizing force on the revolution. The second factor was Kabila's "Katangization" of the regime—the infiltration of the security services, government and financial departments of the state bureaucracy by fellow Katangese—and the reliance on other foreign

---

[14] Interview with Henri Mova, April 2012.
[15] Interview in Kigali, April 2013.

allies, not least Tanzania which gave him a bodyguard to replace his Rwandese minders and which sent troops to train a parallel army in Katanga, outside the control of Kabarebe. The third was the failure to address key grievances that had motivated those from eastern Congo to join the revolution. In this context, we also assess the effect of natural resources extraction on regime stability and find that in contrast to *after* the outbreak of the second war (post-August 1998), this period was characterized by a *lack* of resource exploitation and revenue generation, which may have weakened the economic ties between the coalition partners.

The Constraints of Strategic Interdependence

Cat-and-Mouse over the UN Human Rights Investigation

As discussed in the previous chapter, the international honeymoon of the AFDL revolution quickly turned into the quotidian frustration that characterizes many of the relationships between African states and the Western-led international system. Democratization and the Kabila government's ties with China and Cuba were early sources of acrimony, but no issue would turn out to be more explosive for the Pan-Africanist alliance than human rights. Initially, the controversy served as a consolidating gel between the comrades. Two months after the overthrow of Mobutu, Zimbabwe's president, Robert Mugabe, called for a regional summit in Kinshasa to bolster Kabila.[16] Mugabe, who not been part of the Pan-Africanist grand alliance despite his own formidable reputation in continental liberation politics, felt the Congolese president was being unfairly attacked by the United Nations and former colonial powers, France and Belgium. "Let not the international community try to raise Laurent Kabila as a devil who must be crushed," Mugabe said later at another regional summit. "He must be seen as the savior of the people."[17] In stark contrast to the near-universal boycott of Kabila's regime ten months later, the one-day summit on July 20, 1997, attracted heads of state from eight African countries—Rwanda, Uganda, Zimbabwe, Namibia, Mozambique, Central African Republic, Eritrea and Zambia—as well as presidential envoys from two others—Ethiopia and Gabon.

---

[16] Prunier, *From Genocide to Continental War*, p. 158.

[17] "African Leaders Rally Around Congo Leader Kabila," Associated Press, November 19, 1997.

The most sensitive concern the leaders discussed was the mounting international pressure on the Kabila government to answer allegations of mass killings during the war against Mobutu. As explained in Chapter 6, as the AFDL advanced irresistibly from east to west, RPA forces systematically hunted down those Rwandans who failed to return to Rwanda and continued to flee—whether infants or elderly, famished or sick, armed or unarmed. As the killings of those dismissed by Kagame as "fugitives"[18] mounted, so did the evidence. Reports of massacres prompted the United Nations High Commission for Human Rights in March 1997 to delegate Robert Garreton, UN special rapporteur on the human rights situation in Zaire, to investigate allegations of atrocities in eastern Zaire, a mandate later expanded to include all incidents since the war started in September 1996. Allegations of mass killings reached a peak with the AFDL's seizure of power. In the month after the fall of Kinshasa, Western newspapers carried front-page stories with eyewitness accounts of atrocities against Rwandan refugees, including the killings in Mbandaka and Wendji that occurred mere days before Kinshasa fell.[19]

Thus, at the moment Kabila expected to be basking in international glory for liberating Zaire, he instead found himself facing global opprobrium for the conduct of "his forces" during the war effort and demands to submit to the UN. Privately, Kabila's American allies complained that the human rights issue was derailing reconstruction efforts in the country. As one diplomat said anonymously to *New York Times* journalist Howard French: "We will not hitch the fortunes of this entire nation to an investigation into the fate of a bunch of Rwandan refugees, many of whom were themselves killers."[20] But the

[18] Philip Gourevitch, *Stories from Rwanda: We Wish to Inform You That Tomorrow We Will Be Killed with Our Families*, New York: Picador, 1998, p. 338.

[19] See, for example: Stephen Smith, "Des morts sans nombre dans l'ombre de Kabila," *Libération*, May 20, 1997; Donald G. McNeil Jr, "The Dead Zone: Reports Point to Mass Killing of Refugees in Congo," *New York Times*, May 27, 1997. McNeil Jr, "In Congo, Forbidding Terrain Hides a Calamity," *New York Times*, June 1, 1997. Colin Nickerson, "Refugee Massacre Unfolds in Congo: Witnesses Tell of Slaughter of Hundreds of Kabila's Soldiers," *Boston Globe*, June 1, 1997. Andrew Maykuth, "Rebels Murder Hundreds of Refugees in Congo," *Philadelphia Inquirer*, June 5, 1997. John Pomfret, "Killing Spree Blamed on Troops of New Congo Leader," *Washington Post*, June 8, 1997. Pomfret, "Massacres Were a Weapon in Congo's Civil War," *Washington Post*, June 11, 1997. Jon Swain, "Kabila Troops in Rush to Cover Up Genocide," *Sunday Times* (London), June 15, 1997.

[20] Howard W. French, "Cold Trail: A Special Report—Congo Not Alone in Ending Massacre Inquiry," *New York Times*, May 7, 1998.

outcry over—and eyewitness accounts of—the killings were so strong in those first few weeks that the Americans could not sweep the issue under the rug. And, according to the US ambassador at large for war crimes, David Scheffer, it would become a key point of diplomatic discussions with the Kabila government up until the outbreak of the second war.[21]

In early June 1997, a large US delegation—the largest and most senior to travel to Africa since Mandela's inauguration, including representatives of the Departments of State, Commerce, Defense and Treasury, the National Security Council, the Agency for International Development, the CIA and Congress—held a series of meetings with Kabila and other government officials to strengthen bilateral relations. Bill Richardson, the US representative to the United Nations, who had engaged with Kabila at the end of the first war in a bid to ensure a smooth transition of power from Mobutu, made it clear that aid and economic assistance were to be tied to improvements on the human rights front, especially allowing the UN investigators access to alleged sites of mass killings. As a deal softener, the Clinton administration signaled simultaneously that it was willing to work with Kabila to find a solution that worked for his government, including acceding to Kinshasa's demands that it should have greater say in the scope and leadership of the investigation.[22]

In the meetings, the "Yankee Clipper"—as Richardson nicknamed Kabila upon discovering the rebel leader's improbable love of baseball[23]—agreed to allow the investigation to begin in a month's time (by July 7); in the post-meeting press conference, Richardson celebrated Kabila's pledge as a "major breakthrough."[24] But over the next several weeks the Congolese government continued to deploy a variety of tactics to stonewall the investigation; this included rejecting the participation of Garreton (who was to continue handling the dossier), insisting the inquiry period cover before and during the Rwandan genocide as far back as March 1993, demanding a budget of $1.7 million for

[21] Interview in Williamsburg, Virginia, March 2015.

[22] French, "Cold Trail."

[23] In his first meeting with Kabila in Lubumbashi in late April 1997, Richardson gave Kabila a New York Yankees baseball cap, which the rebel spokesman wore to the joint press conference following the meeting. Bill Richardson and Michael Ruby, *Between Worlds: The Making of an American Life*, New York: Plume, 2007, p. 220.

[24] See Raymond Bonner, "U.S. Envoy in Congo Offers Aid but Wants Progress on Rights," *New York Times*, June 7, 1997. Cindy Shiner, "U.S. Delegation Offers Congo Leader $50 Million If He Pledges Reforms; Kabila Agrees to Form Electoral Panel, Allow Probe of Massacre Reports," *Washington Post*, June 8, 1997.

Congolese minders who traveled with the UN team, and preventing access to important sites. As Kabila dug in his heels, international condemnation increased. On July 16, 1997, the US Senate passed a provision proposed by Senator "Lauch" Faircloth from North Carolina to the Foreign Assistance Appropriation Act that prohibited direct assistance to Kinshasa until the US president "reports in writing to the Congress that the Government of Congo is cooperating fully with the investigators from the United Nations or any other international relief organizations in accounting for human rights violations or atrocities committed in Congo or adjacent countries."[25]

It was against this backdrop of intensifying pressure and deepening aid conditionality that Mugabe called the one-day summit on July 20 to bolster the Kabila government. The African leaders confronted the controversy over the UN war crimes' investigation head-on; according to the summit's communiqué:

> The heads of state and governments noted with dismay the persistent, unsubstantiated disinformation campaign against the Democratic Republic of Congo and other countries in the region ... We view this as an attempt to undermine the leadership of the Democratic Republic of Congo. We therefore condemn this campaign of vilification and unjust pressures that are being made against the Democratic Republic of Congo.[26]

Despite the moral support of the region and demands for an "independent and neutral commission," the international demands for a UN investigation did not go away. Nor did Kabila's intransigence with the UN human rights team. As Bill Richardson describes it, this "merry-go-round" went around again when Richardson traveled to Kinshasa in late October 1997 to secure access for the investigators.[27] Again access was promised and again access was

---

[25] US Senate, "S.955—Foreign Operations, Export Financing, and Related Programs Appropriations Act, 1998," passed July 17, 1997.

[26] Kamanga Mutond, "African Leaders Rally Behind Kabila," Associated Press, July 20, 1997.

[27] Richardson reported on the outcome of the negotiations in a prepared statement to the US House of Representatives International Relations Committee on November 5, 1997: "In Kinshasa [on October 25], I met for more than four hours ... with President Kabila and key aides—including Reconstruction Minister Mbaya—to emphasize the importance of full cooperation with the team. I explained very plainly that while the U.S. wanted to develop a long-term relationship with this government, it would be more difficult to deepen our bilateral ties and increase aid without access for the team. I am pleased to report that after difficult negotiations, the Congolese

impeded. In April 1998, UN Secretary General Kofi Annan withdrew the team, citing the Congolese government's "total lack of cooperation," which ranged from the arrest of UN personnel to local demonstrations and physical intimidation at investigation sites to travel restrictions.[28] In his memoir, Richardson's final assessment of the Yankee Clipper was that "the guy sure behaved as though he had something *big* to hide."[29]

The Logic and Costs of Stonewalling

Kabila did have something big to hide—even if it was not strictly speaking *his* secret but that of his main ally, the RPF. The secret was not its game-changing involvement in the liberation struggle, which at first Kigali steadfastly denied until Rwandan vice-president, minister of defense and RPF supremo Paul Kagame performed a complete U-turn. In his idiosyncratic, somewhat arrogant style, he (accurately) claimed that the Congolese rebels were not "fully prepared to carry [the revolution] out alone. We did continue to take some role because we thought doing it halfway would be very dangerous. We found the best way was to take it to the end."[30] The real secret was what happened in the forests deep inside Congo as the RPF took "it to the end." As we saw earlier, the RPF has never denied that civilians were killed, but Kigali went to great lengths to conceal the scale, scope and systematized-method of the campaign to eliminate those who refused to return to Rwanda.[31]

The RPF thus remained resolute in its insistence that there should not be an international investigation and that, if the UN and the permanent members of the Security Council truly cared for global justice, they could start by examining the shameful record of the Security Council's five permanent members during the Rwandan genocide.[32] From the perspective of the Front, rebuff-

---

Government confirmed acceptance of the team and agreed that it could conduct its investigation without interference throughout the country." "Richardson Outlines U.S. 'Cautious Engagement' in DROC," United States Information Agency, November 5, 1997.

[28] French, "Cold Trail."

[29] Emphasis added. Richardson and Ruby, *Between Worlds*, p. 223.

[30] Kagame interview with John Pomfret of the *Washington Post*, "Defense Minister Says Arms, Troops Supplied for Anti-Mobutu Drive," July 6, 1997.

[31] Reyntjens, *Great African War*, p. 160.

[32] Interviews with James Kabarebe, Emmanuel Ndahiro, Frank Rusagara and Karake Karenzi, January 2010–December 2014.

WHY COMRADES GO TO WAR

ing the UN human rights commission was not about hiding anything; rather, it was about taking a moral and principled stand against the hypocrisy of the international community, which was now trying to be seen to do something to assuage its "guilt"[33] both at having failed to stop the massacres in 1994 and in not addressing the continuation of the genocidal threat in Zaire—and, even worse, having aided and abetted the *génocidaires* in the refugee camps. "It is my strong belief that the United Nations people are trying to deflect the blame for failures of their own making onto us," Kagame said to the *Washington Post* in July 1997. "Their failure to act in eastern Zaire directly caused these problems, and when things blew up in their faces they blamed us. These are people who want to be judges and nobody can judge them."[34]

For the RPF, this position was non-negotiable. And Kigali expected its ally to hold the line against the UN investigation. Kabila dutifully played his part until the very end. As late as June 24, 1998, his government was still adopting RPF-style rhetoric, stating that "France, which bears the specific responsibility of having trained and armed the FAR and Interahamwe militias convicted of genocide, is the chief country supporting anti-DRC media and ex-Mobutists."[35] Kabila's spirited resistance was partially a function of his own view of the United Nations as an imperialist institution designed to advance Western interests, but also of the strategic alliance he struck with the RPF, in which the latter did the heavy lifting to install him in power and Mzee provided cover for the RPF to use Congo's territory to eradicate the *génocidaires*. Just as Kabila leveraged this deal to its maximum—amassing absolute power under the watchful eye of the RPF—the Front did too—ensuring Kabila, and Kabila alone, shouldered the burden of accounting for the Rwandan refugees. This position was made clear in a statement published by Wilson Rutayisire of the Rwanda Information Office after a coalition of human rights groups in May 1998 implicated James Kabarebe in the massacres:

> Congo is a sovereign state with a government capable of taking up responsibility on each and every inch of its territory and therefore remains the only competent authority to come to an understanding with UN investigators and come up with a report on what exactly happened during the war in the Congo.[36]

[33] Kagame's word in interview with Gourevitch. Philip Gourevitch, "Continental Shift: A Letter from the Congo," *New Yorker*, August 4, 1997.

[34] John Pomfret, "Rwandans Led Revolt in Congo," *Washington Post*, July 9, 1997.

[35] Our translation of the original French. Martens, *Kabila et la révolution congolaise*, vol. 1, p. 362.

[36] "Rwanda Denies Involvement in Congo Killings," *New Vision*, May 19, 1998.

As Kigali offloaded responsibility and international pressure escalated, the Congolese president felt trapped. According to Irung Awan, one of Mzee's diplomatic counselors,

> We had nothing to do with this business, but once we got to Kinshasa we got into incredible trouble because of this ... The presence of the Rwandese in Kinshasa made it impossible for us to make the issue go away. Mzee could not accuse those who accompanied us to power. Impossible.[37]

Minister of Justice Mwenze Kongolo offered a similar sentiment: "There was no other way we could deal with it—we couldn't accuse Rwanda, we took the blame on us, even if Congolese were not involved."[38] Accordingly, Kabila, who relished being the public face of the revolution, became the person most associated with the mass killings; "What Kabila Is Hiding"—not what the RPF or Kagame is hiding—was how human rights organizations framed the issue.[39] This not only deflected the blame from the RPF but also increased Kabila's personal stake in preventing a systematic human rights investigation lest he be found culpable.

* * *

The allegations of mass atrocities and Kabila's obstructionism had significant material consequences. In December 1997, the World Bank convened a "Friends of the Congo" meeting in Brussels with seventeen donor governments, nine bilateral and multilateral aid agencies, and the International Monetary Fund. The Congolese government sought debt relief of the $15 billion of foreign debt accrued under Mobutu and $700 million in aid to help fund its $1.68 billion "Economic Stabilization and Recovery Program" for 1998. But the refugee issue continued to loom large: the meeting was only able to take place after Kabila agreed to let the UN investigators back into the country in November after a five-month delay. On the eve of the meeting, Amnesty International released a report, "DRC: Deadly Alliances in Congolese Forests," which accused "the AFDL and its allies ... [of] using various methods, including burning bodies and dumping them in rivers, to conceal evidence of the atrocities."[40] The donors reiterated their position: no aid without access for the UN investigators.

---

[37] Interview with Irung Awan, Kinshasa, August, 2013.
[38] Interview with Mwenze Kongolo, Kinshasa, August, 2013.
[39] This was the name of an October 1997 report by Human Rights Watch. "What Kabila Is Hiding: Civilian Killing and Impunity in Congo."
[40] Amnesty International, "Democratic Republic of Congo: Deadly Alliances in

Because Kabila refused to concede, in 1998 the Congolese government received only $125 million to rebuild the country. The Clinton administration, despite its close coordination with the AFDL in its overthrow of Mobutu (see Chapter 6), was particularly tight-fisted. Constrained by the Faircloth Amendment, it provided virtually no bilateral aid in 1997 and 1998.[41] This stands in stark contrast to the vital military cooperation with the RPA the Pentagon organized and the $294 million in total bilateral aid Washington provided to Rwanda in 1994 and 1995 in the wake of the genocide.[42] The same was true for other donors. DRC received around $3–4 per person in net official development assistance in 1997 and 1998 compared to the $123–4 per person Rwanda received in 1994 and 1995.[43]

Beyond its effect on foreign aid, the refugee issue had important consequences for Kabila's alliance with the RPF. Even as Kabila aggressively criticized the international community for the "embargo" it imposed on Congo on the pretext of "the respect of human rights,"[44] privately Kabila and those close to him resented the RPF for forcing them to shoulder the burden alone. They were not privy to the details of RPA operations against the fleeing refugees and *génocidaires* and had chosen to look the other way, but were denounced as killing machines. "We were focused on the front and not on the camps; the Rwandans kept quiet about it and didn't tell us much, nor did we ask many questions," Henri Mova explained. Yet "we were unjustly blamed for it. [The international community] used the issue as a stick to beat Kabila with,

---

Congolese Forests," December 3, 1997. The Kabila regime dismissed Amnesty as "an enemy of the Congolese people" and part of a French campaign to undermine its government. "DR Congo Calls Amnesty 'Enemy of Congolese People,'" AFP, December 3, 1997.

[41] In fiscal year 1997, the US government earmarked only $10 million to DRC, primarily for immunizations, but all of this aid bypassed the Congolese government. "Richardson Outlines U.S. 'Cautious Engagement' in DROC," United States Information Agency, November 5, 1997. This exasperated Kabila and he chafed at the American conditions. "We won't accept being told to do this or that." "Congo President Dismisses U.S. Aid as Not Enough," AP, December 10, 1997.

[42] Bilateral aid is reported in current US dollars. Source: World Bank, "World Bank Development Indicators," 2015.

[43] Ibid.

[44] Michel Cariou, "DRCongo President Celebrates One Year in Power," AFP, May 17, 1998.

not Kagame."[45] According to Mwenze Kongolo, many Kabila loyalists only learned about the killings after the fact or as the massacres were taking place:

> The Rwandan refugee issue was a nightmare for us. We didn't know the Rwandan army was killing them. Mzee didn't know much. I began to suspect something about the affair in Kisangani. A Tigres Katangais told me—he had been at the front. He told me they were killing their Rwandan brothers. Tingi-Tingi was the crucial moment.[46]

Shé Okitundu, who as shadow foreign minister dealt directly with the refugee issue, asserted that the international community's hypocrisy and the scapegoating of Kabila by Washington and the NGOs in order "not to have to name the Rwandans" was among the primary causes of the split between Kabila and the RPF.[47] Raus Chalwe, the head of intelligence of the Congolese National Police, recalled how "The Hutu refugee affair infuriated Mzee ... He had tense exchanges with the Rwandese for being blamed by the UN. It was an important source of irritation."[48]

At the same time, others acknowledged that Kabila's management of the issue was counter-productive. Irung Awan conceded that "Our management of the refugee file was a total fiasco. We could have found a way of not accusing the Rwandese and still handling the international community." In particular, Richard Mbaya, the minister tasked by Kabila with the refugee dossier, was "very anti-Western and not very experienced," leading to sharp exchanges with the UN interlocutors and damaging the government's reputation with the international community.[49] Nonetheless, for those around Kabila, the RPF was ultimately responsible, and its exploitation of the Mzee to shield itself would have far-reaching consequences. Joseph Kabila's twin sister, Jaynet, summarized how many close to her father felt: "For Rwanda, access to Congo was about killing the Rwandese refugees. The issue became very destabilizing for us. The disagreement over this became one of the causes of the breakdown."[50]

Killing the Golden Goose

Beyond the strains on the Kabila–RPF alliance, the human rights controversy would also have significant effects on the government's economic policies.

[45] Interview in Brussels, April 2012.
[46] Interview with Mwenze Kongolo, Kinshasa, August 2013.
[47] Interview with Shé Okitundu, Kinshasa, August 2013.
[48] Interview in Kinshasa, August 2013.
[49] Interview with Irung Awan, Kinshasa, August 12, 2013.
[50] Interview in Kinshasa, August 2013.

When the AFDL seized power in May 1997, the Congolese economy was in ruins—courtesy of Mobutu's kleptocratic and neo-patrimonial style of governance discussed in Chapter 4. Baudouin Kayokela Kasangula, one of the new regime's central bankers, described how "the Central Bank was empty. It had been completely emptied, there were no more reserves, nothing."[51]

The economy was beset by runaway inflation; the monetary sector had broken down, returning the country to "its precolonial, pre-monetary existence" in which bartering was the principal means of exchange;[52] commercial production had collapsed, especially the principal export, copper, which had declined by more than 90 per cent since the 1970s; the state had virtually no capacity to collect taxes, and a mountain of foreign debt totaling over $12 billion; social support and the healthcare systems had been destroyed; there were virtually no formal job opportunities for a restless youth population; and foreign aid and investment flows had effectively been terminated.

In the heady final days of the war, macro-economic fundamentals did not seem to matter to the mining magnates from around the world who flew into the AFDL's de facto headquarters in Lubumbashi to pay tribute to the soon-to-be king of Africa's richest country. Kabila, himself Katangese of course, made no secret of where he expected a new Congolese economy to emerge from. As the rebels racked up one multi-million-dollar mining deal after another, an irrational exuberance gripped the new Congo. As one South African mining executive said, with no sense of irony, "Cecil Rhodes must be spinning in his grave at the opportunities he is missing."[53]

The most spectacular deal the AFDL concluded during the war was with a new entrant to the Congo mining scene, the US-based company American Mineral Fields (AMF), which signed a contract worth around $900 million to exploit copper and cobalt mines in Katanga.[54] Others followed suit. One Australian mining executive salivated at the investment potential:

> The gap between what this country is producing and what this country is capable of producing is wider than anywhere else in the world ... This country has the capacity to support 200 or 300 mining conventions. It's a ridiculous tragedy. If this new

[51] Interview in Lubumbashi, August 2013.

[52] Prunier, *From Genocide to Continental War*, p. 163.

[53] Sam Kiley, "Mining Giants Sign $3bn-a-Year Deals with Zairean Rebels," *The Times* (London), April 22, 1997.

[54] Howard W. French, "The Great Gold Rush in Zaire," *New York Times*, April 18, 1997.

government comes forward and makes a strong statement that they will support contracts properly, you will see a flood of mining companies coming into Zaire.[55]

* * *

The rule of law seemed anathema to Kabila, however, who thrived on informality and personal control, made little distinction between the private and public sphere, and relished being unpredictable. Justine Kasa-Vubu, the daughter of Congo's first president who was appointed minister of public office and later Congolese ambassador to Belgium by Mzee, wrote a damaging memoir of her twelve months in Kabila's cabinet. Her analysis of Mzee's modus operandi was echoed by friends and foes alike in dozens of interviews we conducted:

> In truth, the man is afraid, to the point that he is capable of annulling an official foreign mission of a Congolese leader, simply because he learns that this person is well regarded in the West. But if that same individual goes there after all, he sends a shadow to receive him there and to follow his mission. Does one, in other words, need to have a certificate of mediocrity and incompetence to be at ease in this regime? The slightest hint of competence is crushed, the slightest popularity squashed. That is what passes for the revolution ... He has conquered a territory and thus working with him means a relationship of master and slave. He stops every initiative and does what he can to discredit it, just to affirm his grip on power.[56]

One of the most damning portraits of Kabila's managerial style was provided by Moïse Nyarugabo, his private secretary who grew increasingly incredulous at his boss's penchant for dysfunctionality, including a total lack of organization and planning; a rejection of bureaucratic procedures; and a preference for verbal orders by letting others deal with signatures and written decrees: "It was nauseating: he managed the country like he was managing the *maquis*."[57] Nyarugabo recalls how, after the AFDL captured Mbuji-Mayi on April 5, 1997, he went with Kabila to meet officials from the state-owned Societé minière de Bakwanga (MIBA). Kabila was given five or six bags of diamonds, which he personally kept in his room before selling them for millions of dollars in cash.[58]

* * *

[55] Emphasis added. James C. McKinley, "Zairian Rebels' New Allies: Men Armed with Briefcases," *New York Times*, April 17, 1997.

[56] Our translation from Z.J.M'Poyo Kasa-Vubu, *Douze mois chez Kabila (1997–1998)*, Brussels: Cri, 1998, p. 62.

[57] Interview with Moïse Nyarugabo, Kinshasa, December 4, 2009.

[58] See also a report in April 1997 by Howard French on this incident, in which an anon-

After the breakneck speed of the campaign and the exuberance resulting from the mining deals, the full extent of the economic challenge of state-building became apparent on May 18, 1997. The AFDL was desperate for cash to pay the country's bills, rebuild its infrastructure and manage the expansive network of Banyamulenge pastoralists, veteran Lumumbists, Swahili-speaking *kadogo*, and others who had jumped on the revolutionary bandwagon as it steamrolled through Congo. The government was hopeful that the same international allies that backed them on the battlefield would now provide the requisite foreign aid needed to stabilize the economy. When the Americans offered a pittance owing to the refugee issue, Kabila was outraged. On the eve of US Secretary of State Madeleine Albright's visit to Kinshasa in December 1997, Kabila derided the $10 million Washington pledged to the "Friends of Congo" Trust Fund. "If they want to help us, let them really help us," he said.[59]

Hungering after cash, the AFDL turned to extorting the very companies on which early hopes for economic revival rested; Kabila let it be known in August 1997 that he was expecting a minimum of US$3 billion in investment. The triannual program published by the government after the "Friends of Congo" meeting increased that amount to US$4.5 billion.[60] But despite paying lip service to the World Bank's demands for "good governance," the AFDL opted in practice for other ways of capturing foreign funds. On the one hand, domestic entrepreneurs were relentlessly harassed, including the repeated arrests of the head of the Congolese employers' confederation, Jeannot Bemba Saolona and his successor José Endundo Bononge who despite paying substantial sums to the AFDL were squeezed for further money.[61] On the other, foreign companies reported Kabila's government was demanding large "down payments" to win mining contracts. As one risk analyst reported in December 1997, "The government is shaking everybody down right now, saying we want you to give us a whole bunch of money up front."[62] Additional funds were even urged from companies that had already paid up in Lubumbashi.[63] The landmark deal with

ymous mining official claimed "The March diamond production was already packed up and awaiting transport to Kinshasa ... Kabila just carted it off." Howard W. French, "The Great Gold Rush in Zaire," *New York Times*, April 18, 1997.

[59] "Congo President Dismisses U.S. Aid as Not Enough," AP, December 10, 1997.

[60] De Villers and Willame, *République démocratique du Congo*, p. 125.

[61] Ibid., p. 106.

[62] Karen Howlett and Madelaine Drohan, "Mining Companies Clash in the Congo," *Globe and Mail* (Canada), December 5, 1997.

[63] Tom Masland, "An African Big Man in Trouble," *Newsweek*, December 15, 1997.

AMF was shipwrecked by the extortion racket. As the contract was to be executed, the Kabila government demanded an additional "large payment into a Kinshasa bank to seal an already signed deal."[64] Simultaneously, Kabila's confidant, Victor Mpoyo, initiated talks with the South African mining giant, Anglo American, for the same property.[65] By January 1998, the president had canceled the tender. Another twelve mining deals signed by the AFDL rebels with foreign companies were scrapped in the following weeks.[66] Reneging on mining contracts and relying on strong-arm tactics had a chilling effect on foreign investors, who feared the direction Kabila was taking Congo. "It's getting impossible to do business here. They're going to kill the goose before it lays the golden egg," said one foreign executive.[67]

* * *

With aid flows blocked and investors exiting as fast as they came jetting in, the economic situation remained dire as the AFDL marked its first year in power. This gravely strained the revolution as the expected windfall from natural resources never materialized.[68] Fewer rents made it harder for Kabila to maintain the sprawling networks he had developed as he rose to power. The disarray in the mining sector also meant that any cross-regional economic integration that might have resulted from the Pan-Africanist campaign never materialized.[69]

One exception that reveals the economic ties some in the coalition envisaged may result from their cooperation against Mobutu was the Banque de Commerce et de Développement (BCD), run by a Rwandan, Alfred Kalisa.[70]

---

[64] Howard W. French, "Though Mobutu Is Buried, Corruption Dies Hard," *New York Times*, November 20, 1997. The payments required may have been in the magnitude of hundreds of millions of dollars. According to Tom Masland, "The major shareholder of one U.S. mining concern told associates last month that a landmark deal he'd secured last April with a 'loan' of $100 million is being held up until he can produce another $100 million." This seems to be a clear reference to American Mineral Fields. Masland, "An African Big Man in Trouble."

[65] French, "Though Mobutu Is Buried, Corruption Dies Hard."

[66] "Congo's Investment Blues," *Mail and Guardian* (Johannesburg), January 30, 1998.

[67] Masland, "An African Big Man in Trouble."

[68] Pierre Lumbi, Daito Amuri Tobakombee, "La Gestion des ressources minières en RCD. 1. Le diamant," Kinshasa: OGT, 2001.

[69] Interview with Yemane Kidane in Addis Ababa, November 2014 and Yemane Gebreab in Asmara, March 2015.

[70] Unlike his Rwandan counterparts, Kalisa did not leave Kinshasa in the lead up to

Kalisa was described by Baudouin Kayokela Kasangula, who worked both at the Central Bank and at the BCD, as "both Mzee's banker and Kagame's banker."[71] According to a 2001 UN Panel of Experts report, Kalisa's other bank, the Banque de commerce du développement et d'industrie (BCDI), based in Kigali, had been a key financial instrument for the AFDL, where companies could make payments to contribute to "the war effort."[72] The BCD was set up in Kinshasa after Mobutu had been overthrown. Like the BCDI, it too was a political instrument for the regime. According to Oscar Mudiay, the chef-de-cabinet of Economy Minister Victor Mpoyo, "all ministers held private accounts [in the bank], plus all taxes levied on petroleum products went into a private account there too."[73] It was also probably the receptacle for payments made from mining companies as they vied for lucrative contracts.[74]

But to Kalisa, who according to one of his Congolese colleagues, "worked for Congo's interests first and took a long-time horizon of thirty years, contrary to his [fellow] Rwandese," the bank was supposed to represent something larger than a slush fund for the new order. This was what the Pan-Africanist support team for the AFDL composed of Haile Menkerios, Claude Dusaidi, Yemane Kidane, Yemane Gebreab and others had envisaged: the centralization of rents to help rebuild a Congolese state with deep linkages to Rwanda, Uganda, Ethiopia and Eritrea.[75] With shareholders from Angola, Rwanda and Congo, the BCD reflected "Kalisa's vision of win–win projects being funded

---

the outbreak of the second war in August 1998. And unlike other Tutsis in the capital, he was protected from frenzied attacks whipped up by Congolese officials after the war started and personally escorted to N'Djili Airport for a safe exit by former minister of finance, Mawampanga Mwana Nanga. Interview with Roger Meece of the US embassy in Kinshasa, January 2010. See also Lynne Duke, "As Congo Jails Suspect Tutsis, One Is Handled with Kid Gloves," *Washington Post*, August 13, 1998.

[71] Interview in Lubumbashi, August 2013.

[72] United Nations, "Report of the Panel of Experts on the Illegal Exploitation of Natural Resources and Other Forms of Wealth of the Democratic Republic of the Congo," S/2001/357.

[73] Interview in Kinshasa, August 2013.

[74] As some Congolese economic analysts described BCD, "it was effectively an alternative bank for official funds that Kabila did not wish to entrust to the state institution in the early days of his rule." Duke, "As Congo Jails Suspect Tutsis, One Is Handled With Kid Gloves."

[75] Interview with Haile Menkerios, Addis Ababa, November 2014.

across the region by and for the liberators of Congo."[76] In July 1997, Mzee in turn visited Eritrea, where he was greatly impressed by the Sawa military camp (where Joseph Kabila briefly underwent training) and the Eritrean system of using militarily trained youngsters in local development projects like building schools, hospitals and roads—very much like the Nyerere model of People's Defense Forces as a "developmental militia." A month earlier, in June, Issayas had traveled to Congo, starting in Kinshasa where he engaged the AFDL government on the idea of Pan-Africanist integration before ending his visit with a regional tour of Katanga and its mines with Kabila and Bizima Karaha, during which potential joint operations and investments were discussed between Congo, Eritrea and other comrade countries.[77] But these regional ventures would be few and far between.

Beyond its stake in the BCD, the 2001 UN Panel of Experts report also noted that after May 1997, Rwanda (and even more so Uganda) increased their exports of valuable minerals, including coltan, diamonds and gold, despite the absence of a corresponding rise in domestic production, which pointed to evidence of "mass looting ... and systematic and systemic exploitation."[78] Crucially, however, this exploitation only reached the level of "mass-scale looting" after the outbreak of the second war in August 1998,[79] when, as Prunier notes, there was the need and the opportunity for Rwanda and Uganda to scale up their extraction of Congo's mineral riches.[80]

However, for the most part, during the interbellum period the RPF stayed out of the economic sphere, which it instead left to Kabila—"No budgetary decision of consequence could be taken without the Mzee."[81] This was a vital part of the implicit deal the Front struck with Kabila—a free hand in the security realm in exchange for his absolute control of Congo's political and economic sectors.[82] This became all the more pressing as the conflict with the *génocidaires* re-intensified in late 1997 as they escalated their attacks inside

[76] Interview with Baudouin Kayokela Kasangula, former administrator in Congolese Central Bank and BCD, Lubumbashi, August 2013.

[77] M'Poyo Kasa-Vubu, *Douze mois chez Kabila (1997–1998)*, pp. 41–3, 65–6.

[78] United Nations, "Report of the Panel of Experts on the Illegal Exploitation of Natural Resources and Other Forms of Wealth of the Democratic Republic of the Congo," p. 3.

[79] Ibid.

[80] Prunier, *From Genocide to Continental War*, p. 220.

[81] Interview with Baudouin Kayokela Kasangula, Lubumbashi, 18 August 2013.

[82] Interview with Shé Okitundu in Kinshasa, August 2013.

Rwanda (see Chapter 9). Ultimately, where the strategic alliance between Kabila and the RPF broke down was not over the economy and resource extraction, but, as we explain in the next section, over control of the state's coercive apparatus.

Katangization and the Creation of a Parallel Army

In May 1997, as the AFDL was poised to take Kinshasa, its political leadership had settled comfortably in Lubumbashi, despite only capturing the city a month before. Kabila felt naturally at home there, but so did several of his Congolese Tutsi lieutenants—Bizima Karaha, Moïse Nyarugabo, Azarias Ruberwa—who had previously studied and lived in Lubumbashi. It was thus from the mineral-rich capital of Katanga, located almost 1,500 miles southeast of Kinshasa, that Kabila held court with international financiers and mining conglomerates, including De Beers, America Mineral Fields and Goldman Sachs; received Congolese politicians, including Patrice Lumumba's son, François; and met American government officials, such as Congresswoman Cynthia McKinney, Clinton's special envoy, Howard Wolpe, and Bill Richardson, US ambassador to the United Nations.[83] And of course it was from Lubumbashi that Kabila issued his controversial proclamation anointing himself president.

Lubumbashi was such to their liking that the rebels raised the possibility of moving the capital there. Such a change was not unprecedented in African history. As part of its nation-building project, in 1973 Nyerere's TANU agreed to relocate Tanzania's capital from coastal Dar es Salaam to the more centrally located Dodoma. Following a similar logic, Nigeria moved its capital from Lagos to Abuja in 1991. The AFDL could not use the same rationale for moving to Lubumbashi; the city was equally as remote from the rest of the country as Kinshasa. The claims of better weather and less corruption were not as specious, but they were still unconvincing. Instead, in a moment of incredible candor, Mwenze Kongolo, a native of Katanga, suggested that "[Moving the capital to Lubumbashi] keeps us farther away from the enemy. It keeps us closer to our friends. It's better to stay here with friendly neighbors."[84]

---

[83] James Rupert, "In Rebel City, the Powers That Would Be; Battlefield Success Has Turned Kabila into Zaire's Main Attraction," *Washington Post*, May 15, 1997.

[84] Andrew Maykuth, "Compared with Kinshasa, It Has Better Weather, Less Corruption: Among Zaire's Rebels, Sentiment for Moving Capital to Lubumbashi," *Philadelphia Inquirer*, May 15, 1997.

This was a stunning statement at a time when the AFDL was on the verge of total victory. On the one hand, it reflected the rebels' anxieties about having to control a large city (Kinshasa) that many comrades, including Kabila, the *famille katangaise* and the Banyamulenge representatives had not lived in or visited for decades; and in which the *kadogo* and the RPF had never even stepped foot in. On the other hand, it also reflected an important ethno-regional dimension to the rebellion that we discussed in Chapter 6. Despite seeking to a build a national revolution representing all marginalized groups in society, two constituencies were pre-eminent in the AFDL—those from the Kivus, especially the Banyamulenge, and those from Katanga. Only one member of the AFDL's ten-person Executive Committee hailed from west of Kasai—Bas Congo native Mawampanga Mwana Nanga. Moreover, most of the fighters were from the east and a fair number of the political leaders were Katangese. In contrast, Mobutu hailed from Equateur, and the leader of the opposition, Tshisekedi, was Kasaien though with strong support in Kinshasa.[85]

When the AFDL resolved that moving the capital to Lubumbashi was impractical at a time when the economy was in a shambles and the state near collapse, Kabila, Kongolo and other members of his inner circle brought their "friends ... and friendly neighbors" to Kinshasa—filling some of the most important positions in the new government with those from the region.[86] If bringing the center of power to Katanga was not feasible, then they would bring Katanga to the center of power. As discussed above, Joseph Kabila became deputy of the FAC; Mzee Kabila appointed his close friend from his childhood days, Gaëtan Kakudji, as minister of interior (described by some as effectively prime minister[87]); Mwenze Kongolo served as minister of justice; his brother-in-law, Célestin Kifwa, was appointed head of the national police. Beyond this top tier, Katangese occupied other influential but less visible positions. John Numbi rapidly advanced within the army to become commander of the 50th Brigade and FAC chief of transmissions and logistics; Colonel Raus Chalwe was anointed head of intelligence in the new national police; former Gécamines director Umba Kyamitala became Minister of Strategic Zones of Development. "*La montée au front du clan katangais*," as one Congolese newspaper put it,[88] was described in conspiratorial terms by the

---

[85] Tshisekedi is also a Baluba, like Kabila, but from Kasai.

[86] Ngolet, *Crisis in the Congo*, pp. 12–16.

[87] "Embattled Kabila," *Africa Confidential*, 39, 14 (July 10, 1998).

[88] "The rise of the Katangese clan"—see *Le Soft International*, pp. 723, 9–15, January 1998. Cited in Reyntjens, *Great African War*, p. 160.

Congolese Tutsi who felt Kabila had used them to overthrow Mobutu and then incrementally and systematically marginalized them. "Katangization was the Mzee's chief tactic to consolidate power," according to one Banyamulenge in the AFDL, "It was one of our earliest, biggest fears, he appointed his co-ethnics everywhere."[89]

Like many African rulers, Kabila was careful to ostensibly and formally draw on representatives from all the major regions and individuals with ties to important political parties or historical figures (e.g., Justine Kasa-Vubu and Juliana Lumumba) to signal the inclusivity of his regime and increase his legitimacy. Nonetheless, Kabila's rivals dismissed these appointments as window-dressing while he created a shadow state composed of the "Katangese mafia" at the expense of his comrades. Few factors contributed more to the outbreak of Africa's Great War than this important shift in the locus of power in the regime from the Banyamulenge (and the RPF) to the Katangese.[90] Consistent with our theoretical framework, we do not attribute this rupture to Kabila's ethnic chauvinism. Instead, the determining factor was the strategic–institutional environment in which Kabila operated, which itself was exploited by his fellow Katangese who, having been marginalized under Mobutu and his coterie from Equateur for more than three decades, felt it was now "our time to rule."

Co-ethnicity and the Power of Networks

In the absence of any type of meritocratic or programmatic basis for making ministerial appointments and other recruitment decisions, and given the weakness of party organs, which would have led to a collective process for filling the new regime, the leadership of the AFDL had a high degree of discretion over hiring and firing decisions. In the early days, the RPF held this discretionary authority and used it to build a movement it felt it could control. But as the rebellion advanced into Congo, it became more and more difficult for the RPF to exercise such authority and they empowered Kabila to make decisions. In turn, Kabila used this opportunity to consolidate his position and insulate himself as much as possible from present and future challengers.

Two considerations were probably utmost in his mind. First, protecting himself against existential challenges necessitated appointing people he could trust,

---

[89] Interview with Thomas Nziratimana, March 2013.

[90] Ngolet, *Crisis in the Congo.*

people he could easily monitor and people who would face high personal costs and social sanctions if they moved against him. In many revolutionary governments, the social and institutional basis of trust is underpinned by the "bonds of solidarity rooted in a shared experience of violent struggle,"[91] and the organizational structures that emerge from the struggle to enforce cooperation; in the absence of organizations enforcing cooperation and reciprocity, these revolutions rarely succeed.[92] In the AFDL, a sense of camaraderie did develop among the revolutionaries. In interviews, Kabila loyalists nostalgically recalled the days fighting with the Front, the brilliant military leadership of "Commander James" and the contribution the Rwandans made to the liberation effort.[93] But this camaraderie was never supported by strong revolutionary organs to which all were equally subordinate. Consequently, there was no impersonal institution that would allocate power, nor settle disputes, nor constrain any one faction from increasing its power at the expense of others.

Unconstrained but also vulnerable, Kabila turned to co-ethnicity and its norms of reciprocity, social sanctioning mechanisms and dense social networks via overlapping family and kinship ties to help him overcome the weakness of the revolution's political institutions and manage this highly uncertain environment.[94] As Reyntjens notes, "The more [Kabila] felt isolated and threatened in a physical context he feared (he did not know nor understand Kinshasa, an environment which intimidated him), Kabila surrounded himself with those close to him, Katangans and Balubakat in particular."[95]

A second obsession for Kabila was to don the presidential laurels without having to rely on external protection or sanction. As the arrest of General Muland of the Tigres Katangais demonstrated during the campaign (see Chapter 6), he knew the RPF would be willing to help him consolidate his power because it would reduce the delegation problems that would arise from the existence of multiple agents. Simultaneously, Mzee was under no illusion that his dependence also meant vulnerability: the RPF could remove him

---

[91] Steven R. Levitsky and Lucan A. Way, "Beyond Patronage: Violent Struggle, Ruling Party Cohesion, and Authoritarian Durability," *Perspectives on Politics*, 10, 4 (2012).

[92] Huntington, *Political Order in Changing Societies*.

[93] Interview with Raphael Ghenda in Kinshasa, 2009.

[94] On social institutions underpinning co-ethnic trust, see James Habyarimana et al., *Coethnicity: Diversity and the Dilemmas of Collective Action*, New York: Russell Sage Foundation, 2009. On the use of these mechanisms to consolidate power in a weak institutional environment, see Roessler, *Ethnic Politics and State Power in Africa*.

[95] Reyntjens, *Great African War*, p. 159.

from power at will and his legitimacy was gravely tarnished. As a nationalist who had been fighting since the 1960s and had never sold out to Mobutu, he resented the fact that he was viewed as a stooge of Kagame. Yet with no army of his own, his liberation dreams would go unfulfilled without the RPF. The need to address these concerns was the bottom-line of most of Kabila's politicking throughout the May 1997–August 1998 period; he was less focused on state- and nation-building than on his own political and even physical survival. This single-minded focus could occasionally reach rather absurd levels, as Jean-Marc, an AFDL intelligence officer from Lubumbashi revealed, "Out of fear of poisoning but also concerned with Mzee's nationalist image, we changed the cooks working for Mzee from the capture of Lubumbashi onwards; Mzee decided to have his own Katangan family cooking for him, rather than having Rwandans feed him like before."[96]

Minister of Transport Henri Mova remembers the pressure Mzee felt from the outset to "Congolize" the rebellion. The liberation struggle could not afford to be branded as a Rwandan operation or a Tutsi-led insurgency; legitimacy in Kinshasa and elsewhere depended on the unambiguously Congolese character of the AFDL. Mova recalls a meeting, before Mzee's self-proclamation as president in May 1997, between Kabila, fellow Katangese Mutomb Tsibal and himself, in which Kabila expressed his fears of how difficult it would be to get rid of the RPF and the Congolese Tutsi who had him under constant surveillance.[97] In May 1998, this obsession with the nexus of perception and security would lead Kabila to demand a change in his bodyguard controlled by RPA officer Francis Gakwerere and his Tutsi forces. James Kabarebe disparagingly recalled: "[for Mzee,] the short people should be brought to replace all those tall guards which people are seeing."[98] While perhaps not the result of ethnic prejudice, Kabila's statement and subsequent actions cut deep into the soul of his Kinyarwanda-speaking comrades. As Kabarebe noted, Kabila's personal guard was composed of Congolese soldiers, not Rwandans.[99] Consequently, as Kabila sought to demonstrate his independence from the RPF, the similarities and differences between Congolese Tutsi and Rwandan Tutsi became a matter of state security. Even if Kabila certainly knew the difference, perceived Tutsi characteristics of height and

---

[96] Interview with a source who requested his name be changed, Kinshasa, August 2013.
[97] Interview in Brussels, April 2011.
[98] Interview in Kigali, April 2013.
[99] Ibid.

facial characteristics would make it hard for the Congolese public to distinguish between the two. Thus if his goal was to distance himself from the RPF for nationalist purposes, he felt he could not be surrounded by Tutsi regardless of their nationality. As he removed Banyamulenge from positions of influence, such as his decision not to retain Moïse Nyarugabo as his office manager after they captured Kinshasa, Mzee alienated a key constituency while, perhaps not intentionally, flaming the anti-Tutsi prejudices that triggered the revolution in the first place. In the words of Nyarugabo: "You want to give us the impression that we fought for nothing ... You think like them: that I am a foreigner ... The war started in my head for me that day."[100]

The marginalization of part of the political base of the AFDL was not merely the result of societal pressure against "foreign rule" but also of Kabila's anxiety over his inability to scrutinize what was happening outside his purview. Being excluded from Tutsi ethnic networks and unable to understand Kinyarwanda increased the monitoring costs of Kabila and his fellow Katangese over Banyamulenge leaders like Bizima Karaha, Moïse Nyarugabo and Azarias Ruberwa. Strong ties between the RPF and the Congolese Tutsi (some of whom had served in the RPA) made Kabila nervous that even as his regime sought to break free of the RPF, the presence of Congolese Tutsi in government, especially in strategic parts of the regime, could serve as a Trojan horse.

Two examples illustrate how ethnic differences increased uncertainty within the regime and how different perceptions of ethnicity's political role shaped the relations between the alliance's main forces. The first example dates back to early 1998 when Mzee suddenly called Kabarebe, Kakudji, Kongolo, Numbi, Joseph Kabila and a handful of others to an urgent National Security Council meeting at the Palais de Marbre. Until the last minute, the participants were kept in the dark about the purpose of the meeting: Kabila revealed that he had received information that six stunningly beautiful Rwandan girls had left from Cyangugu in Rwanda to Bukavu and were now traveling to Kinshasa to seduce and poison Congolese politicians and destabilize the regime. Upon hearing this story—which had long circulated in the region in various guises (and still occasionally makes the rounds), all of them reproducing tropes of "innate" Tutsi power hunger, moral deviance and forbidden sexuality—Kabarebe nearly fell off his chair. Repulsed that the Congolese president would echo such xenophobic conspiracies, he ironically declared: "I will address this security issue." Kabarebe also added that: "But I have a thousand

---

[100] Interview with Moïse Nyarugabo, Kinshasa, December 2009.

troops that could overthrow this government in a second so which one is more urgent according to you?" An awkward silence followed and the meeting was adjourned.[101]

A second example was cited by Minister for Human Rights Shé Okitundu. He recalls traveling abroad with Foreign Minister Bizima Karaha and being picked up at N'Djili Airport upon their return by an RPF officer. Karaha and this official would converse in Kinyarwanda, the lingua franca of Rwanda but foreign to Okitundu, leaving him feeling humiliated and in the dark about potentially important information exchanged.[102] As the power struggle intensified between Kabila and his fellow Katangese on one side and the RPF and the Congolese Tutsi on the other, the barriers to penetrating and monitoring Tutsi networks became a major liability for Kabila and handed the RPF an offensive advantage that the Congolese president felt he could not tolerate.[103]

These dynamics were compounded by the intra-ethnic pressure to which Kabila was subjected. Many Katangese joined the AFDL late in the game— only after the movement captured Lubumbashi or even Kinshasa. They thus lacked the power of those revolutionaries such as Masasu or Bugera, who were around since the beginning; they also understandably did not share the same feelings of camaraderie. In turn, some Congolese Tutsi felt Kabila's co-ethnics manipulated him to bolster their own influence. The particularly poisonous

---

[100] Interview with Jaynet Kabila, August 2013; interview with James Kabarebe in Kigali, April 2013; interview with Abdoulaye Yerodia in Kinshasa, August 2013; interview with Godefroid Tchamlesso in Kinshasa, August 2013.

[102] Interview in Kinshasa, December 2009.

[103] Numerous interviewees (both in the RPF and on Kabila's side) mentioned that Didier Kazadi seemed to be especially influential in shaping Mzee's views on the RPF; he has often been accused in retrospect of inflating the threat posed by the Rwandans. It is important to note that Kazadi speaks Kinyarwanda, having learned the language while in Belgian Ruanda–Urundi, where his father served as a colonial administrator. Kazadi himself claimed to have exploited this knowledge to eavesdrop on Francis Gakwerere who called Paul Kagame five to six times a day. It was through this surveillance that Kazadi claims to have learned Gakwerere was plotting to "assassinate" Kabila. This in turn, Kazadi claimed, prompted Kabila to switch his presidential guard. We have no way to verify Kazadi's charge of a Gakwerere-led assassination plot. But this anecdote does reveal the information challenges posed by different ethnic networks and the power and influence gained by those individuals who could tap into their rival's networks. Interview with Didier Kazadi in Kinshasa, August 2013.

role played by the *famille katangaise* from April 1997 onwards was a ubiquitous complaint of Banyamulenge representatives.[104] Even some of Kabila's co-ethnics admitted as much; in the testimony of Jean-Marc, the Katangese intelligence officer cited earlier: "The clan around Kabila, our people, did feed Mzee false information about coups and rebellions from the moment we came to power. Masasu was a good example. He was not preparing to take over, but the things they told to Mzee were crazy."[105]

Balancing against the RPF: Kabila Creates a Parallel Army

One of the main predicaments Kabila faced, as discussed earlier, was that he came to power with RPF support, and as he lacked his own army he remained dependent on the Rwandans for regime security. The Front was happy to oblige Kabila's request that James Kabarebe and some RPA units stay on in Kinshasa; it gave the RPF incredible latitude to continue to counter the *génocidaires* and ensure a friendly regime controlled Congo. The sensitivity of such an arrangement for Kabila was not lost on Kabarebe and Munyuza, however, and in a bid to assuage concerns, Joseph Kabila was confirmed as FAC deputy chief of staff. While this gesture was important in symbolizing the RPF's goodwill in maintaining cooperative ties, it did not resolve Kabila's strategic dilemma—he remained a ruler without an army of his own. In the highly uncertain environment that prevailed in the post-revolutionary state, especially as rumors of conspiracies swirled around the streets of Kinshasa, Kabila took several steps to buttress his own coercive power.

First, he Katangized the existing security services under the direction of Mwenze Kongolo and Gaëtan Kakudji, who served as minister of interior from January 1998. Second, he created a new Congolese National Police under the leadership of two Katangese loyalists, Célestin Kifwa and Raus Chalwe, who ensured no Rwandans joined the organization.[106] Third, he replaced his presidential guard with Tanzanian-trained soldiers, having told the Mkapa–Kikwete government (suspicious of Kagame in its own right) that he needed autonomy from the RPF.

During the armed struggle, the RPA "volunteered" one of its own specialist operatives, Francis Gakwerere, to head Kabila's bodyguard. As Dan Munyuza

---

[104] Interview with Malick Kijege in Kinshasa, August 2013.

[105] Interview in Kinshasa, August 2013.

[106] Mzee insisted on this; he wanted people he could trust. Interview with Raus Chalwe, Kinshasa, August 2013.

was promoted to chief of intelligence inside Congo, Gakwerere became Kabila's ultimate gatekeeper. He was described by Kongolo as a "tough guy, an excellent bodyguard ... [Gakwerere] was one of the only ones who could and would refuse things to the president."[107] And according to Raus Chalwe, "[He] totally controlled access to the Mzee ... He really made it almost impossible for us to see the president." After becoming president, Kabila chafed at the RPF's tight grip on his personal movement. In searching for alternatives, it was most likely Kabila's national security adviser and later head of Congo's Agence Nationale de Renseignements under Joseph Kabila, Didier Kazadi, who suggested Mzee look to the Tanzanians. Kazadi, a veteran of Kabila's PRP, had developed strong connections with Tanzania's security services in the years he lived in exile in the country, enabling him to exploit their emerging rivalry with Kigali and simultaneously offer his boss the prize he craved for.[108] In May 1998, Mzee was thus finally able to replace Gakwerere and his security personnel.[109] This did not go down well with the RPF, according to Okwiri Rabwoni, one of Museveni's main intelligence liaisons with the AFDL: "Kabila sent some Congolese young men he trusted to Tanzania for training; upon their return they replaced Francis's men, the RPF hated Kabila for doing that, it really infuriated them."[110] According to Kabarebe, Kabila's new protection unit, commanded by Tanzanian advisers who had trained the Katangese guards, was openly hostile to him and the RPA.[111]

This sheds some light on the important albeit often overlooked role of Tanzania's influence on the regional balance of power after the overthrow of Mobutu. According to various interviewees, including high-ranking Tanzanian officials, Tanzania emerged as a vital foil to the RPF during the interbellum period. As discussed in Chapter 4, Kagame and Museveni consulted with Nyerere as they built the AFDL and invited Kabila to join its leadership council. Nyerere, Kagame and Museveni were of one mind about the importance of removing Mobutu. By 1998, however, the elder statesman still retained influence but his physical condition was deteriorating, limiting his travel and workload. Instead, official Tanzanian policymaking was in the hands of indi-

---

[107] Interview in Kinshasa, August 2013.

[108] Interview with Didier Kazadi, Kinshasa, August 2013. The RPF also point a finger at Kazadi on this front. "Kabila was manipulated by the Tanzanians, with a key role for Didier Kazadi as the go between." Interview with Jack Nziza, Kigali, July 2014.

[109] Interview with Mwenze Kongolo in Kinshasa, August 2013.

[110] Interview in Kampala, March 2013.

[111] Interview in Kigali, April 2013.

viduals with which the RPF had strained relations, such as the foreign minister, Jakaya Kikwete, or chief of the Tanzanian People's Defense Forces, General Robert Mboma. Both were known to be highly skeptical of Kagame's regime and were in turn perceived as apologists for Hutu Power by the RPF. Many in the RPF considered Kikwete, a former intelligence colonel, "pro-Hutu" given his threats to arm the Hutu rebels in Burundi if the Tutsi-dominated military regime of Buyoya did not sue for peace.[112] Moreover, during the genocide, senior Tanzanian officials had openly speculated (encouraging certain NGOs and expatriates to make similar claims) that the mass killings in eastern Rwanda in and around Kibungo had been carried out by RPA death squads rather than the Interahamwe. General Mboma's disparaging comments in a meeting with RPF officers in May 1994 at the Tanzania–Rwanda border were a particular sore point. Mboma allegedly showed no sympathy for the victims of the genocide but instead expressed disgust that the dead bodies were contaminating the Akagera River that runs along the two countries' border. According to DMI officer Jack Nziza, who was there at the time, Mboma said, "I don't want to see such dirt in Tanzania" when referring to the bodies of massacred Rwandans.[113]

Nonetheless, in the interest of regional cooperation and sharing the costs of rebuilding the Congo, the RPF initially welcomed the support of Tanzania in helping to train the new Congolese army. The Tanzanians sent some 600 instructors to a military training center in Kamina, Katanga, where they remained until the outbreak of the second war[114]—when the Tanzanian officers stood by and watched as Congolese soldiers in Kamina massacred more than 100 Tutsi officers in training when news of the mutiny of the 10th Brigade in Goma in August 1998 reached their military base.[115]

---

[112] See International Crisis Group, "Burundian Refugees in Tanzania: The Key Factor to the Burundi Peace Process," *ICG Central Africa Report*, no. 12, Brussels: International Crisis Group, 1999.

[113] Interview in Kigali, July 2014. See also Tom Ndahiro, "The Tutsi Genocide and the Ideological River," *New Times*, May 10, 2010. This incident was confirmed by a former high-ranking Tanzanian government official, though he claimed the bodies filling the river were indeed victims of reprisal killings by the RPF. Interview in Dar es Salaam, June 2015.

[114] Prunier, *From Genocide to Continental War*, p. 158.

[115] According to Malick Kijege, Tanzania's inaction was shameful: "Tanzania was an important AFDL ally and could have saved people; its role is thus very grave." Interview in Kinshasa, August 2013.

The way in which training was conducted at the center had begun to raise suspicions soon after the base was established. According to Caesar Kayizari, who was the RPA's deputy force commander in the AFDL campaign, he and Joseph Kabila flew to Kamina in June 1997 as complaints had surfaced about the base, including reports of de facto segregation of troops along ethnic lines, with the Congolese Tutsi not integrated with the others.[116] Kayizari told the Tanzanian officers to change this and get the house in order, but upon his return to Kinshasa, Mzee did not see him, choosing to receive the report on the Kamina situation from his son; the dossier was essentially buried.[117] The segregated training continued and provided Kabila with a parallel military force. As Kabarebe recalls: "[Kabila] had built an army of 30,000 people next to my army."[118] While the size of the Tanzanian-trained force was not that large, it probably numbered 6,000–7,000 men, including 1,000 officers.[119]

Kabila's efforts to balance against the RPF by acquiring a separate force unsettled the Congolese Tutsi, who felt a sense of loyalty to Mzee as their revolutionary leader. As aspiring military cadres, they were disappointed by Kabila's actions as they felt it undermined the professionalism and cohesion of the national army. For Zacharias, a young Banyamulenge battalion commander who felt more personal proximity to Kabila than to the RPA officers:

> If Mzee had had a bit more patience with James, we would have had a good army and everybody would have been better off. But his embrace of Gaëtan Kakudji and John Numbi made him lose track—the Katangan family pushed him in a bad direction. They manipulated him, even if we were ready to die for him. We protected him.[120]

Of course, Kabila's move to raise a parallel army also alarmed Kabarebe as his troops began to be surrounded by what he saw as hostile forces; soon the RPA would no longer be absolutely vital to the president's personal security. Slowly but surely, Kabila gained some of the security he felt he needed to stand on his own and Tanzania felt was necessary to balance against the RPF. Thus, according to Jean-Marc, the Katangese intelligence official close to

---

[116] According to one former Tanzanian military commander, the exclusion of Congolese Tutsi from the training was intentional given their ties with the RPF. Interview in Dar es Salaam, June 2015.

[117] Interview in Kigali, April 2013.

[118] Interview in Kigali, April 2013.

[119] Interview with former high-ranking Tanzanian government official, in Dar es Salaam, June 2015.

[120] Named changed at source's request. Interview in Kinshasa, August 2013.

the Mzee: "When we trained serious security forces from our area [Katanga], later the core of the Republican Guard, and we felt we were ready, we decided the Rwandans had to leave."[121] The comrades-turned-rivals were now fast approaching a point of no return.

The Volcano Rumbles: New and Old Grievances in Eastern Congo

The slide into growing mistrust and open rivalry between the comrades happened not just at the international level, as the Pan-Africanist alliance withered quickly, and in the whirlpool of tempestuous Kinshasa politics, where the RPF and the Katangese power bloc stumbled from close cooperation into a security dilemma. The existential crisis of the AFDL also very much revealed itself in eastern Congo—the movement's ground zero where the spark of the liberation project had been lit. If the first anniversary of the revolution appeared as an elegy in western Congo, in the east martial tunes were increasingly the order of the day.

Caught up in the chess game between Kabila and the RPF were the Congolese Tutsi, once a marginalized, disorganized and stigmatized minority but since May 1997 a politico-military factor on the rise. As explained in Chapter 4, their emergence as one of the liberation project's main constituencies was a function of the political, social and economic storms that ravaged eastern Congo in the 1990s and the lethal identity politics that forced them to fight back. By some accounts, Congolese Tutsi youth made up the bulk of the forces in the AFDL and they were strongly represented in the AFDL Executive Council, claiming half of the ten positions. Yet their prominence in government never equaled that of the period of the struggle during which they were so visible that the AFDL was commonly known in African and Western media as the "Banyamulenge rebellion." According to Moïse Nyarugabo, Kabila refused to appoint more than one Congolese Tutsi to his cabinet for political reasons—to calm anti-Tutsi sentiments in Kinshasa.[122] With that space reserved for Kabila's favorite son from the east—Foreign Minister Bizima Karaha—there was no room for any others. Those close to Kabila reject the notion that the president's cabinet selections were intentionally meant to marginalize the Congolese Tutsi. According to Henri Mova, "Mzee was not a tribal leader and Katanga was if anything underrepresented—it was

---

[121] Interview in Kinshasa, August 2013.
[122] Interview in Kinshasa, December 2009.

the Tutsi who had always been overrepresented!"[123] The arrest of Masasu and Bugera's demotion, however, reinforced the Banyamulenge view that Kabila was sidelining his former foot soldiers from national power.

If the Congolese Tutsi felt they were being purged from the Kinshasa government, the opposite applied in North and South Kivu, where it was alleged that Tutsi now dominated civil service positions.[124] Moreover, the continued presence of RPA troops in the region bred resentment. Complemented by Congolese Army divisions, such as the 10th Brigade, drawing heavily from Congolese Tutsi soldiers, these units aggressively patrolled the hills and forests, seeking to eradicate the ex-FAR/Interahamwe and their local auxiliaries. The perceived "Tutsi domination" of the east, extensive narratives of the looting of cars, furniture and factory parts from towns like Bukavu, and the rumored threats of Rwanda's possible annexation of the region provoked a strong local backlash from non-Tutsi groups, such as the Hunde, Babembe, Nande, Nyanga and others who united against the "occupation" of their lands and the "Tutsification" of local political, judiciary and administrative positions. Anti-Tutsi sentiment was channeled through local militias, known as the Mai Mai, which had originally fought alongside the AFDL but then turned their weapons against the RPA and its Congolese allies.[125] Guerrilla attacks by these Mai Mai, combined with the ongoing conflict between the RPF and the *génocidaires*, ensured that the Kivus continued to experience regular bouts of extreme violence.[126] The local and national political exclusion of the constituencies the Mai Mai represented only deepened the crisis.[127]

Masisi became the focal point for confrontation in August and September 1997 as the return of Tutsi families to the area after the overthrow of Mobutu was violently opposed by local residents; as many as 1,000 people were killed within the space of a few weeks. In response, Rwandan troops reportedly "burned most of the town to the ground in revenge."[128] Another important cause of insecurity in North Kivu, discussed in detail in the following chapter, was the rising number of cross-border attacks into Rwanda by the *génocidaires* and which occasionally included participation of Mai Mai militants. The latter

---

[123] Interview in Brussels, April 2011.

[124] See Reyntjens, *Great African War*, pp. 147–50.

[125] Kisangani, *Civil Wars in the Democratic Republic of Congo*, pp. 135–40.

[126] De Villers and Willame, *République démocratique du Congo*, pp. 258–75.

[127] Kisangani, *Civil Wars in the Democratic Republic of Congo*, pp. 135–40.

[128] Lynne Duke, "Ethnic Violence Grips Eastern Congo," *Washington Post*, October 10, 1997.

also became a tremendous headache in South Kivu for the AFDL. After the public humiliation of the *chef coutumier* (customary chief) of the Batembo—who was forced to serve as a carrier of luggage for Banyamulenge soldiers in July 1997—Mai Mai units went on a rampage, cleansing territories adjacent to Kalehe by Lake Kivu of Tutsi soldiers and civilians. The situation worsened even further when, on December 11, 1997, in the wake of Masasu's arrest and the opening up of a security vacuum in South Kivu, Mai Mai attacked Bukavu at dawn. The clandestine Radio du Patriote broadcast calls for all Tutsis to return to Rwanda and urged the population to capture and surrender all Tutsis to the "resistance," who would ensure their "repatriation."[129] Such propaganda underscored the tightening alliance between Mai Mai militias and the ex-FAR/Interahamwe who were re-importing the genocidal project into north-west Rwanda.

* * *

From the perspective of both the Congolese Tutsi and their enemies, the heart of the problem in eastern Congo remained the nationality question—who was Congolese and who was not, and the repercussions of this on political and socio-economic rights, including the electoral roll and land ownership. This grievance had driven Tutsi participation in the liberation movement and their main priority for the AFDL's policy agenda was the restoration of full citizenship rights to those from tribes, such as the Banyamulenge, that resided on Congolese territory before 1960 but were not considered "indigenous" because many emigrated to Congo during the colonial era.[130] The migrant status of Kinyarwanda-speaking Congolese denied them both formal citizenship rights and customary rights to land. As referred to in Chapter 4, Mobutu promised to resolve the Banyarwanda's ambiguous legal status through his 1972 decree that instituted a less restrictive temporal definition of citizenship and even granted citizenship to those who fled from Rwanda after the 1959–62 Social Revolution and subsequent violence. As the Banyarwanda used their newfound rights to gain greater access to land in North Kivu, popular resistance among the "indigenous" majority increased, leading Mobutu to reverse the decree and exclude those who did not belong to a tribe that resided on Congolese territory in 1885. In 1991, the Conférence Nationale Souveraine endorsed the enforcement of the more restrictive citizenship law. The absence

---

[129] De Villers and Willame, *République démocratique du Congo*, pp. 245–6.

[130] Mamdani, *When Victims Become Killers*. See also Turner, *Congo Wars*, pp. 80–92.

of full citizenship rights left the Banyarwanda vulnerable to the whims of extremist politicians, such as Anzuluni Bembe, the co-speaker of parliament, who signed a resolution in 1995 that identified the Banyamulenge as recent refugees and called for its members to be expelled from the country.[131]

With the overthrow of Mobutu, the Congolese Tutsi in the AFDL lobbied for the nationality question to be resolved quickly. From the outset, Kabila promised to address the issue and a commission was created to draft a new citizenship law. One of the experts consulted was Azarias Ruberwa who stated that "the text that was being prepared definitely went in the right direction"— it specified that if a given tribe was on Congolese territory before 1960, this meant all of its members were Congolese citizens.[132] Kabila and even Kakudji gave several speeches on the subject, emphasizing that the Banyarwanda were inalienably Congolese; they also endorsed civil society initiatives that preached grassroots reconciliation. Ultimately, however, the president never put the new citizenship bill into law. And worryingly, Mzee eventually stopped talking, publicly and privately, about the nationality question altogether—Moïse Nyarugabo recalls that "Kabila was not ready to take any risks for us."[133]

* * *

In late February 1998, with the citizenship issue left unresolved and the insurgents' attacks into Rwanda increasing, 300 Banyamulenge soldiers led by Muller Ruhimbika mutinied, occupying the Ruzizi Plain after weeks of tension in South Kivu. The mutiny was sparked by an order that Muller's soldiers redeploy to Kasai and Katanga but reflected deeper disillusionment with the regime, including the Tutsis' marginalization from the ruling coalition, the lack of progress on the nationality question and the removal of "their" Masasu.[134] According to one independent-minded Tutsi civil society activist, Enock Rubenrangabo Sebineza, the mutiny was also a revolt against the RPA's arrogant behavior for which Congolese Tutsi youth faced harsh reprisals by the Mai Mai and other vigilante groups.[135] In a context in which many Congolese communities continued to downplay the Rwandan genocide and the threat against the Tutsis—present-day grievances vis-à-vis the "occupa-

---

[131] Mamdani, *When Victims Become Killers*, Chapter 8.

[132] Interview in Kinshasa, December 2009.

[133] Interview with Moïse Nyarugabo in Kinshasa, December 2009.

[134] See Manassé Ruhimbika Muller, *Les Banyamulenge (Congo-Zaïre), entre deux guerres*, Paris: Harmattan, 2001.

[135] Interview in Kinshasa, December 2009.

tion" mingled with old stereotypes—the actions taken by Muller represented the mounting anxiety that the Banyamulenge would once again be crushed in-between national power politics and local xenophobia.

However, before the situation escalated further, the AFDL responded swiftly and pragmatically, demonstrating its peacemaking potential when elite cooperation was sustained. Signaling a unified approach to the crisis, Mzee reminded residents of his words in Bukavu four weeks earlier—"The Banyamulenge! They helped us. Are these not the people with whom you lived [in peace] and with whom you built so much?"—and dispatched Kabarebe and his son, Joseph, to negotiate with the mutineers. They granted personal guarantees to Muller that his men's grievances would be addressed, pledging to persuade the president to settle the nationality question, reduce insecurity and maintain homogenous Banyamulenge military units.[136]

The timely intervention ended the mutiny and Kabila urged the Constitutional Commission he had appointed in October 1997 to deal comprehensively with the nationality question. For a few weeks, optimism resurfaced, only to be extinguished once again. At the same time that the Banyamulenge mutiny ended in South Kivu, AFDL units rounded up dozens—possibly hundreds—in Butembo and Walikale in North Kivu to avenge the deaths of some of their own. Kabila thus faced the stinging criticism again that while he was happy to talk to the Tutsi and accommodate their demands for exceptional treatment, ordinary Congolese merely felt the blows of the sword when they rebelled against his faltering government. Increasingly, it became clear that February 1998 would indeed be a key point in the trajectory of eastern Congo. But rather than acting as a catalyst to finally address the nationality question and the grievances of all communities in the region, it above all gave all parties concerned yet more reason to head to the trenches.

Conclusion

The unraveling of the AFDL coalition was not a story that was written in the stars or that seemed in any shape or form inevitable to the protagonists who experienced the rapid disintegration of the project for which they had been willing to sacrifice their lives. This chapter documented the corrosive misunderstandings, errors of judgment and missed opportunities that characterized the vitally important phase that followed the consolidation of the post-

[136] De Villers and Willame, *République démocratique du Congo*, pp. 258–67.

Mobutu order. The peaceful crisis management of the Banyamulenge mutiny—a combustible situation that could easily have blown up—demonstrated the benefits[137] that accrued from continued collaboration between the coalition partners. It also highlighted that such cooperation remained possible despite Masasu's incarceration and despite shifting equilibria within the regime due to policies of Katangization and Kabila's creation of a parallel army. But rather than ushering in renewed partnership in which the AFDL would successfully formulate political answers to the deep-rooted identity and socio-economic conflicts of the region, the dousing of the flames of the mini-insurrection was soon overshadowed by much greater trouble across eastern Congo and northwest Rwanda. Relations between regime factions worsened further over the next couple of months, plagued by the general environment of strategic uncertainty and numerous decisions which different comrades took, without caring much for how these would be perceived by their supposed allies. By May 17, 1998, the first anniversary of the revolution, it was barely still possible to talk of an alliance—let alone of Pan-Africanism. The border war between Ethiopia and Eritrea, and Rwanda's and Uganda's boycott of the anniversary celebrations signaled the disentanglement of regional cooperation among Africa's liberation regimes.

Laurent-Désiré Kabila was openly favoring his own ethno-regional clients and ever less interested in the nationality question which mattered so much to his Congolese Tutsi brethren. The question of the UN investigation into mass atrocities committed during the campaign led the RPF to put immense pressure on the Congolese president to continue to stonewall Roberto Garreton's team, with significant economic consequences for the revolution. Aid flows amounted to a mere trickle, while shambolic governance practices scared investors. In this context of growing irritation, scheming and free-riding among coalition partners, all paid lip service to the idea of the AFDL as their common framework and Congo as a future progressive beacon for Africa; in reality, the comrades looked for other options and a redrawing of the elite bargain at the heart of the liberation project.

The catalyst for the final stages in the unraveling of the alliance would be the return in full force of a foe presumed severely weakened, if not altogether dead. The resurgence of the *génocidaires* in eastern Congo and Rwanda from

---

[137] Joseph Kabila's role in peacefully dealing with the mutiny impressed some actors from eastern Congo, including Azarias Ruberwa; interview in Kinshasa, December 2009.

late 1997 onwards would dramatically raise the stakes again of the Congolese liberation adventure for the RPF and had a massive psychological effect on the RPA in Kigali and in Kinshasa. As we will see in the next chapter, the resumption of the murder of school children, the targeted killings of *rescapés* in rural communities and the renewed extermination attacks on camps for displaced Tutsi ensured that having a functional, pliable and loyal regime in Congo once again manifested itself as an absolute national security imperative for the RPF. The discovery of evidence that seemed to suggest that the new incumbent in Kinshasa, comrade Kabila, was actually partly responsible for the *génocidaire* offensive led Kagame and Kabarebe to a deadly conclusion: Rwandan-orchestrated regime change in Congo was necessary again.

9

BACK AGAINST THE WALL

THE RETURN OF THE *GÉNOCIDAIRE* THREAT

When a Tutsi like me would meet a Hutu, he would immediately think of him as a killer.
And a Hutu who saw a Tutsi would immediately fear him as an RPF guy who might
shoot him.

Caesar Kayizari, army commander of the RPA's 3rd Division.

We wanted to show that the RPF couldn't govern. We knew people in the interior
backed us.

Paul Rwarakabije, chief of staff of the Armée pour la Libération du Rwanda (ALiR).

On the evening of August 18, 1997, just before midnight, Rwandan Hutu
extremists surrounded the homes of almost two dozen Tutsi survivors—so-
called *rescapés*—of the genocide in the municipality of Mutara, northeast of
Gisenyi, right across the border from Congo. For weeks, death threats had
been issued against the Tutsi of Mutara, including the local tax-collector
Faustin Ndagijimana. One such threat explicitly stated that "We will kill all
you *Inyenzi* [cockroaches], especially you, Ndagijimana, we will cut you into
pieces." On August 18, Faustin was not at home, but his new-born baby and
closest relatives were when the ex-FAR and Interahamwe fighters ("*abacengezi*") blew their whistles to signal their arrival. Using grenades, guns and
machetes, the onslaught commenced against the Tutsi families and Hutus

collaborating with the new RPF regime. According to Faustin's wife, Annonciata Nyiramashuri:

> The children were screaming for me to save them but I couldn't. The neighbouring Hutu women were busy stealing our clothes and food from the house ... They are all neighbours. I asked them why they were killing us when we had never refused them anything; we had shared beer with them during the day, laughing. They replied that we must share everything during the day, but at night they had to kill us because we were *Inyenzi*. After saying that they shot me repeatedly in the legs and thighs and hit my head with a hammer. I was really almost dead.[1]

Fifteen people were murdered that night, including four Hutu "collaborators."

The killings of *rescapés* in Mutara in August 1997 traumatized Rwandans and once again evoked the specter of genocidal violence.[2] This attack was not an isolated incident but the latest episode in a campaign to alter the demography of the country through murder and terror. The hope had been that the dismantling of the refugee camps in eastern Congo, the return of more than a million Rwandans and the defeat of the patron of the old regime, Mobutu Sese Seko, would decisively end the war that had raged since 1990 and eradicate the genocidal project. Yet around the time of the fall of Kinshasa, signs of a growing insurgent movement—ironically but not coincidentally largely composed of former Hutu refugees who had traveled back home—could already be seen. Anti-Tutsi pogroms, targeted assassinations of local officials, strikes against RPA soldiers, genocidal propaganda, the murder of the Hutu "accomplices" of RPF rule and even massacres in schools increased rather than decreased after the AFDL came to power in Congo. The insurgency represented a huge psychological shock to the population, but also to the RPF: its hold on power and legitimacy to rule became increasingly tenuous as it failed to protect its citizens and insurgents overran large swathes of the Gisenyi, Ruhengeri and Gitarama prefectures, as well as launching sporadic attacks in Byumba, Butare and Gikongoro. Even the areas around Kigali could not be fully protected.

The Northwest Insurgency marked not only a potentially existential challenge to the RPF's hold on power and its relationship with the Rwandan

---

[1] African Rights, *Rwanda: The Insurgency in the Northwest*, London: African Rights, 1998, pp. 147–51.

[2] United Nations High Commissioner for Human Rights, "Human Rights Field Operation in Rwanda," in *Report of the United Nations High Commissioner for Human Rights*, New York: UN Economic and Social Council, 1998.

population but also highlighted once again the nexus between domestic security and the regional environment. The fact that the *abacengezi* (infiltrators) drew significant military and logistical support from the *maquis* around Masisi in North Kivu, from where they drew recruits and traded in looted goods and animals, and that they could use the volcanic forests of eastern Congo as rear bases to launch attacks, underscored the umbilical connection between the Kivus, Rwanda and the seemingly never-ending war. Moreover, the RPF claimed that its own operations inside Rwanda and the operations carried out by James Kabarebe as head of the Congolese army were being systematically undermined by its supposed Congolese allies. Local officials across North and South Kivu were accused of tolerating and even collaborating with *génocidaire* forces as they brought war back to Rwanda. But most devastatingly of all, the RPF discovered supposed proof of links between Mzee Kabila—the man they had carried on their backs for more than 1,000 miles and brought to power—and the *abacengezi*. As the insurgency resulted in more massacres across Rwanda's northwest as well as open battles between the rebels and the RPA, this further heightened the stakes of the increasingly fractious political game in Kinshasa. At the very moment it was again being challenged at home, it seemed to lose its vital partnership with Congo. In that widening gap, from the perspective of the RPF, lay the road to a new war.

The Ex-FAR/Interahamwe Regroup, November 1996–May 1997

As we saw in Chapter 6, when RPA forces began crossing into eastern Zaire in September–October 1996 under the cover of the AFDL alliance, the overarching strategic objective was to mortally wound its ex-FAR/Interahamwe archenemy in order for the RPF to consolidate the revolution at home and pave the way for its state-building and nation-building agenda. Summarized by Colonel Joseph Karemera, the RPF minister of health and key counsel of Paul Kagame, "we had to neutralize the threat and free the hostages."[3] In concrete, sequential terms, this meant:

1. disrupting the plans for an imminent invasion of Rwanda;
2. repatriating the refugee population to weaken the support base of its enemy, bring to justice those who committed crimes during the genocide, and getting Rwandans back to work to contribute to economic development;

[3] Interview in Kigali, December 2009.

WHY COMRADES GO TO WAR

3. annihilating the rebuilt FAR military machine;
4. disposing of the *génocidaires'* external patron (i.e., overthrowing Mobutu).

After the initial success of the forces commanded by Kabarebe and Kayizari—within mere weeks the camps were overrun, the enemy was killed or forced to flee and a gigantic mass of displaced Rwandans walked home—the RPF's top strategists were triumphant. There had been no external intervention by France or the United Nations to stop the AFDL and the operation seemed to qualitatively shift the political balance, at home and in Congo. Of course, the ex-FAR/Interahamwe fighters who had escaped from the encirclement and were heading for the rainforest with tens of thousands of civilians in their wake would need to be hunted down and Mobutu could yet conjure up a last-minute trump card. But the fall of one Congolese province after another and the evacuation of the *génocidaire* leadership to Brazzaville, Nairobi and Yaoundé, all faraway from Kigali and from possible military rear bases, further increased the self-confidence of Kagame and his colonels. It appeared as if all four objectives of the invasion would be met: the achievement of the short-term imperatives would clear the way for the longer-term state-building project at home and the consolidation of a new regime of regional security. Nevertheless, just as the RPF was preparing to raise the mission-accomplished flag, a number of cracks appeared in their plan and soon the blowback was fast and furious.

The North Kivu Maquis

A number of strategic and informational failures account for the unraveling of their initial success and would lead to a resurrection of the *génocidaires* at a time when the RPF believed that the enemy had nearly been vanquished. The first was a misjudgment of what its operation in the camps had achieved. Intelligence reports seemed to confirm that the enemy's backbone had indeed been broken: hundreds—possibly thousands—of ex-FAR/Interahamwe fighters had perished at the hands of superior RPA tactics and organization. Moreover, the ferocious advance of AFDL troops and RPA special forces had disrupted the command structure of the extremist force as it beat a chaotic withdrawal. DMI briefings anticipated some continued resistance from individual units that sought to slow the AFDL's progress to cover the retreat of the bulk of the surviving force and its senior officer corps, but (correctly) diagnosed that few major battles after the camps were to be expected. The biggest challenge appeared to be to catch ex-FAR/Interahamwe elements in time before they had the chance to be reinforced by Mobutu or to disappear into the forests to make their way to Central African Republic and Sudan in the north, Congo-Brazzaville in the west and Zambia in the south.[4] This explains the frantic pace of Commanders Kabarebe and Kayizari as they moved out of the Kivus and into Zaire's other provinces to neutralize what seemed like a force in full disbandment. What the RPA intelligence failed to detect, however, is the extent of the ex-FAR/Interahamwe forces that did not flee west and instead melted away in the forests of eastern Zaire—less than 100 kilometers from Rwanda.

* * *

Despite Mobutu's hopes that the *génocidaires* would prove his first line of defense given the hopeless state of the FAZ and the much-weakened DSP, the army of the former Rwandan government failed to meaningfully defend any major Zairian cities or strategic junctures. This situation worsened after the initial RPA onslaught. Communication lines had broken down, the evacuated senior command was separated from its ground troops and the AFDL captured much of its heavy artillery and weaponry. Thus thousands of ex-FAR/Interahamwe combatants abandoned any pretense of fighting and fled toward Zaire's borders in search of safety. However, not all gave up and ran away. Some, particularly those who were the last to mount resistance around the giant Mugunga and Katale camps outside Goma and those fleeing the attacks on the camps north of Bukavu, did not trek further north or west in their withdrawal, but instead, on the orders of Lieutenant-Colonels Leonard Nkundiye and Paul Rwarakabije, broke into smaller groups and hid in the forests around the town of Masisi in North Kivu. As the AFDL pushed on and pursued the ex-FAR/Interahamwe and Hutu civilians heading for Walikale and Kisangani, this group of about 1,000 hardened professional soldiers and their civilian dependents lay low as the storm passed on.

As the weeks went by and the AFDL left only a small force to secure the Kivus, the area around Masisi became the nucleus of the rebirth, from the ground up, of the RPF's archenemy. Many survivors of the RPA onslaught across North and South Kivu headed to join Nkundiye, Rwarakabije and their small force in Masisi, but others were asked to stay put so as not to attract too much attention. The most extremist elements, a minority among the reorganizing troops, were told to set their ideological zeal aside for the time being and

---

[4] Interview with Jack Nziza, July 2014.

to wait patiently until enough strength had been gathered for a new assault on the RPF. Ammunition was scarce, but radio-equipment stolen from a local NGO allowed the force to gather and pass on intelligence, as well as to stay mobile. A battalion of Congolese AFDL troops and local self-defense units thought they were tracking down a few hundred *génocidaires*, but never found them: "we drove them crazy. We ran in circles to wear them down in the forest."[5] The evasion maneuvers were so successful that Nkundiye and Rwarakabije managed to build a military training center in early 1997 to prepare the next generation of anti-RPF fighters.[6]

A crucial factor in the reconstitution of the disintegrated ex-FAR/ Interahamwe into a full-fledged army was the extensive support they received from the Congolese population—a classic precondition for a successful guerrilla campaign. The RPF had fixated on the alliance and personal ties between Habyarimana and Mobutu, and on those between the senior FAR officer corps and the leading DSP and FAZ officials, but it failed to appreciate the connections between the bulk of the ex-FAR/Interahamwe and the displaced population on the one hand, and Congolese tribal chiefs, merchants and ordinary families on the other. As analyzed in Chapter 4, the collapse of Mobutu's regime and the unleashing of centrifugal forces throughout the country had contributed to a series of conflicts over local power and land that killed thousands and displaced many more in North Kivu—and the Masisi region especially. Much of the violence was between self-described *autochtones* ("sons of the soil") and the Rwandophone population, Hutu and Tutsi alike. Yet the latter group, the Banyarwanda, was neither militarily nor politically united: the winds of ethnic divisionism that were blowing in Rwanda reached the Kivus too.[7] To counter the RPF's growing pull on Banyarwanda youngsters across eastern Zaire (hundreds traveled to Uganda to join the liberation movement), Habyarimana had supported Hutu cooperatives, trade cartels and local politicians so they could in turn target potential RPF recruits or families sympathetic to the RPF cause.[8] Many of these had retained extensive ties to Rwanda—often traveling between both countries, deepening business and family connections—and thus proved an invaluable resource when well over

[5] Interview in Kigali with Paul Rwarakabije, April 2013.
[6] Human Rights Watch, "Rwanda: Observing the Rules of War?," New York: HRW, 2001.
[7] Vlassenroot, "Citizenship, Identity Formation & Conflict in South Kivu." See also Mamdani, *When Victims Become Killers*.
[8] Prunier, *From Genocide to Continental War*, pp. 50–1.

a million Rwandan soldiers, Interahamwe and civilians arrived in eastern Zaire after the genocide.[9]

Not only did many members of the Congolese Hutu population join forces with the *génocidaires* to cleanse the Kivus of Tutsi communities (and to steal their cattle) between August 1994 and August 1996 but they would also prove vital in surviving the strike on the refugee camps. The influx of ex-FAR/ Interahamwe in 1994 led to the emergence of a new regional coalition in which Rwandan and Congolese Hutus sided with several *autochtone* groups against the Hunde and Tutsi. For a while, as Kabarebe and Kayizari advanced, it seemed as if the resultant local conflicts had been subsumed in the larger struggle between the AFDL and Mobutu. Below the surface, however, these micro-level conflicts persisted and served as pockets of opposition to the AFDL, as well as a basis of local support as Nkundiye and Rwarakabije sought to reorganize their forces. Food, shelter and weapons were all provided to the regrouping troops, all the more so as discontent in the Kivus with the new AFDL order rapidly grew.

One of the main sources of resentment was the shift in the local distribution of power as a result of the revolution. With the Banyamulenge and the Tutsi from North Kivu providing such an important share of AFDL recruits, their leaders began to convert their military contribution into growing local economic and political influence in order to displace the coalition that had terrorized them for half a decade. The designation of Léonard Kanyamuhanga (Tutsi) as governor of North Kivu and Balume Tusi (Hunde) as his deputy was a clear sign of the ethno-political shift in power.[10] Against a background of decades of anti-Tutsi prejudice and discrimination, this further pitted large swathes of the Kivu population against the new government and deepened their collaboration with the resurgent ex-FAR/Interahamwe force.

Zero Screening: Repatriation of the Refugees and Its Security Implications

If the first and second factors underpinning what would become known as Rwanda's Northwest Insurgency were the incomplete defeat of the ex-FAR/ Interahamwe and the support from the Congolese population, the third factor was the return of hundreds of thousands of refugees from Zaire/Congo to Rwanda after the refugee camps had been dismantled (as well as tens of thou-

---

[9] UN Special Rapporteur of the Commission on Human Rights, "Report on the Situation of Human Rights in Rwanda."

[10] De Villers and Willame, *République démocratique du Congo*, pp. 100, 229–32.

sands of others who were later repatriated, through UN–RPF–AFDL collaboration, from Tingi-Tingi and other locations in Congo). While some of
the most ardent critics have accused the RPF of genocide against the Hutu—
systematically massacring civilians to gain and consolidate power in Kigali[11]—
the repatriation of the refugees to Rwanda suggests precisely the opposite: not
only was there no systematic violence against the refugees as they re-entered
in Rwanda but the vast majority of returnees were left in peace (though still
traumatized and terrified) for the first year after their return from Congo. As
mentioned in Chapter 6, the UN special rapporteur for Rwanda wrote to the
Security Council that

> Few cases of deaths or killings were reported during repatriation. By 6 December
> 1996, the Human Rights Operation in Rwanda had received confirmation of 12
> deaths. Those deaths are, of course, to be deplored, but the number, relative to the
> total of 600,000 returnees, was lower than had been feared.[12]

Moreover, according to one estimate by Amnesty International, of the
90,000 detainees in Rwanda at the end of 1996, the number of those who
were returnees from Zaire or Tanzania was in the low thousands—representing less than 1 per cent of the estimated 750,000 returnees.[13] On November
15, 1996, the RPF-led government announced through President Pasteur
Bizimungu a moratorium on arrests of presumed *génocidaires* to give national
reconciliation a chance. Ironically, it would thus be the lack of RPF attention
paid to the communities it welcomed back home that fostered an insurgency
that even set the rural areas around Kigali aflame.

* * *

The planning for the frontal assault on the refugee camps proceeded steadily
throughout the summer of 1996, but the RPA High Command, which had long
resolved to go to war, kept its plans hidden from other parts of the Rwandan
government. Both the cabinet of national unity as well as the RPF-run Ministry

---

[11] Lemarchand, *Dynamics of Violence in Central Africa*, p. 69.
[12] UN Special Rapporteur of the Commission on Human Rights, "Report on the
Situation of Human Rights in Rwanda," p. 37.
[13] The precise number of arrests is unknown because the RPF usurped the repatriation
process from UNHCR and did not register returnees as they crossed the border.
There were reportedly more arrests of those coming from Burundi. Amnesty
International, "Rwanda: Human Rights Overlooked in Mass Repatriation," AI Index:
AFR 47/02/97, January 14, 1997.

of Rehabilitation and Social Welfare, headed by Patrick Mazimhaka and Christine Umutoni, could guess something was afoot, but neither was briefed on the precise timing or scope of the coming operation.[14] Centrally coordinated by Paul Kagame, James Kabarebe and Patrick Karegeya, the RPA feared that any leaks would destabilize its plan of attack. Only when RPA soldiers actually opened fire on the refugee camps in North and South Kivu did the cabinet and the Ministry of Rehabilitation and Social Welfare learn that they would be confronted with the humanitarian, economic and social consequences of the attack in the immediate future. In order to protect the details of the operation, no serious planning had been allowed to take place.

Keeping Mazimhaka, Umutoni and other leading politicians and administrators in the dark may have been deemed necessary for the success of the operation, but it paved the way for serious trouble later. Dealing with the difficult experiences of the first year after the genocide, in particular the teeming camps in the southwest, had proved a steep learning curve for the ministry and the RPF more generally. But in a deeply martial organization like the RPF, the more cautious politicians did not have anywhere near the same influence as the military officers who had been convinced of the need to wage war once again after the debacle at Kibeho: seen from the RPA's perspective, the political failure to convince the rural and refugee population of the good intentions of the Front and its political agenda should be resolved through military action. The blitzkrieg against the *génocidaire* forces was meant to change the psychology of the average Rwandan Hutu—once any hope of a resumption of the genocidal project and/or the return of a Habyarimana-style government had been quashed, surely the population would fall in line and obey its rulers, like it had always done throughout Rwandan history.

The RPF's absolute belief in force as a solution to escape a political impasse thus represented an important reason for the fateful decision by the RPA and the DMI not to organize any screening of the refugee population when it crossed back into Rwanda in November 1996. In much the same way as the Zairian authorities had failed to perform any security checks on the hundreds of thousands of Rwandans crossing into their country as the genocide drew to a close in July 1994, so now RPA soldiers and intelligence officers did not systematically identify, interrogate and arrest returnees, including *génocidaires* or veteran FAR soldiers that joined the hordes returning to Rwanda. The RPF could do as it pleased, having completely usurped refugee resettlement from

[14] Interview in Doha, April 2015.

the UNHCR and stunned its own citizens with this hands-off policy. As Patrick Mazimhaka testified: "We did zero screening of the returnees. They went all over the country."[15] To the great surprise of many of these returning Hutus, indoctrinated by years of hateful propaganda about the RPF as a genocidal organization, neither the RPA troops in the camps, nor those on the border crossings in Gisenyi or Cyangugu, lifted as much as a finger as they silently went home. There were no large-scale massacres, but instead merely orders to go back to their villages and resume agricultural work. It was yet another pivotal moment in Rwanda's modern history.

Part of the rationale for the fateful decision not to organize any screening of the refugees—or extensive follow-up investigations in subsequent days or weeks—was the sheer impossibility of doing so, a point emphasized by Christine Umutoni.[16] DMI operative Jack Nziza concurred, "You could not screen 1.5 million people."[17] It was certainly true that almost no border force in the world could have coped with the sudden return of hundreds of thousands of citizens, many of them traumatized, wounded and/or hungry, and that in the context of the impoverished, overstretched RPF state, the RPA and DMI simply could not spare the manpower to perform even the most rudimentary security checks. But logistical challenges only partially account for the RPF's "zero-screening" policy; it also reflected a bold politico-military gamble made by Minister of Defense Paul Kagame himself.[18]

Kagame was of the opinion that fundamentally altering the mindset of the population was vital to the long-term security of the new RPF order. Kagame argued internally that the Front should risk showing some degree of vulnerability, both towards a critical outside world (which was already denouncing the violence accompanying the liberation of the camps) and vis-à-vis the displaced Hutu, in a bid to get them to switch allegiances, or at least to tacitly accept RPF rule and cease all violent resistance. Allowing them to return in relative peace would be the strongest possible rebuttal of genocidal propaganda imaginable—it would show to everybody the RPF was not a ruthless killing machine, at least when dealing with a remorseful population willing to come back; those who fled westwards out of the camps with the ex-FAR/Interahamwe into the Congolese interior would be treated less magnani-

---

[15] Interview in Kigali, July 2014.
[16] Interview in Asmara, August 2014.
[17] Interview in Kigali, July 2014.
[18] Gourevitch, *Stories from Rwanda*, p. 308.

mously. Kagame's gamble thus fused his total belief in the "shock and awe" effect of Kabarebe and Kayizari's military operations (assumed to significantly reduce the actual security risks of unrepentant *génocidaires*) with an attempt to make a fresh political start at home by letting the refugees resettle and cultivate the fields again. It was an audacious plan. In the words of DMI chief Karake Karenzi: "You take the risk … We took in everyone, including *génocidaires*, but it was worthwhile. We wanted to change them … We weighed the political gains and we concluded that we had more to win politically than we had to lose from a military perspective."[19]

Kayumba, Karenzi and Mazimhaka began implementing the policy from the moment the first camps were dismantled and people started walking across the border. But inside the RPA, the DMI and the Ministry of Rehabilitation and Social Welfare, mid-level and low-ranking officials complained that this perilous gamble unnecessarily exposed the surviving Tutsi, moderate Hutu and other returning Rwandans from the diaspora to the danger of reinserting an unreconstructed enemy into one's midst.[20] What if the intended psychological transformation was not engendered by the military defeat in Congo and the "open arms" policy? Jack Nziza faithfully implemented his bosses' decision but later conceded that his own strategic doubts about the course of action were vindicated when the violence resumed: "We were not surprised by the insurgency; it was inevitable."[21] Karenzi also admitted that, in discussions with RPA and DMI colleagues, some made the comparison between the new policy and the tactical withdrawal which the RPF had staged in 1992–3, during the civil war. By withdrawing from much of the territory it had conquered earlier, the Front had hoped to create goodwill among all political parties, intending to transform the political landscape and debunk Habyarimana's propaganda about the RPF's "winner takes all" strategy. Yet rather than having a positive effect, RPF officers argued that this merely meant that when the genocide began, many more thousands of people died who would have been saved from the Interahamwe had the Front held on to the territory.[22] The fear was that this political gesture would merely help the killers to resume their job; and these warnings ultimately proved to be correct. The RPF "in fact reimported the civil war."[23]

[19] Interview in London, November 2014.
[20] Interviews in Kigali, July 2014.
[21] Ibid.
[22] Interview in London, November 2014.
[23] Reyntjens, *Great African War*, p. 173.

Fighting the Abacengezi: The Insurgency and Counter-Insurgency

Mere days after the killings of Tutsi *rescapés* and Hutu collaborators in Mutara which opened this chapter, only a few kilometers down the road another, even more terrifying massacre unfolded. Around 1 a.m. on August 21, 1997, an unknown number of *abacengezi* attacked the Mudende refugee camp where Congolese Tutsi had been staying for about a year. They set fire to the tents where the displaced were living. In the pitch dark, the ensuing blaze caused a panic, allowing the assailants to hack away at the disoriented community. By the time RPA forces were able to restore order and kill seventeen insurgents, 148 refugees had been murdered—and in many cases mutilated, with their sexual organs and tongues cut away.[24]

The Mudende massacre was the most lethal *abacengezi* attack since the operation against the refugee camps. But it was far from the only one. On April 27, 1997, the Belgian school headmistress Griet Bosmans was bled to death, along with seventeen school girls in Satinsyi, Gisenyi.[25] Twenty-eight Tutsi were murdered with machetes in Mukamira (Ruhengeri Prefecture) on November 24, and another ten were killed with hoes and clubs in Mutura, close to Mudende, on November 30. A few weeks later, school children and students were lynched in the south of Rwanda, along the Gikongoro–Butare road, by a drunken Hutu mob. Across Ruhengeri and Gisenyi, commune offices were besieged in the autumn of 1997, with mayors, councillors, traders and other local RPF "collaborators" murdered in their hundreds. A crowd of more than 300 men and women stormed Giciye in Gisenyi Prefecture on November 17 to liberate ninety-four prisoners, mostly Interahamwe and ex-FAR soldiers. Fears of a repeat of 1994 stalked the land—ever larger expanses of rural Rwanda were considered no-go areas for Tutsi; every Hutu peasant once again became a suspect in the eyes of their fellow citizens. In the words of one Tutsi student at the National University of Rwanda in Butare, Kenny Theophile Nkundwa: "Walking around at night in those days? That would be crazy. No chance. Or if you were walking alone during the day from hill to hill: they would see you and chase you like a chicken. Kill you like a chicken."[26]

---

[24] African Rights, *Rwanda*, pp. 151–8.

[25] "Gunmen Kill Schoolgirls in Rwanda," Associated Press, April 29, 1997. Note that some observers suspect the RPA of having committed this attack. Filip Reyntjens, *Political Governance in Post-Genocide Rwanda*, New York: Cambridge University Press, 2013, p. 109.

[26] Interview in Oxford, December 2012.

On December 10, 1997, the *génocidaire* forces returned to Mudende camp where 17,000 refugees had now assembled. In an attack that continued for at least four hours, people were burned alive or slaughtered with axes and sticks. Gisenyi hospital was overrun with survivors who had suffered the most horrific injuries.[27] While UN and Rwandan government officials estimated that 300 Congolese Tutsi had died,[28] the refugees insisted 1,643 people lost their lives and angrily accused the RPF of betraying them.[29] Written warnings of an imminent massacre had circulated around the camp, and calls for better security—crucial given the deterioration of relations between the Mudende refugees and the hostile local host community—had gone unheeded. Makeshift roadblocks and diversionary attacks on government positions elsewhere in the Mutara area during the butchery diverted RPA troops from where they were needed most—in the middle of the camp. While UN Secretary-General Kofi Annan issued a statement condemning the attack and drawing parallels with the genocide, US State Department spokesman James Rubin also underlined the lapses by the Kigali government in protecting its own people:

> At Mudende Camp there was a marked failure by the RPA to adequately defend the refugees from attack during the night of December 10th. The reasons for this failure by the RPA remain uncertain but point to the local commander's actions. Such a lapse in security arrangements for refugees must not be repeated.[30]

The Insurgent Network of the Armée pour la Libération du Rwanda

The Mudende massacre made public to the world what large swathes of the Rwandan population and the RPF had already learned in previous months: Hutu extremists had returned and were destabilizing the country. The guerrilla campaign sought to demonstrate that the RPF could not control vital parts of its territory, nor protect its own citizens, local officials or soldiers.[31] Through a mixture of propaganda, coercion and the power of example, the insurgent leadership hoped that their attacks would set in motion a cycle that

[27] African Rights, *Rwanda*, pp. 164–77.

[28] UN High Commissioner for Human Rights, "Human Rights Field Operation in Rwanda," p. 8.

[29] African Rights, *Rwanda*, pp. 164–77.

[30] US Department of State, "Rwanda Country Report on Human Rights Practices for 1997," Washington, DC: Bureau of Democracy, Human Rights and Labor, 1998.

[31] Ann M. Simmons, "Rwandan Atrocities Ignite Hatreds," *Los Angeles Times*, December 14, 1997.

would trigger RPA reprisals, further alienation between the government and the population and ultimately spur a general uprising that would culminate in Kagame and his acolytes fleeing Kigali.

To further these aims, the Armée pour la Libération du Rwanda (ALiR) was formed by the hard core of those who orchestrated the genocide and the former Rwandan government, effectively recreating the command structure of the FAR, including its chiefs of staff, departments, training schools and battalion structure. To confuse the outside world, ALiR, its political wing (PALIR) and the politico-humanitarian front organization with which it closely worked (Rassemblement pour le retour des réfugies et la démocratie au Rwanda (RDR)) opted not to appoint internationally known hardliners—like Tharcisse Renzaho, the notorious ex-mayor of Kigali—as its leaders, but rather second-tier figures who were both trusted by insiders and could represent credible interlocutors to external actors.[32] Some of the "Hutu Power" discourse was toned down in favor of nationalist language, presenting the people in the refugee camps and the survivors of the AFDL/RPA onslaught as the real, legitimate bearers of Rwandan nationhood. This was also the objective of the insurgency, at least at the start—not to openly embrace genocidal fantasies, but to claim to legitimately represent popular discontent with RPF overrule.[33]

The official leader of the ALiR rebellion, until his death on August 3, 1998, was a man whose profile suggested a new, more moderate approach: Lieutenant-Colonel Froduald Mugemanyi was not a prominent killer but rather a doctor from Gikongoro who had been in charge of the FAR's medical wing. Mugemanyi had signed the seemingly reasonable "Déclaration de Kigeme" in July 1994 which denounced the genocide and called for the full implementation of the 1993 Arusha Accords, the peace deal extremist ideologues hated. Working with Mugemanyi was Lieutenant-Colonel Paul Rwarakabije, who would lead ALiR from August 1998. He was born in Ruhengeri and trained as a logistics expert in Belgium and France. During the genocide, he had been chief of operations at the gendarmerie but, according to most eyewitnesses, had not been involved in the egregious crimes committed by many of its units.[34] After July 1994, he became the military commander

---

[32] African Rights, "A Welcome Expression of Intent: The Nairobi Communique and the Ex-FAR/Interahamwe," London: African Rights, 2007, pp. 12–15.

[33] Marina Rafti, "Rwandan Hutu Rebels in Congo/Zaire, 1994–2006: An Extra-Territorial Civil War in a Weak State," in Filip Reyntjens and Stefan Marysse (eds), *L'Afrique des Grand Lacs: annuaire 2005–2006*, Paris: L'Harmattan, 2006.

[34] It is worth noting the International Criminal Tribunal for Rwanda never initiated

of the Katale camp in South Kivu, home to many middle-class regime veterans and Hutu Power intellectuals. Mugemanyi and Rwarakabije, a southerner and a northerner, were to be the new faces of anti-RPF resistance.

However, if these two senior officers embodied the Realpolitik wing of the former Hutu Power order, the two other most prominent members of the ALiR High Command had direct links to openly ideological factions of the old regime. This pointed not merely to the continued genocidal ambitions of the insurgency but would also lead to tensions between the supporters of Rwarakabije and Mugemanyi, who tried to mobilize the masses and limit most of the attacks to RPA targets, and their peers who, with the support of Tharcisse Renzaho, took a much broader definition of who the enemy was. The first of these was Lieutenant-Colonel Léonard Nkundiye, ALiR deputy chief of staff. He had headed Habyarimana's presidential guard and, like the late president, hailed from Karago commune in Gisenyi. Following training at the Institut Royal Supérieur de Défense in Brussels, he occupied a number of leading positions in the army in the period prior to the genocide. Nkundiye had been intimately involved in preparing Interahamwe militias in Mutara (Gisenyi) and was seen to have formed part of the *akazu* cabal which dominated the Rwandan state. He was co-responsible for the coup that took place after Habyarimana's death on April 6, and appeared to be a major figure during the genocide, particularly in the crucial first days.[35] Another *abacengezi* commander hailed, like Nkundiye, from Karago (Gisenyi) and led ALiR's military intelligence operations: Apollinaire Hakizimana, a shrewd, high-flying former gendarmerie officer, had been associated with the hate broadcasts of Radio-Télévision Libre des Mille Collines as well as with killings at roadblocks in Kigali. He had coordinated intelligence gathering in Mugunga camp before the October 1996 invasion. He and Nkundiye represented the hard-core hawks and a zero-compromise agenda.

Importantly, three out of four men leading the *abacengezi*—Nkundiye, Rwarakabije and Hakizimana—were from the northwest of Rwanda, the hotbed of early rebel activity (including Mudende) and the region the insurgents

---

any proceedings against him and Alison Des Forges's seminal work for Human Rights Watch does not implicate Rwarakabije personally either. But Paul Rwarakabije was of course institutionally complicit and linked to heinous violence because of his senior role in the FAR and gendarmerie.

[35] Des Forges, *"Leave None to Tell the Story"*, pp. 283, 319.

came closest to capturing.[36] As discussed earlier, it had been Nkundiye and Rwarakabije who had vanished into the North Kivu forests after the AFDL advance and had begun to reconstitute disintegrated FAR units. To do so, they relied on Congolese Hutu and their local allies. But the latter two groups were not merely instrumental in sheltering the ex-FAR from AFDL/RPA reprisals and giving them land to rebuild military camps; they also used their cross-border social and commercial networks to re-establish communication between the Hutu Power force in Congo and the refugees who had been shepherded back to Rwanda by the RPA: messages were sent via pieces of paper or individual messengers rather than radio. ALiR ordered some of its personnel—civilians and military—to return and infiltrate the country (five people for every commune), with a focus on the northwest to which ten people were sent back every week. Slipping across the border, this number rapidly increased to fifty people at a time, traveling mainly at night. In late March 1997, the ALiR command moved from Masisi—where the AFDL, with RPA help, had begun operations against the growing ex-FAR/Interahamwe presence—to the dormant Mount Mikeno volcano south of Rutshuru in North Kivu. Its sights were fixed on an imminent return to Rwanda, less than 10 kilometers away.

A Faltering Push-Back

The RPF's initial response was characterized by a considerable degree of ambiguity and even denial. To this day, some RPF ministers and senior military officers claim that the insurgency remained a menace of limited scope that the Front had under control, that did not represent a broadly supported challenge to its legitimate rule and that the insurgency itself, to a certain extent, was part of their strategy: the RPA and DMI allowed known ex-FAR/Interahamwe to return to Rwanda to defeat them once and for all on home soil, rather than chasing them in Congo's forests. But an investigation of the empirical record and private discussions with high-ranking officials suggest that this is a rather rosy depiction of what actually happened and of the degree to which the RPF was caught unprepared and (later) deeply preoccupied with how close to Kigali the *abacengezi* came.

The zero-screening policy upon returning the masses from the camps had made it difficult for Rwandan intelligence to build a picture of who the insur-

---

[36] Interview with Paul Rwarakabije, April 2013.

gents were, where they were hiding and how much of a threat they might come to represent throughout 1997. Moreover, many of the RPA and DMI's top assets were busy abroad: defeating Mobutu and consolidating the post-Mobutu order; hunting Interahamwe in Congo's interior; and undertaking clandestine missions in the wider region to arrest genocide suspects. Karake Karenzi, who took charge of quashing the insurgency together with Army Chief of Staff Kayumba Nyamwasa, put his finger on the wound when he connected the *abacengezi* strategy with the scarcity of resources available to his services to neutralize the growing menace: "By putting pressure here in Rwanda [the insurgents] were hoping to force us to pull our troops back from Congo. Our pressure inside Congo gave us a lot of intelligence but also led to overstretch."[37] Caesar Kayizari recognized how the enormity of the territory played into the hands of the insurgents, as he lacked the forces to wage war on Mobutu, stabilize Congo and prevent a *génocidaire* resurgence: "For us any area left behind was left behind for good. Our numbers were too small. You could have a battalion in Bukavu and one in Kindu but nothing in-between."[38] With so much of the RPA preoccupied with other fronts and with the High Command believing the dismantling of the camps spelled the end of the organized *génocidaire* threat to Rwanda, the RPF had left its home base dangerously vulnerable to asymmetric warfare. As Rwarakabije noted: "This was our chance."[39]

For most of 1997, the RPF described any security incidents in Rwanda as one-off events that would be confined to the past once Mobutu was overthrown and the AFDL established full control over Congo. While occasional warnings to outsiders about ongoing attacks served the purpose of legitimizing RPA action across the border, the Front was keen to present Rwanda as a country heading towards full normalization and therefore deserving of more international political and financial support. The arms embargo had been lifted by the UN in September 1996, but donors still hesitated to provide substantial military and financial assistance—which greatly irked the RPF. Anything that could derail the trend towards international legitimacy and cooperation was highly unwelcome.[40] This included a number of foreign individuals with potentially damaging information, which if made public would

[37] Interview in Kigali, December 2009.
[38] Interview in Ankara, June 2015.
[39] Interview in Kigali, July 2014.
[40] Reyntjens, "Rwanda, Ten Years On."

undermine the normalization process.[41] One of these was the Canadian priest Guy Pinard, whose critical views of Paul Kagame's government were in all likelihood the reason why he was gunned down on February 2, 1997, while leading Mass in his parish in Ruhengeri.[42] This assassination followed the unsolved murder of three Spanish aid workers of Medicos del Mundo on January 18, 1997. A shroud of mystery also continues to hang over the deaths of five members of the UN Human Rights Field Operation for Rwanda who were ambushed in Cyangugu on February 4, 1997. The Bosnian Franciscan priest Vjeko Curic was later murdered, most likely by DMI operatives, on January 31, 1998, because of his knowledge of RPA war crimes, according to a UN observer who investigated the case.[43]

Yet what the RPF eagerly presented as a passing problem that would soon blow over following the capture of Kinshasa was evolving into a full-blown insurgency by the final quarter of 1997. In early 1997, the Rwanda Demobilization and Reintegration Program had been created, but it initially had only a limited impact. The RPA and DMI scaled up their activities yet continued to lack the fine-grained information required to successfully run a counter-insurgency campaign: through their mixture of anti-RPF propaganda and death threats against the families of unwilling local officials (many of which were carried out), the *abacengezi* had managed to get commune administrators to observe a code of silence regarding the insurgents' growing influence. In many cases, local councillors were actively involved in mobilizing for the Hutu Power cause. RPA policies of keeping large numbers of young Hutu in incommunicado detention, and search operations characterized by indiscriminate violence, only made the problem worse.[44] At least 150 people lost their lives at the hands of RPA soldiers on March 2–3, 1997, in Kigombe commune, southeast of Ruhengeri; scores of civilians were murdered between August 8 and 11, 1997, in Kanama (Gisenyi Prefecture, not far from where the killings documented in Chapter 5 took place in September 1995); and at least fifteen civilians were killed in Rwerere (Gisenyi) when in

---

[41] For reflections on the human rights climate in Rwanda and the RPF's intolerance of even well-meaning critics, see Sibomana, *Hope for Rwanda*.

[42] Geoffrey York and Judi Rever, "Families of Two Canadian Priests Killed in Rwanda Still Wait for Justice," *Globe and Mail*, November 14, 2014.

[43] Interview with Konrad Huber of the UN Human Rights Field Operation in Rwanda, January 2015.

[44] Amnesty International, "Ending the Silence," London: Amnesty International, 1997.

November 1997 an RPA unit took revenge for the assassination of one of their comrades.[45]

Perhaps the worst of all RPF "excesses" took place in Nyakimana Cave in Gisenyi where an unknown number of people—insurgents but also civilians— were massacred between October 23 and 28, 1997, with estimates ranging from a few hundred to many thousands killed.[46] Even the US government, a reliable friend of post-1994 Rwanda, was critical of how the RPA's counter-insurgency was squandering what little popular goodwill existed for the Front's agenda:

> The RPA used excessive force in suppressing the insurgency along the northwestern border ... No complete death total is available, but the U.N. Human Rights Field Office reported that 2,022 persons were killed by the RPA in May and June alone ... This total comprised insurgents and civilians. There were credible reports that the RPA routinely killed suspected insurgent collaborators and their families, including women and children. In early March in Ruhengeri, an RPA regiment reacted brutally in responding to an attack on a government convoy, and systematically executed at least 100—perhaps as many as 400—civilians suspected of collaborating with insurgents. The RPA commanders in Ruhengeri were arrested, court-martialed in November, and sentenced to prison terms. A military court convicted five officers and one sergeant of failure to stop the killings ... Cyabingo commune was the site of much RPA killing. In May an RPA unit searching for infiltrators fired on a communal meeting there, killing 35 civilians. Following an insurgent attack on a military post on May 16, an RPA cordon and search operation killed 175 persons in Muhoro sector. On May 24, the RPA killed some 250 civilians during an identity card check in Rubabi and Ruvumu sectors.[47]

Given the continued widespread sympathies for the genocidal project and a political context in which hardly any space existed for a third way independent from the *génocidaires* and the RPF, this heavy-handed, arbitrary violence served to make the Front even more unpopular than it already was. The post-genocide "Government of National Unity" was totally dominated by the Front. Squeezed from all sides, the civilians in the northwest suffered greatly as violence engulfed them. And the insurgency scaled up: army chief Kayumba Nyamwasa admitted to AFP on November 19 that the RPA faced at least 15,000 fighters. Earlier, in July 1997, the senior leadership of ALiR had crossed into Rwanda. Nkundiye, Rwarakabije and head of political

---

[45] African Rights, *Rwanda*, pp. 264–77.

[46] "Terrible, Anyhow," *The Economist*, December 11, 1997.

[47] US Department of State, "Rwanda Country Report on Human Rights Practices for 1997."

affairs Gaston Iyamuremye moved into Ruhengeri Prefecture, a return that boosted *abacengezi* confidence. Thus when the December attack on Mudende came and significant international attention turned a security crisis into a political one, internal unrest inside the RPF was unavoidable. According to Minister of Reintegration and Social Housing Patrick Mazimhaka, the military overstretch could no longer be maintained.[48] But rather than a frank discussion of the internal decisions and conditions that had helped to create the rebellion—military oversight during the AFDL campaign, the zero-screening order, unpunished RPA crimes, the political climate—the finger was pointed at Congo.

Congo, Kabila and the Génocidaires

By early 1998, at least 5,952 Rwandans had died in massacres and assassinations carried out by the *abacengezi* and in the RPA's counter-insurgency campaign; the actual number was probably much higher.[49] Yet if 1997 had meant greater insecurity for Rwanda's Tutsis and the people of the northeast than at any point since the genocide, 1998 would be even worse. According to the RPF, the driving force behind this escalation was situated outside Rwanda's borders—not just in the Congolese jungles, where insurgents regrouped and received local support, but also in Kinshasa, where Kabila's government ignored the pleas of its allies and, instead, appeared to tolerate and even back the resurgent extremists. In the words of Frank Mugambage, chef-de-cabinet at the Rwandan Presidency: "The thrust of the insurgency was not from within, but from outside."[50] Already in October 1997, Paul Kagame had told Belgian Ambassador to Congo Frank De Coninck that if the international community did nothing about the nexus between extremism in the Kivus and bad governance in Kinshasa, the RPF would feel compelled to take strong action itself.[51]

As we saw earlier, the RPF was right to pinpoint eastern Congo as a major security problem and an exporter of instability to Rwanda. Starting in July 1997, Mai Mai militias—an umbrella term for grassroots movements which trace their roots to the Simba Uprising of the 1960s and are united by nation-

---

[48] Interview in Kigali, July 2014.
[49] UN Office of the High Commissioner for Human Rights, "Human Rights Field Operation in Rwanda."
[50] Interview in Kampala, March 2013.
[51] Interview in Rome, May 2009.

alist sentiment and local grievances—had taken up arms against the AFDL. Many Mai Mai had long blamed eastern Congo's problems on the combination of dictatorship in Kinshasa and foreign influences—and organized on an explicitly anti-Banyarwanda platform. But while they helped combat the ex-FAR/Interahamwe and the last FAZ units defending the towns of Kivu during the AFDL campaign, they had quickly come to resent the rapid rise of Congolese Tutsi to positions of considerable local influence. In battles between forces of the FAC and Mai Mai militias, one observer estimates that more than 2,500 rebels died between July and September 1997 alone, as well as almost 500 of Kabila's men.[52] The Mai Mai uprising played directly into the hands of the *abacengezi*. First, it drained resources away that could have been deployed to contain the Nkundiye–Rwarakabije reorganization. Secondly, it allowed ALiR to widen its Congolese networks and supply itself with weapons and ammunition—a major strategic constraint on *abacengezi* operations in the first year, according to Rwarakabije.[53] Armed with more firepower provided by Congolese allies—former FAZ, Mai Mai, Hutus from North Kivu and even AFDL officers increasingly antipathetic to the RPF and its Banyamulenge allies—the *abacengezi* no longer limited their attacks to the northwest where most of them had family ties. A series of killings of dozens of *rescapés* and their presumed Hutu accomplices rocked Gitarama Prefecture in central Rwanda in the first months of 1998.

The spread of the insurgency to Gitarama, as well as further attacks in Butare, Gikongoro and Kibuye in Rwanda's south and west, underlined that the counterinsurgency was faltering. Patrick Mazimhaka testified that the RPF's social base was doubtful the Front would be able to stop the violence: "Of course the Tutsi resented the RPA. They thought we did not protect them enough."[54] But even as the RPA dramatically reinforced its presence in the northwest, as well as in other affected provinces, the insurgency only gained in strength.[55] Karake Karenzi ordered peasants to cut down their banana trees and to plant short crops so insurgents could no longer ambush RPA patrols from the thick plantations by the side of the roads. But even such draconian orders—directly affecting the livelihoods of people already hostile to RPF rule—made little difference to the rebel advance in the direction of Kigali, as

---

[52] Kisangani, *Civil Wars in the Democratic Republic of Congo*, p. 135.
[53] Interview in Kigali, April 2013.
[54] Interview in Kigali, July 2014.
[55] Paul Jackson, "Legacy of Bitterness: Insurgency in North West Rwanda," *Small Wars & Insurgencies*, 15, 1 (2004).

he admitted: "It was huge ... Even Kigali Rural was affected. [Rebel battalions] were maximum one hour away from the capital. They had not conquered these areas, but operated there."[56]

The Growing Regional Stakes of the Insurgency

As the asymmetric insurgent attacks against its civilian enemies intensified and government reprisals further alienated the population,[57] ALiR felt increasingly confident to face the RPA in open battle. Hundreds of rebels fought in an attempt at not merely thwarting RPF control of rural northern Rwanda, but to allow ALiR to conquer, hold and administer territory itself. While this was not particularly successful in military terms, the AliR's audacity in risking open confrontation with the RPA suggested to the RPF High Command that something important had changed in the outlook of Nkundiye and Rwarakabije. Intelligence reports from ESO and DMI assets in Kinshasa, eastern Congo and northern Rwanda alleging a foreign hand rocked the leadership. The RPF grew convinced that some of Mzee Kabila's closest advisers had, as part of their power struggle with James Kabarebe and the Banyamulenge in Kinshasa, opened channels to financially and militarily support the *abacengezi* with a view to getting Rwandan troops out of Congo and driving a wedge between the Front and its Congolese allies. Perhaps even the Congolese president himself was involved, whispered some, including Dan Munyuza.

It is nearly impossible to establish when exactly this support started— Kabila government officials have always admitted that they armed and supplied the ex-FAR/Interahamwe, but insist that this happened *after* August 1998.[58] The RPF, by contrast, maintains that such flows were occurring from as early as March 1998.[59] Our own investigation did not find conclusive evidence as to whether Laurent-Désiré Kabila personally gave orders to his lieutenants to establish an alliance with his supposed Pan-Africanist comrades' nemesis before the definitive fallout with the RPF. However, based on the evidence, two things seem certain: the ALiR did receive extensive outside

---

[56] Interview in London, November 2014.

[57] Amnesty International, "'Disappearances' and Killings Continue on a Daily Basis," London: Amnesty International, 1998.

[58] Interviews with Raus Chalwe, Mwenze Kongolo, Faustin Munene, Shé Okitundu, Jean-Claude Yav, December 2009–August 2013.

[59] Interviews with James Kabarebe, Joseph Karemera, Patrick Mazimhaka, Emmanuel Ndahiro, December 2009–December 2014.

support prior to August 1998 which boosted its action radius and firepower, and the RPF certainly acted like it believed its own intelligence reports alleging that Kabila was helping the *abacengezi*.

As the insurgency in Rwanda escalated and ambushes happened even on the main road north of Kigali at Shyorongi as well as in Taba west of the capital, where genocide survivors were axed to death, the High Command increased its pressure on Kabarebe's RPA forces in Congo.[60] Anxious messages from Kigali pressured Kabarebe into using his power as FAC chief of staff to launch a major offensive against ALiR in eastern Congo; he was forced to acknowledge that the "triumph" that had established his status as one of Central Africa's most extraordinary officers was not nearly as glorious a victory as initially presented: "We disorganized but did not destroy the ex-FAR. They returned later and reorganized ... [Now,] Half of our country [was] in flames. They had taken the north and a lot of the west."[61] To regain the initiative and control over eastern Congo and northwest Rwanda, in February 1998 Kabarebe gave orders to unleash the FAC's two toughest and largest brigades: the 10th Brigade, which had no fewer than nineteen battalions, would fight in North Kivu, whereas the 22nd Brigade, which was smaller but formidably equipped, attacked the insurgent alliance of *abacengezi* and Mai Mai militias in South Kivu. Congo's best troops, with the best weaponry and best logistical support, were all transferred to the east.

While this maneuver was understandable from a military perspective— much of the insecurity plaguing Rwanda also evidenced itself in the Kivus— politically it further enflamed the tensions between Kabarebe and the Katangese circle around Mzee. The latter argued that the decision undermined efforts by Kabila to be seen as a leader in his own right, putting Congolese interests first; what Kabarebe was doing was playing right into the hands of nationalists like Tshisekedi and their critiques of the AFDL "liberation" regime. As the then Congolese intelligence officer Jean-Claude Yav (later Joseph Kabila's head of presidential security) stressed, the popular perception was that the security interests of a small foreign nation trumped those of the rest of the country: "The west of Congo was emptied of troops for their war in the east."[62] A major rift inside the regime was now widening further because of the Northwest Insurgency.

---

[60] Interview with Caesar Kayizari in Kigali, April 2013.

[61] Interview in Kigali, April 2013.

[62] Interview in Kinshasa, August 2013.

As we saw in the previous chapter, Kabila's Katangization campaign had already set in motion a cold war between the factions around Kabarebe and the Congolese Tutsi on the one hand and the group of Kabila supporters drawn from Katanga, his revolutionary network and old-school nationalists on the other. Kabarebe's move was seen by Mzee's inner circle as a reassertion of control by his Rwandan chief of staff, an attempt by the RPF at underlining who really still pulled the strings in Kinshasa.[63] The *famille katangaise* therefore scaled up and accelerated its counter-mobilization efforts. At the heart of this push-back was a 36-year-old Lubakat hardliner, John Numbi, who had established a reputation for brutality as the chief of the militia of the Jeunesse de l'Union des Fédéralistes et Républicains Indépendants (JUFERI) in South Katanga in the early 1990s; it was under Numbi's aegis that JUFERI militants carried out pogroms against Kasaiens and Katangese with Kasai ancestry, displacing tens of thousands of people and killing at least 5,000—often by placing burning car tires around the necks of their victims.[64] DMI operative Jack Nziza reported soon after the fall of Kinshasa that this man was likely to become a problem for the RPF: "We had a lot of trouble with the communications officer, Numbi ... He was totally unmanageable. He was in charge of security in Kinshasa and had been made brigadier-general without any military experience or skill. We asked Joseph to rein him in, or ask his father. They never did."[65]

Numbi used this JUFERI network to build a separate (non-Tutsi) presidential guard for Kabila, a project he had begun in May 1997, near the old Belgian airbase Kamina in Katanga, together with fellow Katangese officers Eddy Kapend and Eric Lenge. He was also given a leading position in the FAC by the Mzee as head of transmissions and logistics.[66] Protected by the president, Numbi used his job—which involved extensive travel across the country—to identify units dissatisfied with their Rwandan commanders and to instruct young officers to ignore or even sabotage James Kabarebe's policies. This was a high-stakes gamble: "The only reason why he got away with this was because Mzee gave him cover."[67]

[63] Interview with Faustin Munene in Kinshasa, December 2009.
[64] Some of these crimes were documented by Roberto Garreton and his UN human rights team—see Chapter 8.
[65] Interview in Kigali, July 2014.
[66] De Villers and Willame, *République démocratique du Congo*, p. 94.
[67] Interview with Jean-Claude Yav, Kinshasa, August 2013.

Briefed daily by Dan Munyuza, the RPF's chief intelligence officer in Congo, Kabarebe was furious with the overt disobedience in the FAC at this critical time and broached the subject with Kabila, who he assumed was being misled and manipulated by his own inner circle. In March 1998, Mzee Kabila and Kabarebe flew to Goma to discuss the critical security situation in North Kivu, and the resultant threat to Rwanda, with the top military brass of both countries: apart from the Congolese president and his Rwandan chief of staff, Jean-Pierre Ondekane (head of the FAC's 10th Brigade), Faustin Munene (vice-minister of the interior) and Kayumba Nyamwasa, the RPA chief of staff, were also in attendance to debate how the newly launched offensive against ALiR could be made more effective. Yet after Kabarebe and Kayumba finished their one-hour long dissection of how the ex-FAR/Interahamwe threatened both countries, Kabila nonchalantly joked to Munene—"Did they say there was a problem? I don't see any." The comments infuriated Kabarebe and Kayumba. But to Munene, Mzee's joke had exposed Kabarebe's selfish reasons for launching the offensive in the first place: "This operation and its military movement was a big mistake for us. It weakened us militarily. And the Rwandans were never been able to explain the nature of the threat to me. I didn't see the problem."[68]

The calamitous Goma meeting had profound repercussions. Kabarebe refused to reconsider his military strategy and decided to largely ignore Kabila and his Katangese inner circle from then on; it was made clear to junior officers throughout the ranks that the operation itself could not be criticized. Jean-Claude Yav, who served under the Banyarwanda Colonel Laurent Nkunda in Walikale in the 224th Brigade, noted that after the Goma meeting, "It was crazy. Our entire military machine was being directed towards the Interahamwe. We could not speak about or do anything else."[69] Almost simultaneously, the RPF in Kigali shifted into higher gear too. Together with his counterpart David Pulkol in Kampala, Patrick Karegeya, the head of Rwanda's External Security Organization, called an emergency meeting of the regional intelligence chiefs of Rwanda, Uganda, Angola, Burundi, Eritrea, Ethiopia and Tanzania, but pointedly "forgot" to invite Didier Kazadi, Kabila's trusted security chief. Set on the eve of the March 1998 "New African Leaders" summit in Entebbe, it was only a last-minute intervention by Angola and Tanzania that ensured Kazadi was issued an invitation.[70] However, Kazadi's presence by

[68] Interview in Kinshasa, December 2009.
[69] Interview in Kinshasa, August 2013.
[70] Interview with David Pulkol, March 2013.

no means stopped Karegeya (and to a lesser extent Pulkol) from uttering sharp-edged accusations against a Congolese state "unable" and/or "unwilling" to take seriously the festering insecurity in its own country and in Rwanda. Even if little concrete came out of the meeting itself, the battle-lines were increasingly being drawn, with Ethiopia and Eritrea not unexpectedly sympathetic to Karegeya's complaints and Angola and Tanzania more skeptical. The latter two seemed to concur with Kazadi's riposte that with a Rwandan in charge of the Congolese army the RPF should not be complaining about the lack of attention Congo was paying to Rwanda's security.

While Kabarebe supervised the offensive of the 10th Brigade in North Kivu and the 22nd Brigade in South Kivu and while Karegeya tried to rally international support, Mzee Kabila consulted his closest allies. Vice-Minister Munene adamantly dismissed the RPF's alarmism about the insurgency as a pretext used to marginalize the president: "[The] increase in number of attacks by ALiR is a lie."[71] But those on the ground in the forests around Walikale, like Jean-Claude Yav, knew that the situation was terrible: "There were indeed very active Interahamwe and, increasingly, Mai Mai in our area … We had incredible problems. Anything or anyone Rwandese could be ambushed at any moment."[72] Yav himself was at one point ensnared by a number of Mai Mai and ALiR soldiers, but released because of his ethnicity, while his fellow Tutsi officers and soldiers were murdered. When stories like that of Yav began filtering through the Katangese network, it generated a perverse effect: rather than bringing the RPF, the Congolese Tutsi and the Katangese closer, Kabila's inner circle sensed the political possibilities that the insurgency presented them with.

Shaking Hands with the Devil? Kabila's Impossible Wager

According to Étienne,[73] a former Rwandan opposition politician with close ties to the Tanzanian security apparatus and later spokesman in Belgium of the Forces Démocratiques pour la Libération du Rwanda (FDLR, the successor organization to ALiR), security advisers to Mzee—including most likely Didier Kazadi, who had lived in Dar es Salaam for years—reached out to

---

[71] Interview in Kinshasa, December 2009.
[72] Interview in Kinshasa, August 2013.
[73] Name withheld at the request of the interviewee; interview in Liege, December 2009.

330

Tanzanian intelligence officers to discuss the option of further increasing the pressure on Kigali. While he was unable to provide the exact date of these contacts, Étienne (who given his vehement anti-RPF views seems to have little reason to lie about this) insisted that at least from May 1998 onwards elements in the Tanzanian security services began working with their Congolese counterparts to provide financial and arms support to the ex-FAR/Interahamwe.

Étienne recalled partaking in meetings in which the Congolese strategy of giving Kabila more leverage over Kabarebe found an eager partner in the growing irritation that existed in Tanzanian intelligence with the "arrogant Kagame boys." While neither the retired Nyerere nor President Mkapa would have been likely to agree to such actions, Étienne nevertheless underlined that airdrops of weapons and supplies in the Kivus were carried out by Tanzanian pilots, with the knowledge of important security players in Kinshasa and Dar es Salaam, perhaps outside the purview of official Tanzanian government policy.

This was also alleged by Joseph Ngirabanzi,[74] a Belgian-trained former captain in the FAR who was a leading figure in the FDLR until 2005, and Roger,[75] another exiled Rwandan Hutu politician with important financial ties to the anti-RPF resistance. Ngirabanzi said he had not seen proof showing a direct link between Kabila and the ALiR but confirmed that weapons were sold for bargain prices by FAC officers to the Rwandan insurgents and he also asserted extensive support from security circles in Tanzania for the struggle against the RPF and against the Burundese (Tutsi-led) government. Roger, in turn, argued that without external help for the *abacengezi*, the insurgency could never have turned into such a challenge for the RPF—pointing specifically to the Congolese president: "Karenzi was right: ALiR would have been destroyed without Kabila's support."[76]

Paul Rwarakabije, the deputy leader of ALiR until August 1998 and then successor to Nkundiye, confirmed assertions of a link between the Mzee and the ex-FAR/Interahamwe in two long interviews—but only up to a point. This matters greatly because Rwarakabije defected from the FDLR in Congo in November 2003 to Kigali and has since risen to lead the Rwanda Correctional Services—the equivalent of a former Wehrmacht general running Israel's prison system. Rwarakabije has been accused by FDLR holdouts,

---

[74] Interview in Brussels, December 2009.

[75] Name withheld at the request of the interviewee; interview in Brussels, December 2009

[76] Interview in Brussels, December 2009.

fugitive *génocidaires* and diaspora groups of being an RPF puppet who slavishly parrots their official position. However, his testimony to us suggests the truth lies somewhere in the middle between the total denial of Kabila's security advisers and the "Kabila shook hands with the devil" argument of the Front. According to Rwarakabije, the ALiR got wind of the mounting tensions in Kinshasa and eastern Congo between the AFDL comrades and began informal contacts through its diaspora network with several Congolese embassies which, the former ALiR general insisted, initiated the conversation. In his own words: "Making alliances takes time ... Kabila's maneuvers did not occur overnight."[77]

One envoy tasked to do so was the Katangese pastor, Daniel Ngoy Mulunda, who began his mission several months prior to August 1998; the main interlocutor on the ALiR side was Major Emmanuel Neretse, an ex-FAR intellectual based in Kenya and then Belgium, who had useful contacts in the Nairobi diplomatic scene. Neretse was also the officer who would directly link up Mzee Kabila and Augustin Bizimana, the former FAR chief of staff, in August 1998. It was only when the Bizimana–Kabila meeting happened, and when several Congolese embassies confirmed to ALiR cells across Africa and Europe that the Kinshasa regime wanted to build a military partnership with the ex-FAR/Interahamwe, that an actual alliance emerged, according to Rwarakabije. More than 20,000 fighters hiding in Congo-Brazzaville, Central African Republic and Sudan traveled back to eastern Congo to fight the invading RPA. Apart from serving directly on the front, these troops also trained Mai Mai and helped Kabila re-establish an army after the implosion of FAC.[78] Earlier, hundreds of young Rwandan Hutus had started joining ALiR from the Benaco refugee camp in northwest Tanzania (less than an hour drive from the Rwandan border) where the local authorities did not tolerate armed militias inside the camp but looked the other way when extremist recruiters came to enlist youngsters for the insurgency. For Rwarakabije, it was impossible to say whether the Tanzanian government as a whole backed this "don't see, don't tell" policy, but key elements in the security services certainly permitted recruitment.

Rwarakabije's testimony, taken together with that of the "European" ALiR/FDLR network, thus suggests that the *abacengezi* did indeed receive crucial military, financial and logistical support from Congo and Tanzania and that

[77] Interview in Kigali, July 2014.
[78] Interview in Kigali, April 2013.

contacts had indeed been established at a very senior level between the insurgents in the Kivus and northwest Rwanda, the Hutu diaspora network and leading figures in the Congolese and Tanzanian security apparatus. While this assistance was certainly not of the order of magnitude of the formal alliance that the ALiR/FDLR would develop with the Kabila government after August 1998, the existence of such contacts and the support provided to the *abacengezi* set off alarm bells for the RPF, especially given the vehemence of the insurgency. Coming from a man who, in their view, had been forced into retirement before the RPF decided to reactivate him—"we had brought him from a shack in Tanzania to power in Kinshasa," according to one special forces officer[79]—this appeared to be the ultimate betrayal. The RPF did not critically examine its own role in the decline of the Pan-Africanist alliance and its links with the insurgency, or the latter's roots in its own policy failures since coming to power in July 1994. Rather, their scorn and attention was increasingly devoted to Mzee and the cabal around him. For Kagame and his colonels, the *famille katangaise* had crossed the one line that should never be crossed—to deceive an ally and to explore an alliance with their genocidal archenemy. James Kabarebe put it succinctly: "They had betrayed us. The regime was our direct enemy now."[80]

Conclusion: The Northwest Insurgency and the Road to a Second Congo War

As the insurgency peaked in Rwanda in 1998, almost a million Rwandans found themselves displaced. Scores of *rescapés* were killed in Nyamabuye on April 11, 1998, in Kayenzi on April 22, Taba on May 12, in Kavoye on June 8. RPA soldiers butchered more than 130 people in Ruhundo, Ruhengeri, on April 1. Ninety-four Rwandans lost their lives to a machete-wielding mob just outside Gisenyi on May 26. On June 17, Nkamira camp was overrun, with the small RPA force overwhelmed by hundreds of assailants who subsequently burned alive fifty-eight Congolese Tutsi.[81] These incidents only represent a fraction of the daily violence from both sides that terrorized the Rwandan countryside—and the collective psychosis once again gripping the country.

The emergence and rapid spread of a home-grown and externally fed insurgency in Rwanda's northern and western provinces has all too often been

---

[79] Name withheld at the request of the interviewee; interview in Kigali, December 2009.
[80] Interview in Kigali, April 2013.
[81] African Rights, *Rwanda*, pp. 175–96, 279–88.

characterized as a relatively minor historical event, reducible to domestic factors—in essence the last pangs of the Rwandan civil war. What this chapter has suggested is that the Northwest Insurgency was far more severe and far more consequential. While it was indeed in large part a product of the violence during and after the genocide in the Rwandan countryside and while ultimately the RPF would gain the upper-hand less than two years after the *abacengezi* returned to their homeland, we have argued that both a key cause and the most important consequence of the insurgency lay in neighboring Congo. The military failure to resolve the threat of the ex-FAR/Interahamwe and the political failure to forge a new social contract with the Hutu rural masses and the returning combatants from the Kivus produced twenty-four months of horrific conflict at home—which for the Front was both reflective of, and contributed further to, a breakdown of the alliance with Kabila. As the *abacengezi* thrust gained further momentum in the first half of 1998 and reached the hills of Gitarama and the areas surrounding Kigali, the RPF came to believe that a precondition for defeating the rebels was, once again, regime change in Kinshasa.

A furious Kagame kept telling his officers to get a grip on the situation, but whenever the number of incidents seemed to decrease, another spectacular wave of *abacengezi* attacks broke through. On July 12, citizens watching France and Brazil battle for global football hegemony were surprised by Interahamwe:

> Some 34 people were killed in an attack by suspected Hutu militias on a hotel where people had gathered to watch Sunday's World Cup final ... They said the attack took place in Tare, some 35 kilometres northwest of the capital Kigali. Survivors were quoted as saying the attackers used petrol on many of their victims who were burned beyond recognition. Some of the dead were killed with machetes. Others were shot. At least 25 bodies were buried in a communal grave next to the hotel. Others were left around the burnt-out remains of the building.[82]

As we will see in the next chapter, the timing of the Tare attack—barely twenty minutes by car from central Kigali—happened at the very same moment that Kabila asked James Kabarebe to step down as FAC chief of staff: relations had deteriorated to such an extent that cooperation between the RPF and the AFDL was coming to an end. But the fact that Kabila did so at the very instant that the *abacengezi* struck again in the heart of Rwanda and

---

[82] "Rwanda: More than 30 Killed in World Cup Final Attack," UN DHA Integrated Regional Information Network, July 14, 1998.

that the weapons and uniforms discovered on killed insurgents suggested Congolese and Sudanese origins[83] was interpreted by the RPF as a grave escalation of the unfolding power struggle, which like a game of multidimensional chess, was being waged in several theaters at the same time—with allies on one board no longer playing along elsewhere. The RPA intensified its counterinsurgency even further, with Karake Karenzi instructing the burning of banana plantations across Gisenyi and Ruhengeri Prefecture and Kayumba Nyamwasa ordering more strikes by the Hind helicopter gunships which the Front had chartered from eastern Europe to crush the resistance. These reprisals did not fail to have their intended effect: "The Army chased us out once more," Rwarakabije said. "They returned from Congo, and we returned to Congo."[84] AliR was forced to stage a tactical withdrawal from Rwanda, an undeniable setback. But the RPF's conclusion that the Pan-Africanist alliance, which had been created to bring both long- and short-term security to its state-building project, was effectively dead in the water would soon open a new opportunity to attack Rwanda. The final chapter that would lead to the total dissolution of the AFDL and the start of Africa's Great War was about to be written 2,000 kilometers away, in Kinshasa.

[83] Orth, "Rwanda's Hutu Extremist Genocidal Insurgency," p. 95.
[84] Philip Gourevitch, "The Life After," *New Yorker*, May 4, 2009.

10

KABILA'S PRE-EMPTIVE STRIKE

THE KINSHASA ENDGAME

The alternative was never considered: that this man would dupe us. None of us thought of this seriously. We did not have time. That was such a problem.
Dr Emmanuel Ndahiro, political adviser to Paul Kagame.

I was in all meetings. ... It [the rebellion] was meant to be short and internal, no need for war or foreign support ... It was meant to be in Kinshasa too. All over.
Bizima Karaha, minister of foreign affairs of Congo (1997–8).

On the evening of Tuesday, July 28, 1998, as the RPA's elite troops headed back to Kigali from Congo after two extraordinary years, James Kabarebe's phone rang a final time. Dialing his number from China was Joseph Kabila. Like so many in the AFDL, Joseph had barely been able to keep up with the frantic pace of political developments and furtive maneuvering inside the movement and had learned that the Rwandan contingent was leaving Kinshasa with blistering speed. Those close to his father informed him that Kabarebe had been planning the assassination of Mzee for months and that a coup d'état after the latter's trip to Cuba had only just been averted. Despite these tidings, an incredulous Joseph still held out hope that the escalating rift between the father–president and his general could be healed as misunderstandings were cleared up: he knew how prone his father was to conspiratorial thinking and

337

he knew how self-righteous RPA commanders could be when they believed they were right about something. As Kabarebe took Joseph's call, an awkward conversation began. After some initial hesitation, Kabarebe burst out: "You saw this coming, Joseph. You know your father is crazy."[1]

Joseph Kabila tried to reason with his mentor and former superior in the Congolese army, seeking to convince him that the rupture need not be fatal. He suggested that "there is another way," regretting the RPF departure and sounding apologetic—surely Kabila *père* had not meant for things to get so out of hand? Joseph insisted a political solution be found, but Kabarebe rejected his overture: "I've told you so many times what the problem is with your father. You know your father is crazy." Kabarebe hung up the phone. For years, the two men would not speak again. Both knew that the end of the conversation would be followed by war.

* * *

This chapter dissects the final phase in the unraveling of the Pan-Africanist alliance that had overthrown Mobutu and traces how and why this rupture between comrades led not just to the end of the coalition but to a cataclysmic regional war. By June 1998, the AFDL was barely holding together. The UN inquiry into the disappearances of tens of thousands of Rwandan Hutus; international exasperation with Kabila's style of governance; the instrumentalization of the FAC by Kabarebe as he pursued the RPF's obsession with security; the "political assassination" of Masasu; the simmering nationality question; the resurgence of the *génocidaire* threat in Rwanda's hills; and indications of a Faustian pact between Kabila and the ex-FAR/Interahamwe exacted a cumulative toll that was putting enormous strains on the perceived benefits of the AFDL framework.

The speed with which developments were unfolding meant that the protagonists had very little time to think clearly about the implications of a complete break in the alliance. Objectively, they still had much to gain from continued cooperation and a number of symbolic gestures might have helped stem the hemorrhaging of trust, creating a basis for a reworked political partnership that would consolidate Kabila's rule, downscale the Rwandan presence in Congo, address the grievances of the Congolese Tutsi and tackle the ALiR threat. But without the institutions in place to sustain cooperation and coordination even in the midst of deepening mistrust and given the dazzling pace with which different actors took tit-for-tat measures, the situation spiraled out

---

[1] Interview with James Kabarebe, Kigali, April 2013.

of control and reached a point of no return. The end game started thousands of miles away from Africa—in Cuba.

Our Man in Havana: Mzee Goes to Cuba

In response to the malaise in the AFDL in the weeks after the dismal first anniversary of the revolution, Mzee Kabila tried to remain bullish about the emergent new Congo and dismissed rumors of an impending divorce with his international and domestic allies.[2] He announced the formation of a reshuffled "Government of National Salvation" on June 1, which increased the number of ministerial posts across the board, making it possible to give representatives from Province Orientale and Bandundu more seats. He also suspended prominent loyalists, like Raphael Ghenda and Emile Kanengele, who were accused of corruption and other infractions of the law—moves that could reasonably interpreted as signs of goodwill and attempts at getting the revolution back on its feet by addressing the grievances of internal and external partners. Perhaps most remarkably, Mzee chose not to protect "General" Sikatenda against the accusations leveled by Kabarebe and the Congolese Tutsi. Sikatenda was a PRP veteran from the Bembe in South Kivu and had been deeply suspicious of Masasu. He had also been crucial in Kabila's efforts to build a parallel army with John Numbi and Raus Chalwe, but evidence suggested he had been inciting anti-Tutsi sentiment in South Kivu; for the RPF, he was increasingly *persona non grata*. Without Kabila's backing, he lost his position as head of the DEMIAP security service and was court-martialed.[3]

Failed Army Reform and the Sacking of James Kabarebe

Despite these measures, the AFDL comrades remained deeply troubled by Kabila and the direction the government was heading.[4] What the Congolese president seemed to give to them with one hand, he took away with the other: the new government broadened regional representation but also further bolstered the number of Katangan ministers in the cabinet to eight; Gaëtan Kakudji became a veritable deputy leader of the AFDL, a kind of de facto premier, while Déogratias Bugera—relieved in May of his role as AFDL sec-

---

[2] Interview with Mwenze Kongolo, Kinshasa, August 2013.
[3] De Villers and Willame, *République démocratique du Congo*, pp. 171–2.
[4] Interview with Moïse Nyarugabo, Goma, December 2009.

retary-general—held a meaningless ministerial portfolio. Moreover, Kabila loyalists continued to frustrate Kabarebe's orders as FAC chief of staff and spread rumors about conspiracies and plots to undermine his authority.[5] This naturally deepened the mistrust with the RPF, whose intelligence sources became convinced that Kabila's agents—Numbi, Sikatenda, Eddy Kapend of the Tigres, Georges Leta of the ANR—were intensifying outreach to ALiR.[6] In early July, the principal Mai Mai leader, "General" Padiri, openly declared in the Kinshasa press that his militias had been helping the ex-FAR/Interahamwe cross back into Rwanda via Bukavu in April and that they remained committed to working personally with President Kabila.[7] This prompted Kabarebe and Dan Munyuza to confront Mzee directly and warn him of the perils of continuing down this path. Kabila rejected such allegations, emphasizing his loyalty to the Pan-Africanist alliance. Ironically, the RPF's threats merely reinforced the message Kabila was receiving from security advisers like Didier Kazadi and Faustin Munene who claimed to be foiling one Rwandan plot after another to put the AFDL back under their thumb.

Matters came to a head in the first days of July 1998 when James Kabarebe called what would turn out to be his last big meeting at the headquarters of the chiefs of staff in Kinshasa.[8] The issue causing uproar was the structure of the FAC and the question of ranks. Discontent had been bubbling up the hierarchy for months (remember the Banyamulenge mutiny), and in a media interview shortly before the chiefs of staff meeting, Kabarebe had indicated that it was time for both a consolidation of ranks in the FAC and for a more vigorous push for national integration through the restoration of some former FAZ officers to their prior positions. During the meeting, Kabarebe stressed that his plans for comprehensive army reform also implied that some AFDL "commanders" would have to leave the army or be assigned to new positions, in function of their actual military competence, experience and performance—rather than based on their revolutionary service. Few dared to publicly contest the chief of staff and his audacious design for a new FAC—potentially a cornerstone of a reworked elite bargain between the RPF and Kabila—but many of those present immediately went to Mzee to complain

[5] Modeste Mutinga, "Eddy Kapend, virtuel chef d'état major général des FAC," *Le Potentiel*, June 17, 1998.

[6] Interview with James Kabarebe, April 2013.

[7] Martens, *Kabila et la révolution congolaise*, vol. 1, p. 372.

[8] Interviews with James Kabarebe in Kigali, April 2013, and Jean-Claude Yav in Kinshasa, August 2013.

about what they saw as a dangerous power grab. Was reform not merely an excuse for a shift in authority towards RPF friendly cadres, they asked? What had the Mobutist FAZ officers done for Congo, apart from looting it? Almost every move was, by then, seen in terms of how it affected the distribution of power, not of how it could strengthen the initial objectives the revolution had fought for. As Kabarebe put it, "We could no longer share a glass without tension."[9]

Under heavy internal pressure, Kabila felt he had to act. On July 11 Kabila replaced Kabarebe, appointing his brother-in-law, Célestin Kifwa, who had until then been head of the National Police, as the new chief of staff of the Congolese army. Kabarebe's dismissal was much celebrated in the Kinshasa press.[10] But while Kabila sought to reassert control, he was wary of a complete break with the RPF. Thus in an attempt to reassure the RPF, he retained Kabarebe as a special military adviser to the president—a position Mzee claimed would render Kabarebe no less powerful but would merely remove him from the spotlights and help assuage anti-Rwandan sentiments among the population. The move failed to appease Kabarebe; the former commander of the AFDL was livid. He informed Kagame that with this move Kabila had dismantled the last vestiges of their interdependence. What especially enraged Kabarebe is that, from his perspective, rather than standing up to xenophobic anti-Tutsi sentiment and to the nepotistic demands of his advisers, Mzee was emboldening them. Even more, Kabila's refusal to countenance reform of the army jeopardized the gains they made by deposing the Mobutu regime and imperiled regional security. Adding insult to injury was the man who replaced Kabarebe. Better known for his love of alcohol and personal ties to Kabila than for military acumen and strategic skills, Kifwa's takeover of the Congolese army repulsed Kabarebe—who refused to attend the handover ceremony, a slight that did not escape the Congolese press.[11]

Beyond all these other considerations, what most unsettled the RPF were the immediate strategic consequences of losing control of the Congolese army. Kabarebe's demotion occurred at the peak of the insurgency inside Rwanda, right at the time of huge confrontations between the RPA and the *abacengezi* in Gisenyi Prefecture and the day before the massacre in Tare on July 12 dur-

---

[9] Interview in Kigali, April 2013.

[10] "Kabila nomme Kifwa a la tête de l'armée," *La référence plus*, July 14, 1998.

[11] Modeste Mutinga, "James Kabare boude son nouveau poste," *Le potentiel*, July 18, 1998.

ing the World Cup final when scores of victims were burned alive 35 kilometers northwest of Kigali. For the RPF, Kabila's maneuver and the Tare attack were inextricably linked.[12] However, in the eyes of Mzee, it was impermissible for the army to continue to be controlled by someone subverting the country's national interests in favor of a foreign power. These differences in perception and opinion were increasingly irreconcilable.[13]

The Power Vacuum Back Home

For about a week after the Kabarebe–Kifwa switch, there appeared to be a remarkable lull in the politicking in Kinshasa. Conversations with diplomats revealed that the Western-led international community was also confident that, despite its poor recent form, the alliance still held and conflict was not on the horizon.[14] Few public statements were made in Kinshasa, the question of army reform seemed, for now at least, to have been shelved and Kabarebe and Munyuza held their cards close to their chest, even if they refused to attend the official inauguration of Kifwa at the Stade des Martyrs.[15] When the UN Security Council, through its chair Sergei Lavrov of the Russian Federation, issued a statement on July 13, 1998, condemning "the massacres, other atrocities and violations of international humanitarian law committed in Zaire/the Democratic Republic of the Congo" and urging Kinshasa and Kigali "to investigate without delay, in their respective countries, the allegations contained in the report of the Investigative Team,"[16] the Congolese and Rwandan government stood shoulder-to-shoulder in rejecting the June 1998 report of Roberto Garreton,[17] arguing it was based on information provided by barely credible witnesses.

[12] Interview with Jack Nziza, July 2014.

[13] Interview with Jaynete Kabila in Kinshasa, August 2013.

[14] Interview with Clare Short, UK minister for international development, Clare Short, November 2009, and Howard Wolpe, US special envoy for Great Lakes, January 2010.

[15] Modeste Mutinga, "James Kabare boude son nouveau poste," *Le potentiel*, July 18, 1998.

[16] "Security Council Condemns Massacres, Humanitarian Law Violations in Zaire/ Democratic Republic of Congo," UN Security Council Press Release, SC/6545, July 13, 1998. Available at http://www.un.org/press/en/1998/19980713.sc6545.html

[17] United Nations Security Council, "Report of the Investigative Team Charged with Investigating Serious Violations of Human Rights and International Humanitarian Law in the Democratic Republic of Congo."

This pause in alliance infighting did not last long. A trilateral meeting on July 14 between Kabila, Namibian President Sam Nujoma and their Angolan counterpart José Eduardo Dos Santos to discuss the troubled peace process in Angola seemed to re-embed Congo in the regional context, but ten days later a summit was organized by Museveni to discuss defense and foreign affairs cooperation in the Great Lakes in which no Congolese delegation participated.[18] Instead, Mzee had traveled to Cuba, which had sent its presidential plane to Luanda for Kabila to be picked up there on July 17. According to his Cuban-Congolese adviser Godefroid Tchamlesso, the visit was supposed to be private and not political, as evident from the fact that *Maman* Sifa Maanya and Joseph's brother Zoe also traveled in his entourage.[19] On the one hand, Kabila wanted to secretly receive medical treatment for an old gunshot wound;[20] on the other, he yearned to see the leaders of a country he admired and had been supported by during the 1960s, even at the risk of a further deterioration of his already poor relations with Washington. But if the visit yielded a photo-opportunity with Fidel Castro and some technical cooperation agreements negotiated by Congolese Minister for Agriculture Mawampanga Mwana Nanga,[21] Mzee suddenly cut his trip short on Saturday July 25—a day before Cuba's Revolution Day which surely the old Congolese revolutionary was eager to celebrate—and he scrambled home after only three days. The reason for this was the flurry of intelligence reports he had begun receiving as soon as he had left Congo; with every passing hour, these appeared more desperate. Kabila's security operatives—led by Didier Kazadi and John Numbi—warned that the situation in Kinshasa was explosive and that James Kabarebe was using the president's absence to reassert this authority and usurp power.[22] The briefings confirmed Kabila's worst fears.

What exactly was unfolding in Kinshasa at the time is not easy to reconstruct, but the tensions between Kabarebe and Munyuza on the one hand and the hardliners around national security adviser Kazadi and "General" Numbi on the other hand were certainly escalating dangerously. Kazadi explicitly wanted to teach the erstwhile comrades a lesson: "The Rwandans had over-

---

[18] "Kabila renforce sa puissance dissuasive et prépare sa contre-offensive," *La référence plus*, July 14, 1998.

[19] Interview in Kinshasa, August 2013.

[20] Interview with Henri Mova, Brussels, April 2011.

[21] "L.D. Kabila à Cuba," *L'Avenir*, July 26, 1998.

[22] Interview with Mwenze Kongolo, August 2013, and Irung Awan in Kinshasa, August 2013.

stayed their welcome and they were asking too much in return. Their behavior was that of conquerors."[23] Kazadi knew that in Kabila's absence he was in de facto control of the national security apparatus and provocatively called a high-level meeting with Kabarebe, suggesting the latter owed him obedience. When both men sat down with their respective lieutenants, to everyone's surprise Kazadi asked the RPA to leave Congo. He thanked the Rwandan contingent for its help and said the country was ready to stand on its own two feet before adding that Kinshasa was willing to help with any problems Kigali may have. Kabarebe laughed loudly and claimed that Kazadi was acting without presidential authority. In response, Kazadi then established a telephone connection to Havana and Mzee confirmed that it was better for the bulk of the Rwandan troops to go home, but he also asked Kabarebe to stay on in Kinshasa as an individual adviser with perhaps a small group of soldiers as a bodyguard. The Rwandan officer balked at the suggestion and committed to little or nothing in his recollection,[24] preferring to settle the matter when Kabila returned to Congo. Kazadi, by contrast, thought that Kabarebe had gotten the message—a first, de facto expulsion order for the RPF to leave permanently—and would be on his way out soon.[25] He nevertheless continued to monitor any RPF activities in the city and, crucially, did not stop sending alarmist cables to Havana either.

Whereas the initial admonitions about a Rwandan plot sent by Kazadi and Numbi were noted by Kabila but attributed to overly agitated aides, doubts crept in as the severity of the warnings increased. In one of the final messages before his eventual departure, a Rwandan plot was described in which Kabila's plane, upon returning to N'Djili, would be shot out of the sky "*Habyarimana-style*" by Kabarebe's troops[26]—an eerie reference to the Rwandan president whose death heralded the start of the 1994 genocide. It was a devastatingly effective—if false—rumor that led Mzee to head back early, via Luanda, in total secrecy, fearing a conspiracy to assassinate him at the airport. On Sunday, July 26, he landed in Kinshasa and was secretly rushed to the palace.[27] He was about to make a decision that would plunge Central Africa into war.

---

[23] Interview in Kinshasa, August 2013.

[24] Interview in Kigali, April 2013.

[25] Interview in Kinshasa, August 2013.

[26] Interviews with Faustin Munene, Kinshasa, December 2009, and Henri Mova, Brussels, April 2011.

[27] Modeste Mutinga, "Kabila rentre en silence à Kinshasa," *Le potentiel*, July 27, 1998.

The Expulsion Order

A Hot July Night in the Presidential Palace

As the evening grew darker on July 26, 1998, a handful of Kabila loyalists—men he had known for years, sometimes decades—gathered at the Palais de Marbre in Kinshasa for a secret reunion that would change the course of African history. While it remains unclear exactly who attended, Didier Kazadi, Gaëtan Kakudji, Mwenze Kongolo, John Numbi, Abdoulaye Yerodia and François Olenga were certainly all present, as was Laurent-Désiré Kabila. The participants were highly strung; the atmosphere was that of a regime besieged. According to Kongolo, on the previous night Numbi and Kazadi had doubled reinforcements all around the city and deployed units with heavy weaponry, claiming that "James was planning a big operation tonight."[28] Kabarebe had allegedly earlier said to Congo's minister of justice that "those soldiers of yours are playing dangerous games ... Only one platoon of mine can destroy your entire army."[29] Comments like these had fueled the frenzy and the men at the meeting exchanged reports, rumors and sometimes clearly fictitious accounts that galvanized each other of the need for offensive action. Kazadi, unsurprisingly, went the furthest in his allegations: with the aid of Gomair, an aviation society entirely run by Rwandans, Kabarebe had for weeks now been flying armed Tutsi youth into Kinshasa to help him carry out a coup.[30] Should the "Habyarimana-style plot" have failed, a force of at least 500 would have launched a rocket attack on the president. According to Kazadi, who was backed up by others at the meeting, the former FAC chief of staff was determined to kill Mzee.

Despite this treacherous environment, both Kabila and Kabarebe were committed to seeing each other face-to-face. As critical as the situation was, neither had forgotten what they had been through *together* over the previous two years: if they could just rekindle the camaraderie that they once shared, they could stave off war. Kabarebe reopened communications with Mzee for a final time on the morning of July 27 by phone. The Rwandan commander indicated that he considered it indispensable to talk to Kabila bilaterally and not in the presence of the men he held responsible for the destruction of the revolutionary project and the mounting insecurity back home in Rwanda. He

---

[28] Interview in Kinshasa, August 2013.
[29] Ibid.
[30] Ibid.

balked at Mzee's suggestion that Kazadi and other advisers be involved in the talks; to Kabarebe, this sounded like he was to face an inquisition jury rather than ex-comrades trying to find a politico-military solution for the dangerous rift within the alliance.

With all trust completely gone, even the practicalities of arranging a meeting proved nigh-impossible. Kabila insisted that Kabarebe come to the palace without his armed guard. The RPA officer rejected such a suggestion as ludicrous, fearing he would be murdered before reaching the Congolese president. According to Kabarebe and one of his confidants,[31] as Kabila continued to stall, Kabarebe warned his former boss that he was coming, with his armed guard, ready to take on any "surprises" Kazadi had in store for him: "I will fight through the ambush to reach you and you will bear the consequences."[32] The president ultimately relented; Kabarebe reached the Palais de Marbre with his escort without obstacles, though he was forced to give up his weapons as he entered Kabila's office. The two men held a brief but tempestuous meeting during which Mzee offered the RPF logistical assistance to return to Rwanda; Kabarebe, by his own account, responded that as they were no longer wanted they would rather go back themselves—if need be on foot—instead of accepting insincere help.

* * *

As emotions ran high, Kabila too felt the adrenaline coursing through his veins but remained remarkably calm in this chess game. He had come to believe that the stories told to him by his loyal aides were probably not only true, but that even if they were exaggerated there was simply no way back to the partnership—or even co-existence—of the previous months and weeks. Failing to heed the advice of his advisers and continuing to insist on dialogue with the RPF seemed as lethal a choice as confrontation with his former Rwandan comrades. However, Mzee also knew that despite his build-up of a parallel army, his soldiers would be no match for the RPA crack troops and their allies in the FAC. Nor could he count on any foreign support, having alienated his own region and the wider world with his disastrous diplomacy and the exclusive alliance he made with the RPF.

Kabila recognized that an immediate military clash with Kabarebe may not end well, whatever the bellicose advice Mzee's most radical lieutenants whis-

---

[31] Interview in Kigali, name withheld, July 2014.

[32] Interview with James Kabarebe, Kigali, April 2013.

pered into his ear. Kabila did not panic; instead, he calmly played the final trump card he had been saving—his sovereign authority.

Mzee understood that for all his weakness and for as much as he was ridiculed as a puppet of the RPF, he was still the Congolese head of state and possessed the legal command of the country's sovereignty. With both sides seeing no way out of the "strike or die" security dilemma they were trapped in, Kabila thought hard about how he could thwart Kabarebe's coup without triggering a firefight that would destroy his regime. One option that was available to him was the simplest tactic imaginable: he could just ask the RPF to leave. As sovereign, it was his prerogative, and it would create a new situation on the ground that, though not without huge risks, at least offered an alternative to urban warfare. After Mzee had consulted a handful of advisers—Kakudji, Kongolo, Kazadi, Numbi—the idea of the expulsion order gradually took shape.

Thus it was that David Kokolo Longo, chef-de-cabinet at the Ministry of Defense, read out a terse statement on television the following night, shortly before midnight. By formally stating to the Congolese public and to the international community that the order "marks the end of the presence of all foreign military forces in the Congo," Kabila immediately increased the costs the RPF faced of launching a coup d'état—for such a strike would now be viewed as a direct response to the expulsion order—an unacceptable act of international aggression in the face of a sovereign government exercising its most basic legal authority. Miraculously, it worked—there was no coup attempt or armed confrontation in Kinshasa; Kabarebe and his force left Kinshasa.

Kabila's move confounded Kigali. The Congolese president was daring the RPF to act and to be caught before the eyes of the world *in flagrante*, something Kabila knew the secretive Front hated. As Kagame admitted to the US ambassador in Rwanda at the time, Robert Gribbin, "he had agonized over what to do—defy the order, replace Kabila, or depart—but had concluded that Kabila held the upper hand at that moment."[33] It certainly was not a fool-proof gamble by Kabila, but it was better than any alternative Mzee could think of given the military imbalance and the total breakdown of relations between his inner circle and the most potent force on the Congolese territory. This was also the view put forward in a particularly well-informed article in the Kinshasa press (quite probably written by someone in the Palais de

---

[33] Gribbin, *In the Aftermath of Genocide*, p. 274.

Marbre) entitled *"Kabila écarte momentanément le danger"*—Kabila *temporarily* escapes the danger.[34]

Betrayed by Our Comrades: The RPF Pulls Out

By the time the expulsion order was formally announced on Monday night, Kabila's decision did not come as a complete surprise to the RPA force in Kinshasa. The writing had long been on the wall that the Kabila loyalists wanted to get rid of them; in the view of Munyuza and Kabarebe, the Congolese president had completely surrendered to the hardliners around Kazadi and Numbi. But in light of the deteriorating security situation back home and the deepening ties between Kabila and ALiR, the RPF could not back down and let Kabila dictate the security situation.

The question for the RPF was how to hold Kabila to account for his betrayal. A junior DMI officer stationed on the ground testified that even if the RPA contingent in Kinshasa had superior firepower, experience and training, it was also quite small by that time—perhaps only 200 people—and would face a difficult time controlling the city by itself after Kabila was "punished."[35] The balance of forces added to the complexity of the decision before Kagame and Kabarebe. While in the previous months the Rwandan intelligence services had helped prepare a major conspiracy against the man they put in power (see below), such an attempt now—in which they would provide the muscle for a Congolese usurper of Kabila's throne—was allegedly ruled out. According to the RPF, this had nothing to do with the expulsion order or military balance in Kinshasa, but put simply: "because we don't do coups,"[36] or as Patrick Mazimhaka, Kigali's key diplomat at the time said: "A coup d'état and then what? Without liberation movement? You remove power from one person to another—nothing changes."[37] The Front has always insisted that a putsch was never an option. Yet whereas coups are supposedly anathema to the RPF—portrayed as vulgar acts that truly disciplined and committed revolutionaries would not engage in, at home in Rwanda or abroad—it is striking that all other means of irregular regime change explicitly were—and are—considered entirely legitimate when confronted with a political impasse.

[34] Modeste Mutinga, "Kabila écarte momentanément le danger," *Le potentiel*, July 29, 1998.
[35] Interview in Kigali, name withheld, July 2014.
[36] Interview with Karake Karenzi in Kigali, December 2009.
[37] Interview in Kigali, December 2014.

Moreover, the proposition of intrinsic RPF resistance to such an action must be balanced against the alternative hypothesis that the expulsion order had succeeded in raising the costs of a potential sudden strike against the president to prohibitive levels. Thus, more than a deeply held ideological antagonism vis-à-vis a putsch, local realities appeared to determine how the RPF would respond to the perceived treachery of its comrades. As we will see in the next section, Patrick Karegeya of Rwanda's ESO certainly had no qualms with preparing, from early 1998 onwards, a general insurrection against Mzee that was meant to start in Kinshasa and swiftly change the regime—which sounded rather strongly like ... a coup. That this conspiracy never came to fruition points to changing tactical conditions on the ground—above all the impact of expelling "all foreign forces."

* * *

The expulsion order read out by chef-de-cabinet Kokolo on national television on the night of July 27 and the nationalist gloating that followed in the Kinshasa newspapers[38] confirmed to the RPF all the disgust and bitterness it was already feeling vis-à-vis the ungrateful Kabila; in the words of RPA lieutenant (and aide to Kabarebe) Frank Begumisa, "we had brought him from a shack in Tanzania to power in Kinshasa and he does this to us?"[39] The Rwandans packed their bags and assured the Kabila government that they would not require forty-eight hours to leave the country. As the RPA contingent began boarding a chartered Ilyushin plane to leave for Kigali later on July 28, Kifwa, Kabarebe's successor as FAC commander, came to the airport and, depending on one's interpretation, tried to either offer a last bit of decorum to the departing troops who had overthrown Mobutu fifteen months earlier or was rubbing salt into a festering wound with his absurd saluting. Kabarebe largely ignored Kifwa and instead braced himself for some difficult discussions in Kigali about what had gone wrong and what the future might hold. He himself was crystal clear in his conclusions about what Mzee's maneuver meant: "They had betrayed us. The regime was our direct enemy now...When we left, we knew it was war."[40]

---

[38] "Kabila chasse tous les soldats rwandais et autres étrangers du territoire congolais," *La référence plus*, July 28, 1998.

[39] Interview in Kigali, December 2009.

[40] Interview in Kigali, April 2013.

The Conspiracy: From "Plan A" to "Plan B"

Kagame and Kabarebe's Preparations for Regime Change in Kinshasa

As Kabarebe and the RPA troops returned from Kinshasa, the atmosphere in Kigali was frantic. It had long been clear to the RPF's Council of Colonels that the liberation project in Congo was falling far short of its ambitious objectives. The insurgency in northwest (and increasingly central) Rwanda was fed by the malaise in eastern Congo from whence the *abacengezi* infiltrated into the Rwandan countryside. Intelligence reports about support from Kinshasa to the insurgents had dominated discussions for months. But the now accelerated unraveling of the AFDL and the seeming inability of the Front to respond to Kabila's growing audacity and autonomy led to tempestuous internal debates; the strategy hitherto pursued was questioned. Kabarebe himself—and to a lesser extent his lieutenant Munyuza—became the subject of controversy.[41]

Prominent RPF officials underscored that although Congo policy was absolutely essential to Rwanda's national security and the survival of the Tutsi, the Front had essentially entrusted all its hopes and fears to one young, inexperienced officer who had been tasked to stay on in Kinshasa after May 1997. They pointed out that he lacked the political wherewithal to counter the scheming of Kakudji and Kazadi and that it should come as no surprise that Kabila had managed to outmaneuver him. Indirectly, this was a critique of Kagame's decision to stay on after liberation without investing the requisite political resources necessary to help stabilize the post-Mobutu order, firmly anchor the AFDL project in an ideological mode close to that of the RPF, and ultimately secure Rwanda's main interests. The choice of Minister of Defense Kagame to delegate so much to the former head of his personal guard came under fire. The charge was that he had fallen into a classic problem of military intelligence and strategy.[42] Critics highlighted that since May 1997 Kagame himself had pursued a Congo policy that relied too heavily on information provided by the very individuals (Kabarebe and Munyuza) tasked with implementing it; there were no other meaningful sources of intelligence to assess

---

[41] The following section is based on interviews with James Kabarebe, Emmanuel Ndahiro, Patrick Mazimhaka, Jack Nziza and Joseph Karemera, December 2009–December 2014.

[42] John Hughes-Wilson, *Military Intelligence Blunders*, New York: Carroll & Graf, 1999.

the success or failure of the project. These informational asymmetries meant that Kabarebe's advice to Kagame seemed to nearly always dictate official RPF policy, or so it seemed to his critics. With the success of the campaign against Mobutu, Kabarebe's rise appeared unstoppable. But if the march into Kinshasa brought much glory, upon his return in late July 1998 the young officer was subject to withering criticism. One common refrain among his critics was that his own personal biases and career interests prevented him from making the necessary course corrections as things in Kinshasa spiraled out of control. Whatever was to be done next, they suggested it was perhaps better done without the dashing but overly impulsive officer who had burned all bridges with Kabila and possibly with Dos Santos's Angola—and whose staying on in Congo certainly had not prevented the resurgence of the *génocidaire* threat.

It was a powerful internal critique of the last year and a half. Kabarebe's detractors created some momentum for change, yet ultimately failed to substantially shift the policy. However much the RPF could have benefited from a careful and comprehensive assessment of what went wrong, the speed and urgency of events, the informational advantages Kabarebe retained, and the clout the military held in the RPF ensured that Kabarebe fended off his skeptics. Kagame conceded to the Council of Colonels that the military situation at home was critical, that the *abacengezi* menace may well get even worse and that Mzee had turned out to be a treacherous ally who in retrospect should have been left in retirement in Tanzania. Faced with such an ominous outlook, however, necessitated reasserting control of the situation and that was best done using the policy tool it mastered best: war. If the RPF had failed to politically manage its principal interests and was likely to lose itself in a political chess game with Kabila in case of an attempted new elite bargain (in which it had no confidence in any event after Mzee's "betrayal"), a military confrontation was a more natural fit for the martial culture of the Front and appeared to have a much better chance of securing its main objectives. There would obviously be constraints on the options available to engineer regime change in Kinshasa—the RPF's main priority because of the links between the Kabila regime and the ex-FAR/Interahamwe—but Kagame reminded his fellow officers of the RPA's tried and tested ability to create facts on the ground and manage information before others had time to respond or shift the balance in its favor. Kagame calculated that if the RPF moved fast enough and with sufficient determination, this was an utterly winnable war that could wipe out the accident of history that was Laurent-Désiré Kabila.

To accomplish this goal, the RPF jettisoned any pretense of bringing together a multilateral Pan-Africanist coalition. The Front wanted an immediate response to hold Kabila accountable and there was simply not enough time to forge a broad alliance. Moreover, support from the other original allies of the AFDL was likely not forthcoming. Eritrea and Ethiopia had been at war since May 1998 and Angola's relations with Rwanda were frosty since Tshikapa and the subsequent expulsion of the MPLA after the overthrow of Mobutu. The ailing Nyerere was no longer capable of playing a role and Tanzania was much closer to Kinshasa than to Kigali. The RPF also opted against informing its most important partner outside of Africa, the United States, of its plans to imminently return to war. Most of the evidence we have gathered from interviews with Rwandan and American officials and diplomatic cables suggests that the RPF only brought Washington into the loop after August 2, 1998. According to Minister of Health Dr Joseph Karemera, this was because the Front knew American support would not be forthcoming (contrary to the first Congo war when Washington's blessing was unambiguous), or if it came, it would be very different in nature from the assistance in 1996–7: "No green light. The [US-led] international community didn't know what to do with the situation. But it couldn't prevent us from doing some things. Because they gave us no alternatives."[43] This was confirmed in the personal accounts of US Ambassador Gribbin and US Defense Attaché Orth.[44]

The only ally Kagame decided to involve, then, was, not coincidentally, Uganda's NRM. Ties with Museveni were not as tight as they had once been, but Kampala remained by far the closest ally the RPF had. Moreover, Kagame knew that Museveni had also been unhappy with the shambolic first year of the AFDL and the insecurity in eastern Congo—he too had stayed away from the revolution's first anniversary on May 17, 1998. Furthermore, it had been Ugandan ESO boss David Pulkol who had called the meeting of intelligence chiefs in March 1998 in Kampala to raise concerns about the new Congo and to analyze how reactionary spoilers—military-Islamist Sudan, Angola's UNITA, the ex-FAR/Interahamwe and Uganda's own Lord's Resistance Army (LRA) and the Allied Democratic Forces (ADF)—might take advantage of the faltering Congolese state to once again destabilize Central Africa.

Since June 1, Ugandan forces had been pursuing the Khartoum-backed ADF in the Ruwenzori Mountains in Province Orientale.[45] Ugandan–Congolese

---

[43] Interview in Kigali, December 2009.

[44] Gribbin, *In the Aftermath of Genocide*; Orth, "Rwanda's Hutu Extremist Genocidal Insurgency."

[45] M. Sserwanga and J. Nzinjah, "Uganda, Congo in Joint Operations against ADF Rebels," *New Vision*, June 2, 1998.

military cooperation had been difficult to obtain from Mzee and was characterized by stop-and-go protocols; permission for incursions on Congolese territory and joint operations cautiously recommenced only from July 22 onwards in the areas around Kasese and Bundibugyo.[46] According to UPDF Chief of Staff Jeje Odongo, the ADF was more of a political headache than a military threat: "ADF threat did not constitute a danger to Kampala, but it was a security menace which threatened the credibility of the NRM in the eyes of the population."[47] Moses Byaruhanga, the political spin doctor who would go on to help Yoweri Museveni in his re-election as Ugandan president in 2001, 2006 and 2011, underlined that his boss needed the votes of the west of the country to maintain political hegemony and advised him to be highly intolerant of any unrest there: "War in western Uganda affected our legitimacy considerably."[48] This was especially pertinent after the massacre at Kichwamba Technical College on June 8, 1998; at dawn on a Monday morning, ADF insurgents poured petrol over the school buildings and burned eighty students alive, as well as abducting more than 100 others. Extensive press coverage and graphic details of the attack and its aftermath—"The stench of human flesh filled the air. Charred bodies of students littered the floor in three dormitories"[49]—enflamed public opinion and increased the pressure on Museveni's NRM to "solve" the problem of rebels using Congolese rear bases to attack Uganda.

Although it was by no means clear that cooperating with the RPF's imminent push for regime change in Kinshasa would actually prevent atrocities like the Kichwamba attack, Museveni found it convenient to frame enduring insecurity on his own territory in terms of a causal link between the Kabila government's policy and ADF activity. Thus, when James Kabarebe traveled to Gulu in northern Uganda—probably on July 31 or August 1, 1998—to see Museveni, his half-brother Major-General Salim Saleh, his Chief of Staff Jeje Odongo and UDPF Fourth Division Commander James Kazini and to discuss Ugandan involvement in a new Congo war, he found them quite receptive.[50] Even if the actual military assistance the UPDF offered to the RPA was limited and would consist mostly of training and material support to anti-Kabila rebels (the Ugandan army was preoccupied with renewed offensives against the LRA, including infiltrations across the Sudanese border), the

[46] J.B. Thawite, "Congo Joins Uganda to Battle ADF Rebels," *New Vision*, July 23, 1998.
[47] Interview in Kampala, March 2013.
[48] Ibid.
[49] M. Sserwanga, "The Day Terror Struck Kichwamba," *New Vision*, June 15, 1998.
[50] Interview with James Kabarebe in Kigali, April 2013.

meeting reinforced the Ugandan–Rwandan alliance and committed both parties to regime change in Kinshasa. Once again there was comparatively little discussion of what exactly a new Congo would look like after the war or how a post-conflict Congolese political landscape could be better managed then between May 1997 and August 1998. Instead, most of the conversation was devoted to the personal betrayal Mzee had committed. Odongo, commenting on his president's decision to return to war alongside Rwanda in Congo: "Kabila was keen to give the impression that he no longer needed us, he was so full of himself ... He came from a humble place but found himself in an extremely powerful position. Kabila was drunk on power, we all saw it."[51]

Drôle de Guerre: The Run Up to August 2, 1998

If the RPF responded decisively to the disintegration of the alliance by preparing for war, the post-expulsion atmosphere in Kinshasa was more confused—and would remain so until the outbreak of violent conflict. News reports—totally reflective of the political elite's outlook—were initially boisterous about the departure of the RPF and full of *schadenfreude*, rehashing stereotypes about Congo's eastern neighbor. The July 30 edition of *La Référence Plus* went furthest in its mockery; its frontpage stated that "James Kabarehe [*sic*] had been forced onto a plane to Kigali after Congolese soldiers had prevented him from smuggling his luxurious Mercedes onto a Gomair flight." The latter was an airline staffed mostly by Rwandan Tutsi and was said to have been used by commanders' girlfriends, as well as being instrumental in RPF coup plans, according to Didier Kazadi. The newspaper then went on to inform its readers that the Rwandans had been sent back to Kigali with their "[female] handbags, matresses and weapons in the hand ... and with death in their souls." This followed triumphant coverage in previous days of cowardly Rwandans finally having been put in their place. However, some in the Kabila government understood that as elated as they were about having escaped a Rwandan-backed coup and having freed their country from "foreign occupation," such inflammatory language in the press only further augmented the risk of a regional war. Mwenze Kongolo saw the danger presented by those security hawks for whom the expulsion order represented a green light to pay back the Tutsis and who put pressure on newspaper editorialists to fan the flames of demagogic nationalism: "Kifwa was crazy. Too excited about his new job."[52] The minister of justice pushed for more toned down language in other dai-

[51] Interview in Kampala, April 2013.
[52] Interview in Kinshasa, August 2013.

lies—*Le Potentiel* contented itself with stating that "Kabila clarifies his alliance with Rwanda"[53]—and was at pains to emphasize that the expulsion order was not aimed at Congolese Tutsi civilians, only at foreign troops. Thus *La Tempête des Tropiques* had the headline "The Rwandans, Our Brothers" and *Le Potentiel* on July 31 published an article entitled "The Banyamulenge Are Congolese." Kongolo himself stated that the expulsion order was not aimed at Tutsi civilians and urged all Congolese to reject xenophobia vis-à-vis ethnic minorities, cautioning against a witch-hunt. *L'Avenir* commented that "the government … warned all those who would seek to attack foreigners and Rwandophone Congolese citizens."[54]

Confusion and fear of a virulent Rwandan reaction were also evident in the private diplomacy Mzee and his inner circle engaged in. The expulsion order had been a desperate but necessary security measure yet Kabila hoped that, like so often in the recent past, he might get away with his bravado. Following on the heels of Kabarebe's repatriation, he sent his two closest lieutenants, Kongolo and Kazadi, on a mission to Kigali to meet Paul Kagame, so the political temperature in Rwanda could be gauged and a process of normalizing relations could be initiated.[55] The Rwandan minister of defense agreed to see them on Thursday July 30 but barely uttered a word; Kazadi and Kongolo tried to soothe Kagame and stressed Congo's continued commitment to Rwandan security and the Pan-Africanist aspirations of the revolution, but also emphasized that it had been time that the RPA returned home. Offered as a token of Congo's appreciation for the RPF, Kazadi and Kongolo handed a check of US$1 million to Kagame, according to Kongolo for "veterans of the campaign against Mobutu and their families" while Kazadi claimed it was for "orphans growing up in Rwanda after the genocide."[56] A difficult silence ensued, with the RPF leader staring incredulously at the two Congolese envoys.[57] Were they really so cut off from the worldview of their former comrades that they thought the Front could be placated with cash? Or was this one of Kabila's sick jokes, meant to once again insult Rwandan pride and echo stereotypes of a Tutsi's only loyalty being to his money? Kagame concluded

[53] Modeste Mutinga, "Kabila clarifie ses alliances avec les Rwandais," *Le potentiel*, July 30, 1998.

[54] "Halte à la confusion!," *L'Avenir*, July 30, 1998.

[55] Interview with Bizima Karaha in Goma, December 2009, and with Henri Mova in Brussels, April 2011.

[56] Interviews with Kongola and Kazadi in Kinshasa, August 2013.

[57] Interview with Joseph Karemera in Kigali, December 2009.

the meeting with an admonition to the departing Kazadi and Kongolo: "Tell Kakudji that he can begin a war but he can never end it."[58]

Back in Kinshasa, the two envoys briefed Kabila and the cabinet on their trip. Unbelievably, their report was resoundingly optimistic: the RPF had not appreciated the expulsion order and was now sulking, but war was unlikely.[59] Although follow-up missions would be required, their counsel was that a peaceful solution was within reach, provided that the Rwandans were sagaciously managed with flattery and reassurances. The RPF regime seemed too fragile and isolated to take on its big neighbor—music to the ears of the hardliners who had encouraged Mzee to expel Kabarebe and Munyuza a long time ago and who now felt vindicated. Their assessment could not have been further from the truth.

August 2, 1998: The Rebellion-cum-Invasion of Congo

On Sunday, August 2, 1998, less than a week after the expulsion order was issued and the RPA contingent left Congo, Major Sylvain Mbuki of the FAC appeared on Radio-Télévision National Congolaise to announce from Goma that a general rebellion against the Congolese government was underway: "On behalf of government troops, we decry the regime of Laurent-Désiré Kabila ... We the army of the DRC have taken the decision to remove President Laurent-Désiré Kabila from power." As the virtually unknown Mbuki spoke, two specialized RPA commando units, with light support from the UPDF, deployed hundreds of troops to capture Goma airport and other strategic facilities in the city.[60] They joined thousands of soldiers of the FAC's strongest and best armed unit—the 10th Brigade—which controlled much of North Kivu and, as we saw earlier, had been used by Kabarebe as his *force-de-frappe* against ex-FAR/Interahamwe. Also backing the rebellion was the 22nd Brigade based in South Kivu—the FAC's second most potent battalion group. Bukavu and Uvira fell very soon, though hundreds of loyalist soldiers had to be killed to fully secure the cities. On August 3, James Kabarebe himself arrived in Goma and prepared for one of the riskiest maneuvers in modern African military history. Africa's Great War was now underway.

* * *

[58] Interview with Mwenze Kongolo in Kinshasa, August 2013.
[59] Interview with Faustin Munene in Kinshasa, December 2009.
[60] Tom Cooper, *Great Lakes Conflagration: The Second Congo War, 1998–2003*, Solihull, England: Helion, 2013, Chapter 4.

The outbreak of conflict had been feared by the pro-Kabila elites in Kinshasa and Lubumbashi but its exact timing still came as a surprise to Mzee and his advisers; the mission by Kazadi and Kongolo to Kigali had given them a false sense of security which even alarmist intelligence reports from the Kivus in the preceding days had left unaltered. Little action was undertaken to address the possibility of an internal crisis away from the capital. According to Koen Vlassenroot, a Belgian academic who was doing fieldwork in Bukavu at the time, Banyamulenge friends had warned him for at least forty-eight hours prior to the onset of the war that it was best to stay inside because "something big" was coming. During one of his last outings in the city, Vlassenroot personally saw the deputy governor of South Kivu, Benjamin Serukiza, and the mayor of Bukavu helping their family cross the border into Rwanda;[61] during the evenings, Banyamulenge security officials would openly complain about the high numbers of Katangese officers deployed in their region, but then laughed loudly about an "imminent change." What this meant in practice transpired more quickly than expected. When the rebellion finally began, hundreds of FAC recruits, many of them Katangese, were massacred at Kavumu Airport, just outside the city.[62]

Crucially, it was not just the timing that caught Kabila and his aides off guard but the form of the challenge to their rule, which differed from what hawks like Kazadi, Munene and Numbi had foreseen. Throughout 1998, and in particular in July, their focus had rested on a coup d'état—and, initially, rightly so. As early as December 1997, disgruntled AFDL politicians began meeting to assess options to deal with the "problem Kabila": the nucleus of the group was formed by individuals who felt marginalized by Mzee's Katangization policy, his authoritarian style and/or the unresolved nationality question. Moreover, many of them opined that their efforts during the liberation struggle or in previous years were insufficiently recognized and rewarded by Kabila. They were also convinced that the enduring weakness of the AFDL, the concentration of power in the president and the declining influence of the movement's foreign allies meant that conventional routes of trying to correct the mistakes of the revolution were closed; hence they began considering extralegal and even outright clandestine action.

The most outspoken of these "AFDL rebels" was Moïse Nyarugabo who had been Mzee's private secretary and thus a gatekeeper to the spokesman-

---

[61] Interview in Ghent, January 2012.
[62] Reyntjens, *Great African War*, p. 195.

cum-president of the AFDL. After liberation, he had lost much of his power and had been appointed to an anti-corruption agency, a role that required him to confiscate illegally acquired properties—which quickly led to rumors across Kinshasa about Tutsis stealing houses, vehicles and furniture in the name of the state. Moïse resented this personal affront—which he suspected had been inflicted on him because of his ethnicity—and loudly argued with the president: "You want to give us the impression that we fought for nothing ... You think like them: that I am a foreigner."[63] Kabila denied any such motives but did not move against Moïse, well aware of how much the latter knew about his personal routine and of his excellent personal ties with the RPF. Moïse's movements were monitored by Kazadi's agents, who smelled a rat when other sullen politicians reached out to one another to discuss their frustrations: Azarias Ruberwa, the Banyamulenge chef-de-cabinet of Foreign Minister Bizima Karaha who had never forgiven Kabila for declaring himself president in Lubumbashi; Mbusa Nyamwisi, a young and ambitious power-broker of the Nande of eastern Congo, who complained that the new government failed to address the insecurity in the Nande's commercial hinterlands and home region; Lunda Bululu, a former prime minister of Mobutu with an impressive network but who had failed to obtain a position in the government. While these individuals knew that discontent with the AFDL regime was broadly shared, they struggled to formulate a clear strategy to address the growing crisis: "We didn't know how to start a rebellion or a coup d'état. We didn't have a form yet. But Kabila was the problem."[64]

The frustration of Nyarugabo, Ruberwa, Nyamwisi and Bululu took on a more concrete form when foreign intelligence agencies developed a keen interest in finding ways of undermining—possibly even replacing—Kabila from about March 1998 onwards. Both Nyarugabo and Nyamwisi entertained parallel contacts with the Ugandan ESO of David Pulkol and the Rwandan ESO of Patrick Karegeya. In the words of Nyarugabo: "We tried to solve the problem from the inside. Later, we met Museveni, Nyerere and Kagame to solve our problem. We were trying to show to these presidents that we were facing serious problems here."[65] Pulkol and Karegeya worked hard to give their respective bosses additional options to deal with the growing disappointments of the liberation of Congo; while their efforts were certainly not the only

---

[63] Interview in Kinshasa, December 2009.

[64] Interview with Moïse Nyarugabo, December 2009.

[65] Interview in Goma, December 2009.

track pursued by the NRM and RPF to control and mold the Kabila regime, the two intelligence chiefs were given the green light by their bosses to encourage the AFDL rebels financially and organizationally so scenarios for regime change could be developed. Nyamwisi spent most of the March–August 1998 period commuting between Kinshasa, Kampala, Kigali and eastern Congo;[66] Karegeya introduced him to Jean-Pierre Ondekane, commander of the 10th Brigade, as part of intensifying efforts to offset Katangization policies in the security services and to target suspected links between pro-Kabila officers and ALiR. Nyarugabo also contacted Congolese Tutsi in the security services and sounded out Dan Munyuza and other Rwandan commanders about the possibility of ambushing and arresting the Congolese president; a plot to neutralize Kabila in this vein was being prepared but was thwarted before it reached the implementation phase because the presidential bodyguard led by RPA officer Francis Gakwerere was replaced by Tanzanian and Katangese soldiers in May 1998.[67]

Despite the fact that options for a coup or a party revolt were limited as relations between Kabila and the RPF deteriorated further in June–July 1998, the AFDL rebels still looked for a way to foster internal change in Kinshasa. All kinds of scenarios were debated; even the possibility of working with Tshisekedi—that other nationalist lion, who despite all his anti-Rwandan rhetoric held confidential talks with the RPF—and installing him as president was an option.[68] However, the twin blows of the replacement of Kabarebe by Kifwa as FAC chief of staff and, above all, the expulsion order effectively closed down the possibility of a coup, as recognized by Bizima Karaha who, despite being a protégé of Mzee, was a central figure in the anti-Kabila conspiracy: "I was in all meetings. ... It [the rebellion] was meant to be short and internal, no need for war or foreign support ... It was meant to be in Kinshasa too. All over."[69] Lunda Bululu, fully on board with the regime change meetings since April 1998, confirmed Karaha's account: "If July 27 [i.e., the expulsion order] hadn't happened, certain 'events' in August would have taken place."[70] Frustrated with the failure of the conspiracy—his name was often mentioned as a more viable alternative then Tshisekedi, not least because

[66] Interview with Mbusa Nyamwisi in Kinshasa, December 2009.

[67] Interview with Moïse Nyarugabo in Goma, December 2009.

[68] Interview with an RPA officer who was intimately familiar with the discussions with Tshisekedi, Kigali, July 2014.

[69] Interview in Goma, December 2009.

[70] Interview in Kinshasa, December 2009.

Bululu was himself Katangese—the former prime minister blamed it on Rwandan dithering at the last minute, before the Cuba trip: "A coup would have succeeded, if James wanted it to."[71] Faustin Munene, the pro-Kabila vice-minister of the interior, concurred: "A coup was far simpler ... The Rwandans were too angry. They lost their cool ... They could just have grabbed power whenever they wanted to. They could have killed us all."[72] David Pulkol also left little room for ambiguity: "We intended to make a change in Kinshasa without regional involvement. We had prepared people on the inside ... Kabila went to Cuba and kicked them out. He had to save himself from the internal thing James was preparing."[73] In other words, the expulsion order effectively forced the Congolese conspirators and their Rwandan–Ugandan backers to switch from the preferred option of a coup to a much riskier and more protracted societal insurgency.

This so-called "Plan B" was immediately put in motion following the return of Kabila from Havana and the departure of Kabarebe and the RPA contingent from Congo. Karegeya had spent considerably less time preparing for this eventuality, but the same networks that he had in place for a sudden strike in Kinshasa now mobilized to help the Rwandan war effort. The RPF was adamant that its involvement remain veiled for as long as possible to limit international condemnation and so would strive, like with the AFDL, to have a Congolese rebel front pursue regime change but with heavy Rwandan assistance to ensure overall strategic guidance and to prevent a repeat of the Kabila problem. As Mbusa Nyamwisi testified: "Rwanda's Plan B was rebellion. The entire rebellion was orchestrated from and by Kigali."[74]

Thus, when Kabarebe traveled to Gulu to meet Museveni, while RPA Chief of Staff Kayumba Nyamwasa prepared troops to spearhead the coming onslaught and Karake Karenzi intensified the counter-insurgency offensive in Rwanda's northwest, Karegeya told his clandestine network of Congolese contacts to abandon their positions in the AFDL state and head to Kigali to assume the reins of the anti-Kabila rebellion. The key men in Karegeya's network uttered a sigh of relief as they had never believed the Kazadi–Kongolo fiction that the expulsion order would not necessarily lead to war; according to Déogratias Bugera's close aide Thomas Nzaratimana, who left Kinshasa on July 30 to head to Zambia: "It was written all over—war was coming. It was

---

[71] Interview in Kinshasa, December 2009.
[72] Interview in Kinshasa, December 2009.
[73] Interview in Kampala, March 2013.
[74] Interview in Kinshasa, December 2009.

so clear."[75] Throughout the country, AFDL politicians began mysteriously dropping off the radar: Bugera secretly crossed the Congo river to Brazzaville on July 30; Azarias Ruberwa stayed for much longer than expected in Bukavu after a friend's wedding and then drove to Cyangugu; Bizima Karaha refused to return from an OAU summit in Mozambique and instead flew first to Johannesburg and then to Kigali, stunning Congolese Minister of the Environment Edi Angilu who had traveled with him initially and had to return alone to Congo.[76]

Accompanying these disappearances was an exodus out of Kinshasa of ordinary Tutsi and those likely to be seen as their auxiliaries—hundreds boarded boats and flights taking them out of the country. Yet despite the increasingly obvious signs that this was not a coincidence but part of a centrally orchestrated plan, Kabila did very little in response. According to the accounts of insiders like Henri Mova and Edi Angilu, Mzee was particularly in denial about the betrayal of Bizima.[77] According to the president's adjunct chef-de-cabinet Godefroid Tchamlesso, "Bizima was the *chouchou* of the Mzee ... Even some of us veterans could not get so close to him."[78] The head of intelligence of the National Police Raus Chalwe highlighted the personal pain Kabila felt as the evidence became incontrovertible that his protégé was one of the brains behind the rebellion: "Bizima was Mzee's son!"[79]

One by one the AFDL renegades appeared in Kigali, having received instructions to travel to Rwanda but still largely in the dark about the magnitude of Plan B. Most of them were already there when Sylvain Mbuki announced the start of the rebellion from Goma, but it was only on Tuesday, August 4, that the ESO gathered them all in one place in downtown Kigali: many of the individuals who had worked secretly and in parallel now met each other. The dissident university lecturer Arthur Z'ahidi Ngoma showed up, as did Mbusa Nyamwisi, Alexis Thambwe (a former minister under Mobutu), Bizima Karaha, Déogratias Bugera, Moïse Nyarugabo, Emile Ilunga and many others; for the RPF, Patrick Karegeya, Emmanuel Ndahiro, Patrick Mazimhaka and Wilson Rutayisire (chief of Rwanda's Information Office) managed the proceedings. The astonishment of the Congolese participants at seeing one another notwithstanding, the RPF lost no time in laying out its strategy: the

---

[75] Interview March 2013.
[76] Interview in Kinshasa, December 2009.
[77] Interviews in Brussels, April 2011, and Kinshasa, December 2009.
[78] Interview in Kinshasa, August 2013.
[79] Interview in Kinshasa, August 2013.

motley crew of Kabila's adversaries was urged to quickly form a credible political platform to take over the state and govern in a more inclusive and responsible manner.

The Front made it clear that the rebellion should, at all costs, be prevented from being framed as a "Rwandan" insurgency against the nationalist Kabila—the formal political and military leadership should therefore be in the hands of non-Tutsis. Z'ahidi Ngoma and Lunda Bululu (who left Kinshasa only on August 7), the political coordinators of what would soon become known as the Rassemblement Congolais pour la Démocratie (RCD), hailed from Maniema and Katanga respectively. Similarly, the man who had announced the start of the uprising, Sylvain Mbuki, was a disgruntled Katangese officer who has been recruited by Rwanda's External Security Organization in previous months. By contrast, Bizima, Bugera and Moïse were, as the nation's most (in)famous Tutsis, asked to stay out of the spotlight.

However, despite the ESO's strenuous efforts, this ostensibly broad, cross-ethnic and cross-regional coalition was never really given the chance to become an autonomous Congolese force that was credible in the eyes of the population. Part of the reason for this was that the RCD leadership obviously appeared to be an ad hoc alliance of opportunists and the disgruntled who shared even less in ideological terms than the original AFDL comrades did. Part of the reason too was that the Tutsi exodus from Kinshasa and the high-profile defections of Bizima and Bugera in particular made it easy for the Kabila government to brand the insurgents as a fifth column for Tutsi interests. But, as we will see in the next chapter, undoubtedly the most important factor was that on the day that the RCD held its first meeting in Kigali—Tuesday, August 4—James Kabarebe did the unthinkable: not only did Rwanda plunge openly into the war, but Kabarebe personally commandeered four planes with 600 heavily armed RPA soldiers to try to take Kinshasa. The RCD rebellion had been orchestrated and choreographed by the RPF but now the public perception of its actions would inextricably become tied up with the simultaneous assault by Rwandan forces on Congo's capital region.

Conclusion: From Alliance Breakdown to Expulsion Order and Violent Conflict

One year after the overthrow of Mobutu, the AFDL was falling apart. The comrades grappled with what was to be done. The three main constituents of the alliance each put forward a different set of priorities. Mzee Kabila prioritized giving the revolution more nationalist cachet and acquiring political and military autonomy from the RPF. The Congolese Tutsi and other politicians and citizens from the east believed that the movement should first tackle the trickiest problem—the fiendish nationality question; resolving this Gordian know would be a great antidote to the poisonous politics of the region. The RPF, in turn, identified the continued presence of *génocidaire* forces, possibly tolerated or even encouraged by Kabila loyalists, as the overriding objective of the alliance. These different priorities were not necessarily incompatible. But addressing them required a degree of coordination, transparency and institutional constraints to ensure progress on one objective did not come at the expense of any other goal. With no coordinated policy response, however, each faction pursued its own objectives, reducing cooperation and increasing suspicion about each other's commitment to the collective liberation project. As internal politics became fractious, visionary political leadership could have gone a long way to addressing mutual fears, even at the last minute.

Instead the month of July 1998 would turn out to be the *Thermidor* of the AFDL revolution. The major coalition partners did not empathize with one another but developed a worsening obsession with their own diagnosis of the rot. This blinded them to how their knee-jerk reactions were perceived by their comrades.

As the events of July 1998 unfolded, Laurent-Désiré Kabila was increasingly consumed by a vortex of nationalism, paranoia and personal delusion that pushed him into a game of politico-military poker that he was extremely lucky to survive. While returning command of the FAC to Congolese hands and putting Congolese interests first were highly understandable goals, the way in which he went about pursuing these was disastrously—and unnecessarily—inflammatory. His steadfast Katangization of the regime, the cultivation of ties with ALiR at a time of an escalating insurgency in Rwanda, and his replacement of James Kabarebe as chief of staff with the utterly incompetent Célestin Kifwa pushed the RPF to pursue regime change. Kabila's privileging of his co-ethnics and close friends deprived him of alternative sources of information and exacerbated his paranoia. As one (Katangese) ANR intelligence officer, Jean-Marc, stated:

> The clan around Kabila, our people, did feed Mzee false information about coups and rebellions from the moment we came to power. [A case in point was] July 1998. The Rwandans were preparing all kinds of things. For example, James moved all the best guys to the east and reinforced all pro-Rwandese units. But our people,

like Kazadi and Numbi, definitely exaggerated and made the situation worse. Mzee ... was manipulated by them.[80]

Hemmed in by his own policies and the games played by his own aides, Kabila stood back against the wall. His expulsion order was a tactical master-stroke that helped protect his collapsing regime against a swift take-over from within, but exposed it to a devastating insurrection-cum-invasion.

The Congolese comrades critical of Kabila must also shoulder part of the blame for why the calamitous month of July 1998 gave way to an even more devastating August. Some of the AFDL's longest-serving revolutionaries were inevitably disappointed that the revolution did not immediately deliver on its grand promises. Moreover, they were frustrated by their own lack of political skills and experience, as this made it hard to survive and thrive in Kinshasa—a very different environment from the local politics of the Kivus or the diaspora circles they were familiar with. Others, by contrast, had long been consummate Kinshasa insiders who looked from the start at the AFDL for spoils—only to be vengeful when Kabila and the AFDL leadership did not serve them as they had hoped. But above all, key Banyamulenge figures and other eastern-ers failed to appreciate that most of the Kinois—or people living in Kasai, Equateur and Katanga—could not think of the nationality question as the country's top priority. Sorting out land and voting rights in the Kivus, as well as the local authority structures they were intimately linked to, mattered but was surely not the only *raison d'être* for the post-Mobutu order. The impa-tience of certain comrades in the AFDL with the constitutional process that Kabila had set in motion deepened divisions within the movement. The deci-sion by Moïse Nyarugabo, Azarias Ruberwa, Bizima Karaha and others to secretly begin organizing against Kabila within half a year after the formation of a new government undermined the very rule of law they claimed to yearn for. It also made it so much easier to recycle hateful jokes and anecdotes about Tutsi greed and Tutsi plotting. The flames of exclusionary nationalism would once again burn thousands of innocent Congolese citizens as the alliance imploded amid a free-for-all over political power.

Finally, the RPF's controversial political choices and unrelenting militarism provides the last piece of the explanation for why the road to war was chosen over a political solution to the challenges the AFDL faced. If the organization historically prided itself on vigorous internal debates in which the leadership would sometimes be checked and forced to reverse policies, then the Congo

---

[80] Name changed on the source's request; interview in Kinshasa, August 2013.

wars generated some intra-movement discussion but, ultimately, had limited consequences and reduced accountability at the very top. The Kagame–Kabarebe tandem used its advantages in terms of information and hard power to push the Front into highly uncompromising positions that made it seem like the RPF was not dealing with presumed comrades or friends, but rather with undeclared enemies. The RPF representatives in Congo handled the politics of their decision to stay on poorly and did little or nothing to empathize with Kabila or other regime factions; their pitiless prioritization of their own tactical (rather than strategic) security interests was exacerbated by the extensive assistance provided by Karegeya's ESO to renegade Congolese comrades in preparing a power grab. The RPF could not care less that the policies and individuals it sought to impose barely had any support among the majority of Congolese citizens. Kagame and Kabarebe did not attempt to de-escalate the security dilemma into which the AFDL fell; to the contrary, as it reached a crescendo with the expulsion order, they decided to pull the trigger and unleashed war.

Thus the responsibility for the violent explosion of the AFDL liberation project was shared between all protagonists who had formed the regime in May 1997. It was the outcome of the movement's non-existent institutions, an internalization of large-scale violence as a legitimate part of politics and abysmally managed differences in interests and perceptions. But the war that would soon become Africa's deadliest conflict ever would not remain a story of Kabila loyalists, eastern Congolese rebels and RPF military advisers alone—its devastating character was also the product of the collapse of the external elite bargain that the unraveling of the AFDL caused. In the next chapter, we thus tell the story of how the violence took on region-wide dimensions and how Angola's MPLA ended up as Kinshasa's kingmaker.

11

COMRADES GO TO WAR

TRIANGULAR DIPLOMACY BETWEEN KINSHASA, KIGALI AND LUANDA

Kagame was too inflexible with Kabila. If he had been more flexible, we could have handled the situation. If Kagame had looked to the region rather than himself ... it would be different.

Mario Placido Cirilo de Sa "Ita," chief of military intelligence of the Forças Armadas Angolanas.

When we went to Kitona, we thought Angola and Zimbabwe would not intervene. We were taken by surprise when they did.

James Kabarebe, former chief of staff of the Forces Armées Congolaises and commander of the Rwandan Patriotic Army troops invading Congo.

On the morning of Tuesday, August 4, Congolese soldiers at Kitona airbase in Bas Congo—about 400 kilometers southwest of Kinshasa—were astonished to see two civilian aircraft approach the runway, one almost directly after the other. There had been no radio contact between air traffic control and the pilots. As the planes touched down in short succession and began taxying, hundreds of Rwandan special forces jumped onto the tarmac and immediately took control of the airport, overwhelming the astonished Congolese regulars. The swift capture of the site's main buildings enabled two more aircraft to land with further Rwandan forces.[1] Hundreds of soldiers secured Kitona's huge arms depots; hardly any shots were fired. Three out of four planes, which had been hijacked the previous day in Goma and flown over 2,000 kilometers by Congolese pilots, returned to the east to pick up reinforcements and supplies (see Map 5).[2] Coordinating this extraordinary assault—a scaled up version of Israel's daring raid on Entebbe to liberate hostages on Ugandan soil in 1976— was none other than James Kabarebe, the humiliated—but not humbled— former chief of staff of the FAC and now in charge of the RPA offensive against Mzee Kabila. Kabarebe had personally commandeered the planes after moving into Goma with his crack troops the day before and compelled the 3,000 or so FAC troops present at Kitona to join the war effort. Within forty-eight hours of landing, Kabarebe's force swelled to five battalions, an army of 5,000 men. More would be airlifted to Bas Congo over the coming days— even as Kigali denied all accusations of the presence of RPA forces in Congo.[3]

The goal of the Kitona operation, as the plan worked out by Kagame and Kabarebe became known, was simple: prevent a drawn-out war that would give Mzee time to organize his forces and rally the Congolese nation around him—a sudden fatal blow to the heart of the Kabila regime to trigger its implosion. This was not just about firepower but about psychological warfare; in the words of James Kabarebe, the Kitona operation was intended to convince the troops defending the Congolese capital that resistance was futile: "We are so daring ... We can do anything to you."[4] The impending fall of Kinshasa would persuade other loyalist forces across the territory to cease fighting once they saw their cause was hopeless and a new regime had been installed. The insertion of two of the RPA's best battalions in the conflict was meant to swiftly clinch a decisive battlefield victory; the overriding objective was to create a *fait accompli*, both domestically and internationally. There would simply be no time for Kabila to respond militarily and enlist foreign support. Politically, the RPF gambled that it would be able to get away with its de facto invasion of Congo through denial of its involvement, the rapid

---

[1] Cooper, *Great Lakes Conflagration*, pp. 24–5.

[2] Howard French, "Pilot's Account Seems to Confirm Rwanda Role in Congo Strife," *New York Times*, August 10, 1998.

[3] For a one-sided RPF-colored account of the outbreak and the first days of the war see Charles Obyango-Obbo, "RPA Brings Kabila In; With UPDF Try Kicking Him Out," *The Monitor*, April 14, 2000; Charles Obyango-Obbo, "Daring RPA Raid in Congo, Angola; And a Heroic UPDF Unit," *The Monitor*, April 16, 2000.

[4] Interview in Kigali, April 2013.

transfer of power to a new Congolese government and a muted reaction from other African states—most of which had clearly expressed their disappointment in Kabila in previous weeks and months.

However, as we document and analyze below, Kagame and Kabarebe miscalculated the regional response to its gambit—nowhere more so than in Angola. The key to success in liberating Congo from Mobutu had been the alignment of regional forces in search of a new order in Africa's Great Lakes, stemming from the ideological and strategic worldview of the movements participating in the AFDL coalition. In August 1998, in its haste to strike back and overthrow Kabila, the RPF rejected any pretense of a regional coalition, believing it could unilaterally establish facts on the ground that would then be accommodated by its regional comrades. What the RPF miscalculated was not the regional disillusionment towards the Kabila regime—that was real—but the depth of mistrust and uncertainty that prevailed regarding its own intentions. Borne out of the way it built and controlled the first Pan-Africanist coalition and dominated the post-Mobutu order, when round two came, the Front discovered, to its astonishment, that it had fewer allies than Kabila.

Zimbabwe's ZANU-PF was the first to object to this stratagem and to rally behind Mzee, but the most crucial re-alignment would be the MPLA's decision to save Kabila. As we show, Luanda's last-minute intervention was the product of much hesitation on the Angolan side and was certainly not a foregone conclusion, as much of the extant literature claims. Both the Congolese government and Kigali extensively lobbied President Dos Santos to join their side, or at least stay neutral, but seemed unable to move him. However, when the MPLA finally resolved to intervene in Congo, after a long period of trepidation, it could hardly have been more consequential: as Angolan troops defeated James Kabarebe's advance force and stabilized western Congo, the pace of the war slowed and the battlefront moved east and south for three long years. Instead of a brief conflict that could have been concluded within weeks of its outbreak, the Great Lakes of Africa would be submerged in a killing spree responsible for the deaths of hundreds of thousands of people, whether through the barrel of the gun, hunger or disease. This chapter tells the story of that pivotal moment.

From the Kitona Blitzkrieg to Angolan Intervention

By opening a second front, far away from the east, in Kitona—an old Belgian air force base strategically located at the mouth of the Congo River and close

to the ports of Boma and Matadi from whence Kinshasa is supplied—
Rwandan Minister of Defense Paul Kagame and RPA commander James
Kabarebe exploited the latter's inside knowledge of the FAC which he had led
for a year. Kabarebe knew that many of the troops gathered in Kitona were
former soldiers of Mobutu's FAZ who were strongly opposed to Mzee's
Katangization policy. They had appreciated Kabarebe's plea in July 1998 for
some of their officers to be reintegrated into the FAC while maintaining their
FAZ ranks and did not need much prodding to join the assault on Kinshasa—
in the process providing Kabarebe not only with thousands of extra men but
also with a more clearly identifiable Congolese identity and with many light
tanks, machine guns and anti-aircraft equipment. Without delay, the RPA–
FAC force moved out of Kitona. One town after another quickly fell in Bas
Congo: Moanda and Banana on August 6, Boma on August 11, Mbanza-
Ngungu on August 16, almost putting them within striking distance (less than
150 kilometers) of Kinshasa. On August 13, Kabarebe and his troops had also
captured the port of Matadi and the Inga Dam on the Congo River, cutting
off the power supply to the capital. The power outage in Kinshasa had severe
humanitarian repercussions, but it also signaled the seemingly unstoppable
advance of the RPA and its Congolese rebel allies of the RCD on the seat of
political power.[5]

The simultaneous outbreak of war on two fronts—one in the east, where
the RCD mutineers made major gains in the Kivus, and one in the west,
where James Kabarebe was overrunning Bas Congo—stretched the forces
loyal to Kabila to such an extent that they were near breaking point. Mzee and
his advisers had expected the RPF's wrath to be merciless, but not with this
battle plan and not at this speed. On the evening of August 2, many of those
closest to the president had gathered at a house in Kinshasa in the residential
neighborhood of Ma Campagne for a Katangese social evening; among them
was Mwenze Kongolo who had flown with Didier Kazadi to Kigali days earlier and was convinced that a conflict was unlikely and certainly not imminent. According to Deborah, the lady hosting the dinner that night,[6] one by
one, the Katangese politicians and generals received phone calls alerting them
to the events in Goma and Bukavu. Within minutes, the boisterous atmosphere of the evening had morphed into panic, with ministers and their bodyguards frantically pursuing all possible information. The Mzee called a war
council the next day, but several of his ministers and high-ranking FAC offic-

---

[5] Lynne Duke, "War Nears Congo's Center of Power," *Washington Post*, August 14,
1998.

ers did not show up. The situation turned even bleaker when he heard of "disturbances" in Bas Congo and reports of Kinyarwanda-speaking commanders sending troops into battle. Kabila soon learned that James Kabarebe himself had returned to Congo to finish off the man he had made president. Nevertheless, amid the chaos and bad news, some successes were reported as well. After the mutiny on August 2, Kabila's greatest immediate concern had been a coup attempt or revolt inside the capital—he particularly feared the almost 600 Tutsi troops garrisoned in Camp Tshatshi in western Kinshasa under the leadership of Malick Kijege, the Banyamulenge officer who had been a fervent supporter of Mzee (to the point of keeping a photo of him in his wallet). As the president was desperately trying to assess which forces were still loyal to him and which were not, he instructed his aides to assemble all officers, disarmed. When Malick received this order at Camp Tshatshi, he refused, saying that he did not recognize the authority of the low-level commander Kabila had sent.[7] Mzee's forces responded immediately by attacking Malick's garrison, as they had long viewed these "rebels" with suspicion and felt they should be taught a lesson.[8] A gun battle ensued during which the Banyamulenge were initially able to stave off the assault, before deciding to try to fight their way out of the city as they saw no other option to survive. Moving southwards, neighborhood by neighborhood, they reached Kasangulu 40 kilometers southwest of Kinshasa a week later with their ranks severely depleted. Their extrication from the capital marked the cleansing of the city of enemy fighters by the Kabila government, which had by now resorted to the enlistment of volunteers, recruited through incessant nationalist and anti-Tutsi propaganda.[9]

Throughout Kinshasa, pogroms were organized against Kinyarwanda-speaking citizens, or simply those Congolese with a stereotypical "Rwandan morphology" (high cheekbones and hooked noses). Incendiary speeches echoed the metaphors used in 1994 in Rwanda, with officials like the president's chef-de-cabinet, Abdoulaye Yerodia, using extermination rhetoric as early as August 4 on Radio-Télévision National Congolaise, according to witnesses who testified to a Belgian investigative judge:

> The discourse was clear. He spoke of vermin that was to be eradicated methodically. Every time Yerodia was amidst the population of Kinshasa, he repeated the same

[6] Name changed at the request of the source; interview in Kinshasa, August 2013.

[7] Interview with Malick Kijege in Kinshasa, August 2013.

[8] Interview with Raus Chalwe in Kinshasa, August 2013.

[9] Reyntjens, *Great African War*, p. 198.

message. Yerodia spoke these words in a context without the slightest ambiguity. The vermin he referred to were the Tutsi, whether civilians or soldiers.[10]

As Stearns documents, there can be no doubt that this campaign was orchestrated from the top:

> Kabila addressed a march in downtown Kinshasa, where he whipped up the crowd against the Tutsi invaders ... 'They want to create a Tutsi empire,' the president announced ... Tshala Mwana, a famous singer and allegedly the president's mistress, led the parade dressed in white, tugging two goats on a leash with signs identifying them as Deo Bugera and Bizima Karaha.[11]

The goats later had their throats slit as the crowd roared.

Elsewhere in the country, too, an upsurge of patriotism mingling with anti-Tutsi fervor proved a mobilizing impetus that, for a moment, appeared capable of holding the combined forces of the RCD rebels and the RPA at bay. In Kisangani, the most strategic city of eastern Congo whose fall in March 1997 had spelled the end of Mobutu, a mutiny similar to the ones in Goma and Bukavu failed. Commanded by Tango Fort, the son of FAC Chief of Staff Célestin Kifwa, the 6,000-strong Groupe Spécial de Sécurité Présidentielle (GSSP, mostly composed of Kabila's Luba co-ethnics, trained in Kamina) helped secure not only Kinshasa but also crushed rebellious elements of the 25th Brigade at Kisangani airport and in the city; by August 10 the enemy had been routed.[12] Equateur, Bandundu, Kasai and Katanga also seemed to be safely in government hands, as did most of Maniema and Province Orientale.

The apparent stabilization of the conflict in the first week after the mutiny of the 10th Brigade was a dangerous illusion. Kagame and Kabarebe had anticipated that Kabila would incite the Congolese population, but this could not conceal the naked military reality that both the best Congolese units—the 10th and the 222nd Brigade—and the crack troops of the RPA were lined up against Mzee's barely functional army. The replacement of Kabarebe with Kifwa had not just led to a severe weakening of tactical skills at the apex of the armed forces, but together with the mutiny it had also contributed to the unraveling of much of the chain of command, communication systems and sheer firepower that the FAC needed.[13] Reinforcements scrambled to Bas

---

[10] Our translation of witness quoted in Arrondissement de Bruxelles Tribunal De Premiere Instance, "Pro Justicia: Mandat D'Arret International Par Defaut," Dossier 40/99, April 11, 2000, p. 7.

[11] Stearns, *Dancing in the Glory of Monsters*, p. 193.

[12] Interview with a GSSP officer in Kisangani; interview in Kinshasa, August 2013.

[13] Interview with Faustin Munene in Kinshasa, December 2009.

Congo, Province Orientale and the Kivus to push back the enemy, but as the days passed the counter-offensive revealed itself as a complete failure. Bukavu and Uvira remained in rebel hands, Bunia fell to them too on August 12. By August 16, the strategic towns of Walikale and Lubuto were wrested from government forces, as was Kabila's old *maquis* of Baraka. A week later, GSSP resistance in Kisangani collapsed and RCD soldiers marched into northern Katanga. Eastern Congo was now lost.

One factor co-constituting the unmistakable writing on the wall was the increasing involvement of Uganda in Africa's Great War. Similar to the campaign against Mobutu, the brunt of the offensive was born by the RPA and its Congolese auxiliary forces, but Ugandan President Yoweri Museveni had green-lighted a bigger UPDF footprint in the second war. In the interpretation of Kabarebe, who after the expulsion order had gone to see Museveni in northern Uganda, this was because the NRM was critical of the way the RPF had handled the AFDL; it considered itself irreplaceable to ensure this second war was more successful politically: "Uganda wanted to make a statement, that's why they joined the war. They wanted to compensate for missing out on the first war."[14] This was confirmed by UPDF Chief of Staff Jeje Odongo and by Okwiri Rabwoni, the Ugandan intelligence liaison with the AFDL who had served as an officer in the RPA. Both agreed that Museveni had come to the same diagnosis as Kagame with regard to Mzee—"We found common ground on Kabila's erratic nature and unreliability; Kampala came around to seeing Kabila like the Rwandese did."[15] He appeared keen to assume a bigger role in another "Congolese adventure,"[16] but one that he could steer more directly, rather than allowing the Rwandan youngsters to handle the conflict in overly martial ways. The difference between the RPF and NRM revolved around how to achieve the ultimate objective, not what that objective was, according to the Ugandan Minister of Security Wilson Muruuli Mukasa. Museveni was equally determined to rid the region of the "crazy Kabila": "If Kabila has chosen to behave like Mobutu, what do we do? He must go!"[17]

Initially, Museveni had to contend with resistance inside the UPDF and his security services, where there was less enthusiasm for intervening in Congo. One of these skeptics was ESO chief David Pulkol: "We found ourselves in an

---

[14] Interview in Kigali, April 2013.
[15] Interview in Kampala with Okwiri Rabwoni, March 2013.
[16] Interview in Kampala with Jeje Odongo, April 2013.
[17] Interview in Kampala, March 2013.

uncomfortable situation created by Rwanda and Kabila."[18] And according to one senior military intelligence officer, Muruga,[19] Uganda risked falling into a quagmire; the close personal relationship between Museveni and "his Rwandan boys" prevented a more dispassionate appraisal of Kampala's interests: "When they need our help, they come crying. When they are in a good place, they don't want us around." Despite these protestations, Museveni pushed on with his Congo agenda of supporting the RPF and its allies—he had after all been part and parcel of the plot prior to July 28, 1998, to bring about regime change from within and saw no reason to change this policy after Kabila's expulsion order, quite the contrary.[20]

UPDF troops had already been active in Province Orientale prior to the outbreak of war on August 2 (see previous chapter), and owing to their direct assistance to the RCD rebels, the whole sub-region, despite its formidable, expansive terrain, would be brought under the control of the anti-Kabila forces within a month. Kampala also provided some artillery and equipment to the initial contingent Kabarebe took to Bas Congo, as well as sending in a small team of special forces as the fighting intensified there. While we were unable to confirm Tom Cooper and Gérard Prunier's assertions[21] that a large battalion of Ugandan infantry joined the raid on Kitona (top Rwandan and Ugandan sources, including Kabarebe and Odongo, explicitly deny this and claim the UPDF contingent sent to Bas Congo was company sized, or around 100 effectives),[22] there can be little doubt that widely circulating rumors that Museveni was about to openly commit even more troops and break through the last FAC defenses exacted a high psychological toll. Increasingly, there seemed to be no way out, no matter how defiant the bulletins filled with nationalist propaganda disseminated from Kinshasa.[23] Mzee knew that the

---

[18] Interview in Kampala, March 2013. Pulkol's reluctance meant Museveni largely sidelined the ESO and kept him in the dark about Uganda's clandestine support for the Rwandan offensive in the first weeks of the war.

[19] Name changed at the source's request; interview in Kampala, March 2013.

[20] Interview with "Muruga" (name changed) in Kampala, March 2013; interview with Mbusa Nyamwisi in Kinshasa, December 2009; interview with David Pulkol in Kampala, March 2013.

[21] Cooper, *Great Lakes Conflagration*, p. 25; Prunier, *From Genocide to Continental War*, p. 420.

[22] Interviews in Kigali and Kampala respectively, April 2013.

[23] Stephen Smith, "Les dix jours de la bataille de l'Ouest. Ou comment le commandant James a plongé la capitale dans le noir," *Libération*, August 15, 1998.

loss of the east and the fall of Inga Dam in the west were just one step short of total, irrevocable defeat.

To ensure the safety of himself and his main cabinet members and to prepare a possible final stand in Katanga, Mzee secretly flew from Kinshasa to Lubumbashi on Wednesday, August 12, the day before electricity to the capital was cut for the first time.[24] Panicked, he recalled Kifwa as FAC Chief of Staff and instead appointed his son Joseph who had rushed back from China and was now tasked with stopping his former mentor Kabarebe from achieving complete victory. Father and son Kabila entrusted the immediate defense of Kinshasa to Minister of Justice Mwenze Kongolo and Vice-Minister of the Interior Faustin Munene; Mzee relentlessly implored self-defense units to rise up.[25] However, with Kabarebe's force advancing at a pace of 25–30 kilometers a day, this was a desperate move reminiscent of Mobutu who kept insisting that non-existent DSP units and the Congolese people would come to his rescue at the last minute. After the capture of Mbanza-Ngungu on August 16, only three long marches separated the RPA from the ultimate prize. Kabarebe divided his army into two for the final assault: one battalion focused on capturing N'Djili Airport, while other units were to cut off possible escape routes into Bas Congo. In previous days, he had urged Kigali to send more Rwandan reinforcements because of the unreliability of his Congolese soldiers, but unable to wait for more high-quality troops he now threw his men forward, entering the final radius of 100 kilometers around Kinshasa at Kisantu.[26] Kabarebe stood poised to again oust a sitting Congolese regime with another stunning victory.

At the very last minute, however, Angolan fighter jets and Zimbabwean helicopters struck Kabarebe's army on August 21–22, 1998 (see Map 5). Rwandan advance forces had already infiltrated the areas southwest of N'Djili and battled Zimbabwean infantry flown in to defend Kabila on August 19, but the aerial bombardments smashed their frontline offensive and rear guard. Moreover, an Angolan mechanized brigade and several commando units poured across the border from Cabinda engaging RPA and Congolese rebel forces throughout Bas Congo, including in Kitona, Moambe and Kasangulu. Any Angolan intervention promised to decisively reconfigure the balance of power,[27] but how it

---

[24] Interview with Faustin Munene in Kinshasa, December 2009.

[25] Martens, *Kabila et la révolution congolaise*, vol. 1, pp. 385–7.

[26] Interview with James Kabarebe in Kigali, April 2013.

[27] Stephen Smith, "L'Angola entre dans la bataille du Congo: Les troupes angolaises ont pris à revers les rebelles anti-Kabila," *Libération*, August 24, 1998.

altered the course of the war was exactly the opposite of what the RPF had expected. Kabarebe could not believe what he was seeing, nor could the High Command back in Kigali.[28] In the words of Caesar Kayizari, one of the RPA's most senior officers:

> When Angolan tanks rolled into Congo from Cabinda, our troops were cheering. Our battalion thought they were coming to helps us. When they shot at us and bombed us, we tried to point out that they had made a mistake and that Kabila's forces were on the other side. Our soldiers thought the MPLA was on our side. So did we as generals. Angola betrayed the deal we had ...[29]

Luanda had finally entered the conflict, a decisive moment in Africa's Great War. But why did it choose to save Laurent-Désiré Kabila, the Congolese president who had expelled the Angolan forces from his country weeks after liberation in May 1997 and who was distrusted by José Eduardo Dos Santos? How did the MPLA turn its back on the RPF, with whom it had ousted Mobutu? In sum, what can account for Luanda's decision to throw its Forças Armadas Angolanas (FAA) into the biggest foreign operation in its history and thereby considerably raise the stakes of an already lethal war?

The Shadow of the Angolan Civil War

As we saw in Chapter 4, the Angolan civil war was one of Africa's longest running and most brutal conflicts, pitting the MPLA against the rebels of UNITA. Neither the Cold War nor the liberation struggle in South Africa caused the conflict, but both fueled the belligerence, as Havana, Moscow, Pretoria and Washington armed their proxies. The fall of the Berlin Wall and the end of Apartheid led to peace talks and a formal de-internationalization of the war (the pullout of all foreign forces from the conflict theater) but neither side trusted the other. Tens of thousands of people perished after the resumption of hostilities in 1992, until the 1994 Lusaka Protocol froze the conflict for four years; MPLA leader and Angolan President Dos Santos and UNITA chief Jonas Savimbi were supposed to share power in a transitional cabinet, but both parties used the lull in fighting to rearm and position themselves for the next round of battle.[30] The MPLA joined the AFDL regional coalition with around 3,500

---

[28] Interview with Frank Mugambage in Kampala, March 2013; interview with Karake Karenzi in London, November 2014; interview with Emmanuel Ndahiro in Kigali, December 2014.

[29] Interview in Kigali, April 2013.

[30] Christine Messiant, Brigitte Lachartre and Michel Cahen, *L'Angola postcolonial*, Paris: Karthala, 2008, pp. 216–47.

soldiers and heavy artillery to destroy the UNITA rear bases in Zaire used for diamond trafficking from Angola's Cuango Valley and arms smuggling.[31] Whereas actual fighting between the FAA and UNITA on Zairean territory was rare—it was the RPA which broke through Mobutu's final lines of defense, including a company of UNITA soldiers—there could be no doubt that installing a pro-MPLA incumbent in Kinshasa was vital to the ruling party's interests. This would deprive Savimbi of his prime supply routes and his longest-standing ally. According to one senior Angolan officer: "We needed a strong government to control everything inside Zaire."[32]

The consolidation of the post-Mobutu order proved deeply disappointing for Angola. Its attempt at obtaining the Tigres Katangais a prominent position in the new government and army failed miserably with the arrest of Delphin Muland and other Tigres officers in Lubumbashi; the Rwandan–Angolan "cold war" following the Tshikapa incident further locked in the interdependence between the RPF and Kabila, at the expense of Angola. These setbacks abridged whatever influence Luanda hoped to project, but no other immediate options presented themselves. According to General Ita, head of Angola's Military Intelligence:

> Our contradiction started close to Kinshasa: Rwanda wanted to control the country. But we had an understanding that we [both Rwanda and Angola] would not stay in Kinshasa. Kabila asked us to leave but Rwanda imposed their will to stay in Congo ... [He] disillusioned us very quickly, but it was all we had. But what could we do? There was no alternative.[33]

At least Kabila, as Mobutu's nemesis, seemed unlikely to develop any kind of relationship with UNITA, and hence the expectation was that while Congolese–Angolan relations might not become cordial, they would at least be normal and non-hostile.

In the weeks and months after the fall of Mobutu, the MPLA kept its gaze firmly fixed on additional ways of undercutting UNITA, according to Carlos Feijó, Dos Santos's chief legal adviser. The coalition government arrangement was dysfunctional before it was even launched and the cease-fire had merely been a signal for the two sides to put each other on the defensive through other channels.[34] One track to destabilize UNITA emerged from improved relations

[31] James Rupert, "Zaire Reportedly Selling Arms to Angolan Rebels," *Washington Post*, March 21, 1997.

[32] Name withheld at the source's request; interview in Luanda, March 2014.

[33] Interview in Luanda, May 2014.

[34] Interview in Luanda, February 2014.

between the MPLA and Washington.[35] This in turn opened the door to tough UN Security Council action in the form of two resolutions, unanimously adopted, which laid the blame for the faltering peace process squarely on the rebels. Resolution 1127, adopted under Chapter VII of the UN Charter in August 1997, severely restricted the ability of UNITA officials and their families to travel internationally and instituted a no-fly zone over UNITA-held territory. Resolution 1173, also under Chapter VII, tightened the arms embargo on UNITA and instructed member states to freeze UNITA assets as well as to crack down on the export of diamonds from UNITA-controlled areas (mostly near the border with Congo's Bandundu and Kasai provinces).

A second route through which the MPLA sought to weaken its archenemy was via military intervention in Congo-Brazzaville. Since 1992, the Republic of Congo had been led by a former university professor, Pascal Lissouba, but he had struggled to implement promised economic reforms that would deal with the country's debt and a renegotiation of its oil concessions. Lissouba never managed to pacify the streets, where protests and ethno-political violence tarnished his legitimacy and ability to rule. He also clashed with the French petroleum giant Elf (state-owned but later privatized), which towered over economic life in Congo-Brazzaville. Not only did this poison relations with Paris, but Lissouba was ultimately forced to go back cap in hand to Elf for advance payments in exchange for further commercial advantages for the firm. Meanwhile, Elf—and Paris—also funded Lissouba's main rivals.[36] Because of these setbacks, the weakened president turned to two different constituencies in his search for cash and friends: Congolese Tutsi exiles with business connections who had fled the chaos of Zaire in the early 1990s and two Angolan rebel movements—UNITA and the Frente para a Libertação do Enclave de Cabinda (FLEC), which fought for the secession of Angola's oil-producing enclave, Cabinda. While his predecessor as president and rival Denis Sassou-Nguesso had long maintained close ties with the MPLA, Lissouba reactivated his old contacts in FLEC and UNITA, less to dabble in Angolan politics than to garner financial support in the deteriorating electoral climate of 1996–7.[37] But this was not how Dos Santos saw it.

[35] Human Rights Watch, *Angola Unravels: The Rise and Fall of the Lusaka Peace Process*, New York: Human Rights Watch, 1999, pp. 279–80.

[36] Ricardo Soares de Oliveira, *Oil and Politics in the Gulf of Guinea*, New York: Columbia University Press, 2007, pp. 257–8.

[37] Prunier, *From Genocide to Continental War*, pp. 167–8.

When Lissouba sent soldiers to arrest Sassou-Nguesso on June 5, 1997, in his private residence on the pretext of maintaining a parallel army (the infamous Cobras), a civil war erupted during which the Angola-backed Cobras battled the pro-government (and Israeli-trained) Cocoye and Ninja militias.[38] The fighting ravaged urban areas, killed thousands of civilians and displaced about 25 per cent of the country's population as the north was controlled by Sassou-Nguesso and the south by Lissouba.[39] Both sides desperately tried to enlist whatever internal and external assistance they could get their hands on.[40] When Lissouba asked Kabila, recently inaugurated as president in Kinshasa, for help, suggesting his rival had recruited from Mobutu's ex-FAZ, Mzee responded by allowing 600 *kadogo* to cross the Congo River to Brazzaville. In response, Sassou-Nguesso turned to one of Kabila's enemies, the remnants of the FAR, who had sought safety in the Republic of Congo after being chased from the Kivu refugee camps. According to a Rwandan Hutu:

> Informed of the presence of well-trained soldiers among the Rwandan refugees on Congolese soil, Sassou-Nguesso wasted no time sending messengers to wherever we were in the effort to recruit men who had been in the FAR and other volunteers to go fight alongside the Cobra. Without hesitation, many of our former soldiers enlisted in Sassou's army and, every week, boatloads of recruits floated down the river carrying the new recruits to Brazzaville.[41]

Lissouba then struck back by relying on UNITA trainers and weapons experts to bolster his forces. Even if we found no evidence to substantiate one scholar's assertion that the RPF also got involved,[42] this regional proxy war

---

[38] The "Cocoye" militia was trained from 1994 onwards by Israeli advisers of the Lordon–Levdan company who left on the eve of war. Also known as the "Aubevillois" or "Zoulous," the militia was subsequently instructed by a French mercenary contingent and an American major. This force called itself "companies of commandos of intervention" (COCOI, or "Cocoye" in Brazzaville vernacular). South African Executive Outcomes, which offered ex-Apartheid officers and commandos for hire, reportedly provided bodyguards for Lissouba. See Chapter 3 of Brian Wood and Johan Peleman, *The Arms Fixers: Controlling the Brokers and Shipping Agents*, Oslo: International Peace Research Institute, 1999.

[39] Amnesty International, *Republic of Congo: An Old Generation of Leaders in New Carnage*, London: Amnesty International, 1999.

[40] Martine-Renée Galloy and Marc-Eric Gruenais, "Au Congo, le pouvoir par les armes," *Le monde diplomatique*, November 1997.

[41] Pierre-Claver Ndacyayisenga, *Dying to Live: A Rwandan Family's Five-Year Flight across the Congo*, Montréal: Baraka Books, 2012, p. 136.

[42] Prunier, *From Genocide to Continental War*, p. 170.

clearly risked spiraling out of control. UNITA's involvement was a red line for the MPLA in Luanda: direct intervention now became inevitable.

On October 11 and 12, President Dos Santos ordered his air force to commence an aerial bombardment of Ninja and Cocoye positions across the Republic of Congo, as well as committing 1,000 battle-hardened soldiers under the command of FAA Chief of Staff João de Matos to take the coastal stronghold of Pointe Noire and cleanse Lissouba loyalists from Brazzaville.[43] The intervention was brief but met all its objectives. By October 24, Sassou-Nguesso had been restored to the presidency he had been forced to give up five years earlier; his continued loyalty to Luanda was ensured by the watchful eye the FAA garrison in Cabinda kept on Brazzaville and by the mutual commercial interests the Sassou-Nguesso family held in Angola and the MPLA controlled in the Republic of Congo. UNITA lost its last regional patron, a significant setback. Moreover, a wider escalation of this proxy war—from which the rebels would surely have benefited—had been averted by the FAA's decisive action.

The substantial blows the MPLA dealt UNITA through UN resolutions and the substitution of Sassou-Nguesso for Lissouba tilted the balance of forces in the ruling party's favor. However, the wounds inflicted were not mortal and UNITA remained a potent military threat, able to use its clandestine networks in the Gulf of Guinea to maintain an annual revenue stream of hundreds of millions of dollars. Despite the official cease-fire decreed by the Lusaka Protocol, throughout 1997 violations of the agreement occurred, including the razing to the ground of a village of 150 people by UNITA troops in Lunda Norte, home to the diamond mining hotspots and bordering Congo.[44] In July 1997 alone, the UN reported 120 flights dropping off supplies at UNITA airstrips across Angola.[45] Under international pressure, Dos Santos and Savimbi concluded a deal in January 1998 to implement the Protocol's outstanding provisions but little on-the-ground progress ensued. Following the latest round of UN sanctions in June 1998—meant to coerce the rebels into concessions—UNITA officers moved from Luanda back to their stronghold in Bailundo in Central Angola. The clouds of war were gathering again.

---

[43] Howard W. French, "Rebels, Backed by Angola, Take Brazzaville and Oil Port," *New York Times*, October 16, 1997

[44] Human Rights Watch, *Angola Unravels*, pp. 23–4.

[45] UN Security Council, "Progress Report of the Secretary General on the United Nations Observer Mission in Angola (MONUA)," S/1997/640, August 13, 1997, p. 4.

At least 20,000 Angolan refugees crossed the border into Katanga in early July 1998; renewed fighting in Moxico province and elsewhere along the frontier with Congo between the FAA and UNITA would displace tens of thousands more. The MPLA became increasingly worried that, despite its strategy of isolating UNITA regionally and despite ostensible demobilization, the military firepower of the insurgents remained intact:

UNITA's force structure of battalions, columns, special forces platoons, motorized anti-aircraft sub-units and engineer platoons still existed, and were distributed with 9000 men in the north, 11000 in the east, 11000 in central Angola and 4000 in the south. Fresh weapons and ammunition were said to be reaching UNITA from Bulgaria through Mozambique and Congo-Brazzaville.[46]

UNITA had for years been a formidable force, stronger than the standing armies of almost all African states. It could deploy more than 50,000 men, thousands of tons of heavy artillery, excellent technicians and BMP-2 tanks and tank-killer battalions which the FAA feared greatly. Intelligence reports indicated the formation of a potent new mechanized brigade in 1998 by UNITA,[47] a tactical advantage perhaps only offset by the FAA's superior airpower. By the admission of General Ita, "In 1998 the internal situation in Angola was very bad. Very bad."[48] The MPLA and FAA leadership obsessed over when full-scale war would resume. Nothing was to detract from this singular focus.

Triangular Diplomacy

It is against this background of high tension about an impending return to war and a UNITA comeback that the MPLA's reaction to the events in Congo in July and August 1998 must be understood. The MPLA had no priorities beyond preventing Kinshasa from once again supporting its mortal enemy or allowing it to use Congolese territory for its funding and military operations, according to Carlos Feijó;[49] whatever arguments Kabila, the RPF and other protagonists presented, the litmus test would be how they affected the balance of forces inside Angola. When the 10th Brigade rebelled on August 2, 1998, the question for Dos Santos and his advisers was not that of governance in

---

[46] Anthony Clayton, *Frontiersmen: Warfare in Africa since 1950*, London: UCL Press, 1999, p. 150.

[47] Name withheld at the source's request; interview in Luanda, March 2014.

[48] Interview in Luanda, May 2014.

[49] Interview in Luanda, February 2014.

Congo, insecurity in the east or the state of the Congolese mining sector. Rather, it was what a victory of the RCD insurgents and their Rwandan allies would mean for the next chapter of the Angolan civil war.

Angolan Weariness

From the perspective of the MPLA, both the Kabila camp and that of his comrades-turned-foes were deeply flawed prospective partners. Dos Santos certainly did not trust Mzee. He had watched with astonishment how the latter had neutralized "General" Muland of the Tigres Katangais on a flimsy pretext even before becoming president; this was a blow to Angolan aspirations of exerting influence in post-Mobutu Kinshasa through the Katangese officers who had served for years in the Angolan civil war and had battled Mobutu during the Shaba wars of the late 1970s. Furthermore, Kabila's personal contacts with Luanda had failed to impress. Starting with his first visit to Angola as AFDL's spokesman in early 1997, when Dos Santos's confidant for security affairs—General Manuel Helder Vieira Dias Júnior "Kopelipa"—met Mzee, Mwenze Kongolo and Victor Mpoyo, the reports Kopalipa forwarded to Dos Santos were disparaging. These misgivings were only further reinforced by what Angola's ally, Cuba, had to say about the Congolese rebel. Che Guevara's literary ruminations on the catastrophic failure to launch a serious campaign in the South Kivu *maquis* and the inadequacy of Kabila as a revolutionary leader were well known, and other Cuban intelligence sources did not think highly of Mzee either.[50] Kabila had always maintained contacts with (would-be) revolutionaries around the world—Belgian communists, Qaddafi's security services, North Korean diplomats and Congolese Cubans— yet his enduring admiration for Havana notwithstanding, this did not translate into a reciprocal embrace by Cuban officials.

These apprehensions had not stopped Dos Santos from backing the AFDL offensive against Mobutu—a figure so hated that his removal could only be perceived as a victory by the MPLA—but Luanda was keen for other leaders in the alliance to emerge. When that did not happen and, to the contrary, Kabila further consolidated power and asked the MPLA, by sending his trusted adviser Pierre-Victor Mpoyo to Luanda, to leave Congo (the first "expulsion order," see Chapter 7), the Angolan government appeared to write off Mzee altogether. His support for Lissouba in Congo-Brazzaville and his

[50] Interview in Luanda with a senior Angolan intelligence source, May 2014.

marginalization of the Tigres Katangais (who bolstered the new army's numbers but barely featured in the senior officer corps) rendered them deeply pessimistic. Given the bleak odds, the MPLA thus endeavored to develop normal relations with Congo and to dissuade Kabila from developing ties with UNITA, even if nothing else could be agreed upon. The chief of Angola's external intelligence, Fernando Miala, kept a wary eye on Kinshasa and consulted frequently with his regional counterparts with regard to Kabila.[51]

If relations with the Mzee were effectively frozen and the MPLA warned Kinshasa that it would not tolerate any engagement with the UNITA or FLEC rebels after Kabila's initial assistance to Lissouba, Luanda's ties with Kigali were not much better. As noted earlier, the Atlantic Africa and Southern Africa of the MPLA differed strongly from the East Africa that was the habitat of the RPF. The RPF and MPLA hardly knew each other, having emerged as political forces in differing contexts: the latter as a faction of urbanized and detribalized elites that captured state power as the Portuguese Empire unraveled in 1974 and was profoundly molded by its extensive involvement in the Cold War's main African battlefront;[52] the former as a Spartan phalanx of refugees who first helped oust the regime of Obote and Okello in Uganda and then overthrew the Mobutu-supported Rwandan government in the midst of genocide. Both shared a rhetorical commitment to Pan-Africanism and a skepticism of the Western-led international system, but the MPLA's main sources of foreign influence were Castro's Cuba and the

---

[51] Name withheld at the request of the source, who was a senior intelligence officer at the time; interview in Luanda, February 2014.

[52] Soares de Oliveira succinctly summarizes the MPLA's worldview and social base: "The MPLA sees the cultural and political convergence of 'Angola' as a work in progress. Some parts of the country and society represent 'Angola' more than others. Luanda and the long-colonized areas that enjoy privileged access to the outside world constitute the pinnacle of both what is 'modern' and 'national' and the historical 'Angolan' culture favoured by the MPLA. This is undergirded by an unstated standard of civilization whereby some Angolans, by their Portuguese language proficiency and 'cosmopolitan' deportment, hold a higher status, while others whose behavior and culture are, in one word, more 'African' are deemed to be backward and of lesser social import ... Viewing itself as the only movement whose nation-building aspirations transcend exclusionary (that is, ethno-regional and racial) boundaries, the MPLA has a 'visceral belief' in its own legitimacy to guide Angola into the modern world." Ricardo Soares de Oliveira, *Magnificent and Beggar Land: Angola since the Civil War*, London: Hurst, 2015, pp. 18–19.

Soviet Union, while the RPF grew up under the mentorship of Museveni. From the onset of the AFDL adventure in 1996, these divergent historical, sociological and geopolitical experiences combined with the ad hoc and informal organization of the regional campaign undermined the cohesion of the Pan-Africanist alliance. The Tshikapa incident of April 1997—when a stand-off between James Kabarebe and the Angola-backed Tigres almost derailed the coalition—was a function of the comrades' different interests, but also of the absence of practically any mechanisms to coordinate their joint campaign to overthrow Mobutu. The lack of information-sharing merely exacerbated the discord between two allies that did not fully understand each other.

As the MPLA saw it, the RPF was complicit in Kabila's power grab, as it had done nothing to temper his growing authoritarianism as the campaign progressed, whether his self-proclamation as president in Lubumbashi or his denigrating treatment of the Tigres. According to Miguel Neto, Dos Santos's roving ambassador in the Great Lakes, "We cooperated with the RPF until the day we removed Mobutu, then all of the cooperation ceased."[53] Angolan military officers recognized that James Kabarebe was a formidable soldier and that the RPA troops he commanded were qualitatively different from most of the African forces they had encountered in the past. Simultaneously, however, Kabarebe also embodied much of what seemed dangerously wrong with the RPF: the brazen young *afande* substituted arrogance and audacity for experience, behaving with a seeming lack of respect for the more senior Angolan leadership, which had battled the army of Apartheid South Africa for years. Kabarebe and the RPF exuded a sense of entitlement, misplaced confidence and disregard for the fundamental interests of their comrades, according to Angolan Minister of Defense Pedro Sebastião;[54] their attitude of wanting the first and the last word on every issue in the Pan-Africanist coalition generated major tensions, both before and after the fall of Kinshasa.

During the 1997 war in Congo-Brazzaville, Luanda had no qualms about letting its client Denis Sassou-Nguesso recruit hundreds of ex-FAR soldiers into his Cobra militia. The MPLA knew how much the RPF hated these fighters but made it clear to Kigali that Sassou-Nguesso's victory was a non-negotiable outcome for them and that they would do what it took, with whom it could find, to achieve this. It is important to highlight that the Brazzaville conflict began at the same time that Kabila asked the FAA to leave

[53] Interview in London, October 2014.
[54] Interview in Luanda, May 2014.

Congo without delay, allegedly with Rwandan encouragement. The RPF denied these accusations, but the links between the Angolan "expulsion" by the AFDL, the recruitment of the FAR into the Cobras and frosty relations between the Front and the MPLA were obvious. As admitted by Jack Nziza, who on behalf of Rwanda's Department of Military Intelligence spent months in Kisangani alongside FAA artillery and intelligence officers during the campaign: "By the time the Angolans left, they were very negative towards us."[55]

However, as in the case of Kabila, the MPLA was determined not to let its disappointment and frustration with the RPF lead to a complete breakdown in relations. Mobutu's downfall remained an undeniable accomplishment: the number of flights landing at UNITA airstrips from Congo dropped off spectacularly, from more than 100 per month when Mobutu was still in charge to around forty by January–February 1998,[56] with the resupplying of arms now increasingly emanating from criminal networks in South Africa, Zambia and Eastern Europe. There was still much to gain from trying to cooperate.[57] Thus, as Angolan hard muscle brought the civil war in Brazzaville to an end in October 1997, the MPLA exerted some pressure on Sassou-Nguesso to rid himself of the ex-FAR soldiers in his forces and to re-engage the AFDL in Kinshasa. Despite the presence of its archenemies in Brazzaville, the RPF had exercised restraint and had not waded into the conflict; Luanda implicitly recognized this and did not want the Republic of Congo to become a rear base for *génocidaire* forces launching attacks on Kinshasa and the RPA garrison there either. Rwandan and Angolan politicians occasionally still met and intelligence ties endured between the leading figures in both countries: Patrick Karegeya remained in close contact with Fernando Miala—the two had been important background orchestrators of the AFDL campaign—which led to valuable information swaps on the security situation in Congo.

Courtship and Distrust in August 1998

In light of the complex relationships the MPLA had with its erstwhile comrades, since late 1997 Angolan intelligence had been monitoring the rising

---

[55] Interview in Kigali, July 2014.
[56] UN Security Council, "Progress Report of the Secretary General on the United Nations Observer Mission in Angola (MONUA)," S/1998/238, March 13, 1998, p. 4.
[57] Interview with General Ita in Luanda, May 2014.

tensions between Kabila, several of the AFDL's main constituencies and the RPF, but it had not sought to directly take advantage of the widening rift and woo any one party: Dos Santos distrusted the Congolese and Rwandan protagonists too much to do so and believed that more benefits would accrue from keeping the lines of communication open with all sides. That the interdependence between Kabila and the RPF at the heart of the alliance had unraveled dawned more rapidly on the MPLA than on most international diplomats and intelligence services, but the frantic pace and violent escalation of the Kinshasa endgame in late July and early August 1998 surprised Luanda too. Fernando Miala listened to Patrick Karegeya's diatribes about Kabila's betrayal and it had been via Luanda that Mzee had traveled to and from Cuba, but the details of the expulsion order by Kabila and the extent of Karegeya's "Plan A" and "Plan B" remained a mystery to the MPLA.[58]

Hence after the mutiny of August 2 and the Kitona raid of August 4, neither Dos Santos nor his top advisers saw much advantage in prematurely declaring allegiance to one of the belligerents. As noted earlier, most existing scholarship treats the Angolan decision to intervene on the side of Laurent-Désiré Kabila as a foregone conclusion and skims over the behind the scenes diplomacy and the Angolan calculus in coolly responding to the arguments of both parties. Not only was an eventual alignment with either side likely to be tactical rather than strategic in light of the general distrust of Angola's elite vis-à-vis both parties, but a wait-and-see approach was deemed necessary to assess the geopolitical implications of the alliance's collapse, not least on UNITA's position. While Uganda and Zimbabwe quickly let it be known where they laid blame for the conflict, the MPLA, which controlled the strongest military force in Central Africa, opted for silence. This triggered a round of shuttle diplomacy as Kabila and the RPF made overtures to Luanda to back its side.

The first to reach out to the MPLA were Mzee's aides. Kabila tasked three trusted envoys to seek Angolan security guarantees for his beleaguered regime: national security adviser Didier Kazadi, deputy chef-de-cabinet, Godefroid Tchamlesso (who lived in Cuba for more than twenty-five years and had been the Havana trip's main organizer) and diplomatic counselor Irung Awan (formerly with the Tigres in Angola for almost two decades). They began their mission right after the expulsion order of July 28; Kazadi, Tchamlesso and

---

[58] Interviews in Luanda with numerous high-ranking security officials in February and May 2014.

Awan explained the fallout with the RPF to Luanda and proposed a partnership between the AFDL and the MPLA, including mutual assistance in security matters.[59] Mzee had taken the tremendous risk of ordering the RPA out of Congo without any formal promises of foreign allies—which made it a quasi-suicidal wager—and was now urgently trying to protect himself against the possibility of an onslaught from within and from without.[60] The MPLA, however, did not budge, even after the raid on Kitona, which put RPA crack troops and rebels in the strategic Angolan backyard of Bas Congo. According to one of Angola's most senior diplomats, the reason was not that Luanda failed to appreciate the severity of the situation, but that it continued to be suspicious of Kabila; the MPLA leadership was convinced he might be talking to UNITA about assistance as well: "He had a habit of making different arrangements with different people about the same issues."[61]

As Kabila struggled to make progress with the MPLA, the RPF placed its bet on Kabarebe swiftly vanquishing the enemy. The hope was to hide its involvement in the regime change campaign against Mzee and to create a *fait accompli*, inviting others to build a more stable regional order with the Front from a position of great strength.[62] Despite the diplomatic offensive of Kinshasa, not just towards Angola but also vis-à-vis Brazzaville, Pretoria, Windhoek and Harare, Kagame remained skeptical of engaging in such politicking himself; he was under little illusion regarding his regime's popularity in the Great Lakes of Africa, particularly because Ethiopia and Eritrea—besides Uganda, the RPF's best friends in Africa—could not be counted on owing to the war they were fighting against each other. Kigali initially contented itself in having Patrick Karegeya, Patrick Mazimhaka and Emmanuel Ndahiro provide limited intelligence briefs to interlocutors from Zambia, South Africa, Zimbabwe and Angola to counter the Kabila narrative. Most of the more political work was left to the RCD rebels, who used pro-insurgent Congolese diplomatic staff to persuade Africa and the world either not to intervene or to further isolate the Kabila government. Their efforts, however, seemed to bear little fruit.

The first to openly pronounce his support for Kabila in the face of "foreign invasion" was Robert Mugabe, who used his position as chair of the Defense Organ of the Southern African Development Community (SADC) to fulmi-

[59] Interview with Godefroid Tchamlesso in Kinshasa, August 2013.

[60] Interview with Irung Awan in Kinshasa, August 2013.

[61] Name withheld at the request of the source; interview in Luanda, February 2014.

[62] Names withheld at the request of various sources among high-ranking RPA officers and RPF politicians; interviews in Kigali, April 2013 and December 2014.

nate against the RPF and the RCD. Zimbabwe's diplomatic and military assistance to Kinshasa left Rwanda flabbergasted: while only a week earlier he had been in Kigali complaining to the permanent secretary of the Rwandan Ministry of Defense about Kabila's incompetence and the non-payment by the Congolese government of tens of millions of dollars in debts to Zimbabwe Defense Industries,[63] Zimbabwean Minister of Defense Moven Mahachi announced in the press on August 5 that Congo and Zimbabwe had signed a defense agreement and that a handful of Zimbabwean forces was already on Congolese territory to assess their ally's needs. The RPA had sent officers to Zimbabwe for training in 1997 and was completely taken by surprise by Mugabe's sudden shift, according to presidential chef-de-cabinet, Frank Mugambage.[64] The Front's incredulity further grew when Mugabe also convened an SADC emergency summit over the weekend of August 8, with Kabila in attendance, during which the Zimbabwean president sounded the drums of war and made it clear Kigali needed to be cut down to size.[65] *The Herald*, the mouthpiece of ZANU-PF, began publishing vitriolic pieces denouncing the destabilization of Congo and calling for the punishment of the aggressors. On August 12, Armed Forces Day in Zimbabwe, Mugabe declared the readiness of his troops to stabilize the region; according to one source,[66] hundreds of Zimbabwean Special Forces—including the reputed Parachute Regiment which had carried out daring operations during the civil war in Mozambique—were already deploying in and around N'Djili to defend Kinshasa.

---

[63] Interview with Frank Rusagara in London, January 2010.

[64] Interview in Kampala, March 2013.

[65] Of all parties involved in Africa's Great War, the role played by Zimbabwe offers perhaps the greatest credence to the "resource wars" argument so dominant in the literature and policy world. Not having participated in the AFDL liberation struggle, Mugabe and his ZDF sought to engage Kabila from early on with nakedly commercial interests as their main priority—including the arms deal signed between Zimbabwe Defense Industries and the Congolese government. As Prunier documents, Harare had no real strategic stake in Congo but plenty of domestic political–economic problems: enabling his generals and pro-regime businesses to engage in rent-seeking on Congolese territory allowed Mugabe to consolidate his power. As early as November 1998, Mzee appointed Zimbabwean business tycoon Billy Rautenbach as the new head of Gécamines—the dormant giant of the Congolese economy. Prunier, *From Genocide to Continental War*, pp. 191–2. See also Cullen Nutt and MLR Smith, "Muffling the Sound of Murder: Re-interpreting Zimbabwe's Strategic Choices in the Congo," *Civil Wars*, 13, 3 (2011).

[66] Cooper, *Great Lakes Conflagration*, pp. 25–6.

The Zimbabwean Defense Forces (ZDF) had a reputation for toughness and their arrival in Congo augured more serious resistance for the advancing battalions of James Kabarebe, which had cut off electricity to the capital by the time the ZDF fortified its positions. However, there was no reason to assume that if the balances of forces stayed this way, Kabarebe could not triumph. He had momentum behind him and knew that the Congolese forces defending Kinshasa were poorly equipped and still disorganized. Hundreds of Zimbabweans might be able to slow the assault of the RPA and the rebels on the city, but could probably not fend it off for a long time when confronted with an enemy that could field more firepower and had brought even more crack troops to the front. Kabarebe and the officers in Kigali still believed that once the ZDF saw that it was in effect protecting Kinshasa alone, Mugabe would pull them out, rather than face an ignominious defeat.

The Angolan Decision to Go to War

The military situation on August 13 thus made the question of possible Angolan intervention all the more crucial: if the FAA entered the theater, this would surely hand victory to whatever side it fought with; staying out of the war altogether would spell an RPA–RCD victory. No other countries appeared willing to intervene. Tanzania would almost certainly rule out any involvement; despite its hostility vis-à-vis what the Mkapa–Kikwete government saw as the RPF's unilateralism and militarism, it also fiercely disliked Mugabe's bellicose attitude and willingness to divide SADC for the sake of Zimbabwean interests. South Africa too would stay on the fence. Nelson Mandela and his Deputy President Thabo Mbeki had been involved with the Congo dossier since the early days of the AFDL: broadly speaking, Pretoria was sympathetic to Kigali and skeptical of Kabila, whom it blamed for worsening misrule and authoritarianism, which negatively affected the business climate for South African firms in Congo. The relationship between Mbeki and Kabila had been strained since the beginning, as was—increasingly—that between Mandela and Mugabe, as the latter tried to reassert himself as Southern Africa's regional leader. All of these were enabling conditions that meant that South Africa would not support an SADC intervention to save Mzee. The Mandela government was too focused on the challenges at home to contemplate military assistance to the RPF and RCD either, but decided not to allow SADC to formally bless Zimbabwe's interventionist designs.[67]

---

[67] Interview with Welile Nhlapo, South African ambassador to Ethiopia and special envoy to the Great Lakes, in Pretoria, February 2013.

In what seemed like a final bid to stave off an inevitable strike by Kabarebe on Kinshasa now that so little international support seemed forthcoming, Laurent-Désiré Kabila traveled to Luanda on Saturday, August 15. The situation was desperate: Mbanza-Ngungu—the last major town before the capital—was about to fall and the government remained exiled in Lubumbashi. Kabila implored Dos Santos to join Mugabe in mounting a defense of Kinshasa and told the Angolan president that Congo's gratitude would know no boundaries if the MPLA came to the rescue of the Congolese people. By now, Mzee's team of envoys to Angola—who flew in and out to assess what it would take for Luanda to intervene[68]—was spearheaded by Pierre-Victor Mpoyo, an internationally acclaimed painter who had undergone a metamorphosis to become the Kabila government's most powerful figure in economic policy. Mpoyo was a wealthy man with high-level contacts in Havana and Luanda and put a bold proposal on the table: Congolese oil in exchange for Angolan military help. His message, according to a veteran adviser present during the negotiations, was simple: "Angola needs a president who can enforce their oil [claims]. Mzee [is] that man."[69] At stake were both contemporary production of 25,000 barrels of oil per day and the much greater untapped petroleum reserves of Congo—which some experts have estimated to be 6 per cent of Africa's total.[70] Mpoyo warned that if the RPF managed to install a puppet government in Kinshasa, the new regime might not only invite American and British petrogiants to bring Congo's reserves on stream but could also contest the rights of Angolan state-owned oil company Sonangol in concessions along the poorly demarcated Congolese–Angolan border. This nightmare scenario for the MPLA stood in stark contrast with the business opportunities in hydrocarbons the Kabila government readily

---

[68] Didier Kazadi remembers the frantic shuttle diplomacy well: "I flew at least four times with my American pilot Tim to Luanda to persuade them to help us." Interview in Kinshasa, August 2013.

[69] Interview in Kinshasa, August 2013.

[70] Drilling for oil in Congo began in the 1960s along the 22 kilometers of Atlantic coastline—an area bordered by Angola's Cabinda enclave and the Zaire province in northern Angola, both of which are key hydrocarbon producing areas. Congolese oil production has stood since the 1960s at around the same level of 25,000–30,000 barrels of oil per day. In June 1992, Mobutu seized the assets of major Western oil companies like Chevron, Mobil, Shell and Petrofina involved in oil exploitation and exploration. See Kenneth B. Noble, "Zaire Seizes the Assets of Foreign Oil Companies," *New York Times*, June 7, 1992.

offered to Angola. Mpoyo, who ironically had been Mzee's envoy to Luanda to ask Angolan forces to leave Congo in May 1997, now dangled the prospect of a Congolese–Angolan joint venture for the distribution of oil products on the entire Congolese territory before Sonangol directors Joaquim David and Manuel Vicente.[71]

The frantic activity of Kabila's envoys throughout the two weeks following the Kitona raid contrasted with the relative passivity of the RPF, which remained confident of military success. Officially, it still denied its troops were operating in Congo in the hope that this would buy Kabarebe enough time to force a collapse of the Kabila regime; however, the Front was prodded into greater action by Mzee's visit to Luanda on August 15 and statements by the Tanzanian secretary-general of the OAU, Salim Salim, who spoke out against the "aggression" in Congolese territory. According to some present at meetings of the Council of Colonels,[72] Kagame told his senior officers that heated rhetoric in the region would not translate into actual military opposition to the advance of Kabarebe and the RCD rebels—the disillusionment with Mzee ran so deep that the RPF strongman could barely imagine anyone who would want to sacrifice themselves for his survival. Nevertheless, Kagame did order two sizeable delegations of RPF officials to travel to Zambia and Angola to provide them with a more detailed explanation for the outbreak of the second Congo war. In his assessment, assuaging these two countries mattered most for the success of the regime change campaign—both were SADC member and shared hundreds of kilometers of strategic border with Congo (with Bas Congo, Bandundu, Kasai and Katanga respectively)—but such diplomatic maneuvering would not necessarily be difficult. Emmanuel Ndahiro and Patrick Mazimhaka, Kagame's main political advisers, were sent to Luanda; the Rwandan minister of defense himself would lead a bigger and more high-profile delegation to Lusaka, which also included ESO chief Patrick Karegeya. This turned out to be a fatal error of judgment.

According to one of the delegation's most high-profile members, "this was a catastrophic assessment of our priorities."[73] Zambian–Angolan relations were worse than Kagame had assumed and his choice to go to Lusaka rather than Luanda did not go down well in Angola. While the Zambian visit was uneventful and merely confirmed what was already known—that Zambia had

[71] Name withheld at the request of the source; interview in Kinshasa, August 2013.

[72] Names withheld at the request of various sources among high-ranking RPA officers and RPF politicians; interviews in Kigali, April 2013 and December 2014.

[73] Name withheld at the request of the source; interview in Kigali, December 2014.

neither the military capacity nor the will to intervene on either side—the delegation engaging the MPLA faced open hostility. President Dos Santos showed no interest in meeting Ndahiro and Mazimhaka, but instead his right-hand men for security—General Kopalipa and General Miala—and Premier Fernando José de França Dias Van-Dúnem angrily lectured the RPF representatives. Van-Dúnem simply told them that "you can't do this" while Kopalipa repeatedly asked "Why did you not tell us to do this together?"[74] The MPLA appeared incensed at the RPF's assumption it could get away with initiating regime change and leaving Angola to piece together the strategic fallout of such a significant development on its doorstep. The reception of the Rwandan delegation in Luanda was hostile, to say the least. As one RPF delegation member testified: "I flew to Angola to try to explain things after the fact ... I am lucky I came out alive. There was incredible hostility towards me ... When I landed here in Kigali, I got a message: they intervened."[75]

Kagame's decision to fly to Zambia rather than to Angola was of course not the cause of the MPLA's decision to intervene, but it highlighted—in the eyes of Dos Santos and his advisers—how problematic the RPF's regional policy in Central Africa was. For months, representatives of the French government and the Direction Générale de la Sécurité Extérieure (DGSE, France's foreign secret service) had been using their ties with Luanda to push the MPLA towards a complete rupture with Kigali. Whereas France's relations with the RPF remained toxic, as discussed in Chapters 4 to 6 (and as has been well documented by other scholars[76]), Paris had made inroads into Angola despite a turbulent past. Extensive support provided by proxies of Paris—Côte d'Ivoire, Morocco, Togo, Zaire—to UNITA and French sympathy for Cabinda secessionists had damaged diplomatic ties for the first two decades after Angolan independence, even if French petro-giant Elf operated in Angola since 1978. Relations convalesced notably when weapons, helicopters and tanks were sold to the MPLA government for a total of US$790 million in the 1990s through the good offices of Jean-Christophe Mitterrand (the son of the fourth president of the Republic), former Minister of the Interior Charles Pasqua and the formidably well-connected businessman Pierre

---

[74] Interviews with Patrick Mazimhaka and Emmanuel Ndahiro in Kigali, December 2014.

[75] Name withheld at the request of the source; interview in Kigali, December 2014.

[76] Daniela Kroslak, *The French Betrayal of Rwanda*, Bloomington: Indiana University Press, 2007; Andrew Wallis, *Silent Accomplice: The Untold Story of France's Role in the Rwandan Genocide*, London: I.B. Tauris, 2006.

Falcone.[77] The French–Angolan relationship further improved owing to the collaboration in Congo-Brazzaville to oust Lissouba and reinstall Sassou-Nguesso as head of state.[78] Paris's support for Mobutu until the end remained an element of friction between France and Angola, but the resolution of the Brazzaville dossier had instilled greater confidence on both sides. This provided the context for Jacques Chirac's visit to Luanda in June 1998 (the first ever by a French president) and the growing traction of the message conveyed by Chirac and the DGSE about the dangers of RPF influence in Central Africa. According to one senior FAC officer close to Mzee, France's subtle but relentless anti-RPF advocacy (often phrased in terms of Anglo-Saxon threats to Angolan oil interests) was a key factor in strengthening the demands of the Congolese for the FAA to intervene.[79]

Ultimately, on August 19 the MPLA came to the conclusion that it would hold its nose and save Kabila to secure its key interests. As explained before, the overriding priority was twofold: a pro-MPLA regime in Kinshasa and guarantees that UNITA would not regain a foothold in Bas Congo. In principle, these objectives could have been secured through an RCD–RPF victory as well, but the combination of mistrust and uncertainty borne out of the AFDL campaign and the MPLA's expulsion from Kinshasa, damning feedback about the arrogance of RPA officials from his top officers and French spin convinced Dos Santos that Angolan interests would not be safe with Kigali and the rebels. Allowing the RPF to continue playing the role of kingmaker in Kinshasa was a dangerous precedent and perhaps Paris was right in its claims that behind the Rwandan–Ugandan alliance stood Anglo-Saxon oil and its bid to control more of the Atlantic reserves. Even more importantly, Kagame and Kabarebe's astounding audacity combined with its secrecy and a go-it-alone mentality worried the MPLA leadership greatly. The RPF's brazen attempt to initiate regime change with unknown consequences for the regional distribution of power, while essentially ignoring Luanda in its deci-

[77] Karl Laske, *Des coffres si bien garnis: enquête sur les serviteurs de l'etat-voyou*, Paris: Denoël, 2004. "Angola-gate," *The Economist*, November 19, 2008.

[78] As noted in Howard W. French, "Rebels, Backed by Angola, Take Brazzaville and Oil Port," *New York Times*, October 16, 1997: "'France was still smarting from the defeat of Mobutu in Zaire,' an African diplomat, speaking on condition of anonymity, said of the fighting in the neighboring Congo Republic. 'With all of the oil wealth in that little country, there was no way France was going to allow itself to lose Brazzaville too.'"

[79] Name withheld at the request of the source; interview in Kinshasa, August 2013.

sion-making and diplomacy (only then to send envoys to reduce any skepticism), suggested that this was not a partner to be trusted with Angola's vital interests. Even senior Pentagon officials, otherwise outright sympathetic towards the RPF, recognized the Front's main problem: "They got so caught up in their own intelligence and arrogance. This was their problem with Angola."[80] Without informing anyone in the FAA, the RPA had launched a raid on the vital stretch of land connecting Angola's two key oil possessions, Cabinda and Zaire province. Seen through this prism, Kagame's choice to go to Zambia rather than Angola only served to underscore the perception that the RPF had no clue about how Luanda saw Congo and/or simply did not want to understand the Angolan perspective.

It was these strategic considerations—rather than presumed RPF linkages with UNITA or a straightforward commercial *quid pro quo*—that explained Angola's last-minute intervention to salvage the Kinshasa government. None of our MPLA interlocutors alleged, as some scholars have,[81] that there were any serious links between the Angolan rebels and Kigali—it was a red herring that Kabila's envoys talked about but was never believed in Luanda. Business considerations also seemed to have been secondary in Dos Santos's decision to enter the war on the side of the Congolese government. As multiple Angolan sources testified, they probably could have received whatever contracts and monopolies they wanted from the RCD rebels too, in exchange for Luanda's support to overthrow Mzee; as one of them noted, if anything the "more disciplined" Kinyarwanda-speakers would probably have made for more reliable business partners then the chaotic wheeler-dealers of Kinshasa or Katanga.

In other words, commercial alignments between Angola and Congo were certainly a *result* of the war, but cannot explain the *formation* of the Kabila–MPLA entente against the RCD–RPF alliance. Only once the decision to intervene in the war had been taken and Kinshasa had been stabilized did the MPLA turn its attention to business. One shared interest that was spawned by the conflict lay in the oil sector. In October 1998, Sonangol Congo began its operations as a 60:40 joint venture between Sonangol and the Congolese state, initially targeting the marketing, storing and distribution of finished

---

[80] Name withheld at the request of the source, interview in Washington, February 2015. On this point see also Stearns, *Dancing in the Glory of Monsters*, p. 191.

[81] Prunier, *From Genocide to Continental War*, pp. 188–9; Reyntjens, *Great African War*, p. 202.

petroleum products (mostly originating from Angola) but with an eye to moving into oil exploration too. The enterprise emerged from the original proposal by Kabila's confidant for economic affairs, Victor Mpoyo, in the aforementioned discussion with the MPLA in Luanda and helped to finance FAA operations. The holding company appointed by the Kinshasa government to act on its behalf as shareholder of Sonangol Congo was the Générale de Commerce d'Import/Export du Congo (COMIEX), which was mostly owned by President Kabila himself and Mpoyo.[82] Founded back in 1973 as the company charged with the export and import of products to and from the Fizi-Baraka *maquis* of Kabila's PRP, the AFDL campaign breathed new life into the company which became a vital financing mechanism for both the revolution and the personal consolidation of power by Mzee.[83] COMIEX dealt extensively with Alfred Kalisa and the BCDI in Kigali where it held an account (see Chapter 8) and was involved in the earliest contacts between mining companies and the AFDL, even before the fall of Kinshasa. After the events of August 2, 1998, COMIEX not only became the main holding company representing the Congolese state in Sonangol Congo, but also the principal partner for the Zimbabwean army and businessmen close to Robert Mugabe for the exploitation of mineral resources and timber.[84]

Conclusion: "In Total War You Will Even Sleep with the Devil"

Our intervention was meant to stop the military advance of Rwanda. They were almost in Kinshasa. They had occupied the frontier up to Soyo—the oil province. This could bring instability—this is why we intervened after failed diplomatic initiatives. First we took N'Djili Airport with the Zimbabwean troops and then by land we retook Kitona base, Boma, Matadi and Kinshasa itself, where we joined Zimbabwean forces.

So testified Major-General Pedro Sebastião, Angola's minister of defense when Africa's Great War erupted.[85] The mass deployment of FAA ground

[82] United Nations, "Report of the Panel of Experts on the Illegal Exploitation of Natural Resources and Other Forms of Wealth of the Democratic Republic of the Congo," S/2001/357, p. 7.

[83] De Villers and Willame, *République démocratique du Congo*, p. 83.

[84] United Nations, "Addendum to the Report of the Panel of Experts on the Illegal Exploitation of Natural Resources and Other Forms of Wealth of the Democratic Republic of the Congo," S/2001/1072, pp. 10–12, 17–18.

[85] Interview in Luanda, May 2014.

troops and air force into Congo was indeed the decisive moment all parties had expected it would be, resoundingly beating back James Kabarebe's offensive. Yet as this chapter has shown, neither the intervention itself, nor which side Luanda would support, was written in the stars. The impending resumption of the Angolan civil war dominated the calculus of José Eduardo Dos Santos: if the overthrow of Mobutu and Lissouba had created a golden opportunity to further isolate UNITA, the second Congo war could fuel a resurgence of the rebel force. Understood against this background, the MPLA was certainly not spoiling for a fight in the Great Lakes region and would rather stay out to focus on its nemesis. It was extremely reluctant to wade back into Congo after the alliance to overthrow Mobutu had fractured and Luanda's influence in the new Kinshasa had proven limited, following Kabila's first expulsion order. But the strategic imperative was unmistakable once the conflict arrived in the areas adjacent to Angola's oil-producing provinces, UNITA's old rear base; from then on, standing by was simply not an option in the analysis of the FAA generals: "War in Bas Congo is different from war on the Congo–Rwanda border. We had to intervene."[86]

Not only was the fact of intervention not a given after the outbreak of conflict on August 2, 1998, that it would come in defense of the Kabila government was highly uncertain too. Mzee and the *famille katangaise* had given the MPLA plenty of reason to be distrustful, both during the AFDL campaign and the 1997–8 interbellum when he marginalized his erstwhile Angolan comrades and their main Congolese allies. As we have argued throughout this chapter, that the MPLA stepped in with full force to thwart the second capture of Kinshasa by a foreign-backed rebel army in two years was more a function of internal Angolan factors and faltering Rwandan foreign policy than the quality of the alliance Kabila could offer Dos Santos.

The Angolan intervention decisively changed the course of African history. A domestic conflict with one major foreign player was transformed into the biggest regional war Africa has ever seen. Had it not been for the FAA combined air and ground assault, the RPA–RCD force would probably have taken Kinshasa in a matter of days, perhaps even hours, ending the conflict. Despite the deployment of hundreds of Zimbabweans around N'Djili and N'Dolo (a smaller Kinshasa airport) and despite Zimbabwean air capability, these troops could probably not have held out against the thousands of well-armed troops that James Kabarebe commanded. The FAC's main defenses lay shattered, the

[86] Interview in Luanda with General Ita, May 2014.

popular militia the Kabila government had been trying to recruit was a phantom army rather than a real opponent. The rebel force approached to within 35–40 kilometers of the center of Kinshasa and still had tanks and artillery at its disposal, as well as RPA elite units who were known for their ability to advance at great speeds on foot to overwhelm the enemy—this, after all, was how Caesar Kayizari captured the city in May 1997. Adding to the agony of the remaining defenders, reports were coming in from across the capital's southern peripheries that the attackers were infiltrating. This meant that not just one route had to be watched, but that the final, lethal thrust could follow multiple avenues into the heart of Kinshasa.

The FAA began its combat operations on Friday, August 21, seventeen days after the raid on Kitona and eight days after the fall of Inga Dam—an agonizingly long wait for the Kabila regime. While first crossing the border cautiously from Cabinda with a mechanized brigade, more than 2,500 Angolan forces then struck the RPA–RCD force in several places at once. On August 22, rebel supply columns were bombed in Matadi and close to Kasangulu (forty-five kilometers from Kinshasa). Kabarebe had barely brought any air defenses because he did not expect to be needing any in this war and the hapless resupplying units were stunned when they suddenly found themselves under heavy fire; the survivors reported that they had initially thought the Angolan Mi-24 jets had made a mistake and were going to strike FAC targets just down the road. Almost simultaneously, Angolan commandos retook the Kitona base from astonished, unprepared defenders—within days, many of Bas Congo's most crucial points had passed into FAA hands: Boma, Matadi, Kasangulu. The RPA–RCD army was rapidly losing both its supplies and its firepower as missiles rained down on it—in Kigali, the incredulous RPA High Command was livid with what it saw as Angola's betrayal. In the words of James Kabarebe himself: "It was in the bag. But Angola took victory from us."[87]

Faced with this abrupt reversal of fortunes, Kabarebe refused to accept defeat. Desperate for cover and by now without armor but with his attacking force still holding the advantage on the ground, he ordered his troops to rush into the city itself and capture its airports. This was a dangerous gambit, but he saw the alternative—surrender or annihilation from the air—as even worse, dealing a perhaps fatal blow to the anti-Kabila regime change campaign and to the RPF myth of invincibility on the battlefront. Thousands of soldiers surged into the peripheral areas around Kinshasa where for five days an intense

---

[87] Interview in Kigali, April 2013.

battle was waged. Despite grave losses inflicted by aerial bombardments, Kabarebe's force managed to capture most of N'Djili Airport on August 26, seemingly handing him victory after all. However, the sheer firepower unleashed by Angolan and Zimbabwean troops ultimately broke all of the Rwandan officer's offensive aspirations: by Sunday, August 30, following days of vicious urban warfare in which at least 5,000 people died, the battle for Kinshasa was over.[88]

The defeat of the RPA–RCD force was greeted with exhilaration by the Kinois population which had endured such hardships over the preceding month, including the power outage and high numbers of civilian casualties during the fighting between four different national armies.[89] The withdrawal of the rebels from N'Djili and the adjacent Masina neighborhood spawned a re-intensification of the anti-Tutsi pogroms; some soldiers had tried to shed their uniforms and melt into the population, but the nationalist hysteria and persisting paranoia after Kabarebe's defeat led straight into a pitiless manhunt. On August 27, Kabila's chef-de-cabinet Abdoulaye Yerodia once again used genocidal language in a television address to urge the population to identify the fifth column hiding in the city; it was a discourse that would be repeated over the next few days as hundreds of people were killed across the city: "For us, these are pieces of garbage, microbes even, that must be eradicated methodically. We have decided to use the most efficient medication available."[90] While deserting soldiers and innocent civilians were being hunted down, Kabarebe staged an improbable retreat, somehow extracting himself with a considerable force from the impossible situation he had fallen into.

This was partly achieved by the break-out of some units instructed to march in the direction of Pointe Noire in Congo-Brazzaville, which provided some relief to the bulk of the surviving troops—perhaps 2,000 men in total, a mix-

---

[88] For a detailed account of the battle for Kinshasa see Cooper, *Great Lakes Conflagration*. Cooper's account is a great military history, though marred by a number of factual inaccuracies and a too one-sided Zimbabwean account of the battle for Kinshasa which, among other things, analyses the Angolan intervention too disparagingly.

[89] Jean Hatzfeld, "La vie reprend à Kinshasa, où le gouvernement de Kabila crie victoire: 'Les Angolais nous ont sauvés,'" *Libération*, September 1, 1998.

[90] In the original French: "Pour nous, ce sont des déchets et c'est même des microbes qu'il faut qu'on éradiquer [*sic*] avec méthode. Nous sommes décidés à utiliser la médication la plus efficace"; Arrondissement de Bruxelles Tribunal De Premiere Instance, "Pro Justicia: Mandat D'Arret International Par Defaut," Dossier 40/99, April 11, 2000, p. 6.

ture of RPA units, Banyamulenge *afande* like Mustapha Mukiza and Ilunga Kabangi, a handful of Ugandans and ex-FAZ soldiers afraid of summary execution at the hands of the FAC. They traveled under the cover of night towards northern Angola. Having marched more than 200 kilometers, Kabarebe's men stormed the FAA airstrip of Maquela do Zombo in the scarcely populated Uegi province. Exhausted, they fortified their positions in a heavily forested area and linked up with UNITA troops in the region (the first time real collaboration occurred between the Angolan rebels and the RPA–RCD).[91] Kabarebe and his troops anxiously waited for weeks (possibly until November 1998) to be airlifted at night by chartered Antonov 72s: a high-risk operation coordinated through radio with Kigali and in all likelihood only made possible with the help of the Pentagon, which exerted pressure on Angola and Zimbabwe to let the remnants of Kabarebe's force safely be evacuated.[92] Whatever agreement Washington might have negotiated was only respected partially: before approximately 1,750 men were actually airlifted out of Maquela do Zombo, FAA bombardments claimed scores of victims. Those extracted from this ordeal still remember Kabarebe's feat—to which they owe their lives—with deep gratitude and professional admiration: "The evacuation was magnificent. The leadership I saw from James was fantastic … No one else in the region could have evacuated such a big force in enemy territory."[93] However, much of the force's remaining equipment had to be left behind. So were many Congolese soldiers who were told that there was simply no space for them to be evacuated too.[94]

The blitzkrieg operation that had begun with the Kitona raid ended with the spearhead of that same force flying back to Rwanda. As James Kabarebe moved east again, so did the main thrust of the war. The internationalization of the conflict continued rapidly: after the involvement of the Rwandan, Ugandan, Zimbabwean and Angolan armed forces, UNITA, ALiR, ADF, LRA and other rebel groups joined the fray as well, as did, in a limited way,

---

[91] Interview with James Kabarebe in Kigali, April 2013.

[92] Prunier, *From Genocide to Continental War*, pp. 185–6, 419–20.

[93] Interview with Malick Kijege in Kinshasa, August 2013.

[94] According to Malick, the question of who would be able to fly out and who might be left behind greatly vexed the soldiers, who were physically at the end of their wits: "We were all asking the question anxiously: who will be the last to be extricated? What will you do if you are the last to go?" Interview in Kinshasa, August 2013. James Kabarebe appeared to have promised that there would be space for all—*quod non*.

Burundi, Chad, Namibia and Sudan. Diplomatic efforts from Mandela's South Africa failed to create real momentum for a ceasefire. The end of the battle of Kinshasa and the stabilization of western Congo could have provided opportunities for a negotiated solution, but the guns did not fall silent and instead the war moved east.

Too much anger had been unleashed between the former comrades—all of whom felt personally betrayed by the other—for a political settlement to emerge. As one protagonist put it, this was not an ordinary conflict but one where irregular violence against civilians and coalitions with anyone who could help vanquish the enemy became the order of the day. The ethnic cleansing and arbitrary killings that had occurred in Kinshasa would be repeated all over the territory, particularly in the Kivus and Katanga: "Enemy of your enemy is your friend. No matter what he has done. In total war you will even sleep with the devil."[95] Prisoners of war were seldom taken: Tutsi officers and recruits were massacred in Kisangani, Kamina and Kananga, among other places; in North and South Kivu those refusing to join the mutiny or found helping the nationalist resistance met a similar, grizzly fate. The RCD rebels, after having taken Kisangani, also moved into Kabila's old fief of Fizi-Baraka and northern Katanga—Kalemie and Moba—a highly symbolic victory given how close that brought them to his ancestral homeland. The Mzee and his allies struck back by formalizing their entente with ALiR which further polarized eastern Congo along ethnic lines; following the killing of their commanders Leonard Nkundiye and Frodouald Mugemana in Ruhengeri, the *abacengezi* staged a tactical withdrawal from western Rwanda across the Congolese border. There they joined at least 15,000 *génocidaire* forces who were flown or ferried in from Cameroon, Central African Republic, Congo-Brazzaville and Sudan to serve under the aegis of Paul Rwarakabije and Augustin Bizimungu, who only two years earlier had been the military commander of the North Kivu refugee camps. ALiR joined the FAC and Mai Mai militias in attacking RPA units at Goma and Gisenyi and targeted Tutsi civilians and their presumed accomplices. An unknown number of people died in those first five weeks of war on Congolese soil, perhaps as many as 20,000–25,000. Over the next three and a half years, hundreds of thousands more would succumb to the violence, hunger and disease Africa's Great War brought to Congo.

---

[95] Interview with Jean-Claude Yav in Kinshasa, August 2013.

PART IV

CONCLUSION

12

WHY COMRADES GO TO WAR

The Mzee Is Dead

As Angolan and Zimbabwean forces turned the tide against the RPF and RCD rebels, Kabila emerged out of hiding in Lubumbashi and returned to Kinshasa buoyed by a wave of popular support. The government was able to hold the capital and gradually stabilized western Congo but made little headway in retaking the east and lost the north to a new insurgent group, the Mouvement pour la Libération du Congo (MLC), led by Jean-Pierre Bemba from Equateur and heavily backed by Uganda. For almost two years, Congo was divided into different zones—the north controlled by the MLC, the eastern region under the control of different RCD groups and the western and southern parts of the country in government hands. Successive offensives failed to hand a definitive battlefield victory to either Mzee's regime or the Rwanda- and Uganda-supported rebels.

With few prospects for breaking the military stalemate, by mid-2000 Kabila was desperate for some type of political breakthrough. Under pressure from his *kadogo* child soldiers to release Anselme Masasu Nindaga—the still popular *afande* from South Kivu who Mzee had arrested in November 1997, sending shockwaves through the regime—the Congolese president decided to show clemency to his former comrade. After all, thousands of *kadogo* had stayed loyal to the official Congolese government and had not joined Kabarebe's forces in the battle for Kinshasa; moreover, giving Masasu his freedom back could bolster Mzee's support in the Kivus and perhaps cast him in a more favorable diplomatic light too, as relations with almost all major international players were in a terrible state. In April 2000, Kabila overturned Masasu's conviction for charges of threatening state security, treason and forming a private militia. Two-and-a-half years in prison, however, had done little to soften the *afande*'s opposition to the Kabila government. Masasu immediately reached out to the young and disillusioned in eastern Congo and publicly criticized Kabila. Once again rattled by Masasu galvanizing the *kadogo* in the Kivus, Mzee panicked and had him re-incarcerated, which was followed by a "a witch hunt for *kadogo* from the Kivus ... launched in Kinshasa."[1] Meanwhile, Masasu was taken to Pweto in the southeast of Congo, near the active frontline with the RPF, where he was executed, on Katangese soil, on November 27, 2000.[2] But if it was largely paranoia rather than a real existential threat that drove Mzee to kill his former lieutenant, his obsession with protecting his hold on absolute power by politically and physically eliminating any potential menace was about to backfire.

One week after Masasu's execution, the RPA and the RCD rebels crushed the Congolese army and its Zimbabwean allies and seized Pweto on December 3, 2000.[3] It was a humiliating defeat. Joseph Kabila, who rushed back from China after the war broke out and had been appointed FAC chief of staff in August 1998, was forced to flee across the border into Zambia as he was tactically outmaneuvered by the RPA. Mzee was furious and reportedly had his son and the rest of the army command that had fled the battlefield arrested and returned to Congo.[4] Kabila's anger over his officers' incompetence was matched only by the growing frustration of his Angolan allies—the very comrades who reluctantly saved him from Kabarebe's offensive in August 1998. Throughout 2000, Kabila confirmed the Angolans' worst fears about the man whose hold on power they had gone to great lengths to protect: ruining numerous diplomatic opportunities Luanda had opened up; meeting Kagame in Kenya, without Dos Santos's blessing; and engaging, through trusted intermediaries, in diamond trafficking with UNITA in a desperate bid to overcome his government's insolvency. The Angolan forces who had served as part of Kabila's personal protection force since the battle of Kinshasa still lingered, but were no longer at the heart of his bodyguard which now mostly comprised Katangese veterans and *kadogo* Mzee personally liked. As one French intelli-

[1] Stearns, *Dancing in the Glory of Monsters*, p. 279.

[2] Joris, *The Rebels' Hour*.

[3] Karl Vick, "Desperate Battle Defines Congo's Warlike Peace," *Washington Post*, January 2, 2001.

[4] Stearns, *Dancing in the Glory of Monsters*, pp. 276, 79.

gence operative in close contact with Kabila testified, this had been his way of signaling discontent with the lukewarm support he felt Angola provided; the upshot was that it left him dangerously vulnerable: "It was outrageous, we could have killed him twenty times over. I've never seen anything like that. This was no security. We could have brought a tank into the Palais de Marbre. A complete disaster. These were no bodyguards."[5] Livid with Kabila for his second betrayal of the MPLA, the Angolan security services deliberately withheld intelligence reports from their Congolese counterparts indicating there was an imminent threat to Mzee's life.

Two years after the outbreak of Africa's Great War, Kabila managed to do little more than keep the war away from Kinshasa, but his quest for absolute power never brought him the personal and political security he desperately sought. Enraged by Mzee's betrayal of their hero Masasu and the execution of dozens of their comrades in Kinshasa just a day earlier, the *kadogo* struck back.[6] In the early afternoon of Tuesday, January 16, 2001, Rashidi Kasereka— a *kadogo* sub-lieutenant from North Kivu, recruited into the AFDL in late 1996—came to Kabila's office in the Palais de Marbre and stood to attention, as if he had a message to deliver. Kabila invited Rashidi into his office and leaned over to take his question; Rashidi then fatally shot the Mzee two or three times before being killed himself by former Tigres Katangais commander Eddy Kapend.

With the Mzee's assassination—an act of revenge carried out by the *kadogo* and probably permitted by Angolan security operatives[7]—the cannibalism of the revolution was complete. In the end, it was the children of the revolution that devoured their leader.

Why Comrades Went to War

One overriding question has motivated us in this book: *Why did comrades go to war*—first as allies in the war to end all wars and then as enemies in the deadliest conflict since World War II? We have tackled this two-part question in parts two and three of this book respectively.

[5] Name withheld at the request of the source, interview in Brussels, September 2010.
[6] Stephen Smith and Antoine Glaser, "Ces enfants-soldats qui ont tué Kabila ...," *Le monde*, February 9, 2001.
[7] For the best analyses of Kabila's assassination and rival theories see Prunier, *From Genocide to Continental War*, pp. 267–84.

The War to End All Wars

One of the book's main claims is that the war against Mobutu was a function of a regional disequilibrium: Central Africa was split between counter-revolutionary forces—which included Mobutu and his protégé in Rwanda, Juvénal Habyarimana—and revolutionary movements—those under the tutelage of Nyerere that sought to take up the mantle of domestic and regional liberation. The externalization of the Rwandan civil war did not commence with the fleeing of the ex-FAR and Interahamwe into eastern Zaire after the genocide in July 1994, but much before that. The future leaders of the RPF were intimately involved in Museveni's liberation project in Uganda, which in turn served as a launching pad for the liberation of their own homeland they had been exiled from since 1959. The RPF's invasion of Rwanda in October 1990 prompted Mobutu to deploy his elite forces, the Division Spéciale Présidentielle, to defend the Habyarimana regime. As the RPF's top brass said to us, this is when the war with Mobutu began.

The death of Habyarimana and the collapse of the genocidal government that tried to keep the RPF at bay in 1994 traumatized the Zairean president. Feeling encircled by the "sons of Nyerere," Mobutu doubled-down on the counter-revolutionary forces, harboring and supporting the *génocidaires* in eastern Zaire as they attempted to reclaim power in Rwanda. Confronted by this dual counter-revolutionary threat, the RPF decided that nothing short of dismantling the Mobutu regime once and for all would secure its own liberation. To do so, the RPF reached out to Congolese opponents of Mobutu and comrades in Uganda, Tanzania, and Angola as well as those further afield in Ethiopia and Eritrea whose interests and ideologies were aligned against the "neo-colonial relic." Like the RPF, this group of liberation and neo-liberation regimes saw the campaign as an attempt to strengthen their own national security, but it was also something greater than that—a collective effort to remake the regional order and usher in a new era of economic and political integration that Mobutu, in their view, had stymied for years.

* * *

From a theoretical perspective, the framework we advance to account for the emergence of the AFDL and the first Congo war offers new insights into the revolution–war nexus. In contrast to third-image theories that conceive of post-revolutionary war as predominantly a function of systemic factors[8] or first- and

---

[8] Walt, *Revolution and War.*

second-image theories that attribute war to revolutions bringing bellicose personalist rulers to power,[9] we illuminate how these two dimensions are mutually constitutive—regional polarization, revolution and war reproduce each other. Regional polarization between revolutionary and counter-revolutionary forces contributes to the spread of revolution and war as each side seeks to install (or keep) allies in power abroad to safeguard their hold on power at home. Moreover, revolutionary change triggers war and the intensification of regional polarization as reactionary forces, feeling further encircled, become more desperate in a bid to stave off what they see as a looming revolutionary threat.

One puzzle that arises from this is why détente proves impossible. Why not accept each other's sphere of influence and agree not to interfere in each other's affairs? As the story of the Congo Wars illustrates, part of the explanation is the uncertainty that dominates international relations and the inability of either side to credibly commit to such a bargain, especially when coalitions include local agents (e.g., rebel movements or counter-revolutionary organizations) that have their own interests and may stoke domestic conflict as a means to elicit support from foreign patrons. But we have also emphasized the importance of the role that ideology has played and illustrated how it intensified the commitment problem among blocs of rival states—Mobutu and his conservative allies versus Nyerere and his Pan-Africanist disciples—preventing peaceful détente. The root cause of a strategic environment that produces cycles of war and revolution is a regional system divided between ideological foes, which see the existence of the other as a threat to their own existence.

In Africa, the ideological battle that defined the twentieth century was not solely the confrontation between Western capitalism and Soviet socialism, but also the struggle between colonialism/neo-colonialism and Pan-Africanism. We have argued that Pan-Africanism's collective foundations and commitment to the total liberation of Africa has been a key driver in the spread of revolutionary thought and practice. The internalization of the Pan-Africanist identity and the adoption of its ideological worldview ensured that those at the forefront of the struggle could not accept détente with reactionary states, whether Apartheid South Africa or Mobutu's Zaire, because it left them vulnerable to counter-revolutionary forces at home and it implied a betrayal of the movement's core principles.

Nkrumah and Nyerere were integral as norm entrepreneurs—elevating the liberation struggle to a central place in Pan-Africanism and inculcating the

[9] Colgan, "Domestic Revolutionary Leaders and International Conflict." Colgan and Weeks, "Revolution, Personalist Dictatorships, and International Conflict."

norm of solidarity in the fight for independence among leftist elites across the region. One of their disciples was Yoweri Museveni, who did more than anyone to bridge the gap between the original liberation movements and their neo-liberation successors. Museveni's biography personifies the evolution of the liberation struggle in Africa over the past fifty years: from his time at the University of Dar es Salaam, which was a hotbed of revolutionary thought, to his application of Fanon's writings on the Algerian struggle to FRELIMO and NRA/M; and from the liberation of Uganda in alliance with the future leaders of the RPF to his support for the Front in its own struggle and then finally, to the grand alliance with the region's liberation forces against Mobutu.

The Tragedy of Africa's Great War

If the overthrow of Mobutu ended once and for all the regional polarization that had plagued Central Africa since the 1960s, why did it fail to usher in regional peace as the protagonists envisaged and the theory predicts? Why did regional peace give way to the most devastating conflict since World War II—a conflict all the more tragic because it would be caused by the falling out of comrades?

We have argued that the revolution against Mobutu was a pyrrhic victory: the military triumph was breathtaking, but from a political perspective it was an utter failure. Like other cases throughout history, the revolution against Mobutu failed not in the destruction of the *ancien régime* but in the management of the politics of the post-revolutionary order—specifically the uncertainty over how power was to be shared and how the new configuration of power was to be enforced. Again like other post-revolutionary cases, this uncertainty was felt domestically—as rival factions within the AFDL jockeyed for power—but also regionally—as the neighboring states had a major stake in who controlled the new Congo and the degree to which the new regime protected their security interests. As we have argued, however, this two-level game, in which domestic bargaining is connected to the regional balance of power and vice versa, was particularly acute for the AFDL because of the RPF's direct involvement in the post-Mobutu regime. This intensified the two-level game and increased the risk that instability on one dimension would immediately be felt on the other.

The fundamental political flaw of the AFDL and the broader Pan-Africanist alliance was the weakness of the political institutions structuring the rebel movement and the cooperation between regional states. The anti-

Mobutu alliance was an ad hoc creation of the RPF designed to allow it to pursue its strategic objectives in Zaire. Though the RPF was genuinely interested in burden-sharing the war against Mobutu (e.g., inviting the MPLA to become involved in order to strengthen the AFDL's firepower) and the rebuilding of the Congolese state (e.g., asking the Tanzanian army to help with military training), there was no formal, central mechanism for coordination at an operational level on these critical tasks. Moreover, the RPF's partnership with Kabila during the campaign—in which both seemed happy to marginalize other comrades—eroded much of the informal ties and goodwill that should have been used to create new options for a political settlement in the absence of the development of stronger institutions and networks of cooperation. The MPLA felt largely excluded and the Pan-Africanist team for political encadrement of the AFDL, with strong Ethiopian and Eritrean participation, was ignored almost entirely by Mzee.

Paul Kagame delegated a handful of his most talented aides—James Kabarebe, Caesar Kayizari, Dan Munyuza and Francis Gakwerere—to focus on three priorities: the total defeat of the ex-FAR/Interahamwe; the overthrow of Mobutu; and the development of strategic interdependence with Kabila, who they bet on as the future leader of Congo. Other than their direct communication with the leadership in Kigali and occasional consultations with Museveni's envoys, these individuals shared little information with other members of the coalition, whether Congolese or allied regimes that were contributing to the campaign. There was no forum for routine meetings to take place with the contributing countries. This approach could not have been more welcome to Kabila who treated it as an implicit authorization to neutralize political rivals. And as much as the RPF thought they were using Kabila to achieve their own objectives, Mzee was cleverly using the RPF to not only carry him to Kinshasa but to consolidate power in his own hands. The informal pact between the old revolutionary and the young Turks of the Front was cemented with Kabarebe's appointment as head of the Congolese army. This unwritten settlement of power-sharing and mutual dependence became the fulcrum of the post-Mobutu order—both within Congo and within Central Africa.

The path charted by Mzee and the RPF—a mixture of conscious decisions and barely considered ad hoc maneuvers in response to the dazzling pace at which developments took place—effectively dissolved the initially very broad coalition of Congolese and other African forces and replaced it with a duopoly shared between Kabila and the Front. AFDL "founding father" Kisase was assassinated in January 1997; Delphin Muland was incarcerated in May; Angola's

FAA was asked to quit Congo in June; the Ethiopian, Eritrean and Rwandan political advisers of the AFDL had all left by September; Masasu was arrested in November. By January 1998, there was only one Banyamulenge minister left—Bizima Karaha—and AFDL Secretary-General Bugera had lost all influence. This consolidation of power in Kabila and the near total authority enjoyed by James Kabarebe as FAC chief of staff were profoundly destabilizing internally and externally. Every time Kabila expanded his power, he deepened his isolation—and in the context of the unbearable weakness of the Congolese state this meant that the revolution's agenda came unstuck. Within a year of ousting Mobutu, he had squandered any possibility of cooperating with Étienne Tshisekedi, alienated the population of Kinshasa, terrified investors and rendered his old Banyamulenge allies so hostile they were plotting to overthrow him. The RPF, for its part, had tarnished the image of itself in Africa as the most courageous of liberation forces: it was increasingly seen as arrogant, untrustworthy and complicit in the installation of a new dictatorship.

Thus, while Kabila and the RPF had sacrificed the AFDL as a national coalition government and a Pan-Africanist alliance in order to further their own objectives, it also meant that when they increasingly distrusted each other, there were no institutional mechanisms to contain and regulate their disagreements.

As much as Kabila had been willing to manipulate the RPF to capture presidential power, deep down he never trusted the men who were less than half his age, hailing from a country ninety times smaller than his. His dependence exacerbated his long-standing paranoia. He knew it left him vulnerable, not just to criticism from the Congolese that he was a stooge of Kigali, but even more problematically to the whims of the RPF: Kabila knew Kabarebe and Munyuza could remove him from power as easily as they had carried him to Kinshasa. Seen from the RPF's perspective, allowing Kabila to consolidate power in his own hands gave him the ability to reconfigure the regime. As he aggressively promoted his co-ethnics from Katanga and marginalized the Congolese Tutsi, the Front grew ever wearier. The rapidly soaring distrust turned into outright hostility when Kabila intensified his efforts at developing a parallel army to establish military parity with the RPF. Advisers from the Tanzanian People's Defense Force had opened a training center in Kamina which was unambiguously intended to balance against the Front. When, in tandem with Katangization and the creation of a loyal force, Mzee also allowed his trusted aides to engage the ex-FAR/Interahamwe, a red line had been crossed. This was the point of no return where the two-level game of intra-regime and regional bargaining intersected in explosive ways.

With the nationality question unresolved and with mounting insecurity in eastern Congo, as well as a full-blown insurgency at home, the vexed RPF found natural partners in its old ally Museveni in Kampala, the Congolese Tutsis in the Kivus and a host of Kinshasa-based dissident politicians. Kabila remained (according to Kabarebe willfully) blind to the return of the *génocidaire* menace in northwest Rwanda which represented a rude awakening for Kigali: the war against its nemesis was by no means finished and Congo remained as important as ever for the survival of the RPF.

With few mechanisms to hold Kabila accountable or even to voice their grievances, the Congolese Tutsi and the External Security Organizations of Rwanda and Uganda explored options to remove Kabila from power. Rumors of such plotting made their way back to Mzee, which in turn augmented his paranoia and desire to hit back at Kagame by helping ALiR. As this security dilemma intensified, Kabila took the fateful step of replacing Kabarebe as head of the army and expelling "all foreign forces" from Congo: a declaration of war as far as the RPF was concerned.

The mutiny of the 10th Brigade on August 2, 1998, and James Kabarebe's raid on Kitona on August 4 pitted the comrades who had collaborated most closely during the liberation war against each other. Both Kabila and the RPF saw the conflict in existential terms. For the Front, a pro-ALiR regime in Kinshasa was unacceptable and threatened to put it back against the wall, a nightmare scenario given how widespread the violence was in Rwanda at the time. For Kabila, defeat would mean losing the position he had fought for since 1965 and probably death. However, the stakes were not just sky-high for the two central protagonists; because of the nature of the liberation project, the region could not stay out of Congo either: regardless of who would win the war, the domestic shift in power would spell major regional realignments too. In the absence of any credible regional mechanisms to manage disagreements between (neo-)liberation movements, each state watched nervously as the falling out of comrades threatened the regional distribution of power in unknown ways. Museveni's NRM quickly bandwagoned behind the RPF, Mugabe's ZANU-PF chose to defend Mzee—with Tanzania, South Africa and Zambia as uneasy fence-sitters. The defining choice, however, would be that of Angola's MPLA: despite its distrust of Kabila and its pessimism about the durability of any alliance with him, Dos Santos thought it even more critical that Luanda firmly underlined who the real kingmaker in Kinshasa was and would be for the future. The RPF had taken the MPLA for granted and would establish itself as the pre-eminent Central African power if it managed to engineer regime change in Kinshasa for the second time in two years. And thus Angolan intervention transformed what could have been a short and swift conflict into Africa's Great War: a hecatomb that would convulse the continent and rang the death knell for the Pan-Africanist liberation project.

The End of the Pan-Africanist Liberation Project: A Requiem

On May 14 and 15, 1998, a Great Lakes summit of foreign ministers was supposed to coincide with the first anniversary of the liberation of Congo. The chief participants in the campaign to oust Mobutu had earlier been invited to Kinshasa for meetings behind closed doors to address the growing worries that all comrades appeared to have about the direction in which the revolution was heading. As the date approached, it became clear none of the African leaders who had been part of the grand alliance would attend—no Nyerere, Dos Santos or Museveni—but that this would not stop senior diplomats and envoys from intelligence agencies traveling to Kinshasa. Neither Ethiopia's Meles Zenawi nor Eritrea's Issayas Afewerki came, but instead Ethiopian Foreign Minister Seyoum Mesfin and Great Lakes envoys Yemane Kidane, Yemane Gebreab and Haile Menkerios all headed to Congo. As the Eritrean delegation boarded its Ethiopian Airlines flight in Addis Ababa, Gebreab—Issayas's political right-hand—told Haile—the president's diplomatic point person—that he feared their Congo trip might be overshadowed by geopolitics. Both Gebreab and Haile had been deeply involved with the AFDL from 1996 onwards and had taken the lead in trying to sharpen its political organization and ideological program. They had both been gravely worried about the state of the alliance. But the geopolitics they were referring to had little to do with Congo.

As the two Eritrean envoys joined the breakfast buffet at the Intercontinental Hotel in Kinshasa the next morning, they were met by their Ethiopian counterparts, Seyoum Mesfin and Yemane Kidane, who immediately challenged them. The previous day on May 12, 1998, two Eritrean brigades had taken the disputed border town of Badme and dislodged a small Ethiopian force—a dramatic escalation after a week-long stand-off. Seyoum and Kidane's emotions alternated between fury and disbelief; the ruling TPLF in Addis and EPLF/PFDJ in Asmara had together beaten the military "Derg" dictatorship of Mengistu Haile Mariam after two decades of struggle. Their leaderships spoke the same language, shared the same culture and were, in several cases, closely related. As the Ethiopian–Eritrean quartet launched into more discussions about who was responsible for the worsening of relations, they were suddenly interrupted; it was not just time for the Kinshasa summit to start, but news came that the Ethiopian parliament had declared war on Eritrea. The four envoys—and their respective countries—exited Congo to focus on their "War of Brothers."[10] The Ethiopian–Eritrean war, which lasted from May 1998 to May 2000 and killed more than 100,000 people, was triggered by the Badme crisis but caused by a whole range of other issues, including monetary disputes, intra-Tigrayan politics and the tumultuous relationship between Meles and Issayas, who both aspired to become Africa's pre-eminent statesman.[11] It was the first of three conflicts in which liberation movements no longer turned their guns on hated "neo-colonial" regimes, but on each other. Crucially, these three outbreaks of violence happened within eighteen months of one another: comrades went to war along the Ethiopian–Eritrean border in May 1998, in eastern Congo and Kitona in August 1998 and in Kisangani, where Uganda and Rwanda fought their war of brothers in three parts, in August 1999, May 2000 and June 2000. These conflicts signaled the end of the Pan-Africanist liberation project as a collective endeavor. Their quasi-simultaneous occurrence had a huge political and psychological impact on the protagonists. For years, leading figures in Ethiopia and Eritrea had dreamed with RPF envoys about a "Greater Horn of Africa"; in Uganda, Sudan and Congo there was a lot of talk about a "New Africa" and even the Clinton administration had famously spoken of a "new generation of African leaders." Through various configurations, they had worked together for regime change in Uganda (1986), Ethiopia (1991), Eritrea (1991–3), Rwanda (1994) and Congo (1997); the conflict in Sudan, another target of the neo-liberation movements, was still undecided but had remained, until the outbreak of the Ethiopian–Eritrean war, a priority to which Meles, Issayas and Museveni contributed thousands of troops. After May 1998, however, the liberation movements would never

---

[10] Interviews in Addis Ababa and Asmara with Yemane Gebreab, Yemane Kidane and Haile Menkerios, November 2014 and March 2015.

[11] Negash Tekeste and Kjetil Tronvoll, *Brothers at War: Making Sense of the Eritrean–Ethiopian War*, Oxford: James Currey, 2000. Kjetil Tronvoll, *War & the Politics of Identity in Ethiopia: Making Enemies & Allies in the Horn of Africa*, Rochester, NY: James Currey, 2009; Richard Reid, "Old Problems in New Conflicts: Some Observations on Eritrea and Its Relations with Tigray—From Liberation Struggle to Inter-state War," *Africa*, 73, 3 (2003); John Abbink, "Ethiopia–Eritrea: Proxy Wars and Prospects of Peace in the Horn of Africa," *Journal of Contemporary African Studies*, 21, 3 (2003).

fight together again and no neo-liberation movement would succeed in over-throwing another incumbent government.

It is hard to overstate the disappointment and irony of the fact that it was the comrades themselves who conducted and performed the requiem for their collective liberation project at exactly the moment that their biggest enemies finally seemed vanquished and at a time when the United States—historically an adversary of Pan-Africanism—appeared to have accepted the legitimacy of the emerging new order. For Nyerere, officially retired from frontline politics for a decade, it was a particularly bitter pill. As he died of leukemia in October 1999, East Africa was more violent and war-torn than ever before, despite the defeat of so many regimes he resented and despite the rise to power of Dar es Salaam graduates and those, like the Tigrayans and Eritreans, who were not his direct political heirs but were attracted to his worldview and strategic thinking. However, there were good reasons for why the supposed grand finale of the liberation project turned out to be such a violent elegy.

As this book has emphasized, one of the project's great strengths resided in the transnational networks of militarily potent and politically shrewd actors who found each other through a common education, a common reading of geopolitical events (e.g., the Congo crisis of the 1960s) and ultimately a common struggle against different enemies. These networks were flexible and adaptable, in which individuals learned quickly from each other and were inspired by each other's success; thus even those who shared little in terms of history or culture—like the RPF and the EPLF—discovered a common out-look on Africa's predicament and common objectives of African liberation to be worked towards. But the changes rocking the continent in the 1990s—of which the Pan-Africanist neo-liberation movements were both cause and effect—also produced the conditions in which they would fall victim to their own success. On the one hand, the neo-liberation movements successfully consolidated internal order (save, ironically, for Kabila's regime)—none of them has ever fallen prey to a coup or been overturned by a rebellion. On the other, the rapid retreat of the "neo-colonial" forces—Apartheid South Africa, Mengistu, Habyarimana, Mobutu—and Washington's growing embrace of the liberation regimes led to the disappearance of an important factor that had ensured cohesion: a common enemy. The demise of most counter-revolution-ary threats—internally and externally—removed some of the glue that bound these transnational elites together.

The withering of regional polarization would not have been a significant challenge for the movements if, like they did back home, they managed to craft a robust organizational framework to handle disputes, formulate joint policies and specify a long-term vision, embedded within informal arrangements and understandings between comrades. But despite their commitment to trans-border cooperation and solidarity (which was real, as was manifested in the military and human sacrifices made for each other's struggle), the liberation movements failed to build strong Pan-Africanist institutions to further their dreams of a Greater Horn or a New Africa. The OAU was fatally compromised in their eyes, as it had failed to even support a single struggle in East or Central Africa, but the liberation movements produced little of their own in institutional terms; despite numerous summits between their respective leaders, little of substance was formulated that could serve as an alternative to the OAU, or at least seek to reform it from within. This failure was partly caused by the fact that, ultimately, this type of militarized Pan-Africanism remained very much an elite-driven project, the creation of a handful of larger than life individuals, and not a wider societal cause, supported by lobby groups or important constituencies in the populations of various countries. Much was determined by the egos of the movement's leaders; their inflated self-confidence, sense of entitlement and ambition helped win wars, but would also produce the fatal disagreements that resulted in the three wars of brothers: Meles vs Issayas; Kabarebe vs Kabila; Museveni vs Kagame.

Exacerbating all of the above—the weak institutionalization of cooperation, the elite nature of the project and the role of big egos—was the deep militarism that characterizes the liberation movements. As discussed earlier, the internalization of the imperative of the violent struggle had both ideological and pragmatic roots. Because these movements rose to power by decisively vanquishing their foes and then aiding violent regime change elsewhere, a profound belief in the transformative role of war was embedded in their organizational DNA. This has also meant that, in a context where few formal mechanisms exist to regulate the intense informal relations between liberation movements, there was a strong temptation to resort to military means to achieve their objectives. This is especially so because in the absence of a dispassionate, arm's length formal relationship, disagreements between individuals or movements are often understood to be personal insults or affronts, rather than political differences that could, potentially, be resolved without implications for personal ties. As Christine Umutoni, formerly a senior RPF leader, noted on the Front's relationship with the NRM in Uganda:

> We forgot the formalities, even after we became two governing parties of two different countries. There were no formal barriers. There was no formal framework.

We forgot it became a state-to-state relationship, no longer one between movements. During the struggle it is so easy to operate through trust but once in state power it is important to formalize.[12]

As we saw in Chapters 10 and 11, this is also what happened in the run-up to Africa's Great War; the explosive personal relationship between Kabila and Kabarebe—and Joseph Kabila—initially contributed to regime stability before fatally undermining it as personalized disagreements arose. The combination of a militarist sociology, the absence of institutionalized avenues to solve conflicts and the tendency to see disagreements as personal betrayal results in a highly combustible mix that lay at the heart of all three instances where comrades fought one another.

However disappointing and violent the requiem of the Pan-Africanist liberation project proved to be, its denouement did not imply the internal collapse of the movements that captured state power. The three wars of brothers effectively ended their revisionist, revolutionary foreign policies and resulted in their replacement with pragmatic Realpolitik in which the formerly transnational (neo-)liberation movements clothe themselves in nationalist garb and pursue national interests without inhibitions and with considerably less personalized political drama. Of course, Ethiopian–Eritrean, Rwandan–Congolese and Ugandan–Rwandan relations remain special and are often particularly opaque and difficult for outsiders to understand; but as the comrades age and their personal relations become less important to the formulation of policy, these relations too lose some of their emotional salience.

This mutation in the identity of the liberation movements has also had important domestic repercussions. To name the three most prominent examples, Angola's MPLA, Ethiopia's TPLF/EPRDF and Rwanda's RPF have all launched sweeping projects of internal transformation of the political–economic system following the military defeat of their nemesis and the end of their most important foreign entanglements. After 2002, these "illiberal statebuilders"[13] have used their formidable organizational prowess to secure what they consider the foundations of long-term hegemony: to place the commanding heights in key sectors under their control while still growing the economy rapidly; to keep the security services firmly politicized and extensively involved, alongside the ruling party, in the management of economic assets;

---

[12] Interview in Asmara, August 2014.

[13] Will Jones, Ricardo Soares de Oliveira and Harry Verhoeven, "Africa's Illiberal State-Builders," Oxford: Refugee Studies Centre, 2013.

to aggressively promote the social mobility of those groups whose support is seen as crucial to staying in power. The systems these liberation movements have built are explicitly illiberal in that they reject the idea of convergence with Washington Consensus recipes and its predicted end state of liberal democracies and free markets dominating the world; both economically and politically, competition and pluralism are seen as dangerous distractions from the unity of purpose and control that is required to build durable states under the aegis of the movement. The contours of these state-building projects could already be discerned in the first years after coming to power, but the end of the Pan-Africanist thrust of collective liberation has ensured that most of the energy and capital of the movements is now mostly spent internally, rather than on promoting external change.

The implication of the analysis presented in *Why Comrades Go to War* is that Africa's Great War was indeed a unique politico-historical tragedy that will most likely never be repeated. It transformed the continent's international relations and financially and organizationally helped rebuild a number of states that appear stronger and more consolidated than at any other point in recent history, even if Congo remains a notable and dispiriting exception to that trend. It is our conviction that both the first and the second Congo war were the product of a number of structural forces, ideological reveries and personal networks that have since lost their salience: the Pan-Africanist project of collective liberation and emancipation through violent struggle against (neo-)colonialism is dead and buried and the comrades of yesteryear are being or will soon be replaced by a different generation. The consequences, however, of their violent gambles are still with us and will continue to shape the continent in myriad ways. The project to turn Congo into the linchpin of a New Africa failed, ironically but not coincidentally, because the would-be liberators failed to think through the political challenge of liberation. At least one comrade, who as a protégé of Nyerere led the struggle in Mozambique, would perhaps not have been surprised by the outcome. "A soldier without politics is an assassin," Samora Machel often remarked. There is perhaps no more fitting epitaph to the fateful project for continental liberation that inspired millions—and gave Africa its most devastating war.

APPENDIX

METHODOLOGICAL NOTE

On the Elite Interviews of Why Comrades Go to War

Why Comrades Go to War relies heavily for many of its claims on extensive interviews with political and military elites in a range of African countries and senior diplomats from Western states. Many current or former officials who, as far we know, have seldom before testified about their role in and experience of Africa's Great War, spoke to us at length. Thus much of this book does not stem from administrative documents, personal letters or written decrees, but rather from actual human beings, at the very top of the decision-making machinery or at crucial posts in the outer nodes of these networks, remembering, analyzing and (re-)evaluating what their war was about. This brings to life the actual lived experiences of the political concepts used in this book and gives the protagonists of Africa's Great War a voice they lack in much contemporary scholarship in which authors mostly speculate about their motives and patterns of thinking.

While we propose an alternative theoretical framework to understand Africa's Great War and to think more broadly about liberation politics and violent conflict, we do not claim to provide a full, comprehensive picture of how this war was experienced—or what its ramifications have been. There is no one truth about the conflict—nor does there need to be a singular message. As scholars, we have taken it as our task to try to engage with the complexity of the real world and the often contradictory experiences of a number of elites at the very pinnacle of decision-making in Central Africa. We have tried to imagine what it was like to stand in the shoes of Laurent-Désiré Kabila, James

Kabarebe or Paul Rwarakabije and to operate within their worldviews, constrained by informational asymmetries and heavily dependent on a set of instruments and envisaged scenarios that have emerged from their respective historical experiences. Unlike some scholars who claim that the complexity of the human past does not lend itself to generalizable conclusions, we believe that as exceptional as the violence in Africa's Great War has been, the pathway from regional polarization to revolution to war is best understand through an analysis of liberation politics and their organizational bases. Ultimately, it is the reader who decides whether the conversation between social science and history writing that this book has engaged in has been successful.

Because we draw so heavily on interviews to weave together a new narrative of Africa's Great War, to shed light on some of its decisive junctures and to reveal important episodes and discussions for the first time, it is worth taking some time to reflect on our approach. From the onset, we never perceived of the set of elite interviews we hoped to conduct as merely neutral exchanges in which we as interviewers would somehow manage to extract information, recovering an "elusive truth" from a handful of gatekeepers. Rather, we see them as encounters in which knowledge was constructed and story-lines were spun, mediated through a range of human emotions, motivations and foibles, including political calculus, personal biases, fickle memory, confusion, a tendency to rationalize one's actions retrospectively, and so on.

Given the sensitivity and the importance of the subject at hand, subjectivity was inevitable—but also very much the core of what we were interested in. *Why Comrades Go to War* is not the story of all who were implicated in or affected by the conflict; it is also not an aloof dissection of the international politics of Congo in the 1990s. It is explicitly about how the winners of the first war—the campaign to overthrow Mobutu and the dream of a new Central Africa—and the belligerents of the second war—"The Great War"—first came together for the purpose of a transnational revolutionary project and then turned on each other. The prevailing discontent among African elites with the extant discourse on Africa's Great War in particular and with the narratives surrounding post-independence Africa more broadly meant that elaborate counter-narratives were destined to surface. Many of our interlocutors have long felt deeply misunderstood and misrepresented—and therefore seemed to have been enthusiastic to participate in reflective conversation about the events and processes they were involved in and/or observed, offering their own theories and explanations to account for the dynamics under study here. This book cannot tell a neutral, bloodless story: it has to capture the contestation, partiality and agony lived by the protagonists themselves, at the time of great hopes and solidarity, during the fratricidal years and today.

When treated carefully in combination with other sources and methods, allowing a lot of narrative agency to rest with interviewees can provide a wellspring of powerful new insights and of a reconceptualization of what history and social science thought they had established. The title of the book and the message it conveys are cases in point: *Why Comrades Go to War* emerged directly from our conversations with the protagonists. From Luanda to Asmara, we were struck by two things—first, how the protagonists would refer to one another and second, what the wider canvas was on which they painted this story of camaraderie and betrayal. We always let interviewees begin the story of their war at whatever point in history they felt was most suitable. In the vast majority of cases (and almost regardless of the individual's age), this meant leaping back to the late 1950s and early 1960s and the personalities, events and ideas shaking Africa to its core at that particular historical juncture. Almost all of our African interlocutors were adamant that this story, however devastating its outcomes, had to be embedded in the history of revolution and liberation politics. This is not merely a matter of vanity and self-glorification on the part of our interviewees, connecting themselves with Lumumba, Nyerere and the struggle against Apartheid to justify their actions—though such motives may well matter too. The framing chosen by the elites under study here is vitally important for understanding their self-image, their frame of reference, and their normative and political standards. In situating their dramatic personal experiences in the turbulent river of African liberation we apply our own dictum of taking the narratives of our interlocutors seriously. And we enable the reader to think through with us, and with the "comrades" central to this book, what the implications are of applying such a frame and burdening oneself with such historic responsibility.

Many of our subjects have built their lives and careers on unconstitutional ("revolutionary") and violent acts—and many of the events and processes under discussion in this book deal with those acts, their motives and their consequences. Given the particular nature of our interest and research questions, we have engaged in these elite interviews with the full expectation that our interviewees would enact performances, play roles and tell prescribed narratives sanctioned by their respective political organizations. At the same time, we also very much found that our interviewees seldom merely reproduced or blindly copied these storylines and that they rejected being mere mouthpieces of the Rwandan Patriotic Front, the Angolan government or the *famille katangaise.* They put their own spin on these narratives, reinterpreted testimonies of other comrades and sought to change them in some instances. They refracted imperatives of obeying the ruling party, appeasing international legal authorities and pleasing the interviewer through their own personal preferences, doubts and feelings of guilt and pride. It was obvious that many of our subjects improvised in response to some issues but also that some have long been haunted by the main questions asked by *Why Comrades Go to War*.

Our emphasis on narrative agency has meant being sensitive to a range of dynamics that have shaped the evidence we were presented with. Often, interviewees would meet us rather well prepared, having consulted personal notes or accounts of scholars or having spoken to old comrades about the war; sometimes this was the result of personal initiative, at other times it clearly emanated from orders given by their organizational superiors. Contemporary political developments had a particularly big impact: the tensions surrounding the publication in 2010 of the UN Mapping Report on the human rights violations committed in Congo between 1990 and 2013; the 2011 presidential election in Congo; the fracas around Rwandan and Ugandan support for the Congolese rebels of the Congrès National pour la Défense du Peuple (CNDP, 2009) and M23 (2013); and the controversy generated by the BBC documentary *Rwanda's Untold Story* in 2014. Such periods could result in the rapid closing down of space to converse about recent history (not least given how much of that history is connected to present politics), but occasionally also led to a stronger desire to tell their side of the truth, countering the narrative dominant in outside media. When these episodes took place, the interviewees would almost always prepare extensively for the interview. In turn, this sometimes helped make our conversation more detailed and the exchanges more vivid; at other times, it seemed to impede the authenticity of some of what was being remembered and narrated.

An important factor frequently at loggerheads with interviewees' strategies and preparations for our encounters has been the highly emotional character of the conflict and the associated breakdown of human relations and camaraderie. One striking feature of many interviews is that they revealed just how deeply invested in the dreams of revolution (however illusory these later revealed themselves to be) the comrades were. The disappointment, sadness and anger that accompanied the evaporating of these reveries continue to influence both the memories of the AFDL period and contemporary politics: the dynamics between Joseph Kabila and James Kabarebe in particular—from mentorship and camaraderie to personal betrayal to incomplete rapprochement since 2009—merit psychoanalytical study. Especially as our interviews carried on and follow-up discussions were organized, emotions of anger, guilt and hatred regularly led our interviewees to say things that seemed in direct contradiction with their own political interests and with their earlier testimonies regarding pivotal events and personalities. One former Congolese government minister broke down in tears, whispering a prayer for forgiveness "for the crimes we have all been involved in"; an intelligence source in Uganda confessed to having been unable to save a friend of his in Kinshasa because he himself was too focused on undermining Museveni; a Rwandan official became so agitated during an interview that he shouted "of course there was revenge [after the genocide]," accusing us of being blind to the suffering of his family members, some of whom were murdered in 1994.

The interaction between the strategic environment, ideology and emotions therefore had to be placed at the heart of *Why Comrades Go to War*. Decision-makers, and particularly politico-military elites in Central Africa, are often portrayed as maximizers of power, coolly calculating how to best play their cards in a Machiavellian milieu. This book clearly does not contradict this picture, but adds to it: the dynamics of the power politics around Africa's Great War can only be grasped when notions such as "interest," "liberation" and "security" are not solely understood in the light of Realpolitik but also through the full spectrum of human emotions. The events that *Why Comrades Go to War* concentrates on are not just epochal political moments, but some of the most shocking experiences any person can live through. As scholars we have tried to do justice to the scars this history has left. RPF strongman Paul Kagame, not often a man to talk about emotions, spoke for the vast majority of our sources when he voiced his bitter discontent with the dominant narratives of Central Africa's killings fields in the 1990s: "Some people even think we should not be affected. They think we are like animals, when you've lost some family, you can be consoled, given some bread and tea—and forget about it."[1]

In order to gain trust to talk about the interplay between ideology, institutions and sentiments we traveled extensively for six and a half years: lush gardens by Lake Kivu and grungy "Hutu-only" cafés in Brussels; desolate mountain strongholds in Eritrea and leafy suburbs of Washington; the luxury hotel enclaves of Luanda as well as dilapidated schools and sweltering bars in Limete, Yolo Sud and Masina. A key dimension of our encounters in all these places was explicitly recognizing, and where appropriate extensively discussing, our posi-

---

[1] Gourevitch, *Stories from Rwanda*, p. 337.

tionality as researchers. As white American and Belgian males, aged in our thirties and twenties when most of the work was carried out, one might expect some segments of Africa's liberation movements to have engaged more eagerly with us than others: this is especially pertinent in a region where Belgian–American partnerships have done extensive damage to local populations and are still seen to produce deeply unfair political pressures on and narratives about the countries in question. Not engaging those critical of both the history writing by involved outsiders and of Western academia in general would have considerably impoverished our understanding of Africa's Great War.

Embracing our positionality and trying to reflect on it with our interviewees—including explicitly soliciting potential pitfalls we may fall into or asking to be alerted of critical blind spots in our investigations—proved immensely important to researching and writing *Why Comrades Go to War*. We tried to be open about our project and about our eagerness to interview the protagonists and to tell the story through their voices: a story of empathy but not sympathy. In the course of this project we have never misrepresented what we do, who we are or what our objectives have been throughout. We have always believed that, both from an ethical standpoint and from the perspective of our own security and that of our interlocutors, openness and transparency was the only possible route. We did not hide that we already had or would interview their enemies, past and present. We offered them a fair hearing of their side of the story and a representation of their history that is as accurate as possible, though not an acceptance of the veracity of their testimony or any sympathy. The response to this approach has been overwhelmingly positive, bringing protagonists to the point where they were willing to talk about areas often considered no-go terrain: the inner circle of President Kabila talking about its relationship with the ex-FAR/Interahamwe; the RPF addressing the question of war crimes in Congo and in post-genocide Rwanda; dissident Congolese politicians revealing the preparations of a coup plot against their Mzee.

While using this method generated ample support and interest on the part of the people we have spoken to about this research project, we recognize that documenting and analyzing history by relying heavily on these testimonies is not without its problems. We already touched on several major concerns that we wrestled with: selectivity of interviewees (who speaks?); selectivity of topics (what is spoken about and what is left out?); the weakness of human memory (is what is remembered really what happened?); representation and political motivations (how does the present situation influence what memories are shared and what interpretations are given?). All of these are valid and important, but they are not qualitatively different from the usual obstacles faced by social scientists in academic inquiry and the examination of primary sources: questions of selectivity, representation, political motivation and other biases are as much part of the analysis of written documents as they are of oral testimonies.

Moreover, whereas interviews are indeed an essential component of the evidence put forward by this book in order to reconstruct why comrades went to war, we do not rely on them in isolation from contributions made by the impressive secondary literature we survey; from numerous written documents like diplomatic cables that also constitute crucial primary data; from tests of internal coherence and consistency with past testimonies by the same person; and from the claims made by other interviewees. Triangulation is a vitally important strategy deployed throughout the book—we do not provide standalone testimonies or quotes that are not put in context, linked back to secondary sources and/or nuanced or qualified by other witnesses or decision-makers. While this approach probably does not answer all questions there are to be posed about our choice to place elite interviews at the heart of our analysis and narrative, we think our understanding of this turning point of African history is much enriched by the inclusion of these testimonies, filtered through a theoretically informed and empirically rigorous set of checks.

Our focus on narrative agency is perhaps most sensitive to two specific aspects of representation: the faulty nature of human memory—as a trove of cognitive studies have shown, what people remember and how they remember changes over time is highly susceptible to context and interlocutor—and the translation of people's testimonies to us into the central narrative of *Why Comrades Go to War*. The former points once again to the importance of combining multiple sources and different methods: as valuable as individual elite interviews are, to rely on them for, say, exact dates (when exactly was "General" Muland arrested?) or exact numbers (how many people were killed in Mugunga?) would be misguided. Moreover, as two veteran researchers of interviews with Washington politicians underline, elite narratives are often "improvised accounts that overstate the significance of individuals (rather than institutions), personalities (rather than incentives) and processes (rather than contexts)."[2] Helped by a mixed-methods design and a rich conceptual apparatus, we as authors have tried to balance our desire to let our inter-

[2] Matthew N. Beckman and Richard L. Hall, "Elite Interviewing in Washington, DC," in Layna Mosley (ed.), *Interview Research in Political Science*, Ithaca: Cornell University Press, 2013, p. 198.

viewees tell the narrative with a recognition of the inherent cognitive biases of such memory mining and therefore the need for checks and structure.

Such active mediation, or even "co-production" of narratives,[3] highlights the delicate role we as scholars play in managing competing priorities, including faithfully reflecting the words and intentions of interviewees while also trying to establish historical truth. We have attempted, to the best of our ability, to accurately represent the worldviews and interpretations of our interlocutors. We never promised them that we would believe them; all we could guarantee was a serious engagement with their testimonies. Some of our interviewees may well be disappointed with the end result and feel that our conclusions are unfair, or paint their actions in an unfavorable light. We have done our utmost to weigh up, contextualize and situate the controversial decisions, heinous crimes and egregious violence documented in these pages. Many of our interlocutors genuinely appear to regret some of what has been done by their organizations, sometimes in their names, sometimes even by themselves. While it is impossible to say whether such remorse is authentic, there was almost universal recognition that all parties share part of the blame for Africa's Great War: this tragedy must be collectively owned. In many cases, interviewees struggle to publicly say this in their own country's public sphere, but are nevertheless deeply convinced of the need for a much broader conversation about what happened—and how and why Africa's Great War unfolded. We fervently hope that this book makes a meaningful contribution to that dialogue.

We conclude this appendix by providing the reader with a non-exhaustive list of elite interviewees consulted for *Why Comrades Go to War*. As such, we aim to balance the confidentiality of the interviews and interviewees with academic credibility and the importance of referencing our analysis. The claims made about the motivations and actions of elites in Congo and elsewhere in Central Africa are based on many hours of in-depth discussions. Some spoke on condition of anonymity, while others were happy to be cited for research purposes. The list below contains the majority of the senior sources interviewed over a six-year period (2009–15). A substantial number of sources are omitted, at their request, given the sensitivity of the information that they chose to share and the potential consequences for their security, political career or residency status for being linked to certain episodes

---

[3] Jaber F. Gubrium and James A. Holstein, "Narrative Practice and the Transformation of Interview Subjectivity," in Jaber F. Gubrium and James A. Holstein (eds), *Handbook of Interview Research: Context & Method*, Thousand Oaks, CA: Sage, 2002.

reported in the book. This is particularly the case for diaspora communities, not least those Rwandans associated with the old Habyarimana regime and the struggle of the ALiR/FDLR against the RPF. The names below are listed with their most relevant affiliation for the purposes of this research project. While some may have gone on to other illustrious positions, we only include here the formal function they fulfilled during the time period under examination.

We sincerely hope that the end result of our six and a half year odyssey illustrates the merits of the methodological approach pursued.

List of Interviewees

* Homayoun Alizadeh, officer of the UN Human Rights Field Operation in Rwanda, 1995–7
* Edi Angilu, Kabila's minister of the environment
* Irung Awan, diplomatic counsellor to Laurent-Désiré Kabila
* Frank Begumisa, lieutenant in the Rwandan Patriotic Army and close aide to James Kabarebe
* Kizza Besigye, national political commissar for Uganda's National Resistance Movement
* Deogratias Bugera, AFDL secretary general (1996–8)
* Lunda Bululu, former prime minister under Mobutu (1990–1), coordinator of the RCD rebellion
* Winnie Byanyima, MP in Ugandan Parliament
* Moses Byaruhanga, political adviser to the president of Uganda
* Raus Chalwe, head of intelligence of the Congolese National Police
* Manuel Correia de Barros, colonel in the Angolan Military Intelligence Service
* Francisco Da Cruz, political counselor at the Angolan Embassy in Washington, DC
* Frank De Coninck, Belgian ambassador to Rwanda (1994–7) and Congo (1997–2000)
* Luc De Temmerman, defense counsel of the Habyarimana family in the 1990s and of Colonel Théoneste Bagosora of the Forces Armées Rwandaises
* Chikez Diemu, member of the Congolese National Assembly
* Carlos Feijo, chief legal adviser to President Dos Santos
* Gerald Gahima, secretary-general of the Rwandan Ministry of Justice
* Yemane Gebreab, chief political adviser to Eritrean President Issayas Afewerki

* Yemane Gebremeskel, presidential adviser to Issayas Afewerki
* Raphael Ghenda, Kabila's minister of information
* Filippo Grandi, field coordinator of UN humanitarian activities and of the Office of the UN High Commissioner for Refugees in the Democratic Republic of Congo, 1996–7
* Robert Gribbin, US ambassador to Rwanda (1996–9)
* Konrad Huber, officer of the UN Human Rights Field Operation in Rwanda, 1995–7
* Émile Ilunga, one of the founders of the RCD
* Joseph Ilunga, minister for small- and medium-sized enterprises under Mobutu (1993)
* Mario Placido Cirilo de Sa "Ita," head of military intelligence of the Angolan Armed Forces in Congo
* James Kabarebe, colonel in the Rwandan Patriotic Army and chief of staff of the Forces Armées Congolaises
* Jaynet Kabila, daughter of Laurent Désiré Kabila and twin-sister (and political confidante) of Joseph Kabila
* Rose Kabuye, mayor of Kigali (1994–6) and head of protocol at the Office of the President of Rwanda
* Bizima Karaha, Kabila's minister of foreign affairs
* Joseph Karemera, minister of education in the Rwandan government and colonel in the Rwandan Patriotic Army
* Karake Karenzi, head of Military Intelligence of the Rwandan Patriotic Army
* Gideon Kayinamura, Rwandan ambassador to the United Nations (1996–8)
* Caesar Kayizari, deputy force commander of the Rwandan Patriotic Army in Congo (1996–7)
* Baudouin Kayokela Kasangala, administrator at the Congolese Central Bank
* Didier Kazadi, national security adviser to President Kabila
* Yemane Kidane, special envoy for Ethiopia to the Great Lakes (1996–8)
* Célestin Kifwa, inspector-general of the Congolese National Police and, from July 1998, chief of staff of the Forces Armées Congolaises
* Malick Kijege, battalion commander in the Forces Armées Congolaises
* Mwenze Kongolo, Kabila's minister of justice
* Norbert Mao, MP in the Ugandan Parliament
* Ian Martin, head of the United Nations Human Rights Field Operation in Rwanda (1995–6)

* Alexander Mayer-Rieckh, report editor of the UN Human Rights Field Operation in Rwanda, 1995-7
* Patrick Mazimhaka, Rwanda's special envoy to the Great Lakes (1997-2000) and minister of rehabilitation and social welfare (1994-7)
* Baby Mbaye, Kabila's minister of planning and industry
* Roger Meece, deputy chief of mission at the US embassy in Kinshasa (1995-8)
* Haile Menkerios, Eritrean ambassador to the Organization of African Unity and special envoy to the Great Lakes (1991-8)
* Henri Mova Sakanyi, Kabila's minister of transport
* Oscar Mudiay, chef de cabinet of Minister of the Economy and Petroleum Victor Mpoyo
* Frank Mugambage, chef de cabinet of Rwandan President Pasteur Bizimungu
* Wilson Muruuli Mukasa, Ugandan minister of security
* Faustin Munene, vice-minister of the interior in Congo
* Dan Munyuza, head of intelligence for the RPF in Congo (1997-8)
* Faustin Musare, Office of Rwandan President Pasteur Bizimungu (1997-8)
* Joseph Mutaboba, Rwandan ambassador to the United States (1994-8)
* Miguel Neto, Angola's special envoy to the Great Lakes
* Emmanuel Ndahiro, chief political adviser to Vice-President Kagame
* Joseph Ngirabanzi, captain of the Forces Armées Rwandaises and later member of the Executive Committee of the Forces Démocratiques pour la Liberation du Rwanda
* Welile Nhlapo, South African ambassador to the OAU and Ethiopia, 1995-7
* Antepas Mbusa Nyamwisi, organizer of the RCD
* Moïse Nyarugabo, private secretary to Kabila (1997) and one of the main organizers of the RCD
* Jack Nziza, major in Rwanda's Directorate of Military Intelligence
* Jeje Odongo, chief of staff of the Ugandan People's Defense Forces
* Léonard "Shé" Okitundu, Kabila's minister of human rights and top diplomatic adviser
* Philomène Omatuku, speaker of the Congolese National Assembly during the transition
* Rick Orth, US defense attaché to Rwanda (1996-9)
* David Pulkol, head of Uganda's External Security Organization
* Okwiri Rabwoni, MP in Ugandan Parliament and former officer in the Rwandan Patriotic Army (1990-6)

* Azarias Ruberwa, chairman of the RCD and chef de cabinet of Foreign Minister Bizima Karaha
* Frank Rusagara, permanent secretary of the Rwandan Ministry of Defense
* Paul Rwarakabije, chief of staff of the Armée pour la Liberation du Rwanda
* David Scheffer, ambassador at large for war crimes, US State Department
* Pedro Sebastiao, Angolan minister of defense
* Clare Short, British minister for international development
* Jean-Baptiste Sondji, Kabila's minister of health
* Johan Swinnen, Belgian ambassador to Rwanda (1990–4)
* Godefroid Tchamlesso, adjunct chef de cabinet of Kabila
* Tsadkan Tensae, chief of staff of the Ethiopian National Defense Force (1991–2001)
* Mutomb Tshibal, Kabila's minister of sports and youth
* Christine N. Umutoni, Directeur de Cabinet of Rwanda's Ministry of Rehabilitation (1994–7)
* Howard Wolpe, US special envoy to the Great Lakes (1997–2000)
* Jean Claude Yav, head of security for the deputy chief of staff of the Forces Armées Congolaises, Joseph Kabila
* Abdoulaye Ndombasi Yerodia, chef de cabinet of Laurent-Désiré Kabila
* Zemhret Yohannes, Executive Council of Eritrea's (ruling) Party for Freedom, Democracy and Justice

BIBLIOGRAPHY

Abbink, John, "Ethiopia–Eritrea: Proxy Wars and Prospects of Peace in the Horn of Africa," *Journal of Contemporary African Studies*, 21, 3 (2003), pp. 407–26.

Abdul-Raheem, Tajudeen (ed.), *Pan-Africanism: Politics, Economy, and Social Change in the Twenty-First Century*, London: Pluto Press, 1996.

Acemoglu, Daron, and James A. Robinson, *Why Nations Fail: The Origins of Power, Prosperity and Poverty*, New York: Crown Publishers, 2012.

Acemoglu, Daron, Thierry Verdier and James A. Robinson, "Kleptocracy and Divide-and-Rule: A Model of Personal Rule," *Journal of the European Economic Association*, 2, 2–3 (2004), 162–92.

Adelman, Howard, and Govind C. Rao, *War and Peace in Zaire–Congo: Analyzing and Evaluating Intervention, 1996–1997*, Trenton: Africa World Press, 2004.

Adi, Hakim, Marika Sherwood and George Padmore, *The 1945 Manchester Pan-African Congress Revisited*, 3rd edn, London: New Beacon Books, 1995.

African Rights, "'If You Die, Perhaps I Will Live': A Collective Account of Genocide and Survival in Murambi, Gikongoro, April–July 1994." Kigali: African Rights, 2007.

—— *Rwanda: The Insurgency in the Northwest*, London: African Rights, 1998.

—— "A Welcome Expression of Intent: The Nairobi Communique and the Ex-Far/Interahamwe," London: African Rights, 2007.

Akyeampong, Emmanuel Kwaku, and Henry Louis Gates, *Dictionary of African Biography*, vol. 1, New York: Oxford University Press, 2012.

Alexander, Jocelyn, JoAnn McGregor and T.O. Ranger, *Violence & Memory: One Hundred Years in the "Dark Forests" of Matabeleland*, Oxford: James Currey 2000.

Amnesty International, "Amnesty International Condemns Human Rights Violations against Tutsi," London: Amnesty International, 1996.

—— "Deadly Alliances in Congolese Forests," London: Amnesty International, 1997.

—— "'Disappearances' and Killings Continue on a Daily Basis," London: Amnesty International, 1998.

—— "Ending the Silence," London: Amnesty International, 1997.

—— *Republic of Congo: An Old Generation of Leaders in New Carnage*, London: Amnesty International, 1999.

Arden-Clarke, Charles, "Eight Years of Transition in Ghana," *African Affairs*, 57, 226 (1958), pp. 29–37.

Askin, Steve, and Carole Collins, "External Collusion with Kleptocracy: Can Zaïre Recapture Its Stolen Wealth?," *Review of African Political Economy*, 20, 57 (1993), 72–85.

Atumba, Honoré N'Gbanda Nzambo Ko, *Ainsi sonne le glas: les derniers jours du Maréchal Mobutu*, Paris: Groupe International d'Edition et de Publication de Presse économique, 1998.

Autesserre, Séverine, *The Trouble with the Congo: Local Violence and the Failure of International Peacebuilding*, Cambridge and New York: Cambridge University Press, 2010.

Bacquelaine, Daniel, Marie-Thérèse Coenen and Ferdy Willems, "Parlementair onderzoek met het oog op het vaststellen van de precieze omstandigheden waarin patrice lumumba werd vermoord en van de eventuele betrokkenheid daarbij van Belgische politici," Brussels: Belgische Kamer van Volksvertegenwoordigers, 2001.

Bailey, Martin, "Tanzania and China," *African Affairs*, 74, 294 (1975), 39–50.

Barber, James, and John Barratt, *South Africa's Foreign Policy: The Search for Status and Security, 1945–1988*, Cambridge: Cambridge University Press, 1990.

Bayart, Jean-François, *L'etat en afrique: la politique du ventre*, Paris: Fayard, 1989.

Beckman, Matthew N., and Richard L. Hall, "Elite Interviewing in Washington, D.C.," in Layna Mosley (ed.), *Interview Research in Political Science*, Ithaca: Cornell University Press, 2013.

Behrend, Heike, *Alice Lakwena and the Holy Spirits: War in Northern Uganda*, Oxford: James Currey, 1999.

Beit-Hallahmi, Benjamin, *The Israeli Connection: Who Israel Arms and Why*, London: I.B. Tauris, 1987.

Bell, Richard H., *Understanding African Philosophy: A Cross-Cultural Approach to Classical and Contemporary Issues in Africa*, New York: Routledge, 2002.

Berkeley, Bill, "An African Horror Story," *Atlantic Monthly*, 272, 2 (1993), pp. 20–5.

Berman, Eric G., and Katie E. Sams, "The Peacekeeping Potential of African Regional Organizations," in Jane Boulden (ed.), *Dealing with Conflict in Africa: The United Nations and Regional Organizations*, New York: Palgrave, 2003.

Bhebe, Ngwabi, and T.O. Ranger (eds), *Soldiers in Zimbabwe's Liberation War*, Portsmouth, NH: Heinemann, 1996.

Bienen, Henry, *Tanzania: Party Transformation and Economic Development*, Princeton, NJ: Princeton University Press, 1970.

Binet, Laurence, *Rwandan Refugee Camps in Zaire and Tanzania, 1994–1995*, Geneva: Médecins sans Frontières, 2005.

BIBLIOGRAPHY

Bjerk, Paul, *Building a Peaceful Nation: Julius Nyerere and the Establishment of Sovereignty in Tanzania, 1960–1964*, Rochester, NY: University of Rochester Press, 2015.

Blumenthal, Erwin, "Zaïre: rapport sur sa crédibilité financière internationale," *La revue nouvelle*, 77, 11 (1982), pp. 360–78.

Boix, Carles, and Milan W. Svolik, "The Foundations of Limited Authoritarian Government: Institutions, Commitment, and Power-Sharing in Dictatorships," *Journal of Politics*, 75, 2 (2013), pp. 300–16.

Branch, Adam, "Neither Peace nor Justice: Political Violence and the Peasantry in Northern Uganda, 1986–1998," *African Studies Quarterly*, 8, 2 (2005), pp. 1–31.

Brett, Edward A., "Rebuilding Organisation Capacity in Uganda under the National Resistance Movement," *Journal of Modern African Studies*, 32, 1 (1994), pp. 53–80.

Brownlee, Jason, *Authoritarianism in an Age of Democratization*, New York: Cambridge University Press, 2007.

Bulhan, Hussein Abdilahi, *Frantz Fanon and the Psychology of Oppression*, New York: Plenum Press, 1985.

Callaghy, Thomas, "The State as Lame Leviathan: The Patrimonial Administrative State in Africa," in Zaki Ergas (ed.), *The African State in Transition*, New York: St. Martin's Press, 1987.

Callaghy, Thomas, Ronald Kassimir and Robert Latham, *Intervention and Transnationalism in Africa: Global–Local Networks of Power*, New York: Cambridge University Press, 2001.

Chabal, Patrick, *Amílcar Cabral: Revolutionary Leadership and People's War*, Cambridge: Cambridge University Press, 1983.

⸺ (ed.), *Political Domination in Africa: Reflection on the Limits of Power*, New York: Cambridge University Press, 1986.

Chabal, Patrick, and Jean-Pascal Daloz, *Africa Works: Disorder as Political Instrument*, Oxford: James Currey, 1999.

Chafer, Tony, *The End of Empire in French West Africa: France's Successful Decolonisation?*, Oxford: Berg Publishers, 2002.

Chrétien, Jean-Pierre, *Le défi de l'ethnisme: Rwanda et Burundi, 1990–1996*, Paris: Karthala Editions, 1997.

Clapham, Christopher, *Africa and the International System: The Politics of State Survival*, New York: Cambridge University Press, 1996.

⸺ "Introduction: Analysing African Insurgencies," in Christopher Clapham (ed.), *African Guerrillas*, Oxford: James Currey, 1998.

Clark, John F., "The Nature and Evolution of the State in Zaire," *Studies in Comparative International Development*, 32, 4 (1998), pp. 3–23.

Clark, John F. (ed.), *The African Stakes of the Congo War*, New York: Palgrave Macmillan, 2002.

Clayton, Anthony, *Frontiersmen: Warfare in Africa since 1950*, London: UCL Press, 1999.

Coker, Christopher, "The Western Alliance and Africa, 1949–81," *African Affairs*, 81, 324 (1982), pp. 319–35.

Colgan, Jeff D., and Jessica L.P. Weeks, "Revolution, Personalist Dictatorships, and International Conflict," *International Organization* (2015), pp. 1–32.

Colgan, Jeff D., "Domestic Revolutionary Leaders and International Conflict," *World Politics*, 65, 4 (2013), pp. 656–90.

Collier, Paul, *The Bottom Billion: Why the Poorest Countries Are Failing and What Can Be Done About It*, New York: Oxford University Press, 2007.

Collier, Paul, Anke Hoeffler and Måns Söderbom, "Post-Conflict Risks," *Journal of Peace Research*, 45, 4 (2008), pp. 461–78.

Connell, Dan, and Frank Smyth, "Africa's New Bloc," *Foreign Affairs* (1998), pp. 80–94.

Cooper, Tom, *Great Lakes Conflagration: The Second Congo War, 1998–2003*, Solihull, England: Helion, 2013.

Copeland, Dale C., *The Origins of Major War*, Ithaca: Cornell University Press, 2000.

Cosma, Wilungula B., and Jean-Luc Vellut, *Fizi, 1967–1986: Le Maquis Kabila*, Brussels: Institut Africain CEDAF, 1997.

Daly, M.W., *Empire on the Nile: The Anglo-Egyptian Sudan, 1898–1934*, New York: Cambridge University Press, 1986.

David, Steven R., *Choosing Sides: Alignment and Realignment in the Third World*, Baltimore: Johns Hopkins University Press, 1991.

De Villers, Gauthier, and Jean Tshonda Omasombo, "An Intransitive Transition," *Review of African Political Economy*, 29, 93–4 (2002), pp. 399–410.

——— *Zaïre: la transition manquée (1990–1997)*, Paris: Éditions L'Harmattan, 1997.

De Villers, Gauthier, and Jean-Claude Willame, *République Démocratique du Congo: chronique politique d'un entre-deux-guerres, octobre 1996–juillet 1998*, Tervuren and Paris: Institut Africain—CEDAF and Editions L'Harmattan, 1999.

De Witte, Ludo, *Huurlingen, Geheim Agenten En Diplomaten*, Leuven: Uitgeverij Van Halewyck, 2014.

De Witte, Ludo, and Ann Wright, *The Assassination of Lumumba*, London: Verso, 2002.

Des Forges, Alison, *Defeat Is the Only Bad News: Rwanda under Musinga, 1896–1931*, Madison: University of Wisconsin Press, 2011.

——— *"Leave None to Tell the Story": Genocide in Rwanda*, New York: Human Rights Watch, 1999.

Devlin, Larry, *Chief of Station, Congo: Fighting the Cold War in a Hot Zone*, New York: PublicAffairs, 2007.

DuBois, W.E.B., "To the Nations of the World," in David L. Lewis (ed.), *W.E.B. Dubois: A Reader*, New York: H. Holt, 1995.

Dunn, Kevin C., *Imagining the Congo: The International Relations of Identity*, London: Palgrave Macmillan, 2003.

BIBLIOGRAPHY

El Saadawi, Nawal, "President Nyerere Talks to *El Mussawar* (1984)," in Chambi Chachage and Annar Cassam (eds), *Africa's Liberation: The Legacy of Nyerere*, Kampala, Uganda: Pambazuka Press, 2010.

Englebert, Pierre, *Africa: Unity, Sovereignty, and Sorrow*, Boulder, CO: Lynne Rienner, 2009.

Ernesto, "Che" Guevara, *The African Dream: Diaries of the Revolutionary War in the Congo*, London: Havill Press, 2000

Esedebe, P. Olisanwuche, *Pan-Africanism: The Idea and Movement, 1776–1991*, 2nd edn, Washington, DC: Howard University Press, 1994.

Fanon, Frantz, *Black Skin, White Masks*, New York: Grove, 1967.

——— *Les damnés de la terre*, Paris: F. Maspéro, 1961.

——— *The Wretched of the Earth*, trans. Richard Philcox, New York: Grove Press, 2004 (1963).

Fearon, James D., "Rationalist Explanations for War," *International Organization*, 49, 3 (1995), pp. 379–414.

Federation Internationale des Droits de l'Homme, "Forces de fuir: violence contre les Tutsi Au Zaïre," Paris, 1996.

Finnegan, William, *A Complicated War: The Harrowing of Mozambique*, Berkeley: University of California Press, 1992.

Fisher, Jonathan, "Managing Donor Perceptions: Contextualizing Uganda's 2007 Intervention in Somalia," *African Affairs*, 111, 444 (2012), pp. 404–23.

Flint, Julie, and Alexander De Waal, *Darfur: A New History of a Long War*, New York: Zed Books 2008.

French, Howard W., *A Continent for the Taking: The Tragedy and Hope of Africa*, New York: Alfred A. Knopf, 2004.

Fryer, Peter, *Staying Power: The History of Black People in Britain*, London: Pluto Press, 1984.

Gilpin, Robert, *War and Change in World Politics*, New York: Cambridge University Press, 1981.

Gleditsch, Kristian Skrede, "Transnational Dimensions of Civil War," *Journal of Peace Research*, 44, 3 (2007), pp. 293–309.

Gleditsch, Kristian Skrede, Idean Salehyan and Kenneth Schultz, "Fighting at Home, Fighting Abroad," *Journal of Conflict Resolution*, 52, 4 (2008), pp. 479–506.

Gleijeses, Piero, "Moscow's Proxy? Cuba and Africa 1975–1988," *Journal of Cold War Studies*, 8, 4 (2006), pp. 98–146.

Goldstone, Jack A., "Toward a Fourth Generation of Revolutionary Theory," *Annual Review of Political Science*, 4 (2001), pp. 139–87.

Gourevitch, Philip, "Continental Shift," *New Yorker*, August 4, 1997.

——— "The Life After," *New Yorker*, May 4, 2009.

——— *Stories from Rwanda: We Wish to Inform You That Tomorrow We Will Be Killed with Our Families*, New York: Picador, 1998.

Gribbin, Robert E., *In the Aftermath of Genocide: The US Role in Rwanda*, Lincoln, NE: iUniverse, 2005.

Gubrium, Jaber F., and James A. Holstein, "Narrative Practice and the Transformation of Interview Subjectivity," in Jaber F. Gubrium and James A. Holstein (eds), *Handbook of Interview Research: Context & Method*, pp. 27–43, Thousand Oaks, CA: Sage, 2002.

Gunther, John, *Inside Africa*, New York: Harper, 1955.

Habyarimana, James, Macartan Humphreys, Daniel N. Posner and Jeremy M. Weinstein, *Coethnicity: Diversity and the Dilemmas of Collective Action*, New York: Russell Sage Foundation, 2009.

Halliday, Fred, *Revolution and World Politics: The Rise and Fall of the Sixth Great Power*, Durham, NC: Duke University Press, 1999.

Hare, Paul Julian, *Angola's Last Best Chance for Peace*, Washington, DC: United States Institute of Peace Press, 1998.

Harroy, Jean-Paul, *Rwanda: de la féodalité à la démocratie, 1955–1962*, Brussels: Hayez and Académie des Sciences d'Outremer, 1984.

Hatzfeld, Jean, *Into the Quick of Life: The Rwandan Genocide—The Survivors Speak*, London: Serpent's Tail, 2005.

Hechter, Michael, *Alien Rule*, New York: Cambridge University Press, 2013.

Henriksen, Thomas H., *Revolution and Counterrevolution: Mozambique's War of Independence, 1964–1974*, Westport, CT: Greenwood Press, 1983.

Herbst, Jeffrey, "African Peacekeepers and State Failure," in Robert I. Rotberg et al. (eds), *Peacekeeping and Peace Enforcement in Africa*, pp. 16–53, Washington, DC: Brookings Institution Press, 2000.

——— *States and Power in Africa: Comparative Lessons in Authority and Control*, Princeton, NJ: Princeton University Press, 2000.

Hochschild, Adam, *King Leopold's Ghost: A Story of Greed, Terror, and Heroism in Colonial Africa*, Boston: Houghton Mifflin, 1998.

Horne, Alistair, *A Savage War of Peace: Algeria, 1954–1962*, New York: New York Review Books, 2011.

Horowitz, Michael C., and Allan C. Stam, "How Prior Military Experience Influences the Future Militarized Behavior of Leaders," *International Organization*, 68, 3 (2014), pp. 527–59.

Hughes-Wilson, John, *Military Intelligence Blunders*, New York: Carroll & Graf, 1999.

Huliaras, Asteris C., "The 'Anglosaxon Conspiracy': French Perceptions of the Great Lakes Crisis," *Journal of Modern African Studies*, 36, 4 (1998), pp. 593–609.

Human Rights Watch, *Angola Unravels: The Rise and Fall of the Lusaka Peace Process*, New York: Human Rights Watch, 1999.

——— "Attacked by All Sides: Civilians and the War in Eastern Zaire," New York: Human Rights Watch, 1997.

——— "Rwanda: Observing the Rules of War?," New York: Human Rights Watch, 2001.

BIBLIOGRAPHY

———— "What Kabila Is Hiding: Civilian Killing and Impunity in Congo," New York: Human Rights Watch, 1997.

Humphreys, Macartan, "Natural Resources, Conflict, and Conflict Resolution," *Journal of Conflict Resolution*, 49, 4 (2005), pp. 508–37.

Huntington, Samuel P., *Political Order in Changing Societies*, New Haven, CT: Yale University Press, 1968.

Ikos Rukal Diyal, J.E., *La générale de carrières et des mines (gcm): une culture et une civilisation*, Lubumbashi: Editions Baobab, 2007.

International Crisis Group, "Burundian Refugees in Tanzania: The Key Factor to the Burundi Peace Process," *ICG Central Africa Report*, no. 12, Brussels: International Crisis Group, 1999.

———— "How Kabila Lost His Way: The Performance of Laurent Désiré Kabila's Government," Brussels: International Crisis Group, 1999.

Jackson, Paul, "Legacy of Bitterness: Insurgency in North West Rwanda," *Small Wars & Insurgencies*, 15, 1 (2004), pp. 19–37.

Jackson, Robert H., *Quasi-States: Sovereignty, International Relations and the Third World*, Cambridge: Cambridge University Press, 1990.

Jackson, Robert H., and Carl G. Rosberg, *Personal Rule in Black Africa*, Berkeley: University of California Press, 1982.

———— "Why Africa's Weak States Persist: The Empirical and the Juridical in Statehood," *World Politics*, 35, 1 (1982), pp. 1–24.Jervis, Robert, "Cooperation under the Security Dilemma," *World Politics*, 30, 2 (1978), pp. 167–214.

Joint Evaluation of Emergency Assistance for Rwanda, "The Rwanda Experience: International Response to Conflict and Genocide," Copenhagen, 1994.

Jonas, Raymond Anthony, *The Battle of Adwa: African Victory in the Age of Empire*, Cambridge, MA: Belknap Press of Harvard University Press, 2011.

Jones, Will, Ricardo Soares de Oliveira and Harry Verhoeven, "Africa's Illiberal State-Builders," Oxford: Refugee Studies Centre, 2013.

Joris, Lieve, *The Rebels' Hour*, trans. Liz Waters, New York: Grove Press, 2008.

Kalyvas, Stathis N., *The Logic of Violence in Civil War*, New York: Cambridge University Press, 2006.

Kasfir, Nelson, "Guerrillas and Civilian Participation: The National Resistance Army in Uganda, 1981–86," *Journal of Modern African Studies*, 43, 2 (2005), pp. 271–96.

Kennes, Erik, *Essai biographique sur Laurent Désiré Kabila*, Paris: L'Harmattan, 2003.

Keohane, Robert O., *After Hegemony: Cooperation and Discord in the World Political Economy*, Princeton, NJ: Princeton University Press, 1984.

Khadiagala, Gilbert M., *Allies in Adversity: The Frontline States in Southern African Security, 1975–1993*, Athens: Ohio University Press, 1994.

Khan, Shaharyar M., *The Shallow Graves of Rwanda*, London: I.B. Tauris, 2000.

Kibreab, Gaim, "Eritrean–Sudanese Relations in Historical Perspective," in Richard Reid (ed.), *Eritrea's External Relations: Understanding Its Regional Role and Foreign Policy*, pp. 71–97. London: Royal Institute of International Affairs, 2009.

Kindela, Fadjay, and Laurens Rademakers, "Recycling the Past: Rehabilitating Congo's Colonial Palm and Rubber Plantations," http://news.mongabay.com/bioenergy/2006/09/recycling-past-rehabilitating-congos.html

Kinzer, Stephen, *A Thousand Hills: Rwanda's Rebirth and the Man Who Dreamed It*, Hoboken: John Wiley & Sons, 2008.

Kisangani, Emizet F., *Civil Wars in the Democratic Republic of Congo, 1960–2010*, Boulder: Lynne Rienner, 2012.

—— "The Massacre of Refugees in Congo: A Case of UN Peacekeeping Failure and International Law," *Journal of Modern African Studies*, 38, 2 (2000), pp. 163–202.

Kriger, Norma J., *Zimbabwe's Guerrilla War: Peasant Voices*, New York: Cambridge University Press, 1992.

Kroslak, Daniela, *The French Betrayal of Rwanda*, Bloomington: Indiana University Press, 2007.

Krueger, Robert, and Kathleen Tobin Krueger, *From Bloodshed to Hope in Burundi: Our Embassy Years during Genocide*, Austin: University of Texas Press, 2009.

Laidi, Zaki, *The Superpowers and Africa: The Constraints of a Rivalry, 1960–1990*, Chicago: University of Chicago Press, 1990.

Langley, J. Ayodele, *Pan-Africanism and Nationalism in West Africa, 1900–1945: A Study in Ideology and Social Classes*, Oxford: Clarendon Press, 1973.

Larmer, Miles, "Local Conflicts in a Transnational War: The Katangese Gendarmes and the Shaba Wars of 1977–78," *Cold War History*, 13, 1 (2012), 89–108.

Larmer, Miles, and Erik Kennes, "Rethinking the Katangese Secession," *Journal of Imperial and Commonwealth History*, 42, 4 (2014), pp. 741–61.

Laske, Karl, *Des coffres si bien garnis: enquête sur les serviteurs de l'etat-voyou*, Paris: Denoël, 2004.

Le Billon, Philippe, "The Political Ecology of War: Natural Resources and Armed Conflicts," *Political Geography*, 20, 5 (2001), pp. 561–84.

Lemarchand, René, *The Dynamics of Violence in Central Africa*, Philadelphia: University of Pennsylvania Press, 2009.

—— "Foreign Policy Making in the Great Lakes Region," in Gilbert M. Khadiagala (ed.), *African Foreign Policies: Power and Process*, pp. 87–106, Boulder: Lynne Rienner, 2001.

—— *The Dynamics of Violence in Central Africa*, Philadelphia: University of Pennsylvania Press, 2011.

Leonard, David K., and Scott Straus, *Africa's Stalled Development: International Causes and Cures*, Boulder, CO: Lynne Rienner, 2003.

Leslie, Winsome J., *The World Bank and Structural Transformation in Developing Countries: The Case of Zaire*, Boulder: Lynne Rienner, 1987.

—— *Zaire: Continuity and Political Change in an Oppressive State*, Boulder: Westview, 1993.

Levitsky, Steven R., and Lucan A. Way, "Beyond Patronage: Violent Struggle, Ruling

Party Cohesion, and Authoritarian Durability," *Perspectives on Politics*, 10, 4 (2012), pp. 869–89.

——— "The Durability of Revolutionary Regimes," *Journal of Democracy*, 24, 3 (2013), pp. 5–17.

Longman, Timothy, *Christianity and Genocide in Rwanda*, Cambridge: Cambridge University Press, 2009.

——— "Limitations to Political Reform: The Undemocratic Nature of Transition in Rwanda," in Scott Straus and Lars Waldorf (eds), *Remaking Rwanda*, pp. 25–47, Madison: University of Wisconsin Press, 2011.

Lumuna Sando, C.K., *Histoire du Congo: les quatres premiers présidents*, Kinshasa: Editions SECCO & CEDI, 2002.

Lyall, Jason, "Are Coethnics More Effective Counterinsurgents? Evidence from the Second Chechen War," *American Political Science Review*, 104, 1 (2010), pp. 1–20.

M'Poyo Kasa-Vubu, Z.J., *Douze mois chez Kabila (1997–1998)*, Brussels: Cri, 1998.

MacQueen, Norrie, *The Decolonization of Portuguese Africa: Metropolitan Revolution and the Dissolution of Empire*, New York: Longman, 1997.

——— "Peacekeeping by Attrition: The United Nations in Angola," *Journal of Modern African Studies*, 36, 3 (1998), pp. 399–422.

Madsen, Wayne, *Genocide and Covert Operations in Africa, 1993–1999*, Lewiston, NY: Edwin Mellen Press, 1999.

Mamdani, Mahmood, *Citizen and Subject: Contemporary Africa and the Legacy of Late Colonialism*, Princeton: Princeton University Press, 1996.

——— *When Victims Become Killers: Colonialism, Nativism, and the Genocide in Rwanda*, Princeton: Princeton University Press, 2001.

Mandela, Nelson, *Long Walk to Freedom: The Autobiography of Nelson Mandela*, Boston: Little, Brown, 1994.

——— *No Easy Walk to Freedom: Articles, Speeches and Trial Addresses of Nelson Mandela*, London: Heinemann Educational, 1973.

Maoz, Zeev, *Domestic Sources of Global Change*, Ann Arbor: University of Michigan Press, 1996.

Martens, Ludo, *Kabila et la révolution congolaise: panafricanisme ou néocolonialisme?*, vol. 1, Antwerp: EPO, 2002.

Martin, Guy, *African Political Thought*, Basingstoke: Palgrave Macmillan, 2009.

Mathews, K., "Tanzania's Foreign Policy as a Frontline State in the Liberation of Southern Africa," *Africa Quarterly*, 21, 2–4 (1981), pp. 41–61.

Mazrui, Ali A., "Anti-Militarism and Political Militancy in Tanzania," *Journal of Conflict Resolution*, 12, 3 (1968), pp. 269–84.

——— "Seek Ye First the Political Kingdom," in Christophe Wondji and Ali AlAmin Mazrui (eds), *General History of Africa: Africa since 1935*, London: Heinemann, 1993.

McDoom, Omar Shahabudin, "Who Killed in Rwanda's Genocide? Micro-Space,

Social Influence and Individual Participation in Intergroup Violence," *Journal of Peace Research*, 50, 4 (2013), pp. 453–67.

McKinley, Dale T., *The ANC and the Liberation Struggle: A Critical Political Biography*, London: Pluto Press, 1997.

Médecins sans Frontières, "Forced Flight: A Brutal Strategy of Elimination in Eastern Zaire," Geneva: MSF, 1997.

Melvern, Linda, *Conspiracy to Murder: The Rwandan Genocide*, London: Verso, 2006.

Messiant, Christine, Brigitte Lachartre and Michel Cahen, *L'Angola postcolonial*, Paris: Karthala, 2008.

Minter, William, "America and Africa: Beyond the Double Standard," *Current History*, 99, 637 (2000), pp. 200–10.

Morelli, Massimo, and Dominic Rohner, "Resource Concentration and Civil Wars," National Bureau of Economic Research, 2014.

Museveni, Yoweri, "Fanon's Theory on Violence: Its Verification in Liberated Mozambique," in Nathan M. Shamuyarira (ed.), *Essays on the Liberation of Southern Africa*, Dar es Salaam: Tanzania Publishing House, 1975.

——— "The Qaddafi I Know," *Foreign Policy*, 24 (2011).

——— *Sowing the Mustard Seed: The Struggle for Freedom and Democracy in Uganda*, London: Macmillan, 1997.

Mwakikagile, Godfrey, *Life under Nyerere*, Dar es Salaam, Tanzania: New Africa Press, 2006.

——— *Nyerere and Africa: End of an Era*, Pretoria: New Africa Press, 2010.

Mwanke, Augustin Katumba, *Ma vérité*, Nice: Imprimerie Toscane, 2013.

Nayar, Pramod K., *Frantz Fanon*, London and New York: Routledge, 2013.

Ndacyayisenga, Pierre-Claver, *Dying to Live: A Rwandan Family's Five-Year Flight across the Congo*, Montréal: Baraka Books, 2012.

——— *Voyage À travers la mort: le témoignage d'un exilé Hutu du Rwanda*, Montréal: Groupe Ville-Marie Littérature, 2012.

Ndlovu-Gatsheni, Sabelo J., "Pan-Africanism and the International System," In Timothy Murithi (ed.), *Handbook of Africa's International Relations*, London: Routledge, 2014.

Newbury, Catharine, *The Cohesion of Oppression: Clientship and Ethnicity in Rwanda, 1860–1960*, New York: Columbia University Press, 1988.

——— "Ethnicity and the Politics of History in Rwanda," *Africa Today*, 45, 1 (1998), pp. 7–24.

——— "Ubureetwa and Thangata: Catalysts to Peasant Political Consciousness in Rwanda and Malawi," *Canadian Journal of African Studies/La Revue canadienne des études africaines*, 14, 1 (1980), pp. 97–111.

Newbury, David, "Canonical Conventions in Rwanda: Four Myths of Recent Historiography in Central Africa," *History in Africa*, 39 (2012), pp. 41–76.

——— "Precolonial Burundi and Rwanda: Local Loyalties, Regional Royalties," *International Journal of African Historical Studies*, 34, 2 (2001), pp. 255–314.

Ngolet, François, *Crisis in the Congo: The Rise and Fall of Laurent Kabila*, New York: Palgrave Macmillan, 2011.

Nkrumah, Kwame, *Africa Must Unite*, London: Heinemann, 1963.

——— *Ghana: The Autobiography of Kwame Nkrumah*, New York: Nelson, 1957.

——— *Handbook of Revolutionary Warfare: A Guide to the Armed Phase of the African Rvevolution*, New York: International Publishers, 1969.

——— *Neo-Colonialism: The Last Stage of Imperialism*, New York: International Publishers, 1966.

——— *Towards Colonial Freedom: Africa in the Struggle against World Imperialism*, London: Heinemann, 1962.

Nugent, Paul, *Africa since Independence: A Comparative History*, New York: Palgrave Macmillan, 2012.

Nutt, Cullen, and M.L.R. Smith, "Muffling the Sound of Murder: Re-Interpreting Zimbabwe's Strategic Choices in the Congo," *Civil Wars*, 13, 3 (2011), pp. 232–58.

Nyerere, Julius K., "Third World Negotiating Strategy," *Third World Quarterly*, 1, 2 (1979), pp. 20–3.

——— "A United States of Africa," *Journal of Modern African Studies*, 1, 1 (1963), pp. 1–6.

——— "America and Southern Africa," *Foreign Affairs*, 55 (1976), pp. 671–84.

——— *Crusade for Liberation*, Oxford: Oxford University Press, 1978.

Nzongola-Ntalaja, Georges, *The Congo from Leopold to Kabila: A People's History*, London Zed Books, 2002.

Odom, Thomas Paul, *Journey into Darkness: Genocide in Rwanda*, College Station: Texas A&M University Press, 2005.

Orth, Richard, "African Operational Experiences in Peacekeeping," *Small Wars & Insurgencies*, 7, 3 (1996), pp. 308–23.

——— "Rwanda's Hutu Extremist Genocidal Insurgency: An Eyewitness Perspective," *Small Wars and Insurgencies*, 12, 1 (2001), pp. 76–109.

Othman, Haroub, "Mwalimu Julius Nyerere: An Intellectual in Power," in Chambi Chachage and Annar Cassam (eds), *Africa's Liberation: The Legacy of Nyerere*, Kampala, Uganda: Fountain Publishers, 2010.

Pachter, Elise Forbes, "Contra-Coup: Civilian Control of the Military in Guinea, Tanzania, and Mozambique," *Journal of Modern African Studies*, 20, 4 (1982), pp. 595–612.

Pakenham, Thomas, *The Scramble for Africa*, New York: Random House, 1991.

Pearce, Justin, "Control, Politics and Identity in the Angolan Civil War," *African Affairs*, 111, 444 (2012), pp. 442–65.

Powell, Robert, "War as a Commitment Problem," *International Organization*, 60, 1 (2006), pp. 169–203.

Power, Marcus, Giles Mohan and May Tan-Mullins, *China's Resource Diplomacy in Africa: Powering Development?*, New York: Palgrave Macmillan, 2012.

Praeg, Bertus, *Ethiopia and Political Renaissance in Africa*, New York: Nova Science Publishers, 2006.

Prunier, Gérard, *From Genocide to Continental War: The "Congolese" Conflict and the Crisis of Contemporary Africa*, London: Hurst, 2009.

—— "Rebel Movements and Proxy Warfare: Uganda, Sudan and the Congo (1986–99)," *African Affairs*, 103, 412 (2004), pp. 359–83.

—— *The Rwanda Crisis: History of a Genocide*, New York: Columbia University Press, 1995.

—— "The Rwandan Patriotic Front," in Christopher Clapham (ed.), *African Guerillas*, Oxford: James Currey, 1998.

Rafti, Marina, "Rwandan Hutu Rebels in Congo/Zaire, 1994–2006: An Extra-Territorial Civil War in a Weak State," in Filip Reyntjens and Stefan Marysse (eds), *L'Afrique des Grand Lacs: annuaire 2005–2006*, pp. 55–83, Paris: L'Harmattan, 2006.

Reed, W. Cyrus, "Guerrillas in the Midst: The Former Government of Rwanda (FGOR) and the Alliance of Democratic Forces for the Liberation of Congo-Zaire (ADFL) in Eastern Zaire," in Christopher Clapham (ed.), *African Guerrillas*, pp. 134–54, Oxford: James Currey, 1998.

Reid, Richard, "Old Problems in New Conflicts: Some Observations on Eritrea and Its Relations with Tigray, from Liberation Struggle to Inter-State War," *Africa*, 73, 3 (2003), pp. 369–401.

Reno, William, "Sovereignty and Personal Rule in Zaire," *African Studies Quarterly*, 1, 3 (1997).

—— *Warfare in Independent Africa*, New York: Cambridge University Press, 2011.

—— *Warlord Politics and African States*, Boulder, CO: Lynne Rienner, 1998.

Reyntjens, Filip, *The Great African War: Congo and Regional Geopolitics, 1996–2006*, Cambridge: Cambridge University Press, 2009.

—— *Political Governance in Post-Genocide Rwanda*, New York: Cambridge University Press, 2013.

—— *Pouvoir et droit au Rwanda*, Tervuren: Musée Royale de l'Afrique Centrale, 1985.

—— "Rwanda: Genocide and Beyond," *Journal of Refugee Studies*, 9, 3 (1996), pp. 240–51.

—— "Rwanda, Ten Years On: From Genocide to Dictatorship," *African Affairs*, 103, 411 (2004), pp. 177–210.

Richardson, Bill, and Michael Ruby, *Between Worlds: The Making of an American Life*, New York: Plume, 2007.

Rodney, Walter, "How Europe Underdeveloped Africa," in Paula S. Rothenberg (ed.), *Beyond Borders: Thinking Critically about Global Issues*, pp. 107–25, New York: Worth Publishers, 1972.

Roessler, Philip, "The Enemy Within: Personal Rule, Coups, and Civil War in Africa," *World Politics*, 63, 2 (2011), pp. 300–46.

—— *Ethnic Politics and State Power in Africa: The Logic of the Coup–Civil War Trap*, New York: Cambridge University Press, 2016.

Rosenblum, Peter, "Irrational Exuberance: The Clinton Administration in Africa," *Current History*, 101, 655 (2002), pp. 195–202.

Ross, Michael L., "Does Oil Hinder Democracy?," *World Politics*, 53, 3 (2001), pp. 325–61.

—— "The Political Economy of the Resource Curse," *World Politics*, 51, 2 (1999), pp. 297–322.

—— "What Do We Know about Natural Resources and Civil War?," *Journal of Peace Research*, 41, 3 (2004).

Rucyahana, John, *The Bishop of Rwanda*, Thomas Nelson, 2007.

Ruhimbika Muller, Manassé, *Les Banyamulenge (Congo-Zaïre), entre deux guerres*, Paris: Harmattan, 2001.

Rumiya, Jean, *Le Rwanda sous le régime du mandat belge (1916–1931)*, Paris: Editions L'Harmattan, 1992.

Rutinwa, Bonaventure, "The Tanzanian Government's Response to the Rwandan Emergency," *Journal of Refugee Studies*, 9, 3 (1996), pp. 291–302.

Ryckmans, Pierre, "Belgian 'Colonialism,'" *Foreign Affairs*, 34, 1 (1955), pp. 89–101.

—— *Dominer pour servir*, Brussels: Librairie Albert Dewit, 1931.

Salehyan, Idean, "The Delegation of War to Rebel Organizations," *Journal of Conflict Resolution*, 54, 3 (2010), 493–515.

—— *Rebels without Borders: Transnational Insurgencies in Word Politics*, Ithaca, NY: Cornell University Press, 2009.

—— "Transnational Rebels: Neighboring States as Sanctuary for Rebel Groups," *World Politics*, 59 2 (2007), pp. 217–42.

Sapire, Hilary, and Christopher C. Saunders (eds), *Southern African Liberation Struggles: New Local, Regional and Global Perspectives*, Claremont, South Africa: University of Cape Town Press, 2013.

Schatzberg, Michael G., *The Dialectics of Oppression in Zaire*, Bloomington: Indiana University Press, 1988.

—— *Mobutu or Chaos? The United States and Zaire, 1960–1990*, Lanham: University Press of America, 1991.

Scherrer, Christian P., *Genocide and Crisis in Central Africa: Conflict Roots, Mass Violence, and Regional War*, Westport, CT: Praeger, 2002.

Schultz, Kenneth A., "The Enforcement Problem in Coercive Bargaining: Interstate Conflict over Rebel Support in Civil Wars," *International Organization*, 64, 2 (2010), pp. 281–312.

Sebarenzi, Joseph, *God Sleeps in Rwanda*, New York: Atria, 2011.

Sechser, Todd S., "Are Soldiers Less War-Prone Than Statesmen?," *Journal of Conflict Resolution*, 48, 5 (2004), pp. 746–74.

Sharkey, Heather J., *Living with Colonialism: Nationalism and Culture in the Anglo-Egyptian Sudan*, Berkeley: University of California Press, 2003.

Shaw, Bryant P., "Force publique, force unique: The Military in the Belgian Congo, 1914–1939," University of Wisconsin–Madison, 1984.

Shubin, Vladimir, *The Hot Cold War: The USSR in Southern Africa*, London: Pluto Press, 2008.

—— "Unsung Heroes: The Soviet Military and the Liberation of Southern Africa," in Sue Onslow (ed.), *Cold War in Southern Africa: White Power, Black Liberation*, London and New York: Routledge, 2009.

Sibomana, André, *Hope for Rwanda: Conversations with Laure Guilbert and Hervé Deguine*, London: Pluto Press, 1999.

Skocpol, Theda, "Social Revolutions and Mass Military Mobilization," *World Politics*, 40, 2 (1988), pp. 147–68.

—— *States and Social Revolutions: A Comparative Analysis of France, Russia, and China*, Cambridge: Cambridge University Press, 1979.

Soares de Oliveira, Ricardo, "Illiberal Peacebuilding in Angola," *Journal of Modern African Studies*, 49, 2 (2011), pp. 287–314.

—— *Magnificent and Beggar Land: Angola since the Civil War*, London: Hurst, 2015.

—— *Oil and Politics in the Gulf of Guinea*, New York: Columbia University Press, 2007.

Stearns, Jason, *Dancing in the Glory of Monsters: The Collapse of the Congo and the Great War of Africa*, New York: PublicAffairs, 2011.

Stengers, Jean, and Jan Vansina, "King Leopold's Congo," in G.N. Sandersen, J.D. Fage and Roland Oliver (eds), *The Cambridge History of Africa: From 1870 to 1905*, pp. 315–58, Cambridge: Cambridge University Press, 1985.

Strachan, Hew, *The First World War in Africa*, Oxford Oxford University Press, 2004.

Straus, Scott, *The Order of Genocide: Race, Power, and War in Rwanda*, Ithaca: Cornell University Press, 2006.

Svolik, Milan W., *The Politics of Authoritarian Rule*, New York: Cambridge University Press, 2012.

Taylor, Ian, "Conflict in Central Africa: Clandestine Networks & Regional/Global Configurations," *Review of African Political Economy*, 30, 95 (2003), pp. 45–55.

Tekeste, Negash, and Kjetil Tronvoll, *Brothers at War: Making Sense of the Eritrean–Ethiopian War*, Oxford: James Currey, 2000.

Thompson, Carol B., *Challenge to Imperialism: The Frontline States in the Liberation of Zimbabwe*, Boulder, CO: Westview Press, 1986.

Thompson, W. Scott, *Ghana's Foreign Policy, 1957–1966: Diplomacy, Ideology, and the New State*, Princeton, NJ: Princeton University Press, 1969.

Tripp, Aili Mari, *Museveni's Uganda: Paradoxes of Power in a Hybrid Regime*, Boulder: Lynne Rienner, 2010.

Tronvoll, Kjetil, *War & the Politics of Identity in Ethiopia: Making Enemies & Allies in the Horn of Africa*, Rochester, NY: James Currey, 2009.

Turner, Thomas, *The Congo Wars: Conflict, Myth, and Reality*, London: Zed Books, 2007.

Umutesi, Marie Béatrice, *Surviving the Slaughter: The Ordeal of a Rwandan Refugee in Zaire*, Madison: University of Wisconsin Press, 2004.

United Nations Development Programme, *Human Development Report: The Rise of the South*, New York: UNDP, 2013.

United Nations High Commissioner for Human Rights, "Human Rights Field Operation in Rwanda," in *Report of the United Nations High Commissioner for Human Rights*, New York: UN Economic and Social Council, 1998.

United Nations High Commissioner for Human Rights, "Report on the Situation of Human Rights in Zaire," New York: UNCHR, 1997.

United Nations Security Council, "Report of the Investigative Team Charged with Investigating Serious Violations of Human Rights and International Humanitarian Law in the Democratic Republic of Congo," New York: UNSC, 1998.

United Nations Special Rapporteur of the Commission on Human Rights, "Report on the Situation of Human Rights in Rwanda," New York: UN Commission on Human Rights, 1997.

US Department of State, "Massacre at Mudende Refugee Camp, Rwanda," Washington, DC: Office of the Spokesman, 1997.

———— "Rwanda Country Report on Human Rights Practices for 1997," Washington, DC: Bureau of Democracy, Human Rights and Labor, 1998.

Van der Meeren, Rachel, "Three Decades in Exile: Rwandan Refugees, 1960–1990," *Journal of Refugee Studies*, 9, 3 (1996), pp. 252–67.

Van Reybrouck, David, *Congo: Een Geschiedenis*, Amsterdam: De Bezige Bij, 2010.

Vandewalle, Gaston, *De Conjuncturele Evolutie in Kongo En Ruanda–Urundi, Van 1920 Tot 1939 En Van 1949 Tot 1958*, Ghent: Rijks Universiteit, 1966.

Vansina, Jan, *Antecedents to Modern Rwanda: The Nyiginya Kingdom*, Madison: University of Wisconsin Press, 2005.

Verhoeven, Harry, "Nurturing Democracy or into the Danger Zone? The Rwandan Patriotic Front, Elite Fragmentation and Post-Liberation Politics," in Maddalena Campioni and Patrick Noack (eds), *Rwanda Fast Forward: Social, Economic, Military and Reconciliation Prospects*, Basingstoke: Palgrave, 2012.

———— "The Rise and Fall of Sudan's Al-Ingaz Revolution: The Transition from Militarised Islamism to Economic Salvation and the Comprehensive Peace Agreement," *Civil Wars*, 15, 2 (2013), pp. 118–40.

Verhoeven, Harry, and Luke A. Patey, "Sudan's Islamists and the Post-Oil Era: Washington's Role after Southern Secession," *Middle East Policy*, 18, 3 (2011), pp. 133–43.

Verpoorten, Marijke, "The Death Toll of the Rwandan Genocide: A Detailed Analysis for Gikongoro Province," *Population*, 60, 4 (2005), pp. 331–67.

Verwimp, Philip, "Development Ideology, the Peasantry and Genocide: Rwanda

Represented in Habyarimana's Speeches," *Journal of Genocide Research*, 2, 3 (2000), pp. 325–61.

—— "An Economic Profile of Peasant Perpetrators of Genocide: Micro-Level Evidence from Rwanda," *Journal of Development Economics*, 77, 2 (2005), pp. 297–323.

—— "Testing the Double-Genocide Thesis for Central and Southern Rwanda," *Journal of Conflict Resolution*, 47, 4 (2003), pp. 423–42.

Villafana, Frank R., *Cold War in the Congo*, New Brunswick, NJ: Transaction Publishers, 2009.

Villers, Gauthier de, *De Mobutu à Mobutu: trente ans de relations Belgique–Zaïre*, Brussels: De Boeck Université, 1995.

Vlassenroot, Koen, "Citizenship, Identity Formation & Conflict in South Kivu: The Case of the Banyamulenge," *Review of African Political Economy*, 29, 93 (2002), pp. 499–516.

Vlassenroot, Koen, and Timothy Raeymaekers, "The Politics of Rebellion and Intervention in Ituri: The Emergence of a New Political Complex?," *African Affairs*, 103, 412 (2004), pp. 385–412.

Wallerstein, Immanuel Maurice, *Africa: The Politics of Independence and Unity*, Lincoln, NE: University of Nebraska Press, 2005.

Wallis, Andrew, *Silent Accomplice: The Untold Story of France's Role in the Rwandan Genocide*, London: I.B. Tauris, 2006.

Walt, Stephen M., *Revolution and War*, Ithaca: Cornell University Press, 1996.

Walter, Barbara F., "Why Bad Governance Leads to Repeat Civil War," *Journal of Conflict Resolution*, 59, 7 (2014).

Waltz, Kenneth Neal, *Theory of International Politics*, Reading, MA: Addison-Wesley, 1979.

Weeks, Jessica L., "Strongmen and Straw Men: Authoritarian Regimes and the Initiation of International Conflict," *American Political Science Review*, 106, 2 (2012), pp. 326–47.

Weinstein, Jeremy M., *Inside Rebellion: The Politics of Insurgent Violence*, New York: Cambridge University Press, 2007.

Wendt, Alexander, "Anarchy Is What States Make of It: The Social Construction of Power Politics," *International Organization*, 46, 2 (1992), pp. 391–425.

Wilkinson, Ray, "Cover Story: Heart of Darkness," *Refugees Magazine*, 110 (1997).

Williame, Jean-Claude, *L'automne d'un despotisme: pouvoir, argent et obéissance dans le Zaïre Des années quatre-vingt*, Paris: Karthala, 1992.

Williams, Paul D., "The Peace and Security Council of the African Union: Evaluating an Embryonic International Institution," *Journal of Modern African Studies*, 47, 4 (2009), pp. 603–26.

Witness, Global, "Under-Mining Peace: Tin—The Explosive Trade in Cassiterite in Eastern DRC," London: Global Witness, 2005.

Wood, Brian, and Johan Peleman, *The Arms Fixers: Controlling the Brokers and Shipping Agents*, Oslo: International Peace Research Institute, 1999.

Wrong, Michela, *In the Footsteps of Mr Kurtz*, New York: HarperCollins, 2001.

—— *In the Footsteps of Mr Kurtz: Living on the Brink of Disaster in Mobutu's Congo*, London: Fourth Estate, 2000.

York, Geoffrey, and Judy Rever, "Families of Two Canadian Priests Killed in Rwanda Still Wait for Justice," *Globe and Mail*, November 14, 2014.

Young, Crawford, *The African Colonial State in Comparative Perspective*, New Haven, CT: Yale University Press, 1994.

—— "Contextualizing Congo Conflicts: Order and Disorder in Postcolonial Africa," in John F. Clark (ed.), *The African Stakes of the Congo War*, New York: Palgrave Macmillan, 2002.

Young, Crawford, and Thomas Turner, *The Rise and Decline of the Zairian State*, Madison, WI: University of Wisconsin Press, 1985.

Zartman, I. William, "Africa as a Subordinate State System in International Relations," *International Organization*, 21, 3 (1967), pp. 545–64.

Zinzen, Walter, *Kisangani: Verloren Stad*, Leuven: Van Halewyck, 2004.

INDEX